DECISIONS FOR HEALTH

PRENTICE HALL

MIDDLE GRADES MATH
TOOLS FOR SUCCESS

Course 2

*Prentice Hall dedicates
this mathematics program
to all mathematics educators
and their students.*

AUTHORS

Suzanne H. Chapin

Mark Illingworth

Marsha S. Landau

Joanna O. Masingila

Leah McCracken

CONSULTING AUTHORS

Sadie Chavis Bragg

Bridget A. Hadley

Vincent O'Connor

Anne C. Patterson

PRENTICE HALL

MIDDLE GRADES
MATH
TOOLS FOR SUCCESS

Course 2

PRENTICE HALL
Needham, Massachusetts
Upper Saddle River, New Jersey

AUTHORS

Suzanne H. Chapin, Ed.D., Boston University, Boston, Massachusetts Proportional Reasoning and Probability strands, and Tools for Problem Solving

Mark Illingworth, Hollis Public Schools, Hollis, New Hampshire Graphing strand

Marsha S. Landau, Ph.D., Formerly, National Louis University, Evanston, Illinois Algebra, Functions, and Computation strands

Joanna O. Masingila, Ph.D., Syracuse University, Syracuse, New York Geometry strand

Leah McCracken, Lockwood School District, Billings, Montana Data Analysis strand

CONSULTING AUTHORS

Sadie Chavis Bragg, Ed.D., Borough of Manhattan Community College, The City University of New York, New York, New York

Bridget A. Hadley, Mathematics Curriculum Specialist, Hopkinton, Massachusetts

Vincent O'Connor, Formerly, Milwaukee Public Schools, Milwaukee, Wisconsin

Anne C. Patterson, Volusia County Schools, Daytona Beach, Florida

PRENTICE HALL

ISBN: 0-13-434683-1

6 7 8 9 10 04 03 02 01 00 99

We are grateful to our reviewers, who advised us in the development stages and provided invaluable feedback, ideas, and constructive criticism to help make this program one that meets the needs of middle grades teachers and students.

REVIEWERS

All Levels

Ann Bouie, Ph.D., Multicultural Reviewer, Oakland, California

Dorothy S. Strong, Ph.D., Chicago Public Schools, Chicago, Illinois

Course 1

Darla Agajanian, Sierra Vista School, Canyon Country, California

Rhonda Bird, Grand Haven Area Schools, Grand Haven, Michigan

Gary Critselous, Whittle Springs Middle School, Knoxville, Tennessee

Rhonda W. Davis, Durant Road Middle School, Raleigh, North Carolina

Leroy Dupee, Bridgeport Public Schools, Bridgeport, Connecticut

Jose Lalas, Ph.D., California State University, Dominguez Hills, California

Richard Lavers, Fitchburg High School, Fitchburg, Massachusetts

Lavaille Metoyer, Houston Independent School District, Houston, Texas

Course 2

Raylene Bryson, Alexander Middle School, Huntersville, North Carolina

Susan R. Buckley, Dallas Public Schools, Dallas, Texas

Sheila Cunningham, Klein Independent School District, Klein, Texas

Natarsha Mathis, Hart Junior High School, Washington, D.C.

Jean Patton, Clements Middle School, Covington, Georgia

Judy Trowell, Arkansas Department of Higher Education, Little Rock, Arkansas

Course 3

Michaele F. Chappell, Ph.D., University of South Florida, Tampa, Florida

Bettye Hall, Math Consultant, Houston, Texas

Joaquin Hernandez, Barbara Goleman Senior High, Miami, Florida

Steven H. Lapinski, Henrico County Public Schools, Richmond, Virginia

Dana Luterman, Lincoln Middle School, Kansas City, Missouri

Loretta Rector, Leonardo da Vinci School, Sacramento, California

Elias P. Rodriguez, Leander Middle School, Leander, Texas

Anthony C. Terceira, Providence School Department, Providence, Rhode Island

STAFF CREDITS

The people who made up the *Middle Grades Math* team—representing editorial, design, marketing, page production, editorial services, production, manufacturing, technology, electronic publishing, and advertising and promotion—and their managers are listed below. Bold type denotes core team members.
Barbara A. Bertell, Bruce Bond, Therese Bräuer, Christopher Brown, **Judith D. Buice**, Kathy Carter, Linda M. Coffey, Noralie V. Cox, Sheila DeFazio, Edward de Leon, Christine Deliee, Gabriella Della Corte, Jo DiGiustini, Robert G. Dunn, Barbara Flockhart, Audra Floyd, David B. Graham, Maria Green, Kristen Guevara, Jeff Ikler, Mimi Jigarjian, Elizabeth A. Jordan, Russell Lappa, Joan McCulley, Paul W. Murphy, Cindy A. Noftle, Caroline M. Power, Olena Serbyn, Dennis Slattery, Martha G. Smith, Kira Thaler Marbit, Robin Tiano, **Christina Trinchero**, **Stuart Wallace**, **Cynthia A. Weedel**, **Jeff Weidenaar, Mary Jane Wolfe,** Stewart Wood

We would like to give special thanks to National Math Consultants Ann F. Bell and Brenda Underwood for all their help in developing this program.

COURSE 2

Contents

CHAPTER 1

Interpreting Data and Statistics

Problem Solving and Connections

...and More!

Hobbies 5
Business 6
Television 12
Nutrition 22
Math at Work 25
History 30
Environment 37

CHAPTER PROJECT

Theme: Marketing
Too Many to Count

Problem Solving and Connections

...and More!

ASSESSMENT

CHAPTER PROJECT

Theme: Science
Weighty Matters

Algebra: Integers and Equations

Problem Solving and Connections

...and More!

ASSESSMENT

CHAPTER PROJECT

Theme: Recreation
Board Walk

CHAPTER 4

Fractions and Number Theory

Problem Solving and Connections

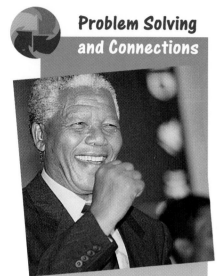

...and More!

ASSESSMENT

Mixed Review in every lesson

CHAPTER PROJECT

Theme: Measurement
Making the Measure

CHAPTER
5 Applications of Fractions

CHAPTER

6 Using Proportions and Percents

Problem Solving and Connections

Crafts	288
Math at Work	290
Physical Therapy	293
Architecture	298
Engineering	315
Statistics	320
History	324

...and More!

ASSESSMENT

CHAPTER PROJECT

Theme: Construction
Raisin' the Roof

CHAPTER 8 Geometry and Measurement

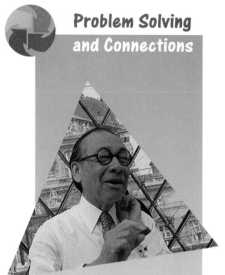

Problem Solving and Connections

...and More!

ASSESSMENT

CHAPTER PROJECT

Theme: Logic
Everybody Wins!

Problem Solving and Connections

ASSESSMENT

CHAPTER PROJECT

Theme: Graphing
Happy Landings

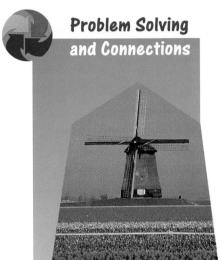

**Problem Solving
and Connections**

...and More!

**CHAPTER
PROJECT**

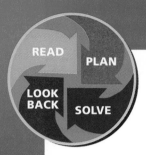

READ
PLAN
LOOK BACK
SOLVE

Tools for Problem Solving... An Overview

CONTENTS

To the Student:

The key to your success in math is your ability to use math in the real world—both now and in the future. To succeed you need math skill and some problem solving tools too. In this Problem Solving Overview, you'll learn how to use a four-step plan for problem solving, how to choose strategies for solving problems, how to best work in groups, and how to apply strategies to standardized tests.

As you work through the book, you'll find plenty of opportunities to improve your problem solving skills. The more you build on a skill, the better you'll get. And the better you get, the more confident you'll become. So keep at it!

Problem Solving Strategies

Draw a Diagram
Guess and Test
Look for a Pattern
Make a Model
Make a Table
Simulate a Problem
Solve a Simpler Problem
Too Much or Too Little
  Information
Use Logical Reasoning
Use Multiple Strategies
Work Backward
Write an Equation

The Four-Step Approach

Problem solving is a skill — a skill that you may use without even knowing it. Problem solving involves logical reasoning, wise decision making, and reflecting on solutions.

How you approach a problem is one skill that can make a difference in whether or not you solve the problem. George Polya, a mathematician, devised a four-step method for solving problems.

POLYA'S FOUR-STEP APPROACH

1. Read and understand the problem.
2. Plan how to solve the problem.
3. Solve the problem.
4. Look back.

As you follow each step of Polya's approach, ask yourself questions about the problem.

SAMPLE PROBLEM............

A gardener has 32 feet of fencing. He wants to fence a rectangular area to have the largest garden possible. If he uses all of the fence material, what dimensions give him the greatest area?

....

READ

Read for understanding. Summarize the problem.

Read the problem again. What information is given? What information is missing? Most importantly, what are you being asked to find or to do?

Organize your information.

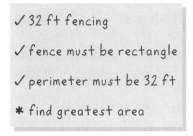

> ✓ 32 ft fencing
>
> ✓ fence must be rectangle
>
> ✓ perimeter must be 32 ft
>
> * find greatest area

PLAN

Decide a strategy.

Consider the strategies you know. Could you use one of them? Have you ever solved a similar problem? If so, try the same approach.

To get a clear idea of the problem, the first thing you might do is draw a diagram.

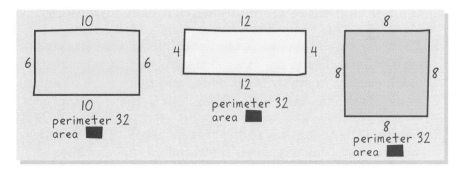

SOLVE

Try the strategy.

Making a table will help you organize your information. Start with length 1 ft.

Length ℓ	Width w	Perimeter $P = 2\ell + 2w$	Area $A = \ell w$
1 ft	15 ft	32 ft	15 ft^2
2 ft	14 ft	32 ft	28 ft^2
3 ft	13 ft	32 ft	39 ft^2
4 ft	12 ft	32 ft	48 ft^2
5 ft	11 ft	32 ft	55 ft^2
6 ft	10 ft	32 ft	60 ft^2
7 ft	9 ft	32 ft	63 ft^2
8 ft	8 ft	32 ft	64 ft^2
9 ft	7 ft	32 ft	63 ft^2

You do not need to continue the table because a 9 ft × 7 ft rectangle is the same as a 7 ft × 9 ft rectangle. The table shows that the area is greatest when the length and width are each 8 ft.

LOOK BACK

Think about how you solved the problem.

This is the most important step in solving problems. Check that you answered the original question. Ask yourself some questions.

• Is your answer reasonable?

• Does your answer make sense?

• Could you have solved the problem another way?

EXERCISES *On Your Own*

Use Polya's four-step method to solve each problem. Remember that there are many ways to solve problems.

1. There are two sizes of tables in the cafeteria. One size seats exactly 5 people and the other size seats exactly 8 people. At lunch exactly 79 students sat down, and there were no empty seats. How many tables of each size are in the cafeteria?

2. *Languages* In one school 65 students speak Spanish and 49 students speak Japanese. If 80 students speak either Spanish or Japanese, how many students speak *both* Spanish and Japanese?

3. *Geometry* How many triangles are in the diagram at the right?

4. *Carpentry* A lumberyard worker cuts a board in half. Then he cuts each piece in half. Then he cuts each of those pieces in half again.
   a. How many cuts did the worker make?
   b. How many pieces of wood are there?

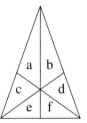

5. *Physical Science* Earth's atmosphere is divided into four regions: the mesosphere, the stratosphere, the thermosphere, and the troposphere. The stratosphere is higher in altitude than the troposphere, but not as high as the thermosphere. The mesosphere is just below the thermosphere. Arrange the regions in order from lowest altitude to highest altitude.

Using Strategies

There are many ways to solve problems. Some of the strategies you have learned in previous math courses are Draw a Diagram, Look for a Pattern, Guess and Test, and Make a Table.

Different students solve problems in different ways. Remember that any method that works is a good method!

SAMPLE PROBLEM..

The town of Lewiston celebrates Founder's Day with a parade of antique vehicles. One kind of vehicle in the parade is the cycle. Some antique cycles have 2 wheels and some antique cycles have 3 wheels.

During the parade, 24 different antique cycles were counted. There were a total of 54 wheels on these 24 cycles.

How many of the cycles in the parade had 3 wheels?

The solutions shown here and on the next page use three strategies to solve the problem. As you examine the solutions, ask yourself, "Which strategy would I use?"

Solution 1

STRATEGIES: *Guess and Test* and *Make a Table*

Use the Make a Table strategy when you use Guess and Test to keep your guesses organized.

2 wheels	3 wheels	Number of Cycles (24)	Number of Wheels (54)	
12	12	24	$(12 \cdot 2) + (12 \cdot 3) = 60$	high
15	9	24	$(15 \cdot 2) + (9 \cdot 3) = 57$	high
17	7	24	$(17 \cdot 2) + (7 \cdot 3) = 55$	high
20	4	24	$(20 \cdot 2) + (4 \cdot 3) = 52$	low
18	6	24	$(18 \cdot 2) + (6 \cdot 3) = 54$	✓

Six antique cycles in the Founder's Day parade had three wheels.

Solution 2

STRATEGY: *Draw a Diagram*

The Draw a Diagram strategy helps you see the relationships in a problem.

All 24 cycles in the parade have *at least* 2 wheels.

Now add wheels until you have 54.

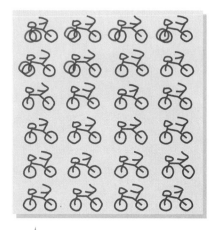

└ You have accounted for 48 wheels.

└─54 wheels in all.

So, 6 cycles have three wheels.

WHAT? A steel penny-farthing bicycle, like the one shown on page xxiii, could weigh as much as 50 or 60 lb. A modern racing bicycle can be a combination of titanium and aluminum and can weigh as little as 19 lb.

1. **Money** Petra and Kim are sisters who baby-sit after school and on weekends. Petra charges $4 per hour and Kim charges $5 per hour. On Saturday they baby-sat a total of 11 hours and together made $47. How much money did each girl earn on Saturday?

2. **Geometry** The diagrams show the diagonals in several figures. How many diagonals are in a figure with 9 sides?

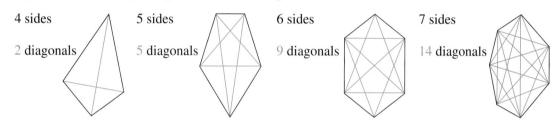

4 sides

2 diagonals

5 sides

5 diagonals

6 sides

9 diagonals

7 sides

14 diagonals

3. **Sports** Students at Maxfield Middle School can choose between two sports in the fall: soccer and track. In the winter the sports are basketball, volleyball, gymnastics, and swimming. In the spring there are two choices: tennis and cross-country. How many different combinations of sports are available to a student who wishes to play one sport each season?

4. A commuter train leaves for the city every 40 min. The first train leaves at 5:20 A.M. What is the departure time closest to 12:55 P.M.?

5. Yesterday, Sam walked from his house to the grocery store. At 3:35 P.M., he passed a mailbox that is three blocks from his house. He passed the town fire station at 3:39 P.M. At that point he was four blocks from the grocery store and half the way there. Suppose Sam walked at the same speed all the way to the grocery store. At what time did Sam arrive at the grocery store? Explain your answer.

6. **Money** Zachary sells juice drinks at sports events. After last weekend's game, he had some $1 bills, some $5 bills, and some $10 bills. He had a total of 17 bills worth a total of $87. How many of each type of bill did he have?

7. **Number Sense** Find the sum of the numbers.

$$1 + 3 + 5 + 7 + \ldots + 295 + 297 + 299$$

Working Together

Have you ever heard the saying "Two heads are better than one"? You may be asked to work in a cooperative group during math class this year. You will have an opportunity to learn new methods and share your ideas as you solve problems with other students.

Solving problems in a group involves responsibility and cooperation. Usually classrooms have individual and group rules.

Individual rules can include the following.

- You are responsible for your own work.
- You are responsible for your own behavior.

Group rules can include the following.

- You must be willing to help other group members.
- Group members should try to answer questions themselves before asking a teacher.

In a cooperative learning group, members work together to solve problems, but some members of the group may also have specific responsibilities.

- The **recorder** takes notes and records information.
- The **researcher** tracks down information that is not immediately available.
- Each member of the group should have general supplies such as paper and pencil, a calculator, and a ruler. The **organizer** makes sure any unusual items, like a stopwatch or masking tape, are available.
- The **presenter** explains the group's solution process to the rest of the class.

Remember that even though members of a group have different jobs, each one must help solve the problem.

EXERCISES *On Your Own*

Solve the following problems with your small group. Assign a job to each member of your group. Switch roles for each problem.

1. *Money* Ahmed has 3 pennies, 2 nickels, 3 dimes, and 2 quarters. How many different amounts of money can Ahmed make by using all the possible combinations of coins?

2. Annie, Ben, Clarisse, and David each sit in one of the four desks in the third row. Each day they sit in a different order. How many days can they do this before they must repeat a previous pattern?

3. *Sports* José can run 5 km in 30 min. In the same amount of time, Juan can run 3 km. How much of a head start does Juan need for both runners to finish an 8-km course at the same time?

4. *Patterns* A marching-band director wanted to arrange the band members in pairs for a parade, but she was one person short. She then tried to arrange the band members by fives and by sevens and was one person short each time. What is the least number of people that are in the band?

5. The clock in the old town hall loses 8 minutes every 3 days. The town residents have decided that eventually it will get back to the correct time on its own. Suppose that the clock is correct at noon on June 10. When will the clock show the correct time again?

Preparing for Standardized Tests

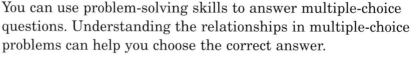

You can use problem-solving skills to answer multiple-choice questions. Understanding the relationships in multiple-choice problems can help you choose the correct answer.

SAMPLE PROBLEM 1...

Cooking Cassandra's recipe for salad dressing calls for 3 tablespoons (tbsp) olive oil and 1 tbsp lemon juice. By mistake, she used 3 tbsp lemon juice and 1 tbsp olive oil. How many more tablespoons of olive oil must she add to have the correct mix?

A. 2   **B.** 8   **C.** 9   **D.** 15   **E.** Not Here

Read and Understand You are asked to find how many more tablespoons of olive oil Cassandra needs.

Keep in mind that Cassandra put in 3 tbsp lemon juice. She only needed 1 tbsp.

Plan an Approach Thinking about the problem logically is a good way to solve it.

Since Cassandra put in three times as much lemon juice as the recipe states, she needs three times as much olive oil.

Solve the Problem

$3 \times$ original amount of olive oil = new amount of olive oil

3×3 tbsp = 9 tbsp

Cassandra needs a total of 9 tbsp olive oil. Since she already put in 1 tbsp olive oil, she only needs 8 more tablespoons.

Choice B is the correct answer.

Look Back When Not Here is an answer choice, you need to check each of the other possible choices before choosing Not Here. For this problem, choice E is not correct. Thinking about the problem logically helps you eliminate choices A, C, and D as possible answers.

Another strategy for answering multiple-choice questions is to Work Backward. You can check each choice to see which results in a correct answer by substituting the values into the problem.

SAMPLE PROBLEM 2..

Money In a pile of dimes and quarters, there are twice as many dimes as quarters. The total value of the coins is $9.45. How many quarters are in the pile?

A. 11   **B.** 18   **C.** 21   **D.** 24

Work Backward Check each answer to see if it works.

A: 11 quarters = 2.75   22 dimes = 2.20   2.75 + 2.20 = 4.95 ✗

B: 18 quarters = 4.50   36 dimes = 3.60   4.50 + 3.60 = 8.10 ✗

C: 21 quarters = 5.25   42 dimes = 4.20   5.25 + 4.20 = 9.45 ✔

Choice C is the correct answer.

EXERCISES *On Your Own*

Use problem-solving strategies to choose the best answer.

1. *Money* In an antique desk Lia found some stamps worth 4¢ and 5¢. The value of the stamps was $1.00. There were 22 stamps in all. How many 5¢ stamps were in the desk?

   A. 3   **B.** 6   **C.** 9   **D.** 12

2. *Number Sense* Find the missing number.
   1 4 16 64 ■ 1,024 4,096

   A. 96   **B.** 192   **C.** 256   **D.** 342   **E.** Not Here

3. *Money* Kate bought some CDs for $80, sold them for $95, bought them back for $120, and sold them again for $130. How much money did she make?

   A. $0   **B.** $15   **C.** $30   **D.** $50   **E.** Not Here

4. Given the numbers 0 and 5, it is *not* reasonable to conclude —

   A. that the sum is greater than the product
   B. that the product is greater than the sum
   C. that the difference equals the sum
   D. that the difference is greater than the product

1

Interpreting Data and Statistics

WHAT YOU WILL LEARN IN THIS CHAPTER

- How to collect, record, and interpret data

- How to construct, read, and interpret tables, charts, and graphs

- How to use technology to graph data

TOO MANY TO COUNT

Chances are there's at least one person in a crowd like this one that has the same birthday as you! How many people do you think have the same favorite food? How many like the same television show? What kinds of cars do the people in the crowd have? Pollsters face questions like these all of the time, and they take surveys to help answer them.

Estimate the Size of a Crowd and Take a Survey For the chapter project you will use averages to estimate the size of a crowd. You will also take a survey and present your results in a graph.

• **How to use logical reasoning to solve problems**

PROBLEM SOLVING

3

1-1 Reporting Frequency

What You'll Learn

1 To display data in a frequency table or a line plot

2 To make a histogram

...And Why

Knowing how to display the frequency of data can help you analyze information.

Here's How

Look for questions that
- build understanding
- ✔ check understanding

THINK AND DISCUSS

1 *Frequency Tables and Line Plots*

Below are the number of letters in each of the words of The Pledge of Allegiance.

1 6 10 2 3 4 2 3 6 6 2 7 3 2 3
8 3 5 2 6 3 6 5 3 11 4 7 3 7 3 3

You can organize and display the data in a line plot or in a frequency table. A **line plot** uses a number line with × marks to represent each data item. A **frequency table** lists each data item together with the number of times it occurs.

■ **EXAMPLE 1**

a. Display the data above in a line plot.

Number of Letters in The Pledge of Allegiance

b. Display the data above in a frequency table.

Number of Letters	1	2	3	4	5	6	7	8	9	10	11
Tally	l	₩	₩₩	ll	ll	₩	lll	l		l	l
Frequency	1	5	10	2	2	5	3	1	0	1	1

Number of Letters in The Pledge of Allegiance

1. ■ *Look Back* Which display do you prefer for the data? Why?

KEN GRIFFEY, JR.

2 Using Histograms

You can use a **histogram** to show frequency. The height of each bar gives the frequency of the data. There are no spaces between consecutive bars.

The information on the horizontal axis of a histogram is grouped into *intervals* of equal size. Intervals must not overlap.

■ **EXAMPLE 2**   *Real-World Problem Solving*

Hobbies Use the data at the left to draw a histogram.

How Many Baseball Cards
Do You Have?

Number	Tally	Number	Tally
11	I	21	I
12	⅏	22	IIII
13	II	23	
14	I	24	III
15	IIII	25	I
16	I	26	
17	II	27	III
18		28	I
19		29	
20	IIII	30	⅏ II

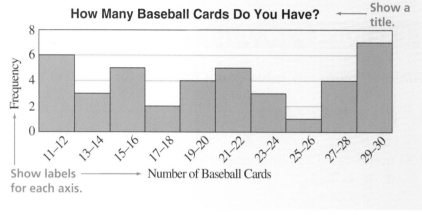

Show a title.

How Many Baseball Cards Do You Have?

Show labels for each axis.

Number of Baseball Cards

2. a. ▪**Analyze** Which interval has the tallest bar? The shortest bar?
   b. What is the difference between the greatest frequency and the least frequency shown in the graph?

3. a. ▪**Reasoning** Would intervals of 0–10, 10–20, and 20–30 be appropriate for the data? Explain.
   b. What are two choices of intervals of equal size for the data?
   c. ✔**Try It Out** Redraw the histogram using one of your answers to part (b).

4. How many people were surveyed?

Work Together

Work in groups to collect data and make a display. Ask twelve people one of the questions at the left.

How many lace holes (eyelets) are in your shoes?

What color are your eyes?

How many pencils do you have with you?

5. Record the responses in a frequency table.

6. Create a histogram for your data.

7. Explain why you chose the interval you used.

8. What response was most frequent? Least frequent?

EXERCISES *On Your Own*

Make a frequency table and a line plot for each set of data.

1. tickets sold per day: 45 48 51 53 50
   46 46 50 51 48 46 45 50 49 46

2. ages of students: 13 12 14 12 11 12
   13 14 13 13 14 11 12 12 13 11 11

3. number of TVs per household: 1 3 2
   2 1 4 1 2 2 1 3 1 3 3 2 2 3 1

4. miles from home to shopping center: 2 4
   10 5 4 6 7 9 5 5 3 1 10 8 6 4 3

5. *Business* Estelle works at a book store. She made the line plot at the right to show the number of books each customer bought one morning.
   a. How many customers did Estelle have?
   b. How many customers bought more than three books?

Number of Books Purchased

```
        ×
  ×     ×
  ×     ×   ×
  ×     ×   ×                ×
  ×     ×   ×   ×   ×   ×
 ─────────────────────────────
  1     2   3   4   5   6
```

The line plot at the right shows responses to a survey.

6. What do the numbers in the line plot represent?

7. How many people answered the survey?

8. *Open-ended* Choose a nursery rhyme or poem. Write the number of letters in each word. Make a line plot of the data.

How Many Times Have You Flown in an Airplane?

```
  ×           ×
  ×     ×     ×
  ×     ×     ×   ×                ×
  ×     ×     ×   ×        ×   ×
 ──────────────────────────────────
  1     2     3   4   5    6   7
```

9. **Entertainment** Use the histogram at the right.

   a. About how many of the people surveyed saw fewer than two movies last summer?

   b. Which interval shows the greatest number of responses? What is the number of responses for this interval?

   c. About how many more people saw 4–5 movies than 10–11 movies?

   d. About how many people answered the survey?

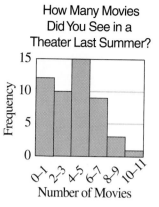

How Many Movies Did You See in a Theater Last Summer?

Number of Movies

10. **Writing** What is an advantage and a disadvantage of displaying information in a histogram?

Use each table of data to make a histogram.

11. How Many Hours Do You Sleep Each Night?

Number of Hours	5–6	7–8	9–10	11–12
Frequency	4	12	9	1

12. How Many Meals Did You Eat Out Last Month?

Number of Meals	0–3	4–7	8–11	12–15
Frequency	8	12	3	7

13. **Health** Gabriel asked 16 people what time they get up in the morning. The data at the right show their answers.

   a. Make a frequency table and a histogram for the data. Use half-hour intervals such as 6:00–6:29 and 6:30–6:59.

   b. Which half-hour interval is the most common?

5:30	6:45	5:45	6:15
6:25	6:20	7:15	7:45
8:00	7:00	8:00	7:30
6:00	7:10	7:50	6:10

Mixed Review

Compare. Use < (is less than), > (is greater than), or = (is equal to). *(Previous Course)*

14. $10 + 2 \blacksquare 15 - 3$ **15.** $7 \times 2 \blacksquare 5 \times 3$ **16.** $9 \times 4 \blacksquare 24 + 8$ **17.** $56 \div 8 \blacksquare 13 - 8$

Use mental math. *(Previous Course)*

18. $58 + 12$ **19.** $638 - 328$ **20.** $594 + 406$ **21.** $702 - 212$

CHAPTER PROJECT

PROJECT LINK: COLLECTING DATA

In a magazine or newspaper, find a picture of a large crowd. Use a sporting event or concert. Guess how many people are in the picture. Save the picture to use later in your project.

Making Bar and Line Graphs

What You'll Learn

1 ▼ To make a bar graph

2 ▼ To make a line graph and use a line graph to make predictions

...And Why

You can analyze graphs to compare amounts and to see changes over time.

Here's How

Look for questions that

▪ build understanding

✔ check understanding

Popular Movies

Movie	Income (in millions)
Apollo 13	$172.1
Batman	$251.2
E.T.	$399.8
Jurassic Park	$357.1
Toy Story	$182.4

Source: *Variety*

THINK AND DISCUSS

1 ▼ *Making a Bar Graph*

You can use a **bar graph** to compare amounts. To make a bar graph, choose an appropriate scale for the vertical axis. Be sure to give your graph a title and to label each axis.

▪ **EXAMPLE 1**   *Real-World Problem Solving*

Entertainment Make a bar graph. Use the table at the left.

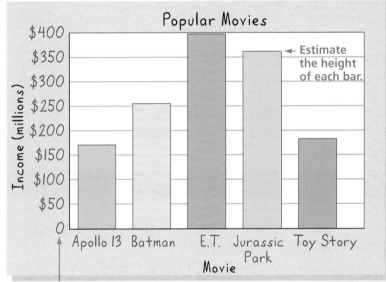

Label the vertical scale using equally spaced intervals.

1. ✔ *Try It Out* Suppose the income for a movie was $340 million. Explain how to estimate the bar height for a graph with the same scale as the one shown in Example 1.

2. ▪ *Reasoning* The year each movie came out is listed below.

Apollo 13	*Batman*	*E.T.*	*Jurassic Park*	*Toy Story*
1995	1989	1982	1993	1995

Do you expect any movie in this list to overtake E.T. in income? Explain.

2 Making a Line Graph

To show how an amount changes over time, make a **line graph.**
You can use a line graph to look for trends and make predictions.

■ **EXAMPLE 2** *Real-World Problem Solving*

Entertainment Use the data at the left. Make a line graph.

Indoor Movie Screens in the United States
(in thousands)

Year	Number
1980	14.9
1984	17.4
1988	21.7
1992	24.2
1996	28.9

Source: Motion Picture Association of America

Graph a point for each data item. Then connect the points.

3. ⚎*Explain* In Example 2, how do you estimate the position of the point for 1980?

4. What trend do you see in the graph in Example 2?

■ **EXAMPLE 3** *Real-World Problem Solving*

Suppose the trend for the number of screens continues. Use the line graph to predict the number of screens in 2000 and 2004.

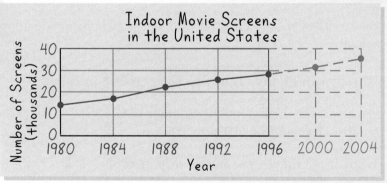

There will be about 32,500 indoor movie screens in 2000.
There will be about 37,000 screens in 2004.

5. ⚎*Reasoning* Is it likely that the number of indoor movie screens in 2000 and 2004 will be exactly what is predicted in Example 3? Explain.

Diorama by Gerard Fritch

1. *Entertainment* The data below show the number of movies made in one year in three countries. Make a bar graph using the data. Be sure your graph has a title and labels on the axes.

Country	France	India	United States
Number of movies	133	806	578

The graph at the right shows cargo traffic for one year at each airport. Use the graph for Exercises 2–5.

2. Which airport has the least cargo traffic?

3. Which airports have more cargo traffic than Kennedy airport in New York City?

4. Estimate the number of metric tons of cargo traffic at the Memphis airport.

5. Rank the airports from most to least busiest.

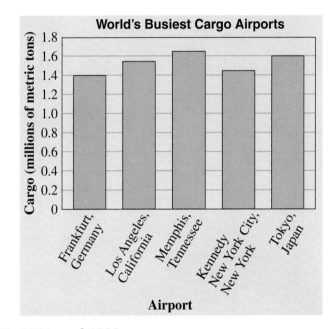

Would you use a line or a bar graph to display each of the following? Why?

6. the population in Alaska in 1950, 1960, 1970, 1980, and 1990

7. the number of boys and the number of girls by grade at your school

Use the graph at the right for Exercises 8 and 9.

8. Estimate the change in the number of CD singles shipped from 1994 to 1995.

9. What trend do you see in the shipment of CD singles?

10. *Research* Find the population of your state or your city for 1960, 1970, 1980, and 1990. Make the appropriate graph of your data. Describe any trends that you see.

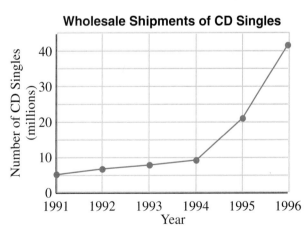

11. **a.** Use the data at the right. Draw a line graph.
    b. Describe the trends you see in your graph.
    c. Extend your graph to predict the shipments of music videos in 1998 and 2000.

12. **a.** *Data Collection* Choose five movies that are showing at movie theaters now. Interview 20 people. Find how many people have seen each movie. Graph your results.
    b. Explain why you chose the graph you used.

13. **Choose A, B, or C.** Suppose you collected data on the number of students attending your school for the past ten years. Which type of graph would be best for your data?

    A. histogram   **B.** line graph   **C.** bar graph

14. *Writing* Is the graph below appropriate for the data? Justify your answer.

Wholesale Shipments of Music Videos

Year	Units shipped (in millions)
1990	1.1
1992	7.6
1994	11.2
1996	16.9

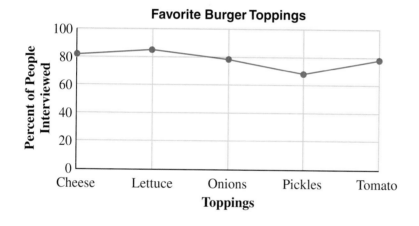

Favorite Burger Toppings

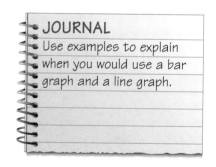

JOURNAL
Use examples to explain when you would use a bar graph and a line graph.

Mixed Review

Use the data at the right for Exercises 15–17.
(Lesson 1-1)

15. How many students are in the class?

16. What is the frequency of each response?

17. Which response is the most common?

Ages of Students in Mr. Harris's Class

Age	Number of Students
12	llll
13	lHt lHt lHt l
14	lHt lHt ll

Calculate. *(Previous Course)*

18. 4×27 **19.** $18 \div 3$ **20.** $84 - 23$ **21.** $37 + 19$ **22.** $63 \div 21$

1-3 Spreadsheets and Data Displays

What You'll Learn

1 To use a spreadsheet to make graphs

2 To interpret and make double bar and double line graphs

...And Why

By analyzing graphs, you can understand information presented in books, magazines, and newspapers.

Here's How

Look for questions that
- build understanding
- ✔ check understanding

THINK AND DISCUSS

1 Understanding Spreadsheets

A **spreadsheet** is a tool for organizing and analyzing data. A **cell** is a box where a row and a column meet.

■ **EXAMPLE 1** *Real-World Problem Solving*

Television What is the value in cell C3?

Households with VCR and Households with Cable TV
(in millions)

	A	B	C	
1	Year	VCR	Cable TV	
2	1986	32.5	42.0	column ↓
3	1988	56.2	48.6	← cell C3 ← row
4	1990	65.4	54.9	
5	1992	70.3	57.2	
6	1994	72.8	59.7	
7	1996	78.8	64.0	

Source: The Motion Picture Association of America and Nielsen

The value in cell C3 is 48.6, which represents 48.6 million households.

1. ✔ *Think About It* What is the value in cell B6?

2. Which cell tells the number of households with VCRs in 1990?

2 Double Bar and Double Line Graphs

You can use a spreadsheet program to create a graph of data. The graphs on the next page show the data above.

A **double bar graph** compares two sets of data. A **double line graph** compares changes over time of two sets of data. The **legend,** or key, identifies the data compared in a graph.

■ EXAMPLE 2

When did the number of households with VCRs exceed 60 million? When did the number with cable TV exceed 60 million?

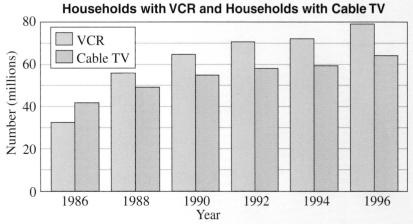

Households with VCR and Households with Cable TV

The number of households with VCRs exceeded 60 million in 1990. The number with cable TV exceeded 60 million in 1996.

■ EXAMPLE 3

Compare the VCR and cable TV data shown in the graph.

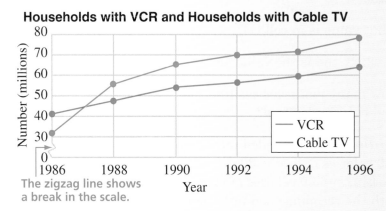

Households with VCR and Households with Cable TV

The zigzag line shows a break in the scale.

The number of households with VCRs exceeded the number with cable TV between 1986 and 1988. After 1988, the number with VCRs continued to be greater than the number with cable TV.

3. ✔*Think About It* Why would it be confusing if the two graphs above did not have a legend?

The first United States space shuttle was named *Enterprise* after NASA received 400,000 requests from *Star Trek* fans.

Work Together
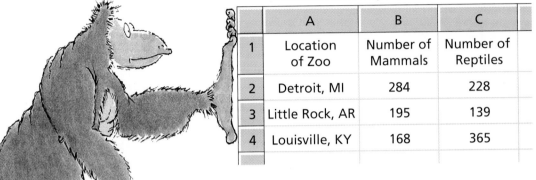

Work in a group. Use the data below.

Mammals and Reptiles in Three Zoos

	A	B	C
1	Location of Zoo	Number of Mammals	Number of Reptiles
2	Detroit, MI	284	228
3	Little Rock, AR	195	139
4	Louisville, KY	168	365

4. **a.** Enter the data in a spreadsheet program if possible. Then graph the data. Explain why you chose the graph you made.

b. *Open-ended* Write a question that could be answered using your graph.

EXERCISES *On Your Own*

Use the spreadsheet at the right for Exercises 1–4.

1. What value is in cell C3?

2. In which cell is the value 46?

3. How many more calories from fat are in cat food than in dog food?

Recommended Nutrition in Dog and Cat Foods
(out of 100 calories)

	A	B	C	D
1	animal	fat	protein	carbohydrates
2	dog	37	26	37
3	cat	46	28	26

4. *Writing* Recommended nutrition for humans in 100 calories of food is 30 calories of fat, 10 calories of protein, and 60 calories of carbohydrates. Compare this with the recommended nutrition for cats and dogs.

5. *Business* The double line graph at the right shows bicycle and automobile production over several years.
   a. In which year are the two lines closest together?
   b. *Reasoning* The two graphs begin to separate widely after the year you identified in part (a). What do you think could account for this?

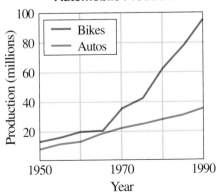

Worldwide Bicycle and Automobile Production

Source: Watchman Institute

Use the graph at the right for Exercises 6–8.

6. Which library circulated the most children's books? The most adults' books?

7. Which library had the greatest total circulation?

8. a. Which library had the greatest difference between the number of adults' books and children's books circulated?

   b. *Reasoning* Suppose you were the librarian in that community. About how many adults' books would you buy for each children's book?

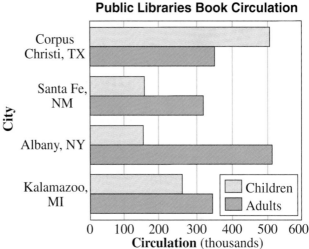

Public Libraries Book Circulation

Draw a graph for each set of data.

9. population of four western states

Population

	A	B	C
1	State	1980	1990
2	ID	943,935	1,006,749
3	NV	800,493	1,201,833
4	OR	2,633,105	2,842,321
5	WA	4,132,156	4,866,692

Source: *The Information Please Almanac*

10. spending on movie and theater/opera tickets

Total Spent on Tickets (in billions)

	A	B	C
1	Year	Movies	Theater/Opera
2	1991	4.7	4.5
3	1992	5.3	6.0
4	1993	5.0	6.8
5	1994	5.5	8.7
6	1995	5.6	9.0

Source: *The World Almanac*

Mixed Review

Money **Use the frequency table at the right for Exercises 11 and 12.** (*Lesson 1-1*)

11. a. Can you tell from the table how many people had exactly 17 pennies in their pockets?
    b. Why or why not?

12. Make a histogram of the data.

Pennies in Pocket

Number	Frequency	Number	Frequency
1–5	12	21–25	5
6–10	6	26–30	6
11–15	10	31–35	0
16–20	7	36–40	4

Dividing Whole Numbers

Before Lesson 1-4

The calculation below indicates the vocabulary associated with division.

$$\begin{array}{r} 7 \quad \leftarrow \text{quotient} \\ \text{divisor} \longrightarrow 6\overline{)45} \quad \leftarrow \text{dividend} \\ -42 \\ \hline 3 \quad \leftarrow \text{remainder} \end{array}$$

You can write the answer as 7 R3.

To divide, first estimate the quotient by rounding the divisor, the dividend, or both. Then use these steps:

Step 1 Find each digit of the quotient by dividing from left to right.

Step 2 Multiply and subtract.

Step 3 Repeat Steps 1 and 2 until the remainder is less than the divisor.

■ EXAMPLE

Find each quotient.

a. $741 \div 8$

Estimate: $720 \div 8 = 90$

$$\begin{array}{r} 93 \\ 8\overline{)744} \\ -72 \\ \hline 24 \\ -24 \\ \hline 0 \end{array}$$

b. $838 \div 43$

Estimate: $800 \div 40 = 20$

$$\begin{array}{r} 19 \; R21 \quad \leftarrow \\ 43\overline{)838} \\ -43 \\ \hline 408 \\ -387 \\ \hline 21 \quad \leftarrow \text{remainder} \end{array}$$

Find each quotient.

1. $4\overline{)60}$
2. $8\overline{)72}$
3. $7\overline{)92}$
4. $3\overline{)845}$
5. $6\overline{)78}$

6. $6\overline{)469}$
7. $3\overline{)653}$
8. $8\overline{)648}$
9. $9\overline{)231}$
10. $4\overline{)415}$

11. $43\overline{)273}$
12. $52\overline{)281}$
13. $69\overline{)207}$
14. $38\overline{)121}$
15. $81\overline{)433}$

16. $94 \div 4$
17. $66 \div 9$
18. $90 \div 5$
19. $68 \div 6$
20. $58 \div 8$

21. $382 \div 72$
22. $580 \div 68$
23. $279 \div 43$
24. $232 \div 27$
25. $331 \div 93$

1-4

Mean, Median, and Mode

What You'll Learn

1 To find mean, median, and mode

2 To choose mean, median, or mode to describe data

...And Why

You can analyze data from surveys using mean, median, and mode.

Here's How

Look for questions that
- build understanding
- ✔ check understanding

20 Responses to "How Many Times a Day Do You Drink from the Water Fountain?"		
0	1	1
5	2	10
2	3	5
1	5	2
2	3	4
3	5	5
2	2	

THINK AND DISCUSS

1 *Finding Mean, Median, and Mode*

To make a general statement about a set of data, you can find the *mean, median,* or *mode* of the data. The **mean** is the sum of the data divided by the number of items in the set of data. The mean is often referred to as the *average*.

■ **EXAMPLE 1**   *Real-World Problem Solving*

▦ *Survey Data*   Find the mean of the data at the left below.

First find the sum of the responses.

63 ⊞ 20 ⊟ 3.15 ← Divide the sum by the number of responses.

The mean is 3.15. These students drink from the water fountain about three times a day.

1. ✔ *Try It Out*   Earl conducted the survey. Suppose he forgot to include his own data. He does not drink from the fountain. What is the mean when you include this data?

The **median** is the middle number in a set of data that is written in order. The median of an even number of data items is the mean of the two middle items.

■ **EXAMPLE 2**

Find the median of the water fountain data in the chart.

First write the data in order from least to greatest.

0 1 1 1 2 2 2 2 2 2 3 3 3 4 5 5 5 5 5 10

⌐⌐⌐ The two middle items are 2 and 3.

2 + 3 = 5   ← Find the mean of the
5 ÷ 2 = 2.5   two middle items.

The median is 2.5.

2. ✔ *Try It Out*   Find the median of the data below.
   71 23 54 65 22 23 71 59 34 37 42

1-4 Mean, Median, and Mode   **17**

Favorite Flowers of Ten People Surveyed

rose	rose
pansy	peony
pansy	daisy
daisy	rose
daisy	orchid

The data item that occurs most often is the **mode.** A set of data may have more than one mode. There is no mode when all the data items occur the same number of times.

■ EXAMPLE 3

Find the mode of the data at the left.

Make a frequency table to organize the data.

rose	pansy	peony	daisy	orchid
III	II	I	III	I

There are two modes, rose and daisy.

3. ✔ *Try It Out* Find the mode(s) of the following data.
   17 15 23 22 12 17 22 25 36 22 17

▼ *Describing Data with Mean, Median, or Mode*

A data item that is far apart from the rest of the data is called an **outlier.** The outlier usually affects the mean of a set of data more than it affects the median or the mode.

4. ✔ *Try It Out* What is the outlier of the following data?
   5 10 12 13 8 9 5 6 26 11 5
   a. Find the mean with and without the outlier.
   b. How did the outlier affect the mean?

■ EXAMPLE 4

Which best describes each situation, the mean, the median, or the mode? Explain.

a. the favorite book of students in the third grade

   Mode; use the mode when the data are not numerical or when choosing the most popular item.

b. the number of students in each class at school

   Mean; use the mean when there are no outliers to distort the data.

c. the number of pets your classmates have

   Mean or median; use the median when there are outliers that may distort the data or use the median to describe the middle value.

Work Together

Work with a partner to collect data on one of the topics at the right or a topic of your own. Collect at least 10 pieces of data.

5. Find the mean, median, and mode of the data.

6. Does the mean, median, or mode best describe the data you collected?

DATA CHOICES

- Number of buttons on people's clothing
- Number of pages in a book
- Number of times the letter "e" appears in a paragraph

EXERCISES *On Your Own*

Find the mean, median, and mode of each set.

1. hours of practice before a concert
2 1 0 1 5 3 4 2 0 3 1 2

2. one team's hockey scores
3 2 1 3 0 3 1 1 2 3 3

3. daily low temperatures (°F) for a week
55 58 62 62 65 67 72

4. number of grocery purchases of the first nine people in an express check-out lane
3 6 2 5 3 4 8 3 2

5. number of seconds for a 200-m run
27 30 25 28 29 33 32 25 25 35

6. number of hours of homework per night
1 2 3 2 3 3 2 3 1 4

7. *Environment* Fifty people live in a state where there is a deposit on aluminum cans. They were asked whether they returned their cans. Their responses are at the right.
   a. What is the mode?
   b. *Reasoning* From the data at the right, is it reasonable to conclude that only one out of fifty people gives to charity?

Do You Return Aluminum Cans?

Response	Frequency
Give them to a charity	1
Never	4
Sometimes	12
Always	33

8. *Data Collection* Roll one number cube 20 times. Make a frequency table to record the number you roll each time. Find the mean, median, and mode of your data.

9. a. The total weight of all the students on a football team is 2,730 lb. The mean is 130 lb. How many students are on the team?
   b. The median weight is 125 lb. Only one student weighs 125 lb. How many students weigh more than 125 lb?

10. *Education* A Jonesburg Middle School seventh-grade social studies class took a test recently. The class scores are shown in the tally at the right.
    a. Find the mean, median, and mode of the data.
    b. What is the outlier in this set of data?
    c. Does the outlier raise or lower the mean?
    d. Which measure—the mean, the median, or the mode—most accurately reflects how the class did as a whole? Justify your answer.

Grade	Tally	Grade	Tally
60	I	85	ᚼᚼᚼ IIII
78	III	87	II
80	ᚼᚼᚼ III	91	I
81	II	94	I

Birthday Bash

The Rose Hill Retirement Home celebrated seven birthdays last Sunday. Mrs. Ullsca turned 102, while the "baby" of the group, Mrs. Hansen, turned a mere 78. Family members and friends gathered for the party. Other birthdays celebrated were Mr. Harlem, 79; Mr. Joyla, 84; Mr. Ajayi, 85; Miss Rugas, 81; and Mrs. Greene, 79.

11. a. Find the mean, median, and mode of the data found in the article above. Round the mean to the nearest whole number.
    b. Is there an outlier? If there is, identify it.
    c. Does the mean, the median, or the mode most accurately reflect the age of those celebrating a birthday? Explain.

12. *Writing* Ten people were surveyed about the number of times a person's teeth should be brushed each day. Their responses are shown in the table at the right. Explain why the mean is not a good representation of this data.

How Many Times a Day Should You Brush Your Teeth?

Response	Frequency
3 times	9
10 times	1

13. **Choose A, B, C, or D.** Dominic's test grades in his Spanish class are 89, 94, 82, 84, 98. What score must Dominic make on his next exam to average 90 points?

    A. 100   B. 97   C. 93   D. 90

14. *Open-ended* Find the number of books ten people read last summer. Find the mean, median, and mode of the data.

15. **a.** *Science* Calculate the mean life expectancy for the animals in the table.
   b. What is the median of the data? What is the mode?
   c. *Reasoning* Does the mean, median, or mode describe the data the best? Explain.

Average Life Expectancy of Some Hoofed Animals

Animal	Years	Animal	Years
Bison	15	Goat	8
Cow	15	Horse	20
Deer	8	Moose	12
Donkey	12	Pig	10
Elk	15	Sheep	12

Mixed Review

Would you use a double bar graph or a double line graph to display each of the following. Why? *(Lesson 1-3)*

16. the change in taxes for the average household for two cities over the last ten years

17. the cost of seven different items at two different grocery stores

Estimate. *(Previous Course)*

18. 197×3 19. 42×19 20. $359 \div 60$ 21. $88 - 32$ 22. $128 + 98$

23. *Choose a Strategy* Find two numbers that have a sum of 30 and a product of 81.

✓ CHECKPOINT 1 *Lessons 1-1 through 1-4*

1. Make a frequency table and a line plot of the data below.
   5 7 8 3 5 4 6 7 8 9 1 2 5 4 2 1 3

Find the mean, median, and mode of the data below.

2. *Sports* golf scores for 18-hole games
   120 112 130 128 124
   117 118 117 121 113

3. *Cars* average miles per gallon
   25 28 23 27 21 22 25
   24 25 27 28 29 22 24

4. Graph the data below. Explain why you chose the graph you drew.

Art Show Attendance

Day	Sun.	Mon.	Tues.	Wed.	Thur.	Fri.	Sat.
Number of Adults	54	29	22	28	12	15	49

Stem-and-Leaf Plots

What You'll Learn

1 To organize and display data using stem-and-leaf plots

2 To find range using stem-and-leaf plots

...And Why

Stem-and-leaf plots give you a visual picture of data while displaying the data values.

Here's How

Look for questions that
- build understanding
- ✔ check understanding

THINK AND DISCUSS

1 *Displaying Data Using Stem-and-Leaf Plots*

A **stem-and-leaf plot** is a display that organizes your data by showing each item in order. The leaf is the last digit to the right. The stem is the remaining digit or digits.

leaf ————→
10.6
stem ————↑

leaf ————→
27
stem ————↑

■ **EXAMPLE 1** *Real-World Problem Solving*

Nutrition Use the table at the left below. Draw a stem-and-leaf plot of the data.

Choose the stems. For this data, the stems are made using the values in the ones place. Draw a line to the right of the stems.

stems ——→
$$\begin{array}{c|} 0 \\ 1 \\ 2 \end{array}$$

For this data, the leaves are the values in the tenths place.

$$\begin{array}{c|cccc} 0 & 7 & 7 & 9 \\ 1 & 1 & 6 & 4 & 5 \quad \longleftarrow \text{leaves} \\ 2 & 6 & 1 & 6 \end{array}$$

Arrange the leaves from least to greatest. Include a key to explain what your stems and leaves represent.

$$\begin{array}{c|cccc} 0 & 7 & 7 & 9 \\ 1 & 1 & 4 & 5 & 6 \\ 2 & 1 & 6 & 6 \end{array}$$
$0\,|\,7$ means 0.7 ←—key

1. ✔ *Try It Out* Make a stem-and-leaf plot of the data below.

Wind Speeds Recorded During a Storm
(in miles per hour)

9   14   30   16   18   25   29   25   38   34   33

Iron in Three Ounces of High-Protein Foods

Food	Iron (in milligrams)
Clams	2.6
Crab meat	1.1
Salmon	0.7
Tuna	1.6
Ground beef	2.1
Steak	2.6
Lamb	1.4
Ham	0.7
Chicken	0.9
Turkey	1.5

Source: *Home and Garden Bulletin, No. 72*

▼2 Finding Range

The **range** of a set of data is the difference between the greatest and least data items.

■ EXAMPLE 2

Find the range of the data in the stem-and-leaf plot.

```
12 | 4   4   8        ← least data item
13 | 3   7   8   8
14 |
15 | 2   7   9        ← greatest data item
     12 | 4 means 12.4
```

15.9 − 12.4 = 3.5

The range of the data is 3.5.

2. ✔ **Try It Out** What is the range of the data in Example 1?

You can also find the range of data in a list.

3. ✔ **Try It Out** What is the range of the data given below?
Alaska mountain heights (ft): 16,390 14,573 20,320
16,550 15,885 14,163 14,831 16,237 17,400 16,286

Work Together _____ *Using Stem-and-Leaf Plots*

Social Studies Work with a partner.

4. Make a stem-and-leaf plot.

5. Find the mean, median, and mode of the data. Round the mean to the nearest whole number.

6. Does the mean, the median, or the mode best describe the data?

7. What is the range of the data?

8. ♣ *Open-Ended* Write a question that you could answer using your stem-and-leaf plot.

Counties in Western States

State	Number of Counties
Arizona	15
California	58
Colorado	63
Idaho	44
Montana	56
Nevada	16
New Mexico	33
Oregon	36
Utah	29
Washington	39
Wyoming	23

Source: *The World Almanac*

Create a stem-and-leaf plot for each set of data.

1. sales of twelve companies (millions of dollars)
   1.3   1.4   2.3   1.4   2.4   2.5
   3.9   1.4   1.3   2.5   3.6   1.4

2. heights of giant sunflowers (in inches)
   98   99   94   87   83   74
   69   88   78   99   100   87   77

3. high temperatures (°F) in the desert
   99   113   112   98   100   103   101
   111   104   108   109   112   113   118

4. heights of ceilings in older homes (in feet)
   9.7   12.3   10.2   11.5   14.1   9.6
   13.7   14.4   11.5   9.7   11.6   11.5

Use the stem-and-leaf plot at the right for Exercises 5–8.

5. How many data items are there?

6. What is the least value given? The greatest value given?

7. How many values are greater than 65?

8. **Choose A, B, C, or D.** Which of the following is most likely the source of the data in the stem-and-leaf plot?

   A. test scores for a class
   B. average monthly temperatures in Dallas (in °F)
   C. depth of 12 swimming pools (in feet)
   D. numbers of books in New York City libraries

```
4 | 3  6  7
5 | 1  2
6 | 1  7
7 | 1  8
8 | 2  6  8
      8 | 2 means 82
```

The stem-and-leaf plot at the right shows kilometers walked during a benefit walk. Use it for Exercises 9–13.

9. What place values are the leaves?

10. How many data items are there?

11. How many people walked more than 19 km?

12. Find the range.

13. *Writing* How would you find the median?

14. *Data Collection* Measure the width of the hands of at least ten people. Measure using metric units. Make a stem-and-leaf plot of the data you collect.

```
16 | 1  1  2  3  5  5
17 | 0  2  2
18 | 4  5  8  9
19 | 3  6  7  9  9  9
      19 | 3 means 19.3
```

15. Sports The table at the right shows the career wins for ten women who had won the most golf tournaments during their careers as of 1996.

  a. Make a stem-and-leaf plot of the data.

  b. Find the range of the data.

Career Wins for Top Women Golfers

Name	Wins	Name	Wins
Kathy Whitworth	88	Nancy Lopez	47
Mickey Wright	82	JoAnne Carner	42
Patty Berg	57	Sandra Haynie	42
Betsy Rawls	55	Carol Mann	38
Louise Suggs	50	Patty Sheehan	35

Source: *Sports Illustrated Sports Almanac*

Mixed Review

Estimate. *(Previous Course)*

16. $122 + 237$ **17.** $393 - 27$ **18.** 48×47 **19.** 9×119 **20.** $5,250 - 4,798$

Compare. Use <, >, or =. *(Previous Course)*

21. $12 \times 3 \; \blacksquare \; 45 - 9$ **22.** $24 \div 2 \; \blacksquare \; 3 \times 6$ **23.** $9 \times 6 \; \blacksquare \; 8 \times 7$ **24.** $81 \div 3 \; \blacksquare \; 9 \times 4$

25. Choose a Strategy A student is standing in the middle of a line of students. There are 23 students ahead of him. How many students are in the line?

Math at Work

POLLSTER

Pollsters interview people to find out their opinions and their preferences. Pollsters use math to analyze data, finding the mean, median, mode, and range to get an overall look at the data they collect. They often graph data to display their findings.

Visit this Gallup Web site for more information: www.gallup.com

EXPLORATION

Box-and-Whisker Plots

After Lesson 1-5

A box-and-whisker plot is another way to display data. A **box-and-whisker plot** shows you how the data are distributed. The diagram at the right identifies the important features of a box-and-whisker plot.

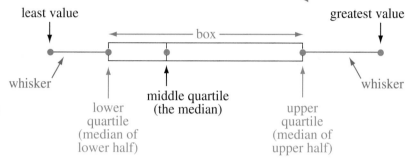

least value | greatest value

box

whisker

whisker

lower quartile (median of lower half)

middle quartile (the median)

upper quartile (median of upper half)

■ EXAMPLE

The director of a computer center recorded the number of users each hour for one day. The results were 13, 14, 22, 25, 30, 29, 27, 18, 19, 14, 18, 19. Draw a box-and-whisker plot of the data.

least value → 13 14 14 18 18 19 19 22 25 27 29 30 ← greatest value

List the data in order.

The lower quartile is 16.   The middle quartile is 19.   The upper quartile is 26.

Find the quartiles.

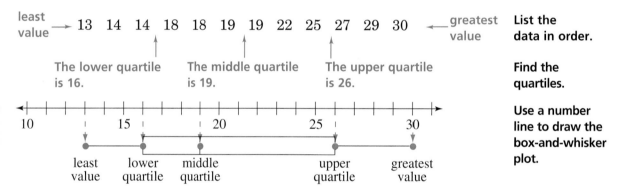

least value   lower quartile   middle quartile   upper quartile   greatest value

Use a number line to draw the box-and-whisker plot.

1. **Reasoning** In the Example, why is the middle quartile not in the middle of the box?

Create a box-and-whisker plot for each data set.

2. 2 3 5 7 7 8 8 10 14
   14 15 15

3. 32 34 34 36 40 42 42 42
   46 54 54 56

4. 8 11 11 13 14 14 16
   16 16 17 19 22 24

5. 62 55 60 86 62 65 68 70 55
   60 65 62 58 60 62 68 65

6. **a.** In Exercise 5, what is the outlier?
   b. **Reasoning** How does the outlier affect the way the box-and-whisker plot looks?

1-6 Use Logical Reasoning

Problem Solving Strategies

Draw a Diagram
Guess and Test
Look for a Pattern
Make a Model
Make a Table
Simulate a Problem
Solve a Simpler Problem
Too Much or Too Little
  Information
✔ Use Logical Reasoning
Use Multiple Strategies
Work Backward
Write an Equation

THINK AND DISCUSS

Have you ever solved a logic puzzle? They can be fun — if you know a good strategy!

Sample Problem ....

Keesha, Frieda, Pascal, Jered, and Mika are each studying different foreign languages. Mika gave Mr. Sanchez, his neighbor, the following information.

- The woman studying Italian is not Keesha. Also, Keesha is not studying German.

- Frieda and Pascal do not study Mandarin Chinese, but one of them does study French.

- Keesha, Frieda, and Jered drive to their classes together. One of them studies German, one studies Spanish, and one studies Italian.

Mr. Sanchez thought for a while, used paper and pencil to organize the information, and told Mika exactly what language each person was studying. Who is studying which language?

Bonjour!

Buon giorno!

Guten Tag!

¡Buenos dias!

你好嗎

....

READ

Read for understanding. Summarize the problem.

Think about what you are being asked.

1. What information are you given?

2. What information do you need to find?

PLAN

Decide on a strategy.

Logical reasoning can help you eliminate impossibilities, organize alternatives, and find a solution. Consider the first clue.

3. **a.** Is Keesha studying Italian? German?
   b. Is she studying French? What information gives you the answer?
   c. What language is Keesha studying? Which clues did you use?

 **SOLVE**
Try the strategy.

A table can help you organize your thoughts. Consider each piece of information separately. Write an X for choices you eliminate, and a dot when you know what language a person is studying.

	French	German	Italian	Mandarin Chinese	Spanish
Keesha	X	X	X	X	●
Frieda	▪	▪	▪	▪	X
Mika	▪	▪	▪	▪	X
Pascal	▪	▪	▪	▪	X
Jered	▪	▪	▪	▪	X

4. In the row for Keesha, there is an X in every box but one. Why?

5. In the column for Spanish, there is an X in every box but one. Why?

6. Copy and complete the table. Find the language each person is taking.

 LOOK BACK
Think about how you solved the problem.

7. How did the table help you solve this problem?

EXERCISES *On Your Own*

Use logical reasoning to solve.

1. *Sports* Three lockers contain the school's basketballs, footballs, and soccer balls. Each locker contains only one type of ball, but the labels on them are incorrect. The locker marked "footballs" has basketballs. Which balls are in the locker labeled "basketballs," and which are in the locker labeled "soccer balls"?

2. Skye's class sold calendars to raise money for a field trip. The top four sellers were Skye, Amalie, Mandela, and Scott. Skye sold more calendars than Amalie, but fewer than Mandela. Scott also sold more than Amalie, but fewer than Skye. Who sold the most calendars in the class?

Use any strategy to solve each problem. Show your work.

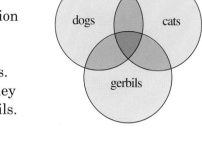

dogs cats

gerbils

3. Use a diagram like the one at the right and the information below to determine how many students had no pets.
   • Of 50 students surveyed, 30 had cats and 25 had dogs.
   • Sixteen students had both cats and dogs, but no gerbils.
   • Five reported that they had only gerbils. Four noted they had both dogs and gerbils. Two had both cats and gerbils.
   • Only one student had all three pets mentioned.

4. Mato has 10 loose identical red socks and 10 loose identical blue socks in his sock drawer. What is the least number of socks he would have to choose to be sure to find a matched pair?

5. The African pavilion at the zoo has ostriches and zebras. The number of legs is 14 more than twice the number of heads. Find the number of zebras.

6. Popsville is 20 mi from Topsville. Mopsville is 5 mi from Popsville along the same road. How far could Mopsville be from Topsville?

Mixed Review

Use the stem-and-leaf plot at the right for Exercises 7–9. *(Lesson 1-5)*

7. What number has stem 1 and leaf 0?

8. Find the mean, median, and mode.

9. Which measure in Exercise 8 could Trinh use to convince her parents that she has plenty of time left for homework?

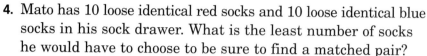

Miles Trinh Biked per Day

0	5 5 7 8 8 9 9
1	0 0 0 1 2 7 8
2	2 5 8 8 9 9

2 | 5 means 25

Find the value of each expression. *(Previous Course)*

10. $123 - 75$ 11. 24×8 12. $60 \div 4$ 13. $292 + 41$ 14. 57×3

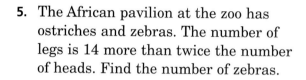

CHAPTER PROJECT

PROJECT LINK: ANALYZING

Use the picture you found for the Project Link on page 7. To estimate the number of people in the crowd, first divide the picture into equal rectangular sections. Count the number of people in several sections. Be careful! The people in the front of the picture appear larger than those in the back. Find the mean (average) number of people in a rectangle. Use your average to estimate the number of people in the picture.

What You'll Learn

1 To identify a random sample

2 To write survey questions

...And Why

Candidates for public office use samples and surveys to measure public opinion.

Here's How

Look for questions that
- **∷** build understanding
- ✔ check understanding

Work Together _____ *Analyzing a Survey*

Work with a partner to analyze the situation below.

1. **∷** *Analyze* In the presidential election of 1948, Thomas Dewey and Harry Truman were candidates for president. On the day of the election, the people taking election polls said that Mr. Dewey had won. The polling was done by telephone. Why do you think the pollsters were wrong?

THINK AND DISCUSS

1 *Identifying a Sample*

In the presidential election of 1948, the people taking polls could not survey all 50 million voters. To collect data from a whole group, or **population**, is usually impractical. A sample of the population can often provide enough information.

2. **∷** *Reasoning* Suppose you are studying the eating habits of college students. What question could you ask to decide if Joe Smith is a member of the population you are studying?

You can use a **random sample** to predict the responses of a population. A sample is random if the members of the population have an equal chance of being selected.

■ EXAMPLE 1

Suppose you are surveying customers at a mall to find which stores they shop at the most. Would you get a random sample of customers if you stood at one entrance to the mall?

Customers entering at one entrance may be shopping at only the stores that are near that entrance. So this would not be a random sample.

3. For Example 1, how could you get a random sample?

President Truman celebrated his victory by showing a headline written before the vote was counted.

▼2 *Writing Survey Questions*

Biased questions are unfair questions. They can make assumptions that may or may not be true or make one answer seem better than another.

■ **EXAMPLE 2** *Real-World Problem Solving*

Television Which of the following questions is biased? Which is fair? Why?

a. "Do you think the extreme violence of Saturday morning cartoons affects young, impressionable children?"

This question is biased. It assumes cartoons are violent. Also the words "extreme" and "young, impressionable" may influence responses.

b. "Is there violence in some Saturday morning cartoons?"

This question is fair. It does not make any assumptions about cartoons or the people watching them.

4. ✔ *Try It Out* Write a fair survey question about the time of day your school starts. Then write a biased question.

EXERCISES *On Your Own*

1. *Public Transportation* Jeremy is an urban planner. He wants to know how the city's bus drivers are affected by work crews in the streets. How can he survey a random sample?

You want to survey teenagers in Idaho about their snacking habits. Tell whether each of the following will give you a random sample. Justify each of your answers.

2. You ask five teenagers in a group to name their favorite snack.

3. For three mornings you stand at the same place on Broadway Avenue in Boise, Idaho. You survey all the teenagers who pass you.

4. You select teenagers from lists of middle school and high school students in each Idaho county. You survey them by telephone.

5. Suppose you are gathering information about visitors to Yosemite National Park. You survey every tenth person entering the park. Would you get a random sample of visitors? Why or why not?

6. *Writing* Tell how you would find a random sample of the students in your school.

Tell whether the following questions are biased or fair. Explain.

7. Do you prefer getting invigorating exercise or being a couch potato?

8. Do you prefer to exercise or watch television?

9. Do you prefer rock music or jazz?

10. Do you prefer, harsh rock music or soothing jazz?

11. Explain how you can tell if a survey question is biased.

Mixed Review

Find the mean, median, and mode of each set of data. Identify any outliers and tell how they affect the mean. *(Lesson 1-4)*

12. 122   114   113   116   120
123   119   117   123   111

13. 54   99   50   49   55   50
49   50   58   47   55

14. Inez surveyed a group of students at Midtown Middle School about the number of books they read over the summer. Her results are at the right. *(Lesson 1-1)*
  a. What should be the title of the histogram?
  b. What should be the label of each axis?
  c. How many people answered Inez's survey?

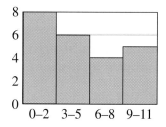

CHAPTER PROJECT

PROJECT LINK: SURVEYING

Suppose you want to know what kinds of foods people might buy during a sporting event or a concert. Write a fair survey question. Survey a random sample of the students in your grade. Use a graph to display your results.

Extra Practice, Lesson 1-7, page 514

PROBLEM SOLVING PRACTICE

Choose the best answer.

1. A sports reporter rounded the attendance at a professional basketball game to the nearest thousand. How did he report the attendance of 14,538 people?

   A. 10,000   **B.** 14,000
   C. 14,500   **D.** 15,000

2. Danzell went on a five-day fishing trip with his family. The number of fish that he caught each day was 6, 4, 7, 2, and 6. What was the mean (average) number of fish that he caught each day?

   F. 2   **G.** 3
   H. 4   **J.** 5

3. Mario's Sandwich Shop received orders from people at three different addresses on the same street: 2525, 2432, and 2784. In which of the following ways should the orders be delivered to take the least time?

   A. 2432   2525   2784
   B. 2525   2432   2784
   C. 2784   2432   2525
   D. 2432   2784   2525

Please note that items 4–8 have *five* answer choices.

4. Jim has a part-time job. He works 8 to 12 hours each week. Is it reasonable to assume that during four weeks he will work –

   F. less than 30 hours
   G. exactly 30 hours
   H. more than 30 hours
   J. exactly 50 hours
   K. more than 50 hours

Favorite Juice Drink

Juice	Number of Students
Orange	11
Apple	8
Pineapple	3
Grapefruit	2
Tomato	5

5. The table above shows the results of a survey on students' favorite juice drinks. How many flavors of juice were chosen by more than 5 students?

   A. 1   **B.** 2   **C.** 3
   D. 4   **E.** 5

6. Use the table above. Which type of juice is the mode?

   F. Orange
   G. Apple
   H. Pineapple
   J. Grapefruit
   K. Tomato

7. Maria was reading a novel for a book report. After four days, she had read 340 pages. On the fifth day, Maria read 88 pages. A reasonable conclusion would be that Maria read —

   A. less than 55 pages each day
   B. between 55 and 79 pages each day
   C. between 80 and 95 pages each day
   D. more than 96 pages each day
   E. Not Here

8. Which set of data has 24 for the median?

   F. 24, 24, 22, 23   **G.** 23, 27, 25, 22
   H. 22, 24, 27, 20   **J.** 23, 27, 20, 28
   K. Not Here

Using Data to Persuade

What You'll Learn

1 To recognize how presentation of data can influence opinion

...And Why

You can evaluate displays of data for their accuracy and determine if the displays are trying to influence you.

Here's How

Look for questions that
- ⊞ build understanding
- ✔ check understanding

Work Together

Analyzing Data

Business You and your partner are struggling to make ends meet on a peanut farm. You decide to look for outside investors. You compile the data below. Decide how you will go about convincing people to invest in your peanut farm.

Peanut Facts

Average size of farm: 100 acres Peanut seeds planted: 100 pounds/acre Cost of seed: $.70/pound Average yield: 2,705 pounds/acre Average profit: $63/acre	548 peanuts make one 12-ounce jar of peanut butter. 30,000 peanut butter sandwiches can be made from one acre of peanuts. 800 million pounds of peanut butter are expected to be eaten each year.	In two tablespoons of peanut butter • there are 210 calories. • there are 0 mg of cholesterol. • there are 16 g of fat. • there are 7 g of protein.

Source: Peanut Advisory Board

1. ⊞*Analyze* Which data would convince investors to invest in your farm?

2. Which data would you not present to possible investors?

3. One investor heard that peanut butter is high in cholesterol. How would you respond to this?

THINK AND DISCUSS

Data is often presented to influence you. As you look at data displays, consider these questions: Is the information shown accurately? Is the presentation trying to influence you?

■ **EXAMPLE 1** *Real-World Problem Solving*

Business Which graph is more likely to convince someone to invest in a peanut farm? Why?

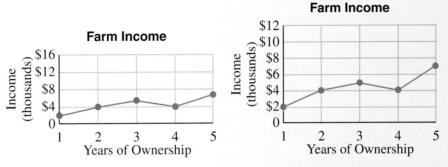

The second graph is more persuasive. The vertical scale makes the farm income seem greater, which makes the farm look like a good investment.

4. ✔*Try It Out* Suppose you do not want to emphasize that the income decreased one year. Which graph from Example 1 would you use? Why?

5. ⊞*Reasoning* What can you look for to tell if a graph was made to influence you?

■ **EXAMPLE 2** *Real-World Problem Solving*

Business The poster at the left is part of an ad campaign at Harry's Hamburger Heaven. Below are data about Harry's hamburgers. Is the ad misleading?

Item	Calories	Fat (g)	Average Number Sold Daily
Kiddie Burger	480	35	80
Hamburger Plus	575	42	68
Health Burger	580	40	65
Golden Fried Hamburger	660	57	43
Burger Deluxe	700	55	75

Most of the types of hamburgers made and most of the ones sold have more than 500 calories. So, the ad is misleading.

6. ⊞*Reasoning* How would you change the ad to better reflect the data?

1. **Sports** Use the data at the right.
   a. Make a line graph that shows little change in the number of people running in the Boston Marathon.
   b. Make a second line graph that shows great change in the number of people running the Boston Marathon.
   c. **Advertising** You want the sponsors of the Boston Marathon to increase their contributions. Which of your graphs would you use? Explain.

Boston Marathon Entrants

Year	Women	Men
1989	1,743	5,320
1991	1,562	7,124
1993	1,861	7,069
1995	2,175	7,241
1997	2,998	7,473

2. a. **Open-ended** Find a graph in a newspaper or magazine. Describe the data presented.
   b. Is the graph trying to influence you? Explain.

3. **Television** Use the data at the right to make two different histograms. One will show that there is little relationship between income and hours of television watched. The other will show that there is a strong relationship between income and hours of television watched.

Television Viewing and Income

Annual Income	Hours of TV per Week
Under $30,000	53
$30,000 to $39,999	49
$40,000 to $49,999	48
$50,000 to $59,999	47
$60,000 and more	46

4. **Nutrition** Farnaz asked students at her school, "What's your favorite pizza topping?" She drew the double bar graph below. Explain why the graph is misleading.

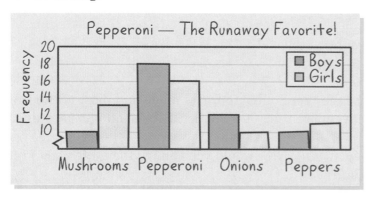

5. Chantay has a 93, 83, 76, 92, and 76 on her social studies exams.

    a. Chantay wants to show her parents how well she is doing in her class. Does the mean, the median, or the mode make her grades look the best?

    b. Should her teacher use the mean, the median, or the mode to encourage Chantay to study harder?

6. *Medicine* The graph below and the data at the right show measles cases in the United States over several years.

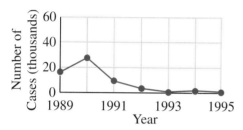

    a. *Reasoning* What does this graph seem to say about the outbreak of measles in 1990?

    b. Draw a better graph. Give your graph a title.

Measles Cases Reported in the United States

Year	Number of Cases (in thousands)
1989	18.2
1990	27.8
1991	9.6
1992	2.2
1993	0.3
1994	1.0
1995	0.3

Source: *Statistical Abstract*

Environment **Use the graphs below.**

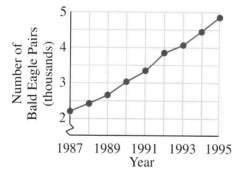
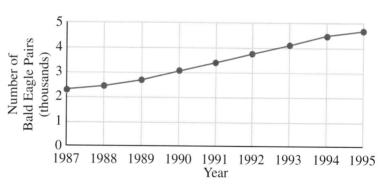

7. What is the first graph trying to tell you about the change in the number of bald eagle pairs? Write a title for the graph.

8. What is the second graph trying to tell you about the change in the number of bald eagle pairs? Write a title for the graph.

9. Estimate the range of the data.

10. *Writing* Does either graph accurately show the change in the number of bald eagle pairs without being misleading? Explain.

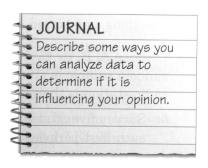

JOURNAL
Describe some ways you can analyze data to determine if it is influencing your opinion.

2 *Interpreting Scatter Plots*

You can use scatter plots to look for *trends*, or relationships. In the bookbag graph there is a relationship between the number of books in a bag and the weight of the bag. As the number of books increases, the weight of the bag generally increases.

You can examine a scatter plot to see whether there is a trend and what kind of trend is shown.

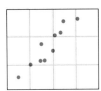 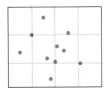

Positive trend

As one set of values increases, the other set tends to increase.

Negative trend

As one set of values increases, the other set tends to decrease.

No trend

The points show no relationship.

■ **EXAMPLE** *Real-World Problem Solving*

Describe the trend in the scatter plot.

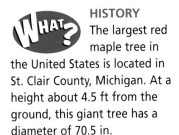

HISTORY
The largest red maple tree in the United States is located in St. Clair County, Michigan. At a height about 4.5 ft from the ground, this giant tree has a diameter of 70.5 in.

Source: *The Guinness Book of Records*

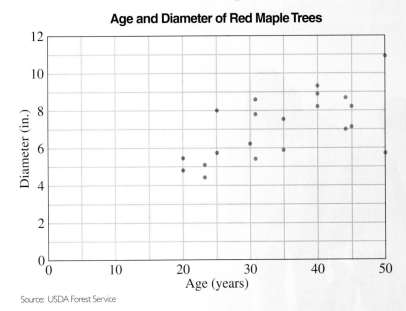

Source: USDA Forest Service

There is a positive trend between the age of a red maple tree and its diameter.

3. ✔ *Try It Out* What kind of trend do you see in the bookbag scatter plot on page 39?

Work Together

Work with a partner.
Use the data at the right.

4. Make a scatter plot using the average cost of a ticket and the number of people attending movies.

5. a. What labels did you choose for the axes?
   b. What intervals did you choose for the axes?

6. ⚒*Analyze* What sort of trend do you see?

Movie Attendance

Year	Average Ticket Cost (dollars)	Admissions (millions)
1982	2.94	1,175
1984	3.36	1,199
1986	3.71	1,017
1988	4.11	1,085
1990	4.23	1,189
1992	4.15	1,173
1994	4.18	1,292
1996	4.42	1,339

Source: Motion Picture Association of America

EXERCISES *On Your Own*

Biology **Use the data at the right.**

1. Can you see any pattern in the wolf population? In the moose population?

2. a. Make a scatter plot to compare the moose population and wolf population.
   b. *Reasoning* Do you see any relationship between the two populations? Explain.

Tell what trend you would expect to see in scatter plots comparing the following sets of data. Explain your reasoning.

3. the number of children in a family and the number of pets

4. hours spent watching television and hours spent studying

5. area of a state and the number of governors the state has had

Moose and Wolf Populations on Isle Royale, Michigan

Year	Wolf	Moose	Year	Wolf	Moose
1980	50	664	1989	11	1,397
1981	30	650	1990	15	1,216
1982	14	700	1991	12	1,313
1983	23	900	1992	12	1,600
1984	24	811	1993	13	1,879
1985	22	1,062	1994	15	1,770
1986	20	1,025	1995	16	2,422
1987	16	1,380	1996	22	1,178
1988	12	1,653			

Source: National Park Service, Isle Royale, Michigan

6. *Social Studies* Use the data at the right.
   a. Make a scatter plot showing the relationship between the number of households and number of people per household.
   b. *Writing* Do you see a trend in your scatter plot? Support your answer.

7. **Choose A, B, or C.** Carmella made a scatter plot comparing the daily temperature and the number of people at a beach. Which of the three scatter plots below most likely represents the data? Explain your choice.

Households in the United States

Year	Number of Households (in millions)	Number of People per Household
1950	43.6	3.37
1960	52.8	3.33
1970	63.4	3.14
1980	80.8	2.76
1990	93.3	2.63

Source: *Statistical Abstract of the United States*

A.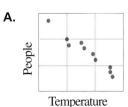

B.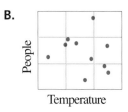

C.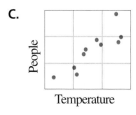

8. Make a scatter plot of the data below. Describe any trends you see in the data.

Average Temperature in Northern Latitudes

Latitude (°)	0	10	20	30	40	50	60	70	80
Temp. (°F)	79.2	80.1	77.5	68.7	57.4	42.4	30.0	12.7	1.0

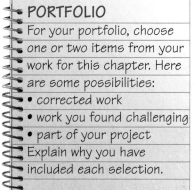

PORTFOLIO
For your portfolio, choose one or two items from your work for this chapter. Here are some possibilities:
• corrected work
• work you found challenging
• part of your project
Explain why you have included each selection.

Mixed Review

Make a stem-and-leaf plot for each set of data. *(Lesson 1-5)*

9. number of students per teacher
   27   29   34   24   29   19
   30   19   25   22   27   15

10. depths at different points in pond (in feet)
    3.7   9.6   9.4   8.4   8.6   7.5   6.8
    8.8   7.9   9.2   10.3   10.1   7.8

11. Is the question "Do you prefer summer or fall?" biased? Explain. *(Lesson 1-7)*

12. *Choose a Strategy* Valerie had three bags of fruit. The first was labeled "peaches," the second "plums," and the third "pears." No bag had a correct label. Valerie reached into the bag marked "plums" and picked out a peach. Match each bag's label with the fruit in the bag.

Estimate the Size of a Crowd and Take a Survey The Project Link questions on pages 7, 29, 32, and 38 should help you to complete your project. Here is a checklist to help you gather together the parts of your project.

✔ a crowd picture with your estimate of its size

✔ your survey question and a graph that displays the results of your survey

✔ an estimate of survey results using the size of the crowd in your picture

Use your estimate of the crowd size and your survey results to plan what type of concessions you would have at a new stadium or arena.

Be sure all of your work is neat and clear. You want to impress the city planners!

Reflect and Revise

Review your project with a friend or someone at home. Is your method for finding the estimate of the size of the crowd clear? Do you explain how you chose your random sample? If necessary, make changes to improve your project.

Web Extension
Prentice Hall's Internet site contains information you might find helpful as you complete your project. Visit www.phschool.com/mgm2/ch1 for some links and ideas related to taking surveys.

Collecting and Reporting Data

To organize data, you can make a frequency table and use it to create a line plot or a histogram.

Cooked	Frequency
0–2	11
3–5	8
6–8	4
9–11	2

1. Frances surveyed her classmates to see how many times a month each cooked dinner at home. The frequency table at the right shows their responses. Make a line plot or a histogram of the data.

Displaying Data

Spreadsheets can be useful tools for organizing data. You can create graphs from a spreadsheet. A **bar graph** compares amounts and a **line graph** shows changes in data over time.

2. The spreadsheet shows the population (in millions) for two age groups in the United States.
   a. What is the value in cell B3?
   b. Which cell has the value 82.1?

	A	B	C
1	year	0–19 yr	20–39 yr
2	1980	72.5	72.4
3	1985	70.3	80.6
4	1990	71.7	82.1
5	1995	75.8	81.0

3. a. Make a graph of the data at the right.
   b. Estimate the population in 2000 for people ages 0–19 years old.

The **mean, median** and **mode** of a set of data, along with any **outliers,** reflect the characteristics of the data.

You can use a **stem-and-leaf** plot to organize a set of data.

4. Meredith plays the French horn. At the right is a record of her practice time in minutes for two weeks.
   a. Find the mean, median, and modes of the data.
   b. What is the outlier? How does it affect the mean?
   c. Meredith wishes to impress her teacher with how much she has practiced. Will Meredith show her teacher the mean, median, or one of the modes of her daily practice time?

Week 1	Week 2
25	0
15	10
35	20
15	25
15	30
40	40
75	40

5. Make a stem-and-leaf plot of the data in the table.

6. Sam, Katie, and Martin went to a costume party as a spider, a fox, and a fish. Each brought a treat to the party. The fish did not bring oatmeal cookies. The spider brought apples. Martin was the fox, and Katie made popcorn. Which costume did each person wear and what treat did each person bring?

Samples and Surveys and Using Data to Persuade   1-7, 1-8

A **random sample** is selected if the members of the population have an equal chance of being selected.

Biased questions are unfair questions. They make assumptions that may or may not be true or make one answer seem better than another.

7. *Writing* The editor of the school newspaper has asked you to write an article on what improvements students would like to see in the school bus service.
   a. Write a fair question for your survey.
   b. How would you choose your random sample?

8. *Open-ended* Describe an advertisement you have seen in which data were used to persuade.

Scatter Plots   1-9

Scatter plots show the relationship between two sets of data.

9. a. Make a scatter plot of the data at the right.
   b. Is there a relationship between the weight of an animal and its pulse? Explain.

10. **Choose A, B, or C.** Which of the scatter plots below shows a positive trend?

A.  B. 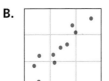 C.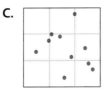

Average Weights and Pulse Rates of 9 Animals

Animal	Weight (in pounds)	Pulse (in beats/min)
Carp	17	59
Cat	9	130
Cod	11	48
Fox	10	240
Mink	2	340
Porcupine	15	300
Rabbit	3	150
Salmon	6	38
Squirrel	1	390

1. Twenty people were asked about the amount of time it takes them to commute to work.
   a. Make a frequency table for the data.
   b. Choose intervals for the data. Make a histogram.

"How Many Minutes Do You Spend Commuting to Work?"

0	60	25	10
15	45	35	30
25	50	90	20
35	10	60	30
40	30	50	45

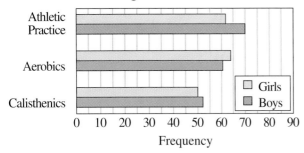

Teenagers' Preferred Exercise

2. Use the graph above to answer the following questions.
   a. Who gets more exercise through athletic practice?
   b. Who gets less of their exercise through calisthenics?
   c. Which form of exercise do teenagers do most?
   d. About how many girls were surveyed?

3. The Summer Street School holds a crafts fair every year. Their profits for the last five years are $425, $355, $390, $400, and $360. Make a line graph representing the profits.

4. a. What kind of graph is better for showing changes over time?
   b. What kind of graph is better for comparing data?

5. **Choose A, B, C, or D.** To best describe the favorite subject of seventh grade students, which measure would you use?
   A. mean   B. median
   C. mode   D. range

6. Mark Lenzi and Xiong Ni competed for the gold medal at the 1996 Summer Olympic men's diving competition. Use the scores to create an appropriate graph to compare the two diver's scores for the six final dives.

Dive	Lenzi	Xiong
1	75.60	75.60
2	68.40	77.19
3	62.10	72.00
4	79.05	78.30
5	79.20	79.20
6	92.40	87.72

7. Find the mean, median, mode, and range of the weights, in ounces, of one-month-old hamsters: 4, 1, 3, 2, 2, 2, 1, 1, 2, 1, 2, 3.

8. Ella, Sara, and Tim have the last names Ellis, Syrio, and Trang. Syrio is Trang's nephew. No one has a first and a last name that begin with the same letter. What is the full name of each person?

9. Create a stem-and-leaf plot for the following junior league bowling scores: 45, 56, 34, 55, 78, 21, 38, 66, 56, 41.

10. Suppose you want to conduct a survey on how long people wait in doctors' offices. Would you have a random sample if you called all of Dr. Mengesha's patients? Explain.

11. *Writing* What are some ways in which a graph may be misleading?

Choose the best answer.

1. Use the line plot. How many families own at least three bicycles?

Number of Bicycles in a Family

```
                      ×
            ×    ×    ×
            ×    ×    ×
       ×    ×    ×    ×    ×    ×
       ×    ×    ×    ×    ×    ×
   ←———————————————————————————————→
       0    1    2    3    4    5
```

A. 11   **B.** 13   **C.** 15   **D.** 19

2. What is the range of the data in the stem-and-leaf plot?

A. 88   **B.** 22
C. 104   **D.** 110

```
 8 | 8
 9 | 1 6
10 | 3 4 4 5
11 | 0
        8 | 8 means 88
```

3. What could the data in the stem-and-leaf plot above most likely represent?

   A. High temperatures for 8 days
   B. Number of hours 8 people spent watching television in one day
   C. Weight in pounds of Chicago Bears football players
   D. Number of books read in one week by members of the Mystery Club

4. Which symbol makes the sentence true?

$$3 \times 5 - 2 = 7 + (3 \blacksquare 2)$$

   A. +   **B.** −   **C.** ×   **D.** ÷

5. What is the mode of the data below?
3 7 7 9 2 4 3 8 8 7 0 6

   A. 6.5   **B.** 7   **C.** 8   **D.** 9

6. What is the best estimate of 12×37?

   A. 250   **B.** 300   **C.** 350   **D.** 400

7. When the soccer team stopped for lunch, eight players ordered pasta and salad while three players ordered salad only. There are 20 players on the team, and each player ordered at least one of these two items. How many players ordered pasta but no salad?

   A. 5   **B.** 12   **C.** 9   **D.** 17

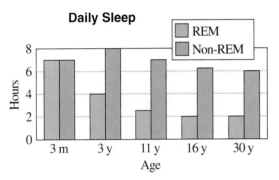

Daily Sleep

8. Use the bar graph above to compare the total number of hours slept daily by a 3-month-old to the total hours slept by a 30-year-old.

   A. about half as much
   B. about twice as much
   C. about the same
   D. about three times as much

9. Use the bar graph to estimate the REM sleep for each age group. What is the mean of the data?

   A. 3.5   **B.** 2   **C.** 5   **D.** 2.5

10. In the bar graph, about how many more hours does a 3-month-old spend in REM sleep than a 30-year-old?

   A. 2   **B.** 3   **C.** 4   **D.** 5

11. What is the median of the data below?
5 2 8 10 4 6 3 9 12 8

   A. 5   **B.** 6.7   **C.** 7   **D.** 8

Applications of Decimals

2

THEME:
SCIENCE

Weighty Matters

Have you ever loved a pet so much that you wanted a statue made of it? Imagine a statue of your pet on the front steps of your home. "Gee, what a wise way to spend hard-earned money," your admiring neighbors would say. Or maybe not. In addition to being expensive, these statues would also be heavy. For instance, a 35-lb dog cast in gold would weigh about 670 lb.

Using Specific Gravity For the chapter project, you will find the weight of different animals and the weight of different metals. Your final project will be a table of animals with their weights, the weight of their statues in different materials, and the cost of the statues.

• How to analyze problems with too much or too little information

PROBLEM SOLVING

2-1 Comparing and Rounding Decimals

What You'll Learn

1. To compare and order decimals
2. To round decimal numbers

...And Why

You can compare speed records and weather data.

Here's How

Look for questions that
- build understanding
- ✔ check understanding

THINK AND DISCUSS

▼ 1 Comparing and Ordering Decimals

In 1920, a gasoline-powered Dusenberg car set a one-mile speed record in auto racing at 155.046 mi/h (miles per hour). In 1997, a jet-propelled Thrust set the all-time record of 763.04 mi/h.

To read a decimal, find the value of the last digit on the right.

155.046 ◄——The last digit is in the thousandths' place.

Read the decimal point as "and."

You read 155.046 as "one hundred fifty-five and forty-six thousandths."

hundreds	tens	ones	.	tenths	hundredths	thousandths	ten-thousandths	hundred-thousandths
1	5	5	.	0	4	6		
7	6	3	.	0	4			

1. **▪ Reasoning** The digit 6 appears twice in the place value chart at the left. What is the value of the 6 each time it appears?

2. Dina read 12.0045 as "twelve and forty-five thousandths." Was she correct? Why or why not?

You can compare decimal numbers using models or a number line.

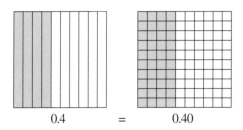

0.4   =   0.40

The numbers 0.4 and 0.40 are **equivalent decimals.** They name the same amount.

3. ⬛ *Modeling* Draw models of 0.58 and 0.6. Which is greater?

■ **EXAMPLE 1**

Order 0.5, 0.8, and 0.25 from least to greatest. Use a number line.

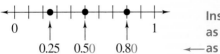

Insert a zero so each is written as hundredths. Numbers increase ←as you move to the right.

From least to greatest, the numbers are 0.25, 0.5, and 0.8.

4. ✔ *Try It Out* Order the numbers from least to greatest.
   a. 2.6, 2.3, 2.7   **b.** 7.58, 7.59, 7.54   **c.** 4.9, 4.84, 4.87

You can also compare numbers using place value.

■ **EXAMPLE 2**   *Real-World Problem Solving*

Average Yearly Rainfall

City	Amount (in.)
Amarillo, TX	19.8
San Francisco, CA	19.0
Fargo, ND	19.3

Source: *The Weather Almanac*

Weather Use the data at the left. Order the cities according to the average yearly rainfall.

Compare the numbers 19.8, 19.0, and 19.3.

19.8   19.0   19.3 ← The digits in the tens and ones places are the same.

Digits in the tenths place are different.

0 < 3 < 8 ←Compare the digits in the tenths place.

Therefore, 19.0 < 19.3 < 19.8.

Ranked from least to greatest rainfall, the cities are San Francisco, Fargo, and Amarillo.

5. ⬛ *Number Sense* Which decimal place must you use to compare 44.0174 and 44.0147?

▼ *Rounding Decimal Numbers*

Rounding decimal numbers is similar to rounding whole numbers.

QUICKreview

Round up if the digit to the right is 5 or greater. Round down if the digit to the right is 4 or less.

■ **EXAMPLE 3**

Round 1.73628 to the nearest hundredth.

1.73628 ←Look at the digit to the right of the hundredths place.

3 → 4 ←Since 6 > 5, round the hundredths digit up.

1.74 ←Write the rounded number.

Need Help? For practice in rounding decimals, see Skills Handbook page 534.

The symbol ≈ means "is approximately equal to." To the nearest hundredth, 1.73025 ≈ 1.73. To the nearest thousandth, 1.73025 ≈ 1.730.

6. Which is 1.37602 rounded to the nearest ten-thousandth, 1.3760 or 1.37600? Why?

7. ✔ *Try It Out* Round each number to the indicated place.
    a. 3.5̲71   **b.** 19.07̲362   **c.** 8.0̲15   **d.** 4.751̲8

EXERCISES *On Your Own*

1. a. *Modeling* Look at the models at the right. Write the value of the shaded area of each model in words and as a decimal.
    b. Write a statement that compares the decimals from part (a) using <, >, or =.

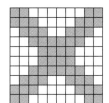 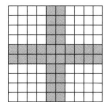 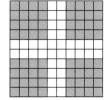

Use a number line to order the decimals from least to greatest.

2. 3.5, 3.2, 3.3   **3.** 9.4, 9.7, 9.42   **4.** 4.04, 4.01, 4.02   **5.** 0.32, 0.38, 0.29

6. 6.1, 6.3, 6.12   **7.** 1.6, 1.74, 1.30   **8.** 0.9, 1.38, 1.04   **9.** 5.43, 5.42, 5.51

Sports **Use the table at the right to answer Exercises 10–12.**

10. Who had the highest batting average? The lowest?

11. List the players in order from highest to lowest batting average.

12. *Reasoning* Suppose you rounded each batting average to the nearest hundredth. Could you accurately order the players from highest to lowest? Why or why not?

American League Batting Champions

Year	Player	Batting Average
1991	Julio Franco, Texas	.341
1992	Edgar Martinez, Seattle	.343
1993	John Olerud, Toronto	.363
1994	Paul O'Neill, New York	.359
1995	Edgar Martinez, Seattle	.356
1996	Alex Rodriguez, Seattle	.358

Source: *The Information Please Sports Almanac*

Open-ended **Write five numbers between the given numbers.**

13. 40 and 50   **14.** 18 and 19   **15.** 3.7 and 3.8   **16.** 7.08 and 7.09

Compare using <, >, or =.

17. 0.167 g ▮ 0.16 g

18. 3.1309 m ▮ 3.1903 m

19. 45.715 mm ▮ 45.175 mm

20. 1.34 mL ▮ 1.27 mL

21. 2.6289 in. ▮ 3.2895 in.

22. 3.09725 mi ▮ 3.07926 mi

23. *Writing* Explain how you would determine which decimal is greater, 16.75 or 16.746.

24. *Biology* The smallest spider is a male *Patu marplesi* that is 0.017 in. across, about the size of a period. The largest spider is a male goliath bird-eating spider that is 11.020 in. across.
   a. Write each number in words.
   b. Round each number to the nearest hundredth.

25. Suppose you rounded 1.73648 to the nearest thousandth and wrote 1.736. Did you make a mistake? Why or why not?

The goliath bird-eating spider is found in the rain forests of South America. This male is shown $\frac{1}{4}$ of its normal size.

Identify the place value of the underlined digit. Then round each decimal to the indicated place.

26. 0.769̲49

27. 5.194̲38

28. 0.5643̲91

29. 0.6̲134

30. 3.245̲5

31. 415̲.78201

32. 8.7̲247

33. 15.619̲403

34. *Open-ended* Write five decimals that round to 7.26.

35. **a.** Give an example of a situation when a rounded number is appropriate.
   b. Give an example of a situation when it is not appropriate to use a rounded decimal.

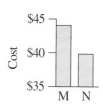

JOURNAL
Find a newspaper article that has a decimal. Do you think the decimal was rounded? Explain your reasoning.

Mixed Review

Find the mean, median, and mode of the given data. *(Lesson 1-4)*

36. 6 3 7 4 2 3 6 3 2

37. 0.2 0.8 0.2 0.4 0.5 0.5 0.2

38. **a.** Does Brand M cost twice as much as Brand N? Explain.
   b. Is this graph misleading? Explain. *(Lesson 1-2)*

39. *Choose a Strategy* A list of consecutive whole numbers begins with 1 and ends with 113. How many digits are on the list?

Problem Solving: Using Estimation Strategies

What You'll Learn

1 To estimate sums and differences

2 To estimate products and quotients

...And Why

You can check reasonableness of answers.

Here's How

Look for questions that
- build understanding
- ✔ check understanding

THINK AND DISCUSS

1 Estimating Sums and Differences

You can estimate an answer before you calculate it to make sure your answer is reasonable. If the answer is close to the estimate, it is probably correct. Sometimes, an estimate is all you need.

You can use *rounding* to estimate sums and differences.

■ **EXAMPLE 1**   *Real-World Problem Solving*

Food Use the menu board. Estimate the cost of a grilled cheese sandwich and a frozen yogurt.

$1.89 + 1.49 \approx 2 + 1.5$ ←—Round to the nearest half-dollar.
$= 3.5$ ←—Add.

The cost is about $3.50.

1. ▪**Look Back** Is this estimate more or less than the exact cost? How do you know?

2. Estimate the difference between the prices of a taco and a grilled cheese sandwich to the nearest half-dollar.

3. ✔ **Try It Out** If you have $6, can you buy a taco, a frozen yogurt, and a large juice? Explain.

Another method of estimating is *front-end estimation*.

■ **EXAMPLE 2**

Estimate the cost of a slice of pizza and yogurt with granola.

Add the
front-end digits. ——→ $\left.\begin{array}{r} 1.45 \\ +\ 1.39 \end{array}\right\}$ ←— Estimate the total amount of cents to the nearest dollar.

$2 + 1 = 3$ ←—**Add.**

The total cost is about $3.

4. ▪*Reasoning* In Example 2, do you get the same answer if you use rounding? Why or why not?

SEASIDE SNACKS

Taco	$3.29
Grilled Cheese	$1.89
Yogurt & Granola	$1.39
Slice of Pizza	$1.45
Frozen Juice Bar	$1.39
Frozen Yogurt	$1.49
Juice	sm $ .69
	lg $1.29

5. ✔ *Try It Out* Which method of estimation would you use to find how much more a large juice costs than a small juice? Explain why you chose that method.

▼2 *Estimating Products and Quotients*

You can use rounding to estimate products.

■ **EXAMPLE 3**   *Real-World Problem Solving*

Home Decorating Estimate the area of a living room that is 10.5 ft × 9.25 ft.

$$10.5 \approx 11$$
$$9.25 \approx 9$$ Round each factor.
$$11 \times 9 = 99$$ ←——Multiply.

The area of the living room is about 99 ft^2.

6. ✔ *Try It Out* Estimate 7.65 × 3.12.

7. ⬝⬝*Reasoning* You want to paint a wall that is 9.75 ft × 8.25 ft. Do you need to find an estimate or the exact area to decide how much paint to buy?

Estimate quotients using two compatible numbers. **Compatible numbers** are numbers that are easy to divide mentally.

■ **EXAMPLE 4**   *Real-World Problem Solving*

Music You've saved $50.25. Based on the chart at the left, about how many CDs from category D could you buy?

$$7.95 \approx 8$$ ←——Round.

$$50.25 \approx 48$$ ←—— Choose a number that is close to 50.25 and divisible evenly by 8.

$$48 \div 8 = 6$$ ←——Divide.

You can buy about 6 CDs from category D.

8. ✔ *Try It Out* About how many CDs in category B can you buy? Explain your choice of compatible numbers.

9. **a.** Is an estimate of the price good enough to decide if you have enough money to buy the CDs you want? Explain.
   b. Is an estimate of the price good enough when you pay for your CDs? Why or why not?

QUICKreview

Area of a rectangle = length × width

CD Price List

Category	Price
A	$23.95*
B	$15.95
C	$12.95
D	$ 7.95

*Double CD

Work Together

A science teacher is building shelves for the bins that hold equipment for 8 lab activities. Each shelf holds 55 lb.

Bin Weights

Activity	Bin Weight (lb)
Activity 1	16.8
Activity 2	16
Activity 3	12
Activity 4	14.98
Activity 5	15.26
Activity 6	13.8
Activity 7	17.1
Activity 8	15.04

10. **a.** Estimate the least number of shelves the teacher needs.
    b. Explain which method you chose to estimate part (a) and why you chose that strategy.

11. **⁂ Reasoning** Which bins should share a shelf to distribute the weight as evenly as possible?

12. Is it reasonable to use estimates in this situation? Explain.

EXERCISES *On Your Own*

Estimate by rounding to the nearest half dollar.

1. $10.13
    + 1.46

2. $9.82
    − 1.76

3. $11.53
    + 7.23

4. $14.17
    − 10.92

5. $21.18
    − 17.92

6. *Weather* In Chicago, Illinois, the average wind speed is 10.4 mi/h. In Great Falls, Montana, the average wind speed is 13.1 mi/h. About how much greater is the average wind speed in Great Falls than in Chicago?

Use front-end estimation to find each sum.

7. $5.429 + 2.665$ 8. $3.602 + 2.309$ 9. $2.174 + 5.891$ 10. $4.39 + 9.57$

11. *Writing* Suppose you used a calculator to find $362.9 + 42.8 + 35.46$. Your display reads 826.36.
    a. Describe how you could have gotten this answer.
    b. How could estimation help you discover your mistake?

12. **Choose A, B, C, or D.** The correct estimate of a sum is 900. Which numbers could have been used to get this estimate?

    A. $682.14 + 65.21 + 142.65$

    B. $734.3 + 201.79 + 55.22$

    C. $421.5 + 337.948 + 275.801$

    D. $225.06 + 275.8 + 269.7$

13. **Open-ended** Write a problem you could solve using front-end estimation.

The sample below shows the estimation technique called clustering. Use clustering to estimate each sum in Exercises 14–16.

Sample: $2.8 + 2.6 + 2.2 + 2.4 + 2.5 \approx 2.5 + 2.5 + 2.5 + 2.5 + 2.5$

$5 \times 2.5 = 12.5$ ←—Multiply.

14. $6.3 + 5.9 + 6.09 + 6.33 + 5.68 + 6.1$

15. $\$14.25 + \$13.75 + \$14.53 + \$13.69$

16. $33.15 + 37.95 + 34.63 + 36.29 + 34.08$

17. **Cooking** It took 75.75 lb of shredded cheese to make the world's largest burrito. Estimate how many 10-lb boxes of shredded cheese the cooks needed.

18. **Travel** One of the world's fastest trains is France's TGV (*train à grande vitesse*, or train of great speed). It averages 132 mi/h. About how far could it travel in 4.75 h?

France

19. **Money** Apples cost $.69 per pound. Estimate the cost of a 3.75-lb bag of apples.

Use any estimation strategy to calculate. Tell which strategy you used and why.

20. $71.43 - 28.098$

21. 24.32×179.12

22. $345.124 \div 8.98$

23. $726.27 + 685.8 + 699.05$

24. $3.963 \div 1.79$

25. 4.27×1.6

26. $9.355 - 0.8$

27. $24.71 + 16.03$

28. $7.59 \div 2.143$

29. **Weather** Six students measured rainfall at their homes and plotted the data in the stem-and-leaf plot at the right.
    a. Estimate the range of the rainfall.
    b. Estimate the mean rainfall for the area.

Rainfall (in.)

0	5 9
1	6 7 3
2	4

2 | 4 means 2.4

30. **Sports** A bowling ball weighs 5.61 kg and a bowling pin weighs 1.57 kg. About how many bowling pins would it take to equal the weight of the bowling ball?

▼2 *Properties of Addition*

You can use the properties of addition to add decimals mentally. You can make general statements of properties using letters. This shows that a property is true for any value.

PROPERTIES OF ADDITION
Identity Property The sum of zero and a is a. **Arithmetic:** $5.6 + 0 = 5.6$ **Algebra:** $a + 0 = a$
Commutative Property Changing the order of the addends does not change the sum. **Arithmetic:** $1.2 + 3.4 = 3.4 + 1.2$ **Algebra:** $a + b = b + a$
Associative Property Changing the grouping of the addends does not change the sum. **Arithmetic:** $(2.5 + 6) + 4 = 2.5 + (6 + 4)$ **Algebra:** $(a + b) + c = a + (b + c)$

■ **EXAMPLE 3**

Use the properties of addition to find $0.7 + 12.5 + 1.3$ mentally.

$$0.7 + 12.5 + 1.3 = 12.5 + 0.7 + 1.3 \quad \longleftarrow \text{Commutative Property}$$
$$= 12.5 + (0.7 + 1.3) \quad \longleftarrow \text{Associative Property}$$
$$= 12.5 + 2$$
$$= 14.5$$

5. ✔ *Try It Out* Explain which properties you would use to find $4.4 + 5.3 + 0.6$. Then find the sum.

6. ⬛ *Mental Math* Use mental math and the properties of addition to find each sum.
   a. $5.2 + 0 + 3.8$ b. $7.4 + 1.9 + 2.6$

Find each sum or difference.

1. 4.56 + 2.9   **2.** 5.3 − 0.12   **3.** 12.46 − 7.2   **4.** 3.061 + 1.8

5. 0.56 + 0.8 + 3.1   **6.** 25.1 − 15.06   **7.** 3.102 − 0.89   **8.** 7 + 0.582

9. 102.8 + 3   **10.** 0.008 − 0.0002   **11.** 0.1305 − 0.066   **12.** 0.75 + 3.8 + 4

13. *Hobbies* The width of the tracks determines the size of model trains. Use the information at the right.
   a. *Estimation* Estimate the difference between the widths of the smallest gauge track and the largest gauge track.
   b. *Decision Making* Suppose you plan to buy a train for a 5-year-old child. Which train would you purchase? Why?

14. *Cars* In 1976, Kitty Hambleton set the women's land-speed record. The mean of her two runs was 512.710 mi/h. Her faster run was at 524.016 mi/h. What was the difference between her fastest speed and her mean speed?

N gauge
0.79375 cm wide

0 gauge
3.175 cm wide

Geometry **Find the perimeter of each figure.**

15.

6.13 m

8.7 m

16.

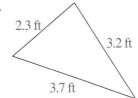

2.3 ft

3.2 ft

3.7 ft

17. *Entertainment* Lisa, Ana, and Lisa's brother Jacob went roller skating. Admission was $3.50 for those 12 and older, and $1.75 for those under 12. The roller skates rented for $2.75 a pair. Lisa and Ana are 13 years old, and Jacob is 10.
   a. How much more did Lisa pay than Jacob?
   b. What was the total cost of admission?
   c. How much did it cost for them all to rent roller skates?

G gauge
5.3975 cm wide

Identify each property shown.

18. (46.8 + 32.7) + 7.3 = 46.8 + (32.7 + 7.3)   **19.** 60.2 + 0 = 60.2

20. 1.97 + 31.2 − 1.97 = 31.2 + 1.97 − 1.97   **21.** 1.3 + (5.8 + 3.91) = (1.3 + 5.8) + 3.91

22. *Writing* How could you use the identity property to find
5.238 − 5.238 + 17.9?

Use the properties of addition to find the value of each expression. State which properties you used.

23. 16.2 + 23.5 + 3.8   **24.** 24.4 + (5.6 + 11)   **25.** 27.4 + 0 + 12.1

26. 6.1 + 8.4 + 1.6   **27.** 9.2 + 1.8 + 0   **28.** (4.7 + 10.6) + 0.3

29. 8.5 + 6.3 + 1.5   **30.** (6.4 + 0.3) + 0.7   **31.** 7 + 3.2 + 3

Mixed Review

Tell whether the questions are biased or fair. *(Lesson 1-7)*

32. Do you prefer tuna sandwiches or chicken sandwiches?

33. Do you like long, warm days of summer or dark, cold days of winter?

Find the value of each expression. *(Previous Course)*

34. 17 − 8 + 2   **35.** 15 − 11 + 4 − 3   **36.** 8 + 56 − 8   **37.** 18 − 2 − 5 + 1

38. *Consumer Issues* When you join the Teen Tape Club, you
get 6 tapes for 1¢ each. You must buy 8 more tapes for $7.99
each. What is the average price of each tape? *(Lesson 1-4)*

✓ CHECKPOINT 1   *Lessons 2-1 through 2-3*

Compare using <, >, or =.

1. 4.406 ■ 4.4060   **2.** 6.621 ■ 6.612   **3.** 10.01 ■ 0.101   **4.** 5.034 ■ 5.304

5. a. Round to estimate $3.07 + $3.48 + $4.24.
   b. Use front-end estimation to find the sum again.
   c. Explain which strategy you would use when buying items.

6. Choose A, B, C, or D. Which property is shown?
7.65 + 1.43 + (1.07 + 8.92) = 7.65 + (1.43 + 1.07) + 8.92

   A. Identity   **B.** Commutative   **C.** Associative   **D.** Not Here

Find each sum or difference.

7. 89.32 − 23.073   **8.** 2.99 + 3.08 + 18.5642   **9.** 9.7418 − 4.603

EXPLORATION

Mental Math: Compensation

You can use compensation to find sums and differences. You use compensation to make problems easier to calculate mentally.

A sum remains the same if you add a number to one addend and subtract it from another addend.

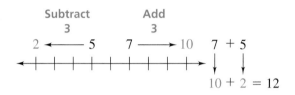

$$10 + 2 = 12$$

The difference between two numbers remains the same if you add (or subtract) the same number from both numbers.

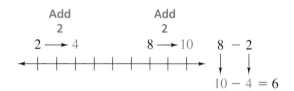

$$10 - 4 = 6$$

■ EXAMPLE

Find each sum or difference.

a. $4.6 + 3.9$

$4.6 + 3.9 + 5.4$

$+0.4 \qquad -0.4 \leftarrow$ Add 0.4 to one addend and subtract 0.4 from another addend.

$5 + 3.9 + 5 = 13.9$

b. $6.1 - 1.3$

$6.1 - 1.3$

$+0.7 \qquad +0.7 \leftarrow$ Add 0.7 to both numbers.

$6.8 - 2 = 4.8$

Use compensation to find each sum or difference.

1. $\begin{array}{r} 0.9 \\ + 1.4 \\ \hline \end{array}$

2. $\begin{array}{r} 22 \\ 29 \\ + 38 \\ \hline \end{array}$

3. $\begin{array}{r} 10.5 \\ 7.1 \\ + 2.9 \\ \hline \end{array}$

4. $\begin{array}{r} 72 \\ + 14 \\ \hline \end{array}$

5. $\begin{array}{r} 2.5 \\ + 9.1 \\ \hline \end{array}$

6. $\begin{array}{r} 117 \\ + 96 \\ \hline \end{array}$

7. $\begin{array}{r} 72.3 \\ 8.1 \\ + 6.7 \\ \hline \end{array}$

8. $\begin{array}{r} 3.8 \\ + 1.7 \\ \hline \end{array}$

9. $38 - 11$

10. $9.3 - 6.1$

11. $102 - 77$

12. $41.6 - 0.7$

13. $11.7 - 6.9$

14. $69 - 31$

15. $984 - 852$

16. $8.4 - 6.9$

17. $53 + 81 + 69$

18. $74.6 - 35.8$

19. $0.4 + 7.8$

20. $12.4 - 8.3$

2-4

Too Much or Too Little Information

Problem Solving Strategies

Draw a Diagram
Guess and Test
Look for a Pattern
Make a Model
Make a Table
Simulate a Problem
Solve a Simpler Problem
✔ Too Much or Too Little
    Information
Use Logical Reasoning
Use Multiple Strategies
Work Backward
Write an Equation

THINK AND DISCUSS

Some problems may not contain enough information for you to solve them. Others may have more information than you need.

SAMPLE PROBLEM...

Holdfield Middle School is sponsoring a Family Day. The seventh grade will be selling lemonade.

The class hopes to sell at least 100 cups of lemonade. Four 64-oz pitchers were borrowed to serve the lemonade. Three packages of 50 paper cups at $1.50 per package and fourteen 12-oz cans of frozen lemonade were bought for $.89 each. Each can makes 48 oz.

The charge for a 6-oz cup of lemonade is $.30. How much was spent on supplies?

....

READ

Read for understanding. Summarize the problem.

1. Think about what is asked, the information given, and which information to use.
   a. What do you need to find?
   b. Do you need all the facts to solve the problem? Explain.

PLAN

Decide on a strategy.

To find the total cost of supplies, decide what the supplies are, and how much was spent on them.

2. How much was spent on lemonade?

3. How much was spent on paper cups?

4. How much was spent on pitchers?

SOLVE

Try the strategy.

Use this information to solve the problem.

5. What was the total cost of supplies?

LOOK BACK

Think about how you solved the problem.

To solve the problem, you selected some facts and ignored the rest.

6. What information didn't you need?

7. Could you find the profit for the day? Why or why not?

EXERCISES *On Your Own*

Solve if possible. If not, tell what information is needed.

1. *Sewing* A group of friends made a 4-yd long rectangular banner. They paid $3.75 per yard for the fabric and $9 for the trim to go around the banner's 10-yd perimeter. What was the width of the banner?

2. *Hobbies* A pet store has 32 tropical fish. The store charges $2.45 per fish and $5.00 for a fish bowl. How much will a fish bowl and some fish cost?

3. *Travel* The four members of the Coy family drove eight hours a day for three days. What is the average number of miles the family traveled each day?

Use any strategy to solve each problem. If it is not possible to solve, tell what information is missing.

4. *School Fair* Central Middle School is having a heritage fair. Ed, Daria, Jarel, and Liz are each presenting an item. The items are maracas from Mexico, a sari from India, a game from Ghana, and a ram's horn from Israel. Jarel did not bring an item from Ghana or India. Daria did not bring an item from Ghana. Ed brought maracas. What items did the other students bring?

5. *Money* Lamarr sold frozen slush at a fair from 12 noon to 5 P.M. He charged $.50 for a small slush and $.75 for a large one. Twelve children bought a total of 15 small slushes and 24 adults bought a total of 28 large slushes. How much money did Lamarr collect?

6. *Biology* The Chinese giant panda lives in bamboo forests. It spends about 10–12 h each day eating. About every 50 years, bamboo forests flower, seed, and die. As a result, many pandas die since the panda mainly eats bamboo. In 1983, before the most recent bamboo forest seeding and dying, about 1,000 pandas were alive. How many are left?

China

The giant panda is about 6 in. long and weighs about 3 lb at birth. Adult pandas can weigh up to 300 lb and stand 5 ft tall when upright.

7. James, Emily, and Marcia are working on a history project. One student is interviewing, one is researching, and one is writing. Their last names are Brown, Johnson, and Wong, but not in that order.

- Emily's last name is not Brown.
- The student whose last name is Wong and the girl who is doing research are neighbors.
- James is not interviewing.
- The student whose last name is Johnson likes to go camping with his father.

What is each student's full name and what part of the history project is each working on?

Mixed Review

Estimate each sum or difference. *(Lesson 2-2)*

8. $52.039 + 12.99$ **9.** $9.37 - 8.4$ **10.** $1.562 - 0.91$ **11.** $9.1 + 0.578$

Make a stem-and-leaf plot for each set of data. *(Lesson 1-5)*

12. 29 27 37 40 46 48   **13.** 1.3 2.2 1.7 1.4 1.3   **14.** 21 19 16 23 18 16

CHAPTER PROJECT

PROJECT LINK: RESEARCHING

Specific gravity describes how many times heavier a metal is than the weight of an equal volume of water. For example, the specific gravity of gold is about 19.3. If a cup of water weighs 8 ounces, then a cup of gold would weigh 8×19.3 ounces, or 154.4 ounces. Since mammals are made mostly of water, their specific gravity is about 1. Use an encyclopedia to find the specific gravity of four of these metals: lead, copper, zinc, aluminum, silver, iron, or nickel.

2-5 Multiplying Decimals

What You'll Learn

1 To multiply decimals

2 To use the properties of multiplication

...And Why

You use decimals in calculations involving money and sports.

Here's How

Look for questions that
- build understanding
- ✔ check understanding

Need Help? For practice in multiplying whole numbers or decimals, see Skills Handbook pages 530 and 535.

Work Together 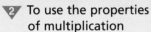 _Modeling Decimal Multiplication_

Work with a partner to model multiplication of decimals. For example, the product of 0.7 and 0.4 is 0.28.

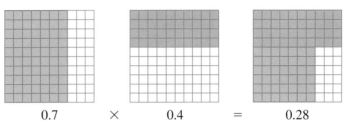

0.7	×	0.4	=	0.28

1. Draw models for 0.2×0.9, 0.3×0.5, and 0.8×0.2.

2. **Draw a Conclusion** In Exercise 1, is each product greater or less than each factor? What can you conclude about the product of decimals less than one?

THINK AND DISCUSS

1 _Multiplying Decimals_

When you multiply decimals, first multiply as if the factors were whole numbers. Then count the decimal places in both factors to find where to place the decimal point in the product.

■ EXAMPLE 1

Find each product.

a. 243×25

$$
\begin{array}{r}
243 \\
\times\ 25 \\
\hline
1215 \\
486 \\
\hline
6075
\end{array}
$$

b. 2.43×2.5

$$
\begin{array}{r}
2.43 \quad \leftarrow \text{two decimal places} \\
\times\ 2.5 \quad \leftarrow \text{one decimal place} \\
\hline
1215 \\
486 \\
\hline
6.075 \quad \leftarrow \text{three decimal places}
\end{array}
$$

The products are 6,075 and 6.075.

3. ✔ *Try It Out* Find each product.
   a. 37×9 **b.** 1.43×0.81 **c.** 8.732×5.4

There are several ways to use symbols to indicate multiplication. Four ways to write "Multiply 3.4 by 5" are shown below.

3.4×5 $3.4 \cdot 5$ $3.4(5)$ $(3.4)(5)$

4. ▪ *Think About It* Suppose you are indicating multiplication using a dot. Why is it important to use a *centered* dot?

▼2 *Using Properties of Multiplication*

The properties of multiplication can help you find products mentally.

PROPERTIES OF MULTIPLICATION

Identity Property

The product of one and a is a.

Arithmetic: $5 \times 1 = 5$ Algebra: $a \times 1 = a$

Zero Property

The product of zero and any number is zero.

Arithmetic: $5 \times 0 = 0$ Algebra: $a \times 0 = 0$

Commutative Property

Changing the order of factors doesn't change the product.

Arithmetic: $5 \times 2 = 2 \times 5$ Algebra: $a \times b = b \times a$

Associative Property

Changing the grouping of factors doesn't change the product.

Arithmetic: $(3 \times 2) \times 5 = 3 \times (2 \times 5)$
Algebra: $(a \times b) \times c = a \times (b \times c)$

---

5. ▪ *Reasoning* Carmela found the answer to $3.625 \times 58.42 \times 0$ in less than one second. How did she do it?

■ EXAMPLE 2

Find $0.25 \times 3.58 \times 4$.

$$\begin{aligned}
0.25 \times 3.58 \times 4 &= 3.58 \times 0.25 \times 4 &\longleftarrow \text{Commutative Property} \\
&= 3.58 \times (0.25 \times 4) &\longleftarrow \text{Associative Property} \\
&= 3.58 \times 1 \\
&= 3.58 &\longleftarrow \text{Identity Property}
\end{aligned}$$

6. ✔ *Try It Out* Use the commutative property to find $2.5 \times 6.3 \times 4$.

7. ⬛ *Think About It* What property would you use first when finding $4.3 \times 2.5 \times 2$? Explain your reasoning.

EXERCISES *On Your Own*

Rewrite each equation with the decimal point in the correct place in the product.

1. $1.2 \times 49 = 588$

2. $27 \times 1.3 = 351$

3. $3.7 \times 6.4 = 2368$

▦ *Choose* **Use a model, paper and pencil, or a calculator to find each product.**

4. 0.2×0.7

5. $0.4 \cdot 0.6$

6. $0.3 \cdot 0.5$

7. 27×817

8. 145×26

9. 1.3×0.05

10. $0.008(1.25)$

11. $(41)(7.5)$

12. $2.41 \cdot 0.17$

13. $8.7(0.45)$

14. $(1.02)(3.6)$

15. 0.45×1.5

16. *Sports* The International Tennis Federation (ITF) requires that a new tennis ball bounce between 0.53 and 0.58 of its original height when dropped on a hard surface.
    a. A new tennis ball is dropped from a height of 200 cm. Find the range of acceptable heights after the first bounce.
    b. A tennis ball dropped from a height of 150 cm reached 79 cm after one bounce. Does the ball meet ITF standards?

17. *Open-ended* Write a problem that you could solve using multiplication of decimals. Include your solution.

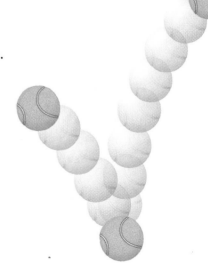

18. *Food* Rice costs $.69 per pound. Jerry bought 1.3 lb. How much did he pay?

19. *Exercise* Monina walks 3.5 mi/h. She took a 1.2 h walk. How far did she walk?

20. a. *Calculator* Find 0.5×0.3, 0.5×0.5, 0.5×0.2, and 0.5×0.4 without a calculator and then with a calculator.
  b. When the final digit in a decimal product is a zero, what does your calculator do?

21. a. *Reasoning* Suppose the decimal point key on your calculator is not working. How could you use the calculator to find the area of a room that is 12.5 ft $\times$ 15.75 ft?
  b. Find the area of the room.

Complete. Name the property of multiplication shown.

22. $3.6 \times \blacksquare = 0$ **23.** $\blacksquare \times 1 = 25.5$ **24.** $\blacksquare \times 4 = 4 \times 3$ **25.** $7.8 \times \blacksquare = 7.8$

26. $(2.5 \times \blacksquare) \times 2.3 = 2.5 \times (1.4 \times 2.3)$ **27.** $9.1 \times (6.5 \times 2.7) = (9.1 \times \blacksquare) \times 2.7$

Mental Math **Use the properties of multiplication to find the value of each expression.**

28. $0.2 \times 3.41 \times 5$ **29.** $1.09 \times 23.6 \times 0$ **30.** $(2.3 \times 0.5) \times 4$ **31.** $5 \times (4.3 \times 1)$

32. *Writing* How are the identity properties of multiplication and of addition similar? How are they different?

33. Choose A, B, C, or D. Which example shows the commutative property of multiplication?
  A. $(8.76 \times 5.4) \times 3.9 = 8.76 \times (5.4 \times 3.9)$ **B.** $5.61 \times 1.4 \times 8.9 = 5.61 \times 8.9 \times 1.4$
  C. $4.8 \times 0 \times 7.91 \times 5.742 \times 6.108 = 0$ **D.** $0.53 \times 7.159 \times 1 = 0.53 \times 7.159$

Mixed Review

Round each decimal to the indicated place. *(Lesson 2-1)*

34. $33.51\underline{6}23$ **35.** $0.61\underline{8}736$ **36.** $5.62\underline{8}49$ **37.** $10.\underline{4}53$

38. Use the line plot at the right. *(Lesson 1-4)*
  a. Find the mean, median, and mode of the data.
  b. Which measure is the greatest?
  c. Which measure is the least?

Textbooks Brought Home

```
                              X
              X   X   X   X
              X   X   X   X
      X   X   X   X   X   X
    ←─────────────────────→
      1   2   3   4   5   6
```

39. *Choose a Strategy* Devon earns $25.50 per day working in a shoe store. His boss pays him $.50 extra for each package of sports socks he sells. After 5 days of work, Devon earned $157.50. How many packages of sports socks did he sell?

PROBLEM SOLVING PRACTICE

Read each question and choose the best answer.

1. The restaurant bill for Sam and four of his friends was $47.84. In order to determine the tip, Dave rounded this amount to the nearest dollar. What is this amount rounded to the nearest dollar?

   A. $40.00   **B.** $47.00
   C. $48.00   **D.** $50.00

2. The table shows the number of hours of homework that each of six students did in one week. What was the median number of hours of homework?

   Hours of Homework

Student	Number of Hours
Lisi	4.5
Jareem	8
Marisa	10
Camille	6
Tyler	9.25
Lindy	5.5

   F. 6.5   **G.** 7   **H.** 7.5   **J.** 8

3. Use the table above. What was the range of hours of homework?

   A. 4.5   **B.** 5   **C.** 5.5   **D.** 6

Please note that items 4–9 have *five* answer choices.

4. A bottle of apple juice holds 3.79 L. A bottle of orange juice holds 1.89 L. How much more does the bottle of apple juice hold?

   F. 0.8 L   **G.** 0.9 L   **H.** 1.8 L
   J. 1.9 L   **K.** 2.9 L

5. A bookstore received a carton that contained 12 copies of a dictionary. Each dictionary weighed 2.3 kg, and the carton weighed 1.3 kg. What is the total weight of the filled carton?

   A. 26.3 kg   **B.** 27.6 kg   **C.** 27.9 kg
   D. 28.9 kg   **E.** Not Here

6. For a class party, the student council purchased 42 balloons at $1.85 each. What is the best estimate of the total amount the student council paid for the balloons?

   F. $70.00   **G.** $75.00   **H.** $80.00
   J. $90.00   **K.** $95.00

7. Jenny saved part of her allowance for four weeks. The first week Jenny saved $4.20, the second week she saved $3.85, the third week she saved $2.50, and the fourth week she saved $3.30. What was the total amount Jenny saved?

   A. $12.85   **B.** $13.75   **C.** $13.85
   D. $13.86   **E.** Not Here

8. The hiking club went on a 7-day trip. Each day they hiked between 5.5 and 7.5 miles. It is reasonable to assume that during the 7 days the club hiked —

   F. less than 35 miles
   G. between 35 and 55 miles
   H. exactly 55 miles
   J. more than 55 miles
   K. Not Here

9. Esther used rounding to estimate the sum of two prices. Her sum was $5. What numbers could she have added?

   A. $4.23 + $7.80   **B.** $3.95 + $2.25
   C. $2.37 + $2.07   **D.** $2.35 + $2.73
   E. $3.59 + $2.78

2-6 Dividing Decimals

What You'll Learn

1 To divide decimals by whole numbers

2 To divide decimals by decimals

...And Why

You can find how to share costs when you buy items with others.

Here's How

Look for questions that
- build understanding
- ✔ check understanding

THINK AND DISCUSS

1 *Dividing a Decimal by a Whole Number*

Recall the names of the parts of a division problem.

$$\text{divisor} \longrightarrow 6\overline{)18} \begin{array}{l} \longleftarrow \text{quotient} \\ \longleftarrow \text{dividend} \end{array}$$

$$\phantom{\text{divisor} \longrightarrow 6\overline{)1}}3$$

Estimation can help you avoid errors when you divide decimals.

■ **EXAMPLE 1**   *Real-World Problem Solving*

Computers You and two friends are buying a new computer game for $40.95. How much is your share?

Estimate: 40.95 ÷ 3 ≈ 42 ÷ 3 = 14   ←—Use compatible numbers.

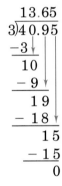

$$
\begin{array}{r}
13.65 \\
3\overline{)40.95} \\
-3 \\
\hline
10 \\
-9 \\
\hline
19 \\
-18 \\
\hline
15 \\
-15 \\
\hline
0
\end{array}
$$

←—Place the decimal point in the quotient. Then divide.

Your share is $13.65.

1. ✔ *Try It Out* Find each quotient.
   a. 20.65 ÷ 5   **b.** 9.868 ÷ 2   **c.** 20.93 ÷ 7

2 *Dividing a Decimal by a Decimal*

Can you divide by zero? Consider these related problems.

6 ÷ 3 = 2   6 ÷ 0 $\stackrel{?}{=}$ 0 ←— $\stackrel{?}{=}$ means deciding if equal or not.

2 × 3 = 6   0 × 0 ≠ 6 ←— ≠ means not equal to.

The related division and multiplication problems show that division by zero does not make sense! So division by zero is undefined.

Before you begin to divide decimals, rewrite the problem so the divisor is a whole number.

Need Help? For practice in dividing decimals, see Skills Handbook pages 537 and 539.

■ **EXAMPLE 2**   *Real-World Problem Solving*

Exercise Suppose you ride your bicycle 25.75 mi in 2.5 h. Find your average speed in miles per hour.

Estimate: 25.75 ÷ 2.5 ≈ 25 ÷ 2.5 = 10

$$2.5\overline{)25.75} \rightarrow 25\overline{)257.5}$$

$$\begin{array}{r} 10.3 \\ 25\overline{)257.5} \\ -25 \\ \hline 07\,5 \\ -7\,5 \\ \hline 0 \end{array}$$

← Multiply the divisor and dividend by 10.

← Since 7 is less than 25, put a zero in the quotient. Then bring down both 7 and 5.

Your average speed is 10.3 mi/h.

2. ■*Reasoning* If you multiplied 2.5 and 25.75 by 100 in the example above, will this affect the answer? Explain.

When you divide by a decimal, sometimes you need to use extra zeros in the dividend, the quotient, or both.

■ **EXAMPLE 3**

Find 0.14 ÷ 0.04.

$$0.04\overline{)0.14} \rightarrow 4\overline{)14.0}$$

$$\begin{array}{r} 3.5 \\ 4\overline{)14.0} \\ -12 \\ \hline 2\,0 \\ -2\,0 \\ \hline 0 \end{array}$$

← Multiply the divisor and dividend by 100.

← Insert a zero after the dividend.

Check 0.04 × 3.5 = 0.14✓ ← Multiply the quotient by the original divisor.

3. ✔ *Try It Out* Find $3.2\overline{)17.6}$. Check your answer.

EXERCISES *On Your Own*

Find each quotient. Check each answer.

1. 22.2 ÷ 3

2. $5\overline{)16.5}$

3. 14.49 ÷ 7

4. $4\overline{)5.16}$

5. 79.599 ÷ 13

6. $83\overline{)15.272}$

7. 22.568 ÷ 26

8. 0.0882 ÷ 6

9. **Movies** Akiko bought five tickets for $23.75. How much did each ticket cost?

10. **Food** The longest parsnip grown was 171.72 in. long. How long was it in yards?

Choose Use mental math, paper and pencil, or a calculator.

11. $10.8 \div 2.7$

12. $0.04\overline{)10}$

13. $0.3\overline{)135.6}$

14. $0.04\overline{)1}$

15. $59.2 \div 0.8$

16. $0.003 \div 0.6$

17. $0.34\overline{)0.00119}$

18. $0.054 \div 0.72$

19. $1.2\overline{)0.078}$

20. $2.245 \div 0.05$

21. $0.04\overline{)0.1}$

22. $2.8 \div 0.25$

23. **a.** Find each quotient.

    i. $75\overline{)300}$ **ii.** $7.5\overline{)300}$ **iii.** $0.75\overline{)300}$

  b. **Patterns** Describe what happens to a quotient when the dividend remains the same and the divisor decreases.

Mental Math **Find each quotient.**

24. $0.9 \div 100$

25. $236.7 \div 0.1$

26. $5.02 \div 0.01$

27. $0.7 \div 10$

28. **Gardening** After digging up lilac bushes in his garden, Julio used sod to cover the dirt. The sod cost $2.25/yd^2. He paid $31.50. How much sod did he buy?

29. **Reasoning** Last week Sue's father drove 283.4 mi on 16.2 gal of gasoline. Sue says that he averaged about 1.75 mi/gal. Is her answer reasonable? Explain.

30. **Hobbies** Nikia bought 3.2 yd of fabric for a total price of $13.92. How much did the fabric cost per yard?

31. **Writing** Do you think there is a commutative property of division? Why or why not? Give examples.

Mixed Review

Find each sum. *(Lesson 2-3)*

32. $8.56 + 3.11$

33. $9.843 + 8.2$

34. $6.4 + 7.024$

35. $17.1 + 3.09$

36. **a.** Use the data below to draw a scatter plot. Graph the number of classes on the horizontal axis and hours of homework on the vertical axis.

Number of Classes	6	7	5	7	6	6	5	6	7	4	5
Hours of Homework	3	4	3.5	4.5	3.5	4	3	5	6	2	4

  b. Do you see a trend? Explain. *(Lesson 1-9)*

SKILLS REVIEW

The Metric System

After Lesson 2-6

The basic unit of length in the metric system is the meter. All the other units are based on the meter. In the chart below, each unit is 10 times the value of the unit to its left.

Unit	millimeter	centimeter	decimeter	meter	decameter	hectometer	kilometer
Symbol	mm	cm	dm	m	dam	hm	km
Value	0.001 m	0.01 m	0.1 m	1 m	10 m	100 m	1,000 m

The same prefixes are used with gram for measures of mass and liter for measures of capacity. For example, one thousand grams (symbol g) is a kilogram (symbol kg). One thousandth of a liter (symbol L) is a milliliter (symbol mL). (*Note:* A *capital* L is used for liters to avoid confusion with the number 1.)

To change a measure from one unit to another, start by finding the relationship between the two units.

■ EXAMPLE

Complete each equation.

a. 245 mL = ■ L
1 mL = 0.001 L
245 × 0.001 = 0.245 ← To change mL to L, multiply by 0.001.
245 mL = 0.245 L

b. 2.3 kg = ■ g
1 kg = 1,000 g
2.3 × 1,000 = 2,300 ← To change kg to g, multiply by 1,000.
2.3 kg = 2,300 g

Complete each statement.

1. ■ L = 90 mL

2. ■ g = 8 mg

3. 0.6 mL = ■ L

4. ■ mg = 2.7 kg

5. 1,200 mL = ■ kL

6. ■ km = 620,000 mm

7. 58 L = ■ mL

8. 7,800 g = ■ kg

9. ■ m = 850 cm

10. ■ cg = 80 g

11. 2.46 km = ■ mm

12. ■ L = 0.47 kL

13. ■ km = 309,000 cm

14. 240 kL = ■ L

15. 7 m = ■ km

16. *Language* Use a dictionary to find the meaning of each prefix in the chart above.

2-7 Terminating and Repeating Decimals

What You'll Learn

1. To investigate division using a calculator
2. To classify decimals as terminating or repeating

...And Why

You can understand how your calculator's memory retains calculations.

Here's How

Look for questions that
- build understanding
- ✔ check understanding

THINK AND DISCUSS

1 *Investigating Division on a Calculator*

Do you know how a scientific calculator's memory affects the answers it gives you? You can learn more about a calculator by exploring division.

1. Suppose you divide 8 by 6, then multiply the product by 6. What will be the result?

2. a. ⊞ *Calculator* Use your calculator to find $8 \div 6$.
   b. Clear your calculator. Enter the result to part (a) and multiply by 6.
   c. Does your answer to part (b) match your answer to Question 1?

3. Now find $8 \div 6 \times 6$ using these keystrokes: 8 ÷ 6 × 6.

When you find $8 \div 6$, the calculator's memory holds more digits in its memory than are shown on the screen. When you continue calculations, you use all these digits without re-entering them.

4. a. ⊞ *Calculator* Use each method to find $6 \div 9 + 5 \div 15$.

   (6 ÷ 9) + (5 ÷ 15) =   6 ÷ 9 + 5 ÷ 15 =

   b. Are your results for both methods the same?

2 *Classifying Quotients*

When you divide decimals, if the quotient stops it is a **terminating decimal.** When a digit or sequence of digits keeps repeating, it is a **repeating decimal.** You can write 0.666. . . as $0.\overline{6}$.

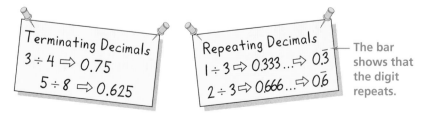

Terminating Decimals
$3 \div 4 \Rightarrow 0.75$
$5 \div 8 \Rightarrow 0.625$

Repeating Decimals
$1 \div 3 \Rightarrow 0.333... \Rightarrow 0.\overline{3}$
$2 \div 3 \Rightarrow 0.666... \Rightarrow 0.\overline{6}$

The bar shows that the digit repeats.

■ **EXAMPLE**

Find each quotient. Tell if the quotient is terminating or repeating.

a. 1 ÷ 4

```
    0.25
4)1.00
   −8
   20
  −20
    0  ←── There is no
           remainder.
```

b. 9 ÷ 11

```
     0.8181
11)9.0000
   −88
    20
   − 11
    90
   − 88
    20
   − 11
     9  ←── There will
              always be a
              remainder.
```

1 ÷ 4 = 0.25,
a terminating decimal.

9 ÷ 11 = 0.8181 . . . or 0.$\overline{81}$,
a repeating decimal.

 The number 142857 is called "roundabout." Does it look familiar? Check what happens when it's multiplied by 2. How about 3? What happens when it's multiplied by 7?

Source: *The Kids' World Almanac of Amazing Facts About Numbers, Math, and Money*

5. ✔ *Try It Out* Find each quotient. Put a bar over any repeating digit(s).
   a. 5 ÷ 6   **b.** 4 ÷ 9   **c.** 7 ÷ 8   **d.** 50 ÷ 11

6. **a.** Find 1 ÷ 7. What digits repeat?
   b. Write the quotient of 1 ÷ 7 using a bar.
   c. ▪ *Calculator* Use a calculator to find 1 ÷ 7. How many of the digits can you see repeating in the display?

EXERCISES *On Your Own*

Use a calculator to find each quotient.

1. 7 ÷ 12 + 4 ÷ 24   2. 5 ÷ 9 − 8 ÷ 36   3. 7 ÷ 11 − 3 ÷ 22   4. 5 ÷ 7 + 10 ÷ 35

5. 6 ÷ 13 + 1 ÷ 26   6. 41 ÷ 17 − 14 ÷ 34   7. 5 ÷ 7 + 14 ÷ 49   8. 23 ÷ 60 − 2 ÷ 15

Choose **Use a calculator or paper and pencil to find each quotient. Use a bar to show repeating decimals.**

9. 3 ÷ 8   10. 12 ÷ 13   11. 10 ÷ 3   12. 155 ÷ 11   13. 2 ÷ 7

14. 12 ÷ 5   15. 60 ÷ 11   16. 42 ÷ 28   17. 50 ÷ 6   18. 16 ÷ 5

19. **a. Patterns** Look at the division problems at the right. What pattern do you see in the divisors?

   b. Copy the table. Find the missing divisors. Find each quotient.

   c. Reasoning As the divisor gets closer and closer to zero, what happens to the quotient? Why?

20. **a. Patterns** Use your calculator to find 4 ÷ 99, 5 ÷ 99, and 6 ÷ 99. What pattern do you see?

   b. Use your pattern to find 7 ÷ 99, 8 ÷ 99, and 9 ÷ 99 without a calculator.

21. Divide 1 by each whole number from 10 to 20.

   a. For which divisors do the digits in the quotients repeat? For which divisors do the digits terminate?

   b. For which divisors can't you tell if the digits of the quotient terminate or repeat? Why can't you tell?

Dividend		Divisor		Quotient
50	÷	100	=	■
50	÷	10	=	■
50	÷	1	=	■
50	÷	0.1	=	■
50	÷	0.01	=	■
50	÷	0.001	=	■
50	÷	■	=	■
50	÷	■	=	■
50	÷	■	=	■

SLICES OF *Pi*

CIRCLES, computers, and "Star Trek" are all linked to one number, *pi. Pi,* or π, defines the relationship between a circle and its diameter.

Different approximations have been used for π. The Egyptians believed it to be 256 ÷ 81. The Chinese used 355 ÷ 113, and one estimate used in India was 62,832 ÷ 20,000. The Greek mathematician Archimedes proved that π is between 22 ÷ 7 and 223 ÷ 71.

In 1767, Johann Lambert proved that π is a decimal that neither terminates nor repeats. Because π never terminates nor repeats, the Star Trek crew used it to keep an evil computer busy until it could be disarmed.

Use the article to answer Exercises 22–24.

22. Is the Indian estimate a terminating or repeating decimal?

23. Which of the two estimates of π given by Archimedes is closer to the value your calculator gives?

24. **Open-ended** Find two numbers not mentioned in the article whose quotient is about equal to π.

25. **Writing** Is the number 3.03003000300003. . . a repeating decimal? Why or why not?

26. **Mental Math** Find 7 ÷ 12. Use it to find 70 ÷ 12.

Mixed Review

Find each difference. *(Lesson 2-3)*

27. $9.8 - 7.02$ **28.** $190.76 - 178.5$ **29.** $18.4 - 9.57$ **30.** $10 - 4.139$

Compare using <, >, or =. *(Lesson 2-1)*

31. $3.012 \blacksquare 3.12$ **32.** $79.284 \blacksquare 79.28$ **33.** $35.009 \blacksquare 35.01$

34. a. *Business* Use the line graph at the right. Find the change from Monday to Friday for each stock.
  b. You buy one stock on Monday and sell it on Friday. Which stock is the better choice? Explain. *(Lesson 1-3)*

35. A penny weighs about 0.1 oz. How much is a pound of pennies worth? *(Lesson 2-5)*

Change in Stock Prices

PROJECT LINK: CALCULATING

Use the weights of the different animals and the specific gravities of the different metals. Find the weight of a statue of each animal in each metal.

✓ CHECKPOINT 2   *Lessons 2-4 through 2-7*

Find each product or quotient. Use a bar to show repeating decimals.

  1. 6×8.2 **2.** $4.5 \div 3$ **3.** $9.1 \cdot 2.4$ **4.** $8.7 \div 4$ **5.** $9.35 \div 6$ **6.** 10.3×5.7

  7. $7 \div 4.8$ **8.** $17 \cdot 0.61$ **9.** $9.8 \div 3.7$ **10.** 1.36×8.94 **11.** $15 \div 0.11$ **12.** $11.5 \div 3$

13. a. *Open-ended* Write an expression with division and decimals.
  b. Find the value of your expression. Is it a terminating decimal or a repeating decimal?

14. Each seventh-grade student is in one activity. Twelve of the students are on the student council. One is the president and one is the treasurer. Another 25 play sports, and 19 are in the band. Seven students work on the school paper. How many students are in seventh grade?

2-8 Order of Operations and the Distributive Property

What You'll Learn

1 To use the order of operations

2 To use the distributive property

...And Why

You can use the distributive property to find products mentally.

Here's How

Look for questions that

▪ build understanding

✔ check understanding

Work Together

Exploring Area

Set Design Luther, Zia, Jon, and Rashanda painted scenery screens for the school play. Each screen was a rectangle 9 ft tall that could combine with other screens to make different scenes.

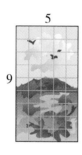 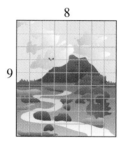 

Work in pairs. Use graph paper to draw rectangles that have the following dimensions.

$$9 \times 4 \qquad 9 \times 5 \qquad 9 \times 6 \qquad 9 \times 7 \qquad 9 \times 8$$

1. Cut out the rectangles. Find the area of each rectangle.

2. ▪ *Number Sense* Combine any two rectangles. How does the area of the combined rectangle compare with the sum of the areas of the two original rectangles?

THINK AND DISCUSS

1 *Using the Order of Operations*

Suppose you combine the 9×4 and 9×5 scenery screens. You can find their area using $9 \times 4 + 9 \times 5$.

You use the order of operations to know what to do first in an expression with more than one operation.

ORDER OF OPERATIONS

1. Do all operations within grouping symbols first.
2. Multiply and divide in order from left to right.
3. Add and subtract in order from left to right.

■ EXAMPLE 1

Find the value of each expression.

a. $30 \div 3 + 2 \cdot 6$

$30 \div 3 + 2 \cdot 6$ ←——Divide and multiply.

$10 + 12$ ←——Add.

22

b. $30 \div (3 + 2) \cdot 6$

$30 \div (3 + 2) \cdot 6$ ←——Do operations within grouping symbols.

$30 \div 5 \cdot 6$ ←——Divide.

$6 \cdot 6$ ←——Multiply.

36

3. ✔ Try It Out Find the value of each expression.

a. $7 \cdot (0.5 + 2) - 1$ **b.** $8 - 4 \times 1.5 + 3$

▼ 2 Using the Distributive Property

5 4

9

Another way to find the total area of the combined rectangles is to add the widths and multiply by the length.

4. a. What is the width of the combined rectangles?
   b. A numerical expression that describes the area by combining the widths first is $9 \cdot (4 + 5)$, or $9(4 + 5)$. Using the order of operations, what should you do first?
   c. What is the area of the combined rectangles?

You can rewrite $9 \cdot 4 + 9 \cdot 5$ as $9(4 + 5)$ because they are equal expressions. This is an example of the distributive property. You can use the distributive property to evaluate expressions that have a number multiplying a sum or a difference.

DISTRIBUTIVE PROPERTY

Arithmetic:

$9(4 + 5) = 9 \cdot 4 + 9 \cdot 5$

$5(8 - 2) = 5 \cdot 8 - 5 \cdot 2$

Algebra:

$a(b + c) = a \cdot b + a \cdot c$

$a(b - c) = a \cdot b - a \cdot c$

---

5. ✔ Try It Out Rewrite $9(4.2 - 2)$ without parentheses.

You can use the distributive property to multiply numbers mentally.

■ **EXAMPLE 2**

Find 6×53 mentally.

To find 6×53 mentally, think of 53 as $50 + 3$.

$$6 \times 53 = 6(50 + 3)$$
$$= 6 \cdot 50 + 6 \cdot 3 \quad \longleftarrow \text{Use the distributive property.}$$
$$= 300 + 18 \quad \longleftarrow \text{Add.}$$
$$= 318$$

6. ✔ *Try It Out* Find each product mentally using the distributive property.
   a. 8×21 **b.** 14×9 **c.** 48×6 **d.** 7×92

You can also use the distributive property to multiply a whole number by a decimal.

■ **EXAMPLE 3**

Find $7(5.9)$ mentally.

To find 7×5.9 mentally, think of 5.9 as $6.0 - 0.1$.

$$7 \times 5.9 = 7(6.0 - 0.1)$$
$$= 7 \cdot 6.0 - 7 \cdot 0.1 \quad \longleftarrow \text{Use the distributive property.}$$
$$= 42 - 0.7 \quad \longleftarrow \text{Subtract.}$$
$$= 41.3$$

7. ✔ *Try It Out* What steps would you use to find 4×12.1 mentally using the distributive property and addition?

8. **a.** ▪*Explain* Why does $3(2.5 + 5) = (2.5 + 5)3$?
   b. Complete: $(2.5 + 5)3 = (2.5)\blacksquare + (5)\blacksquare$

EXERCISES *On Your Own*

Find the value of each expression.

1. $6 + 1 \times 5$ 2. $4 \div 2 + 9$ 3. $5 - 8 \div 4$ 4. $3 - 0 \cdot 11$

5. $12 \div 6 - 1$ 6. $100 - 7 \cdot 9$ 7. $9 \div 2 + 8$ 8. $19 \div 4 \times 3$

9. *Open-ended* Write an expression with three operations. Find the value of your expression.

10. **Choose A, B, C, or D.** Which expression has the greatest value?

   A. $(5 + 2) \div 7 + 9 \times 0.5 - 3$ **B.** $9 - 4 \cdot 2 + 1 \times 1.5 \div 0.3$
   C. $7 \div 2 + 1.4 \times 3 - 6$ **D.** $8 + 1 - 10 \div 4 - 12 \div 4$

Insert $+$, $-$, $\times$, or $\div$ to make each equation true.

11. $5 \ \blacksquare\ 3 + 2 = 17$
12. $1.1 \ \blacksquare\ 6 \times 0.3 = 2.9$
13. $30 - 6 \ \blacksquare\ 6 = 29$

14. $23.1 \div 7 \ \blacksquare\ 3.3 = 6.6$
15. $48 \ \blacksquare\ 12 + 11 = 15$
16. $21 \div 7 \ \blacksquare\ 4 = 12$

Place parentheses to make each statement true.

17. $4 + 4 \div 4 - 4 = 1$
18. $4 \times 4 \div 4 + 4 = 2$
19. $4 + 4 + 4 \div 4 = 3$

20. $4 \times 4 - 4 + 4 = 4$
21. $4 + 4 \times 4 - 4 = 28$
22. $4 + 4 \times 4 - 4 = 0$

23. *Advertising* Rashaun made a large poster for his school rummage sale. The poster measured 20 in. $\times$ 28.5 in.
   a. Use the distributive property to write an expression to find the area of the poster using mental math.
   b. Find the area of Rashaun's poster.

Find the missing numbers.

24. $4(7 + 8) = 4(\blacksquare) + 4(\blacksquare)$
25. $3(8.2 - 1.5) = (\blacksquare)8.2 - (\blacksquare)1.5$

26. $\blacksquare(4.8) = 6(5) - 6(\blacksquare)$
27. $\blacksquare(2.8 + 6.5) = 7(2.8) + 7(6.5)$

28. Dustin and five of his friends went to the science museum. The admission fee was \$5.25 per person. The planetarium was an additional \$4.75 per person.
   a. Show how you would use the distributive property to find the admission fee for all of them.
   b. Use the distributive property to find the additional planetarium cost.
   c. How much did Dustin and his friends pay altogether?
   d. *Research* Find the total admission fees to a local museum for three adults and four children.

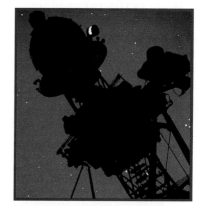

Planetarium projectors are used to simulate views of the night sky.

Calculate mentally using the distributive property.

29. $6(3.9)$ 30. $10.3(4)$ 31. $7(2.6)$ 32. $11.6(9)$

Geometry **Write two expressions to find the total area of each figure. Find the area.**

33.

1
3

8

34.

3

5   5

35.

5

2   3

36. *Money* A caterer is buying lilies to use in centerpieces. Each centerpiece will have 3 lilies. There are a total of 10 tables. After a discount, each lily costs $.92. Use mental math to find the cost of the lilies.

37. *Mental Math* You want to buy 4 notebooks at $.89 each. Use mental math to find the total cost.

38. *Writing* Explain how you could use the distributive property to calculate 4(110.5) two different ways.

> **PORTFOLIO**
> For your portfolio, choose one or two items from your work for this chapter. Here are some possibilities:
> • a journal entry
> • corrected work
> • part of your project
> Explain why you have included each selection.

Mixed Review

Find each quotient. *(Lesson 2-6)*

39. $2.21 \div 1.7$ **40.** $0.75 \div 0.5$ **41.** $62 \div 2.5$ **42.** $3.8 \div 4$ **43.** $7.1 \div 0.8$

Use the data at the right for Exercises 44–46. *(Lessons 1-1, 1-2)*

44. Make a line plot and a histogram of the data.

45. How many students are in the class?

46. What is the range of ages of the students?

47. *Patterns* Find the product of 4.2×10, 4.2×100, and $4.2 \times 1,000$. Predict $4.2 \times 1,000,000$. *(Lesson 2-5)*

Student Ages in a History Class

Age	Number of Students
12	6
13	15
14	8

CHAPTER PROJECT

PROJECT LINK: CALCULATING

Find the price of the different metals you used. Include the source of your information. Use this data to calculate how much each statue would cost.

CHAPTER PROJECT

Weighty Matters

Using Specific Gravity The Project Link questions on pages 58, 66, 79, and 84 should help you to complete your project. Here is a checklist to help you gather together the parts of your project.

- ✓ the list of animals and their weights
- ✓ the list of different metals' specific gravity
- ✓ the weight of each statue in each metal
- ✓ the cost of each statue in each metal

Choose your favorite statue. Pretend that you are going to present this statue as a gift to a city, museum, or park. Explain why you chose that statue. How much would it weigh? How much would it cost?

Reflect and Revise

Review your project with a friend or someone at home. Are your lists complete? Are your calculations accurate? Are your numbers realistic? If necessary, make changes to improve your project.

Web Extension
Prentice Hall's Internet site contains information you might find helpful as you complete your project. Visit www.phschool.com/mgm2/ch2 for some links and ideas related to specific gravity.

Rounding and Ordering Decimals — 2-1

To compare numbers, start from the left. Compare the first set of digits that are not the same.

When rounding numbers, round up if the digit to the right is 5 or greater. Round down if the digit to the right is 4 or less.

Compare using <, >, or = .

1. 0.168 ▧ 0.1680   **2.** 5.6 ▧ 5.592   **3.** 1.83 ▧ 2.032   **4.** 11.26 ▧ 11.206

Round each number to the underlined place value.

5. 17.8$\underline{5}$2   **6.** 0.10$\underline{3}$8   **7.** 1$\underline{0}$9.71   **8.** 1.$\underline{3}$601   **9.** $\underline{5}$.4972   **10.** 8.194$\underline{6}$5

Estimation Strategies — 2-2

You can estimate decimals using rounding, front-end estimation, or compatible numbers.

Use any estimation strategy to calculate. Then tell which strategy you used.

11. 50.3 ÷ 6.9   **12.** 1.46 + 4.38   **13.** 98.52 − 46.9074   **14.** 6.9 × 8.92

15. $37.63 ÷ $7.19   **16.** 0.167 + 0.902   **17.** 7.981 − 3.0189   **18.** 1.7 × 78.43

19. *Writing* Explain when you would use compatible numbers to estimate the value of an expression.

Addition and Subtraction of Decimals — 2-3

When adding or subtracting decimals, align the decimal points.

Use the **commutative property** to change the order in an expression. Use the **associative property** to change the grouping.

Find each sum or difference.

20. 8.62 + 9.4   **21.** 10.87 − 6.9   **22.** 4.6 − 3.87   **23.** 8.04 + 9.1

24. 7.4 + 9.2   **25.** 11.47 − 9.03   **26.** 0.54 + 0.027   **27.** 3.09 − 2.975

Problem Solving Strategies 2-4

Before you try to solve a problem, you must decide if you have too much or too little information.

Solve if possible. If not, tell what information is needed.

28. *Sports* In doubles tennis, the width of the court is 10.97 m. The net is between 0.91 m and 1.07 m tall. The court is 23.77 m long. Find the area of the court.

29. *Clothing* Tamika bought a sweater on sale for half of the original $36 price. She also bought jeans on sale for $15. How much did she save by buying sale items?

Multiplication of Decimals and the Order of Operations 2-5, 2-8

When you multiply decimals, put the decimal point in the proper place in the product.

Use the **order of operations** to simplify an expression. Use the **distributive property** to evaluate expressions that have a number multiplying a sum or a difference.

Find the value of each expression.

30. $7 \div 2 + 3 \times 4 - 10$

31. $8.1 - (4.2 \times 0.25) \div 5$

32. $(7.3 + 4) \div 4 + 0.3 \times 2$

33. $(11.94 - 7.621) \times (3.45 + 6.1)$

34. $8 - 6.2 \div 5 + 0.7 \times 0.91$

35. $61.152 \div 9.8 - (2.1 + 1.8) + 0.5$

36. **Choose A, B, C, or D.** Which property is illustrated below?
$8.4 \times (7.23 \times 4.915) = (8.4 \times 7.23) \times 4.915$

A. Identity property
B. Distributive property
C. Associative property
D. Commutative property

Dividing Decimals 2-6, 2-7

When you divide decimals, if the quotient ends it is a **terminating decimal.** When a digit or sequence of digits keep repeating, it is a **repeating decimal.**

Find each quotient. Use a bar to indicate repeating digits.

37. $9.8 \div 5$

38. $3.52 \div 0.6$

39. $1.67 \div 1.5$

40. $7 \div 4.4$

41. $8.25 \div 0.25$

42. $2.54 \div 6.4$

43. $5.38 \div 11$

44. $18.5 \div 3.52$

1. Round each number to the underlined place value.
   a. 0.571034
   b. 26.095
   c. 501.9386
   d. 18.419
   e. 467.15
   f. 43.577

2. Order the numbers from least to greatest: 8.05, 8.5, 8.059, 8.049, 8.0499.

3. Use any method to estimate the value of each expression.
   a. 289.76 − 52
   b. 8.7891 − 3.493
   c. 68.5 ÷ 7.02
   d. 97.60 · 3.4
   e. 7.532 + 2.19
   f. 5.4 × 9.5

4. Use front-end estimation to estimate the sum of the following grocery item prices: $7.99, $2.79, $4.15, $2.09.

5. Find each sum or difference.
   a. 9.53 + 3.29
   b. 8 − 6.1273
   c. 10.5 − 9.67
   d. 0.57 + 1.825
   e. 9 − 5.018
   f. 8.51 + 4

6. **Money** On her last bank statement, Rhea Medeiros had a balance of $213.15 in her checking account. She wrote one check for $68.94 and another for $128.36. What is her current balance?

7. Identify each property shown.
   a. 9.5 + 6.1 + 2.3 = 9.5 + 2.3 + 6.1
   b. 7.2 × (1.6 × 3.9) = (7.2 × 1.6) × 3.9
   c. 8.329 + 0 + 1.74 = 8.329 + 1.74
   d. 5.1(7.4 − 3.1) = 5.1(7.4) − 5.1(3.1)

8. Find each quotient. Use a bar to show repeating decimals.
   a. 1.9 ÷ 1.8
   b. 5.1 ÷ 3
   c. 1.2 ÷ 0.3
   d. 1.58 ÷ 1.1

9. **Writing** You have a choice of two jobs for the summer. You can work at a gas station at $5.20/h for 18 h/wk or you can babysit at $3.75/h for 25 h/wk. Which job should you choose? Explain your reasoning.

10. Find the value of each expression.
    a. 9.5 − 7.1 + 2.4 × 0.5 − 1.3
    b. 8.25 ÷ 4 × (0.6 − 0.54) + 8.3
    c. (7.2 + 3.6) ÷ 5 + 8.4 × 0.6
    d. 5.82 + 10.24 ÷ 3.2 − 4.195

11. **Choose A, B, C, or D.** The weights of four bags of apples were 3.5, 3.8, 4.2, and 3.5 lb. What was the median weight?

    A. 3.5   B. 3.65   C. 3.75   D. 3.8

12. Use the distributive property to find the value of each expression.
    a. 6(10.5)
    b. 3(98)
    c. (7.3)6

13. Solve the problem or tell what information is needed to solve.

    At the 1996 Summer Olympics, Denis Pankratov of Russia swam the 100-m butterfly in 52.27 seconds to win the gold medal. At the 1972 Summer Olympics, Mark Spitz won the same event. Who had the faster time, and how much faster was it?

14. Solve the problem or tell what information is needed to solve.

    You bought a case of 30 toys for your store at $3.95 each. They were delivered on Wednesday. A customer bought 3 toys for $4.99 each. How much profit did you make on the 3 toys?

Choose the best answer.

1. Laura bought several tennis items at the sports store. She purchased a racket on sale for $49.50, socks for $8.50, and 3 cans of tennis balls for $12.95. On sale, sunglasses were $8.99. Laura spent $4.89 more on a shirt than on a pair of shorts. What else do you need to know to determine how much Laura spent in all?

   A. the cost of the pair of shorts
   B. the number of tennis balls in each can
   C. the number of socks purchased
   D. the original price of the racket

2. In the problem above, what information is not needed to solve the problem?

   A. the cost of the tennis balls
   B. the original price of sunglasses
   C. the sale price of the racket
   D. how much more the shirt cost than the shorts

3. What does the stem-and-leaf plot *not* tell you?

1	3 4 9
2	1 2 4 4
3	0 3

   2 | 5 means 25

   A. The greatest number is 33.
   B. The mode is 24.
   C. The median is 22.
   D. There are 12 items of data.

4. Which kind of graph would best show the change in population of the United States from 1935 to 1995?

   A. line graph   B. bar graph
   C. scatter plot   D. stem-and-leaf plot

5. Rendell bought 1.2 lb of peanuts at $2.89/lb, 0.7 lb of cashews at $4.59/lb, and two one-pound boxes of raisins for $2.39 each. How much did he spend?

   A. $9.87   B. $12.26
   C. $11.46   D. $12.31

6. What is the greatest number of movie tickets you can buy if you have $33.48 and each movie ticket costs $6.75?

   A. 3   B. 4   C. 5   D. 6

7. Eulalia received $25.00 for her birthday. She paid $6.89 for two magazines and repaid her brother $4.25. How much money did Eulalia have left?

   A. $20.75   B. $18.11   C. $12.86
   D. $11.14   E. Not Here

8. What information is *not* given by the bar graph below?

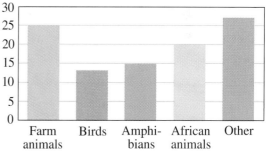

Number of Zoo Animals

   A. There are about the same number of birds as amphibians at the zoo.
   B. There are more farm animals than African animals.
   C. Reptiles are included in the "other" category.
   D. There are fewer birds than farm animals at the zoo.

Algebra: Integers and Equations

3

Board Walk

What makes a board game so much fun? You have challenges like road blocks or false paths that make you backtrack. Then you land on a lucky square that lets you leap forward past your opponent. Best of all, you are with your friends as you play!

Create a Board Game For this chapter project, you will use integers to create a game. Then you will play your game with friends or family for a trial run. Finally you will decorate your game and bring it to class to play.

• **How to solve problems by making a table**

3-1 Evaluating and Writing Variable Expressions

What You'll Learn

1 To evaluate variable expressions

2 To write variable expressions

...And Why

You can use variables and variable expressions to find the cost of a purchase of video tapes.

Here's How

Look for questions that
- build understanding
- ✔ check understanding

Work Together

Collecting Data

Work in a group. Find the number of times your heart beats in 15 s by taking a 15-s reading of your pulse. Each beat corresponds to one beat of your heart.

1. Record each person's 15-s rate. Calculate the beats per minute.

2. a. Use the heart rates you found in Question 1. How many times would each person's heart beat in 5 minutes? In 1 day? In 1 week?

   b. **Reasoning** Explain how you found the expected number of heartbeats in 5 minutes and in 1 day.

THINK AND DISCUSS

1 Evaluating Variable Expressions

A **variable** is a symbol that stands for a number. A **variable expression** is a group of numbers, variables, and operations.

$$\text{variables} \longrightarrow \quad g \qquad z \qquad x$$
$$\text{variable expressions} \longrightarrow \quad 13 - g \qquad z \div 2 \qquad 3x + 8$$

You can use a variable expression to describe data. Suppose your heart beats 72 times in one minute.

variable represents number of minutes

$72m$ } ← variable expression represents number of heartbeats in m minutes

The variable expression $72m$ means $72 \times m$ or $72 \cdot m$. To evaluate a variable expression, replace the variable with a number.

$$72m = 72 \cdot 3 \quad \longleftarrow \text{Substitute 3 for } m \text{ to find the number of heartbeats in three minutes.}$$

$$= 216 \quad \longleftarrow \text{Multiply.}$$

EXAMPLE 1   *Real-World Problem Solving*

Entertainment Suppose you want to buy two video tapes and a $7 cassette tape. Use the variable expression $2v + 7$. Find the total cost of your purchase if the tapes cost $9.95 each.

$$2v + 7 = 2 \cdot 9.95 + 7 \quad \longleftarrow \text{Substitute 9.95 for } v.$$
$$= 19.9 + 7 \quad \longleftarrow \text{Multiply.}$$
$$= 26.9 \quad \longleftarrow \text{Simplify.}$$

The total cost of your purchase is $26.90.

3. ✔ *Try It Out* Suppose the video tapes from Example 1 cost $17.95 each. Find the total cost.

▼2 *Writing Variable Expressions*

The table shows some of the key words you can use in word phrases for variable expressions.

Key Words	Operation	Key Words	Operation
add	+	minus	−
plus	+	difference	−
sum	+	subtract	−
total	+	less than	−
increased by	+	less	−
more than	+	decreased by	−
product	×	quotient	÷
times	×	divide	÷
multiply	×		

Below are three ways you can write a word phrase for $x + 2$.

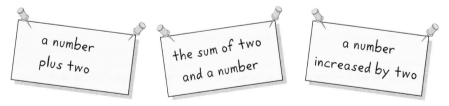

a number plus two

the sum of two and a number

a number increased by two

4. Write a word phrase for each variable expression.
   a. $5 + n$ **b.** $p \div 3$ **c.** $50.75 - c$

5. Choose A, B, or C. Which variable expression corresponds to "3 less than a number"?

   A. $n - 3$ **B.** $3 - n$ **C.** $3 < n$

51. *Estimation* This section of a page from a telephone directory shows 11 names in 1 in. Each page has four 10-inch columns. Write a variable expression for the approximate number of names in p pages of the directory.

52. **a.** There are b books on one shelf in the library. Write a variable expression for the number of books on 275 shelves.
    b. Evaluate your expression for 25 books per shelf.

53. *Biology* An adult human heart pumps about 599.4 gal of blood per hour.
    a. Write a variable expression for the number of gallons an adult heart pumps in h hours.
    b. Find the gallons of blood the heart pumps in one day.

54. *Writing* Write each variable expression at the right as a word phrase. Then make up a situation for each expression.

$$3 \div n \quad n \div 3 \quad 3n \quad 3 - n$$

55. **Choose A, B, C, or D.** What operations are in the variable expression for "twice a number increased by three"?

    A. $+$ and $-$ **B.** $\times$ and $-$ **C.** $\times$ and $+$ **D.** $\times$, $+$, and $-$

56. *Business* Erik can mow one lawn each weekday after school and two lawns on Saturday.
    a. How many lawns can Erik mow in one week?
    b. Write a variable expression for the number of lawns he can mow in w weeks.
    c. Suppose Erik earns an average of $6 for each lawn. How much money can he make in one week?
    d. Write a variable expression for the amount of money he can make in w weeks.

Mixed Review

Find the value of each expression. *(Lesson 2-8)*

57. $3(4 + 5) + 2(4 + 5)$ 58. $3 + 7(1.2) + 7(0.5)$ 59. $5(0.25 \times 40)$

Estimate each answer. *(Lesson 2-2)*

60. $239.6 - 118.43$ 61. $26.92 + 13.267$ 62. $765.7 - 66.7$ 63. $29.5 + 32.3$

64. *Choose a Strategy* Karisha has read the first 79 pages of a book. When she has read 17 more pages, she will have read half of the book. How many pages are in the book?

Comparing and Ordering Integers

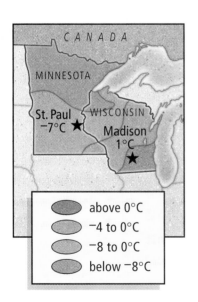

THINK AND DISCUSS

1 *Graphing and Ordering Integers*

In January, the average daily high temperature measured in Celsius (°C) in Louisville, Kentucky, is about five degrees above zero. The average daily low temperature is about five degrees below zero.

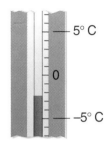

You can write the temperature above zero as +5°C or 5°C. You write the temperature below zero as −5°C. You read the numbers 5 and −5 as *positive* 5 and *negative* 5.

■ **EXAMPLE 1** *Real-World Problem Solving*

Weather Use the map at the left. Which city is colder, St. Paul or Madison?

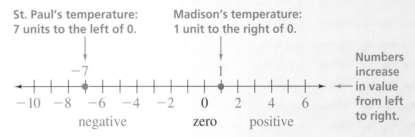

St. Paul's temperature: 7 units to the left of 0.

Madison's temperature: 1 unit to the right of 0.

Numbers increase in value from left to right.

It is colder in St. Paul than it is in Madison.

---

1. **a.** ✔ *Try It Out* Graph the numbers −8 and 2 on a number line. Which number has the lesser value? Explain.

   b. Choose >, <, or =. Write a number sentence to compare −8 and 2.

2. ■ *Think About It* Which number is greater, 247 or −247? Use a number line to explain your reasoning.

3. ■ *Go a Step Further* Use a number line. Order −9, 6, 0, −4, and 1 from least to greatest.

▼2 *Finding Absolute Value*

The numbers 3 and −3 are *opposites*. **Integers** are the set of whole numbers and their opposites. The **absolute value** of an integer is its distance from 0 on a number line. Distance is always positive. You write "the absolute value of −3" as |−3|.

■ EXAMPLE 2

Find |−3| and |3|. Use a number line.

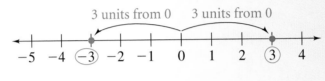

|−3| = 3; |3| = 3

4. ✔ *Try It Out* Write |−4| in words. Then find |−4|.

5. What two numbers have an absolute value of 1?

6. ▪*Reasoning* Can the absolute value of a number be −7? Why or why not?

WEATHER For snowboarding you need snow! The average January snowfall for the cities listed at the right ranges from 23.7 inches in Caribou, Maine, to 2.2 inches in Barrow, Alaska.

Work Together ──────────── *Comparing Temperatures*

Weather Work with a partner. Use the table below of normal high and low temperatures in January for selected cities.

7. Draw a number line. Use the normal high temperature for January. Arrange the cities above the number line from coldest to warmest.

8. Use the normal low temperature for January. Arrange the cities below the number line from coldest to warmest.

Normal Temperatures for January (°F)

City	High	Low
Barrow, AK	−7	−19
Bismarck, ND	20	−2
Caribou, ME	19	−2
Duluth, MN	16	−2
Omaha, NB	31	11

Source: National Climatic Data Center

9. ▪*Analyze* Which city has the least variation in normal temperatures in January? Which has the greatest? How do you know?

Name the integer represented by each point on the number line.

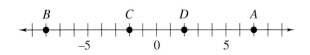

1. *A*   **2.** *B*   **3.** *C*   **4.** *D*

5. On the number line above, which two points are opposites?

Write an integer to represent each situation.

6. *Geography* The city of New Orleans, Louisiana, is 8 ft below sea level.

7. *Temperature* In Miami, Florida, the average July temperature is 83°F.

8. *Astronomy* The surface temperature on the light side of the moon is 270°F.

9. *Geography* The Dead Sea is 1,312 ft below sea level.

Write the absolute value represented by each diagram.

10. Distance is 5 units from 0.

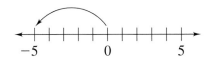

11. Distance is 7 units from 0.

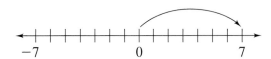

Compare. Use <, >, or =.

12. $0 \ \blacksquare \ -2$ **13.** $|-6| \ \blacksquare \ -3$ **14.** $-14 \ \blacksquare \ 14$

15. $-23 \ \blacksquare \ 0$ **16.** $-4 \ \blacksquare \ -5$ **17.** $17 \ \blacksquare \ -18$

18. $7 \ \blacksquare \ -12$ **19.** $10 \ \blacksquare \ |-10|$ **20.** $5 \ \blacksquare \ -1$

21. *Writing* Suppose a friend does not know how to order integers. Write an explanation for how to order the numbers from least to greatest: $-32, 12, 0, -4, 22, -5$.

22. *Science* Use the information at the right. Write integers to represent the temperatures on Mars. Label each temperature as high or low.

23. *Research* Write integers to represent the high and low surface temperatures of two other planets.

The "Sojourner" robot investigated the surface of Mars in 1997. Scientists know that the surface temperature ranges from 68 degrees below zero during the day to 176 degrees below zero at night.

Graph each integer and its opposite on a number line.

24. 2   **25.** -9 **26.** 12   **27.** -5

Find the value of each expression.

28. $|8|$ **29.** $|-11|$ **30.** $|-16|$ **31.** $|-1|$ **32.** $|4|$

33. $|4| + 3$ **34.** $|-4| + 3$ **35.** $|-1| + 3$ **36.** $|-5| - 3$ **37.** $|-2| + 2$

Open-ended **Write an integer to make the statement true.**

38. $-7 < \blacksquare$ **39.** $|12| < \blacksquare$ **40.** $-15 > \blacksquare$

41. $|-4| < \blacksquare$ **42.** $\blacksquare = |-13|$ **43.** $0 > \blacksquare$

44. $-357 < \blacksquare$ **45.** $|-253| < \blacksquare$ **46.** $\blacksquare > |-6| + 1$

JOURNAL
How is comparing and ordering integers similar to and different from comparing and ordering decimals? Give examples.

47. Which integer is greater, -43 or 22? Which has the greater absolute value? Explain your reasoning.

48. a. *Open-ended* Write three numbers that are between -3 and -4.
     b. Are the numbers you wrote integers? Why or why not?

Mixed Review

Find each quotient. *(Previous Course)*

49. $8\overline{)296}$ **50.** $5\overline{)3,245}$ **51.** $93\overline{)6,882}$ **52.** $82\overline{)22,960}$ **53.** $71\overline{)39,902}$

54. *Recreation* A family of four spends an average of $189.70 per day while on vacation. *(Lesson 3-1)*
     a. Write a variable expression to express the amount a family would spend in any number of days.
     b. Use your expression to find the amount a family would spend in nine days.

CHAPTER PROJECT

PROJECT LINK: MAKING A DECISION

Choose a setting for your game board. Is the game in a cave, in a castle, in a person's digestive tract? Decide whether you want players to move by selecting cards, rolling number cubes, or both. Do you want the end of the game to be determined by the number of points someone has or by moving to an end square?

Exploring Inequalities

After Lesson 3-2

An *inequality* is a statement that compares two expressions. Sometimes an inequality contains a variable, like $x \geq 2$. All the values that make the inequality true are solutions of the inequality.

Inequality Symbols

$<$	less than
$>$	greater than
$\leq$	less than or equal to
$\geq$	greater than or equal to

■ EXAMPLE 1

Tell whether each number is a solution of $x \leq 2$: $-3, 0, 2, 4.5$.

$$x \leq 2 \qquad \longleftarrow \text{Use the inequality.}$$

$$-3 \leq 2 \quad 0 \leq 2 \quad 2 \leq 2 \quad 4.5 \leq 2 \qquad \longleftarrow \begin{array}{l}\text{Replace } x \text{ with each} \\ \text{number.}\end{array}$$

$$\uparrow \qquad \uparrow \qquad \uparrow \qquad \uparrow$$

true   true   true   false

The numbers -3, 0, and 2 are solutions of $x \leq 2$. The number 4.5 is not a solution.

You can graph solutions of an inequality on a number line.

■ EXAMPLE 2

Graph each inequality on a number line.

a. $x \geq -3$

b. $x < 7$

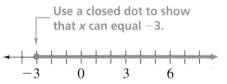
Use a closed dot to show that x can equal -3.

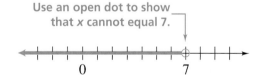
Use an open dot to show that x cannot equal 7.

Which numbers are solutions of each inequality?

  1. $x < 0$; $-3, 0, 5$ **2.** $x > -4$; $-4, -2, 5$ **3.** $x \geq -7$; $-9, 0, 6$ **4.** $x \leq 5$; $3, -1, -5$

Graph each inequality on a number line.

  5. $x \geq 8$ **6.** $x < -2$ **7.** $x \leq 1$ **8.** $x > -10$ **9.** $x < 3$ **10.** $x \geq -4$

11. *Writing* In your own words, tell how to graph an inequality on a number line.

Using Models: Adding Integers

What You'll Learn

▼1 To use models to add integers

▼2 To use absolute value to add integers

...And Why

You can add integers to find how much you owe someone or how high a temperature is.

Here's How

Look for questions that
- build understanding
- ✔ check understanding

THINK AND DISCUSS

▼1 *Adding Integers Using Models*

Algebra tiles can help you understand integers.

◻ 1   ◼ −1

positive   negative

1. **⊞ Modeling** Write the integer represented by each set of tiles.
   a. ◻◻   **b.** ◼◼◼   **c.** ◻◻◻   **d.** ◼

2. Draw a set of tiles to represent each integer and its opposite.
   a. −2   **b.** 4   **c.** −7   **d.** 5

An equal number of positive and negative tiles represents zero.

◻◼ ◂— a zero pair

You can write this as the number sentence $1 + (-1) = 0$.

3. **⊞ Think About It** Suppose you have 8 positive tiles. How many negative tiles do you need to represent zero?

4. Suppose you have 5 negative tiles. How many positive tiles do you need to represent zero?

◼ EXAMPLE 1

Add $-8 + 3$.

$-8 =$ ◼◼◼◼ / ◼◼◼◼

$3 =$ ◻◻◻   ◂— Use tiles to represent each integer.

◂— Group and remove zero pairs.

$-8 + 3 \quad = -5$ ◂— Simplify.

5. **✔ Try It Out** Use tiles to find each sum.
   a. $5 + (-3)$ **b.** $2 + (-5)$ **c.** $-4 + (-3)$

You can also use a number line to add integers.

■ **EXAMPLE 2**

Use a number line to find $-6 + 4$.

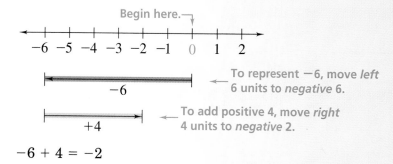

Begin here.

To represent -6, move *left* 6 units to *negative 6*.

To add positive 4, move *right* 4 units to *negative 2*.

$-6 + 4 = -2$

PROBLEM SOLVING HINT

The first arrow below the number line represents the first integer in the expression.

6. ✔ *Try It Out* Draw a number line to find each sum.

   a. $-4 + 5$ **b.** $2 + (-5)$ **c.** $-1 + (-7)$

▽ *Addition Using Absolute Value*

You can use absolute values to find the sum of two integers.

ADDING INTEGERS

The sum of two positive numbers is positive. The sum of two negative numbers is negative.

Examples: $3 + 5 = 8$ $-3 + (-5) = -8$

To add two numbers with different signs, find the *difference* between their absolute values. The sum has the same sign as the number with the greater absolute value.

Examples: $-3 + 5 = 2$ $3 + (-5) = -2$

 January is the coldest month of the year in Fairbanks, Alaska, with an average daily temperature of $-10°F$. The average daily temperature in January in Honolulu, Hawaii, is $73°F$.

Source: National Climatic Data Center and USA Today Weather Almanac

■ **EXAMPLE 3**   *Real-World Problem Solving*

Weather During the day, the temperature in Fairbanks, Alaska, rose $17°F$. The low temperature for the day was $-18°F$. What was the high temperature for the day?

$|-18| > |17|$ ←Compare the absolute values.

$|-18| - |17| = 18 - 17 = 1$ ←Find the difference.

$-18 + 17 = -1$ ← Because $|-18|$ is greater than $|17|$, the sum is negative.

The high temperature for the day was $-1°F$.

7. ✔ *Try It Out* Use absolute values to find each sum.

    a. $-19 + 34$ **b.** $21 + (-39)$ **c.** $-97 + (-65)$

Work Together

Playing an Integer Game

Work with a partner. You will need two number cubes and a bag containing algebra tiles. Take turns rolling the number cubes.

The number you roll is the number of tiles you draw. For example, if you roll a 6 and a 1, you draw seven tiles from the bag. Place the tiles on the table without looking.

8. a. Write the number represented by the tiles. Record it in a chart like the one at the right. Use $<$, $>$, or $=$ to compare the values.

Player 1	Player 2	Integer Sentence
-5	3	$-5 < 3$
▩	▩	▩

The person with the lesser value scores 1 point.

b. Repeat the activity until one of you has 10 points.

EXERCISES *On Your Own*

Write an expression for each model. Then find the sum.

1.

2.

3.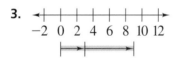

4.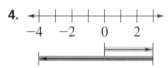

5. A set of tiles represents the integer 7. The set contains 4 negative tiles. How many positive tiles does it contain?

Find each sum.

  6. $-5 + (-4)$ **7.** $2 + (-8)$ **8.** $-6 + 7$ **9.** $12 + (-7)$ **10.** $3 + (-3)$

11. $-8 + (-1)$ **12.** $7 + (-2)$ **13.** $3 + (-12)$ **14.** $-14 + 16$ **15.** $-10 + 7$

Open-ended **Sketch tiles to represent each integer in three different ways.**

  16. 8   **17.** -1 **18.** -6 **19.** 2   **20.** 0   **21.** -9

22. Nina uses the expression $t + 3$ to find the time in New York, where t stands for the time in Los Angeles. Find the time in New York when it is 5 P.M. in Los Angeles.

23. *Entertainment* How far below ground level will the roller coaster go?

24. *Writing* Explain how you would find the sum of two integers that have different signs.

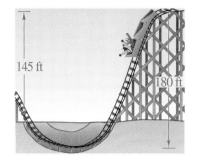

145 ft

180 ft

Mental Math **Find the value of each expression.**

25. $4 + 7 + (-2)$ **26.** $|-3| + 5 + (-3)$ **27.** $28 + (-12) + (-26)$

Evaluate each expression for $n = 6$.

28. $3.4 + n$ **29.** $-3.4 + n$ **30.** $-n + 3.4$ **31.** $-n + (-3.4)$

Use the associative property of addition to simplify.

32. $-3 + (-7 + 13)$ **33.** $5 + (-5 + 12)$ **34.** $-12 + (-8 + 6)$ **35.** $(-4 + 10) + (-10)$

▦ *Choose* **Use a calculator, paper and pencil, or mental math. Write an expression for each situation. Find the value of the expression.**

36. *Money* On Friday Rosa borrowed $10 from her sister. The next day she paid back $5. Then on Monday she borrowed $4 more. How much does Rosa owe?

37. *Weather* At midnight, the temperature was $-12°$F. By 6 A.M. the next morning the temperature had risen 19 degrees. What was the temperature at 6 A.M.?

Find each sum.

38. $27 + (-24)$ **39.** $42 + (-42)$ **40.** $-15 + 20$ **41.** $-13 + 7$ **42.** $28 + (-32)$

43. $126 + (-92)$ **44.** $68 + (-72)$ **45.** $-99 + 137$ **46.** $-50 + 48$ **47.** $74 + (-25)$

Mixed Review

Make a stem-and-leaf plot for each data set. *(Lesson 1-5)*

48. 39, 37, 47, 50, 56, 58

49. 2.43, 2.44, 2.48, 2.57, 2.49, 2.62, 2.53, 2.50

Compare. Use <, >, or =. *(Lesson 3-2)*

50. -4 ▪ -10 **51.** 5 ▪ -6 **52.** $|-3|$ ▪ $|3|$ **53.** $|16|$ ▪ $|-23|$

54. *Choose a Strategy* The pages of a book are numbered from 1 to 128. How many page numbers contain the digit 6?

What You'll Learn

▼ To use models to subtract integers

▼ To use a rule to subtract integers

...And Why

You can subtract integers to find the difference in temperatures.

Here's How

Look for questions that
- build understanding
✔ check understanding

THINK AND DISCUSS

▼ *Using Models to Subtract Integers*

The coldest recorded temperature for Sacramento is $-5°$C. The coldest recorded temperature for San Diego is $-2°$C. To find the difference in temperature of these California cities, you subtract.

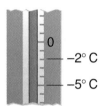

1. Which expression describes subtracting -2 from -5: $-2 - (-5)$ *or* $-5 - (-2)$?

Algebra tiles can help you understand how to subtract integers.

■ EXAMPLE 1

Use algebra tiles to find $-5 - (-2)$.

■ ← Start with 5 negative tiles.

■ ← Take away 2 negative tiles. There are 3 negative tiles left.

$-5 - (-2) = -3$

2. ✔ **Try It Out** Use algebra tiles to find each difference.
   a. $-7 - (-2)$ b. $5 - 3$ c. $-5 - (-4)$

■ EXAMPLE 2

Find $4 - 6$.

■ ← Start with 4 positive tiles.

 ← There are not enough positive tiles to take 6 away. Add 2 zero pairs.

■ ← Take away 6 positive tiles. There are 2 negative tiles left.

$4 - 6 = -2$

3. ✔ *Try It Out* Use algebra tiles to find each difference.
   a. $4 - 7$ **b.** $-1 - 5$ **c.** $7 - (-5)$ **d.** $-6 - 10$

▼2 *Using a Rule to Subtract Integers*

To subtract integers, look for a pattern in related addition and subtraction problems.

4. ▪*Modeling* Use algebra tiles to find each difference and sum.
   a. $5 - 3$ **b.** $-9 - (-6)$ **c.** $4 - (-5)$
      $5 + (-3)$ $-9 + 6$ $4 + 5$

5. ▪*Patterns* What do you notice about the sums and differences in Question 4?

The patterns you investigated in Questions 4 and 5 lead to a rule for subtraction.

SUBTRACTING INTEGERS

To subtract an integer, add its opposite.

Examples: $3 - 5 = 3 + (-5) = -2$
                  $-3 - 5 = -3 + (-5) = -8$

■ **EXAMPLE 3**   *Real-World Problem Solving*

Temperature The highest temperature recorded in the United States was 134°F, measured at Death Valley, California. The coldest temperature, -80°F, was recorded at Prospect Creek, Alaska. What is the difference between these temperatures?

   $134 - (-80) = 134 + 80$ ◀—To subtract -80, add its opposite, 80.
              $= 214$

The difference between the highest and lowest temperatures recorded in the United States is 214 degrees.

6. ✔ *Try It Out* Find each difference.
   a. $3 - 7$ **b.** $-2 - (-8)$ **c.** $17 - 9$ **d.** $-23 - 18$

7. Temperatures in Verkhoyansk, Russia, have ranged from a low of -90°F to a high of 98°F. Find the temperature range in Verkhoyansk.

Draw models to find each difference.

1. $-4 - (-2)$ 2. $-4 - (-6)$ 3. $3 - 9$ 4. $9 - (-11)$

5. $-7 - (-1)$ 6. $-8 - 12$ 7. $6 - (-6)$ 8. $0 - 11$

Find each difference.

9. $12 - (-4)$ 10. $-7 - 3$ 11. $-15 - 2$ 12. $-3 - (-3)$ 13. $2 - 5$

14. $1 - (-7)$ 15. $-5 - (-9)$ 16. $270 - 35$ 17. $47 - 151$ 18. $-3 - 9$

19. $17 - (-8)$ 20. $20 - (-8)$ 21. $-14 - (-14)$ 22. $-100 - 150$ 23. $-10 - (-18)$

24. $589 - 635$ 25. $-121 - 98$ 26. $0 - (-22)$ 27. $-54 - 82$ 28. $-8 - (-12)$

29. **Choose A, B, C, or D.** At 8 P.M. the wind speed was 10 miles per hour (mi/h). The wind-chill temperature was $-9°F$. One hour later, the wind speed had increased to 25 mi/h. The wind-chill temperature had fallen to $-29°F$. Which number sentence below shows this change?

    A. $29 + (-9) = 20$ **B.** $-29 - (-9) = -20$ **C.** $-9 - (-29) = 20$ **D.** $-29 - 9 = -38$

30. *Temperature* A scientist measured the temperature at the surface of a 7-inch-deep snowbank. The temperature was $-27°F$. At ground level the temperature was $24°F$. How much warmer was the temperature at ground level?

Write the related addition expression for each subtraction expression. Then find its value.

31. $-9 - (-6)$ 32. $6 - 11$ 33. $5 - (-3)$

34. $-2 - (-5)$ 35. $1 - (-9)$ 36. $-16 - 17$

37. *Finance* The chart at the right shows the changes in a stock price each day.
    a. The opening price of the stock on Monday was $25. What was the closing price on Tuesday?
    b. How much did the stock price change during the week?
    c. What was the average daily change?

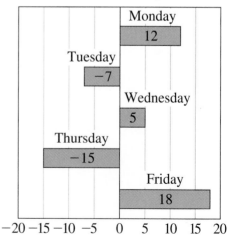

Stock Activity

Mental Math **Find the value of each expression.**

38. $-4 + 5 - (-4)$ **39.** $-3 - (-3) + (-6)$ **40.** $7 + (-7) + 5$ **41.** $6 - 13 - (-13)$

42. $-8 + 4 - (-8)$ **43.** $-2 + (-3) - (-5)$ **44.** $-11 - (-3) + 11$ **45.** $-3 + 10 + (-7)$

46. $21 - 12 + (-21)$ **47.** $7 - (-4) - (-3)$ **48.** $19 - (-7) + 1$ **49.** $2 + 8 - (-2)$

Without calculating, determine whether each difference is positive or negative.

50. $-18 - 25$ **51.** $9 - (-2)$ **52.** $46 - (-65)$ **53.** $-7 - (-13)$

Estimation **Round each number. Then estimate the sum or difference.**

54. $124 - 238$ **55.** $-53 + (-110)$ **56.** $122 - 16$ **57.** $22 - (-7)$

58. $-74 - 52$ **59.** $-1,302 - 2,305$ **60.** $16 - 23$ **61.** $-52 - (-104)$

62. $-78 + (-97)$ **63.** $258 + (-167)$ **64.** $-38 + 17$ **65.** $-295 - (-82)$

Science **Use the data at the right for Exercises 66–69.**

66. How much less than the boiling temperature of carbon is the boiling temperature of gold?

67. How much greater than the boiling temperature of chlorine is the boiling temperature of iodine?

68. How much less than the boiling temperature of mercury is the boiling temperature of helium?

69. How much greater than the boiling temperature of helium is the boiling temperature of chlorine?

Boiling Point

Element	Temperature (Celsius)
Carbon	4827
Chlorine	−34.6
Gold	2807
Helium	−268.934
Iodine	184.35
Mercury	356.58
Water	100

Source: *Information Please Almanac*

70. *Writing* In your own words, explain how you add and subtract integers. Use examples.

71. *Reasoning* Tell if each of the subtraction sentences would *always*, *sometimes*, or *never* be true. Support your answer with examples.
   a. (positive) − (positive) = (positive)
   b. (negative) − (positive) = (negative)
   c. (negative) − (negative) = (positive)
   d. (positive) − (negative) = (negative)
   e. (negative) − (positive) = (positive)
   f. (positive) − (positive) = (negative)

Mixed Review

Find each sum. *(Lesson 3-3)*

72. $-9 + 6$ **73.** $15 + (-4)$ **74.** $90 + (-73)$ **75.** $-50 + (-22)$ **76.** $84 + (-38)$

Divide. *(Lesson 2-6)*

77. $1.2 \div 0.6$ **78.** $39 \div 1.3$ **79.** $14.7 \div 3.5$ **80.** $45.14 \div 3.7$ **81.** $174.22 \div 3.1$

82. *Choose a Strategy* Dwana is in training for a marathon. The first week she runs 1 mi each day, the second week 2 mi each day, and the third week 3 mi each day. If she continues in this way, how many total miles will she have run at the end of 5 weeks?

CHAPTER PROJECT

PROJECT LINK: DESIGNING

Make a draft of your game board. Add details. Use integers to determine positive and negative points or positive and negative movement on the game board. Think of adventures and misadventures for your game like "Catch a falling star. Get +10 points" or "Fall off a cliff. Move −7 spaces."

✓ CHECKPOINT 1

Lessons 3-1 through 3-4

Use the data from the table at the right.

1. **a.** Write a variable expression to find the plums in p boxes.
   b. Evaluate the expression from part (a) for $p = 4$; $p = 10$.

2. Write a variable expression for the sum of the number of apples in a bags and the number of tomatoes in t boxes.

Farmer's Market Produce

Produce	Package
Apples	10 per bag
Daisies	12 per bunch
Green beans	2-lb bag
Plums	6 per box
Tomatoes	8 per box

Evaluate each expression for $p = 7$ and $q = 6$.

3. $4(p - 2)$ 4. $18 - 3q$ 5. $pq \div 14$ 6. $3.2(p + q)$

Find the value of each expression.

7. $-5 + 9$ 8. $-6 + (-3)$ 9. $8 + (-4)$ 10. $-27 + 4$ 11. $14 + (-23)$

12. $3 - (-2)$ 13. $-7 - (-4)$ 14. $-17 - 12$ 15. $14 - 19$ 16. $-23 - (-29)$

TECHNOLOGY

Using Spreadsheets

After Lesson 3-4

You can use a computer spreadsheet to keep track of the balance in a checking account. You add deposits and subtract checks. You can compute values in cells in a spreadsheet.

■ EXAMPLE

Use the spreadsheet. Find the balance after each entry.

	A	B	C	D
1	Date	Deposits	Checks	Balance
2				$350
3	4/29	$100		■
4	4/30		$400	■

Use the formula $= D2 + B3$.
The computer finds 350 + 100 = 450.

Use the formula $= D3 - C4$.
The computer finds 450 − 400 = 50.

The first balance is $450. The second balance is $50.

Use the spreadsheet at the right.

1. Find the account balance after each entry. Write the formulas you used.

2. **Choose A, B, C, or D.** Which formula could you use to find the balance in cell D9 regardless of whether a check had been written or a deposit had been made?

   A. $= D8 - B9 + C9$ **B.** $= D8 - B9 - C9$
   C. $= D8 + B9 + C9$ **D.** $= D8 + B9 - C9$

3. *Reasoning* Suppose the balance in cell D9 is $130.34. Was the amount of a deposit entered into cell B9, or was the amount of a check entered into cell C9? Support your answer.

4. *Writing* Consider your answer to Exercise 2. Explain why the formula you chose works, and give examples.

	A	B	C	D
1	Date	Deposits	Checks	Balance
2				$250
3	11/3		25.98	■
4	11/9		239.40	■
5	11/10	122.00		■
6	11/13		54.65	■
7	11/20	350.00		■
8	11/29		163.80	■

Multiplying and Dividing Integers

What You'll Learn

▼ To multiply integers
▼ To divide integers

...And Why

Stockbrokers use integers to describe changes in the price of stock.

Here's How

Look for questions that
⁘ build understanding
✔ check understanding

QUICKreview

Commutative Property
$ab = ba$

$$-4(3) = \blacksquare$$
$$-4(2) = \blacksquare$$
$$-4(1) = \blacksquare$$
$$-4(0) = \blacksquare$$
$$-4(-1) = \blacksquare$$
$$-4(-2) = \blacksquare$$
$$-4(-3) = \blacksquare$$

THINK AND DISCUSS

▼ *Multiplying Integers*

Suppose a cave explorer descends 4 ft/min for 3 min. You can use negative tiles to model the explorer's descent. Show 3 groups of 4 negative tiles.

$3(-4) = -12$. The explorer descends 12 ft.

You can use the commutative property to find $-4(3)$.

$$-4(3) = 3(-4) = -12$$

To use tiles to find $-2(5)$, think $-2(5) = 5(-2)$. Then model $5(-2)$. Show 5 groups of 2 negative tiles.

$5(-2) = -10$, so $-2(5) = -10$.

1. ✔ *Try It Out* Use tiles to find each product.
   a. $-6(4)$ **b.** $3(-3)$ **c.** $4(-5)$

2. Choose the correct word to complete the following statement:

   The sign of the product of two integers with different signs is *negative / positive*.

Patterns can help you find the product of two negative integers.

3. **a.** Copy and complete the table at the left.
   b. ⁘*Patterns* Describe the pattern you see in the products as you go from $-4(3)$ to $-4(-3)$.
   c. Write a pattern like the one on the left to find $-2(-5)$. Start with $-2(3)$.
   d. Complete the following statement:

   The sign of the product of two negative integers is __?__.

MULTIPLYING INTEGERS

When you multiply two integers with the same sign, the product is positive.

Examples: $2 \cdot 6 = 12$ $-2(-6) = 12$

When you multiply two integers with different signs, the product is negative.

Examples: $-2 \cdot 6 = -12$ $2(-6) = -12$

■ **EXAMPLE 1**

Find each product.

a. $5(3)$ $5(3) = 15$ ← Both factors are positive, so the product is positive.

b. $5(-3)$ $5(-3) = -15$ ← One factor is negative, so the product is negative.

c. $-5(3)$ $-5(3) = -15$ ← One factor is negative, so the product is negative.

d. $-5(-3)$ $-5(-3) = 15$ ← Both factors are negative, so the product is positive.

4. ✔ *Try It Out* Find each product.
   a. $-6 \cdot 2$ b. $15(-8)$ c. $-12 \cdot 6$ d. $22(-41)$

Lechuguilla Cave in New Mexico is the deepest cave discovered in the United States.

Source: *The Guinness Book of Records*

❷ Dividing Integers

You can use tiles to divide integers. To find $-6 \div 2$, use 6 negative tiles and make 2 equal groups.

So, $-6 \div 2 = -3$.

5. ✔ *Try It Out* Use tiles to find each quotient.
   a. $-8 \div 2$ b. $-6 \div 3$ c. $-10 \div 5$

Multiplication and division are *inverse operations*.

6. a. ♣ *Patterns* Use inverse operations to find each quotient.

   i. $3 \cdot 4 = 12$ ii. $3(-4) = -12$ iii. $(-3)(-4) = 12$
   $12 \div 4 = \blacksquare$ $-12 \div (-4) = \blacksquare$ $12 \div (-4) = \blacksquare$
   $12 \div 3 = \blacksquare$ $-12 \div 3 = \blacksquare$ $12 \div (-3) = \blacksquare$

   b. When two integers have the same sign, what is the sign of the quotient? When two integers have different signs, what is the sign of the quotient?

   c. Rewrite the Rules for Multiplying Integers to include dividing integers.

Some problems may require you to use more than one operation.

■ **EXAMPLE 2** *Real-World Problem Solving*

Stock Market In one week, the Dow Jones Industrial Average rose 1 point on Monday, fell 3 points on Tuesday, rose 4 points on Wednesday, fell 4 points on Thursday, and fell 3 points on Friday. What was the average daily change?

$$\frac{1 + (-3) + 4 + (-4) + (-3)}{5} = \frac{-5}{5} \longleftarrow \text{Find the sum of the changes and divide by 5.}$$

The average daily change was −1 point, or down 1 point.

7 ✔ *Try It Out* Find the average of these winter temperatures.
−12° −8° −6° −3° 0° 3° 5°

EXERCISES *On Your Own*

Use tiles to find each product.

1. $7(-4)$ **2.** $-4(4)$ **3.** $-4(9)$ **4.** $6(-3)$ **5.** $3(-2)$ **6.** $12(-1)$

Multiply.

7. $-2(-13)$ **8.** $-6 \cdot 12$ **9.** $-5(-6)$ **10.** $4(-9)$ **11.** $12(-4)$

12. $-15(-3)$ **13.** $-36 \cdot 2$ **14.** $102(-6)$ **15.** $-35(24)$ **16.** $27 \cdot 31$

17. *Hobbies* Suppose a scuba diver is 180 ft below sea level and rises to the surface at a rate of 30 ft/min. How long will it take the diver to reach the surface?

Open-ended **Complete each number sentence. Then write two examples to illustrate each relationship.**

18. (positive) · (positive) = ■   **19.** (positive) · (negative) = ■

20. (negative) · (positive) = ■   **21.** (negative) · (negative) = ■

22. (positive) ÷ (positive) = ■   **23.** (positive) ÷ (negative) = ■

24. (negative) ÷ (positive) = ■   **25.** (negative) ÷ (negative) = ■

Use tiles to find each quotient.

26. $-15 \div (5)$ **27.** $-12 \div 6$ **28.** $-9 \div 9$ **29.** $-16 \div (2)$ **30.** $-20 \div (4)$

Mental Math **Divide.**

31. $36 \div (-12)$ **32.** $72 \div 9$ **33.** $39 \div (-3)$ **34.** $0 \div (-2)$ **35.** $(-4 \cdot 6) \div (-3)$

36. $15 \div (-3)$ **37.** $-50 \div (-5)$ **38.** $66 \div (-11)$ **39.** $-72 \div 8$ **40.** $-27 \div 9$

41. Write two related division sentences for $7(-3) = -21$.

42. *Business* The price of a stock fell $2 each day for 8 days.
   a. What was the total change in the price of the stock?
   b. Before the price of the stock started falling, its value was
      $38. What was the price of the stock after the drop?

Estimation **Estimate each product or quotient.**

43. $-24 \cdot 35$ **44.** $428 \div (-58)$ **45.** $-108(-55)$ **46.** $-58 \div (-9)$ **47.** $12 \cdot (-15)$

48. $-265 \div (-129)$ **49.** $-72 \cdot 68$ **50.** $64 \cdot 93$ **51.** $19 \div 4.7$ **52.** $-12(-14)$

Find the point on the number line that shows each product or quotient.

53. $-2 \cdot 0$ **54.** $-16 \div (-2)$ **55.** $(-1)(-1)$ **56.** $-4(2)$ **57.** $32 \div (-8)$

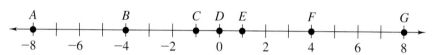

Use the table at the right for Exercises 58 and 59.

58. *Nutrition* Suppose you swam for 25 min. Then you
   ate 1 c of tomato soup, 3 oz of cheddar cheese, and
   8 crackers.
   a. Find the number of calories you used while
      swimming and the number of calories you
      ate during lunch.
   b. Find the net gain or loss of calories.

59. *Open-ended* Select some foods for lunch and an
   activity for 40 min of exercise. Find the total number of
   calories you would eat during lunch. Find the number
   of calories you would use during exercise. What would
   be your net gain or loss of calories?

60. *Writing* Explain how to find the sign of the product or
   quotient of any two integers.

Food	Calories
Apple (1)	80
Banana (1)	100
Cheddar cheese (1 oz)	115
Lettuce, iceberg (1c)	5
Mayonnaise (1 tbsp)	100
Milk, skim (1 c)	85
Orange juice (1 c)	120
Crackers (4)	50
Tomato soup (1 c)	90
Tuna (3 oz)	170

Activity	Calories used per minute
Walking	3
Skating	4
Tennis	5
Swimming	6

Mixed Review

Find each difference. *(Lesson 3-4)*

61. $8 - 1$ **62.** $3 - (-6)$ **63.** $-4 - (-9)$ **64.** $86 - (-17)$ **65.** $-23 - 9$

Evaluate for $m = 1.8$ and $n = 4.6$. *(Lesson 3-1)*

66. $4m - n$ **67.** $4(n + m)$ **68.** $n - 5$ **69.** $mn + 13$ **70.** $mn \div 2.3$

71. *Choose a Strategy* In how many ways can you order the letters A, B, C, and D? Do not repeat a letter in any arrangement.

CHAPTER PROJECT

PROJECT LINK: DESIGNING

Add details to your game board that require multiplication of integers. Use illustrations and color, and put a cardboard backing on the game board.

Math at Work

SOFTWARE DEVELOPER

Software developers create programs for computers. Computer software can consist of operating systems, which control the computer, or applications programs, which adapt the computer to perform a specific task, such as figuring a payroll, modeling a machine part, or running a video game.

To find out more about computer software, visit this Web site:

http://www.yahooligans.com/Computers__ Games__and_Online/Software/

Choose the best answer.

Balance Beam Competition

Gymnast	Score
Ruth	9.45
Davida	9.5
Shante	9.4
Lupe	9.55
Aun	9.05

1. The gymnasts' names will be posted on the bulletin board in order based on their scores from greatest to least. In what order will the names be listed?

   A. Davida, Ruth, Lupe, Shante, Aun
   B. Lupe, Shante, Ruth, Davida, Aun
   C. Lupe, Davida, Ruth, Shante, Aun
   D. Aun, Shante, Ruth, Davida, Lupe

2. The marching band does a formation in which there are 48 students in the first row, 42 students in the second row, and 36 students in the third row. If the pattern continues, how many students are in the *seventh* row?

   F. 24   **G.** 18   **H.** 12   **J.** 6

Please note that items 3–7 have *five* answer choices.

3. At the grocery store, Dan bought hamburger that weighed 1.42 lb, sausage that weighed 2.16 lb, and chicken that weighed 3.73 lb. How many pounds of meat did Dan purchase in all?

   A. 3.58 lb   **B.** 5.89 lb   **C.** 6.31 lb
   D. 7.31 lb   **E.** 7.41 lb

4. Tanya started her road trip with a full tank of gas. She drove 318 miles and then put 12 gallons of gas in her car. What was the average number of miles per gallon?

   F. 26.5   **G.** 26
   H. 25.5   **J.** 25
   K. Not Here

5. At the gardening store, Ellen bought weed killer on sale for $4.97 a bottle, a gardening rake and a shovel for $8.25 each, and several bags of soil that cost a total of $37.50. Ellen had $85 before she made her purchases. What additional information do you need to find the total cost of her purchases?

   A. the price of the rake
   B. the price of the shovel
   C. the original price of the weed killer
   D. the number of bags of soil
   E. the number of bottles of weed killer purchased

6. In the problem above, what information is *not* needed to solve the problem?

   F. the sale price of the weed killer
   G. the combined cost of the rake and shovel
   H the total cost of the bags of soil
   J. the amount of money Ellen had before making the purchases
   K. Not Here

7. After 4 weeks, Kono had $25 in his savings account, after 5 weeks he had $31.25, and after 6 weeks he had $37.50. If the pattern continues, how much money will he have after 9 weeks?

   A. $62.50   **B.** $56.25   **C.** $54.25
   D. $50.00   **E.** $43.75

Solving Equations by Adding and Subtracting

What You'll Learn

▼ 1 To use models to solve equations

▼ 2 To use inverse operations to solve equations

...And Why

You can solve equations to find a predicted number of jobs.

Here's How

Look for questions that
- ⊞ build understanding
- ✔ check understanding

THINK AND DISCUSS

▼ 1 Using Models to Solve Equations

Solving an equation is like balancing a scale. A scale balances when the weights on both sides are equal. An equation is true when the values on both sides are equal.

The green rectangular tile in the model at the right represents the variable in an equation. The value of the variable that makes the equation true is the **solution.**

1. ⊞ **Analyze** How would you remove weights to get the variable alone but keep the scale balanced?

To find the value of a variable, you need to get it alone on one side of the equal sign.

■ EXAMPLE 1

Use models to solve $x + 3 = 7$.

Model the equation.   Remove 3 tiles from each side.

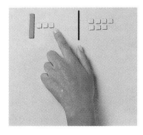  

$$x = 4$$

2. ✔ **Try It Out** Model and solve each equation.
   a. $x + 3 = 5$ b. $y + 5 = 8$ c. $7 + a = 12$

3. ⊞ **Go a Step Further** Complete each step of the equation at the right.

   $x + 7 = 24$
   $x + 7 - \blacksquare = 24 - \blacksquare$
   $x = \blacksquare$

A model can be especially helpful when you solve equations involving subtraction or negative integers.

■ EXAMPLE 2

Model the equation $n - 4 = -1$ and solve.

$n - 4 = -1$
$n + (-4) = -1$ ←— Subtracting is the same as adding the opposite.

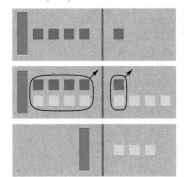

←— Represent the equation.

←— Add 4 positive tiles to each side. Remove zero pairs.

←— Simplify.

4. ✔ *Try It Out* Model each equation. Then solve.
   a. $x - 4 = 5$ **b.** $y - 2 = 8$ **c.** $a - (-5) = -3$

▼2 *Using Inverse Operations*

Addition and subtraction are inverse operations. You can add to undo subtraction and subtract to undo addition.

You can add or subtract the same number from each side of an equation. The result is an equation having the same solution.

■ EXAMPLE 3

Solve $-4 = x - 3$. Check your answer.

$$-4 = x - 3$$
$$-4 + 3 = x - 3 + 3$$ ←— Since 3 is subtracted from the variable, add 3 to both sides of the equation.
$$-1 = x$$ ←— Simplify.

Check: $-4 = x - 3$ ←— Start with the original equation.
$-4 \overset{?}{=} -1 - 3$ ←— Replace x with -1.
$-4 = -4$ ✔ ←— Simplify.

5. ⬛ *Error Alert* Stephen solved $x - 5 = -3$. His solution was $x = -8$. Find his mistake.

The following properties summarize how you can add or subtract to rewrite an equation.

PROPERTIES OF EQUALITY
Addition
You can add the same value to each side of an equation.
Arithmetic: Since $\frac{20}{2} = 10$, $\frac{20}{2} + 3 = 10 + 3$.
Algebra: If $a = b$, then $a + c = b + c$.
Subtraction
You can subtract the same value from each side of an equation.
Arithmetic: Since $\frac{20}{2} = 10$, $\frac{20}{2} - 3 = 10 - 3$.
Algebra: If $a = b$, then $a - c = b - c$.

6. State which property you would use to solve each equation. Then state what you would add or subtract.
   a. $x + 19 = 36$ b. $x - 54 = -28$ c. $x - (-15) = -4$

EXERCISES *On Your Own*

Write the equation represented by each model. Then solve.

1.

2.

3.

4.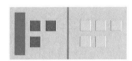

Use a model to solve each equation.

5. $x + 4 = 5$

6. $x - 3 = -2$

7. $x + 1 = -4$

8. $-1 = 4 + n$

9. $y + 1 = 9$

10. $3 = a - 5$

11. $2 + n = -3$

12. $8 = p + 7$

13. $-8 = (-7) + b$

14. $-2 + m = -9$

15. $d - (-1) = 5$

16. $x - (-5) = 3$

Mental Math **Solve each equation.**

17. $x + 6 = -6$

18. $x - 6 = -6$

19. $x + 6 = 6$

20. $x - 6 = 6$

21. $x - 3 = 0$

22. $-5 = p + 8$

23. $q - 6 = 4$

24. $7 = 9 + y$

25. $x - 2 = 1$

26. $-7 = k + 4$

27. $m - 4 = 12$

28. $17 = 19 + t$

Solve each equation.

29. $16 = c + (-5)$ **30.** $-11 = a - (-6)$ **31.** $-7 + g = 10$ **32.** $r + (-2) = -4$

33. $9 + x = -4$ **34.** $p + (-3) = 8$ **35.** $5 + e = -7$ **36.** $3 = -2 + k$

37. $12 = q - (-7)$ **38.** $8 + b = 0$ **39.** $-1 = h - 5$ **40.** $r - 54 = 74$

▦ *Choose* **Use a calculator, paper and pencil, or mental math. Solve each equation and check the solution.**

41. $n - 35 = 84$ **42.** $166 = m + 97$ **43.** $x + 25 = 16$ **44.** $-17 = x + 6$

45. *Business* The bar graph at the right shows the projected changes in employment for selected occupations.

   a. Which occupation expects the greatest increase in jobs from 1994 to 2005? Which expects the greatest decrease?

   b. Which equation could you use to find the occupation that expects 17 more jobs per 100 than mathematician, $n - 17 = 5$ or $n + 17 = 5$?

   c. Which occupation expects 17 more jobs per 100 than mathematician?

46. *Reasoning* Can you rewrite the equation $5 + x = 4$ to become the equation $3 + x = 2$? Explain.

47. *Writing* Explain how you could use the Addition Property of Equality to solve the equation $x + 15 = 34$.

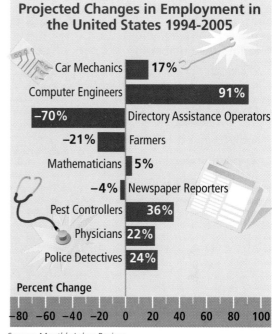

Projected Changes in Employment in the United States 1994-2005

Car Mechanics **17%**
Computer Engineers **91%**
−70% Directory Assistance Operators
−21% Farmers
Mathematicians **5%**
−4% Newspaper Reporters
Pest Controllers **36%**
Physicians **22%**
Police Detectives **24%**

Percent Change

−80 −60 −40 −20 0 20 40 60 80 100

Source: *Monthly Labor Review*

Mixed Review

Find each answer. *(Lesson 3-5)*

48. $54 \div (-9)$ **49.** $-24 \div 3$ **50.** $4(5)(-3)$ **51.** $(15 \div 3)(-6)$

52. *Choose a Strategy* The 16 teams in the summer softball league held a tournament. A team was eliminated after a single loss. How many games were played to determine the league championship?

Solving Equations by Multiplying and Dividing

What You'll Learn

1 To solve equations by dividing

2 To solve equations by multiplying

...And Why

You can solve equations to find the number of days a library book was late.

Here's How

Look for questions that
- build understanding
- ✔ check understanding

THINK AND DISCUSS

1 *Solving Equations by Dividing*

You can use algebra tiles to solve some equations that involve multiplication.

■ **EXAMPLE 1**

Use algebra tiles to solve the equation $3x = 21$.

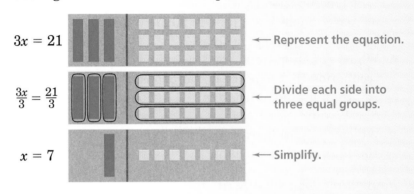

$3x = 21$ ← Represent the equation.

$\frac{3x}{3} = \frac{21}{3}$ ← Divide each side into three equal groups.

$x = 7$ ← Simplify.

1. ✔ *Try It Out* Write the equation for each model. Then use algebra tiles to solve.

a.

b.

Since multiplication and division are inverse operations, you can use division to undo multiplication.

■ **EXAMPLE 2**

Solve $-12x = 84$.

$$-12x = 84$$
$$\frac{-12x}{-12} = \frac{84}{-12}$$ ← Divide each side by -12.
$$x = -7$$ ← Simplify.

2. ✔ Try It Out Solve each equation.

   a. $12x = 84$ **b.** $12x = -84$ **c.** $-12x = -84$

■ **EXAMPLE 3**   *Real-World Problem Solving*

Money Suppose you return an overdue library book. Your fine is 78¢. The library charges 6¢ per day. Solve the equation $6d = 78$ to find the number of days the book was overdue.

$$6d = 78 \quad \longleftarrow \text{Since 6 multiplies } d, \text{ divide each side of the equation by 6.}$$
$$\frac{6d}{6} = \frac{78}{6} \quad \longleftarrow \text{Simplify.}$$
$$d = 13$$

Check: $6d = 78 \quad \longleftarrow \text{Replace } d \text{ with 13.}$

          $6 \cdot 13 \stackrel{?}{=} 78 \quad \longleftarrow \text{Simplify.}$

             $78 = 78 ✔$

The book was 13 days overdue.

3. ✔ Try It Out David's library charges 7¢ per day for overdue books. David has a fine of 98¢. Solve the equation $7d = 98$ to find the number of days his book was overdue. Check your answer.

▼2 *Solving Equations by Multiplying*

Just as you use division to undo multiplication, you can use multiplication to undo division.

■ **EXAMPLE 4**

Solve $\frac{s}{-4} = -5$.

$$\frac{s}{-4} = -5$$
$$(-4)\frac{s}{-4} = (-4)(-5) \quad \longleftarrow \text{Since } -4 \text{ divides } s, \text{ multiply each side of the equation by } -4.$$
$$s = 20 \quad \longleftarrow \text{Simplify.}$$

4. Check the solution to Example 4.

5. ✔ Try It Out Solve and check each equation.

   a. $\frac{x}{8} = 9$ **b.** $\frac{x}{6} = -15$ **c.** $\frac{x}{-5} = -23$

The following properties summarize how you can use division and multiplication to rewrite equations.

PROPERTIES OF EQUALITY

Multiplication

You can multiply each side of an equation by the same value.

Arithmetic: Since $\frac{12}{2} = 6$, $\frac{12}{2} \cdot 2 = 6 \cdot 2$.

Algebra: If $a = b$, then $a \cdot c = b \cdot c$.

Division

You can divide each side of an equation by the same nonzero value.

Arithmetic: Since $3(2) = 6$, $3(2) \div 2 = 6 \div 2$.

Algebra: If $a = b$, then $a \div c = b \div c$.

6. Would you use the Division Property of Equality or the Multiplication Property of Equality to solve each equation?
   a. $5x = 95$ **b.** $\frac{x}{-12} = -24$ **c.** $-3x = 42$

EXERCISES *On Your Own*

Write the equation represented by each model. Then solve and check the equation.

1.

2.

Choose **Use models, paper and pencil, or mental math to solve each equation.**

3. $5b = -20$ **4.** $35 = -7h$ **5.** $-52 = 13e$ **6.** $8p = -40$ **7.** $12 = 6t$

8. $2x = 4$ **9.** $3x = -27$ **10.** $-7y = -28$ **11.** $7 = d \div 4$ **12.** $\frac{m}{-5} = 3$

13. $-6 = \frac{r}{10}$ **14.** $z \div 8 = -3$ **15.** $-14 = q \div -2$ **16.** $m \div -3 = 9$ **17.** $\frac{t}{8} = 120$

18. *Estimation* What equation would you use to estimate the solution of $12x = -38$? Explain your choice. Then estimate the solution.

19. *Entertainment* Dr. H. Howard Hughes of Fort Worth, Texas, saw 6,136 plays in 31 years. Solve the equation $31p = 6{,}136$ to find the average number of plays p he saw per year.

20. *Reasoning* For what values of x is $5|x| = 10$ true?

▦ *Choose* **Use a calculator, paper and pencil, or mental math to solve each equation.**

21. $27 = -9w$
22. $-3k = -18$
23. $\frac{c}{6} = -1$
24. $\frac{y}{-4} = -12$
25. $\frac{n}{-5} = 11$

26. $t \div 6 = -10$
27. $\frac{q}{-5} = 30$
28. $8n = 112$
29. $-4 = -2r$
30. $-4y = 24$

31. $-7 = 7m$
32. $3g = 42$
33. $d \div 7 = -8$
34. $\frac{n}{3} = 4$
35. $-5 = \frac{a}{-9}$

36. $\frac{n}{3} = -42$
37. $\frac{r}{-4} = -104$
38. $7 = \frac{n}{9}$
39. $\frac{x}{18} = -40$
40. $\frac{x}{-78} = -63$

41. *Writing* Susan's solution for the equation $\frac{n}{-6} = 12$ is $n = -2$. Explain how Susan may have found this solution and how you would help her correct her mistake.

42. George Adrian of Indianapolis, Indiana, picked 15,830 pounds of apples in 8 hours. Solve $8a = 15{,}830$ to find the number of pounds of apples a he picked per hour.

43. **Choose A, B, C or D.** Which equation would you use to represent the following situation? A growing tree absorbs about 26 lb of carbon dioxide a year. How many years y would it take the tree to absorb 390 lb of carbon dioxide?

   A. $26 + y = 390$
   B. $\frac{y}{26} = 390$
   C. $26y = 390$
   D. $\frac{26}{y} = 390$

Mixed Review

Name the property shown. *(Lessons 2-3, 2-5, and 2-8)*

44. $3(4 + 8) = 12 + 24$
45. $21 \cdot 1 = 21$
46. $0(17.56) = 0$
47. $3 + 4 = 4 + 3$

Evaluate each expression for *m* = 12. *(Lesson 3-1)*

48. $32 - 2m$
49. $5 + 6m$
50. $2m + 10$
51. $7m$
52. $125 - 4m$

53. *Choose a Strategy* A clock gains 4 min every hour. One day it is set to the correct time at 9:00 A.M. What is the correct time when the clock shows 1:00 P.M.?

Writing Equations

THINK AND DISCUSS

You can use what you learned about writing expressions to write equations. A word sentence translates to an equation the way a word expression translates to a mathematical expression.

■ EXAMPLE 1

Write and solve an equation for "Four times a number is ten."

Let n = the unknown number. ◄— Identify the variable.

$$4n = 10$$ ◄— Write an equation.

$$\frac{4n}{4} = \frac{10}{4}$$ ◄— Divide each side by 4.

$$n = 2.5$$ ◄— Simplify.

1. ✔ **Try It Out** Write and solve an equation for each sentence.
   a. Three less than a number is twelve.
   b. A number divided by three equals twelve.

You can write equations to solve some real-world problems.

■ EXAMPLE 2 *Real-World Problem Solving*

Architecture The 553-m CN Tower in Toronto is 110 m taller than the Sears Tower in Chicago. Write and solve an equation to find the height of the Sears Tower.

| Words | • | height of CN Tower | is | 110 m | more than | height of Sears Tower |

• Height of CN Tower = 553
  Let s = height of Sears Tower

Equation • 553 = 110 + s

$$553 = 110 + s$$ ◄— Set up the equation.

$$553 - 110 = 110 + s - 110$$ ◄— Subtract 110 from each side.

$$443 = s$$ ◄— Simplify.

The Sears Tower is 443 m tall.

HISTORY The first true skyscraper was built in Chicago in 1885 for the Home Insurance Corporation. It had 10 stories. The Sears Tower has 110 stories.

Source: *American Art and Architecture*

2. ✔ *Try It Out* On Tuesday, 80 students were absent from Hartwell Middle School. There were 478 students present. Write and solve an equation to find how many students attend the school.

Work Together

Work with a partner. Match each word sentence with an equation.

3. Five less than a number equals three.

4. Three times a number is negative five.

5. A number minus three is five.

6. Five is three more than a number.

7. Three equals a number divided by negative five.

8. The product of a number and five is negative three.

9. Five plus a number is three.

A. $5 = 3 + n$

B. $3 = \frac{n}{-5}$

C. $m - 3 = 5$

D. $5n = -3$

E. $p - 5 = 3$

F. $5 + 3 = n$

G. $3n = -5$

H. $5 + a = 3$

I. $y - 5 = -3$

EXERCISES *On Your Own*

Write a word sentence for each equation.

1. $67 = n + 15$

2. $13n = 69$

3. $\frac{n}{2} = 17$

4. $n - 16 = 12$

5. $18 = \frac{n}{3}$

6. $n - 2 = 34$

7. $-55 = 5n$

8. $17 + n = -12$

Write an equation. Then solve.

9. The sum of 52 and a number is 75.

10. A number divided by 6 equals 8.

11. Five times some number is 45.

12. Fifty-six is fourteen less than a number.

13. Ten times a number is sixty.

14. Negative two is ten less than a number.

15. The product of negative one and a number is eight.

16. Seven equals a number divided by negative three.

Use the given word model to write an equation for each problem. Then solve the equation.

17. Environment The world's fastest-moving glacier is the Quarayaq in Greenland, which can flow 72.5 ft in one week. About how far can the glacier flow in one day?

distance per week	÷	days in one week	=	distance per day

18. Entertainment You and three friends go to lunch and a matinee movie. The total cost of the outing is $37. How much should each person contribute to share the cost evenly?

number of people	×	cost per person	=	total cost

Write an equation for Exercises 19–26. Then solve.

19. Four times what number is 52?

20. Seven subtracted from what number is 29?

21. What number increased by 12 is 61?

22. Six is what number divided by 9?

23. What number added to 3 is −2?

24. Twenty-seven is 3 times what number?

25. Thirteen times what number is 91?

26. Twelve is −7 plus what number?

27. Astronomy Ptolemy, an astronomer who lived from about A.D. 85 to about A.D. 165, named 48 constellations. Today, there are 88 named constellations. How many constellations were *not* named by Ptolemy?

28. Education Hillary spends 3 h a week at soccer practice. She spends 2.5 times as long on her homework. How much time does she spend on her homework?

29. You are putting glasses on display shelves. You have 120 glasses. You know that each shelf holds 30 glasses. How many shelves will you need?

30. Writing One gum tree reached a height of 150 ft in 15 years. Cathy and Darla wrote different equations to find the yearly average growth of the tree, g. Cathy wrote $15g = 150$. Darla wrote $150 ÷ 15 = g$. Do these equations have the same solution? Explain.

JOURNAL
Write a problem you would use an equation to solve. Solve the problem. Explain the steps you used.

Write each number in words. *(Previous Course)*

31. 836,001   **32.** 4,900,456   **33.** 312,291,745   **34.** 2,933,458,695   **35.** 25,785,456

Find the value of each expression. *(Lessons 2-3, 2-5, and 2-6)*

36. $6.2 + 7.4$ **37.** $8.3 - 2.9$ **38.** $2.4(5.2)$ **39.** $12.9 \div 4.3$ **40.** $2.7(3.4 - 1.9)$

41. *Estimation* Dalen bought three paperbacks at a used-book store. They cost $2.53, $2.65, and $2.39. *(Lesson 2-2)*
  a. About how much does each paperback cost?
  b. Explain how you would estimate the total cost.

CHAPTER PROJECT

PROJECT LINK: ORGANIZING

Finish your game board, and write the rules of your game. Organize everything needed to play your game.

✓ CHECKPOINT 2   *Lessons 3-5 through 3-8*

Multiply or divide.

  1. $6(-7)$ **2.** $-3(-4)$ **3.** $15 \div (-3)$ **4.** $-28 \div 4$ **5.** $-9(6)$ **6.** $-32 \div (-8)$

  7. $12(6)$ **8.** $-93 \div (-31)$ **9.** $106 \div 2$ **10.** $-8(11)$ **11.** $-12(-4)$ **12.** $84 \div (-12)$

Solve each equation.

  13. $t \div 4 = 16$ **14.** $-5y = -50$ **15.** $\dfrac{p}{-3} = -6$ **16.** $f + (-6) = -13$

  17. $r \div 7 = -6$ **18.** $-8d = 72$ **19.** $s + (-4) = 17$ **20.** $g - (-4) = -3$

  21. **Choose A, B, C, or D.** Which equation means "Fifteen is three less than a number"?
    A. $15 = 3 - n$ **B.** $15 = n - 3$ **C.** $15 - 3 = n$ **D.** $3 - 15 = n$

Write an equation. Then solve.

  22. Twenty is nine more than a number.   **23.** Six less than a number is fifteen.

  24. Twice a number is sixty-two.   **25.** A number divided by thirteen is seven.

3-9 Solving Two-Step Equations

What You'll Learn

▼ To solve two-step equations

...And Why

Understanding how to solve two-step equations allows you to apply your knowledge of algebra to more situations.

Here's How

Look for questions that

⊞ build understanding

✔ check understanding

THINK AND DISCUSS

You can use algebra tiles to solve some two-step equations. The tiles below show how to solve $2x + 1 = 7$.

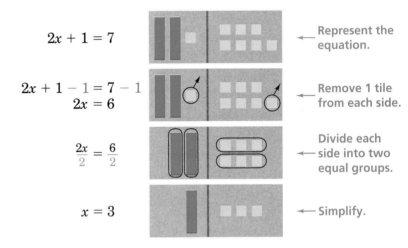

$2x + 1 = 7$ ← Represent the equation.

$2x + 1 - 1 = 7 - 1$
$2x = 6$ ← Remove 1 tile from each side.

$\dfrac{2x}{2} = \dfrac{6}{2}$ ← Divide each side into two equal groups.

$x = 3$ ← Simplify.

1. ✔ **Try It Out** Use algebra tiles to solve each equation.
   a. $3x - 1 = 8$ **b.** $4x + 2 = 14$ **c.** $2x - 3 = -9$

You can use inverse operations to solve two-step equations.

SOLVING A TWO-STEP EQUATION

Step 1 Undo addition or subtraction.

Step 2 Undo multiplication or division.

■ EXAMPLE 1

Solve $5n - 7 = -22$.

$5n - 7 = -22$
$5n - 7 + 7 = -22 + 7$ ← Add 7 to each side.
$5n = -15$ ← Simplify.
$\dfrac{5n}{5} = \dfrac{-15}{5}$ ← Divide each side by 5.
$n = -3$ ← Simplify.

2. ✔ *Try It Out* Solve each equation.

    a. $2n + 5 = 7$ **b.** $2n = 5 + -7$ **c.** $2n - 5 = 7$

■ EXAMPLE 2

Solve and check $\frac{n}{3} + 2 = 6$.

$$\frac{n}{3} + 2 = 6$$

$$\frac{n}{3} + 2 - 2 = 6 - 2 \quad \longleftarrow \text{Subtract 2 from each side.}$$

$$\frac{n}{3} = 4 \quad \longleftarrow \text{Simplify.}$$

$$(3)\frac{n}{3} = (3)(4) \quad \longleftarrow \text{Multiply each side by 3.}$$

$$n = 12 \quad \longleftarrow \text{Simplify.}$$

Check: $\frac{n}{3} + 2 = 6$

$$\frac{12}{3} + 2 \stackrel{?}{=} 6 \quad \longleftarrow \text{Replace } n \text{ with 12.}$$

$$6 = 6 ✔ \quad \longleftarrow \text{Simplify.}$$

3. a. ⚏*Reasoning* Which two operations would you use to solve $\frac{n}{3} - 2 = 6$?

    b. Solve $\frac{n}{3} - 2 = 6$.

To solve an equation like $\frac{n}{3} + 2 = 6$ using a calculator, think of the equation like this.

$$\frac{n}{3} + 2 - 2 = 6 - 2 \quad \longleftarrow \text{Subtract 2 from each side.}$$

$$(3)\frac{n}{3} = (3)(6 - 2) \quad \longleftarrow \text{Multiply each side by 3.}$$

$$n = (3)(6 - 2) \quad \longleftarrow \text{Simplify the left side.}$$

3 ⊠ 〖 6 ⊟ 2 〗 ▤ 12 $\longleftarrow$ Use a calculator.

4. ✔ *Try It Out* Show the calculator sequence you would use to solve each equation.

    a. $2n + 3 = 11$ **b.** $\frac{n}{5} - 2 = 8$ **c.** $3n + 17 = -4$

5. ⚏*Explain* Describe how you would use a calculator to solve $12x - 35 = 76$.

HISTORY
The earliest mathematical records that archaeologists have found come from Babylon, now central Iraq. About 300 clay tablets, dating about 2100 B.C. to A.D. 300, include many equations and their solutions.

EXERCISES *On Your Own*

Write and solve the equation represented by each model.

1.

2.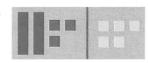

3.

Use a model to solve each equation. Then check your solution.

4. $2n + 6 = -8$ **5.** $2x - 6 = 18$ **6.** $y - 11 = -36$ **7.** $3x - 2 = 4$

Mental Math **Solve each equation.**

8. $\frac{x}{3} + 9 = 9$ **9.** $3x + 6 = 12$ **10.** $2y - 10 = -2$ **11.** $10t - 10 = 90$

12. $5c + 5 = 0$ **13.** $5d - 8 = 12$ **14.** $4g + 7 = 35$ **15.** $2p - 7 = 13$

16. Choose A, B, C, or D. Which calculator sequence shows how to find the solution to $5x + 12 = 67$?

A. 〔 67 ⊟ 12 〕 ÷ 5 ▤

B. 67 ⊟ 12 ÷ 5 ▤

C. 67 ▤ 5 ⊟ 12 ▤

D. 67 ⊞ 12 ✕ 5 ▤

Solve each equation. Then check your solution.

17. $8r - 8 = -32$ **18.** $\frac{n}{4} + 2 = 4$ **19.** $-9h + 5 = 32$ **20.** $5t + 12 = 67$

21. $\frac{m}{-11} + 1 = -10$ **22.** $\frac{n}{8} + 4 = 13$ **23.** $7r - 6 = -104$ **24.** $4k + 5 = 41$

25. $3t - 6 = -15$ **26.** $-6y + 2 = -4$ **27.** $10q + 3 = -27$ **28.** $-5h - 2 = 8$

29. $8a - 1 = 23$ **30.** $\frac{m}{-10} - 5 = 9$ **31.** $\frac{x}{-7} + 3 = -2$ **32.** $\frac{b}{-8} - 4 = 3$

▦*Calculator* **Write a calculator sequence to solve each equation. Then solve.**

33. $4n - 6 = -12$ **34.** $\frac{w}{2} - 7 = -1$ **35.** $\frac{n}{3} + 5 = 10$ **36.** $-2g + 8 = 12$

Match each sentence with a two-step equation.

37. Half a number plus three equals five.

38. Three times a number minus four equals twelve.

39. Twice a number plus three equals negative 1.

40. Two less than a number divided by three equals negative five.

41. Ten less than negative two times a number equals twenty.

42. Seventeen more than a number times negative three equals twelve.

A. $2c + 3 = -1$

B. $3x - 4 = 12$

C. $\frac{3}{z} - 4 = 8$

D. $\frac{b}{3} - 2 = -5$

E. $\frac{n}{2} + 3 = 5$

F. $-3a + 17 = 12$

G. $-2y - 10 = 20$

43. *Jobs* Jim earns $5/h helping a disabled man. He pays $1 in bus fare each way. To find the number of hours he must work to make $20, solve the equation $5h - 2 = 20$.

44. *Travel* Best Deal Auto Rental offers a daily rate of $38 plus $.30/mile. After a one-day rental, the bill was $74. Solve the equation $38 + 0.3m = 74$ to find the number of miles driven.

45. *Entertainment* Movie Madness video rental rents movies at $3.95 for the first night, plus $1.25 for each additional night. When he returned his movie, Ravi paid $7.70. Solve the equation $3.95 + 1.25n = 7.7$ to find the number of extra nights Ravi kept the movie.

Write an equation. Then solve.

46. Two times a number plus five equals seventeen.

47. Three times a number minus fifty-one equals zero.

48. Three less than five times a number equals twenty-seven.

49. Five less than half a number equals negative fifteen.

50. *Writing* Suppose a friend was absent from today's class. Write a note to your friend explaining how to solve the equation $5x - 23 = -13$.

Mixed Review

Find the value of each expression. *(Lesson 2-8)*

51. $36 \div (2 + 4) \times 4 - 5$

52. $36 \div 2 + 4 \times 4 - 2$

53. $36 \div 2 + 4 \times (4 - 2)$

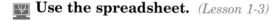 **Use the spreadsheet.** *(Lesson 1-3)*

54. Which cell contains the value 12?

55. What is the value in cell B3?

	A	B	C
1	3	6	12
2	7	14	28
3	11	22	44

56. *Choose a Strategy* Every white cat at a pet show was long-haired. Half of all black cats were long-haired. Half of all long-haired cats were white. There were 40 black cats and 30 white cats. How many long-haired cats were neither black nor white?

3-10

Make a Table

Problem Solving Strategies

Draw a Diagram
Guess and Test
Look for a Pattern
Make a Model
✔ Make a Table
Simulate a Problem
Solve a Simpler Problem
Too Much or Too Little
  Information
Use Logical Reasoning
Use Multiple Strategies
Work Backward
Write an Equation

THINK AND DISCUSS

When a problem requires you to look at a lot of possibilities, you can organize the information in a table.

SAMPLE PROBLEM...

Sheila works at a variety store after school. Three children bought the same items. Sheila gave each child 45¢ in change. She used a different combination of coins each time. Then Sheila wondered how many ways she could make 45¢ in change without using pennies.

 READ

Read for understanding. Summarize the problem.

1. Restate what you are to find in your own words.

2. What information will you need to use to solve the problem?

 PLAN

Decide on a strategy.

Making a table of the coins and their values will help you find all the possible coin combinations that total value 45¢. A table will also help you avoid using the same combination more than once.

 SOLVE

Try the strategy.

3. **a.** Copy and complete the table. Extend the table until you have found all possible combinations.

Coin	Number of Coins (Value)			
Quarter	1(25¢)	1(25¢)	1(25¢)	0(0¢)
Dime	0(0¢)	1(10¢)	2(20¢)	■
Nickel	4(20¢)	2(10¢)	0(0¢)	■
Total value	45¢	45¢	45¢	■

b. How many different ways can Sheila make 45¢ in change without using pennies?

 LOOK BACK

Think about how you solved the problem.

4. How did the table help you organize the information?

5. Make a table to show all the ways of making 60¢ in change without using pennies.

Make a table to solve each problem.

1. Each day Jamal selects a pair of jeans and a sweatshirt from his wardrobe.
   a. How many different combinations of jeans and sweatshirts can Jamal make with his clothes?
   b. Describe any patterns or shortcuts you found that helped you solve the problem.

2. Karen remembers that the three digits in her locker combination are 3, 5, and 7, but she has forgotten the order of the numbers. What is the maximum number of combinations she must check in order to open her lock?

3. The local library sponsored a used book sale to raise money. The books were priced at $.60 for paperback books and $1.00 for hardcover books. Kim spent $4.40. How many of each kind of book did she buy?

Use any strategy to solve each problem. Show all your work.

4. Hanon and Oliver collected $29 for tickets to the science museum. Adult's tickets cost $7, and children's tickets cost $5. How many adults and how many children plan to visit the museum?

5. a. The town of Dornville is 15 mi south of Chester. Topson is 12 mi north of Dornville. Ludberg is 4.5 mi north of Topson. What is the order of the towns from north to south?
   b. What is the distance between Dornville and Ludberg?

6. Without looking, Ruben drew one marble at a time from a bowl containing red, green, blue, and white marbles. He was told to stop when he had one marble of each color. What is the least number of marbles he could have selected?

7. A science teacher discovered that students had used, and misplaced, several of his weights. He can find the 9 mg, 7 mg, 2 mg, and 5 mg weights. How can he use these weights to find out if a piece of copper wire weighs 1 mg?

8. **Biology** In spring, a female crocodile lays 30 to 70 eggs. After 90 days the eggs hatch. Baby crocodiles are about 12 in. long when they hatch and grow about 10 in. a year. How old is a crocodile that is about 32 in. long?

9. **Physical Science** A ball drops 16 ft and hits the ground. It bounces one-half its previous height on each bounce. The ball is caught when the height of its bounce is 2 ft. What is the total vertical distance the ball travels?

10. **Sports** A weight lifter can lift 80 kg plus the weight of the bar. He has 5 kg, 10 kg, and 25 kg weights. The bar will hold up to seven weights on each side. Each side must have the same weights. How many different combinations of weights can be placed on the bar for a total of 80 kg?

11. During a 10-minute period in a busy office building, an elevator started at the ground floor, rose 8 floors, rose 7 floors, descended 3 floors, rose 5 floors, descended 1 floor, rose 2 floors, rose 8 floors, and descended 11 floors. On which floor was the elevator at the end of the 10-minute period?

12. Jaleesa has three pen pals. She writes back the same week that she gets a letter. Robby writes every four weeks, Emma every three weeks, and Takashi every five weeks. Jaleesa wrote to all of her pen pals this week. How many weeks will it be before she writes to them all in the same week again?

PORTFOLIO

Select one or two items from your work for this chapter. Consider:
- work with manipulatives
- work you found challenging
- cooperative work

Explain why you have included each selection that you make.

Mixed Review

13. a. **Data Analysis** Use the data to find the mean, median, and mode. *(Lesson 1-4)*
    b. Suppose you were a worker earning $14,000. Would you use the mean or the median to convince your boss that you should be given a raise? Why? *(Lesson 1-8)*

Order from least to greatest. *(Lesson 2-1)*

14. 0.234, 0.243, 0.23, 0.24

15. 0.368, 0.3681, 0.36792, 0.3

16. **Weather** Between 1862 and 1866 British scientist James Glaisher made 28 balloon flights to gather weather data. During one flight, temperature went from 19°C to −8°C. What was the temperature range? *(Lesson 3-4)*

Yearly Salary

Name	Salary
Sylvia	$ 14,000
Jose	$ 23,000
Yukiko	$ 27,000
Brisa	$ 14,000
Elki	$ 65,000
Anitha	$104,000

CHAPTER PROJECT

Create a Board Game The Project Link questions on pages 100, 110, 116, and 129 should help you complete your project. Here is a checklist to help you gather together the parts of your project.

✔ the setting for your game, and how moves and the end of game are determined

✔ the rough draft of your game board with ways to use integers

✔ the details for using multiplication of integers

✔ the final game board and the rules for your game

Play your game so you can make final revisions before bringing it to school. Is the game too easy or too hard? Is the game interesting enough? What should you add or change?

Reflect and Revise

Work (or play) in small groups to test each other's games. Point out to each other the features of the games that you think are well-designed. What part of the mathematics of the game works well? What do you like about playing the game? Revise your game based on comments from your group.

Web Extension

Prentice Hall's Internet site contains information you might find helpful as you complete your project. Visit www.phschool.com/mgm2/ch3 for some links and ideas related to creating a board game.

3 WRAP UP

Variable Expressions

3-1

A **variable** is a symbol that stands for a number. A **variable expression** contains at least one variable. To evaluate an expression, you replace the variable with a number and simplify.

Evaluate each expression for $x = 3$ and $y = 5$.

1. $6x + 9$ **2.** $3 + 8y$ **3.** xy **4.** $2x + y$ **5.** $3x - y$ **6.** $2y - 3x$

Write a variable expression for each word phrase.

7. n less than 8   **8.** the product of 6 and c **9.** 6 more than twice n

Integers, Opposites, and Absolute Value

3-2

Opposites are two numbers that are the same distance from 0 on a number line, but in opposite directions. The set of **integers** is the set of whole numbers and their opposites. The **absolute value** of an integer is its distance from 0 on a number line.

10. What integer represents 9°F below zero?   **11.** Draw a model for zero using 6 tiles.

12. Write the absolute value of each integer.
a. -5 **b.** 2 **c.** -17

13. Order the integers from least to greatest.
$7 \quad -6 \quad 0 \quad -3 \quad 1$

Compare. Use <, >, or =.

14. $-7 \ \blacksquare\ 7$ **15.** $|-3| \ \blacksquare\ |3|$ **16.** $-12 \ \blacksquare\ 0$ **17.** $|-9| \ \blacksquare\ -4$ **18.** $8 \ \blacksquare\ -15$

19. Choose A, B, C, or D. Which number of tiles could you use to model -5?
A. 4 tiles   **B.** 9 tiles   **C.** 10 tiles   **D.** 12 tiles

Adding and Subtracting Integers

3-3, 3-4

The sum of two positive integers is positive. The sum of two negative integers is negative. To find the sum of two integers with *different* signs, *subtract* their absolute values. The sum has the same sign as the integer with the greater absolute value.

To subtract an integer, add its opposite.

Write an expression for each model. Then find its value.

20. ⬛⬛ + ⬛⬛⬛
     ⬛⬛   ⬛⬛⬛

21. ⬜⬜⬜ + ⬜⬜
     ⬜⬜   ⬛⬛

22.
$$\overset{\longleftarrow\;|\;\;|\;\;|\;\;|\;\;|\;\;|\;\;|\;\;|\;\;|\;\;|\;\longrightarrow}{\underset{-6\quad\;-4\quad\;-2\quad\;\;0}{}}$$

Find each sum or difference.

23. $-4 + 7$ 24. $-14 + (-8)$ 25. $3 - 8$ 26. $17 - (-12)$ 27. $15 + (-18)$

Multiplying and Dividing Integers   3-5

The product or quotient of two integers with the *same* sign is *positive*.

The product or quotient of two integers with *different* signs is *negative*.

Find each product or quotient.

28. $-5 \cdot 6$ 29. $-14 \cdot (-6)$ 30. $125 \div (-5)$ 31. $-98 \div (-49)$ 32. $-15 \div 3$

33. *Writing* Explain how to determine the signs of each of the following: the sum of -5 and 8 and the product of -5 and 8.

Solving Equations with Integers   3-6, 3-7, 3-8, 3-9

To solve an equation using addition or subtraction, add or subtract the same value from both sides of the equation.

To solve an equation using multiplication or division, multiply or divide both sides of the equation by the same nonzero value.

Choose **Use models, a calculator, or paper and pencil to solve and check.**

34. $x - (-2) = -4$ 35. $2y = 8$ 36. $\dfrac{q}{5} = 7$ 37. $3m + 4 = -2$

38. $t + 4 = -5$ 39. $\dfrac{w}{2} = -7$ 40. $-8g = -24$ 41. $3d - 4 = 17$

42. Write an equation for the statement "Four more than a number is negative seven." Solve the equation.

Problem Solving Strategies   3-10

You can use the strategy Make a Table to solve problems.

43. Tadeo sold banners for a school fund raiser. Small banners cost $1.25. The large ones cost $1.75. How many of each size could he sell for $20? Write all the possible solutions.

1. *Open-ended* Complete with an integer that makes each statement true.
   a. $-1 <$ ▪
   b. ▪ > -7
   c. $|-13| >$ ▪
   d. $-17 <$ ▪

2. Draw models to represent each integer in two different ways.
   a. 8   b. -1 c. -5 d. 0

3. Write the integers in order from least to greatest.
   $$-2 \quad 5 \quad 0 \quad -7 \quad -3$$

4. Find each sum.
   a. $7 + (-1)$
   b. $-3 + 2$
   c. $-4 + (-2)$
   d. $-11 + (-5)$
   e. $-8 + (-5)$
   f. $5 + (-7)$

5. *Mental Math* Find the value of each expression.
   a. $-3 + 5$
   b. $-2 + (-2)$
   c. $-4 - 9$
   d. $-11 + 15$
   e. $8 + (-8) + 4$
   f. $7 - 13 + (-7)$

6. Find the value of each expression.
   a. $6(-11)$
   b. $-63 \div (-7)$
   c. $48 \div (-3)$
   d. $-8(-9)$
   e. $22(4) \div -8$
   f. $(-2 \cdot 8) \div 4$

7. *Writing* Explain the steps you would use to solve the equation $5y + 2 = 17$.

8. **Choose A, B, C, or D.** Kira had $58.25 after buying a calculator. Which equation could you use to find how much money Kira had to start with if the calculator cost $13.45?
   A. $m - \$13.45 = \$58.25$
   B. $m + \$13.45 = \$58.25$
   C. $m + \$58.25 = \$13.45$
   D. $\$58.25 - \$13.45 = m$

9. Solve each equation.
   a. $x + 3 = 9$
   b. $a - 4 = -1$
   c. $c - 2 = 5$
   d. $y + 1 = -12$
   e. $n + (-4) = -10$
   f. $z - (-2) = -8$

10. Write an equation. Then solve.
    a. A number divided by 7 equals 3.
    b. Six less than a number is 52.
    c. A number times 6 equals -48.
    d. Five more than a number is -14.

11. Solve each equation.
    a. $6n = -42$
    b. $m \div 8 = 8$
    c. $g \div 2 = -11$
    d. $-9x = -180$
    e. $-12c = -132$
    f. $\frac{h}{7} = -14$

12. A submarine was at a depth of 250 m below sea level. It rose 75 m. Then it dove 20 m. Use an integer to describe the new depth of the submarine.

13. Jamie has a coordinated wardrobe consisting of four blouses, three skirts, and two pairs of slacks. How many different two-piece outfits can she make?

14. Solve each equation.
    a. $4d - 3 = 9$
    b. $7z + 2 = -19$
    c. $9g + 1 = 82$
    d. $\frac{x}{5} - 8 = -1$
    e. $49 + 6t = 25$
    f. $7 + 13m = 13.5$

15. **Choose A, B, C, or D.** Which equation has the same solution as $5a - 1 = 9$?
    A. $10a - 15 = -4$
    B. $6a + 4 = 8$
    C. $13a + 1 = 14$
    D. $2a - 1 = 3$

16. Evaluate for $b = -3$ and $c = 4$.
    a. $b + c$
    b. $-2b$
    c. $3c - 10$
    d. bc
    e. $c - b$
    f. $b - c$
    g. $\frac{b}{c}$
    h. $2c - 13$
    j. $-4 - b$

Choose A, B, C, or D.

1. *Entertainment* Zoom Video charges $3.75 per day for overdue videos. Carli had a video that was due on Sunday. She returned it the following Friday. How much did she owe?

   A. $3.75 **B.** $22.50 **C.** $18.75 **D.** $15

2. *Estimation* Estimate to determine which sum is between 21 and 22.

   A. $13.71 + 1.5 + 8.2$
   B. $6.75 + 9.02 + 5.838$
   C. $5.99 + 2.69 + 15.49$
   D. $3.772 + 12.04 + 4.009$

3. Which set of tiles does *not* represent the integer -2?

   A. ▨ ■ ■ ■

   B. ▨ ▨ ▨ ■
   ■ ■ ■ ■

   C. ■ ■

   D. ▨ ▨ ■ ■

4. What is the solution of the equation $-15 = m - 9$?

   A. -6 **B.** -24 **C.** 24 **D.** 6

5. Which is the best survey question to find how much time students spend on their math homework?

   A. How long did your homework take you last night?
   B. How many hours did you spend on math homework last week?
   C. Which homework takes you more time, math or history?
   D. Did you do last night's math homework?

6. Which expression *cannot* be rewritten using the distributive property?

   A. $3(2 + 8)$ **B.** $9(14 - 6)$
   C. $5(2 \cdot 3)$ **D.** $(18 - 9)7$

7. *Cooking* Suppose s represents the cups of sugar in a recipe. The amount of flour is one-half cup more than twice the amount of sugar. Which variable expression represents the amount of flour?

   A. $\frac{1}{2} + s$ **B.** $\frac{1}{2} + \frac{s}{2}$
   C. $2(s + \frac{1}{2})$ **D.** $\frac{1}{2} + 2s$

8. *Money* Kali has $3. How many different lunches of one sandwich and one drink can he order?

Tuna	$2.50
Hot dog	$1.75
Roast Beef	$2.95
Milk	$.60
Lemonade	$.50

   A. 3   **B.** 4   **C.** 5   **D.** 6

9. What variable expression is described by the word phrase "increase r by 2"?

   A. $2r$ **B.** $r - 2$ **C.** $r + 2$ **D.** $r \cdot 2$

10. In the stem-and-leaf plot below, the stem represents the tens digit. What does the stem and leaf plot *not* tell you?

1	3 4 9
2	1 2 4 4
3	0 3

    1 | 3 means 13

    A. The greatest number is 33.
    B. The mode is 24.
    C. The median is 22.
    D. There are 12 items of data.

11. The mean of six numbers is 6. Five of the numbers are 5, 9, 3, 1, and 10. What is the sixth number?

    A. 0   **B.** 4   **C.** 8   **D.** 12

12. What is the best estimate of $12(-17)$?

    A. -200 **B.** -150 **C.** 150 **D.** 200

F ractions and Number Theory

4

making the measure

I n the high jump, as in most sports, a consistent system of measurement allows athletes to make comparisons. It took the decree of a king to create one such system!

Back in the 12th century, King Henry I of England decided that a yard was the distance from the tip of his nose to the end of his thumb. How far is it from the tip of your nose to the end of your thumb? Is it more than a yard or less? Is it the same distance for everyone?

Invent Your Own Ruler For the chapter project, you will design a new system for measuring distance. Your final project will be a new ruler, together with a report on its usefulness.

• **How to solve problems by looking for a pattern**

PROBLEM SOLVING

4-1 Relating Fractions to Models

What You'll Learn

1. To use models to explore fractions

2. To model mixed numbers

...And Why

Models can help you understand the meaning of fractions and mixed numbers.

Here's How

Look for questions that

- build understanding
- ✔ check understanding

Work Together

Modeling Fractions

Work with a partner. You can use pattern blocks to explore fractions that are part of a whole. A yellow hexagon represents one whole.

1. **a.** How many trapezoids make up one hexagon?
   b. What part of a whole is one trapezoid?

2. **a.** How many triangles make up one hexagon?
   b. What part of a whole is one triangle?

3. **a.** How many parallelograms make up one hexagon?
   b. What part of a whole is one parallelogram?

hexagon

trapezoid

triangle   parallelogram

THINK AND DISCUSS

1 *Fractions and Models*

Fractions describe parts of a whole or members of a group.

■ **EXAMPLE 1**

Write the fraction that each model represents.

a.

Three parts of a whole that has four parts is represented by $\frac{3}{4}$.

b.

Three members of a group of four items is also represented by $\frac{3}{4}$.

4. ✔ *Try It Out* Draw two models, one that shows $\frac{2}{3}$ as parts of a whole, and one that shows $\frac{2}{3}$ as part of a group.

▼ *Modeling Mixed Numbers*

You can use models to represent fractions that are mixed numbers. A **mixed number** is the sum of a whole number and a fraction.

■ **EXAMPLE 2**

Write the mixed number that the model represents.

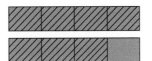 ←—Represents 1.

 ←—Represents $\frac{3}{4}$.

The model represents $1\frac{3}{4}$.

5. ✔ *Try It Out* Write the mixed number that each model represents.

a.

b.

EXERCISES *On Your Own*

Write a fraction for each model.

1.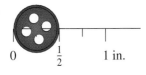

2.

3.

4. a. *Quilting* What fraction of each quilt square is purple?
b. What fraction of each quilt square is blue?

5. *Open-ended* Design a quilt square in which $\frac{1}{3}$ of the square is green.

Square A   Square B   Square C

6. *Writing* Jason described the shaded region at the right as $\frac{1}{3}$ of a circle. Is he correct? Why or why not?

Write a fraction or a mixed number for each model.

7.

8.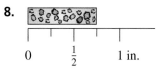

9.

10. **a.** *Music* List the denominators of the fractions in the table.

Symbol						
Name	whole note	half note	quarter note	eighth note	■	■
Value	1	$\frac{1}{2}$	$\frac{1}{4}$	$\frac{1}{8}$	■	■
Model	◯	◐	⊕	✳	■	■

    b. *Patterns* Describe the pattern of the denominators. Based on this pattern, what do you think are the names of the last two notes in the table?

    c. Copy and complete the last two rows of the table.

Mixed Review

Write a variable expression for each phrase. *(Lesson 3-1)*

11. twice a number decreased by four

12. three more than half a number

Compare. Use <, >, or =. *(Lessons 3-2, 3-3, 3-4, 3-5)*

13. $5 - (-8)$ ■ 13

14. $3.5(-3)$ ■ $7 - 11$

15. $6 \div (-2)$ ■ -4

16. -1 ■ $-5 - 6$

17. A team of bakers at the Shiwassee County Fairgrounds, Michigan, created a 100-tier cake. At 30.85 m, it was the tallest in the world. About how tall was each tier? *(Lesson 2-2)*

4-2 Equivalent Fractions

What You'll Learn

1. To find the factors and multiples of a number
2. To write equivalent fractions

...And Why

Using factors and multiples, you can find many ways to write one fraction.

Here's How

Look for questions that
- build understanding
- ✔ check understanding

THINK AND DISCUSS

1 Identifying Factors and Multiples

Suppose you and a friend do volunteer work at the animal shelter. Both of you are at the shelter today. You volunteer every third day and your friend volunteers every fourth day. After how many days will you both be at the center on the same day?

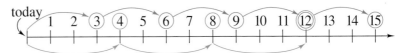

You will see each other at the shelter 12 days from today.

The diagram above shows multiples of 3 and 4. A **multiple** of a number is the product of the number and a nonzero whole number.

The **least common multiple (LCM)** of two numbers is the least number that is a multiple of both. The LCM of 3 and 4 is 12.

■ EXAMPLE 1

Find the least common multiple of 6 and 9.

multiples of 6: 6, 12, 18, 24, 30, 36 ← ┐ List the first several
multiples of 9: 9, 18, 27, 36 ← ┘ multiples of 6 and 9.

The LCM of 6 and 9 is 18.

1. Find the first four multiples of each number.
   a. 5   b. 8   c. 11

2. ✔ *Try It Out* Find the LCM of each pair of numbers.
   a. 4, 10   b. 5, 7   c. 12, 15

3. ■ *Reasoning* Zero is not considered a multiple of a number other than itself. Why does this make sense?

A **factor** is a whole number that divides another whole number with no remainder.

■ EXAMPLE 2

Find the factors of 30.

$$30 = 1 \times 30, 2 \times 15, 3 \times 10, \text{ and } 5 \times 6 \leftarrow$$ Find all the pairs of numbers with a product of 30.

The factors of 30 are 1, 2, 3, 5, 6, 10, 15, and 30.

4. ✔ *Try It Out* Find the factors of 8.

❷ *Writing Equivalent Fractions*

Fractions that are equal are **equivalent fractions.**

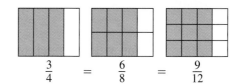

$$\frac{3}{4} = \frac{6}{8} = \frac{9}{12}$$

You can find equivalent fractions by multiplying the numerator and denominator by the same number.

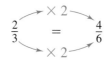

■ EXAMPLE 3

Use a table of multiples to find three fractions equivalent to $\frac{3}{4}$.

	× **2**	× **3**	× **4**
3	6	9	12
4	8	12	16

Multiples in the same column will form fractions equivalent to $\frac{3}{4}$.

Three fractions equivalent to $\frac{3}{4}$ are $\frac{6}{8}$, $\frac{9}{12}$, and $\frac{12}{16}$.

5. ✔ *Try It Out* Find two other fractions equivalent to $\frac{3}{4}$.

6. ⚓ *Open-ended* You can write 2 as the fraction $\frac{2}{1}$. Write three other fractions equivalent to 2.

7. ⚓ *Error Analysis* Shana wrote that $\frac{5}{6} = \frac{5+4}{6+4} = \frac{9}{10}$. Is her answer reasonable? Explain.

Another way to find equivalent fractions is to divide the numerator and the denominator by the same nonzero number.

■ EXAMPLE 4

Find three fractions equivalent to $\frac{24}{30}$.

Factors of 24: 1, 2, 3, 4, 6, 8, 12, 24 ⟶ Find common factors.
Factors of 30: 1, 2, 3, 5, 6, 10, 15, 30 ⟵

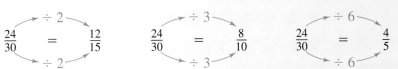

Three fractions equivalent to $\frac{24}{30}$ are $\frac{12}{15}$, $\frac{8}{10}$, and $\frac{4}{5}$.

8. ✔ *Try It Out* Use division to find two fractions equivalent to $\frac{30}{36}$.

EXERCISES *On Your Own*

Mental Math **List the factors of each number.**

1. 17   **2.** 18   **3.** 32   **4.** 42   **5.** 23   **6.** 70

Write the first five multiples of each number.

7. 7   **8.** 4   **9.** 9   **10.** 13   **11.** 18   **12.** 32

13. Describe the relationship between 15, 5, and 3 using the words *factor* and *multiple*.

14. *Number Sense* What number is a factor of all other numbers?

15. Mr. Quaid's class has 24 students, and Mrs. Carlson's class has 30 students. Each class is divided into several teams. What is the greatest number of people on a team if both classes have teams that are equal in size?

16. *Number Theory* A number n is a multiple of 2. Is $n + 1$ a multiple of 2? Explain using examples.

Find the LCM of each pair of numbers.

17. 4, 6   **18.** 9, 12   **19.** 8, 5   **20.** 14, 21   **21.** 3, 8   **22.** 2, 5

23. 5, 10   **24.** 15, 18   **25.** 10, 6   **26.** 15, 9   **27.** 12, 16   **28.** 24, 8

Write two equivalent fractions for each model.

29.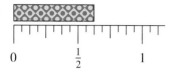

30.

31.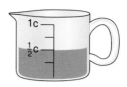

32. **a.** Write the first four multiples of 8 and 12.
  b. Use multiples to write three fractions equivalent to $\frac{8}{12}$.
  c. Find the factors of 8 and 12. What are the common factors?
  d. Use common factors to find two fractions equivalent to $\frac{8}{12}$.

33. **a.** Takala had 20 homework problems. She finished 15 of them while she was at the library. What fraction of the problems did she have left to do at home?
  b. Write a fraction equivalent to your answer in part (a) using common factors.

Use the multiplication table below for Exercises 34–38. Find the number that makes each statement true.

	1	2	3	4	5	6	7	8	9
5	5	10	15	20	25	30	35	40	45
6	6	12	18	24	30	36	42	48	54
7	7	14	21	28	35	42	49	56	63
8	8	16	24	32	40	48	56	64	72

34. $\frac{5}{6} = \frac{20}{\blacksquare}$

35. $\frac{25}{40} = \frac{\blacksquare}{32}$

36. $\frac{7}{8} = \frac{35}{\blacksquare}$

37. $\frac{\blacksquare}{72} = \frac{30}{48}$

38. $\frac{20}{28} = \frac{\blacksquare}{49}$

Find each missing number.

39. $\frac{18}{\blacksquare} = \frac{6}{7}$

40. $\frac{5}{8} = \frac{\blacksquare}{32}$

41. $\frac{\blacksquare}{6} = \frac{4}{1}$

42. $\frac{5}{7} = \frac{25}{\blacksquare}$

43. $\frac{\blacksquare}{72} = \frac{7}{8}$

44. $\frac{\blacksquare}{49} = \frac{3}{7}$

45. $\frac{\blacksquare}{64} = \frac{5}{8}$

46. $\frac{6}{7} = \frac{\blacksquare}{28}$

47. $\frac{35}{\blacksquare} = \frac{7}{8}$

48. $\frac{10}{\blacksquare} = \frac{5}{8}$

49. $\frac{7}{8} = \frac{21}{\blacksquare}$

50. $\frac{35}{\blacksquare} = \frac{7}{1}$

51. **Choose A, B, C, or D.** Which square does *not* have the same fraction shaded as the others?

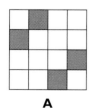 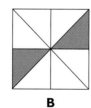 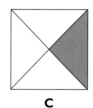 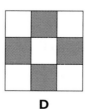

A   B   C   D

52. Writing Explain to someone who has been absent from class how to find fractions equivalent to $\frac{6}{18}$.

53. Open-ended Write a fraction. Then find two fractions equivalent to your fraction.

54. a. Measure the thickness of the door at the right to the nearest $\frac{1}{4}$ inch.

 b. Measure the thickness of the door to the nearest $\frac{1}{8}$ inch.

 c. Reasoning You have a sliding door with the thickness shown at the right. Would you use your answer to part (a) or part (b) if you were making a track for the door to slide in? Explain.

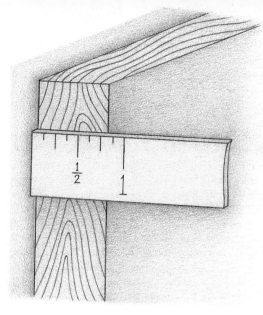

Mixed Review

Solve each equation. *(Lesson 3-9)*

55. $8m + 3 = 19$ **56.** $-5t + 7 = 62$ **57.** $\frac{s}{2} - 4 = 11$ **58.** $\frac{n}{3} + 2 = -4$

Find each sum or difference. *(Lesson 2-3)*

59. $14.02 + 3.6$ **60.** $0.83 - 0.75$ **61.** $45.79 - 2.3$ **62.** $7.077 + 25.3$ **63.** $25.98 - 8.89$

Math at Work

PEDIATRICIAN

A pediatrician uses math skills when reading a patient's medical profile and to interpret test results. Logical reasoning and problem-solving skills are essential to make a diagnosis and determine the proper treatment for a child who is ill.

Visit this Web site on Pediatrics to find more information:

www.yahoo.com/Health/Medicine/Pediatrics

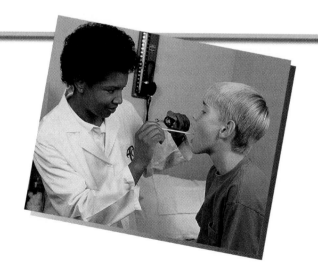

4-3 Comparing and Ordering Fractions

What You'll Learn

1 To compare fractions

2 To order fractions

...And Why

You can compare amounts in recipes.

Here's How

Look for questions that

- build understanding
- ✔ check understanding

THINK AND DISCUSS

1 Comparing Fractions

1. Name the fractions represented by the fraction models below.

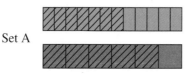

Set A

Set B

2. a. Use greater than (>) to compare the fractions in set A.
   b. Use less than (<) to compare the fractions in set B.

A number line helps you compare fractions too.

As you can see, if the denominators are the same, the numerators determine which is greater. So $\frac{7}{10} < \frac{9}{10}$, or $\frac{9}{10} > \frac{7}{10}$.

To compare fractions with different denominators, write them using the same denominator. Then, compare the numerators.

The **least common denominator (LCD)** of two fractions is the least common multiple of their denominators.

■ EXAMPLE 1   Real-World Problem Solving

Do people remember more of what they say or do?

Rewrite $\frac{3}{4}$ and $\frac{9}{10}$ using the LCD. The LCD of 4 and 10 is 20.

$$\frac{3}{4} = \frac{3 \cdot 5}{4 \cdot 5} = \frac{15}{20}$$

$$\frac{9}{10} = \frac{9 \cdot 2}{10 \cdot 2} = \frac{18}{20}$$

← Write equivalent fractions.

Since $15 < 18$, $\frac{15}{20} < \frac{18}{20}$, and $\frac{3}{4} < \frac{9}{10}$.

People remember more of what they do than what they say.

3. ✔ *Try It Out* Compare each pair of fractions.

   a. $\frac{3}{4} \blacksquare \frac{5}{6}$ b. $\frac{1}{6} \blacksquare \frac{2}{9}$ c. $\frac{4}{10} \blacksquare \frac{3}{8}$

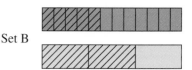

People remember:
- three fourths of what they say
- one tenth of what they hear
- nine tenths of what they do

Oatmeal Bread

Ingredients:

$2\frac{1}{4}$ teaspoons yeast

$2\frac{1}{2}$ cups water

$\frac{1}{2}$ cup sugar

$\frac{2}{3}$ cup oatmeal

$\frac{1}{4}$ cup oil

9 cups flour

❷ Ordering Fractions

You can use the LCD to order more than two fractions.

■ **EXAMPLE 2** . *Real-World Problem Solving*

Cooking Compare the amounts of sugar, oatmeal, and oil in the recipe at the left. Which has the greatest? The least?

Order $\frac{1}{2}$, $\frac{2}{3}$, and $\frac{1}{4}$.

The LCD of the denominators 2, 3, and 4 is 12.

$\frac{1}{2} = \frac{1 \cdot 6}{2 \cdot 6} = \frac{6}{12}$
$\frac{2}{3} = \frac{2 \cdot 4}{3 \cdot 4} = \frac{8}{12}$ ⟵ Use the LCD to find equivalent fractions.
$\frac{1}{4} = \frac{1 \cdot 3}{4 \cdot 3} = \frac{3}{12}$

$\frac{3}{12} < \frac{6}{12} < \frac{8}{12}$ so $\frac{1}{4} < \frac{1}{2} < \frac{2}{3}$.

Oatmeal has the greatest amount, and oil has the least.

4. ✔ *Try It Out* Order from least to greatest.

a. $\frac{3}{8}, \frac{1}{2}, \frac{2}{5}$ b. $\frac{6}{9}, \frac{1}{3}, \frac{7}{12}$ c. $\frac{1}{5}, \frac{2}{6}, \frac{1}{15}$

EXERCISES *On Your Own*

Write two fractions for the models and compare them.

1.

2.

Compare. Use <, >, or =.

3. $\frac{5}{12} \; \blacksquare \; \frac{7}{12}$ **4.** $\frac{5}{6} \; \blacksquare \; \frac{3}{6}$ **5.** $\frac{1}{3} \; \blacksquare \; \frac{3}{4}$ **6.** $\frac{5}{6} \; \blacksquare \; \frac{3}{5}$ **7.** $\frac{3}{8} \; \blacksquare \; \frac{2}{3}$

8. $\frac{6}{7} \; \blacksquare \; \frac{4}{5}$ **9.** $\frac{2}{3} \; \blacksquare \; \frac{5}{8}$ **10.** $\frac{5}{6} \; \blacksquare \; \frac{7}{10}$ **11.** $\frac{3}{8} \; \blacksquare \; \frac{3}{5}$ **12.** $\frac{7}{12} \; \blacksquare \; \frac{5}{9}$

13. $\frac{3}{8} \; \blacksquare \; \frac{5}{8}$ **14.** $\frac{2}{3} \; \blacksquare \; \frac{3}{5}$ **15.** $\frac{1}{8} \; \blacksquare \; \frac{3}{16}$ **16.** $\frac{3}{4} \; \blacksquare \; \frac{3}{10}$ **17.** $\frac{4}{5} \; \blacksquare \; \frac{2}{3}$

Which fractional part would you prefer? Explain.

18. $\frac{2}{3}$ or $\frac{2}{5}$ of an apple to eat   **19.** $2\frac{1}{2}$ or $2\frac{3}{4}$ h of homework   **20.** $\frac{1}{6}$ or $\frac{1}{12}$ year for vacation

21. *Writing* Describe an easy way to compare two fractions that have the same *numerator*, like $\frac{4}{5}$ and $\frac{4}{7}$.

22. *Reasoning* You want to nail a board that is $\frac{1}{2}$ in. thick onto a wall. You can choose from nails that are $\frac{3}{8}$ in. long and $\frac{3}{4}$ in. long. Which size nail is the better choice? Explain.

Order from least to greatest.

23. $\frac{3}{4}, \frac{2}{3}, \frac{5}{6}$ **24.** $\frac{3}{8}, \frac{1}{4}, \frac{2}{3}$ **25.** $\frac{4}{9}, \frac{2}{3}, \frac{1}{2}$ **26.** $\frac{1}{3}, \frac{5}{6}, \frac{3}{8}$ **27.** $\frac{1}{8}, \frac{1}{6}, \frac{1}{9}$ **28.** $\frac{9}{16}, \frac{3}{6}, \frac{5}{8}$

29. $\frac{3}{15}, \frac{3}{10}, \frac{3}{5}$ **30.** $\frac{5}{8}, \frac{7}{9}, \frac{3}{4}$ **31.** $\frac{3}{5}, \frac{1}{2}, \frac{2}{3}$ **32.** $\frac{6}{10}, \frac{7}{12}, \frac{5}{8}$ **33.** $\frac{5}{6}, \frac{4}{5}, \frac{3}{4}$ **34.** $\frac{8}{9}, \frac{7}{12}, \frac{3}{4}$

Estimation **Match each fraction with a point on the number line.**

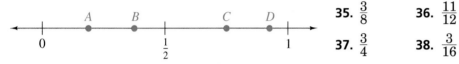

35. $\frac{3}{8}$ **36.** $\frac{11}{12}$

37. $\frac{3}{4}$ **38.** $\frac{3}{16}$

39. *Reasoning* For a party, a class ordered the same number of cheese pizzas, vegetable pizzas, and meatball pizzas. The leftovers were $\frac{5}{8}$ of a cheese pizza, $\frac{2}{3}$ of a vegetable pizza, and $\frac{3}{4}$ of a meatball pizza. Which type was most popular? Explain.

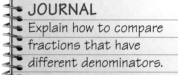

JOURNAL
Explain how to compare fractions that have different denominators.

Mixed Review

Find each sum. *(Lesson 3-3)*

40. $-3 + 7$ **41.** $5 + (-2)$ **42.** $6 + (-8)$ **43.** $-9 + (-4)$ **44.** $-1 + 7$ **45.** $3 + (-7)$

Find each product or quotient. *(Lessons 2-5, 2-6)*

46. 9.4×0.3 **47.** $1.02 \div 0.3$ **48.** 8.07×14.2 **49.** $85.92 \div 4.8$ **50.** $63.18 \div 8.1$

51. *Choose a Strategy* In a science class the number of bacteria in a jar doubles each day. If the jar is full on the 28th day, on what day was it half full?

CHAPTER PROJECT

PROJECT LINK: DESIGNING

Design a new unit for measuring length. What will you call it? Make a ruler one unit long based on your new measurement. Use it to measure the length of a classroom door. Estimate the length of your classroom using your measuring unit. What is the length of a bicycle or a car?

4-4

Exponents and Order of Operations

What You'll Learn

▼ To write numbers with exponents

▼ To evaluate expressions with exponents using the order of operations

...And Why

Using exponents is an efficient way of writing products of the same factor.

Here's How

Look for questions that

⬚ build understanding

✔ check understanding

Work Together

Exploring Exponents

Luis and Sofia suggested that their allowance be changed. They wanted 2¢ the first week, with their allowance to be doubled each week. Their parents investigated the suggestion using this table.

Week	Cents	
one	2	= ▪
two	2×2	= ▪
three	$2 \times 2 \times 2$	= ▪
four	$2 \times 2 \times 2 \times 2$	= ▪

1. **a.** Complete the table to find how many cents Luis and Sofia would be paid each of the first four weeks.

   b. How much would they be paid the seventh week? The tenth week?

2. ⬚ *Reasoning* Do you think their parents will agree with their suggestion? Explain.

THINK AND DISCUSS

▼ *Standard and Exponential Forms*

In the Work Together you multiplied 2 by itself several times. You can use an **exponent** to indicate repeated multiplication.

$$\text{base} \rightarrow 2^{\overset{\displaystyle\frown\ \text{exponent}}{4}} = \underbrace{2 \times 2 \times 2 \times 2}$$

The base is used as a factor four times.

A number expressed using an exponent is a **power.** You read 2^4 as "two to the fourth power." Both 2^4 and 16 have the same value.

exponential expression $\longrightarrow 2^4 = 16 \longleftarrow$ the value of the expression

3. ✔ *Try It Out* What are the base and the exponent of each expression?
   a. 10^2 **b.** 3^5 **c.** 12^7

There are special exponent keys on a scientific calculator. These can help you find the value of an exponential expression.

Gibraltar

Gibraltar is the smallest colony in the world. It is located at the mouth of the Mediterranean, off the coast of Spain.

■ **EXAMPLE 1** *Real-World Problem Solving*

Gibraltar has an area of $(1.5)^2$ mi^2. Evaluate $(1.5)^2$.

1.5 $\boxed{x^2}$ 2.25 ←— Use the $\boxed{x^2}$ key to square numbers.

The area of Gibraltar is 2.25 mi^2.

You can use the $\boxed{y^x}$ key to raise a number to any power.

$4^3 \longrightarrow$ 4 $\boxed{y^x}$ 3 $\boxed{=}$ *64*

4. ⬚ *Think About It* Describe three ways you can use your calculator to find the value of 2.3^2.

▼2 *Using the Order of Operations*

To evaluate expressions that contain exponents, you must include exponents in the order of operations.

> **ORDER OF OPERATIONS**
>
> 1. Do all operations within grouping symbols first.
> 2. Evaluate any term with exponents.
> 3. Multiply and divide in order from left to right.
> 4. Add and subtract in order from left to right.

■ **EXAMPLE 2**

Simplify $3^4 \times (7 - 2)^3$.

$$3^4 \times (7 - 2)^3 = 3^4 \times 5^3 \quad \longleftarrow \text{Do operations in parentheses.}$$
$$= 81 \times 125 \quad \longleftarrow \text{Evaluate exponential expressions.}$$
$$= 10{,}125 \quad \longleftarrow \text{Multiply.}$$

5. ✔ *Try It Out* Which operation happens first? Explain.
   a. $(3^2 + 5) - 2$ **b.** $3^2 + 5 - 2$ **c.** $(3 + 5)^2 - 2$

A scientific calculator follows the order of operations. Here are the keystrokes to find the value of the expression in Example 2.

3 $\boxed{y^x}$ 4 $\boxed{\times}$ $\boxed{(}$ 7 $\boxed{-}$ 2 $\boxed{)}$ $\boxed{y^x}$ 3 $\boxed{=}$ *10125*

⊞ 6. ✔ *Try It Out* What key strokes would you use to find the value of $(1.5 + 21)^2 \div 72$?

When you use an exponent with a negative number as the base, it is important to use grouping symbols to avoid confusion.

■ EXAMPLE 3

Simplify each expression.
a. $(-5)^4 = (-5)(-5)(-5)(-5)$ b. $-5^4 = -(5 \cdot 5 \cdot 5 \cdot 5)$
          $= 625$ $= -625$

7. ✔ Try It Out Simplify each expression.
a. -2^3 b. $(-2)^3$ c. -2^4 d. $(-2)^4$

EXERCISES *On Your Own*

Write each expression using exponents.

1. $7 \times 7 \times 7$ 2. $4 \times 4 \times 4 \times 4 \times 4 \times 4$ 3. $0.3 \times 0.3 \times 0.3 \times 0.3 \times 0.3$

**Write each expression as a product of repeated factors.
Then evaluate each expression.**

4. 4^5 5. 5^3 6. 13^6 7. 0.2^4 8. 3^3 9. 9^6

10. 11^3 11. 6^5 12. 1.7^3 13. 8^4 14. 5^5 15. 0.6^2

16. a. *Geometry* How many small squares are on one side of the square at the right?
    b. How many small squares make up the whole square?
    c. *Language* Why do you think 3^2 is referred to as "3 squared"?

17. a. Copy and complete the table at the right.
    b. *Patterns* What pattern do you see with powers of 10?
    c. Use your pattern to find the value of 10^{12}.

18. *Calculator* Use a calculator. Find 5^1, 17^1, and 3.2^1. What do you notice?

19. *Open-ended* Write two numbers using exponents that are between the values of 5^2 and 5^3.

20. a. Without calculating, predict which is greater, 2^6 or 6^2.
    b. *Calculator* Find 2^6 and 6^2. Was your prediction correct? Explain.

	Value	Number of Zeros
10^1	▨	1
10^2	▨	▨
10^3	▨	▨
10^4	▨	▨
10^5	▨	▨

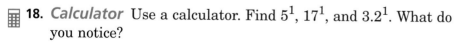

4-4 Exponents and Order of Operations

Match the fact with the power.

21. wheels on a unicycle

22. planets in the solar system

23. freezing point of water in °F

A. 2^5

B. 3^2

C. 1^{17}

24. **a.** Look at the chart below. What exponent completes it?

Value	16	8	4	2	1
Power of 2	2^4	2^3	2^2	2^1	$2^{\blacksquare}$

   b. *Calculator* Check your prediction on your calculator.
   c. *Patterns* Find 3^0, 4^0, 5^0, 10^0. What do you notice?
   d. *Writing* Write a general rule to describe your discovery.

Choose **Use your calculator, paper and pencil, or mental math to evaluate each expression.**

25. $2^5 \times 4^2$

26. $12 + 5^3$

27. -7^4

28. $3(0.5 + 2.5)^2$

29. $(-5)^5$

30. $10^2 + 6^2$

31. $(10 + 6)^2$

32. $8 + 3^4$

33. $3(4^2 - 10)$

34. $(5 - 2^2) - 1$

35. $4^3 + 14 \div 7$

36. $(20 \div 10)^2$

Evaluate each expression for $m = 3$, $n = 2$, and $r = 4$.

37. $m^2 + n^2$

38. $(m + n)^2$

39. $(-r)^3$

40. $-m^3$

41. $m^4 - r^2$

42. $n^2(m + r)$

43. **a.** What is the base of $(7 - 9)^4$? The exponent?
   b. Evaluate $(7 - 9)^4$.

Mixed Review

Find the value of each expression *(Lesson 2-8)*

44. $12 + 3 - 6$

45. $2 - 5 \times 3 \times 3$

46. $27 - 2 \times 8 \div 2$

47. $17 - (2 + 6) \times 2$

Compare. Use <, >, or =. *(Lesson 2-1)*

48. $22.168 \ \blacksquare \ 22.1168$

49. $3.899 \ \blacksquare \ 3.8899$

50. $9.3742 \ \blacksquare \ 9.3842$

51. *Biology* A honeybee hive contains 35,000 cells. How many cells are there in 50 hives? *(Lesson 3-5)*

Divisibility Tests

Before Lesson 4-5

You can use divisibility tests to simplify fractions. A number is *divisible* by another if the remainder is zero. You can combine divisibility tests to develop tests for other numbers.

Number	Divisibility Test
2	The ones digit is 0, 2, 4, 6, or 8.
3	The sum of digits is divisible by 3.
4	The number formed by the last two digits is divisible by 4.
5	The ones digit is 0 or 5.
8	The number formed by the last three digits is divisible by 8.
9	The sum of digits is divisible by 9.
10	The ones digit is 0.

■ EXAMPLE

Use the divisibility tests to determine by which numbers 30 is divisible.

The ones digit of 30 is 0, so 30 is divisible by 2, 5, and 10. The sum of the digits is $3 + 0 = 3$, so it is divisible by 3.

Test whether each number is divisible by 2, 3, 4, 5, 8, 9, and/or 10.

1. 36   2. 324   3. 150   4. 840   5. 2,235   6. 2,724

7. 6,168   8. 810   9. 3,864   10. 1,430   11. 2,421   12. 6,720

13. 875   14. 81,816   15. 7,848   16. 625   17. 4,725   18. 4,104

19. a. Complete: Since 54 is divisible by 2 and 3, it must also be divisible by ■.
    b. *Reasoning* Write a divisibility test for 15.
    c. *Reasoning* Write a divisibility test for 12.

20. *Writing* In her notes, Michiko wrote "14 can be divided by 4, but 14 is not divisible by 4." Is she correct? Explain.

4-5

Prime Factorization

What You'll Learn

▼**1** To find the prime factorization of a number

▼**2** To find the greatest common factor (GCF) of two numbers

...And Why

Learning how to find the greatest common factor of two numbers will help you compute with fractions.

Here's How

Look for questions that
⚓ build understanding
✔ check understanding

Work Together

Finding Factors

Work with a partner. The 4 by 6 and the 6 by 4 rectangles in the photograph are considered the same.

1. **a.** Use graph paper. Draw all the rectangles with an area of 24 square units.
   b. List the dimensions of the rectangles.

2. **a.** Now draw all the rectangles with an area of 7 square units.
   b. List the dimensions of the rectangles.

3. ⚓ *Explain* How do the dimensions you found relate to the factors of each number?

THINK AND DISCUSS

▼**1** *Finding Prime Factorization*

As you saw in the Work Together, twenty-four has more than two factors. It is a **composite** number. Seven has exactly two factors, 1 and itself. It is a **prime** number. The number 1 has exactly one factor, 1, and is neither prime nor composite.

4. Tell whether each number is prime or composite.
   a. 11   **b.** 12   **c.** 13   **d.** 14   **e.** 15

5. ⚓ *Reasoning* Are all even numbers composite? Explain.

To write the **prime factorization** of a composite number, you write the number as the product of its prime factors. A *factor tree* can help you find the prime factors of a number.

■ EXAMPLE 1

Use a factor tree to write the prime factorization of 60.

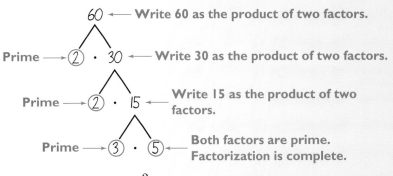

$60 = 2 \cdot 2 \cdot 3 \cdot 5$, or $2^2 \cdot 3 \cdot 5$

6. a. ✔ *Try It Out* Use a factor tree to write the prime factorization of 28.
   b. Write the prime factorization of 28 using exponents.

▼2 *Finding the GCF*

The greatest number that is a factor of two or more numbers is the **greatest common factor** or **GCF.** You can use the prime factorizations of two numbers to find their GCF.

■ EXAMPLE 2

Find the GCF of 24 and 36.

Step 1 Write the prime factorization of each number. Identify the common prime factors.

$24 = 2 \cdot 2 \cdot 2 \cdot 3$ ⎤ Both 24 and 36 have
$36 = 2 \cdot 2 \cdot 3 \cdot 3$ ⎦ the factors $2 \cdot 2 \cdot 3$.

Step 2 Find the product of the common prime factors.

$2 \cdot 2 \cdot 3 = 12$

The GCF of 24 and 36 is 12.

7. ✔ *Try It Out* Use prime factorizations to find the GCF of each pair of numbers.
   a. 16, 24   **b.** 15, 25   **c.** 9, 45   **d.** 10, 8

8. ⬧ *Go a Step Further* Write two pairs of numbers with a GCF of 4.

Another way to find the GCF is to list the factors of each number.

■ EXAMPLE 3

What is the greatest common factor of 28 and 42?

List the factors of 28 and 42 to find the GCF.

Factors of 28: 1, 2, 4, 7, 14, 28

Factors of 42: 1, 2, 3, 6, 7, 14, 21, 42

14 is the greatest common factor.

The GCF of 28 and 42 is 14.

9. ✔ *Try It Out* List the factors to find the GCF of 54 and 72.

EXERCISES *On Your Own*

Mental Math **Is each number prime or composite?**

1. 104   **2.** 88   **3.** 165   **4.** 47   **5.** 77   **6.** 69

7. *Number Sense* List all the prime numbers less than 50.

Use a factor tree to write the prime factorization of each number. Write the prime factorization using exponents where possible.

8. 45   **9.** 64   **10.** 84   **11.** 111   **12.** 100   **13.** 52

14. 65   **15.** 132   **16.** 48   **17.** 60   **18.** 72   **19.** 75

20. *Writing* Sal and Marla made the two factor trees at the right of the prime factors of 24. Are both correct? Explain.

21. *Number Theory* If n is a number, is $2n$ prime or composite? Justify your answer.

22. *Reasoning* What is the GCF of two prime numbers?

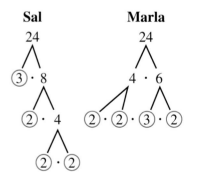

Sal   Marla

Find the GCF of each pair of numbers.

23. 75, 90   **24.** 38, 76   **25.** 100, 75   **26.** 12, 15

27. 77, 121   **28.** 32, 18   **29.** 54, 80   **30.** 22, 121

31. 16, 80   **32.** 10, 85   **33.** 98, 105   **34.** 52, 26

35. *Reasoning* The prime factors of 18 and 24 are at the right.

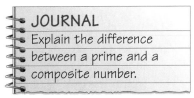

a. Find the product of the factors that are in the intersection of both circles. Is this the GCF or the LCM?
b. Find the product of the factors in both circles. Is this the GCF or the LCM?

36. *Reasoning* Find two composite numbers with a GCF of 1.

37. *Number Sense* Will a prime number and a composite number always have a GCF of 1? Explain.

JOURNAL
Explain the difference between a prime and a composite number.

Mixed Review

Find the value of each expression. *(Lessons 3-3, 3-4)*

38. $8 - (-14)$

39. $-25 + 46$

40. $-31 - (-18)$

41. $29 + (-74)$

42. *Charity* In 1997, Princess Diana auctioned some of her dresses to raise money for charity. *(Lessons 1-4, 1-5, 2-3)*
a. The highest price for a dress was $222,500, and the lowest price was $19,000. What was the range of prices?
b. The 97 dresses sold for a total of $3.25 million. What was the mean price? Round your answer to the nearest dollar.
c. Sales of the catalog raised another $2.5 million for charity. What was the total amount that was raised for charity?

✓ CHECKPOINT 1   *Lessons 4-1 through 4-5*

Write two fractions equivalent to the given fraction.

1. $\frac{3}{4}$ **2.** $\frac{16}{32}$ **3.** $\frac{15}{20}$ **4.** $\frac{7}{9}$ **5.** $\frac{4}{5}$ **6.** $\frac{6}{8}$

7. Choose A, B, C, or D. Which fraction has the greatest value?

A. $\frac{5}{8}$ **B.** $\frac{7}{10}$ **C.** $\frac{8}{12}$ **D.** $\frac{12}{15}$

Find the value of each expression.

8. $8^2 + 11$ **9.** $5^3 - 7^2$ **10.** $(9 - 3)^2$ **11.** $(-2)^4$ **12.** $(-5)^3$ **13.** -3^4

Tell whether each number is prime or composite. Then find the GCF of each pair of numbers.

14. 12, 9   **15.** 121, 11   **16.** 15, 3   **17.** 6, 8   **18.** 9, 27   **19.** 3, 45

4-6

Simplifying Fractions

What You'll Learn

1 To write fractions in simplest form

2 To use the greatest common factor (GCF) to write fractions in simplest form

...And Why

You can use fractions in surveys.

Here's How

Look for questions that
⬛ build understanding
✔ check understanding

THINK AND DISCUSS

1 *Writing Fractions in Simplest Form*

Social Studies Jeremy conducted a survey for his social studies class. He asked 24 people to identify the country each of the people in the table below are from. The frequency table shows the number of correct responses. (Try it yourself. The answers are at the bottom left of the page.)

World Leader Survey	LEADER	FREQUENCY
	Jacques Chirac	15
	Benjamin Netanyahu	16
	Ernesto Zedillo	20
	King Hussein	12
	Bill Clinton	24
	Nelson Mandela	21
	Jean Crétien	18

1. Jeremy wrote the fraction $\frac{12}{24}$ to report the fraction of people who identified that King Hussein is from Jordan. Jeremy's brother thinks he should use the fraction $\frac{1}{2}$. Which fraction do you think Jeremy should use? Why?

A fraction is in simplest form when the only factor common to both the numerator and the denominator is 1.

⬛ **EXAMPLE 1**

Simplify $\frac{12}{24}$.

$$\frac{12 \div 2}{24 \div 2} = \frac{6}{12} \qquad\longrightarrow\qquad \frac{6 \div 6}{12 \div 6} = \frac{1}{2}$$

Divide the numerator and denominator by a common factor.

If necessary, divide again by another common factor.

In simplest form, $\frac{12}{24}$ is $\frac{1}{2}$.

(Jacques Chirac: France; Ernesto Zedillo: Mexico; Benjamin Netanyahu: Israel; King Hussein: Jordan; Bill Clinton: United States; Nelson Mandela: South Africa; Jean Crétien: Canada)

2. ✔ *Try It Out* Write each fraction in simplest form.

a. $\frac{6}{8}$ b. $\frac{8}{12}$ c. $\frac{10}{15}$ d. $\frac{7}{14}$

3. Use the table in Example 1. What fraction of the people recognized the countries that Ernesto Zedillo and Nelson Mandela are from? Write each fraction in simplest form.

② *Using the GCF to Simplify Fractions*

You can divide the numerator and the denominator of a fraction by their GCF to write the fraction in simplest form in one step.

■ **EXAMPLE 2**

Simplify $\frac{18}{30}$.

$18 = 2 \cdot 3 \cdot 3$
$30 = 2 \cdot 3 \cdot 5$ ← The GCF is 2 · 3, which is 6.

$\frac{18 \div 6}{30 \div 6} = \frac{3}{5}$ ← Divide the numerator and denominator by the GCF.

4. ✔ *Try It Out* Write $\frac{36}{96}$ in simplest form by using the GCF of 36 and 96.

You can also simplify a fraction using the prime factorization of the numerator and denominator.

■ **EXAMPLE 3**

Write $\frac{42}{105}$ in simplest form.

$\frac{42}{105} = \frac{2 \cdot 3 \cdot 7}{3 \cdot 5 \cdot 7}$ ← Write the prime factorization of the numerator and the denominator.

$= \frac{2 \cdot \overset{1}{\cancel{3}} \cdot \overset{1}{\cancel{7}}}{\underset{1}{\cancel{3}} \cdot 5 \cdot \underset{1}{\cancel{7}}}$ ← Divide numerator and denominator by the common factors.

$= \frac{2}{5}$ ← Write the fraction in simplest form.

5. ✔ *Try It Out* Use prime factorization to write each fraction in simplest form.

a. $\frac{18}{48}$ b. $\frac{99}{132}$ c. $\frac{60}{75}$

6. ⠿ *Think About It* When would you prefer to simplify a fraction by dividing by the GCF? When would you prefer to use prime factorization?

Pictured above are Ernesto Zedillo (top) and Nelson Mandela.

Write each fraction in simplest form.

1. $\frac{24}{32}$ 2. $\frac{18}{27}$ 3. $\frac{20}{24}$ 4. $\frac{10}{12}$ 5. $\frac{33}{39}$ 6. $\frac{8}{18}$

7. $\frac{16}{28}$ 8. $\frac{21}{28}$ 9. $\frac{18}{30}$ 10. $\frac{25}{35}$ 11. $\frac{9}{15}$ 12. $\frac{6}{28}$

13. *Writing* Which of the following fractions is in simplest form: $\frac{9}{16}, \frac{10}{24}, \frac{14}{35}$? Explain how you know.

14. *Entertainment* Larry surveyed some students to find their music preferences. His results are at the right. Larry wanted to write the results in fraction form for a news article. What fractions should Larry use?

Student Music Preferences	
Musical Format	**Number**
Rock	18
Country/Western	8
Classical	4

15. On an average school day, Josephina spends 7 hours in school, 1 hour delivering newspapers, 2 hours doing her homework, 3 hours reading or talking on the phone, and 8 hours asleep. Write a fraction in simplest form to express how much time she spends on each activity each day.

Find the GCF of the numerator and denominator of each fraction. Then write each fraction in simplest form.

16. $\frac{27}{72}$ 17. $\frac{42}{63}$ 18. $\frac{35}{49}$ 19. $\frac{12}{75}$ 20. $\frac{24}{60}$ 21. $\frac{15}{105}$

22. $\frac{12}{57}$ 23. $\frac{28}{96}$ 24. $\frac{75}{125}$ 25. $\frac{108}{120}$ 26. $\frac{63}{81}$ 27. $\frac{125}{200}$

28. $\frac{42}{64}$ 29. $\frac{35}{95}$ 30. $\frac{25}{80}$ 31. $\frac{18}{48}$ 32. $\frac{20}{54}$ 33. $\frac{17}{51}$

34. *Anatomy* An adult has 206 bones. Of these, 106 are in the feet, ankles, wrists, and hands. What fraction of the bones are in the feet, ankles, wrists, and hands? Write your answer in simplest form.

35. **Choose A, B, C, or D.** Which fraction is *not* in simplest form?

   A. $\frac{5}{16}$ B. $\frac{7}{35}$ C. $\frac{9}{70}$ D. $\frac{10}{169}$

36. *Error Alert* Alex used the method below to write $\frac{54}{64}$ in simplest form. Is he correct? Explain.

   $$\frac{54}{64} = \frac{5\cancel{4}}{6\cancel{4}} = \frac{5}{6}$$

The Global Village

Think of Earth as a global village of only a thousand people. Then 605 of those people would be from Asia, 128 from Africa, 126 from Europe, 84 from Latin America, 52 from North America, and 5 from Australia and New Zealand.

Only 70 people in the village would be over 65, but 320 would be under 15.

37. What fraction of the people in the global village are from each area? Write each fraction in simplest form.

38. What fraction of the people are under 15? Adults over 65? Adults under 65? Write each fraction in simplest form.

Mixed Review

Open-ended **Write a fraction equivalent to the given fraction.** *(Lesson 4-2)*

39. $\frac{3}{4}$ **40.** $\frac{12}{15}$ **41.** $\frac{45}{63}$ **42.** $\frac{6}{9}$ **43.** $\frac{7}{14}$ **44.** $\frac{3}{8}$

Find the value of each expression. *(Lessons 3-2, 4-4)*

45. $(2 + 5)^2$ **46.** $-|10|$ **47.** $2^4 + (3 \cdot 5)$ **48.** $(4 - 7)^3$ **49.** $|-8|$

Choose **Use a calculator or paper and pencil to find each quotient. Use a bar to show repeating decimals.** *(Lesson 2-7)*

50. $9 \div 4$ **51.** $11 \div 3$ **52.** $34 \div 8$ **53.** $37 \div 6$ **54.** $21 \div 4$

55. *Choose a Strategy* Mrs. Brown has retired to Florida. Her children enjoy visiting her. Melvin visits her every three months, Lillian every four months, and Whitney every five months. If all the children visited her in June, in how many months will they all visit her in the same month again?

CHAPTER PROJECT

PROJECT LINK: MEASURING

So you can measure very short lengths with your ruler, mark it to show equal fractions of a unit. What fractions do the marks on your ruler show? Explain why you chose them. Use the fractions on your ruler to measure several small objects.

4-7 Look for a Pattern

Problem Solving Strategies

Draw a Diagram
Guess and Test
✓ Look for a Pattern
Make a Model
Make a Table
Simulate a Problem
Solve a Simpler Problem
Too Much or Too Little
 Information
Use Logical Reasoning
Use Multiple Strategies
Work Backward
Write an Equation

THINK AND DISCUSS

You can solve a problem by solving a series of simpler problems. Then you look for a pattern.

SAMPLE PROBLEM

What is the ones digit of 3^{50} when you find the value of the expression?

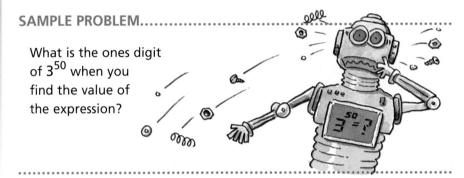

READ

Read for understanding. Summarize the problem.

Think about the information you are given.

1. a. What is the meaning of the expression 3^{50}?
 b. Why is it not easy to evaluate 3^{50} with paper and pencil?
 c. What happens when you try to evaluate 3^{50} with a calculator?

PLAN

Decide on a strategy.

Look for a pattern of the ones digits of the powers of 3 instead of using paper and pencil or a calculator.

2. What is the ones digit in 3^2, 3^3, and 3^4?

SOLVE

Try the strategy.

You need to look for a pattern, so it is a good idea to organize your answers in a table.

3. a. Copy and complete the table at the right.
 b. Circle the ones digit of each number in the Value column. What pattern do you see?
 c. What is the fiftieth number in the pattern?
 d. What is the ones digit of 3^{50}?

Power	Value	Power	Value
3^1	■	3^6	■
3^2	■	3^7	■
3^3	■	3^8	■
3^4	■	3^9	■
3^5	■	3^{10}	■

LOOK BACK
Think about how you solved the problem.

4. How did looking for a pattern help in solving this problem?

5. Explain how you can find the ones digit of any power of 4.

EXERCISES *On Your Own*

Look for a pattern to solve each problem. Show your work.

1. a. Find a pattern for the ones digits of the powers of 7. Describe the pattern you find.
   b. What is the ones digit of 7^{21}?

2. a. Find the sum of the first one hundred odd numbers. That is, find the sum $1 + 3 + 5 + 7 + \ldots + 199$.
   b. Describe how you solved part (a).

3. What is the value of $(-1)^{427}$?

Use any strategy to solve each problem. Show your work.

4. Choose A, B, C, or D. How long is one side of the seventh square in this pattern?

| 225 square units | 196 square units | 169 square units | 144 square units |

A. 121   **B.** 81   **C.** 40.5   **D.** 9

5. Cars A new car comes in five different exterior colors and three different interior colors. How many different color combinations are available?

6. Nita, a six-year-old, can stretch her legs to take two steps at one time. How many different ways can she climb the six steps on her porch using any combination of one or two steps?

7. Jiro has four ways to walk to school and two ways to walk to his after-school job. He does not like to take the same path every day. How many school days elapse before Jiro must repeat a path if he goes to his job every day?

8. *Entertainment* The Drama Club presented two performances of the play *The Wizard of Oz*, one on Friday night and one on Saturday night. Twice as many people came to see the play on Saturday as on Friday. If 495 people saw the play altogether, how many came on each night?

9. It takes two minutes to make one cut through a log. How long will it take to cut a ten-foot log into four equal pieces?

10. There are two blinking neon signs on one block. One blinks on every 10 s, while the other blinks on every 6 s. How many times per minute do they blink together?

11. Show how to cut a round pizza into eleven pieces with exactly four straight cuts.

12. In a class of 30 students, 18 students study Spanish, 15 study French, and 5 study neither Spanish nor French. How many students study both Spanish and French?

13. Five pears weigh the same as three apples and two strawberries. An apple weighs the same as 21 strawberries. How many strawberries weigh the same as a pear?

14. Suppose three students fill four Thanksgiving food baskets in twelve minutes. How many baskets can four students fill in eighteen minutes?

15. *Health* Suppose that in 1 hour a 125-lb person burns 110 calories by walking 2 mi/h, 180 calories by walking 3 mi/h, or 260 calories by walking 4 mi/h. How many calories do you think a 125-lb person would burn in 1 hour by walking 5 mi/h?

Mixed Review

Solve each equation. *(Lesson 3-7)*

16. $x \div 50 = 4$ 17. $-2z = -12$ 18. $-7y = 105$ 19. $-10x = 10$ 20. $y \div 9 = -3$

Estimate. Use any method. *(Lesson 2-2)*

21. $4.29 + 3.88 + 1.01$ 22. $5.7621 - 2.497$ 23. $2.4 + 2.71 + 2.359$

24. Write an equation for the statement "two times n plus seven equals eleven." Solve the equation. *(Lesson 3-9)*

Choose the best answer.

1. Which equation is equivalent to
   $8p + 4.5 = 32$?

   A. $8p + 4.5 = 32 + 4.5$
   B. $8p = 36.5$
   C. $8p = 27.5$
   D. $6p = 32 - 2$

2. Which expression is equivalent to
   $9m + 9n$?

   F. $18(m + n)$ **G.** $(m + n)$
   H. $m + n$ **J.** $9(m + n)$

3. Scores in a golf tournament were reported
   by the number of strokes each player
   was above or below par. The scores for
   6 players at the end of the tournament
   were $-12, +2, -7, +4, -4,$ and -3. What
   are the golfers' scores in order from the
   least number under par to the greatest
   number over par?

   A. $-12, -7, -4, -3, +2, +4$
   B. $+2, -3, -4, +4, -7, -12$
   C. $+4, +2, -3, -4, -7, -12$
   D. $-3, -4, -7, -12, +2, +4$

4. The cost for renting a boat for a day is
   found by using this formula:

   $$C = 15 + 10h,$$

   where C is the total cost of renting the
   boat, $15 is the maintenance fee for the
   boat, and h is the number of hours the
   boat is rented. Using this formula, what
   would it cost to rent a boat for 6 hours?

   F. $100   **G.** $75   **H.** $60   **J.** $45

5. If $4t + 13.7 = 29.9$, what is the value of t?

   A. 64.8   **B.** 10.5   **C.** 4.05   **D.** 3.55

6. What factors represent $2^3 \times 4^2$?

   F. $3 \times 3 \times 2 \times 2$
   G. 6×8
   H. $2 \times 2 \times 2 \times 4 \times 4$
   J. $2 \times 2 \times 4 \times 2$

7. Which numbers are between 6^3 and 6^4?

   A. 3^6 and 4^6 **B.** 5^3 and 5^4
   C. 7^2 and 7^3 **D.** 4^5 and 5^4

**Please note that items 8–10 have _five_
answer choices.**

8. Mountain climbers hiked down 1,800 feet
   from the top of a mountain every day.
   How far down from the top of the
   mountain are the climbers after six
   days?

   F. 1,806 ft   **G.** 12,600 ft
   H. 10,800 ft   **J.** 9,000 ft
   K. Not Here

9. Medium beverages cost $1.39 and small
   beverages cost $.89. Which equation could
   be used to find the total cost in dollars d
   of any number of medium beverages m
   and any number of small beverages s?

   A. $d = (\$1.39 + m) \times (\$.89 + s)$
   B. $d = (m \times \$.89) + (s \times \$1.39)$
   C. $d = (m \times \$1.39) + (s \times \$.89)$
   D. $d = (\$.89 + \$1.39) \times (m \times s)$
   E. $d = (\$1.39 + \$.89) + (m \times s)$

10. What is the prime factorization of 6,000?

   F. $10 \cdot 20 \cdot 30$ **G.** $10^2 \cdot 60$
   H. $2^2 \cdot 3 \cdot 5^4$ **J.** $2^4 \cdot 3 \cdot 5^3$
   K. Not Here

4-8 Mixed Numbers and Improper Fractions

THINK AND DISCUSS

1 *Mixed Numbers to Improper Fractions*

An **improper fraction** has a numerator that is greater than or equal to its denominator. You can use models to understand the connection between mixed numbers and improper fractions.

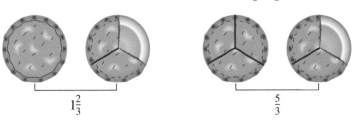

$1\frac{2}{3}$ $\frac{5}{3}$

A number line can also help you understand improper fractions and mixed numbers. The number line shows that $1\frac{1}{4} = \frac{5}{4}$.

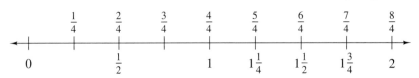

1. Use the number line to write two other mixed numbers as improper fractions.

You can change a mixed number to an improper fraction using equivalent fractions.

■ EXAMPLE 1

Write $2\frac{3}{4}$ as an improper fraction.

$2\frac{3}{4} = 2 + \frac{3}{4}$ ←— Write the mixed number as a sum.

$= \frac{8}{4} + \frac{3}{4}$ ←— Write 2 as the fraction $\frac{8}{4}$.

$= \frac{8 + 3}{4}$ ←— Add the numerators.

$2\frac{3}{4} = \frac{11}{4}$

---

2. ▪▪ ***Look Back*** Why is $\frac{8}{4}$ a good choice as the equivalent fraction for $\frac{2}{1}$?

3. ✔ *Try It Out* Write each mixed number as an improper fraction.

a. $1\frac{2}{3}$ **b.** $2\frac{2}{3}$ **c.** $3\frac{2}{3}$ **d.** $4\frac{2}{3}$

4. ⬩ *Patterns* Describe the pattern you see in the numerators of the fractions you wrote for Question 3.

Here is another way to write mixed numbers as improper fractions.

■ **EXAMPLE 2**

Write $4\frac{2}{3}$ as an improper fraction.

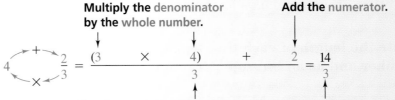

Multiply the **denominator** by the **whole number**.

Add the **numerator**.

$$4\,\frac{2}{3} = \frac{(3 \times 4) + 2}{3} = \frac{14}{3}$$

Write the result over the **denominator**, which stays the same.

5. ✔ *Try It Out* Write each mixed number as an improper fraction.

a. $3\frac{4}{5}$ **b.** $2\frac{5}{8}$ **c.** $3\frac{1}{4}$ **d.** $1\frac{7}{8}$

2 *Improper Fractions to Mixed Numbers*

To change an improper fraction to a mixed number, divide the numerator by the denominator.

■ **EXAMPLE 3**

Write $\frac{30}{8}$ as a mixed number in simplest form.

denominator →
$$\begin{array}{r} 3 \\ 8\overline{)30} \\ \underline{24} \\ 6 \end{array}$$
← whole number

← remainder

$\frac{30}{8} = 3\frac{6}{8}$ ← Write $\frac{\text{remainder}}{\text{denominator}}$.

$= 3\frac{3}{4}$ ← Simplify the fraction.

6. ✔ *Try It Out* Write each fraction as a mixed number.

a. $\frac{12}{5}$ **b.** $\frac{8}{6}$ **c.** $\frac{15}{12}$ **d.** $\frac{25}{4}$

Write each mixed number as an improper fraction.

1. $2\frac{3}{8}$ 2. $5\frac{3}{4}$ 3. $1\frac{1}{12}$ 4. $4\frac{3}{5}$ 5. $1\frac{3}{7}$ 6. $4\frac{5}{8}$

7. $3\frac{2}{5}$ 8. $2\frac{11}{12}$ 9. $5\frac{2}{3}$ 10. $3\frac{1}{4}$ 11. $2\frac{4}{9}$ 12. $4\frac{7}{10}$

13. $4\frac{7}{8}$ 14. $3\frac{1}{6}$ 15. $8\frac{3}{7}$ 16. $2\frac{5}{12}$ 17. $6\frac{1}{7}$ 18. $3\frac{5}{12}$

19. *Writing* How can you tell if a fraction is an improper fraction?

20. *Research* Find a mixed number in a newspaper. State your source, then write it as an improper fraction.

Write the length of each line segment below as a mixed number and as an improper fraction.

21.

22.

23.

24.

Write each improper fraction as a whole number or a mixed number in simplest form.

25. $\frac{16}{3}$ 26. $\frac{21}{3}$ 27. $\frac{42}{4}$ 28. $\frac{31}{12}$ 29. $\frac{32}{8}$ 30. $\frac{49}{6}$

31. $\frac{84}{7}$ 32. $\frac{45}{10}$ 33. $\frac{18}{3}$ 34. $\frac{15}{8}$ 35. $\frac{9}{2}$ 36. $\frac{42}{7}$

37. $\frac{22}{5}$ 38. $\frac{17}{6}$ 39. $\frac{27}{4}$ 40. $\frac{19}{12}$ 41. $\frac{18}{4}$ 42. $\frac{21}{9}$

43. *Reasoning* A recipe calls for $1\frac{3}{4}$ c of flour. Darrell and Tanisha have only a quarter cup measure. How many times will they fill it for the recipe?

44. *Carpentry* Pearl kept track of the time she worked on her carpentry project. She worked a total of 345 min. Use mixed numbers to write Pearl's time in hours.

45. *Travel* It took the Brook family 3 h 45 min to travel from their home to their cousins' home for Thanksgiving. Write the time as a mixed number and as a fraction in simplest form.

46. *Cooking* A cooking class served $25\frac{1}{4}$ loaves of banana bread at a faculty breakfast. Each loaf was cut into eight equal slices. How many slices of banana bread did they serve?

47. Choose A, B, C, or D. A length of material measures between 3 and $3\frac{1}{4}$ feet. What length could it be?

A. $\frac{26}{7}$ **B.** $\frac{11}{3}$ **C.** $\frac{25}{8}$ **D.** $\frac{18}{5}$

48. Each pizza delivered to a class party was divided into 8 equal slices. After the party, there were 2 slices from one pizza, 3 slices from each of two other pizzas, and 5 slices from another pizza left on the table. Write the amount of leftover pizza as a mixed number.

49. *Reasoning* Use the digits 2, 5, and 9 to write a fraction with the greatest possible value. Then write the fraction as a mixed number.

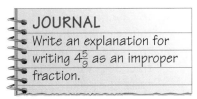

JOURNAL
Write an explanation for writing $4\frac{5}{9}$ as an improper fraction.

Mixed Review

Find each sum or difference. *(Lessons 3-3, 3-4)*

50. $6 + (-7)$ **51.** $8 - (-5)$ **52.** $-12 + (-3)$ **53.** $-20 - 4$ **54.** $-5 - (-1)$

55. Alan has lumber 63 in. long, 84 in. long, and 105 in. long. He plans to cut all the lumber into pieces of equal length. What is the longest length he can cut without having any left over? *(Lesson 4-5)*

✓ CHECKPOINT 2

Lessons 4-6 through 4-8

Write each fraction in simplest form.

1. $\frac{36}{48}$ **2.** $\frac{42}{63}$ **3.** $\frac{30}{45}$ **4.** $\frac{18}{20}$ **5.** $\frac{12}{54}$ **6.** $\frac{35}{50}$

Write each improper fraction as a mixed number and each mixed number as an improper fraction.

7. $\frac{29}{6}$ **8.** $\frac{82}{5}$ **9.** $4\frac{1}{9}$ **10.** $1\frac{9}{10}$ **11.** $\frac{33}{12}$ **12.** $2\frac{5}{6}$

13. a. *Writing* Would you prefer to list factors or use prime factorization to simplify $\frac{375}{1,000}$? Why?
   b. Use your choice to simplify $\frac{375}{1,000}$.

14. A street has a building for every number. How many buildings are on the odd-numbered side of a street that starts at number 107 and ends with 189?

What You'll Learn

1 To change fractions to decimals

2 To change decimals to fractions in simplest form

...And Why

Fractions and decimals are used to compute statistics.

Here's How

Look for questions that
- build understanding
- ✔ check understanding

Work Together

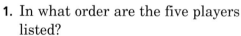

Ordering Fractions

The white blur of the softball speeds toward you. Your body leans, your arms and wrist snap the bat around. Pow! The ball rockets into center field for a hit.

It doesn't happen every time at bat. In fact, few players get a hit more than $\frac{1}{3}$ of the time.

Top Five Georgia Bulldogs Hitters, 1997

Player	Hits	Times at Bat	Fraction of Times Player Got a Hit
Jessi Cerra	47	164	$\frac{47}{164}$
Chrissy Gavin	35	137	$\frac{35}{137}$
Heather Boyer	32	93	$\frac{32}{93}$
Sabrina Touchberry	30	100	$\frac{30}{100}$
Caroline Patrick	23	85	$\frac{23}{85}$

1. In what order are the five players listed?

2. Who had more times at bat, Sabrina Touchberry or Heather Boyer?

3. Do you think Sabrina Touchberry or Heather Boyer had hits a greater fraction of her times at bat? Why?

4. *Explain* Was Sabrina Touchberry or Heather Boyer more likely to get a hit when she came to bat?

THINK AND DISCUSS

1 ► *Writing Fractions as Decimals*

Batting averages are usually expressed as decimals. Change the fraction $\frac{hits}{times\ at\ bat}$ to a decimal by dividing the numerator by the denominator.

■ **EXAMPLE 1**   *Real-World Problem Solving*

Sports Write Heather Boyer's batting average as a decimal. Round your answer to the nearest thousandth.

Heather Boyer got a hit $\frac{32}{93}$ of the time.

32 ■ 93 ▤ *0.344086021* ◄─── Use a calculator to divide the numerator by the denominator.

≈ 0.344 ◄─── Round to the nearest thousandth.

Heather Boyer's batting average is .344.

5. **a.** ✔ *Try It Out* Change the fraction for each of the other players' batting averages on page 176 to a decimal. Round each average to the nearest thousandth.

 b. List the five players in order from highest to lowest batting average.

 c. ⬤ *Think About It* Is it easier to compare batting averages in fraction form or in decimal form? Why?

6. ⬤ *Reasoning* Why do you need to know what place to round the decimal to in Example 1?

Sometimes when you change a fraction to a decimal, the result is a repeating decimal. To show that a decimal repeats, you use a bar over the digits that repeat.

■ **EXAMPLE 2**

Change each fraction to a decimal.

 a. $\frac{5}{11}$ **b.** $\frac{2}{3}$

 $\frac{5}{11} = 5 \div 11$ $\frac{2}{3} = 2 \div 3$

 $= 0.454545454\ldots$ $= 0.666666666\ldots$

 $= 0.\overline{45}$ $= 0.\overline{6}$

7. ✔ *Try It Out* Write each fraction as a decimal. Use a bar to show repeating digits.

a. $\frac{2}{11}$ b. $\frac{5}{15}$ c. $\frac{5}{9}$ d. $\frac{7}{12}$

▼ 2 *Changing Decimals to Fractions*

QUICKreview

A terminating decimal is a decimal that ends.

You can change a terminating decimal to a fraction by writing the decimal as a number over some power of 10, like 10, 100, or 1,000.

■ EXAMPLE 3

Write 1.325 as a fraction in simplest form.

Read the number as one and three hundred twenty-five *thousandths*. The number in the denominator is *1,000*. Write $1\frac{325}{1,000}$.

$$1\frac{325}{1,000} = 1\frac{325 \div 25}{1,000 \div 25} \quad \longleftarrow \quad \text{Use the GCF to write the fraction in simplest form.}$$
$$= 1\frac{13}{40}$$

8. ✔ *Try It Out* Write each decimal as a fraction in simplest form.

a. 0.6   b. 2.48   c. 0.79   d. 0.525

EXERCISES *On Your Own*

▦*Choose* **Use a calculator, paper and pencil, or mental math to write each fraction as a decimal. Use a bar to show any repeating digits.**

Greenland

1. $\frac{2}{5}$ 2. $\frac{5}{6}$ 3. $\frac{3}{20}$ 4. $\frac{3}{8}$ 5. $\frac{11}{12}$ 6. $\frac{3}{2}$

7. $\frac{6}{8}$ 8. $\frac{4}{15}$ 9. $\frac{5}{12}$ 10. $\frac{6}{11}$ 11. $\frac{1}{6}$ 12. $\frac{4}{5}$

13. $\frac{25}{33}$ 14. $\frac{9}{16}$ 15. $\frac{21}{30}$ 16. $\frac{10}{45}$ 17. $\frac{72}{80}$ 18. $\frac{5}{24}$

19. **Science** About 12,500 icebergs break away from Greenland each year. Of these, about 375 float into the Atlantic Ocean.
   a. What fraction of the icebergs that break away from Greenland each year float into the Atlantic Ocean? Write your answer in simplest form.
   b. Change your answer from part (a) to a decimal.
   c. What fraction of the icebergs *don't* float into the Atlantic Ocean? Write your answer in simplest form.

20. Use the table at the right.

a. Write a fraction showing $\frac{\text{number of people under 18}}{\text{total population}}$ for each state.

b. *Estimation* For most of the states, would $\frac{1}{2}$, $\frac{1}{3}$, or $\frac{1}{4}$ best describe the fraction of the population that is under 18?

c. *Calculator* Change each fraction from part (a) to a decimal. Round to the nearest thousandth.

d. Write the states from least to greatest based on the part of the population that is under 18.

21. Choose A, B, C, or D. Which has the greatest value?

A. 0.668   **B.** $\frac{4}{6}$ **C.** $\frac{5}{7}$ **D.** 0.68

22. a. *Calculator* Change each fraction in the table below to a decimal. Use a bar to show repeating decimals.

Population Chart

State	Total Population (thousands)	Number of People Under 18 (thousands)
ME	1,235	310
NY	18,055	4,366
OH	10,939	2,819
CA	30,380	8,163
MD	4,860	1,201
KY	3,713	875
OK	3,175	875
WY	460	154
AK	570	180
FL	13,277	2,998

Source: *Statistical Abstract of the United States*

Basketball Players' Statistics

Player	Free Throws	Attempts	Fraction
A	52	96	$\frac{52}{96}$
B	75	120	$\frac{75}{120}$
C	51	99	$\frac{51}{99}$
D	92	150	$\frac{92}{150}$

b. List the players in order from highest to lowest free-throw average.

23. *Writing* Describe some everyday situations in which you need to change fractions to decimals.

24. a. Write $3\frac{5}{8}$ as an improper fraction.

b. Change your answer from part (a) to a decimal.

Write each decimal as a fraction in simplest form.

25. 0.6   **26.** 0.125   **27.** 0.66   **28.** 2.5   **29.** 3.75   **30.** 0.32

31. 0.19   **32.** 0.8   **33.** 0.965   **34.** 1.6   **35.** 4.305   **36.** 1.27

37. 0.65   **38.** 0.394   **39.** 1.690   **40.** 0.78   **41.** 0.568   **42.** 0.35

43. Write in order from least to greatest.
$\frac{2}{3}$, 0.67, $\frac{5}{9}$, 0.58, $\frac{7}{12}$

44. In an experiment with seeds from wild plants, a botanist gathered the data below on the number of seeds planted and the number that sprouted for each variety.

Seed Type	A	B	C	D	E	F	G	H	I
Number Sprouted	15	5	22	17	18	21	14	18	8
Number Planted	48	20	44	35	52	63	55	35	15

a. *Calculator* Write a fraction showing $\frac{\text{number sprouted}}{\text{number planted}}$, then change the fraction to a decimal. Round to the nearest hundredth.

b. Place the seed types into 3 groups: those that sprout about $\frac{1}{2}$ of the time, those that sprout about $\frac{1}{3}$ of the time, and those that sprout about $\frac{1}{4}$ of the time.

c. Which type(s) of seeds would you prefer to plant? Why?

45. In 1990, the average number of people per household was 2.63. Write this number as a mixed number and as an improper fraction.

PORTFOLIO

For your portfolio, choose one or two items from your work for this chapter. Here are some possibilities:
• cooperative work
• work you found challenging
• part of your project
Explain why you have included each selection.

Mixed Review

Write each mixed number as an improper fraction. *(Lesson 4-8)*

46. $1\frac{2}{3}$ **47.** $2\frac{4}{5}$ **48.** $6\frac{4}{9}$ **49.** $3\frac{1}{12}$ **50.** $4\frac{2}{7}$ **51.** $2\frac{3}{11}$

Find each quotient. *(Lesson 2-6)*

52. $0.45 \div 9$ **53.** $0.64 \div 0.8$ **54.** $1.75 \div 0.05$ **55.** $3.06 \div 0.3$

56. Find the mean, median, and mode of the following scores: 93, 80, 77, 93, 69, 90, 85, 88. *(Lesson 1-4)*

57. *Choose a Strategy* Six building blocks are cubes with edges of 1 cm, 2 cm, 3 cm, 4 cm, 5 cm, and 6 cm. Can you use all the blocks to make two towers of the same height? Explain.

CHAPTER PROJECT

PROJECT LINK: ANALYZING

Is your system as good as the other systems you have used to measure lengths? What are the advantages and disadvantages of your system and the other systems?

CHAPTER PROJECT

making THE measure

Invent Your Own Ruler The Project Link questions on pages 154, 167, and 180 should help you to complete your project. Here is a checklist to help you gather together the parts of your project.

- ✔ the actual ruler
- ✔ the name of your unit of measurement
- ✔ the list of objects and their lengths that you have measured with your unit
- ✔ an explanation of how to measure in fractional units
- ✔ your analysis of measurement systems

Be prepared to demonstrate your ruler to the class. Show how to measure a wide range of lengths using your ruler. Include some actual measurements to show how useful your system is.

Reflect and Revise

Discuss the usefulness of your ruler with a friend or family member. Does it allow you to measure long and short lengths? Can you measure in fractions of units? If necessary, make changes to improve your project.

Web Extension

Prentice Hall's Internet site contains information you might find helpful as you complete your project. Visit www.phschool.com/mgm2/ch4 for some links and ideas related to measurement.

The Meaning of Fractions 4-1

Fractions are used to describe parts of a whole and members of a group.

Write a fraction for each model.

1. **2.** 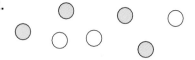 **3.**

Inches   1

Equivalent Fractions and Comparing Fractions 4-2, 4-3

To find **equivalent fractions,** multiply or divide the numerator and denominator by the same nonzero number. To compare fractions, first find a common denominator.

Order from least to greatest.

4. $\frac{3}{8}, \frac{1}{2}, \frac{1}{4}$ **5.** $\frac{3}{4}, \frac{7}{12}, \frac{1}{6}$ **6.** $\frac{2}{5}, \frac{1}{3}, \frac{7}{15}$ **7.** $\frac{6}{10}, \frac{4}{5}, \frac{8}{20}$ **8.** $\frac{6}{7}, \frac{8}{10}, \frac{3}{4}$ **9.** $\frac{4}{6}, \frac{9}{12}, \frac{3}{5}$

10. Choose A, B, C, or D. Which fraction is *not* equivalent to $\frac{4}{7}$?

   A. $\frac{24}{42}$ **B.** $\frac{48}{74}$ **C.** $\frac{16}{28}$ **D.** $\frac{20}{35}$

Exponents 4-4

You use an **exponent** to show repeated multiplication.

Write each expression as a product of repeated factors. Then evaluate each expression.

11. 2^3 **12.** -3^4 **13.** 6^2 **14.** 0.2^3 **15.** 0.12^2 **16.** $(-3)^4$

Prime Factorization and Simplifying Fractions 4-5, 4-6

A **prime number** has exactly two factors, 1 and the number itself. If a number has more than two factors, then it is **composite.**

To write the **prime factorization** of a composite number, you write the number as the product of its prime factors.

A fraction is in **simplest form** when the only factor common to both the numerator and the denominator is 1.

Identify each number as prime or composite. Then write the prime factorization of each number.

17. 73   **18.** 110   **19.** 16   **20.** 87   **21.** 121   **22.** 28

Write each fraction in simplest form.

23. $\frac{24}{48}$ **24.** $\frac{33}{132}$ **25.** $\frac{54}{72}$ **26.** $\frac{24}{60}$ **27.** $\frac{32}{36}$ **28.** $\frac{84}{144}$

Problem Solving Strategies   4-7

You can use patterns to help you solve problems.

29. A grocer is stacking boxes of cereal as part of a display. Each row has one less than the row beneath it. The top row will have one box. How many boxes will be in 20 rows?

Mixed Numbers and Improper Fractions   4-8

The numerator of an **improper fraction** is greater than or equal to the denominator.

Write each mixed number as an improper fraction and each improper fraction as a mixed number in simplest form.

30. $4\frac{5}{8}$ **31.** $\frac{23}{5}$ **32.** $5\frac{7}{9}$ **33.** $3\frac{2}{3}$ **34.** $\frac{15}{8}$ **35.** $\frac{28}{6}$

36. *Writing* Explain how to write an improper fraction as a mixed number in simplest form. Include an example.

Fractions and Decimals   4-9

To write a fraction as a decimal, divide the numerator by the denominator.

To write a decimal as a fraction, first write a fraction with a denominator that is a power of ten. Then, simplify the fraction.

Write each fraction as a decimal, and each decimal as a fraction in simplest form.

37. 0.05   **38.** $\frac{75}{100}$ **39.** 0.24   **40.** $\frac{7}{8}$ **41.** 2.96   **42.** $\frac{5}{6}$

1. What fraction does the shaded part of the model represent?

2. Draw models to represent $\frac{3}{4}$ and $2\frac{3}{5}$.

3. Write two fractions equivalent to each given fraction.
   a. $\frac{1}{3}$ b. $\frac{15}{24}$ c. $\frac{4}{5}$ d. $\frac{16}{28}$

4. Compare. Use $<$, $>$, or $=$.
   a. $\frac{2}{9} \blacksquare \frac{8}{9}$ b. $\frac{5}{16} \blacksquare \frac{3}{8}$ c. $\frac{13}{20} \blacksquare \frac{5}{8}$

5. Find the value of each expression.
   a. $(3^2 + 1) \div 5$ b. $5^2 - 7^2$
   c. $(6 - 9)^3$ d. $54 \div 3^2$

6. List the factors of each number.
   a. 27   b. 36   c. 100   d. 25

7. Tell whether each number is prime or composite.
   a. 17   b. 75   c. 49   d. 83

8. Find the GCF of each pair of numbers.
   a. 32, 40   b. 55, 15
   c. 36, 57   d. 24, 68

9. **Choose A, B, C, or D.** Which statement is *always* true?
   A. Two is a composite number.
   B. Any factor of a whole number is greater than any multiple of a whole number.
   C. A number is divisible by 3 if its last digit is divisible by 3.
   D. One is neither a composite nor a prime number.

10. Use a factor tree to write the prime factorization of 42.

11. Write the first four multiples of 27.

12. *Writing* Explain how to use prime factorization to write a fraction in simplest form.

13. Write each fraction in simplest form.
    a. $\frac{12}{18}$ b. $\frac{27}{54}$ c. $\frac{36}{96}$ d. $\frac{7}{42}$

14. The Fair-Share Salvage crew found a sunken pirate ship that had a chest containing 168 gold and 200 silver coins. All crew members received an equal share of each kind of coin. There were no coins left over. What is the greatest possible number of crew members? How many of each type of coin does each crew member get?

15. Write each mixed number as an improper fraction.
    a. $5\frac{2}{3}$ b. $4\frac{5}{6}$ c. $8\frac{7}{10}$ d. $3\frac{2}{5}$

16. Write each improper fraction as a whole number or a mixed number.
    a. $\frac{12}{5}$ b. $\frac{30}{9}$ c. $\frac{48}{12}$ d. $\frac{42}{30}$

17. Write each fraction as a decimal.
    a. $\frac{2}{16}$ b. $\frac{6}{15}$ c. $\frac{5}{4}$ d. $\frac{8}{25}$

18. Write each decimal as a fraction.
    a. 0.2   b. 1.3   c. 0.35   d. 3.62

19. Find the value of the expression $1 - 2 + 3 - 4 + 5 - \ldots - 50$. Explain how you found your answer.

20. In one week, $\frac{5}{8}$ of the mail the Franklin family received was advertisements and $\frac{1}{5}$ of the mail was from friends. What is the least number of pieces of mail they could have received?

Choose the best answer.

1. A hexagon represents one whole. Which mixed number is shown?

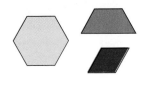

   A. $3\frac{2}{3}$　　**B.** $5\frac{1}{2}$　　**C.** $2\frac{1}{3}$　　**D.** $1\frac{5}{6}$

2. How much will a $3.99 sandwich and $1.19 juice cost?

   A. $5.18　　　**B.** $4.18
   C. $5.08　　　**D.** $4.08

3. You have data about the age and height of some trees. How would you display the data to find a relationship between the age and height of a tree?

   A. double bar graph
   B. frequency table
   C. scatter plot
   D. line plot

4. Which expression represents "3 less than w"?

   A. $3 - w$　　　**B.** $w \div 3$
   C. $3 \div w$　　　**D.** $w - 3$

5. Which fraction is *not* equivalent to $\frac{9}{12}$?

   A. $\frac{24}{32}$　**B.** $\frac{6}{8}$　**C.** $\frac{15}{20}$　**D.** $\frac{16}{24}$

6. Which statement is *false*?

   A. The GCF of two prime numbers is 1.
   B. Any fraction with composite numbers in the numerator and denominator is *not* in simplest form.
   C. More than half of the numbers between 1 and 100 are composite.
   D. The GCF of a number and twice that number is the number itself.

7. You want to buy two tickets that regularly cost $354 each. From which airline should you buy your tickets?

Airline	Price Offer
A	"Buy 1 ticket, get the 2nd at $\frac{1}{2}$ off"
B	"$\frac{1}{4}$ off the price of all tickets"
C	"Get $\frac{1}{2}$ off any ticket over $400"
D	"$89 off each ticket"

8. How is the product $5 \times 5 \times 5 \times 5$ expressed as a power?

   A. 5^4　**B.** 4^5　**C.** 4×5　**D.** 10^2

9. What is the next fraction in the pattern $\frac{1}{2}, \frac{3}{4}, \frac{9}{8}, \frac{27}{16}, \cdots$?

   A. $\frac{36}{24}$　**B.** $\frac{81}{32}$　**C.** $\frac{54}{48}$　**D.** $\frac{40}{25}$

10. If $\frac{b}{6} - 3 = 9$, what is the value of b?

    A. 2　　**B.** 24　　**C.** 36　　**D.** 72

11. A video store offered movies on sale at 3 for $42.50. Scott wants to purchase 5 videos. It is reasonable to assume that the cost of the 5 videos is

    A. exactly $42.50
    B. between $40 and $60
    C. between $60 and $80
    D. more than $80

12. The book sale at Meyer Middle School made $552.78. This money will be divided equally among three grades. What is the best estimate of the amount each class will receive?

    A. $170　**B.** $180　**C.** $190　**D.** $200

Applications of Fractions

5

Toss and Turn

Did you ever make pancakes? The recipe can be pretty simple—an egg, some pancake mix, milk, and maybe some oil. Or forget the mix and start from scratch! Either way, you can vary the ingredients to suit your tastes. Do you want to include some wheat germ? How about some pecans, or maybe some fruit? Bananas are always in season!

Write Your Own Recipe For the chapter project, you will write your own recipe for pancakes. Your final product will be a recipe that will feed everyone in your class.

Steps to help you complete the project:

p. 196   Project Link: *Interviewing*
p. 209   Project Link: *Researching*
p. 224   Project Link: *Calculating*
p. 225   *Finishing the Chapter Project*

• How to solve problems by working backward

Estimating with Fractions and Mixed Numbers

THINK AND DISCUSS

1 *Estimating Sums and Differences*

To estimate sums and differences of fractions, round them to 0, $\frac{1}{2}$, or 1. You can think of a number line as you round the fractions.

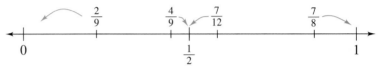

Round to 0 when the numerator is very small compared to the denominator.

Round to $\frac{1}{2}$ when the denominator is about twice the numerator.

Round to 1 when the numerator and denominator are nearly equal.

■ EXAMPLE 1

Estimate $\frac{7}{8} + \frac{4}{9}$.

$$\frac{7}{8} + \frac{4}{9} \approx 1 + \frac{1}{2} = 1\frac{1}{2}$$ ←—Round each fraction. Then add.

1. ✔ *Try It Out* Estimate each sum or difference.

   a. $\frac{5}{12} + \frac{1}{15}$ **b.** $\frac{3}{5} - \frac{1}{8}$ **c.** $\frac{7}{8} + \frac{7}{9}$ **d.** $\frac{7}{8} - \frac{5}{9}$

When a sum or difference involves mixed numbers, you get a reasonable estimate by rounding to the nearest whole number.

■ EXAMPLE 2   *Real-World Problem Solving*

Swimming In the week before the swim meet, Paulo practiced by swimming $8\frac{1}{5}$ mi. Allen swam $4\frac{1}{2}$ mi. About how many more miles did Paulo swim?

Estimate $8\frac{1}{5} - 4\frac{1}{2}$.

$$8\frac{1}{5} - 4\frac{1}{2}$$ ←—If the fractional part is greater than or equal to $\frac{1}{2}$, round up.

$$8 - 5 = 3$$

Paulo swam about 3 mi farther.

2. ✔ *Try It Out* Estimate each sum or difference.

  a. $7\frac{4}{5} + 2\frac{1}{3}$ **b.** $1\frac{7}{8} + 3\frac{2}{5}$ **c.** $4\frac{1}{8} - 1\frac{8}{9}$ **d.** $8\frac{9}{16} - 3\frac{7}{8}$

▼2 *Estimating Products and Quotients*

To estimate a product of mixed numbers, round to the nearest whole number.

■ EXAMPLE 3

Estimate $2\frac{2}{5} \cdot 6\frac{1}{10}$.

$$2\frac{2}{5} \cdot 6\frac{1}{10} \qquad \longleftarrow \text{Round.}$$

$$2 \ \cdot \ \ 6 = 12 \quad \longleftarrow \text{Multiply.}$$

3. ✔ *Try It Out* Estimate each product.

  a. $3\frac{5}{6} \cdot 5\frac{1}{8}$ **b.** $8\frac{1}{8} \cdot 5\frac{11}{12}$ **c.** $2\frac{3}{5} \cdot 1\frac{2}{5}$ **d.** $5\frac{3}{4} \cdot 4\frac{11}{12}$

4. ⁑ *Look Back* Is the actual product in Example 3 *greater than* 12 or *less than* 12? Explain.

QUICK review

$$72 \div 9 = 8$$

dividend divisor quotient

To estimate a quotient of mixed numbers, you can use compatible numbers. First round the divisor. Then find a compatible number for the dividend.

■ EXAMPLE 4

Estimate $43\frac{1}{4} \div 5\frac{7}{8}$.

$$43\frac{1}{4} \div 5\frac{7}{8} \qquad \longleftarrow \begin{array}{l} 5\frac{7}{8} \text{ rounds to 6. 42 is compatible with 6,} \\ \text{and is close to } 43\frac{1}{4}. \end{array}$$

$$42 \ \div \ \ 6 = 7 \quad \longleftarrow \text{Find the quotient.}$$

5. ⁑ *Think About It* What compatible numbers would you use to estimate each quotient?

  a. $21\frac{1}{2} \div 5\frac{1}{5}$ **b.** $34\frac{1}{3} \div 6\frac{5}{8}$ **c.** $42\frac{1}{3} \div 7\frac{1}{4}$ **d.** $70\frac{3}{5} \div 9\frac{2}{5}$

6. ✔ *Try It Out* Estimate each quotient.

  a. $35\frac{3}{4} \div 5\frac{11}{12}$ **b.** $22\frac{7}{8} \div 3\frac{5}{6}$ **c.** $44\frac{1}{8} \div 6\frac{1}{2}$ **d.** $8\frac{1}{8} \div 3\frac{1}{8}$

7. *Reasoning* Victor estimated $87\frac{3}{4} \div 10\frac{5}{8}$. His answer was 8. Is this answer reasonable? Explain.

Estimate each sum or difference.

1. $\frac{1}{7} + \frac{3}{8}$ **2.** $\frac{2}{3} + \frac{9}{10}$ **3.** $9\frac{1}{11} - 3\frac{7}{9}$ **4.** $5\frac{3}{5} + 3\frac{2}{3}$ **5.** $4\frac{1}{2} - 1\frac{24}{25}$

6. $\frac{3}{5} - \frac{1}{2}$ **7.** $7\frac{2}{3} - 2\frac{11}{12}$ **8.** $\frac{1}{7} + \frac{3}{8}$ **9.** $\frac{3}{4} + \frac{5}{6}$ **10.** $\frac{3}{4} - \frac{1}{5}$

Music **Use the table for Exercises 11–13. The table shows the weight of the bells of Boston's Old North Church. The bells are in order from smallest to largest.**

Tone	F	E	D	C	B flat	A	G	low F
Weight in tons	$\frac{3}{10}$	$\frac{3}{10}$	$\frac{7}{20}$	$\frac{2}{5}$	$\frac{11}{25}$	$\frac{19}{40}$	$\frac{3}{5}$	$\frac{3}{4}$

11. Estimate the total weight of the two largest bells.

12. Estimate the total weight of all eight bells.

13. Estimate the difference in the weights of the largest and smallest bell.

14. a. Estimate $\frac{1}{8} + \frac{2}{5}$ by rounding each fraction to the nearest whole number.

 b. Estimate the sum by rounding each fraction to $0, \frac{1}{2}$, or 1.

 c. *Reasoning* Why is the estimation method used in part (b) more appropriate than the method used in part (a)?

Estimate each product or quotient.

15. $2\frac{1}{8} \cdot 3\frac{6}{7}$ **16.** $5\frac{2}{9} \cdot 4\frac{9}{10}$ **17.** $10\frac{7}{8} \div 3\frac{1}{9}$

18. $7\frac{3}{5} \div 1\frac{1}{2}$ **19.** $3\frac{2}{5} \cdot 7\frac{9}{20}$ **20.** $3\frac{3}{8} \cdot 5\frac{1}{6}$

21. $36\frac{1}{3} \div 4\frac{2}{5}$ **22.** $1\frac{7}{10} \cdot 8\frac{1}{12}$ **23.** $5\frac{3}{4} \cdot 2\frac{2}{3}$

24. *Weather* The average annual rainfall in Nashville, Tennessee, is about $47\frac{3}{10}$ in. Estimate the average monthly rainfall.

HISTORY Lanterns were set in the Old North Church to signal Paul Revere to start his ride in April of 1775. This was the start of the American Revolution.

25. Writing Write two mixed numbers. Explain how you would estimate their sum, difference, product, and quotient.

26. Cooking You want to make three kinds of pasta salad. One recipe requires $\frac{2}{3}$ c. Another requires $\frac{3}{4}$ c. The third requires $1\frac{2}{3}$ c. You have 4 c of pasta. Do you have enough? Explain.

Estimate each answer.

27. $5\frac{1}{8} - 2\frac{6}{7}$ **28.** $1\frac{5}{8} \cdot 3\frac{1}{3}$ **29.** $\frac{5}{6} + \frac{7}{9}$ **30.** $16\frac{1}{7} \div 3\frac{3}{5}$ **31.** $4\frac{2}{3} \cdot 5\frac{1}{3}$

32. $7\frac{1}{6} + \frac{8}{10}$ **33.** $\frac{8}{9} \div \frac{19}{20}$ **34.** $6\frac{2}{9} - 5\frac{9}{10}$ **35.** $29\frac{5}{6} \cdot 1\frac{13}{25}$ **36.** $20\frac{7}{8} \div 1\frac{1}{12}$

37. $\frac{49}{50} - \frac{1}{2}$ **38.** $9\frac{3}{5} \div 4\frac{1}{2}$ **39.** $\frac{5}{12} - \frac{2}{5}$ **40.** $3\frac{2}{3} \cdot 5\frac{1}{2}$ **41.** $\frac{27}{50} + \frac{47}{99}$

42. Jogging Suppose you jog $16\frac{1}{4}$ times around an indoor track that is 125 yd long. Have you jogged more than a mile? Explain. (*Hint:* 1 mi = 1,760 yd)

43. Cooking Your recipe for a loaf of bread calls for $2\frac{3}{4}$ c of flour. You want to triple the recipe. The label on a two-pound bag of flour says that it contains about 7 c. Will that be enough flour to make three loaves of bread? Explain.

44. School Fair Donnat and Alex are making place mats for a school fair. Each mat uses $14\frac{3}{4}$ in. of fabric. They have fabric that is $89\frac{3}{4}$ in. long. About how many place mats can they make?

JOURNAL Describe a situation where it would be appropriate to find a sum by using estimation.

45. Choose A, B, C, or D. Which is between 6 and 7?
   A. $\frac{1}{2} \cdot 14\frac{1}{2}$ **B.** $2 \cdot 3\frac{15}{16}$ **C.** $5\frac{11}{12} + \frac{24}{25}$ **D.** $7\frac{8}{9} - \frac{1}{2}$

Mixed Review

Divide. (*Lesson 2-6*)

46. $0.768 \div 1.6$ **47.** $8.19 \div 9$ **48.** $74.2 \div 0.53$ **49.** $760.38 \div 0.38$ **50.** $903.6 \div 25.1$

Explain why you would or would not expect to see a trend in the scatter plots described in Exercises 51–53. (*Lesson 1-9*)

51. height and age   **52.** height and income   **53.** age and income

54. Fund-Raising The school band sold 116 tickets to their concert. They spent $50 on refreshments and ended up with $327. How much did each ticket cost? (*Lesson 2-6*)

Using Fraction Models

You can use models to add and subtract fractions.

■ EXAMPLE 1

Find $\frac{3}{10} + \frac{1}{10}$.

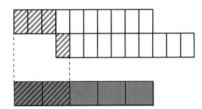

To add, align the right side of the shaded part of the first model with the left side of the second one.

Find a model that represents the sum of the shaded parts. If you have more than one model to choose from, use the one with the largest sections.

$$\frac{3}{10} + \frac{1}{10} = \frac{2}{5}$$

■ EXAMPLE 2

Find $\frac{3}{4} - \frac{1}{3}$.

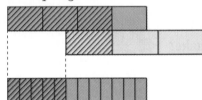

To subtract, align the right ends of the shaded part of each model.

Find the model that represents the difference.

$$\frac{3}{4} - \frac{1}{3} = \frac{5}{12}$$

Write a number sentence for each model.

1.

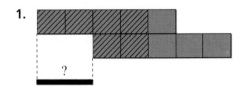

?

2.

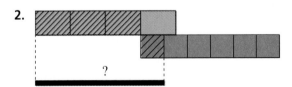

?

Use models to find each sum or difference.

3. $\frac{3}{8} + \frac{3}{8}$ **4.** $\frac{5}{6} - \frac{1}{6}$ **5.** $\frac{9}{10} - \frac{7}{10}$ **6.** $\frac{1}{6} + \frac{5}{6}$ **7.** $\frac{2}{5} + \frac{1}{2}$ **8.** $\frac{3}{4} + \frac{1}{8}$

9. $\frac{4}{5} - \frac{1}{2}$ **10.** $\frac{7}{10} - \frac{1}{5}$ **11.** $\frac{5}{6} + \frac{1}{2}$ **12.** $\frac{5}{8} + \frac{1}{4}$ **13.** $\frac{2}{3} - \frac{1}{6}$ **14.** $\frac{9}{10} - \frac{1}{2}$

What You'll Learn

▼ **1** To add fractions

▼ **2** To subtract fractions

...And Why

When using customary units, you frequently use fractions.

Here's How

Look for questions that

⊞ build understanding

✔ check understanding

Need Help? For practice in adding and subtracting fractions, see Skills Handbook page 540.

Work Together

Using Models

Work with a partner. Use the models shown to answer the questions below.

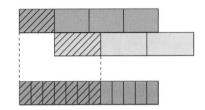 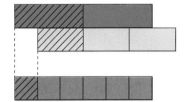

1. Which model shows addition? Subtraction?

2. Write a number sentence for each model.

3. ⊞ *Modeling* Use fraction models to find two or more sums or differences that equal $\frac{1}{3}$.

THINK AND DISCUSS

1 *Adding Fractions*

To find the sum of two fractions that have the same denominator, you add their numerators.

■ **EXAMPLE 1**

Find $\frac{2}{9} + \frac{4}{9}$.

Estimate: $\frac{2}{9} + \frac{4}{9} \approx 0 + \frac{1}{2} = \frac{1}{2}$

$$\frac{2}{9} + \frac{4}{9} = \frac{2+4}{9} \quad \longleftarrow \text{Add the numerators.}$$

$$= \frac{6}{9}$$

$$= \frac{2}{3} \quad \longleftarrow \begin{array}{l}\text{Simplify the fraction. The answer} \\ \text{is close to the estimate.}\end{array}$$

4. ✔ *Try It Out* Find each sum.

    a. $\frac{2}{5} + \frac{2}{5}$ **b.** $\frac{1}{8} + \frac{3}{8}$ **c.** $\frac{1}{3} + \frac{2}{3}$ **d.** $\frac{9}{10} + \frac{3}{10}$

HISTORY The ancient Egyptians represented all fractions, except $\frac{2}{3}$, as a *unit fraction* or the sum of unit fractions. A unit fraction, such as $\frac{1}{2}$, is a fraction with a numerator of 1. The Egyptians would write $\frac{3}{4}$ as $\frac{1}{2} + \frac{1}{4}$.

To find the sum of two fractions that have different denominators, you first find their LCD.

■ **EXAMPLE 2**

Find the sum $\frac{4}{5} + \frac{2}{3}$.

Estimate: $\frac{4}{5} + \frac{2}{3} \approx 1 + \frac{1}{2} = 1\frac{1}{2}$

$$\frac{4}{5} = \frac{4 \cdot 3}{5 \cdot 3} = \frac{12}{15}$$
$$\frac{2}{3} = \frac{2 \cdot 5}{3 \cdot 5} = \frac{10}{15}$$

⟵ The LCD is 15. Write the fractions with the same denominator.

$$= \frac{22}{15}$$ ⟵ Add the numerators.

$$= 1\frac{7}{15}$$ ⟵ Write the answer as a mixed number. The answer is close to the estimate.

5. ✔ Try It Out Find each sum.

a. $\frac{1}{3} + \frac{1}{8}$ **b.** $\frac{3}{4} + \frac{3}{8}$ **c.** $\frac{1}{4} + \frac{5}{6}$ **d.** $\frac{2}{3} + \frac{3}{5}$

2 Subtracting Fractions

You also use the LCD to subtract fractions with different denominators.

■ **EXAMPLE 3**   *Real-World Problem Solving*

Carpentry A cabinet maker needs a board that is $\frac{11}{16}$ in. thick. How much must he decrease the thickness of a board that is $\frac{7}{8}$ in. thick?

Find $\frac{7}{8} - \frac{11}{16}$.

Estimate: $\frac{7}{8} - \frac{11}{16} \approx 1 - \frac{1}{2} = \frac{1}{2}$

$$\frac{7}{8} - \frac{11}{16} = \frac{7 \cdot 2}{8 \cdot 2} - \frac{11}{16}$$

⟵ The LCD is 16. Write the fractions with the same denominator.

$$= \frac{14}{16} - \frac{11}{16}$$

$$= \frac{3}{16}$$ ⟵ Subtract the numerators. The answer is close to the estimate.

The cabinet maker should decrease the thickness of the board by $\frac{3}{16}$ in.

6. ✔ Try It Out Find each difference.

a. $\frac{3}{4} - \frac{1}{8}$ **b.** $\frac{4}{5} - \frac{2}{3}$ **c.** $\frac{5}{6} - \frac{1}{4}$ **d.** $\frac{3}{4} - \frac{3}{5}$

Find each sum.

1. $\frac{1}{7} + \frac{4}{7}$ 2. $\frac{1}{5} + \frac{3}{5}$ 3. $\frac{2}{3} + \frac{1}{2}$ 4. $\frac{7}{12} + \frac{1}{6}$ 5. $\frac{3}{3} + \frac{5}{8}$

6. $\frac{4}{5} + \frac{7}{8}$ 7. $\frac{1}{2} + \frac{4}{5}$ 8. $\frac{4}{3} + \frac{2}{3}$ 9. $\frac{3}{2} + \frac{1}{4}$ 10. $\frac{5}{6} + \frac{7}{8}$

11. One third of the students in your class got an A on a test. One fourth of them got a B.
   a. What fraction of the students got an A or a B?
   b. Did a majority of the students get As and Bs? Explain.

12. *Error Analysis* What is the error in $\frac{2}{8} + \frac{3}{8} = \frac{5}{16}$?

13. Allen and Meda have recipes for three kinds of cookies. The recipes call for $\frac{1}{2}$ c, $\frac{2}{3}$ c, and $\frac{3}{4}$ c of sugar. They have 2 c of sugar. Allen says that isn't enough sugar for one batch of each recipe. Is he correct? Explain.

Find each difference.

14. $\frac{4}{5} - \frac{1}{5}$ 15. $\frac{7}{10} - \frac{1}{10}$ 16. $\frac{7}{10} - \frac{1}{6}$ 17. $\frac{7}{10} - \frac{1}{5}$ 18. $\frac{9}{10} - \frac{2}{5}$

19. $\frac{2}{3} - \frac{1}{4}$ 20. $\frac{5}{6} - \frac{1}{3}$ 21. $\frac{11}{12} - \frac{3}{4}$ 22. $\frac{3}{5} - \frac{1}{4}$ 23. $\frac{7}{6} - \frac{3}{4}$

24. Hal is using nails that are $\frac{5}{6}$ in. long to nail $\frac{1}{4}$-in. thick plywood to a beam. How much of the nail extends into the beam?

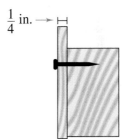

$\frac{1}{4}$ in. →

25. a. You rowed two thirds of a mile. Your friend rowed eight tenths of a mile. Who rowed farther? How much farther?
   b. Which operation did you use to solve the problem? Why?

Find each sum or difference.

26. $\frac{7}{12} - \frac{1}{12}$ 27. $\frac{1}{4} + \frac{1}{3}$ 28. $\frac{2}{3} - \frac{1}{8}$ 29. $\frac{1}{3} - \frac{1}{4}$ 30. $\frac{1}{3} + \frac{5}{12}$

31. $\frac{5}{6} + \frac{3}{4}$ 32. $\frac{1}{5} + \frac{3}{10}$ 33. $\frac{1}{2} - \frac{1}{8}$ 34. $\frac{1}{2} + \frac{5}{6}$ 35. $\frac{7}{6} - \frac{3}{4}$

36. $\frac{1}{2} - \frac{1}{3}$ 37. $\frac{3}{5} + \frac{3}{4}$ 38. $\frac{1}{3} - \frac{1}{5}$ 39. $\frac{1}{5} + \frac{3}{8}$ 40. $\frac{3}{4} - \frac{3}{10}$

41. Sally has to walk $\frac{7}{10}$ mi from her home to the bus stop. She has to walk $\frac{1}{4}$ mi from her home to the subway station. How much farther is it to the bus stop than to the station?

42. Use the circle graph at the right.

   a. What fraction of takeout food is eaten at home or in a car?

   b. How much greater is the fraction of takeout food eaten at home than at work?

   c. What fraction of the takeout food is eaten at home, in a car, or at work?

   d. *Writing* Describe two ways to get the answer to part (c).

Where Takeout Food Is Eaten

Home $\frac{1}{2}$

Other $\frac{3}{20}$

Work $\frac{3}{20}$

Car $\frac{1}{5}$

Reasoning **Use what you know about addition of integers to predict whether each sum will be positive, negative, or zero. Explain your reasoning.**

43. $-\frac{2}{3} + \frac{5}{6}$ **44.** $-\frac{4}{5} + \frac{8}{10}$ **45.** $-\frac{7}{8} + \frac{3}{4}$ **46.** $-\frac{3}{4} + \frac{3}{5}$

47. *Calculator* You can use this key sequence to find $\frac{3}{5} + \frac{1}{4}$.

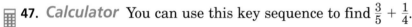

3 ÷ 5 + 1 ÷ 4 =

The answer the calculator displays, *0.85*, can be rewritten as the fraction $\frac{85}{100}$ which simplifies to $\frac{17}{20}$.

   a. Write the key sequence you could use to find $\frac{7}{8} - \frac{3}{5}$.

   b. Use your key sequence to find $\frac{7}{8} - \frac{3}{5}$.

Mixed Review

Multiply or divide. *(Lesson 3-5)*

48. $5 \cdot (-11)$ **49.** $-84 \div 12$ **50.** $-3 \cdot (-9)$ **51.** $-13 \cdot 5$ **52.** $-63 \div (-7)$

Find the value of each expression. *(Lesson 2-8)*

53. $7 \cdot 3 + 8 \cdot 2$ **54.** $8 - 2 + 3 \cdot 4$ **55.** $82 - 43 - 6 \div 6$

56. *Choose a Strategy* Find the ways a clerk can give change for a dollar for a $.35 purchase without using pennies.

CHAPTER PROJECT

PROJECT LINK: INTERVIEWING

Interview some people who know how to make pancakes or start with a recipe in a cookbook. Use that information to write your own recipe. Most of the ingredients should involve fractions. Include things that you like, such as fruits or nuts.

Adding and Subtracting Mixed Numbers

What You'll Learn

▼ To add mixed numbers

▼ To subtract mixed numbers

...And Why

You can find the space needed for newspaper ads.

Here's How

Look for questions that
- build understanding
- ✔ check understanding

THINK AND DISCUSS

▼ Adding Mixed Numbers

To add mixed numbers that have common denominators, you add the whole numbers and then you add the fractions.

■ EXAMPLE 1

Find $1\frac{2}{5} + 2\frac{4}{5}$.

Estimate: $1\frac{2}{5} + 2\frac{4}{5} \approx 1 + 3 = 4$

$$1\frac{2}{5}$$
$$+\ 2\frac{4}{5}$$
$$=3\frac{6}{5} \quad \longleftarrow \text{Add the whole numbers. Add the fractions.}$$
$$=3 + 1\frac{1}{5} \quad \longleftarrow \text{Rename } \frac{6}{5}\colon \frac{6}{5} = \frac{5}{5} + \frac{1}{5} = 1\frac{1}{5}$$
$$=4\frac{1}{5} \quad \longleftarrow \begin{array}{l}\text{Add the whole numbers.}\\ \text{The answer is close to the estimate.}\end{array}$$

1. ✔ **Try It Out** Find $6\frac{3}{8} + 4\frac{7}{8}$.

Fractions in mixed numbers may have different denominators. Use the LCD to rewrite the fractions with common denominators.

■ EXAMPLE 2   *Real-World Problem Solving*

Hiking You hiked $2\frac{2}{3}$ mi from the campground to Jewel Pond and then $3\frac{1}{4}$ mi to Lookout Ledge. How far did you hike?

Find $2\frac{2}{3} + 3\frac{1}{4}$.

Estimate: $2\frac{2}{3} + 3\frac{1}{4} \approx 3 + 3 = 6$

$$2\frac{2}{3} + 3\frac{1}{4} = 2\frac{8}{12} + 3\frac{3}{12} \quad \longleftarrow \text{The LCD is 12.}$$
$$=5 + \frac{11}{12} \quad \longleftarrow \begin{array}{l}\text{Add the whole numbers.}\\ \text{Add the fractions.}\end{array}$$
$$=5\frac{11}{12} \quad \longleftarrow \text{The answer is close to the estimate.}$$

You hiked $5\frac{11}{12}$ mi.

2. ✔ *Try It Out* Find each sum.

    a. $4\frac{3}{4} + 3\frac{1}{2}$ **b.** $1\frac{5}{6} + 4\frac{2}{3}$ **c.** $2\frac{1}{3} + 6\frac{4}{5}$ **d.** $3\frac{1}{6} + 8\frac{7}{8}$

▼2 *Subtracting Mixed Numbers*

When you subtract mixed numbers, you may need to rename before subtracting.

■ EXAMPLE 3

Find the difference $6\frac{1}{8} - 2\frac{3}{4}$.

Estimate: $6\frac{1}{8} - 2\frac{3}{4} \approx 6 - 3 = 3$

$$6\frac{1}{8} - 2\frac{3}{4} = 6\frac{1}{8} - 2\frac{6}{8} \quad \longleftarrow \text{The LCD is 8.}$$

$$= 5\frac{9}{8} - 2\frac{6}{8} \quad \longleftarrow \text{Rename } 6\frac{1}{8}: 6\frac{1}{8} = 5 + 1\frac{1}{8} = 5\frac{9}{8}.$$

$$= 3\frac{3}{8} \quad \longleftarrow \text{Subtract the whole numbers. Subtract the fractions. The answer is close to the estimate.}$$

3. ✔ *Try It Out* Find each difference.

    a. $5\frac{1}{2} - 3\frac{3}{4}$ **b.** $2\frac{7}{8} - 1\frac{1}{4}$ **c.** $6\frac{1}{2} - 1\frac{7}{8}$ **d.** $10\frac{1}{3} - 7\frac{3}{4}$

EXERCISES *On Your Own*

Find each sum.

1. $6\frac{2}{5} + 1\frac{4}{5}$ **2.** $5\frac{2}{3} + 7\frac{1}{3}$ **3.** $9\frac{1}{2} + 9\frac{1}{3}$ **4.** $7\frac{1}{6} + 8\frac{1}{8}$ **5.** $6\frac{1}{2} + 4\frac{5}{6}$

6. $8\frac{3}{4} + 8\frac{1}{8}$ **7.** $5\frac{5}{9} + 9\frac{1}{3}$ **8.** $8\frac{2}{3} + 5\frac{1}{4}$ **9.** $17\frac{3}{4} + 3\frac{3}{8}$ **10.** $17\frac{2}{5} + 11\frac{3}{4}$

11. *Masonry* A brick is $1\frac{7}{8}$ in. high. How high is a stack of 2 bricks? A stack of 4 bricks?

12. *Writing* Explain the steps you would use to find $3\frac{2}{3} + 4\frac{1}{2}$.

Find each difference.

13. $8\frac{4}{5} - 4\frac{1}{5}$ **14.** $3\frac{1}{3} - 1\frac{2}{3}$ **15.** $7\frac{2}{3} - 1\frac{1}{6}$ **16.** $15 - 3\frac{3}{4}$ **17.** $15\frac{3}{4} - 8\frac{3}{8}$

18. $9\frac{1}{2} - \frac{2}{3}$ **19.** $14 - 5\frac{1}{5}$ **20.** $6\frac{9}{10} - 3\frac{2}{5}$ **21.** $15\frac{1}{3} - 9\frac{1}{2}$ **22.** $6\frac{3}{8} - 2\frac{3}{4}$

23. *Mechanic* A piece of tubing $8\frac{5}{8}$ in. long is cut from a piece $23\frac{1}{2}$ in. long. How much is left?

24. One bag of corn chips contains $1\frac{5}{8}$ oz. Another contains $1\frac{3}{4}$ oz. Which contains more? How much more does it contain?

Find the value of each expression.

25. $8\frac{2}{5} - 5\frac{3}{5}$ **26.** $12\frac{7}{8} + 8\frac{1}{4}$ **27.** $4\frac{2}{3} - \frac{5}{6}$ **28.** $13\frac{5}{8} + 5\frac{1}{2}$ **29.** $1\frac{3}{4} + 5\frac{1}{3}$

30. $2\frac{1}{8} + 4\frac{7}{8}$ **31.** $10 - \frac{5}{6}$ **32.** $3\frac{5}{8} + 2\frac{1}{4}$ **33.** $18\frac{1}{8} - 9\frac{3}{4}$ **34.** $16\frac{7}{8} - 14\frac{3}{4}$

35. $24 - 9\frac{3}{5}$ **36.** $19\frac{3}{4} + 6\frac{2}{5}$ **37.** $25\frac{1}{4} - 11\frac{2}{5}$ **38.** $30\frac{2}{3} + 12\frac{3}{4}$ **39.** $25\frac{7}{8} - 9\frac{4}{5}$

40. $4\frac{2}{3} + 6 + 3\frac{1}{3}$ **41.** $8\frac{2}{5} - 3\frac{2}{3} + 2$ **42.** $8\frac{2}{5} - (3\frac{2}{3} + 2)$ **43.** $3\frac{1}{3} - 1\frac{1}{4} - 1\frac{1}{5}$

44. a. *Advertising* A company placed ads in a newspaper that require $4\frac{1}{2}$ c.i. (column inches), $5\frac{3}{4}$ c.i., $3\frac{1}{4}$ c.i., $4\frac{3}{4}$ c.i., and $5\frac{3}{4}$ c.i. What is the total number of column inches?

   b. At $20 per column inch, what is the total cost of the ads?

45. *Construction* A bolt must go through a sign that is $\frac{5}{8}$ in. thick and a support that is $1\frac{1}{2}$ in. thick. An additional $\frac{5}{16}$ in. is needed for the washer and nut. How long should the bolt be?

46. Your punch bowl holds 6 qt. Is it large enough to hold all the ingredients called for in the recipe at the right? Explain.

Lemon Raspberry Fizz

$1\frac{1}{2}$ qt lemonade
$2\frac{1}{4}$ qt ginger ale
$1\frac{2}{3}$ qt lemon sherbet
$\frac{1}{2}$ qt raspberry juice

47. *Calculator* You can use this key sequence to find $5\frac{1}{2} + 4\frac{3}{4}$.

> (5 + 1 ÷ 2) + (4 + 3 ÷ 4) = *10.25*

The calculator display 10.25 can be written as $10\frac{1}{4}$.

a. Write a key sequence you can use to find $4\frac{1}{8} - 1\frac{3}{4}$.

b. Use your key sequence to find $4\frac{1}{8} - 1\frac{3}{4}$.

Mixed Review

Write the prime factorization of each number. *(Lesson 4-5)*

48. 54   **49.** 104   **50.** 128   **51.** 70   **52.** 100

Order from least to greatest. *(Lesson 2-1)*

53. 0.438, 0.431, 0.4, 0.43   **54.** 11.2, 11.02, 11.201, 11.1   **55.** 75.3, 75.09, 75.98

56. *Choose a Strategy* An ice machine makes 50 ice cubes/h. Each ice cube uses 0.025 L of water. How much water is used to make ice cubes in one day?

5-4 Solving Equations with Fractions by Adding and Subtracting

What You'll Learn

1 To solve one-step equations by adding

2 To solve one-step equations by subtracting

...And Why

Knowing how to solve more kinds of equations allows you to use algebra in more situations.

Here's How

Look for questions that
- build understanding
- ✔ check understanding

Work Together — Modeling Equations

1. At the right is a model of one of the following equations. Which equation do you think it is?

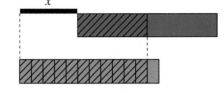

A. $x + \frac{11}{12} = \frac{1}{2}$ **B.** $x + \frac{1}{2} = \frac{11}{12}$ **C.** $x - \frac{1}{2} = \frac{11}{12}$

2. What is the solution of the equation modeled above?

3. a. Complete: The model at the right represents the equation $x - \blacksquare = \blacksquare$.
   b. What is the solution of the equation?

4. **Modeling** Model and solve the equation $x - \frac{7}{12} = \frac{1}{4}$.

THINK AND DISCUSS

1 *Solving Equations by Adding*

If an equation involves subtraction, use addition to "undo" it.

QUICKreview

Addition and subtraction are inverse operations. Addition "undoes" subtraction, and subtraction "undoes" addition.

■ EXAMPLE 1

Solve $n - \frac{1}{2} = 4\frac{3}{4}$.

$n - \frac{1}{2} = 4\frac{3}{4}$

$n - \frac{1}{2} + \frac{1}{2} = 4\frac{3}{4} + \frac{1}{2}$ ←Add $\frac{1}{2}$ to each side.

$n = 4\frac{3}{4} + \frac{2}{4}$ ←Find a common denominator.

$n = 4\frac{5}{4} = 5\frac{1}{4}$ ←Add the numerators. Rewrite $4\frac{5}{4}$ as $5\frac{1}{4}$.

5. ✔ **Try It Out** Solve each equation.
   a. $g - \frac{1}{4} = 3\frac{1}{2}$ **b.** $2\frac{1}{2} = k - 4\frac{1}{3}$ **c.** $x - \frac{2}{5} = \frac{5}{6}$

▼ Solving Equations by Subtracting

Use subtraction to "undo" addition.

■ **EXAMPLE 2**

Solve $s + \frac{1}{3} = 2\frac{1}{6}$.

$$s + \frac{1}{3} = 2\frac{1}{6}$$

$s + \frac{1}{3} - \frac{1}{3} = 2\frac{1}{6} - \frac{1}{3}$ ←—Subtract $\frac{1}{3}$ from each side.

$s = 2\frac{1}{6} - \frac{2}{6}$ ←—Find a common denominator.

$s = 1\frac{7}{6} - \frac{2}{6}$ ←—Rewrite $2\frac{1}{6}$ as $1\frac{7}{6}$.

$= 1\frac{5}{6}$ ←—Subtract.

6. ✔ *Try It Out* Solve each equation.

a. $r + 4\frac{2}{5} = 9\frac{7}{10}$ **b.** $2\frac{2}{3} = p + \frac{1}{4}$ **c.** $\frac{1}{4} = \frac{1}{6} + m$

You use fractions in equations to solve many everyday problems.

■ **EXAMPLE 3** *Real-World Problem Solving*

Commercial Fishing A fisherman caught $1\frac{1}{4}$ tons of fish. His boat holds $2\frac{3}{4}$ tons. How many more tons can he catch?

Words • | tons of fish to be caught | + | tons of fish already caught | = | capacity of boat |

• Let t = tons of fish to be caught

Tons of fish already caught $= 1\frac{1}{4}$

Capacity of boat $= 2\frac{3}{4}$

Equation • $t + 1\frac{1}{4} = 2\frac{3}{4}$

$$t + 1\frac{1}{4} = 2\frac{3}{4}$$

$t + 1\frac{1}{4} - 1\frac{1}{4} = 2\frac{3}{4} - 1\frac{1}{4}$ ←—Subtract $1\frac{1}{4}$ from each side.

$t = 1\frac{2}{4}$

$t = 1\frac{1}{2}$ ←—Simplify $1\frac{2}{4}$.

The fisherman can catch $1\frac{1}{2}$ tons more of fish.

7. ▪*Look Back* Suppose the boat holds $3\frac{3}{8}$ tons. How many tons more could the fisherman catch if he already has $1\frac{1}{4}$ tons of fish?

Estimate each answer.

1. $\frac{1}{2} + \frac{2}{5}$

2. $\frac{1}{8} + \frac{5}{12}$

3. $4\frac{2}{5} - 1\frac{1}{4}$

4. $8\frac{1}{3} \cdot 2\frac{4}{5}$

5. $28\frac{3}{4} + 2\frac{7}{8}$

Find each sum or difference.

6. $\frac{3}{4} + \frac{7}{8}$

7. $\frac{2}{3} - \frac{5}{8}$

8. $\frac{1}{6} + \frac{3}{8}$

9. $\frac{5}{6} - \frac{1}{9}$

10. $\frac{1}{2} + \frac{1}{6}$

11. $7\frac{1}{2} - 3\frac{3}{7}$

12. $\frac{4}{5} + 3\frac{2}{3}$

13. $13\frac{3}{8} - 7\frac{1}{2}$

14. $7\frac{2}{5} - 1\frac{2}{3}$

15. $5\frac{1}{2} + 7\frac{5}{8}$

Write an equation for each model.

16.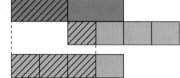

17.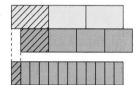

18.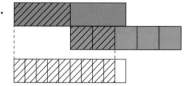

Solve each equation.

19. $\frac{3}{8} = t - \frac{3}{4}$

20. $n + 2\frac{1}{3} = 3\frac{4}{5}$

21. $3\frac{1}{2} + a = 5\frac{3}{10}$

22. $p - 3\frac{3}{4} = 15\frac{1}{8}$

23. $b + \frac{1}{2} = \frac{3}{5}$

24. $\frac{3}{8} + f = \frac{7}{12}$

25. $5\frac{3}{5} = d - 2\frac{1}{4}$

26. $h - 8\frac{1}{3} = 1\frac{4}{5}$

Math at Work

SONGWRITER

Songwriters need to know what types of music are "in" and compose songs that will sell. Then the songwriter must find a publisher willing to find an artist to record it. Producers and record companies decide if they will promote a song as a potential hit.

Songwriters use mathematics to understand complex rhythms and produce lyrics to all kinds of music.

To learn more, check out this Web site on Songwriting, Composition, and Performing: www.studyweb.com/music/songs.htm

Choose Use a calculator, paper and pencil, or mental math to find each product.

25. $3 \cdot 2\frac{3}{8}$ **26.** $\frac{3}{4}$ of 20   **27.** $10 \cdot 1\frac{4}{5}$ **28.** $6\frac{2}{3} \cdot 3\frac{1}{3}$ **29.** $2 \cdot 3\frac{2}{3}$

30. $\frac{1}{2}$ of $6\frac{1}{2}$ **31.** $\frac{1}{3} \cdot 2\frac{2}{5}$ **32.** $\frac{7}{8} \cdot 32$ **33.** $\frac{1}{2} \cdot \frac{4}{5}$ **34.** $3\frac{1}{6} \cdot 4\frac{3}{4}$

35. $4\frac{3}{8} \cdot \frac{5}{7}$ **36.** $3\frac{4}{9} \cdot 2\frac{1}{4}$ **37.** $2\frac{1}{4} \cdot 5\frac{1}{6}$ **38.** $4\frac{3}{8} \cdot 16$ **39.** $1\frac{7}{8} \cdot \frac{8}{15}$

Find the area of each rectangle.

40.
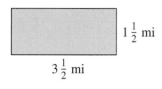
$1\frac{1}{2}$ mi
$3\frac{1}{2}$ mi

41.
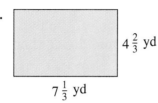
$4\frac{2}{3}$ yd
$7\frac{1}{3}$ yd

42.
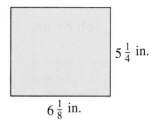
$5\frac{1}{4}$ in.
$6\frac{1}{8}$ in.

43. *Calculator* Write a key sequence to find $1\frac{1}{4} \cdot 3\frac{1}{5}$.

44. *Writing* How does multiplying two fractions differ from adding them?

45. *Cooking* A recipe for Sloppy Joes serves 100 people. It calls for $11\frac{1}{2}$ lb of tomato puree. How much puree would you need to serve 300 people?

46. *Jogging* A track around a football field is about $\frac{1}{4}$ mi. Franklin jogged around the track $3\frac{3}{4}$ times. What distance did he jog?

Mixed Review

Estimate. *(Lesson 2-2)*

47. $19.5 + 56.13$ **48.** $34.3 - 18.9$ **49.** 26.7×9.9 **50.** $119 \div 23$ **51.** $204 \div 0.48$

52. *Choose a Strategy* You regularly buy a monthly magazine at a newsstand for $3.99. The subscription rate is $1.50 per issue. How much can you save in a year by subscribing?

CHAPTER PROJECT

PROJECT LINK: RESEARCHING

Test your recipe by making pancakes for your family. (You may ask some cooks to review your recipe if you do not have an opportunity to cook.) Revise if necessary. Adjust quantities so you have the right amount to feed your family.

Dividing Fractions and Mixed Numbers

What You'll Learn

1. To divide fractions
2. To divide mixed numbers

...And Why

You can find the number of costumes you can make from a piece of fabric.

Here's How

Look for questions that
- build understanding
- ✔ check understanding

THINK AND DISCUSS

1 ▼ Dividing Fractions

"What is $4 \div \frac{2}{3}$?" is the same as asking, "How many two thirds are in four wholes?" To find how many two thirds are in 4, draw 4 rectangles and divide them into thirds.

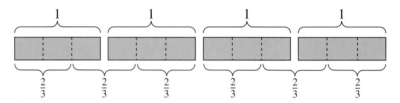

You can see that there are 6 two thirds in four wholes.

1. Complete each statement.

   a. $4 \div \frac{2}{3} = \blacksquare$　　　**b.** $4 \cdot \frac{3}{2} = \blacksquare$　　　**c.** $4 \div \frac{2}{3} = 4 \cdot \frac{\blacksquare}{\blacksquare}$

The numbers $\frac{2}{3}$ and $\frac{3}{2}$ are **reciprocals** because their product is 1. To divide by $\frac{2}{3}$, you can multiply by $\frac{3}{2}$. To find the reciprocal of a fraction, interchange the numerator and denominator.

2. ✔ *Try It Out* Find the reciprocal of each fraction.

   a. $\frac{3}{5}$　　　**b.** $\frac{1}{2}$　　　**c.** $\frac{9}{4}$　　　**d.** $\frac{5}{2}$

To divide by a fraction, multiply by the reciprocal of the fraction.

■ EXAMPLE 1

Find $\frac{2}{3} \div \frac{5}{6}$.

$$\frac{2}{3} \div \frac{5}{6} = \frac{2}{3} \cdot \frac{6}{5}$$ ◄——Multiply by the reciprocal of $\frac{5}{6}$ which is $\frac{6}{5}$.

$$= \frac{2 \cdot \cancel{6}^2}{{}_1\cancel{3} \cdot 5}$$ ◄——The GCF is 3.

$$= \frac{4}{5}$$ ◄——Simplify.

3. ✔ *Try It Out* Find each quotient.

   a. $\frac{3}{4} \div \frac{1}{4}$　　　**b.** $\frac{3}{10} \div \frac{3}{5}$　　　**c.** $\frac{3}{4} \div \frac{1}{8}$　　　**d.** $\frac{2}{3} \div \frac{2}{3}$

To divide with fractions and whole numbers, first write the whole number as a fraction with a denominator of 1. Then multiply by the reciprocal of the divisor. For example,

$$\frac{3}{5} \div 2 = \frac{3}{5} \div \frac{2}{1} = \frac{3}{5} \cdot \frac{1}{2} = \frac{3}{10}$$

4. ✔ *Try It Out* Find each quotient.

  a. $\frac{3}{4} \div 3$ **b.** $\frac{3}{4} \div 6$ **c.** $10 \div \frac{3}{5}$ **d.** $2 \div \frac{4}{3}$

▼2 *Dividing Mixed Numbers*

To divide mixed numbers, rewrite them as improper fractions.

■ **EXAMPLE 2**   **Real-World Problem Solving**

Sewing Joanne has $13\frac{1}{2}$ yd of material to make costumes. Each costume takes $2\frac{1}{4}$ yd. How many costumes can she make?

You need to find the quotient of $13\frac{1}{2} \div 2\frac{1}{4}$.

Estimate: $13\frac{1}{2} \div 2\frac{1}{4} \approx 14 \div 2 = 7$

$$13\frac{1}{2} \div 2\frac{1}{4} = \frac{27}{2} \div \frac{9}{4}$$ ← Write the mixed numbers as improper fractions.

$$= \frac{27}{2} \cdot \frac{4}{9}$$ ← Multiply by the reciprocal of $\frac{9}{4}$.

$$= \frac{^{3}27 \cdot 4^{2}}{_{1}2 \cdot 9_{1}}$$ ← Divide 27 and 9 by 9, their GCF. Divide 4 and 2 by 2, their GCF.

$$= \frac{6}{1} = 6$$ ← Simplify.

Joanne can make six costumes.

5. ✔ *Try It Out* Another costume takes $2\frac{2}{3}$ yd of material. How many can be made from $13\frac{1}{3}$ yd of material?

EXERCISES *On Your Own*

Find the reciprocal of each number.

1. $\frac{3}{4}$ **2.** 5 **3.** $\frac{1}{7}$ **4.** $\frac{5}{4}$ **5.** $2\frac{1}{6}$ **6.** $4\frac{5}{8}$

Mental Math **Find each quotient.**

7. $8 \div \frac{1}{2}$ **8.** $5 \div \frac{1}{3}$ **9.** $2 \div \frac{1}{9}$ **10.** $10 \div \frac{1}{10}$ **11.** $\frac{3}{2} \div \frac{1}{2}$

Find each quotient.

12. $\frac{4}{5} \div \frac{1}{4}$ **13.** $15 \div \frac{3}{4}$ **14.** $\frac{7}{8} \div 3$ **15.** $\frac{2}{9} \div \frac{2}{3}$ **16.** $\frac{3}{4} \div \frac{8}{9}$

17. $\frac{3}{4} \div \frac{3}{5}$ **18.** $6 \div \frac{1}{7}$ **19.** $\frac{5}{16} \div \frac{1}{2}$ **20.** $\frac{5}{6} \div \frac{3}{4}$ **21.** $42 \div \frac{7}{9}$

22. A new gas line will be installed along a $\frac{3}{4}$-mi. long street. It takes a day to install $\frac{1}{8}$ mi. How long will the project take?

23. *Writing* Explain how to find the reciprocal of a fraction or whole number.

▤ *Choose* **Use a calculator, paper and pencil, or mental math to find each quotient.**

24. $2\frac{1}{6} \div \frac{5}{6}$ **25.** $\frac{3}{4} \div 3$ **26.** $\frac{1}{4} \div \frac{2}{3}$ **27.** $4\frac{3}{4} \div 1\frac{1}{4}$ **28.** $\frac{7}{12} \div 2\frac{1}{6}$

29. $1\frac{1}{5} \div 2\frac{3}{10}$ **30.** $\frac{7}{9} \div \frac{1}{4}$ **31.** $\frac{2}{3} \div 4\frac{1}{12}$ **32.** $8\frac{1}{3} \div 2\frac{1}{2}$ **33.** $2\frac{2}{3} \div 5\frac{1}{9}$

34. $8\frac{2}{5} \div \frac{3}{10}$ **35.** $4\frac{7}{8} \div 3\frac{1}{4}$ **36.** $11 \div \frac{1}{9}$ **37.** $1\frac{2}{3} \div \frac{9}{10}$ **38.** $\frac{2}{5} \div \frac{4}{7}$

39. *Biology* A killer whale can swim 40 mi in $1\frac{1}{4}$ h. How far can the whale swim in 1 h?

40. *Meal Planning* One serving of cereal contains $1\frac{1}{2}$ oz. How many servings are in a $19\frac{1}{2}$-oz box?

▤ **41.** *Calculator* You can use this key sequence to find $2\frac{1}{2} \div \frac{5}{6}$.

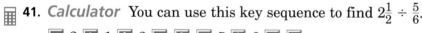

Write and use a key sequence to find $13\frac{7}{8} \div 6\frac{1}{6}$.

Mixed Review

Write each fraction as a decimal. Use a bar to indicate any repeating digits. *(Lesson 4-9)*

42. $\frac{4}{5}$ **43.** $\frac{3}{8}$ **44.** $\frac{2}{9}$ **45.** $\frac{8}{3}$ **46.** $\frac{2}{32}$ **47.** $\frac{7}{24}$

Write each decimal as a fraction in simplest form. *(Lesson 4-9)*

48. 0.4   **49.** 0.625   **50.** 5.75   **51.** 2.38   **52.** 0.55   **53.** 4.305

54. *School Store* At the school store, notebooks cost $1.75, pencils $.05, pens $1, and folders $.75. How much would two notebooks and four pencils cost? *(Lessons 2-3, 2-5)*

TECHNOLOGY

Using a Fraction Calculator

After Lesson 5-6

You can use a fraction calculator to compute with fractions.
A fraction calculator will give you your result in fraction form.

■ EXAMPLE 1

Find $3\frac{4}{5} + 2\frac{5}{8}$.

3 [UNIT] 4 [/] 5 [+] 2 [UNIT] 5 [/] 8 [=] $5\textsf{u}57/40$ [A$^\text{b/c}$] $6\textsf{u}17/40$

The sum is $6\frac{17}{40}$.

To simplify an answer, you may need to use [SIMP] [=] more than
once.

■ EXAMPLE 2

Find $9\frac{3}{8} \cdot 4\frac{2}{3}$.

9 [UNIT] 3 [/] 8 [×] 4 [UNIT] 2 [/] 3 [=]

$1050/24$ [A$^\text{b/c}$] $43\textsf{u}18/24$ [SIMP] [=] $43\textsf{u}9/12$ [SIMP] [=] $43\textsf{u}3/4$

The product is $43\frac{3}{4}$.

■ EXAMPLE 3

Find $5\frac{3}{4} \div 1\frac{7}{8}$.

5 [UNIT] 3 [/] 4 [÷] 1 [UNIT] 7 [/] 8 [=]

$184/60$ [A$^\text{b/c}$] $3\textsf{u}4/60$ [SIMP] [=] $3\textsf{u}2/30$ [SIMP] [=] $3\textsf{u}1/15$

The product is $3\frac{1}{15}$.

Find the value of each expression.

1. $8\frac{7}{10} + 9\frac{1}{5}$
2. $14\frac{5}{12} - 6\frac{5}{8}$
3. $11\frac{4}{5} + 8\frac{1}{4}$
4. $9\frac{3}{4} \cdot 4\frac{5}{6}$
5. $17\frac{3}{8} \div 5\frac{3}{4}$

6. $13\frac{5}{12} - 4\frac{7}{8}$
7. $7\frac{2}{3} \cdot 10\frac{1}{4}$
8. $18\frac{3}{10} \div 10\frac{1}{2}$
9. $17\frac{11}{12} \cdot 21\frac{3}{8}$
10. $28\frac{7}{16} - 19\frac{5}{8}$

11. a. *Writing* Suppose a student calculated $4\frac{2}{3} + 5\frac{3}{4}$. The
   student's answer was $17\textsf{u}11/12$. Why is this answer not
   reasonable?
   b. What error may the student have made when entering
   the fractions in the calculator?

5-7 Work Backward

Problem Solving Strategies

Draw a Diagram
Guess and Test
Look for a Pattern
Make a Model
Make a Table
Simulate a Problem
Solve a Simpler Problem
Too Much or Too Little
 Information
Use Logical Reasoning
Use Multiple Strategies
✔ Work Backward
Write an Equation

THINK AND DISCUSS

To solve some problems, you may need to work backward.

SAMPLE PROBLEM................................

Mrs. Ruiz is taking her son Javier and his friends to dinner, and then to a concert that starts at 8:00 P.M. It will take $\frac{3}{4}$ h to pick up his friends and get to the restaurant next to the theater and $1\frac{1}{4}$ h to eat and walk to the theater. They want to be at the theater 15 min before the concert starts. When should they leave home?

READ

Read for understanding. Summarize the problem.

1. Think about the information you are given.
   a. At what time does the concert start?
   b. What activities are planned between the time Mrs. Ruiz and Javier leave home and the time the concert starts?
   c. What amount of time is planned for each activity?
   d. Summarize the goal of the problem in your own words.

PLAN

Decide on a strategy.

You know that a series of events must *end* at 8:00 P.M. It makes sense to work backward to find when the events must *begin*.

SOLVE

Try the strategy.

2. a. Write the time for each event.

concert starts   arrive at theater   arrive at dinner   leave home

b. What is the solution to the problem?

LOOK BACK

Think about how you solved the problem.

3. Show how to check your solution by working *forward*.

4. **a.** Think of 15 min as $\frac{1}{4}$ h. Find the sum $\frac{3}{4} + 1\frac{1}{4} + \frac{1}{4}$.

   b. How could you use your answer to part (a) to solve the problem in a different way?

EXERCISES *On Your Own*

Work backward to solve each problem.

1. Look back at the Sample Problem.
   a. Suppose that the concert starts at 8:30 P.M. At what time should Mrs. Ruiz and Javier leave home?
   b. Suppose that the concert starts at 8:00 P.M., but it takes only 20 min to pick up Javier's friends. At what time should Mrs. Ruiz and Javier leave home?

2. **a.** *Entertainment* The new movie that opened yesterday was so boring that $\frac{1}{2}$ of the people in the theater at the start of the movie left after the first 45 min. In the next 15 min, $\frac{1}{2}$ of the remaining people left. In the next $\frac{1}{4}$ h, 18 more people left. Only 36 of the people who were there at the start stayed to see the end of the movie. How many people were in the theater at the start of the movie?
   b. Which parts of the given information were not needed to solve the problem?

3. If you start with a number, add 5, then multiply by 7, the result is 133. What was the original number?

Use any strategy to solve each problem. Show your work.

4. Mia has ten coins that have a total value of $.65. She has no pennies. None of the coins is greater than a quarter. What are the coins?

5. **a.** *Business* The manager of a department store plans to make an electronic game shop in a section of the store that is 12 ft wide and 20 ft long. Using the pattern shown at the right, the manager wants to cover the floor with tiles that measure 1 ft on each side. How many black tiles will be needed? How many white tiles will be needed?
   b. How can you use areas of rectangles to check that you found the correct number of tiles?

BASKETBALL CARD BONANZA
Single cards
$9.00
• • •
Buy three cards, get a fourth for $7.00
• • •
Buy five cards for $44.50

6. *Money* Rosita saved $60 to spend on basketball cards. She plans to buy the cards at the sale advertised on the sign at the right. What is the least expensive way to buy five cards?

7. Darren spent one third of his money on lunch. At lunch, his friend gave him $2.50 to repay a loan. Then Darren spent $3.25 for a movie ticket and $.75 for a snack. He had $4.90 left. How much money did Darren have before lunch?

8. *Sports* Janelle practiced gymnastics 28 h in one week. Each day she practiced one hour more than the day before. How many hours did she practice on the fifth day?

9. Chloe and Lavanna started work on the same day. Chloe will earn a salary of $28,000 the first year. She will then receive a $4,000 raise each year that follows. Lavanna's salary for the first year is $41,000, followed by a $1,500 yearly raise. In what year will Chloe's salary be more than Lavanna's?

10. At a fund-raising event attended by 150 people, $2,000 was collected for charity. Suppose 25 people gave nothing. How much was the average donation from those who gave?

11. *Money* Lydia went shopping with $35 in her wallet. She bought a sweater that was on sale for half price, using a coupon for an additional $5 off the sale price. Lydia had $10.50 left. What was the original price of the sweater?

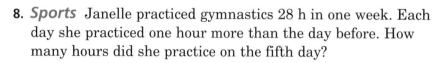

Mixed Review

Find each sum or difference. *(Lessons 5-2, 5-3)*

12. $\frac{3}{8} + \frac{2}{5}$ **13.** $3\frac{3}{4} - 2\frac{5}{8}$ **14.** $9\frac{1}{4} + 7\frac{5}{6}$ **15.** $11\frac{7}{8} - 2\frac{2}{3}$ **16.** $10 - 8\frac{1}{6}$

Evaluate each expression for $a = 4$, $b = 6$, and $c = 5.6$. *(Lesson 3-1)*

17. $8c$ **18.** $3a + 7a$ **19.** $\frac{c}{a}$ **20.** $3b - a$ **21.** $2(c - a)$ **22.** $\frac{b - c}{8}$

23. *Food* You go out to lunch with two friends. Together you order a plate of nachos for $6.99 and a large pizza for $11.97. *(Lessons 2-3, 2-6)*
   a. How much does this lunch cost?
   b. What is your share?

Choose the best answer.

1. For the first half of the baseball season, Karen got a hit $\frac{11}{35}$ of the times she was at bat. To the nearest thousandth, what is this fraction expressed as a decimal?

   A. 0.310   **B.** 0.314   **C.** 0.315   **D.** 0.320

2. After three hours, the biking club had ridden $35\frac{1}{4}$ miles, after four hours they had ridden 47 miles, and after five hours they had ridden $58\frac{3}{4}$ miles. If this pattern continues, how many miles will they have ridden after seven hours?

   F. $70\frac{1}{2}$ miles   **G.** $75\frac{3}{4}$ miles

   H. $82\frac{1}{4}$ miles   **J.** 94 miles

3. If $d - \frac{5}{8} = 4\frac{3}{4}$, what is the value of d?

   A. $3\frac{2}{3}$ **B.** $5\frac{3}{8}$

   C. $5\frac{5}{8}$ **D.** $5\frac{23}{24}$

4. The cost for a museum tour is found by using the formula:

   $$(s \times 1.25) + (t \times 2.25) + 40$$

   In this formula s is the number of students, t is the number of teachers, and $40 is the basic cost of the tour. Using the formula, what would it cost for 35 students and 3 teachers to take the tour?

   F. $50.50   **G.** $83.75

   H. $90.50   **J.** $98.44

5. Which expression is equivalent to $6.5 + (4.6 \times 8.2)$?

   A. $(6.5 + 4.6) \times 8.2$
   B. $6.5 \times (4.6 + 8.2)$
   C. $(6.5 + 4.6) \times (6.5 \times 8.2)$
   D. $(8.2 \times 4.6) + 6.5$

6. Dorie has plants with heights $4\frac{5}{8}$ in., $4\frac{3}{16}$ in., $4\frac{3}{4}$ in., $4\frac{13}{16}$ in., and $4\frac{1}{2}$ in. She wants to arrange the plants on her windowsill from tallest to shortest. Which is the correct order?

   F. $4\frac{13}{16}$ in., $4\frac{5}{8}$ in., $4\frac{3}{4}$ in., $4\frac{3}{16}$ in., $4\frac{1}{2}$ in.

   G. $4\frac{3}{4}$ in., $4\frac{5}{8}$ in., $4\frac{1}{2}$ in., $4\frac{13}{16}$ in., $4\frac{3}{16}$ in.

   H. $4\frac{13}{16}$ in., $4\frac{3}{4}$ in., $4\frac{5}{8}$ in., $4\frac{1}{2}$ in., $4\frac{3}{16}$ in.

   J. $4\frac{13}{16}$ in., $4\frac{3}{16}$ in., $4\frac{5}{8}$ in., $4\frac{3}{4}$ in., $4\frac{1}{2}$ in

7. Jeff is making a taco pie using a recipe that calls for $1\frac{1}{8}$ pounds of ground turkey. Jeff buys a package of ground turkey that is labeled 1.17 pounds. In order to determine if he has enough meat, Jeff writes $1\frac{1}{8}$ as a decimal. Which decimal is equivalent to $1\frac{1}{8}$?

   A. 1.125   **B.** 1.25

   C. 1.8   **D.** 1.875

Please note that items 8–9 have *five* answer choices.

8. Jose needs a board that measures $2\frac{3}{4}$ ft to make a shelf. He has a board that is 5 ft long. What length is left after he cuts the board?

   F. $2\frac{1}{4}$ ft   **G.** $3\frac{1}{4}$ ft   **H.** $7\frac{1}{4}$ ft

   J. $7\frac{3}{4}$ ft   **K.** Not Here

9. During a four-week period, Laron earned $12.75, $31.43, $27.89, and $21.14 at his part-time job. The best estimate of the amount of money he earned during the four weeks is—

   A. $70   **B.** $80   **C.** $90

   D. $100   **E.** $110

5-8 Changing Units in the Customary System

What You'll Learn

▼1 To change units of length and capacity

▼2 To change units of weight

...And Why

To use the customary system of measurement, you must be able to change units.

Here's How

Look for questions that

▪▪ build understanding

✔ check understanding

Customary Units of Measure

Length
12 inches (in.) = 1 foot (ft)
3 feet = 1 yard (yd)
5,280 feet = 1 mile (mi)

Weight
16 ounces (oz) = 1 pound (lb)
2,000 pounds = 1 ton (T)

Capacity
8 fluid ounces (fl oz) = 1 cup (c)
2 cups = 1 pint (p)
2 pints = 1 quart (qt)
4 quarts = 1 gallon (gal)

THINK AND DISCUSS

▼1 Changing Units of Length and Capacity

When a measure involves mixed units, it may be helpful to change to a mixed number involving just one unit.

■ **EXAMPLE 1** *Real-World Problem Solving*

Carpentry Sarah has a board that is 10 ft long. She plans to cut a piece that is 5 ft 3 in. long from the board. What will be the length of the remaining piece?

You need to subtract 5 ft 3 in. from 10 ft.

$$5 \text{ ft } 3 \text{ in.} = 5\frac{3}{12} \text{ ft} = 5\frac{1}{4} \text{ ft}$$ ◀——Write 3 in. as a fraction of a foot.

$$10 - 5\frac{1}{4} = 9\frac{4}{4} - 5\frac{1}{4}$$ ◀——Write 10 as $9\frac{4}{4}$. Then subtract.

$$= 4\frac{3}{4}$$

The remaining piece will be $4\frac{3}{4}$ ft long.

1. ✔ *Try It Out* Suppose Sarah cut 8 ft 5 in. from the 10 ft board. What would be the length of the remaining piece?

To change from a smaller unit to a larger unit, you *divide*.

■ **EXAMPLE 2** *Real-World Problem Solving*

How many one-cup servings are in a 36-fl oz bottle of juice?

Think of the relationship between fluid ounces and cups.   8 fl oz = 1 c ↘ ÷ 8 ↗

To change 36 fl oz to cups, divide 36 fl oz by 8.

$$36 \div 8 = 4.5$$ ◀——Use mental math.

There are $4\frac{1}{2}$ one-cup servings in the 36-fl oz bottle.

2. ✔ *Try It Out* How many one-cup servings are in a 50-fl oz bottle of juice?

▼2 *Changing Units of Weight*

To change from a larger unit to a smaller unit, you *multiply*.

■ **EXAMPLE 3**   *Real-World Problem Solving*

The lighter the frame of a mountain bike, the easier it is to cycle. Which bike shown in the ad will be easier to cycle?

Think of the relationship between pounds and ounces.

$$1\,lb = 16\,oz$$
$$\times 16$$

To change $4\frac{1}{4}$ lb to ounces, multiply $4\frac{1}{4}$ lb by 16.

$$4\frac{1}{4} \cdot 16 = \frac{17}{{}_1\cancel{4}} \cdot \frac{\cancel{16}^4}{1} \quad\longleftarrow\quad \text{Write } 4\frac{1}{4} \text{ as an improper fraction.}$$
$$\qquad\qquad\qquad\qquad\text{Then multiply.}$$
$$= 68$$

The $4\frac{1}{4}$-lb bike weighs 68 oz, so it is lighter than the 76-oz bike.

3. ✔ *Try It Out*   Find the number of ounces for each weight.
   a. $4\frac{5}{8}$ lb   b. $3\frac{7}{16}$ lb   c. $9\frac{3}{4}$ lb

Work Together _____ *Adjusting a Recipe*

Cooking Work in pairs. Suppose that you operate a catering service. You have a basic recipe for split pea soup that serves eight. Copy and complete the chart below to adjust the recipe for 16, 24, 32, and 48 servings. Whenever possible, change an amount to a larger unit of measure.

		Number of Servings				
	Ingredient	**8**	**16**	**24**	**32**	**48**
4.	Dried split peas	$2\frac{1}{4}$ c	▨	▨	▨	▨
5.	Water	2 qt	▨	▨	▨	▨
6.	Chopped onion	$\frac{3}{4}$ c	▨	▨	▨	▨
7.	Chopped celery	1 c	▨	▨	▨	▨
8.	Ham shank	2 lb	▨	▨	▨	▨
9.	Sliced carrot	$\frac{1}{4}$ lb	▨	▨	▨	▨

Tell whether you would *multiply* or *divide* to change from one unit of measure to the other.

1. gallons to quarts   **2.** cups to pints   **3.** quarts to cups   **4.** fluid ounces to cups

Mental Math **Complete.**

5. 4 ft 6 in. = ■ ft   **6.** $\frac{3}{4}$ lb = ■ oz   **7.** 500 lb = ■ T   **8.** $1\frac{1}{5}$ T = ■ lb

9. Yung Mi has three packages of walnuts that weigh 12 oz, 32 oz, and $1\frac{1}{2}$ lb. How many pounds of walnuts does she have altogether?

■ *Choose* **Use a calculator, paper and pencil, or mental math to change from one unit of measure to the other.**

10. $5\frac{1}{4}$ gal = ■ qt   **11.** 5,250 lb = ■ T   **12.** 4 yd 2 ft = ■ yd   **13.** ■ gal = 36 pt

14. 26 in. = ■ ft   **15.** 4 c = ■ fl oz   **16.** 68 oz = ■ lb   **17.** 36 oz = ■ lb

18. $3\frac{1}{2}$ mi = ■ ft   **19.** 16 ft = ■ yd   **20.** $4\frac{1}{2}$ qt = ■ c   **21.** 2,800 lb = ■ T

22. 1 ft 9 in. = ■ ft   **23.** ■ pt = 14 fl oz   **24.** 3 lb 12 oz = ■ lb   **25.** 7 pt = ■ qt

26. *Geography* The length of the Amazon River in South America is about 4,000 mi. How many feet is this?

27. Will 4 gal of milk make 64 one-cup servings? Explain.

28. *Hobbies* Jim has a pattern that requires $1\frac{3}{4}$ yd of 60-in. canvas. At a sale, he finds a remnant of 60-in. canvas that is $5\frac{1}{2}$ ft long. Will this be enough? Explain.

29. *Writing* Explain why you multiply to change from a larger unit to a smaller unit and divide to change from a smaller unit to a larger unit. Include examples.

■ **30. a.** *Calculator* In one day, people in the United States discard an average of 200,000 tons of food. Suppose that a garbage truck can hold 12,000 lb of this food. How many trucks are needed to haul all of it?
   b. Suppose that garbage trucks carrying all the discarded food are lined up bumper to bumper. Each truck is 25 ft long. About how long is the line of trucks in miles?

The Amazon River Basin contains $\frac{1}{5}$ of the world's fresh river water and $\frac{1}{3}$ of its forests. It may produce up to $\frac{1}{2}$ of the oxygen added to the atmosphere each year.

Source: *Curious Facts*

Climb or Dive?

WHAT IS THE TALLEST MOUNTAIN IN THE WORLD? Mount Everest can claim the world's highest elevation above sea level. As shown at the right, however, Hawaii's Mauna Kea is truly the world's tallest mountain, although much of it is hidden in the Pacific Ocean.

So what is the *lowest* elevation on Earth? Located between Israel and Jordan, the Dead Sea is 1,312 ft below sea level. For the oceans, the lowest elevation is the Marianas Trench. It lies 36,198 ft below the surface of the Pacific Ocean. If Mount Everest were placed in the Marianas Trench, its peak would be about $1\frac{1}{3}$ mi below sea level.

13,796 ft sea level
19,204 ft
Mauna Kea

29,028 ft
sea level
Mount Everest

---

31. a. *Earth Science* How many miles high is Mauna Kea?
  b. About how many miles taller than Mount Everest is Mauna Kea?

32. About how many miles in elevation separate the highest and lowest elevations on Earth?

Mixed Review

Solve using mental math. *(Lesson 3-5)*

33. $x + 42 = 83$ **34.** $b - (-2) = 7$ **35.** $z - 92 = 138$ **36.** $m + 4 = -4$

37. *Canoeing* Laura and Leslie rented a canoe for $3\frac{1}{2}$ hours. The canoe rental is $2.20 per hour. How much should each pay? *(Lessons 5-5, 5-6)*

✓ CHECKPOINT 2   Lessons 5-5 through 5-8

Find each product or quotient.

1. $\frac{4}{5} \cdot \frac{5}{8}$ **2.** $\frac{1}{3} \div \frac{4}{9}$ **3.** $\frac{5}{6} \div 6\frac{2}{3}$ **4.** $7\frac{1}{2} \cdot 3\frac{4}{7}$ **5.** $8\frac{1}{2} \div \frac{1}{4}$

6. Alicia has a job interview at 8:30 A.M. She needs 15 min to eat breakfast, $\frac{1}{2}$ h to get dressed, and 40 min to drive to the interview. What is the latest time that she should get up?

Complete.

7. 28 in. = ■ ft   **8.** $8\frac{1}{2}$ lb = ■ oz   **9.** 15 qt = ■ gal   **10.** 7 yd 2 ft = ■ yd

5-9 Solving Equations with Fractions by Multiplying and Dividing

What You'll Learn

1 To solve equations using multiplication

2 To solve equations using division

...And Why

You can extend your knowledge of how to solve equations.

Here's How

Look for questions that
- ⊞ build understanding
- ✔ check understanding

THINK AND DISCUSS

1 Solving Equations by Multiplying

You have solved equations using multiplication and division. Now apply your knowledge to equations with fractions.

■ **EXAMPLE 1**   *Real-World Problem Solving*

Money Paper money is printed in sheets of 32 bills. Inspectors check about one fourth of the sheets. If an inspector checked 44 sheets, how many sheets were printed?

Words • | one fourth | of | sheets printed | = | sheets checked |

• Let s = number of sheets printed

Equation • $\frac{1}{4}s = 44$

$$\frac{s}{4} = 44 \qquad \longleftarrow \text{Write } \frac{1}{4}s \text{ as } \frac{s}{4}.$$

$$4 \cdot \frac{s}{4} = 4 \cdot 44 \qquad \longleftarrow \begin{array}{l}\text{Since } s \text{ is divided by 4, multiply} \\ \text{each side by 4.}\end{array}$$

$$s = 176$$

176 sheets were printed.

1. ✔ Try It Out Solve each equation.

a. $\frac{1}{3}s = 5$ **b.** $\frac{1}{2}s = \frac{3}{4}$ **c.** $\frac{s}{8} = 2\frac{1}{3}$ **d.** $\frac{s}{8} = 6\frac{3}{4}$

2 Solving Equations by Dividing

The solution of an equation may be a fraction or a mixed number.

■ **EXAMPLE 2**

Solve $32c = 130$.

$$32c = 130$$

$$\frac{32c}{32} = \frac{130}{32} \qquad \longleftarrow \text{Divide each side by 32.}$$

$$c = \frac{65}{16} = 4\frac{1}{16} \qquad \longleftarrow \text{Simplify and write as a mixed number.}$$

2. ✔ *Try It Out* Solve each equation.

a. $5x = 43$ b. $8a = 50$ c. $32 = 6d$ d. $4r = 3$

EXERCISES *On Your Own*

Solve each equation.

1. $\frac{y}{6} = 5$ **2.** $\frac{1}{8}d = 5\frac{1}{4}$ **3.** $\frac{t}{5} = 3\frac{7}{10}$ **4.** $16 = \frac{1}{3}e$ **5.** $8\frac{3}{4} = \frac{p}{6}$

6. *Business* On a recent day, a store manager noted that 65 customers bought at least eight items. This was one fifth of the total number of customers that day. Write and solve an equation to find the total number of customers.

7. *Sports* It took Ruthene $\frac{1}{4}$ h to run 2 mi. What was her average speed?

8. *Open-ended* Write a problem that can be solved using the equation $\frac{1}{5}x = 28$.

Solve each equation.

9. $4a = 9$ **10.** $2q = 17$ **11.** $6g = 16$ **12.** $10w = 4$ **13.** $8n = 15$

Mental Math **Solve each equation.**

14. $\frac{x}{6} = 2$ **15.** $3p = 9$ **16.** $12f = 2$ **17.** $\frac{1}{3}b = 12$ **18.** $12k = 8$

19. *Estimation* Carl and Ed each estimated the solution of $20g = 49$. Carl's estimate was $\frac{2}{5}$. Ed's estimate was $2\frac{1}{2}$.
    a. Whose estimate is correct? How do you think he made the estimate?
    b. What error do you think the other person made?

▤ *Choose* **Use a calculator, paper and pencil, or mental math to solve each equation.**

20. $\frac{1}{5}s = 16$ **21.** $9a = 20$ **22.** $48q = 36$ **23.** $\frac{1}{28} = \frac{1}{4}z$ **24.** $3w = 5$

25. $14n = 60$ **26.** $\frac{s}{8} = 128$ **27.** $88 = 22c$ **28.** $\frac{w}{7} = 628$ **29.** $36m = 4$

30. $37p = 407$ **31.** $\frac{1}{55}b = 78$ **32.** $\frac{n}{12} = 10$ **33.** $117 = \frac{1}{9}u$ **34.** $5 = \frac{w}{10}$

35. *Writing* How is solving the equation $4y = 24$ similar to solving $24y = 4$? How is it different?

Estimation **Estimate the solution of each equation.
Explain how you made your estimate.**

36. $23q = 400$ **37.** $9a = 121$ **38.** $\frac{1}{21}n = 12$ **39.** $82 = \frac{1}{9}t$ **40.** $2\frac{5}{6} = \frac{1}{7}x$

Solve each problem by writing and solving an equation.

41. Mount McKinley, the tallest mountain in North America, is 20,320 ft tall. The Petronas Tower in Kuala Lampur, the world's tallest building, is 1,483 ft tall. About how many times as tall as the Petronas Tower is Mount McKinley?

42. *Geography* About one eighth of the total area of the New England states is covered by water. This is about 9,000 mi². What is the total area of the New England states?

43. *Open-ended* Write two different equations that have the solution $5\frac{1}{2}$. One should require division to solve, and one should require multiplication to solve.

> PORTFOLIO
> Select one or two items
> from your work for this
> chapter. Consider:
> • cooperative work
> • work you found challenging
> • part of your project
> Explain why you have
> included each selection
> that you make.

Mixed Review

Estimate each answer. *(Lesson 5-1)*

44. $12\frac{1}{2} - 5\frac{2}{3}$ **45.** $16\frac{1}{2} \div \frac{3}{4}$ **46.** $\frac{1}{2} + \frac{5}{12}$ **47.** $21\frac{1}{8} \cdot 3\frac{1}{3}$ **48.** $\frac{7}{8} - \frac{1}{6}$

Compare. Use <, >, or =. *(Lesson 3-2)*

49. $-15 \ \blacksquare \ 0$ **50.** $7 \ \blacksquare \ -7$ **51.** $23 \ \blacksquare \ |-23|$ **52.** $-5 \ \blacksquare \ -6$ **53.** $|10| \ \blacksquare \ -10$

54. *Videos* In a video store, $\frac{1}{4}$ of the movies are comedies, $\frac{1}{6}$ are romances, and $\frac{1}{2}$ are thrillers. What fraction of the movies are not comedies, romances, or thrillers? *(Lesson 5-2)*

CHAPTER PROJECT

PROJECT LINK: CALCULATING

Now that you have a good pancake recipe for feeding your family, adjust it to serve the number of people that are in your class. Remember to keep the number of eggs as a whole number, even though most of the other ingredients use fractions. Did you multiply fractions or divide fractions to get the class recipe? Explain.

Extra Practice, Lesson 5-9, page 518

CHAPTER PROJECT

Toss and Turn

Write Your Own Recipe The Project Link questions on pages 196, 209, and 224 should help you complete your project. Here is a checklist to help you gather together the parts of your project.

- ✔ the people you interviewed
- ✔ your recipe for feeding your family
- ✔ your recipe for feeding the whole class

Present your recipe to your class. Sell them on how tasty your pancakes are!

Reflect and Revise

With an adult, make a batch of your pancakes for your family. Get their comments and change your recipe as needed.

Think about the math that you used to complete this project. What have you learned in this chapter that helped you? What advice did you get from others to create a great recipe?

Web Extension

Prentice Hall's Internet site contains information you might find helpful as you complete your project. Visit www.phschool.com/mgm2/ch5 for some links and ideas related to cooking.

5 WRAP UP

Estimating with Fractions and Mixed Numbers   5-1

To estimate sums and differences of fractions, round to 0, $\frac{1}{2}$, or 1.

To estimate sums, differences, products, and quotients of mixed numbers, round to the nearest whole number.

Estimate each answer.

1. $\frac{1}{8} + \frac{4}{5}$ 2. $\frac{5}{8} + 1\frac{2}{3}$ 3. $\frac{2}{5} - \frac{1}{4}$ 4. $3\frac{1}{8} \cdot 9\frac{9}{10}$ 5. $12\frac{2}{5} \div 3\frac{8}{9}$

Adding and Subtracting Fractions   5-2, 5-3

To add or subtract fractions, first find a common denominator and then add or subtract the numerators.

To add or subtract mixed numbers, add or subtract the whole numbers and then add or subtract the fractions. You may need to rename a mixed number before subtracting.

Find each sum or difference.

6. $\frac{3}{5} + \frac{3}{5}$ 7. $\frac{3}{4} - \frac{1}{8}$ 8. $\frac{1}{2} + \frac{2}{5}$ 9. $\frac{5}{8} - \frac{3}{16}$ 10. $\frac{2}{3} + \frac{3}{4}$

11. $2\frac{1}{3} + \frac{3}{4}$ 12. $16\frac{4}{5} - 9\frac{2}{3}$ 13. $8\frac{1}{6} + 7\frac{3}{12}$ 14. $11\frac{5}{6} - 5\frac{3}{8}$ 15. $3\frac{1}{3} - 2\frac{3}{4}$

Solving Equations with Fractions by Adding and Subtracting   5-4

Use addition to "undo" subtraction and use subtraction to "undo" addition.

16. $1\frac{7}{8} + n = 3\frac{3}{4}$ 17. $q - 3\frac{1}{5} = 5\frac{3}{10}$ 18. $1\frac{1}{2} = \frac{2}{5} + a$ 19. $2\frac{7}{10} = g - 2\frac{1}{4}$

20. $m - \frac{3}{10} = \frac{4}{5}$ 21. $9\frac{1}{3} = k + \frac{3}{4}$ 22. $2\frac{1}{3} = x - 5\frac{1}{4}$ 23. $4\frac{1}{2} + m = 6\frac{2}{5}$

Multiplying and Dividing Fractions and Mixed Numbers   5-5, 5-6

To multiply fractions, you multiply their numerators and then multiply their denominators.

To divide fractions, you multiply by the **reciprocal** of the divisor. To find $\frac{2}{3} \div \frac{5}{6}$, you multiply $\frac{2}{3} \cdot \frac{6}{5}$.

Find each product or quotient.

24. $\frac{3}{5} \cdot \frac{1}{2}$ **25.** $\frac{2}{3} \cdot \frac{3}{8}$ **26.** $\frac{3}{5} \cdot 1\frac{1}{2}$ **27.** $2\frac{2}{3} \cdot 3\frac{3}{8}$ **28.** $8\frac{5}{6} \cdot 10\frac{3}{4}$

29. $\frac{2}{5} \div \frac{4}{5}$ **30.** $\frac{2}{3} \div \frac{4}{3}$ **31.** $5\frac{1}{4} \div \frac{7}{8}$ **32.** $4\frac{4}{5} \div 1\frac{1}{3}$ **33.** $1\frac{1}{3} \div 4\frac{4}{5}$

Problem Solving Strategies   5-7

To solve some problems you may have to work backward.

34. Lien wants to be at school at 7:30 A.M. It takes her $\frac{3}{4}$ h to get dressed, $\frac{1}{2}$ h to fix and eat breakfast, and 15 min to walk to school. What time should she get up?

35. John bought a pair of shoes during a "$\frac{1}{4}$-off" sale. The original price was $34. After he paid for the shoes he had $14.26. How much money did he start with?

Changing Units in the Customary System   5-8

To change from a larger unit to a smaller unit, you *multiply*. To change from a smaller unit to a larger unit, you *divide*.

Complete.

36. 30 in. = ▧ ft   **37.** 54 oz = ▧ lb   **38.** 20 yd = ▧ ft   **39.** $3\frac{1}{2}$ c = ▧ fl oz

40. 4 ft 8 in. = ▧ ft   **41.** $3\frac{3}{4}$ tons = ▧ lb   **42.** 2 lb 4 oz = ▧ lb   **43.** 78 in. = ▧ ft

Solving Equations with Fractions by Multiplying and Dividing   5-9

Use multiplication to "undo" division and use division to "undo" multiplication.

Solve each equation.

44. $\frac{1}{5}g = 10$ **45.** $\frac{3}{4} = 3t$ **46.** $5p = 18$ **47.** $\frac{x}{5} = \frac{1}{4}$ **48.** $\frac{7}{8} = \frac{s}{4}$

49. $\frac{x}{7} = 3$ **50.** $12p = 78$ **51.** $\frac{1}{4}t = 3\frac{5}{8}$ **52.** $15 = 18d$ **53.** $\frac{1}{10}y = \frac{2}{5}$

54. Write an equation and solve. The 70 students graduating are $\frac{1}{5}$ of the total school population. How many students attend the school?

1. Estimate each answer.
   a. $\frac{7}{8} + \frac{15}{16}$ b. $\frac{3}{5} - \frac{1}{2}$
   c. $7\frac{1}{8} + 2\frac{3}{4}$ d. $8\frac{3}{8} - 5\frac{1}{3}$
   e. $4\frac{5}{8} \cdot 2\frac{1}{10}$ f. $43\frac{1}{2} \div 5\frac{1}{5}$
   g. $23\frac{1}{3} \div 6\frac{2}{5}$ h. $2\frac{1}{2} \cdot 10\frac{1}{4}$

2. You jog $8\frac{1}{2}$ times around the block. The distance around the block is 770 yd. About how many miles have you jogged? (1 mi = 1,760 yd)

3. Find each sum or difference.
   a. $\frac{15}{16} - \frac{3}{16}$ b. $\frac{1}{4} + \frac{2}{3}$
   c. $\frac{1}{2} - \frac{3}{8}$ d. $\frac{2}{3} + \frac{5}{6}$
   e. $8\frac{2}{5} + 5\frac{3}{5}$ f. $7\frac{5}{8} - 4\frac{1}{8}$
   g. $4\frac{3}{4} + 5\frac{1}{5}$ h. $9\frac{3}{8} - 5\frac{1}{4}$
   i. $1\frac{2}{3} - \frac{3}{4}$ j. $4\frac{2}{3} + 1\frac{5}{6}$

4. **Choose A, B, C, or D.** In which equation is the value of x less than 1?
   A. $\frac{3}{8} = x - \frac{3}{4}$ B. $x - \frac{1}{3} = \frac{3}{4}$
   C. $x - 1\frac{1}{3} = 2\frac{1}{3}$ D. $x + 1\frac{1}{5} = 1\frac{3}{5}$

5. Jake worked $12\frac{1}{2}$ h at $4.50 per hour. After he was paid, he spent $24 for a shirt. He now has $89.23. How much money did he have before he was paid?

6. In March, a puppy weighed $4\frac{3}{4}$ lb. In August, it weighed $5\frac{7}{8}$ lb. How much weight did the puppy gain?

7. Pamela is planning to make a dress. She needs to buy $2\frac{3}{4}$ yd of fabric that costs $8 per yard and $1\frac{2}{3}$ yd of fabric that costs $6 per yard. How much will the fabric cost?

8. Martha rides her bicycle $1\frac{1}{2}$ mi to school. At the end of the day, she stops at a park that is on her way home. The park is $\frac{7}{9}$ mi from school. How far is it from Martha's house?

9. Find each product or quotient.
   a. $\frac{4}{5} \cdot \frac{1}{4}$ b. $\frac{4}{5} \div \frac{1}{4}$
   c. $\frac{3}{4} \cdot \frac{2}{3}$ d. $\frac{1}{4} \div \frac{4}{5}$
   e. $1\frac{2}{3} \cdot 1\frac{1}{4}$ f. $1\frac{2}{3} \div 1\frac{1}{4}$
   g. $150 \div 2\frac{2}{3}$ h. $5\frac{3}{8} \cdot 3\frac{3}{4}$

10. Complete.
    a. 38 in. = ▇ ft b. 60 oz = ▇ lb
    c. $3\frac{3}{4}$ qt = ▇ c d. $1\frac{2}{3}$ mi = ▇ ft
    e. $5\frac{1}{2}$ yd = ▇ in. f. 50 fl oz = ▇ c

11. Solve.
    a. $15k = 33$ b. $12 = 8x$
    c. $\frac{y}{12} = 2\frac{1}{2}$ d. $\frac{1}{4}m = 10$
    e. $w + 4\frac{3}{5} = 6\frac{1}{2}$ f. $k - 2\frac{3}{4} = 9$
    g. $7\frac{1}{3} = 4\frac{1}{2} + p$ h. $10\frac{3}{4} = n - \frac{5}{8}$

12. You are an employee at a store that is having a "$\frac{1}{3}$-off" sale. Employees get an additional $\frac{1}{5}$ off the sale price. How much would you pay for a jacket that originally cost $60?

13. A brick is $1\frac{7}{8}$ in. high. Mortar that is $\frac{3}{8}$ in. thick is spread on each row of bricks. How many rows of bricks are needed to reach the top of a $7\frac{1}{2}$ ft doorway?

14. Kimo has $1\frac{1}{2}$ lb of salmon. He wants each person to get a 6-oz serving. How many people can he feed?

Choose the best answer.

1. Which sum is closest to 1?

   A. $\frac{1}{3} + \frac{1}{5}$ B. $\frac{5}{8} + \frac{5}{9}$

   C. $\frac{2}{3} + \frac{4}{11}$ D. $\frac{3}{4} + \frac{3}{5}$

2. You want to buy some birthday presents for your little brother. You have $21. You know you will need about $1 for sales tax. What should you buy?

   A. book and video
   B. model and video
   C. book and soccer ball
   D. model and soccer ball

   Possible Gifts

Item	Cost
Book	$7.95
Model	$8.99
Video	$11.49
Soccer ball	$12.50

3. Which expression has the greatest value?

   A. $3.4 \cdot 7 + 3.4 \cdot 9$ B. $3.4\,(7 + 9)$
   C. $3.4 \cdot 8 + 3.4 \cdot 8$ D. $3.4\,(17)$

4. Which expression has a value that is closest to -10?

   A. $3 - (-6)$ B. $-6 - 3$
   C. $6 - (-3)$ D. $-3 - (-6)$

5. Which decimal is *not* 4.01 when rounded to the nearest hundredth?

   A. 4.0086   B. 4.0049
   C. 4.0149   D. 4.0140

6. Henry plans to build a set of steps for his attic stairway. The steps must reach a height of $8\frac{1}{2}$ ft. Each step can be no more than $7\frac{3}{4}$ in. high. What is the least number of steps he must build?

   A. 11   B. 12
   C. 13   D. 14

7. Estimate $6\frac{3}{4} \cdot 3\frac{1}{5}$.

   A. 18   B. 21   C. 24   D. 27

8. The swimmers in the 100-meter backstroke finished with times of 59.27, 59.32, 58.72, 58.8, and 58.99 seconds. The times will be announced in order from the fastest (least) time to the slowest (greatest) time. In what order will the times be announced?

   A. 58.99, 58.8, 58.72, 59.32, 59.27
   B. 59.32, 59.27, 58.99, 58.8, 58.72
   C. 58.99, 58.8, 58.72, 59.32, 59.27
   D. 58.72, 58.8, 58.99, 59.27, 59.32

9. Which pair of numbers has a product that is greater than their sum?

   A. $-1, -3$ B. $-1, 3$
   C. $1, -3$ D. $1, 3$

10. Which variable expression can be described by the word phrase "*r* increased by 2"?

    A. $2r$ B. $r - 2$ C. $r + 2$ D. $r \cdot 2$

11. Which expression has the greatest value?

    A. $-5 + |-4|$ B. $|-5| + -4$
    C. $-5 + -4$ D. $|-5| + |-4|$

12. The chart shows the changes in Bill's weight over 6 months. What was his average weight change per month?

    A. -3 lb
    B. -2 lb
    C. -1 lb
    D. 2 lb

Month	Weight change (lb)
Jan.	-5
Feb.	$+2$
Mar.	-6
Apr.	$+3$
May	-5
June	-1

6

Using Proportions and Percents

chills and thrills

Your world is spinning. You are screaming. And you are loving every minute of it! Even though you are scared, you know that you will come to a safe stop at the end of the ride.

Clearly, a successful amusement park attraction like the one shown here, which is Paramount Park's ride Top Gun, must be both fun and safe. Planners of amusement parks use a lot of math to create thrills but avoid any spills.

Take a Survey For the chapter project you will decide which rides are likely to be most popular. Your final product will be a recommendation about which rides to include in a proposed amusement park for your town.

• **How to use multiple strategies to solve problems**

6-1 Exploring Ratios Using Data

What You'll Learn

1. To write ratios
2. To find equal ratios

...And Why

You can use a ratio to describe a group of people in terms of age and gender.

Here's How

Look for questions that
- build understanding
- ✔ check understanding

THINK AND DISCUSS

1 *Writing Ratios*

A **ratio** is a comparison of two numbers by division. You can write a ratio three ways.

$$3 \text{ to } 4 \qquad 3 : 4 \qquad \frac{3}{4}$$

The table below shows the ratio of males to females for different years and different age groups.

Ratio of Males to Females by Age Group

Year	10–14	30–34	60–64
1970	104 : 100	97 : 100	88 : 100
1980	104 : 100	99 : 100	86 : 100
1990	105 : 100	100 : 100	87 : 100

Source: *Statistical Abstract of the United States*

1. ⬛ *Think About It* Write each ratio for the year 1990 in two other ways.

■ EXAMPLE 1 *Real-World Problem Solving*

Data Analysis The United States Census Bureau predicts that in the year 2010 there will be about 64 males for every 100 females who are 75 years old or older. Write this information as a ratio in three ways.

$$
\begin{aligned}
\text{males} &\longrightarrow \ 64 \text{ to } 100 \ \longleftarrow \text{females} \\
\text{males} &\longrightarrow \ 64 : 100 \ \longleftarrow \text{females} \\
&\quad \frac{64}{100} \ \begin{array}{l}\longleftarrow \text{males} \\ \longleftarrow \text{females}\end{array}
\end{aligned}
$$

2. ⬛ *Error Alert* A student reported the ratio of males to females as 100 : 64. Explain why this is incorrect.

3. ✔ *Try It Out* The United States Census Bureau predicts that by the year 2010 there will be about 73 million people under the age of 18 and 39 million people 65 and older. Use this information to write a ratio in three ways.

You can use a decimal to express and compare ratios.

■ **EXAMPLE 2**   *Real-World Problem Solving*

Social Studies An official United States flag has a length-to-width ratio of 19 : 10. The largest U.S. flag measures 505 ft by 255 ft. Is this an official U.S. flag?

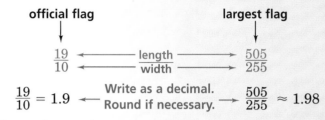

The ratio 1.98 is not equal to the ratio 1.9, so the largest flag is not an official United States flag.

4. ✔*Try It Out* Express each ratio as a decimal. Round to the nearest hundredth, if necessary.
   a. $\frac{3}{4}$ b. 16 to 5   c. 8 : 9   d. $\frac{7}{3}$

The largest United States flag is shown on the Ellipse in Washington, D.C., on Flag Day, June 14. It weighs 2,720 lb.

Source: The Guinness Book of Records

❷ *Writing Equal Ratios*

To find equal ratios, multiply or divide the numerator and denominator of the ratio by the same nonzero number.

■ **EXAMPLE 3**

Find two ratios equal to $\frac{12}{15}$.

Multiply both numerator and denominator by 2.

$$\frac{12}{15} = \frac{24}{30}$$
×2

Divide both numerator and denominator by 3.

$$\frac{12}{15} = \frac{4}{5}$$
÷3

Two ratios equal to $\frac{12}{15}$ are $\frac{24}{30}$ and $\frac{4}{5}$.

5. ✔*Try It Out* Write two ratios equal to $\frac{10}{16}$.

6. ▪*Go a Step Further* Use what you know about fractions. Tell which ratio in Example 3 is written in simplest form.

■ **EXAMPLE 4**   *Real-World Problem Solving*

Biology A brown bear weighs about 325 lb. A polar bear weighs about 1,000 lb. Write a ratio in simplest form to compare the weights of the bears.

$$\frac{325}{1,000} = \frac{325 \div 25}{1,000 \div 25} = \frac{13}{40} \longleftarrow$$ Divide the numerator and the denominator by 25.

The ratio of the weight of the brown bear to the weight of the polar bear is 13 to 40.

7. ✔ *Try It Out* Write each ratio in simplest form.

    a. $\frac{25}{75}$ **b.** $\frac{110}{20}$ **c.** 42 : 66   **d.** 84 to 48

Work Together
Finding Ratios Using Data

8. **a.** ❧*Data Collection* Survey your class to find the month of each person's birthday.
   b. Write the ratio of the number of people born in each month to the number of people in class.
   c. How do you think you could use the data to estimate the number of students in your school who were born in August?

EXERCISES *On Your Own*

Write the ratio for each situation in three ways.

1. About 1 out of 4 people swims at least six times each year.

2. About 24 out of 25 Californians live in a metropolitan area.

Write each ratio in two other ways.

3. 12 : 4   **4.** 8 to 10   **5.** $\frac{5}{4}$ **6.** 13 : 8   **7.** 21 : 28   **8.** $\frac{8}{18}$

9. **Choose A, B, C, or D.** A bag contains red, blue, and yellow marbles. The ratio of red marbles to blue marbles is 1 : 4. The ratio of blue marbles to yellow marbles is 2 : 5. What is the ratio of red marbles to yellow marbles?

    A. 1 : 5   **B.** 1 : 10   **C.** 1 : 2   **D.** 1 : 12

Write each ratio in three ways.

10. A baseball team won 7 out of 15 games.
    a. wins to total games
    b. wins to losses

11. A running club has 23 girls and 19 boys.
    a. girls to boys
    b. boys to total number

12. *Writing* Sara's math class included 15 girls and 10 boys. Sara said the ratio of girls to boys was 3 to 2. Two new students, a girl and a boy, enrolled in the class. Sara says the ratio is still 3 to 2. Is she correct? Why or why not?

Express each ratio as a decimal. Round to the nearest tenth, if necessary.

13. $7 : 8$

14. 18 to 5

15. $\frac{8}{3}$

16. $\frac{14}{19}$

17. $12 : 25$

18. $\frac{110}{105}$

19. *Transportation* Train A can travel 225 miles in 3 hours. Train B can travel 455 miles in 7 hours.
    a. Write a ratio of miles : hours for each train.
    b. Express each ratio as a decimal.
    c. Write a sentence to compare Train A to Train B.

20. *Sports* A softball diamond measures 65 ft by 65 ft. A baseball diamond measures 90 ft by 90 ft. Write a ratio in simplest form for each of the following.
    a. the length of a side of a softball diamond to the length of a side of a baseball diamond
    b. the area of a softball diamond to the area of a baseball diamond
    c. *Reasoning* Why do you think the ratio of the sides and the ratio of the areas are not the same?

Open-ended **Write two other ratios equal to each ratio.**

21. $26 : 54$

22. 12 to 44

23. $\frac{212}{100}$

24. $\frac{21}{3}$

25. $\frac{18}{36}$

26. $1 : 6$

Write each ratio in simplest form.

27. $25 : 10$

28. 7 to 63

29. $\frac{2}{100}$

30. 48 to 12

31. $17 : 34$

32. $\frac{9}{27}$

33. *Cars* A jack for a car requires a force of 120 lb to lift a 3,000 lb car. What is the ratio of the car's weight to the force required to lift the car? Write the ratio in simplest form.

34. Use the chart below.

	Room 101	Room 104	Room 107
Girls	12	9	9
Boys	16	20	12

    a. Which two rooms have the same ratio of girls to boys?

    b. The students in Room 101 and Room 104 have one class together. What is the ratio of girls to boys for the combined class? Write the ratio in simplest form.

35. *Cars* Antifreeze protects a car's radiator from freezing during the winter. One brand of antifreeze recommends mixing at least 2 parts antifreeze with every 1 part water for protection to $-82°F$.

    a. Which of the ratios of antifreeze to water at the right provide protection to $-82°F$?

    b. *Reasoning* A car's radiator can hold 15 qt. How much antifreeze and how much water should be added to give protection to $-82°F$?

Ratio of Antifreeze to Water

Antifreeze (qt) : Water (qt)		
8	:	4
7.5	:	3
12	:	8
3.5	:	1
9	:	18

Mixed Review

Estimate. *(Lesson 2-2)*

36. $412 \cdot (83)$ **37.** $654 \div 48$ **38.** $28.7 \div 5.4$ **39.** $22.7 + 23.5 + 23.1$

Solve. *(Lessons 3-6, 3-7)*

40. $72 = 8x$ **41.** $6 + y = 51$ **42.** $-5 = \frac{q}{7}$ **43.** $-3 + r = -57$ **44.** $x - 34 = -37$

45. *Money* A swimsuit that has a regular price of $38.00 is now on sale for $\frac{1}{4}$ off. What is its sale price? *(Lesson 5-5)*

CHAPTER PROJECT

PROJECT LINK TAKING A SURVEY

What's your favorite amusement park ride? Conduct a survey to find out which rides are most popular. Keep track of the number of people you survey as well as their responses.

Unit Rates and Proportional Reasoning

What You'll Learn

1 To find unit rates
2 To compare unit prices

...And Why

People compare prices to make wise purchasing decisions.

Here's How

Look for questions that
▪ build understanding
✔ check understanding

Work Together   *Comparing Ratios*

Suppose you plan to try out for a part in a radio advertisement. The casting director is looking for someone who can speak clearly but also very fast.

1. Work with a partner. Time each other as you read a newspaper article aloud as clearly and as fast as you can. After two minutes, count the number of words that you read.

2. ▪*Analyze* Write a ratio comparing the number of words you read to your time. Then write a ratio for your partner's reading. Which ratio is greater? Explain how you know.

THINK AND DISCUSS

▼ *Finding Unit Rates*

A **rate** is a ratio that compares two quantities measured in different units. In the Work Together, suppose you read 233 words in two minutes. Your reading rate would be $\frac{233 \text{ words}}{2 \text{ min}}$.

A **unit rate** is a rate that has a denominator of 1.

$$\frac{\text{words}}{\text{minutes}} \longrightarrow \frac{233}{2} \overset{\div 2}{\underset{\div 2}{=}} \frac{116.5}{1}$$

The unit rate is $\frac{116.5 \text{ words}}{1 \text{ min}}$, or 116.5 words/min (words per minute).

3. a. ✔ *Try It Out* Use the data you collected in the Work Together. Find the unit reading rates for your partner and yourself.
   b. Suppose you and your partner continued reading for 5 min. About how many words would each of you read?

4. ▪*Go a Step Further* You measure the speed of a car in miles per hour. How is speed an example of a rate?

HISTORY
During a speech in December, 1961, President John F. Kennedy delivered a passage at the rate of 327 words/min. At the time, this was the fastest rate recorded for a public speaker.

Source: *The Guinness Book of Records*

Sometimes measures are written in mixed units. For example, time may be written in *minutes* and *seconds*. To find a unit rate of time, you first need to change the total time to seconds.

■ **EXAMPLE 1**   *Real-World Problem Solving*

Sports At the 1993 World Championships, Maria Mutola of Mozambique set a new world record for the women's 1,000-meter race. Her time was 2 min 29.34 s. About how fast was her average speed?

2 min 29.34 s = 2 × 60 s + 29.34 s ←— Write the time in seconds.
= 149.34 s

Write the ratio of meters to seconds. Find the unit rate.

$\dfrac{\text{meters}}{\text{seconds}} \longrightarrow \dfrac{1{,}000}{149.34}$ = 1,000 ⬛ 149.34 ⬛ **6.696129637**

≈ 6.70 m/s ←— Round to the nearest hundredth.

Maria Mutola's average speed was about 6.7 m/s.

5. ✔ Try It Out Write the unit rate for each situation.
a. earn $34 in 8 h   b. type 6,750 words in 2 h 30 min

▼2 *Comparing Unit Prices*

A **unit price** is the price per unit of an item. To calculate a unit price, divide the price of the item by the size of the item.

■ **EXAMPLE 2**   *Real-World Problem Solving*

Consumer Issues A 10.2 fl oz bottle of Shine shampoo costs $5.98. The 16 fl oz bottle costs $9.95. Which size is the better buy?

$\dfrac{\text{price}}{\text{size}} \longrightarrow \dfrac{\$5.98}{10.2 \text{ fl oz}}$ ≈ $.59/fl oz ⎤
                                                        ⎥ Find the unit price of each item.
$\dfrac{\text{price}}{\text{size}} \longrightarrow \dfrac{\$9.95}{16 \text{ fl oz}}$ ≈ $.62/fl oz ⎦

Since $.59 < $.62, the 10.2 fl oz bottle is the better buy.

6. ✔ Try It Out You can buy 28 fl oz of fruit juice for $1.69 or 64 fl oz for $3.19. Which size is the better buy?

Write the unit rate for each situation.

1. travel 1,200 mi in 4 h

2. score 98 points in 6 games

3. earn $145 in 25 h

4. write 11 pages in 2 h

5. run 400 m in 1 min 32 s

6. make 686 cars in 56 days

Find each unit price.

7. $12 for 4 yd

8. $9 for 5 fl oz

9. $9.87 for 3 gal

10. $3.45 for 2 lb

11. 4 m for $10

12. 20 lb for $7

13. 7 oz for $6.65

14. 3 qt for $4.49

▦ *Choose* **Use a calculator, paper and pencil, or mental math.**

15. A 17-min telephone call from Boston to Chicago costs $2.38. What is the cost per minute?

16. A plane travels 2,250 km in 3 h. What is its average speed?

Find each unit price. Then determine the better buy.

17. detergent: 32 fl oz for $1.99
    50 fl oz for $2.49

18. crackers: 12 oz for $2.69
    16 oz for $3.19

19. juice: 48 fl oz for $2.15
    64 fl for $2.89

20. popcorn: 15 oz for $1.69
    30 oz for $2.99

21. ribbon: 1 yd for $.49
    3 yd for $1.95

22. walnuts: 1 lb for $3.49
    10 oz for $2.49

23. a. *Geography* *Population density* is the average number of people per unit of area. Alaska has the lowest population density of any state in the United States. What is its population density? Round to the nearest person per square mile.

    b. *Reasoning* New Jersey has 1,071 people/mi^2. It has the highest population density of any state. Can you conclude that 1,071 people live in every square mile in New Jersey? Explain.

    c. *Writing* Explain how you could find the population density of your city or town.

ALASKA
population:
604,000
area:
570,374 mi^2

24. A school has 35 teachers and 945 students. What is the student-to-teacher ratio? Write your answer as a unit rate.

25. *Sports* Use the table below.

Running Records

Distance	Time	Record Holder
200 m	19.32 s	Michael Johnson, USA
400 m	43.29 s	Butch Reynolds, USA
800 m	1 min 41.24 s	Wilson Kipketer, Kenya

Source: *ESPN*

   a. Find the average speed for each record holder. Round to the nearest hundredth of a meter per second.

   b. *Reasoning* Is it fair to compare the speeds? Explain.

26. *Consumer Issues* One brand of cereal costs $1.79 for a 7.2-oz box. A larger box that weighs 1 lb 4.25 oz costs $3.69. Which size is the better buy? Why?

27. a. *Consumer Issues* The 64-oz bottle of Stain-Free detergent is on sale this week for $4.99. The 36-oz bottle is not on sale. It costs $3.29. Which is the better buy?

   b. The 12-oz bottle of Stain-Free detergent costs $.75 every day. Of the three bottles, which is the best buy?

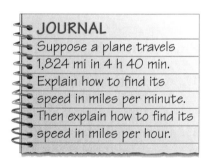

JOURNAL
Suppose a plane travels
1,824 mi in 4 h 40 min.
Explain how to find its
speed in miles per minute.
Then explain how to find its
speed in miles per hour.

28. *Data Collection* Have a member of your family count the number of times you blink in 3 min.

   a. What is your blinking rate in blinks per minute?

   b. About how many times will you blink in an hour?

Mixed Review

Round to the nearest hundredth. *(Lesson 2-1)*

29. 4.883   **30.** 6.1252   **31.** 21.457   **32.** 124.309   **33.** 1.0008   **34.** 7.90345

Draw a model for each fraction or mixed number. *(Lesson 4-1)*

35. $\frac{7}{8}$ **36.** $\frac{3}{5}$ **37.** $1\frac{1}{4}$ **38.** $1\frac{2}{3}$ **39.** $3\frac{1}{2}$ **40.** $2\frac{3}{8}$

41. *Choose a Strategy* A class of 23 students includes 11 students who are in the Computer Club and 14 who are in the Math Club. Five students belong to both clubs. How many students are not members of either club?

6-3 Proportions

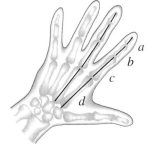

 The bones in your fingers are examples of a very special ratio called the golden ratio. For the bones, the following proportion is true:

$$\frac{a}{b} = \frac{b}{c} \text{ and } \frac{b}{c} = \frac{c}{d}$$

Source: *Fascinating Fibonaccis*

THINK AND DISCUSS

1 Using Cross Products

A **proportion** is an equation stating that two ratios are equal. The equation $\frac{6}{8} = \frac{9}{12}$ is a proportion.

1. a. ⚓*Number Sense* Write both sides of the proportion $\frac{6}{8} = \frac{9}{12}$ as fractions in simplest form. What do you notice?

   b. Find the product of 6 and 12; of 8 and 9. What do you notice?

In the proportion $\frac{6}{8} = \frac{9}{12}$, the products 6×12 and 8×9 are called **cross products.** The cross products of a proportion are always equal. You can use cross products to find if two ratios form a proportion.

■ EXAMPLE 1

Which pairs of ratios could form a proportion?

a. $\frac{5}{9}, \frac{30}{54}$

$\frac{5}{9} \stackrel{?}{=} \frac{30}{54}$ ← Write a proportion. →

$5 \cdot 54 \stackrel{?}{=} 9 \cdot 30$ ← Write cross products. →

$270 = 270$ ← Multiply. →

Yes, $\frac{5}{9}$ and $\frac{30}{54}$ form a proportion.

b. $\frac{7}{8}, \frac{55}{65}$

$\frac{7}{8} \stackrel{?}{=} \frac{55}{65}$

$7 \cdot 65 \stackrel{?}{=} 8 \cdot 55$

$455 \neq 440$

No, $\frac{7}{8}$ and $\frac{55}{65}$ do not form a proportion.

2. ✔ *Try It Out* Which pairs of ratios could form a proportion?

a. $\frac{3}{8}, \frac{6}{16}$ b. $\frac{6}{9}, \frac{4}{6}$ c. $\frac{4}{8}, \frac{5}{9}$ d. $\frac{6}{10}, \frac{9}{15}$

2 Solving Proportions

You can use cross products to solve a proportion that contains a variable.

Physical Science **Use the data at the right. Round your answers to the nearest pound.**

28. NASA designed two *Viking* spacecraft to travel to Mars and send information about the planet back to Earth. *Viking 1* weighed 275 lb and *Viking 2* weighed 272 lb on Earth. Use proportions to find how much they weighed on Mars.

29. *Open-ended* Choose three other planets. Find how much each *Viking* spacecraft would have weighed on each planet.

Weight Comparison Chart	
Planet	Weight (lb)
Earth	100
Mercury	37
Venus	88
Mars	38
Jupiter	264
Saturn	115
Uranus	117
Neptune	118
Pluto	5

Mixed Review

Find the mean and median of each set of data. *(Lesson 1-4)*

30. 14 20 5 17 15 16 17 18 13 17

31. 2.7 3.5 7.8 9 2.1 3.2 5.7 5 6.9

Compare. Use >, <, or =. *(Lesson 4-3)*

32. $\frac{3}{4}$ ▦ $\frac{5}{16}$ 33. $\frac{3}{5}$ ▦ $\frac{2}{3}$ 34. $\frac{1}{2}$ ▦ $\frac{7}{14}$ 35. $\frac{8}{12}$ ▦ $\frac{4}{6}$ 36. $\frac{1}{5}$ ▦ $\frac{2}{12}$ 37. $\frac{6}{8}$ ▦ $\frac{5}{9}$

38. *Choose a Strategy* Jenny, Bruce, and Mia ate salad, chicken, or tofu for lunch. Mia didn't eat chicken or tofu. Bruce didn't eat chicken. What did each person eat?

✓ CHECKPOINT 1   *Lessons 6-1 through 6-3*

Write two ratios equal to each ratio.

1. $2 : 50$ 2. $\frac{3}{5}$ 3. 4 to 12   4. $\frac{6}{9}$ 5. $\frac{20}{3}$ 6. $100 : 25$

Solve each proportion.

7. $\frac{3}{8} = \frac{57}{d}$ 8. $\frac{4}{3} = \frac{m}{21}$ 9. $\frac{x}{15} = \frac{5}{6}$ 10. $\frac{30}{c} = \frac{5}{4}$ 11. $\frac{15}{20} = \frac{4}{t}$ 12. $\frac{21}{7} = \frac{g}{20}$

13. **Choose A, B, C, or D.** Which has the most calories per ounce?

   A. beef: 185 calories in 3 ounces   B chicken: 240 calories in 6.2 ounces
   C. cheese: 230 calories in 2 ounces   D. yogurt: 230 calories in 8 ounces

14. *Travel* A train in Japan takes 50 min to travel 106.3 mi from Morica to Sendi. Suppose a train travels 416 mi from Washington, D.C., to Boston, MA, at the same rate. How long would the trip take? Round to the nearest minute.

6-4 Using Similar Figures

What You'll Learn

1 To discover the properties of similar figures

2 To use proportions to find missing lengths in similar figures

...And Why

Proportions and similar triangles can help you find lengths that you cannot measure directly.

Here's How

Look for questions that
- build understanding
- ✔ check understanding

THINK AND DISCUSS

1 Discovering Properties of Similar Figures

The word **similar** is often used in everyday language to compare things. Explore the figures below to discover the mathematical definition of similar.

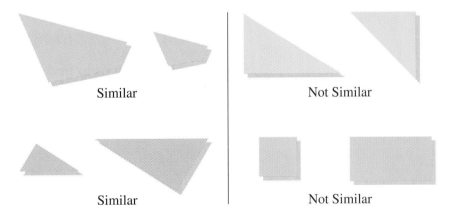

Similar   Not Similar

Similar   Not Similar

1. a. ▪ *Visual Thinking* Are similar figures the same shape?
   b. Do similar figures have to be the same size?

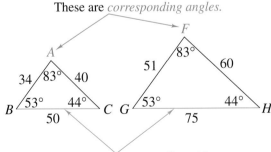

These are *corresponding angles.*

These are *corresponding sides.*

2. a. Look at the similar triangles at the left. What appears to be true of corresponding angles?
   b. List the pairs of corresponding angles.
   c. ▪ *Draw a Conclusion* Complete the sentence: The measures of the corresponding angles of similar figures are ___?___ .

△ABC refers to triangle ABC. You write the segment from B to C as $\overline{BC}$.

3. a. List all the pairs of corresponding sides of the triangles.
   b. Write the ratios of the length of each side of △ABC to the length of the corresponding side of △FGH. What is true of these ratios?
   c. ▪ *Draw a Conclusion* Complete the sentence: The ratios of the lengths of corresponding sides of similar figures are ___?___ .

SIMILAR FIGURES

Similar figures have two important properties.

● The corresponding angles have the same measure.

● The ratios of the lengths of corresponding sides are equal.

The symbol for *is similar to* is ~. For the triangles on page 245 you can write $\triangle ABC \sim \triangle FGH$. The length of $\overline{AB}$, written AB, is the distance from A to B.

▼ Finding Measures Using Proportions

You can use proportions to find missing measures in similar figures since the corresponding sides are proportional.

■ EXAMPLE 1

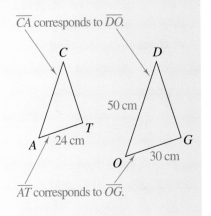

$\triangle CAT \sim \triangle DOG$. Find CA.

$\dfrac{CA}{DO} = \dfrac{AT}{OG}$ ◄—— Write a proportion.

$\dfrac{x}{50} = \dfrac{24}{30}$ ◄—— Substitute.

$30x = 50 \cdot 24$ ◄—— Write the cross products.

$\dfrac{30x}{30} = \dfrac{1{,}200}{30}$ ◄—— Divide each side by 30.

$x = 40$ ◄—— Solve for *x*.

$\overline{CA}$ corresponds to $\overline{DO}$.

$\overline{AT}$ corresponds to $\overline{OG}$.

CA is 40 cm.

4. ✔ *Try It Out* Use the diagram in Example 1.
   a. AT corresponds to ■.
   b. $\dfrac{AT}{OG} = \dfrac{CT}{■}$
   c. Suppose CT is 36 cm. Find the length of its corresponding side.
   d. Is the ratio of the perimeters of $\triangle CAT$ and $\triangle DOG$ equal to the ratio of a pair of corresponding sides? Explain.

Gottfried Liebniz (1646–1716) was the first person to use the symbol ~ to mean similarity. He taught himself Latin at age 8 and began studying Greek at age 12.

Source: *The History of Mathematics*

You can use proportions and similar triangles to measure distances that you would be unable to measure directly.

■ **EXAMPLE 2**   *Real-World Problem Solving*

Measurement A 6-ft-tall man standing near a geyser has a shadow 4.5 ft long. The geyser has a shadow 15 ft long. What is the height of the geyser?

Draw and label a diagram.

x corresponds to 6 ft.

$\frac{x}{6} = \frac{15}{4.5}$ ⟵ Write a proportion.

$4.5x = 6 \cdot 15$ ⟵ Write the cross products.

$\frac{4.5x}{4.5} = \frac{6 \cdot 15}{4.5}$ ⟵ Divide each side by 4.5.

$x = 20$ ⟵ Solve for *x*.

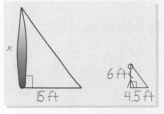

15 ft corresponds to 4.5 ft.

The height of the geyser is 20 ft.

5. ✔ *Try It Out* Suppose a 6-ft-tall man has a shadow 5 ft long and a geyser has a shadow 30 ft long. How tall is the geyser?

Work Together

Exploring Similar Rectangles

Similar figures can nest inside of each other like the rectangles at the right. The diagonals of similar figures will align.

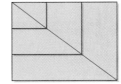

6. **a.** Draw rectangles with the dimensions 2 in. by 3 in., 4 in. by 5 in., 1 in. by $1\frac{1}{2}$ in., 4 in. by 6 in., and 6 in. by $7\frac{1}{2}$ in.

b. ▪*Analyze* Cut out the rectangles and stack them to determine which rectangles are similar. Make a list for each group of similar rectangles.

c. Use proportions to confirm that the rectangles in each of your lists are similar.

1. Judging by appearance, is *LMNO ~ PQRS*? Justify your answer.

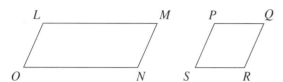

Explain why each pair of figures *are* similar or *are not* similar.

2.

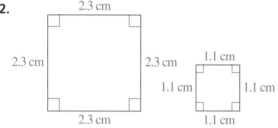

3.

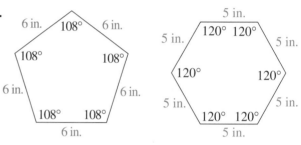

4.

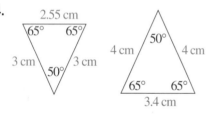

5.

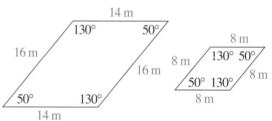

6. △*ABC ~* △*PQR*. Complete.
  a. ∠*A* corresponds to __?__ .
  b. ∠*Q* corresponds to __?__ .
  c. $\overline{AC}$ corresponds to __?__ .
  d. $\overline{PQ}$ corresponds to __?__ .
  e. What is the ratio of the lengths of the corresponding sides?

C

21

R

14

B

12

Q

A

P 8

7. *Writing* Give three examples of real-world objects that are similar.

8. *Social Studies* Students at the Horace Mann Middle School want to enlarge a copy of the flag of the Philippines. To enlarge the flag so that the longest side measures 6 ft, how wide will the students need to make the flag?

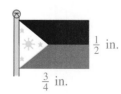

$\frac{1}{2}$ in.

$\frac{3}{4}$ in.

Philippines

9.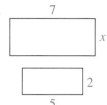

10.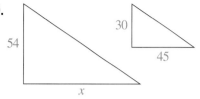

11.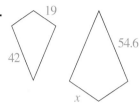

12. Isabel wants to know the height of a Saguaro cactus. The triangle formed by the cactus and its shadow is similar to the triangle Isabel forms with her shadow. How tall is the cactus?

13. *Reasoning* The ratio of the corresponding sides of two similar triangles is 4 : 9. The sides of the smaller triangle are 10 cm, 16 cm, and 18 cm. Find the perimeter of the larger triangle.

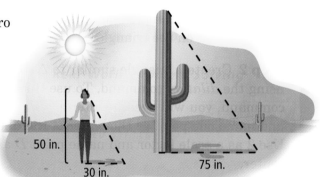

Mixed Review

Solve each equation. *(Lesson 3-6)*

14. $x - 4 = -12$ **15.** $-8 = y + 6$ **16.** $p - (-2) = 5$ **17.** $11 = 17 + q$

Write each number as an improper fraction. *(Lesson 4-8)*

18. $3\frac{1}{5}$ **19.** $2\frac{3}{4}$ **20.** $3\frac{7}{8}$ **21.** $2\frac{1}{6}$ **22.** $4\frac{5}{12}$ **23.** $3\frac{4}{7}$

24. *Estimation* Keisha earns $4.95 an hour and works 19 hours a week. Estimate her pay for the week. *(Lesson 2-2)*

CHAPTER PROJECT

PROJECT LINK: GRAPHING

Use the survey results from the Project Link on page 236. Decide which type of graph will best display your results. Then graph your data. Add a title and any other necessary information to your graph.

You can use the GCF to find the scale of a drawing.

■ **EXAMPLE 2**   *Real-World Problem Solving*

Drafting The actual length of the wheel base for the all-terrain vehicle is 234 cm. Find the scale of the drawing.

$$\frac{\text{scale length}}{\text{actual length}} \longrightarrow \frac{3}{234} = \frac{1}{78} \longleftarrow \begin{array}{l}\text{Divide both measures} \\ \text{by the GCF, 3.}\end{array}$$

The scale is 1 cm : 78 cm.

234 cm

2. ✔ *Try It Out* Suppose the length of a room in an architectural drawing is 10 in. Its actual length is 15 ft. What is the scale of the drawing? (*Hint:* Convert feet to inches before finding the scale.)

Work Together
Exploring Scale Drawings

Work in a group. Make a scale drawing of your classroom.

3. ▪Reasoning How did you decide on the scale for your drawing?

4. ▪Analyze Compare your group's drawing with those of other groups. Do the scale drawings have the same shape even if the scales are not the same? Explain.

EXERCISES *On Your Own*

The scale of a map is 2 cm : 15 km. Find the actual distances for the following map distances.

1. 8 cm   **2.** 1.3 cm   **3.** 5 mm   **4.** 24.4 cm   **5.** 8 mm   **6.** 15.5 cm

A scale drawing has a scale of $\frac{1}{2}$ in. : 10 ft. Find the length on the drawing for each actual length.

7. 20 ft   **8.** 15 ft   **9.** 5 ft   **10.** 45 ft   **11.** $1\frac{1}{2}$ ft   **12.** 13.5 ft

13. *Reasoning* Ramon is drawing a map of his town on a sheet of paper that is 11 in. × 17 in. From east to west the town is 13 mi. From north to south the town is 19 mi. To make the map as large as possible, what scale should Ramon use?

14. *Architecture* The scale drawing shows the first floor of a house. The dimensions of the carport are 20 ft by 25 ft.
    a. Complete: The scale is ■ : 5 ft.
    b. Copy the floor plan on your paper. Write the actual dimensions in place of the scale dimensions.

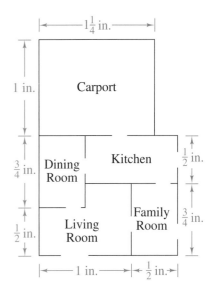

15. *Writing* Describe what you would do to draw a map of the route from your home to school. What scale would you use?

16. *Research* Find an item that someone would want a scale drawing of.
    a. Make a scale drawing of your item. Include the scale on the drawing.
    b. Write a paragraph describing the item and the reasons a scale drawing of it is useful.

17. *Geography* The cities of Indianapolis, Indiana, and Brownsville, Texas, are 1,166 mi apart.
    a. A map of the United States has a scale of 1 in. : 250 mi. How far apart are the cities on the map?
    b. Suppose the cities are 6 in. apart on a map. What is the scale of the map?

Far-Out Clothes

Computers help designers improve space suits for future space travelers.

Clothes designed for space must allow astronauts to move and breathe in an airless environment. An astronaut's suit must protect the astronaut from the sun's harsh rays.

For a computer image that is $\frac{1}{8}$ of the actual size, the designer knows that all other dimensions will have the same ratio.

Use the article for Exercises 18 and 19.

18. Suppose the computer image of the pants of a space suit is 5 in. long. How long are the pants?

19. An astronaut's arm is 24 in. long. Find the arm length in the computer image for a space suit.

Measure the length of the segment shown in each figure. Find the scale of each drawing.

20.

|← 30 in. →|

21.

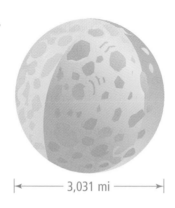

|← 3,031 mi →|

22.

|← 2.5 cm →|

Mixed Review

23. *Geometry* Find the values of x and y in the similar triangles at the right. *(Lesson 6-4)*

Solve each equation. *(Lesson 3-9)*

24. $3x + 2 = 17$ **25.** $\frac{x}{5} + 5 = 21$ **26.** $2a - 4 = -8$

27. *Choose a Strategy* Jordan has a collection of nickels, dimes, and quarters totaling 8 coins. More than $\frac{1}{2}$ of his coins are quarters and less than $\frac{1}{4}$ are dimes. What are the possible amounts of money Jordan has?

Math at Work

AMUSEMENT PARK DESIGNER

An amusement park designer considers the architecture and technology of the rides, the landscape of the park, lighting, and sound. To create exciting rides and interesting fun parks, a designer creates scale drawings and models.

Find out more about amusement park opportunities at this Web site:
http://www.napha.org

Choose the best answer.

1. A blue shark swam 7.26 miles in ten minutes. What is the speed of the shark in miles per hour (mi/h)?

   A. 0.726 mi/h   B. 43.56 mi/h
   C. 48.16 mi/h   D. 72.6 mi/h

2. Carlos bought school supplies with a $10 bill. He received $1.82 in change. How much did the supplies cost?

   F. $8.18   G. $8.28
   H. $9.28   J. $11.82

3. Franklin volunteers time at the local library. Before returning books to the shelves, he puts them in order from least to greatest book number. Which list shows the correct order?

   A. 808.81, 808.8, 813.082, 813
   B. 808.81, 808.8, 813, 813.082
   C. 813.082, 813, 808.81, 808.8
   D. 808.8, 808.81, 813, 813.082

4. Sandra scored 97, 88, 79 and 92 on four math tests. What was her mean (average) score?

   F. 84   G. 89   H. 91   J. 92

5. On Monday, 30 students were in math class. On Tuesday, only 25 students were in math class. What is the ratio of Tuesday's attendance to Monday's attendance?

   A. 6 to 5   B. 5 to 6   C. 5 to 11   D. 11 to 5

6. Litisha went to 12 movies in three months. Each movie admission cost $5.25. Which is the best estimate of the total amount Litisha paid for admission?

   F. $50   G. $55   H. $60   J. $70

Please note that items 7–10 have *five* answer choices.

7. For a party, Andrew paid $1.29 for streamers, $.39 for each package of balloons, $2.58 for two gallons of fruit punch, and $1.35 each for four packages of crackers. What additional information do you need to find how much Andrew spent?

   A. the price of one gallon of punch
   B. the number of packages of balloons
   C. the number of packages of streamers
   D. the price of two packages of cookies
   E. the number of students in the class

8. Carmela cut a length of ribbon into three equal pieces. Each piece measured $\frac{3}{4}$ yd. How long was the original length of ribbon?

   F. $\frac{1}{4}$ yd   G. $1\frac{1}{2}$ yd
   H. $2\frac{1}{4}$ yd   J. 3 yd
   K. Not Here

9. Which of the following is true for the given data? 1, 2, 5, 3, 9, 7, 2

   A. mean < mode   B. median < mean
   C. mode > median   D. mean = mode
   E. median = mean

10. Luisa was reading a biography for her history class. After five days she had read 325 pages. On the sixth day, Luisa read 57 pages. A reasonable conclusion would be that Luisa read —

   F. less than 50 pages each day
   G. between 50 and 60 pages each day
   H. between 55 and 65 pages each day
   J. more than 60 pages each day
   K. Not Here

What You'll Learn

1. To model percents
2. To write percents using equal ratios

...And Why

Reporters use percents to describe consumer trends.

Here's How

Look for questions that
- build understanding
- ✔ check understanding

THINK AND DISCUSS

1 *Modeling Percents*

A **percent** is a ratio that compares a number to 100. You can write the ratio $\frac{25}{100}$ as 25%.

■ EXAMPLE 1

The figure at the right contains 100 squares. Write a ratio and a percent to describe each shaded part.

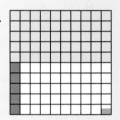

yellow: $\frac{50}{100} = 50\%$ blue: $\frac{5}{100} = 5\%$

red: $\frac{0.5}{100} = 0.5\%$

1. ■ **Go a Step Further** Write a ratio and a percent to describe the unshaded part of the figure in Example 1.

You can model percents even when you divide a figure into fewer than 100 parts.

QUICKreview

To find equal ratios, multiply the numerator and denominator by the same non-zero number.

$$\frac{a}{b} = \frac{a \cdot c}{b \cdot c}$$

■ EXAMPLE 2

What percent does each shaded area represent?

a.
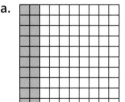

b.
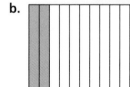

c.
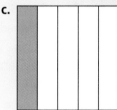

a. $\frac{20}{100} = 20\%$ b. $\frac{2}{10} = \frac{20}{100} = 20\%$ c. $\frac{1}{5} = \frac{20}{100} = 20\%$

2. ✔ **Try It Out** What percent does the shaded area represent in the figure at the right?

You use more than one figure to model percents greater than 100%.

Biology The number of nesting pairs of bald eagles in the lower 48 states increased 185% between 1963 and 1981. Draw a model to represent 185%.

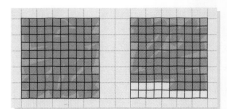

1. Draw two figures.
2. Shade one whole figure. Shade 85% of the second figure.

3. ✔ *Try It Out* Between 1981 and 1994 the number of nesting pairs of bald eagles increased 275%. Use graph paper to model 275%.

▼2 *Writing Percents Using Equal Ratios*

Other than 1, the factors of 100 are 2, 4, 5, 10, 20, 25, and 50. Ratios that have these numbers as the denominator are easy to write as percents by finding equal ratios.

■ **EXAMPLE 4**

Write $\frac{3}{5}$ as a percent.

$$\frac{3}{5} = \frac{3 \cdot 20}{5 \cdot 20} \longleftarrow \text{Since } 5 \cdot 20 = 100, \text{ use } 20 \text{ to write a ratio equal to } \frac{3}{5}.$$

$$= \frac{60}{100} \longleftarrow \text{Multiply.}$$

$$= 60\% \longleftarrow \text{Write as a percent.}$$

4. ✔ *Try It Out* Write each ratio as a percent.

   a. $\frac{6}{25}$ b. $\frac{3}{4}$ c. $\frac{1}{50}$ d. $\frac{19}{20}$

5. ⚬ *Go a Step Further* According to a news report, the prices on consumer goods rose a tenth of a percent during the month of March. Write the percent in numerals.

Write the percent of each figure that is shaded.

1.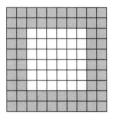

2.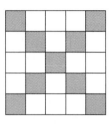

3.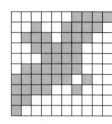

4.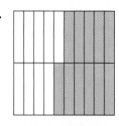

5.

6.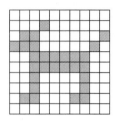

7.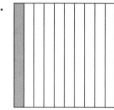

8.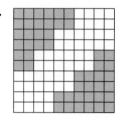

Find what percent of a dollar each set of coins makes.

9. 2 quarters

10. 5 quarters and 2 dimes

11. 3 quarters, 2 dimes, and 1 nickel

Estimate the percent that is shaded in each figure.

12.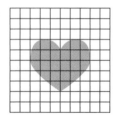

13.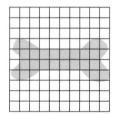

14.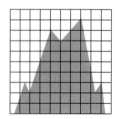

15.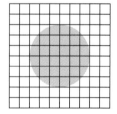

Draw figures on 10 × 10 squares of graph paper to represent each of the following percents.

16. 234%   17. 17%   18. 35%   19. 78%   20. 187%   21. 10%

22. 1.5%   23. 65.5%   24. 115%   25. 8%   26. 25%   27. 90.5%

28. a. *Open-ended* Draw and shade the first letter of your name on a 10 × 10 square of graph paper so that *more than* 30% is shaded.

   b. Draw and shade the last letter of your name on a 10 × 10 square of graph paper so that *less than* 30% is shaded.

29. *Writing* Describe one situation that requires a percent less than 1% and one that requires a percent greater than 100%.

Write each ratio as a percent.

30. $\frac{19}{25}$ **31.** $\frac{3}{5}$ **32.** $\frac{1}{2}$ **33.** $\frac{21}{25}$ **34.** $\frac{7}{10}$ **35.** $\frac{7}{20}$

36. $\frac{24}{25}$ **37.** $\frac{4}{5}$ **38.** $\frac{1}{4}$ **39.** $\frac{3}{10}$ **40.** $\frac{3}{25}$ **41.** $\frac{1}{5}$

42. $\frac{11}{20}$ **43.** $\frac{7}{8}$ **44.** $\frac{9}{50}$ **45.** $\frac{2}{5}$ **46.** $\frac{9}{10}$ **47.** $\frac{7}{50}$

48. a. What percent of the square at the right does the yellow part represent? the green part?
   b. Write ratios to represent each section.

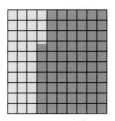

Write each percent in numerals.

49. *Money* Over a six-month period the price of gasoline rose six tenths of a percent.

50. *Education* Between 1974 and 1994 the cost of four years of education at a public university rose almost one hundred thirty-four percent.

51. *Volunteering* Since 1984, job inquiries to the Peace Corps have increased one hundred seventy-six percent.

Mixed Review

Find each sum or difference. *(Lesson 5-3)*

52. $7\frac{4}{5} + 9\frac{7}{10}$ **53.** $17\frac{2}{9} - 12\frac{1}{3}$ **54.** $8\frac{1}{12} + 12\frac{6}{11}$ **55.** $21\frac{2}{5} + 15\frac{1}{4}$ **56.** $9\frac{3}{11} - 8\frac{3}{8}$

Complete. *(Lessons 3-3, 3-4, and 3-5)*

57. $-4 \cdot 3 = 3 \cdot \blacksquare$ **58.** $5 - (-2) = 5 + \blacksquare$ **59.** $4 + 7 + (-4) = 7 + \blacksquare$

60. *Automobiles* The gas tank of Gina's car holds 13.5 gal of gas. The gas tank of Karen's car holds 13.25 gal of gas. Whose car holds more gas? How many more quarts of gas does it hold? *(Lessons 2-1 and 5-8)*

61. *Choose a Strategy* Seven teams are in the tennis-doubles playoffs. Each team plays every other team twice. What is the total number of matches played?

Percents, Fractions, and Decimals

THINK AND DISCUSS

▼ **1** Rewriting Percents and Fractions

You can write any ratio or fraction as a percent.

■ **EXAMPLE 1** *Real-World Problem Solving*

Nutrition Forty-five calories in a slice of cheese pizza are from fat. There are 160 total calories in a slice of cheese pizza. What percent of the calories are from fat?

$$\frac{45}{160} = 45 \div 160 \quad \longleftarrow \text{Write the ratio as a division sentence.}$$

$$= 0.28125 \quad \longleftarrow \text{Divide.}$$

$$= 28.125\% \quad \longleftarrow \text{Express as a percent.}$$

Fat accounts for about 28% of the calories in one slice of cheese pizza.

1. ✔ *Try It Out* Write each fraction as a percent.

   a. $\frac{8}{25}$ **b.** $\frac{3}{5}$ **c.** $\frac{9}{75}$ **d.** $\frac{45}{50}$

You can rewrite a percent as a fraction.

■ **EXAMPLE 2** *Real-World Problem Solving*

Biology An elephant sleeps about 15% of a day. What fraction of a day does an elephant sleep?

$$15\% = \frac{15}{100} \quad \longleftarrow \begin{array}{l}\text{Write 15\% as a fraction with 100}\\\text{as the denominator.}\end{array}$$

$$= \frac{15 \div 5}{100 \div 5} \quad \longleftarrow \begin{array}{l}\text{Divide the numerator and}\\\text{denominator by the GCF, 5.}\end{array}$$

$$= \frac{3}{20} \quad \longleftarrow \text{Simplify the fraction.}$$

An elephant sleeps about $\frac{3}{20}$ of every day.

2. ✔ *Try It Out* Express each percent as a fraction in simplest form.

   a. 95%   **b.** 8%   **c.** 79%   **d.** 4.5%

Need Help? For practice in multiplying or dividing by a power of 10, see Skills Handbook p. 538.

▼ *Percents and Decimals*

To write a decimal as a percent, multiply it by 100, or move the decimal point two places to the right.

$$0.45 \times 100 \longrightarrow 0.45. \longrightarrow 45\%$$

■ EXAMPLE 3

Write each decimal as a percent. Round to the nearest tenth of a percent, if necessary.

a. 0.4 $0.4 \times 100 = 40$, so $0.4 = 40\%$

b. 0.7593 $0.7593 \times 100 = 75.93$, so $0.7593 = 75.9\%$

c. 1.05 $1.05 \times 100 = 105$, so $1.05 = 105\%$

3. ✔*Try It Out* Write each decimal as a percent.
   a. 0.31   b. 0.67328   c. 2.34   d. 0.001

To write a percent as a decimal, divide it by 100, or move the decimal point two places to the left.

$$264.5\% \longrightarrow 264.5 \div 100 \longrightarrow 2.64.5 \longrightarrow 2.645$$

■ EXAMPLE 4

Write each percent as a decimal.

a. 2% $2 \div 100 = 0.02$, so $2\% = 0.02$

b. 67.5% $67.5 \div 100 = 0.675$, so $67.5\% = 0.675$

c. 125% $125 \div 100 = 1.25$, so $125\% = 1.25$

4. ✔*Try It Out* Write each percent as a decimal.
   a. 3%   b. 0.7%   c. 98%   d. 275%

EXERCISES *On Your Own*

Choose **Use paper and pencil or mental math to write each percent as a fraction in simplest form.**

1. 45%	**2.** 62.5%	**3.** 180%	**4.** 12%	**5.** 6%	**6.** 20%
7. 7.5%	**8.** 240%	**9.** 0.1%	**10.** 56%	**11.** 85%	**12.** 37.5%

13. **Choose A, B, C, or D.** Use the figure at the right. Which set of numbers below represents the shaded area?

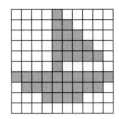

A. $3.8\%, \frac{38}{100}, 0.38$ B. $38\%, \frac{38}{100}, 0.38$

C. $38\%, \frac{38}{100}, 0.038$ D. $0.38\%, \frac{38}{100}, 0.038$

Write each fraction as a percent. Round to the nearest tenth of a percent, if necessary.

14. $\frac{27}{50}$ 15. $\frac{17}{20}$ 16. $\frac{33}{40}$ 17. $\frac{5}{8}$

18. $\frac{8}{50}$ 19. $\frac{19}{4}$ 20. $\frac{125}{625}$ 21. $\frac{101}{100}$

22. $\frac{18}{36}$ 23. $\frac{7}{8}$ 24. $\frac{3}{17}$ 25. $\frac{6}{10}$

26. $\frac{67}{68}$ 27. $\frac{4}{50}$ 28. $\frac{8}{5}$ 29. $\frac{10}{12}$

30. *Nutrition* Runners usually eat foods high in carbohydrates before a race. A gram of fat has 9 calories. A gram of protein and a gram of carbohydrates each have 4 calories.
    a. How many calories does one serving of macaroni and cheese have? How many does one serving of spaghetti with meatballs have?
    b. What percent of the calories in each meal is carbohydrates? Round to the nearest percent.
    c. Which meal is the better choice for a runner? Why?

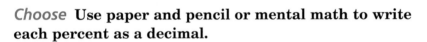

31. *Writing* Does 0.4 equal 0.4%? Explain.

Choose **Use paper and pencil or mental math to write each percent as a decimal.**

32. 130%   33. 32%   34. 2.5%   35. 88%   36. 125%   37. 345%

38. 34.678%   39. 3%   40. 0.95%   41. 12%   42. 19.1%   43. 0.09%

44. *Nutrition* The Deluxe brand vitamin tablet supplies 0.5% of the *recommended daily allowance* (RDA) for phosphorus.
    a. Write the percent as a fraction.
    b. Write the percent as a decimal.
    c. Which way do you prefer to see the number for the Recommended Daily Allowance for phosphorus, as a fraction, as a decimal, or as a percent? Why?

Mental Math **Write each number as a percent.**

45. 0.5   **46.** 0.9002   **47.** 0.0028   **48.** 1.25

49. 0.0033   **50.** 2.89   **51.** 0.375   **52.** 2.5

53. 0.987   **54.** 10.05   **55.** 0.009   **56.** 0.155

57. 10   **58.** 0.00675   **59.** 67.8   **60.** 37.5

61. *Nutrition* The label at the right gives nutritional information for one serving of oatmeal.
  a. Write each percent as a fraction and as a decimal.
  b. How many servings of oatmeal would you need to eat in order to have all the recommended vitamin A for a day?

62. *Open-ended* Find five examples of percents used in a newspaper. Display your examples in class.

Grandma's Oatmeal	
Nutrient	**RDA***
Iron	10%
Calcium	15%
Vitamin A	4%
Vitamin C	2%
Sodium	3%
*With ½ c. fortified skim milk	

Mixed Review

Find the number with the given prime factorization.
(Lessons 4-4 and 4-5)

63. $5^2 \cdot 7^2$ **64.** $2^4 \cdot 3$ **65.** $2 \cdot 5^3 \cdot 13$ **66.** $2^2 \cdot 5 \cdot 7$ **67.** $3 \cdot 5^2$

Solve. *(Lesson 3-7)*

68. $-13t = 52$ **69.** $-5x = -30$ **70.** $-2 = \frac{x}{24}$ **71.** $2f = -9$ **72.** $\frac{g}{-17} = -51$

73. *Choose a Strategy* There are 43 students in the chorus. Ten of them also play in the orchestra. There are 52 students in the orchestra. Eight orchestra members belong to both the chorus and the chess club. How many students belong to both the orchestra and the chorus but *not* to the chess club?

PROJECT LINK: CALCULATING

Use the results of your survey from the Project Link on page 236. Write ratios of the number of people who prefer each ride to the total number of people surveyed. Find the percent of people who prefer each ride.

6-8 Use Multiple Strategies

Problem Solving Strategies

Draw a Diagram
Guess and Test
Look for a Pattern
Make a Model
Make a Table
Simulate a Problem
Solve a Simpler Problem
Too Much or Too Little
  Information
Use Logical Reasoning
✓ Use Multiple Strategies
Work Backward
Write an Equation

THINK AND DISCUSS

Sometimes you may need to use more than one strategy to solve a problem.

SAMPLE PROBLEM..

Jack and his cousin Sam live in Texas. Their homes are 40 mi apart. One day, Jack suggested that they ride their bicycles to a state park halfway between their homes. Sam averages 10 mi/h on his bicycle, and Jack averages 12 mi/h. To meet at 1 P.M., what time should each boy leave home?

....

READ

Read for understanding. Summarize the problem.

Read the problem carefully.

1. **a.** How far apart do Jack and Sam live?
   b. What rate does each boy average when riding his bicycle?

PLAN

Decide on a strategy.

Decide on strategies.

Write an equation to find how long each boy should ride. Work backward to find what time each boy should leave his home.

SOLVE

Try the strategy.

Each boy travels halfway, which is 20 mi. Let x represent the number of hours that Jack should ride his bicycle.

$$12x = 20$$
$$\frac{12x}{12} = \frac{20}{12}$$
$$x = 1\frac{2}{3}$$

Jack should ride his bicycle $1\frac{2}{3}$ h, which is 1 h 40 min.

Work backward to find what time Jack should leave home.

Jack should leave at 11:20 A.M.

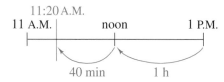

2. When should Sam leave his home to meet Jack?

LOOK BACK
Think about how you solved the problem.

3. Did you solve the problem correctly? Add the traveling time to the starting time for Jack and Sam. Will both boys arrive at the state park at 1:00 P.M.? You will have to think, "One hour past 12:00 can be expressed as 1:00 or 13:00."

EXERCISES *On Your Own*

Use multiple strategies to solve each problem. Show all your work.

1. a. A fenced-in rectangular area has a perimeter of 40 ft. The fence has a post every 4 ft. How many posts are there?
  b. There must be a post at each corner. What do you think the length and width of the field are?
  c. Are there any other possible answers to part (b)? Explain.

2. A kite and its tail total 27 ft in length. The tail is five times as long as the body. How long is the kite's tail?

3. A grocer stacks oranges in the shape of a square pyramid. How many oranges will she use if one side of the base has 6 oranges?

Use any strategy to solve each problem. Show your work.

4. *Consumer Issues* Susan, the Science Club treasurer, found that the bill for 18 sweatshirts ordered by the club had two digits blurred by water damage. Susan was sure that the first and last digits were the same. What do you think the total price is? Explain your choice.
    $■68.9■

5. *Social Studies* At the beginning of every new term, each of the nine judges on the Supreme Court shakes hands with every other judge. How many handshakes take place?

6. *Geometry* How many triangles are in the design at the right?

7. *Cooking* A recipe that makes 2 dozen raisin bars calls for $\frac{3}{4}$ c. of flour. How much flour will be needed to make 5 dozen?

Aerodynamics The smaller the ratio of the weight of a kite to its surface area, the better the kite will fly.

8. *Jobs* Carla and Tanya were paid $45.00 for painting a fence. Carla worked 6 h, and Tanya worked 9 h. How much is Tanya's share of the money?

9. *Patterns* Examine the list at the right and look for a pattern.
 a. Write the sixth row.
 b. What is the last number in the 11th row? in the 23rd row?
 c. What is the sum of the numbers in the 4th row? in the 10th row?
 d. *Reasoning* How can you find the sum of any row when you know the row number?

row 1	1
row 2	1 3
row 3	1 3 5
row 4	1 3 5 7
row 5	1 3 5 7 9
row 6	■

10. *Money* Trevor has $8 in his savings account and adds $1 each week. Aretha has $12 in her savings account and adds $3 each week. After how many weeks will Aretha's account have twice as much money as Trevor's?

11. Alvin, Breon, and Carl work as an artist, a banker, and a conductor. Alvin and the artist play tennis together. The conductor helped Carl plant his garden. Breon is not the conductor, and he does not know Alvin. What does each person do for a living?

12. A box contains the five disks below. Suppose you draw three disks at random and add the numbers together. How many different totals are possible? What are they?

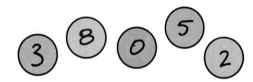

Mixed Review

Find each product. *(Lesson 5-5)*

13. $\frac{2}{5} \cdot \frac{5}{12}$ **14.** $\frac{6}{14} \cdot \frac{12}{18}$ **15.** $\frac{3}{7} \cdot 15$ **16.** $\frac{4}{5} \cdot 2\frac{3}{4}$ **17.** $2\frac{2}{3} \cdot 2\frac{1}{4}$

Write as a ratio in three ways. *(Lesson 6-1)*

18. 3 students to 8 students   **19.** 2 wins to 11 losses   **20.** 180 lb to 150 lb

21. a. Mariko found *s* shells on the beach. She shared them equally with her brother. The variable expression to show the number of shells each person had is $s \div$ ■.
 b. Evaluate the expression for $s = 14$. *(Lesson 3-1)*

6-9 Finding Percent of a Number

What You'll Learn

1 To use a percent to find part of a whole

2 To find discount prices

...And Why

Retail store managers use proportions and survey data to predict customer buying patterns.

Here's How

Look for questions that
- build understanding
- ✔ check understanding

THINK AND DISCUSS

1 *Using Percents to Find Part of a Whole*

You can use a graph to present percent data.

1. What did most people have on their gift list?

2. What do about $\frac{1}{3}$ of the people have on their list? $\frac{1}{4}$ of the people?

3. How many people answered the survey?

4. Why do you think the sum of the percents is greater than 100%?

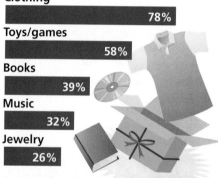

Gifts Holiday Shoppers Plan to Buy

Clothing — 78%
Toys/games — 58%
Books — 39%
Music — 32%
Jewelry — 26%

Survey of 1,012 adults
Source: *USA Today*

■ **EXAMPLE 1**   *Real-World Problem Solving*

Consumer Issues Use the graph above. Find the number of the people surveyed who have clothing on their gift lists.

$$78\% = 0.78 \quad \longleftarrow \text{Change the percent to a decimal.}$$

$$0.78 \times 1,012 = 789.36 \quad \longleftarrow \text{Multiply.}$$

About 789 people have clothing on their gift lists.

---

5. ✔ *Try It Out* Use the graph. About how many people have music on their gift list?

6. ■ *Go a Step Further* Would a department store manager be more interested in the percents or in the actual number of people who responded in each category? Explain.

7. a. Write 25% as a decimal and a fraction.
   b. Use both the decimal and the fraction to find 25% of 44.
   c. ■ *Reasoning* When would you use a decimal to find a percent? When would you use a fraction?

In 1996, toy sales in the United States totaled $20.7 billion, or about $357 per person. In Japan, toy sales totaled $7.9 billion, or about $390 per person.

Source: U.S. Toy Manufacturers Association

Price cut 40%

Was $24

2 Finding Discount Prices

Advertisements that say "40% off" or "Price reduced 40%" tell you the percent a price was reduced. This is the sale price or discount price.

■ **EXAMPLE 2**   *Real-World Problem Solving*

Consumer Issues Find the sale price of the telephone. Round to the nearest cent.

$100\% - 40\% = 60\%$ ◀── The sale price is 60% of the original price.

$60\% = 0.6$ ◀── Write the percent as a decimal.

$0.6 \times 24 = 14.4$ ◀── Multiply.

The sale price of the telephone is $14.40.

8. ✔ *Try It Out* Sneakers that cost $48.99 go on sale for 25% off.
   a. What percent of the original price is the sale price?
   b. What is the sale price? Round to the nearest cent.

EXERCISES *On Your Own*

Find each answer.

1. 6% of 90
2. 125% of 64
3. 12.5% of 56
4. 12% of 230
5. 75% of 240

6. 18% of 90
7. 3% of 12
8. 150% of 17
9. 7% of 300
10. 60% of 120

11. 11% of 121
12. 27% of 120
13. 98% of 65
14. 20% of 80
15. 15% of 45

▦ *Choose* **Use a calculator, paper and pencil, or mental math to solve each problem.**

16. Find 37.5% of 12.
17. What is 8% of 25?
18. Find 30% of 40.

19. What is 25% of 95?
20. Find 190% of 13.
21. What is 20% of 20?

22. Find 30% of 120.
23. Find 12% of 33.
24. What is 120% of 34?

25. *Social Studies* Mesa, Arizona, is one of the fastest-growing cities in the United States. In 1994, the population was almost 500% of its 1970 total of 63,000.
   a. Write an expression to find the population in 1994.
   b. Find the population in 1994.

26. a. *Reasoning* The number of students in this year's seventh grade class is 110% of the number in last year's class. When you write 110% as a ratio, what number is in the denominator? Why?

b. Do you think there will be more or fewer students in this year's class? Why?

c. There were 260 students in last year's class. How many students are in this year's class?

27. *Data Analysis* 150 high school students were surveyed about their foreign language classes. The graph at the right shows their responses.

a. How many students take French? What percent of the 150 students surveyed is that?

b. Find the percent of students taking each language.

c. *Estimation* The high school population is 2,500. Use the percents you found in parts (a) and (b). Estimate the total number of students at the school taking each language.

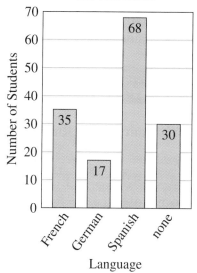

28. *Technology* The regular price of a calculator is $15.40. It is on sale for 30% off of the regular price. Find the sale price.

29. Choose A, B, C, or D. Which expression will *not* help you find the price of a $60 item on sale for 25% off?

A. $60 - 0.25(60)$ **B.** $0.75(60)$

C. $60(1 - 0.25)$ **D.** $60 - 0.75(60)$

Hobbies **Use the advertisement at the right for Exercises 30–33.**

30. a. What percent of the original price of the calico fabric is the sale price?

b. What is the sale price?

31. What is the sale price of the children's patterns?

32. Find the sale price of the scissors.

33. Which costs less on sale, the calico or the cotton knit fabric? How much less?

34. *Open-ended* Find a sale circular. Choose five items from the circular. Calculate the sale price of each item based on the original price of the item and the percent discount.

35. *Writing* Write a word problem about finding the sale price of an item. Solve your problem.

36. *Technology* The price of a new version of a computer game is 120% of the price of the original version. The original version cost $48. What is the cost of the new version?

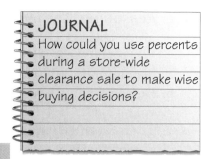

JOURNAL
How could you use percents during a store-wide clearance sale to make wise buying decisions?

Mixed Review

Write each fraction in simplest form. *(Lesson 4-6)*

37. $\frac{8}{10}$ **38.** $\frac{4}{12}$ **39.** $\frac{5}{100}$ **40.** $\frac{16}{24}$ **41.** $\frac{10}{70}$ **42.** $\frac{18}{54}$

Complete. *(Lesson 5-8)*

43. 6 ft 3 in. = ▧ ft   **44.** 4 lb 2 oz = ▧ oz   **45.** $5\frac{1}{2}$ c = ▧ fl oz   **46.** 3 yd = ▧ ft

47. *Choose a Strategy* A student spends $\frac{3}{8}$ of her money on a sweatshirt and $\frac{1}{2}$ of the remaining amount on a cassette. She now has $15. How much money did she have originally?

✓ CHECKPOINT 2   *Lessons 6-4 through 6-9*

Write each fraction as a percent.

1. $\frac{4}{5}$ **2.** $\frac{1}{250}$ **3.** $\frac{1}{3}$ **4.** $\frac{14}{25}$ **5.** $\frac{13}{25}$ **6.** $\frac{3}{15}$

Write each percent as a decimal and as a fraction.

7. 17%   **8.** 29%   **9.** 135%   **10.** 77%   **11.** 98%   **12.** 45%

Find each answer.

13. What is 29% of 58?   **14.** 60 is what percent of 35?   **15.** What is 90% of 16?

16. *Geometry* $\triangle ABC \sim \triangle FDE$. Find x and y.

17. *Maps* A map's scale is 1 in. : 15 mi. Two towns are 3.5 in. apart on the map. What is the actual distance?

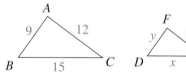

18. A club has 100 members. Each of the 5 officers calls 6 other members to help them decorate for a club party. What percent of the club members help decorate?

6-10

Using Proportions with Percents

What You'll Learn

1 To find what percent one number is of another

2 To find a number when you know a percent and a part

...And Why

Business people use percents to advertise sales.

Here's How

Look for questions that
⬛ build understanding
✔ check understanding

THINK AND DISCUSS

1 *Finding a Percent*

You can use models to understand the relationship of one number to another. You can use your model to write a proportion to express the relationship as a percent.

⬛ **EXAMPLE 1** *Real-World Problem Solving*

Hiking Eighteen students in a class of 25 students plan to go on a class hiking trip. What percent of the students plan to go on the trip?

Model the relationship.

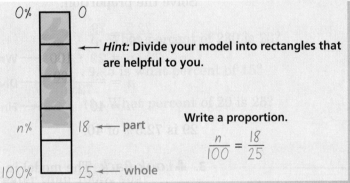

0%   0

← *Hint:* **Divide your model into rectangles that are helpful to you.**

n%   18 ← part   **Write a proportion.**
$$\frac{n}{100} = \frac{18}{25}$$
100%   25 ← whole

Solve the proportion.

$$\frac{n}{100} = \frac{18}{25}$$ ← Simplify by multiplying each side by 100.

$$n = \frac{1800}{25}$$ ← Divide.

$$n = 72$$

72% of the class plan to go on the trip.

1. **⬛Look Back** The model in Example 1 has five equal rectangles. What percent does each rectangle represent?

2. **✔Try It Out** Draw a model for each problem. Then solve.
   a. What percent of 90 is 36?
   b. What percent of 60 is 15?

7. ▲ *Think About It* Find each percent of change. State whether the change is an increase or a decrease.
   a. 5 to 2   **b.** 7 to 9   **c.** 6 to 14   **d.** 19 to 3

Work Together

Exploring Percent of Change

Work in pairs. Measure the length of a rubber band. Hang several different weights on the rubber band, one at a time, and measure the new length of the rubber band each time.

8. Record your results in a table. Make a graph of the data of weights to length of the rubber band.

9. Find the percent of change in the rubber band's length for each weight. Round to the nearest percent.

EXERCISES *On Your Own*

Find each percent of increase. Round to the nearest tenth.

1. 60 to 75   **2.** 88 to 99   **3.** 120 to 240   **4.** 75 to 90   **5.** 15 to 35

6. 2 to 7   **7.** 12 to 63   **8.** 15 to 18   **9.** 120 to 125   **10.** 0.6 to 2.2

11. 15 to 60   **12.** 135 to 200   **13.** 4 to 5   **14.** 12 to 18   **15.** $13\frac{1}{2}$ to 25

16. *Business* The Tots and Tykes Toy Store opened five years ago. The owner uses a computer to track yearly income, but the program she uses has a bug. Some cells print @@@ instead of numbers. Copy and complete the spreadsheet.

	A	B	C	D	
1	Year	Sales ($)	Change from Last Year ($)	Change from Last Year (%)	
2	1	200,000	(not open last year)	(not open last year)	
3	2	240,000	40,000	@@@	
4	3	300,000	@@@	@@@	
5	4	330,000	@@@	@@@	

Find each percent of increase. Round to the nearest tenth.

17. *Social Studies* The population of Fresno, California, was 578,000 in 1980. In 1994, the population was 835,000.

18. *Medicine* Heart surgeons performed 62 heart transplants in 1981. They performed 2,342 in 1994.

19. *Business* A restaurant worker earning $5.15/h receives a raise. He now earns $6.00/h.

20. *Aquaculture* Fish farms in Dutch Harbor, Alaska, raised 106.3 million fish in 1985. In 1993, the same farms raised 793.9 million fish.

Find each percent of decrease. Round to the nearest tenth.

21. 150 to 147   22. 60 to 54   23. 75 to 25   24. 8.4 to 6.3   25. 480 to 300

26. 10 to 7   27. 25 to 12   28. 85 to 60   29. 5 to 3   30. 29 to 25

31. 9 to 2   32. 110 to 88   33. 1000 to 643   34. 100 to 85   35. 70 to 63

36. a. *Business* The My-T-shirt store bought 5 dozen T-shirts for $4.29 each. The store owner decided to sell the T-shirts for $6.59 each. What was the percent of increase in the price of the T-shirts?

  b. *Consumer Issues* After a month, the remaining 2 dozen T-shirts went on sale for $4.59 each. What was the percent of decrease in the price of the T-shirts?

Find each percent of decrease. Round to the nearest tenth.

37. *Mining* In 1990, the value of all the lead mined in the United States was $491 million. In 1994, the value was $286 million.

38. *Social Studies* George Bush won the 1988 presidential election with 48,881,221 votes. He lost the 1992 election with 38,117,331 votes.

39. *Nutrition* In 1970, the average person in the United States ate 79.6 lb of beef. In 1994, each person ate 63.6 lb of beef.

40. *Sports* A football player gained 1,200 yd last season and 900 yd this season.

Find each percent of change. Round to the nearest tenth. State whether the change is an *increase* or a *decrease*.

41. 50 to 45   42. 75 to 70   43. 530 to 600   44. 25 to 35   45. 13 to 15

46. 56 to 78   47. 900 to 630   48. 6 to 9   49. 89 to 110   50. 12.5 to 8.4

51. 27 to 20   52. 16 to 54   53. 105 to 76   54. 16 to 100   55. 30 to 16

56. *Entertainment* The local community theater keeps track of the attendance at their productions. Copy and complete the table below for two weeks of shows.

Day	Number	Change	% Change
F	125	opening night	no change
Sa	130	+5	▩
Su	120	−10	▩
Th	100	▩	▩
F	130	▩	▩
Sa	150	▩	▩

57. *Writing* Describe how you would find the percent of change in the number of students in your school from last year to this year.

Mixed Review

Evaluate for $m = 8$ and $n = -2$. *(Lessons 3-1 and 3-3)*

58. $6m + 8 + 5n$ **59.** $18 - 3(m + n)$ **60.** $-mn + 2$ **61.** $n - (m - 3)$

Write each fraction as a decimal. Use a bar to indicate any repeating digits. *(Lesson 4-9)*

62. $\dfrac{19}{25}$ **63.** $\dfrac{2}{10}$ **64.** $\dfrac{8}{12}$ **65.** $\dfrac{3}{18}$ **66.** $\dfrac{7}{9}$ **67.** $\dfrac{4}{6}$

Write the unit rate. *(Lesson 6-2)*

68. 408 mi traveled on 12 gal of gasoline   **69.** $16.45 for 7 lb of fish

70. A student is participating in a 50-mi fund-raising walk. She walks 40% of the distance the first day and $\frac{1}{3}$ of the remaining distance the second day. How many more miles does she have to walk? *(Lessons 6-7, 5-5)*

CHAPTER PROJECT

PROJECT LINK: RESEARCHING

Find the number of students in your school. Assuming that all the students in your school visit the park, predict how many students would choose each ride as their favorite.

chills and thrills

Take a Survey The Project Link questions on pages 236, 249, 263, and 280 should help you to complete your project. Here is a checklist to help you gather together the parts of your project.

- ✔ the results of your survey
- ✔ the graph of your results
- ✔ the percent of people who preferred each ride
- ✔ the projected number of people who would prefer each ride

Pretend that your town has a limited amount of space for rides in a proposed amusement park. Which rides would you recommend they include? Explain your reasoning.

Be sure all of your work is neat and clear. After all, you *do* want the town to use your recommendations!

Reflect and Revise

Review your project with a friend or someone at home. Is your graph complete? Are your calculations accurate? Are your projections realistic? If necessary, make changes to improve your project.

Web Extension
Prentice Hall's Internet site contains information you might find helpful as you complete your project. Visit www.phschool.com/mgm2/ch6 for some links and ideas related to amusement parks.

Ratios, Rates, and Proportions
6-1, 6-2, 6-3

A **ratio** is a comparison of two numbers.

A **rate** is a ratio comparing two quantities that are measured in different units.

A **proportion** is an equation stating that two ratios are equal.

1. In the 1996 Summer Olympics, the United States won 101 medals, including 44 gold medals. Write the ratio of gold medals to total medals in three ways.

2. A 10-oz box of cereal costs $2.79. A 13-oz box of the same brand of cereal costs $3.99. Find the unit price for each item and tell which is the better buy.

Find the value of *n* in each proportion.

3. $\frac{3}{7} = \frac{n}{28}$

4. $\frac{3}{5} = \frac{15}{n}$

5. $\frac{n}{18} = \frac{12}{72}$

6. $\frac{32}{n} = \frac{4}{17}$

7. $\frac{1.5}{1.2} = \frac{5}{n}$

8. A local lumberyard sells a total of 250,000 board feet of hardwood each year. The ratio of softwood to hardwood is 5 : 3.
   a. Write and solve a proportion to find the amount of softwood sold per year.
   b. Write and solve a proportion to find the total amount of lumber sold per year.

Similarity and Scale Drawings
6-4, 6-5

If two figures are **similar,** corresponding angles are congruent and the ratios of the lengths of corresponding sides are equal.

A **scale drawing** is an enlarged or reduced drawing of an object.

Each pair of figures is similar. Find *x* and *y*.

9.

10.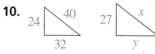

11. The scale on a map is 1.5 in. : 500 mi. The map distance from Chicago to Tokyo is 12 in. Find the actual distance between the cities.

12. A drawing's scale is 0.5 in. : 10 ft. A room is 15 ft long. How long is the room in the drawing?

A **percent** is a ratio that compares a number to 100.

13. Write $\frac{3}{8}$ as a percent.   **14.** Write 1.8% as a decimal.   **15.** Write $62\frac{1}{2}$% as a fraction.

Write a proportion and solve.

16. What percent of 40 is 28?   **17.** 38 is 80% of what number?   **18.** What is 60% of 420?

19. 80% of 15 is what number?   **20.** 54 is 75% of what number?   **21.** 36 is what percent of 180?

22. *Consumer Issues* A bicycle store is having a sale. Zara buys a bike marked 15% off. She pays $45 less than the original price. What was the original price of the bicycle?

Sometimes you use more than one strategy to solve a problem.

23. Choose A, B, C, or D. A rectangular lot is worth $9,000. What is the value of a similar lot whose length and width are each 50% greater than the dimensions of the first lot?

   A. $2,250   **B.** $4,000   **C.** $13,000   **D.** $20,250

A **percent of change** is the percent something increases or decreases from its original measure or amount.

Find the percent of change. State whether the change is an *increase* or a *decrease*. Round to the nearest percent.

24. old: $90; new: $75   **25.** old: 3.5 ft; new: 4.2 ft   **26.** old: 120 lb; new: 138 lb

27. *Writing* When you find percent of change, how do you know whether the percent of change is an increase or a decrease?

28. An answering machine costs $54 on sale. The original price is $80. Find the percent of change.

29. The sale price of a game is $24.95. Its original price was $36.00. Find the percent of change. Round to the nearest percent.

1. Write a ratio for the following information in three ways: 49 out of 50 homes have at least one television.

2. Engineers tested four cars to find their fuel efficiency. Which car gets the most miles per gallon?

Car	Miles	Gallons Used
A	225	14
B	312	15
C	315	10
D	452	16

3. Find each unit rate.
   a. Dontay runs 2.3 km in 7 min.
   b. Carol earns $36.00 in 9 h.
   c. Sumako pays $5.89 for 60 lb.

4. Find the value of n in each proportion.
   a. $\frac{6}{5} = \frac{n}{7}$
   b. $\frac{3}{7} = \frac{8}{n}$
   c. $\frac{n}{4} = \frac{9}{32}$
   d. $\frac{3.5}{n} = \frac{14}{15}$

5. The ratio of teachers to students in Jefferson Middle School is 2 to 25. There are 350 students in the school. Find the number of teachers.

6. A map with a scale 2 in. : 350 mi shows two cities to be 5 in. apart. How many miles apart are the cities?

7. A hot-air balloon is 2,100 ft above the ground. The balloon can descend at the rate of 1.5 ft/s. If the balloon is scheduled to land at 3:30 P.M., when should the balloonist start descending?

8. Write each decimal as a percent and each percent as a decimal.
   a. 5%
   b. 0.3
   c. 125%
   d. 0.0045
   e. 0.39%
   f. 3.4

9. Write each fraction as a percent and each percent as a fraction in simplest form.
   a. 35%
   b. $\frac{3}{4}$
   c. 2%
   d. $\frac{7}{8}$
   e. 125%
   f. $\frac{6}{5}$

10. Use graph paper to model each percent.
   a. 34%
   b. 285%
   c. $12\frac{1}{2}\%$

11. The two triangles are similar. Find x and y.

12. Draw a model and write a proportion to find 25 percent of what number is 30.

13. **Writing** The price of a popular cassette was $8.95 last week. This week the price is $7.16. Explain how to find the percent of decrease in price.

14. Write a proportion and solve.
   a. Find 35% of 150.
   b. What percent of 80 is 50?
   c. 40 is what percent of 25?
   d. 60 is 80% of what number?
   e. What is 225% of 15?
   f. 400 is 150% of what number?

15. Shea bought a sweater for $18.75, which was 25% off the original price. What was the original price?

16. In 1994 there were about 2.1 million registered nurses in the United States. By the year 2005, the United States Labor Department predicts there will be 2.4 million registered nurses. What is the percent of change? Round to the nearest tenth of a percent.

Choose the best answer.

1. Which equation is represented by the model shown?

   A. $x + 3 = 2$ B. $-3x = -2$
   C. $x - 3 = -2$ D. $x + 3 = -2$

2. Which number is closest to 35% of 1,291?

   A. 400   B. 450   C. 500   D. 550

3. Which equation is *not* equivalent to $2x - 3 = 5$?

   A. $2x = 8$ B. $4x - 3 = 10$
   C. $2x - 4 = 4$ D. $x - 1.5 = 2.5$

4. Which expression equals $3 \times 3 \times 3 \times 3$?

   A. 3^4 B. 4^3 C. 5×3 D. 3^3

5. Which point on the number line shows the product $\left(1\frac{7}{8}\right)\left(2\frac{1}{5}\right)$?

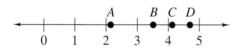

6. Find the median of the data in the stem-and-leaf plot.

7	0 0 5 8
8	1 5 6 9 9
9	4

   7 | 0 means 70.

   A. 81.7   B. 89   C. 85   D. 83

7. Which expression has the greatest value?

   A. $32 - (-12)$ B. $32 - |-12|$
   C. $-32 - (-12)$ D. $|-32 - (-12)|$

8. Which fraction is closest in value to 0.46?

   A. $\frac{19}{50}$ B. $\frac{22}{50}$ C. $\frac{25}{50}$ D. $\frac{28}{50}$

9. Which type of graph would best display the following data on the number of viewers (in millions) watching television during prime time?

   Mon., 91.9   Tue., 89.8   Wed., 93.9
   Thu., 93.9   Fri., 78.0   Sat., 77.1
   Sun., 87.7

   A. scatter plot   B. double line
   C. bar   D. double bar

10. Dyani paid for food at a delicatessen with a $10 bill. She bought a sandwich for $2.45, a salad for $1.25, and a drink for $.89. How much change did she receive?

    A. $4.59   B. $5.41   C. $6.30   D. $14.59

11. Which statement is *not* true?

    A. $\frac{12}{16} = \frac{9}{12}$ B. $\frac{12 + 16}{16} = \frac{9 + 12}{12}$

    C. $\frac{12}{9} = \frac{16}{12}$ D. $\frac{12 + 1}{16} = \frac{9 + 1}{12}$

12. What is $\frac{5}{8}$ written as a percent?

    A. 16%   B. $62\frac{1}{2}\%$ C. 160%   D. 625%

13. Write the numbers 0.361×10^7, 4.22×10^7, and 13.5×10^6 in order from least to greatest.

    A. 13.5×10^6, 0.361×10^7, 4.22×10^7
    B. 4.22×10^7, 13.5×10^6, 0.361×10^7
    C. 0.361×10^7, 13.5×10^6, 4.22×10^7
    D. 13.5×10^6, 4.22×10^7, 0.361×10^7

14. Find the value of $\frac{2m}{m + 2n}$ when $m = -4$ and $n = 3$.

    A. -8 B. -4 C. 0   D. 4

15. Which is the best estimate of $92.56 \cdot 37.1$?

    A. 2,700   B. 3,600   C. 4,000   D. 4,500

Investigating Geometry

WHAT YOU WILL LEARN IN THIS CHAPTER

- How to classify geometric figures

- How to make circle graphs

- How to construct bisectors

Raisin' the Roof

*L*ook around you. Triangles are everywhere in construction! You see them in bridges, in buildings, in scaffolding; even in bicycle frames! This project will give you a greater appreciation of the importance of triangles in construction. You might also develop a taste for raisins!

Build a Tower For the chapter project, you will use toothpicks and raisins to build geometric shapes. Your final product will be a tower strong enough to support a baseball.

• How to solve problems by drawing diagrams

PROBLEM SOLVING

Work Together _____ *Extending Geometric Patterns*

1. a. Sketch the next figure for this pattern.

b. What might be the eighth and ninth figures in the pattern? Can you sketch more than one possibility? Explain.

2. a. Sketch the next two figures for this pattern.

b. What might be the ninth and tenth figures in the pattern?

THINK AND DISCUSS

Many patterns involve geometric figures.

▪ **EXAMPLE**   *Real-World Problem Solving*

Crafts Three parts of a quilt square called Dutchman's Puzzle are shown at the right. What design completes the quilt square?

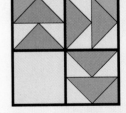

The triangle pattern is turned 90° clockwise going from A to B, from B to C, and from C to D.

3. ✔ *Try It Out* Draw the next two figures for each pattern below.

a.

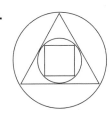
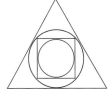

b.

1. a. Draw the next two figures for the pattern.

b. *Writing* Describe the twentieth figure for the pattern.

Choose the figure that continues each pattern.

2.

A. **B.** **C.** **D.**

3.

A. **B.** **C.** **D.**

4. Copy the figures on dot paper. Draw two figures that continue the pattern.

5. Copy the first four figures of the patterns in the Work Together activity. Decide on a way to continue the pattern that is different from Questions 1 and 2. Draw at least the next four figures in your pattern.

6. *Open-Ended* Draw the first four figures of your own pattern of geometric figures.

Mixed Review

Write each fraction in simplest form. *(Lesson 4-6)*

7. $\frac{10}{25}$ **8.** $\frac{14}{32}$ **9.** $\frac{9}{21}$ **10.** $\frac{48}{80}$ **11.** $\frac{28}{35}$ **12.** $\frac{20}{60}$

Find the percent of change. State whether the change is an increase or a decrease. Round to the nearest percent. *(Lesson 6-11)*

13. old: $5.75; new: $6.25   **14.** old: 380 ft; new: 320 ft   **15.** old: 3.95 lb; new: 4.25 lb

16. *Choose a Strategy* Jareem has two pairs of slacks to wear with any of three shirts. How many outfits does he have?

Math at Work

ARCHITECT

Do you have an eye for design? If you choose a career as an architect, then you will design buildings such as homes, schools, and offices. After consulting with a client, an architect uses creativity to plan a beautiful and useful building. In preparing complex blueprints, an architect needs to understand spatial relationships.

Find out more about architecture at the Web site: http://arc.futurescan.com/

7-2 Classifying and Measuring Angles

What You'll Learn

1 To measure and classify angles

2 To work with pairs of angles

...And Why

Measuring angles is important in careers like carpentry and physical therapy.

Here's How

Look for questions that

⚬ build understanding

✔ check understanding

THINK AND DISCUSS

1 *Measuring and Describing Angles*

Recall that segments and rays are both parts of lines.

$\overleftrightarrow{AB}$ (line *AB*) $\overrightarrow{AB}$ (ray *AB*)

$\overline{AB}$ (segment *AB*) $\overrightarrow{BA}$ (ray *BA*)

An **angle** is made up of two rays (the *sides* of the angle) with a common endpoint (the *vertex* of the angle). You can call the angle shown $\angle DCE$, $\angle ECD$, $\angle C$, or $\angle 1$.

1. ⚬ *Reasoning* Can you call the angle $\angle CDE$? Explain.

You can use a protractor to measure angles. You can write the "measure of $\angle X$" as $m\angle X$.

■ EXAMPLE 1

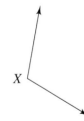

What is the measure of $\angle X$ at the left?

Step 1 Place the center point of your protractor on the vertex of the angle.

Step 2 Make sure that one side of the angle passes through zero on the protractor scale.

Step 3 Read the scale where it intersects the second side of the angle.

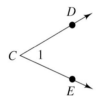

$$m\angle X = 110°$$

2. ⚬ *Think About It* Why was the scale reading of 110° on the protractor chosen rather than 70°?

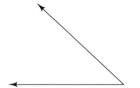

3. **♣ Think About It** How would you measure an angle with sides that do not extend to the scale of the protractor?

4. a. **♣ Estimation** Estimate the measure of the angle at the left.
   b. ✔ **Try It Out** Measure the angle.

You can classify angles by their measures.

  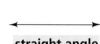

acute angle
measures less than 90°

right angle
measures 90°

obtuse angle
measures greater than 90° and less than 180°

straight angle
measures 180°

QUICKreview

The symbol ⌐ indicates a right angle.

5. ✔ **Try It Out** Use your protractor to draw a 140° angle. Then classify the angle.

▼2 *Pairs of Angles*

Two **adjacent angles** share a vertex and one side but have no common interior points. ∠ABD and ∠DBC are adjacent angles.

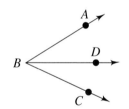

6. ✔ **Try It Out** Are ∠ABD and ∠ABC adjacent angles? Why or why not?

If the sum of the measures of two angles is 90°, the angles are **complementary.**

If the sum of the measures of two angles is 180°, the angles are **supplementary.**

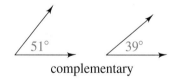

complementary

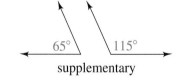

supplementary

7. ✔ **Try It Out** The measure of ∠1 is 56°. What is the measure of its complement? Of its supplement?

8. Name the pairs of adjacent angles in the figure at the left.

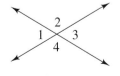

The pairs of angles that are not adjacent are *vertical angles.* ∠1 and ∠3 are vertical angles. ∠2 and ∠4 are vertical angles.

9. **♣ Analyze** Measure the angles in the figure at the left. Make a conjecture about the measures of vertical angles.

Chapter 7 Investigating Geometry

■ EXAMPLE 2

Find the measures of ∠1, ∠2, and
∠3 if $m\angle 4 = 128°$.

$m\angle 1 + 128° = 180°$ ← ∠1 and ∠4 are supplementary.
$m\angle 1 = 180° - 128°$
$m\angle 1 = 52°$
$m\angle 2 = 128°$ ← ∠2 and ∠4 are vertical angles.
$m\angle 3 = 52°$ ← ∠1 and ∠3 are vertical angles.

10. ✔ *Try It Out* The measure of an angle formed by two intersecting lines is 40°. What are the measures of the other three angles?

EXERCISES *On Your Own*

Classify each angle as acute, right, obtuse, or straight.

1. $m\angle A = 45°$
2. $m\angle B = 180°$
3. $m\angle C = 90°$
4. $m\angle D = 150°$

Estimate the measure of each angle. Then classify the angle.

5.

6.

7.

8.

9. *Physical Therapy* Physical therapists use *goniometers* to measure the amount of motion a person has in a joint, like an elbow or a knee. The goniometer has a built-in protractor. Estimate the measure of the angle in the photograph.

Use dot paper or graph paper to draw angles with the following measures *without* using a protractor.

10. 90°
11. 180°

12. 45°
13. 135°

Use the figure at the right to name the following.

14. four lines

15. three segments

16. four rays

17. four right angles

18. two pairs of adjacent supplementary angles

19. two pairs of obtuse vertical angles

20. two pairs of complementary angles

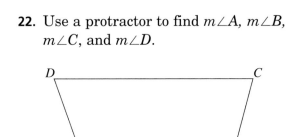

21. *Writing* One student measured ∠*ABC* and said that *m*∠*ABC* = 60°. Explain the mistake that he made.

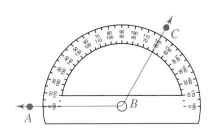

22. Use a protractor to find *m*∠*A*, *m*∠*B*, *m*∠*C*, and *m*∠*D*.

23. ∠*A* and ∠*B* are supplementary angles. If *m*∠*A* = 15°, what is *m*∠*B*?

24. ∠*C* and ∠*D* are complementary angles. If *m*∠*C* = 50°, what is *m*∠*D*?

25. Use a protractor to draw two complementary angles, one of which has measure 25°.

26. Use a protractor to draw two supplementary angles, one of which has measure 55°.

27. ∠1 and ∠2 are vertical angles. If *m*∠1 = 75°, what is *m*∠2?

28. Draw vertical angles, ∠1 and ∠2, that are complementary.

Tell whether the estimate for each angle measure is reasonable. If it is not reasonable, give a better estimate.

29. 120°   **30.** 60°   **31.** 45°   **32.** 90°

JOURNAL

Describe the use of acute angles and obtuse angles in buildings.

IVORY ID

VORY SMUGGLERS try to slip illegal elephant ivory into the United States by labeling the ivory as mammoth tusks. Ed Espinoza of the United States Fish and Wildlife Service has found a way to identify whether ivory tusks are from prehistoric mammoths or from elephants.

The flat edges of tusks contain distinctive markings. When Ed Espinoza and a team of scientists photocopied and measured these markings, they found that markings from mammoth tusks create angles that measure 90° or less. Markings from elephants create angles that measure 115° or more.

33. These are photocopies of two ivory tusks. Identify which comes from a mammoth and which comes from an elephant.

a.

b.
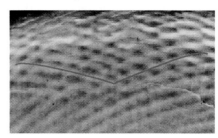

Mixed Review

Find each product. *(Lesson 5-5)*

34. $\frac{4}{5} \cdot \frac{2}{5}$ **35.** $\frac{8}{14} \cdot \frac{7}{8}$ **36.** $\frac{5}{6} \cdot 14$ **37.** $\frac{8}{9} \cdot \frac{11}{12}$ **38.** $\frac{5}{16} \cdot \frac{2}{5}$ **39.** $\frac{8}{9} \cdot \frac{3}{4}$

40. Jack, Barbara, Sally, and Michelle have 25 dimes, 35 nickels, 267 pennies, and 7 quarters, respectively. Who has the most money? The least? *(Lessons 3-2, 3-5)*

PROJECT LINK: RESEARCHING

Find pictures of structures such as bridges and towers that use triangles in their construction. Use the pictures to get ideas for the design of your tower.

EXPLORATION

Parallel Lines

After Lesson 7-2

You can use a piece of notebook paper and your protractor to investigate the angles formed by a line that crosses two parallel lines.

Parallel lines are lines in a plane that do not intersect no matter how far they are extended. You can think of a plane as a flat surface. The lines on notebook paper are parts of parallel lines.

On a clean sheet of notebook paper, draw a diagram like the one at the right. The diagram shows two parallel lines and a *transversal* that crosses them.

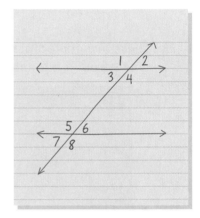

1. Use your protractor to measure each numbered angle.

2. Which angles have the same measure as ∠1?

3. Which angles are supplementary to ∠1?

4. **a.** Draw another pair of parallel lines. Use your protractor to draw a transversal that makes a right angle with one of your parallel lines.
   b. Measure all of the angles. What do you notice?

In each diagram, lines ℓ and m are parallel. Which numbered angles have the same measure as ∠1? Which numbered angles are supplements of ∠1?

5.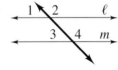

6.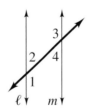

7.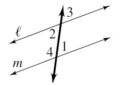

8.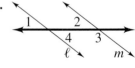

9. In the diagram at the right, lines ℓ and m are parallel and lines n and q are parallel. The measure of ∠4 is 58°. Find the measures of the numbered angles.

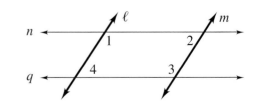

7-3 Triangles

What You'll Learn

1 To classify triangles by sides and by angles

2 To find the measure of one angle of a triangle, given the other two measures

...And Why

Triangles and the measures of their angles appear everywhere, from architecture to designing flags.

Here's How

Look for questions that
- build understanding
- ✔ check understanding

QUICKreview

Congruent segments are segments that have the same length. Congruent angles are angles that have the same measure.

Work Together
Investigating Angles of a Triangle

Cut out a paper triangle that is a different shape from those of the other members of your group.

Step 1 Number the angles of the triangle and tear them off the triangle.

Step 2 Place the three angles side-by-side to form adjacent angles with no angles overlapping.

1. Compare your results with those of your group. Make a conjecture about the sum of the angles.

THINK AND DISCUSS

1 Classifying Triangles

You can classify triangles by the number of congruent sides or by angle measures.

scalene triangle
no congruent sides

isosceles triangle
at least two
congruent sides

equilateral triangle
three congruent sides

right triangle
one right angle

acute triangle
three acute angles

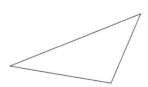
obtuse triangle
one obtuse angle

■ **EXAMPLE 1**   *Real-World Problem Solving*

Architecture The building in the center of this photograph is the Transamerica Building in San Francisco. Classify the front of the Transamerica Building.

The front of the Transamerica Building is an acute isosceles triangle.

2. ✔ *Try It Out* Classify each triangle by its sides.

a. 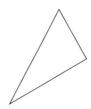   b.

c.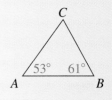

3. ✔ *Try It Out* Classify each triangle in Question 2 by its angles.

▼2 *Angles and Triangles*

In the Work Together activity you discovered that the following statement is true for all triangles.

The sum of the measures of the angles of a triangle is 180°.

■ **EXAMPLE 2**

Find the measure of ∠C.

$$m\angle C + 53° + 61° = 180°$$
$$m\angle C + 114° = 180°$$
$$m\angle C = 180° - 114°$$
$$m\angle C = 66°$$

4. ✔ *Try It Out* The measures of two angles of a triangle are 48° and 37°. What is the measure of the third angle?

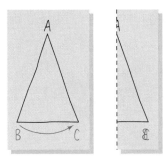

The diagram at the left shows the two congruent sides of an isosceles triangle folded on top of one another. When two sides of a triangle are congruent, two angles are congruent.

■ **EXAMPLE 3**

Triangle ABC is isosceles. Side AB is congruent to side AC, so $\angle B$ is congruent to $\angle C$. Find the measure of $\angle A$.

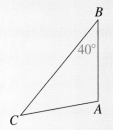

Since $\angle B$ is congruent to $\angle C$, $\angle C$ has the measure 40°.

$$m\angle A + 40° + 40° = 180°$$
$$m\angle A + 80° = 180°$$
$$m\angle A = 180° - 80°$$
$$m\angle A = 100°$$

5. ✔ *Try It Out* One angle of an isosceles triangle has the measure 120°. Find the measure of the two congruent angles.

6. a. ⬖ *Make a Model* Trace the equilateral triangle at the left. Fold the triangle so that one side matches another side. What is true of the angles that match?

b. If you fold the triangle so that a different pair of sides match, do you get the same result? What is true of the three angles of an equilateral triangle?

c. ⬖ *Draw a Conclusion* What is the measure of each angle of an equilateral triangle? Explain.

EXERCISES *On Your Own*

Judging by appearance, classify each triangle by its sides. Name any congruent sides.

1.

2.

3.

4.

Judging by appearance, classify each triangle above by its angles. Name any obtuse or right angles.

5. Exercise 1

6. Exercise 2

7. Exercise 3

8. Exercise 4

9. *Music* In an orchestra, a triangle is a percussion instrument that is made of a thin steel rod. Does a musical triangle look like a scalene triangle, an isosceles triangle, or an equilateral triangle?

10. Choose A, B, or C. The measures of two angles of a triangle are 35° and 50°. Classify the triangle.

    A. acute   **B.** right   **C.** obtuse

Find each missing angle measure.

11.

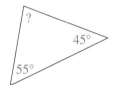

12.

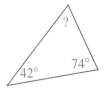

13.

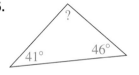

14.

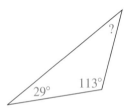

15.

16.

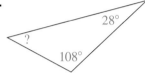

17. *Social Studies* Classify the triangles in the flag of Guyana.

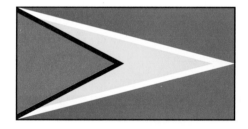

18. a. *Writing* Can an equilateral triangle be a right triangle? Why or why not?
    b. Can an obtuse triangle have a right angle? Why or why not?

Guyana

19. *Reasoning* The measures of the angles of a triangle are 50°, 60°, and 70°.
    a. Classify the triangle by its angles.
    b. Can the triangle be equilateral? Why or why not?
    c. Can the triangle be isosceles? Why or why not?
    d. Can you classify the triangle by its sides? Why or why not?

20. The triangles shown at the right are all right triangles.
    a. What is the sum of the measures of the two acute angles in each triangle?
    b. What is the relationship of the two acute angles in these triangles? Is this true for all right triangles? Explain.

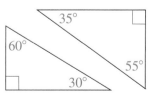

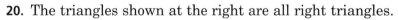

Find the missing angle measures for each isosceles triangle.

21.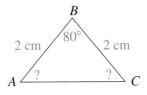

22.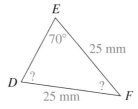

23.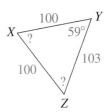

24. *Open-Ended* Use your protractor to draw acute, right, and obtuse triangles that each contain a 40° angle. Label the triangles and the 40° angles.

Mixed Review

Evaluate each expression. *(Lesson 4-4)*

25. 4^3 26. 2^6 27. 7^2 28. 6^4 29. 5^7 30. 10^6

Write each quotient as a decimal. Use a bar to show repeating decimals. *(Lesson 2-7)*

31. $5 \div 3$ 32. $7 \div 16$ 33. $15 \div 18$ 34. $10 \div 6$ 35. $21 \div 8$

36. *Transportation* A taxi charges $2.10 for the first $\frac{1}{5}$ mi and $.50 for each additional $\frac{1}{5}$ mi. Find the cost of a 10-mi ride. *(Lessons 5-3, 5-5)*

✓ CHECKPOINT 1   *Lessons 7-1 through 7-3*

1. Draw the next figure for the pattern at the right.

Classify the angle with the given measure.

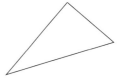

2. 23°   3. 117°   4. 90°   5. 180°

Judging by appearance, classify each triangle by its sides and angles.

6.

7.

8.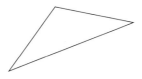

7-4 Draw a Diagram

Problem Solving Strategies

✔ Draw a Diagram
  Guess and Test
  Look for a Pattern
  Make a Model
  Make a Table
  Simulate a Problem
  Solve a Simpler Problem
  Too Much or Too Little
   Information
  Use Logical Reasoning
  Use Multiple Strategies
  Work Backward
  Write an Equation

THINK AND DISCUSS

Drawing a diagram can help you visualize the relationships described in a problem. Be sure to read the problem carefully. There may be more than one diagram that satisfies the given information.

SAMPLE PROBLEM..

A furniture maker is designing a table for a customer who likes his furniture to be mathematical! So the furniture maker plans to make the table top an isosceles triangle. One angle of the table top measures 30°. What are the measures of the other two angles of the table top?

READ

Read for understanding. Summarize the problem.

1. Think about the information you are given and what you need to find.
   a. What is the measure of one angle of the triangle?
   b. What kind of triangle is involved in this problem?
   c. What is special about the angles of this kind of triangle?
   d. Summarize the goal of this problem.

PLAN

Decide on a strategy.

A good strategy to use here is to *draw a diagram*. The 30° angle could be one of the two congruent angles in the triangle or it could an angle that is not congruent to another angle.

SOLVE

Try the strategy.

2. Draw a diagram that shows the 30° angle as one of the two congruent angles.
   a. What is the measure of the angle that is congruent to the given angle?
   b. What is the measure of the third angle?

3. Draw a diagram that shows the 30° angle in a different location. What are the measures of the other angles?

4. Are there any other ways an isosceles triangle can have a 30° angle? Why or why not?

5. Write a solution to the original question by summarizing what you have found.

LOOK BACK
Think about how you solved the problem.

6. Describe how drawing a diagram helped you solve the problem.

EXERCISES *On Your Own*

Draw a diagram to help you solve each problem.

1. Each morning Jacob walks to school. At 8:20 A.M. he passes a stoplight that is two blocks from home. He walks another block and reaches the town library at 8:24 A.M. At this point he is three blocks from school and half the way there. If Jacob walks at the same pace all the way to school, at what time does he arrive at school? Explain your answer.

2. At the first meeting of the Table Tennis Club, the seven members decided to have a tournament in which every player will play a game against every other player. How many games will there be in the tournament?

Use any strategy to solve each problem. Show your work.

3. The diagram shows part of a design made by using toothpicks to form triangles. The top row uses three toothpicks. The second row uses six toothpicks. The third row uses nine toothpicks, and so on.
 a. If you decide to continue the design so that it has seven rows, how many toothpicks do you need altogether?
 b. Which row will use 24 toothpicks?

4. Suppose you buy several pencils at a discount store. All the pencils are the same price, and you buy as many pencils as the cost (in cents) of each pencil. The pencils cost a total of $1.44. How many pencils did you buy?

5. *Gardening* Each year Brandon plants tulip bulbs in a square flower bed. This year Brandon's flower bed has 29 more bulbs than it had last year. If the flower bed is still square, how many tulip bulbs are in it this year?

6. Shana climbed a set of stairs and stopped at the middle step. She then walked down 2 steps, up 4 steps, down 3 steps, and up 5 steps, and she was at the top of the stairs. How many steps are in the set of stairs?

7. Rosa, Alberto, and Vernesha are in a band together. They play guitar, piano, and drums. Alberto is the cousin of the guitar player. Rosa lives next door to the drummer and two blocks from the guitar player. Who plays which instrument?

8. Raphael has $1.55 in dimes and quarters. Find all the possible combinations of coins that Raphael might have.

9. How many angles are shown in the figure at the right? How many of them are obtuse?

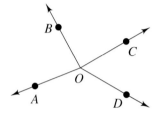

10. The Martin Luther King School library has 8 tables and 42 chairs. There are several small tables with 4 chairs each and some large tables with 6 chairs each. How many tables of each type are in the library?

11. How many triangles are shown in the figure at the right?

Mixed Review

Find each quotient. *(Lesson 5-6)*

12. $\frac{2}{3} \div \frac{8}{9}$ **13.** $3\frac{3}{4} \div \frac{5}{6}$ **14.** $12 \div 3\frac{1}{2}$ **15.** $1\frac{5}{9} \div 2\frac{1}{3}$ **16.** $7\frac{1}{4} \div 8\frac{1}{3}$

Solve each equation. *(Lesson 3-9)*

17. $6x + 7 = 13$ **18.** $-3d + 5 = 17$ **19.** $4r - 12 = -2$ **20.** $-6p - 8 = -20$

21. *Choose a Strategy* Bicycling burns 11 calories/minute, running 14 calories/minute, and dancing 8 calories/minute. Would you burn more calories by running for 15 minutes 3 days a week or bicycling 40 minutes 2 days a week?

CHAPTER PROJECT

PROJECT LINK: ANALYZING

Use toothpicks and raisins to build a triangle and a square. Gently wiggle each figure. Which is more rigid? Add toothpicks to strengthen the weaker one. Describe how you did it.

Congruent Triangles

What You'll Learn

▼ To identify and work with congruent figures

...And Why

Congruent figures are used in crafts and manufacturing.

Here's How

Look for questions that
▪ build understanding
✔ check understanding

Work Together   *Exploring Congruent Figures*

1. Match the figures that appear to have the same size and shape.

a. ◯   b. ◯   c. △   d. ◯

e. ▭   f. ▽   g. ◯   h. ▯

2. How could you check that your answers to Question 1 are correct?

3. Suppose you trace a polygon and match your tracing with another polygon that has the same size and shape. What would be true of the matching angles and segments?

THINK AND DISCUSS

Figures that have the same size and shape are **congruent.** In the pinwheel at the left, all the triangles of the same color are congruent.

A *polygon* is a closed plane figure formed by three or more line segments that do not cross. **Congruent polygons** have congruent *corresponding parts* (sides and angles). You can write the symbol ≅ for "is congruent to."

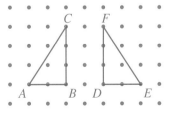

$\overline{AB} \cong \overline{ED}$ $\angle A \cong \angle E$

$\overline{BC} \cong \overline{DF}$ $\angle B \cong \angle D$

$\overline{CA} \cong \overline{FE}$ $\angle C \cong \angle F$

$\triangle ABC \cong \triangle EDF$

You name corresponding vertices in the same order.

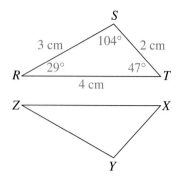

■ EXAMPLE

a. The triangles shown at the left are congruent. Write six congruences involving corresponding parts of the triangles.

$$\angle X \cong \angle T \qquad \angle Y \cong \angle S \qquad \angle Z \cong \angle R$$
$$\overline{XY} \cong \overline{TS} \qquad \overline{ZY} \cong \overline{RS} \qquad \overline{ZX} \cong \overline{RT}$$

b. Find ZY and $m\angle X$.

$ZY = 3$ cm ← Because $\overline{ZY} \cong \overline{RS}$, $ZY = RS$.

$m\angle T = 47°$ ← Because $\angle X \cong \angle T$, $m\angle X = m\angle T$.

4. a. ✔ *Try It Out* Write six congruences involving corresponding sides and angles.

b. $\triangle DEF \cong$ ■

c. $\triangle EFD \cong$ ■

d. $\triangle DFE \cong$ ■

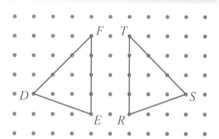

EXERCISES *On Your Own*

1. List the pairs of triangles that appear to be congruent.

a.

b.

c.

d.

e.

f.

Complete. (Be sure that you name corresponding vertices in the same order.)

2. $\triangle ABC \cong$ ■

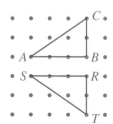

3. $\triangle ABC \cong$ ■

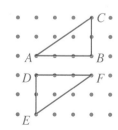

4. $\triangle ABC \cong$ ■

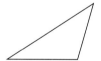

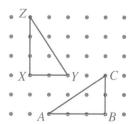

5. $\triangle DEF \cong \triangle CLK$. Complete each congruence statement.

a. $\angle D \cong$ ▨
b. $\angle E \cong$ ▨
c. $\angle F \cong$ ▨
d. $\overline{DE} \cong$ ▨
e. $\overline{EF} \cong$ ▨
f. $\overline{DF} \cong$ ▨

6. *Open-ended* Describe a real-life application of congruent figures.

7. Assume that $\triangle XYZ \cong \triangle RBP$. Write six congruences involving corresponding sides and angles.

8. *Writing* $\triangle ABC \cong \triangle WPQ$. Explain how you can find the measure of an angle and of a side of $\triangle WPQ$.

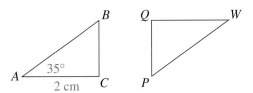

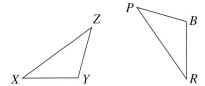

9. Complete in as many correct ways as you can: $\triangle ABC \cong$ ▨

10. $\triangle RST \cong \triangle EFG$. Find as many angle measures and side lengths for $\triangle EFG$ as you can.

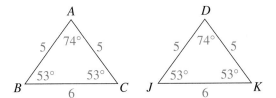

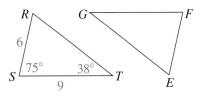

11. **Choose A, B, C, or D.** $\triangle RST$ and $\triangle XYZ$ are congruent equilateral triangles. Which angle or angles must be congruent to $\angle R$?

A. $\angle X$ only
B. $\angle S$ and $\angle T$
C. $\angle X$, $\angle S$, and $\angle T$
D. $\angle S$, $\angle T$, $\angle X$, $\angle Y$, and $\angle Z$

Mixed Review

Write each fraction as a decimal. Use a bar to show repeating decimals. *(Lesson 4-9)*

12. $\frac{1}{2}$
13. $\frac{4}{5}$
14. $\frac{6}{8}$
15. $\frac{1}{3}$
16. $\frac{33}{50}$
17. $\frac{18}{12}$

Write equations for Exercises 18 and 19. Then solve. *(Lesson 3-8)*

18. A number divided by 8 equals 9.

19. Fifteen added to a number equals 45.

20. *Choose a Strategy* Thieu worked 3 h per day on a jigsaw puzzle. It took him 13 h to complete the puzzle. If he started the puzzle on Saturday, on what day did he finish the puzzle?

Polygons and Quadrilaterals

What You'll Learn

▼ 1 To classify polygons and identify regular polygons

▼ 2 To work with special quadrilaterals

...And Why

Polygons and quadrilaterals are all around you, from architecture to signs.

Here's How

Look for questions that
- ▪▪ build understanding
- ✔ check understanding

THINK AND DISCUSS

▼ 1 Classifying Polygons

You name *polygons* by the number of sides.

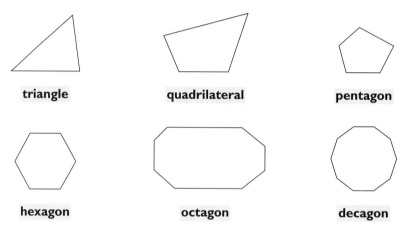

triangle   quadrilateral   pentagon

hexagon   octagon   decagon

1. How many sides does a pentagon have? A hexagon? An octagon? A decagon?

2. What shape is the gazebo in this landscape designer's sketch? What is the shape of the flower beds? Of the path?

A **regular polygon** has all sides congruent and all angles congruent.

3. Which of the labeled polygons above appear to be regular?

4. What is another name for a regular triangle?

☑ Special Quadrilaterals

parallel lines

Some quadrilaterals have special names. Recall that two lines are **parallel** if they lie in the same plane (a flat surface) and do not intersect.

A **trapezoid** has exactly one pair of parallel sides.

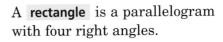

A **parallelogram** has both pairs of opposite sides parallel.

A **rectangle** is a parallelogram with four right angles.

A **rhombus** is a parallelogram with four congruent sides.

A **square** is a parallelogram with four right angles and four congruent sides.

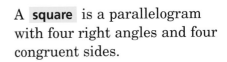

5. What is another name for a regular quadrilateral?

■ EXAMPLE

Draw each of the following figures on dot paper.

a. parallelogram *ABCD* that is not a rectangle or a rhombus

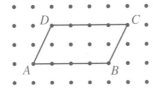

b. rhombus *EFGH* that is not a square

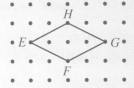

6. ✔ *Try It Out* Use dot paper to draw a trapezoid.

7. ⬥ *Think About It* Can a trapezoid have three right angles? Draw a diagram to support your answer.

Every quadrilateral has two pairs of opposite sides and two pairs of opposite angles.

8. Name two pairs of opposite sides.

9. Name two pairs of opposite angles.

The **diagonals** of quadrilateral *ABCD* are $\overline{AC}$ and $\overline{BD}$.

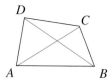

Work Together

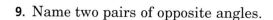

- Start with a parallelogram that is a different shape from those of the other members of your group.
- Draw one diagonal of your parallelogram.
- Cut out the parallelogram and then cut along the diagonal.

10. **a.** Are the two triangles that are formed congruent? Why or why not?
    b. Were the opposite sides of your parallelogram congruent? Why or why not?
    c. What have you shown about two opposite angles of your parallelogram? Suppose you had cut along the other diagonal. What do you think would have been the result?

11. Compare your results with those of your group. What can you conclude about parallelograms? Do your conclusions also apply to rectangles, squares, and rhombuses? Why or why not?

EXERCISES *On Your Own*

Classify each polygon by the number of sides. Then state whether it appears to be a regular polygon.

1.

2.

3.

4.

Judging by appearance, write all the correct names for each quadrilateral. Then circle the best name.

5.

6.

7.

8.

Open-ended **Use dot paper to draw each of the following.**

9. a pentagon

10. a regular quadrilateral

11. an octagon

12. a rhombus

13. two congruent rectangles

14. a trapezoid

15. two regular quadrilaterals that are not congruent

16. two noncongruent trapezoids that have a pair of congruent sides

17. a trapezoid with two right angles

18. a trapezoid with two congruent adjacent sides

19. a trapezoid with two congruent opposite sides

20. a. *Social Studies* Write all the names that can be used for the shape of the bottom Australian road sign. Circle the best name.
    b. Write all the names that can be used for the shape of the top sign. Circle the best name.

21. *Reasoning* Can a quadrilateral be both a rhombus and a rectangle? Explain.

22. **Choose A, B, C, or D.** Which statement or statements are false?
    I. Every trapezoid is a quadrilateral.
    II. Every rectangle is a square.
    III. Every parallelogram is a rhombus.

    A. II only
    B. III only
    C. II and III
    D. I, II, and III

23. *Writing* Write a sentence that uses the word *all* and some of the following words: trapezoids, parallelograms, rectangles, rhombuses, squares. Repeat for the word *some* and then for the word *no*.

Australia

Judging by appearance, classify each quadrilateral. Then name the congruent sides and angles.

24.

25.

26.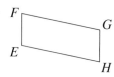

27.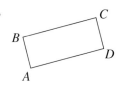

28. **a.** Draw a quadrilateral with exactly one pair of opposite angles that are congruent.
    b. Draw a quadrilateral with exactly one pair of opposite sides that are congruent.

List all additional side lengths and angle measures you can find for each quadrilateral. (*Hint:* Draw a diagram.)

29. parallelogram $ABCD$, $AB = 6$ cm, $m\angle A = 65°$

30. square $EFGH$, $EF = 3$ m

31. rhombus $WXYZ$, $WX = 4$ cm

32. rectangle $JKLN$, $KL = 5$ in.

33. trapezoid $PQRS$, $QR = 10$ cm, $m\angle Q = 65°$

Mixed Review

Estimate each answer. (*Lesson 5-1*)

34. $12\frac{1}{2} - 5\frac{2}{3}$ 35. $16\frac{1}{2} \div 4\frac{3}{4}$ 36. $\frac{1}{2} + \frac{5}{12}$ 37. $3\frac{7}{12} \cdot 2\frac{2}{5}$ 38. $\frac{7}{12} - \frac{3}{10}$

State whether each number is prime or composite. If composite, write its prime factorization. (*Lesson 4-5*)

39. 15   40. 29   41. 333   42. 6,453   43. 146   44. 31

CHAPTER PROJECT

PROJECT LINK: CREATING

Use toothpicks and raisins to build a cube. How many of each are needed? Use additional toothpicks to strengthen the cube. Describe how you did it.

Sum of the Measures of the Angles of a Polygon

After Lesson 7-6

You can use a computer and geometry software to investigate the angles of polygons. We shall consider only convex polygons.

Draw a pentagon like the one shown.

 1. a. Use the computer program to measure each angle. Find the sum of the measures.
   b. Change the pentagon's shape, but keep it convex. Find the sum of the angle measures.
   c. *Draw a Conclusion* What is the sum of the measures of the angles of a pentagon?

2. a. Sketch a pentagon and divide it into triangles by drawing all the diagonals from one vertex.
   b. Multiply the number of triangles you drew by the sum of the angle measures of a triangle.

3. What relationship do you find between your answers to Questions 1(c) and 2(b)?

4. a. Sketch a hexagon. Divide the hexagon into triangles by drawing all the diagonals from one vertex.
   b. Multiply the number of triangles you drew by 180°.

 5. Draw a hexagon using a computer. Measure the angles and find their sum. Change the shape of your hexagon. What do you notice about the sum of the angle measures?

6. Tell how many sides each polygon has and the number of triangles that you can form by drawing all the diagonals from one vertex.
   a. quadrilateral   **b.** pentagon   **c.** hexagon   **d.** octagon

7. *Writing* What is the relationship between the number of sides of a figure and the number of triangles you can form?

8. What is the sum of the measures of the angles of a 12-sided polygon?

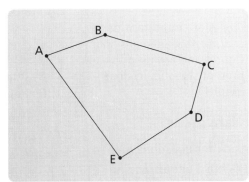

Convex Polygon

Nonconvex Polygon

All diagonals are inside.   A diagonal is outside.

THINK AND DISCUSS

▼ *Parts of a Circle*

A **circle** is the set of points in a plane that are all the same distance from a given point, called the *center*. You name a circle by its center. Circle *O* is shown at the right.

A **radius** is a segment that has one endpoint at the center and the other endpoint on the circle.

$\overline{OB}$ is a radius of circle *O*.

A **diameter** is a segment that passes through the center of a circle and has both endpoints on the circle.

$\overline{AC}$ is a diameter of circle *O*.

A **central angle** is an angle with its vertex at the center of a circle.

$\angle AOB$ is a central angle of circle *O*.

A **chord** is a segment that has both endpoints on the circle.

$\overline{AD}$ is a chord of circle *O*.

■ **EXAMPLE 1**

Name all the radii, diameters, and chords shown for circle *O*.

The radii are $\overline{OA}$, $\overline{OB}$, $\overline{OC}$, and $\overline{OD}$.

The diameter is $\overline{AC}$.

The chords are $\overline{AB}$, $\overline{BC}$, $\overline{CD}$, $\overline{DA}$, and $\overline{AC}$.

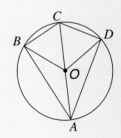

QUICKreview

Radii is the plural of radius.

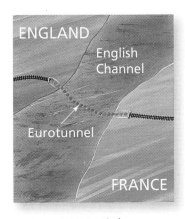
1. ✔ *Try It Out* Name all the radii, diameters, and chords shown in circle *P*.

2. ⬛ *Think About It* Can a radius also be a chord? Explain.

3. Must a diameter also be a chord? Explain.

4. How do the lengths of a radius and a diameter compare?

5. Name the isosceles triangles in the diagram for Example 1. How do you know they are isosceles?

6. **a.** Name four *non-overlapping* central angles of circle *O* in Example 1.
   b. What is the sum of the measures of the four non-overlapping central angles? Explain.

An **arc** is part of a circle. A **semicircle** is half a circle.

arc   semicircle

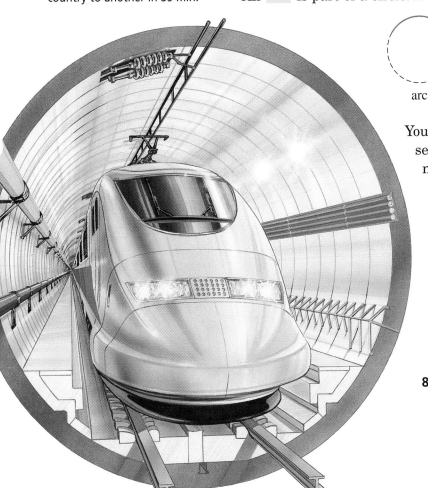

You use three letters to name a semicircle. The first and third letters name the *endpoints* of the semicircle. One semicircle in Example 1 is $\overset{\frown}{ADC}$ (read "arc *ADC*"). You use two letters to name an arc shorter than a semicircle.

7. **a.** ✔ *Try It Out* Name another semicircle in Example 1.
   b. Why do you need to use three letters to name a semicircle?

8. ✔ *Try It Out* $\overset{\frown}{AB}$ is one arc of circle *O* in Example 1. Name the other arcs that are shorter than a semicircle.

A **compass** is a geometric tool used to draw circles and arcs.

9. Use a compass to draw and label a circle P. Label a semicircle as $\overparen{RST}$ and a shorter arc as $\overparen{XY}$.

② Inscribed Polygons

You call a polygon whose sides are chords of a circle an **inscribed polygon**.

■ **EXAMPLE 2**

Name the polygons inscribed in circle P.

The inscribed polygons are $\triangle RST$ and $\triangle STW$.

10. ✔ *Try It Out* Name the polygons that are inscribed in circle O.

11. What is true of all the vertices of an inscribed polygon?

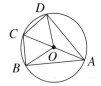

Work Together — *Exploring Inscribed Quadrilaterals*

Work in a group. Inscribe several quadrilaterals in circles.

12. Measure the angles of the quadrilaterals. Make a conjecture about the sum of the measures of the opposite angles of an inscribed quadrilateral.

To draw a circle or an arc with a SAFE-T-COMPASS®, use the center hole of the white dial as the center.

EXERCISES *On Your Own*

Name each of the following for circle O.

1. two or more chords

2. three radii

3. a diameter

4. several central angles

5. two semicircles

6. several arcs

7. the longest chord shown

8. an isosceles triangle

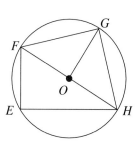

9. Name all the radii, diameters, and chords shown in the figure at the right.

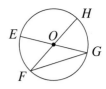

10. a. *Open-ended* Draw a circular design that includes an inscribed quadrilateral.
   b. *Writing* Describe your design so someone could draw it without looking at your drawing.
   c. Ask a family member or friend to use your description to draw your design. Rewrite the description if necessary.

11. Choose A, B, C, or D. Which of the following is *not* an inscribed polygon?

A.   **B.**   **C.**   **D.**

Reasoning **Draw several different diagrams that fit each description. Then make a conjecture.**

12. an inscribed quadrilateral whose vertices are the endpoints of two diameters

13. an inscribed triangle that has a diameter as one of its sides

14. Do the following to inscribe a regular hexagon in a circle.
   • Use a compass to draw a circle.
   • Keeping the compass set to the same width, put the tip on the circle and make a small arc that intersects the circle.
   • Move the tip of the compass to the intersection. Make another small arc. Continue around the circle.
   • Join each pair of consecutive arcs.

Mixed Review

Solve each equation. *(Lesson 5-4)*

15. $p - \frac{4}{7} = 5\frac{1}{14}$ **16.** $3\frac{1}{2} = x - 1\frac{3}{4}$ **17.** $t = 12\frac{9}{10} - 10\frac{2}{3}$ **18.** $\frac{1}{2} = w - 4\frac{5}{12}$

Find each missing number. *(Lesson 4-2)*

19. $\frac{15}{50} = \frac{3}{\blacksquare}$ **20.** $\frac{4}{\blacksquare} = \frac{20}{35}$ **21.** $\frac{18}{32} = \frac{\blacksquare}{16}$ **22.** $\frac{\blacksquare}{40} = \frac{4}{5}$ **23.** $\frac{10}{25} = \frac{2}{\blacksquare}$

24. *Shopping* A $39.95 sweater and a $19.65 skirt were on sale for 40% off. What is the total cost for the sweater and skirt? *(Lesson 6-9)*

7-8 Circle Graphs

THINK AND DISCUSS

▼**1** *Reading Circle Graphs*

Circle graphs present data as percents or fractions of a total. The total must be 100% or 1.

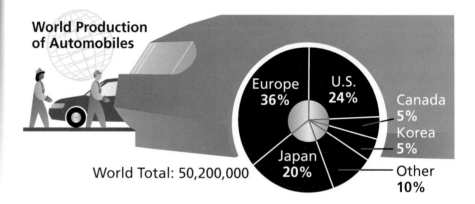

World Production of Automobiles

Europe 36%
U.S. 24%
Canada 5%
Korea 5%
Other 10%
Japan 20%

World Total: 50,200,000

1. ✔ *Try It Out* Use the graph above. Where were the most automobiles produced?

2. Canada's production was what fraction of Japan's production?

3. ▪▪*Predict* About how many automobiles were produced in the United States? in Japan?

4. ▪▪*Number Sense* What is the sum of the percents in the graph?

▼**2** *Making Circle Graphs*

A circle graph is divided into sectors. Each sector is determined by a central angle.

5. **a.** What is the sum of the measures of the central angles in the circle at the right?

   b. What percent of the circular region is each sector?

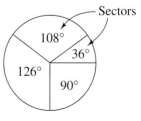

Sectors
108°
36°
126°
90°

Population Statistics The table below shows the number of people in the United States who have at least one grandchild under the age of 18. Draw a circle graph for the data.

Number of Grandparents

Age	People (Millions)
44 and less	3.6
45-54	10.3
55-64	15.0
65 and more	18.2

First add to find the total number.

$$3.6 + 10.3 + 15.0 + 18.2 = 47.1 \text{ (million)}$$

For each central angle, set up a proportion to find the measure. Use a calculator to solve.

$$\frac{3.6}{47.1} = \frac{a}{360°} \qquad \frac{10.3}{47.1} = \frac{b}{360°} \qquad \frac{15.0}{47.1} = \frac{c}{360°} \qquad \frac{18.2}{47.1} = \frac{d}{360°}$$

$$a \approx 27.5° \qquad b \approx 78.7° \qquad c \approx 114.6° \qquad d \approx 139.1°$$

Use a compass to draw a circle. Draw the central angles with a protractor.

Label each sector. Add any necessary information.

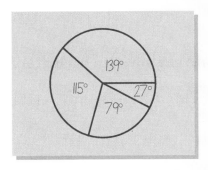

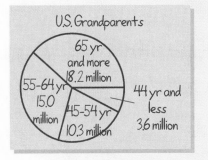

6. a. ✔ *Try It Out* Draw a circle graph to show the ways apples are used.
   b. Did you have to calculate the measure of each central angle? Why or why not?

Uses of Apples

Use	Percent
Juice	41
Fresh	41
Applesauce	9
Other	9

1. The age for obtaining a driver's license without a driver's education course varies by state. The circle graph shows the percent of states requiring the indicated minimum ages.
   a. The graph does not tell the total number of states. Do you think the total should be part of the graph? Explain.
   b. What is the most common minimum age for obtaining a license without a driver's education course? How many states require this age?

Minimum Driving Ages

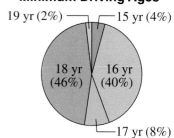

Use the graph at the right for Exercises 2 and 3. In the graph, the angle measure for the portion of the graph that represents 4 people in a vehicle is 20°.

2. What fraction of the circle represents the given number of people in a vehicle?
   a. 1 person   b. 2 people   c. 3 people   d. 4 people

3. How many vehicles contained 4 people? Why must you round your answer?

Number of People in Vehicles

Each digit indicates the number of people in one vehicle.

Total Vehicles: 536

4. **Choose A, B, C, or D.** Which circle graph shows 25%, 5%, 40%, and 30%?

A.   B.   C.   D.

Number Sense **Find the missing measures in each graph.**

5.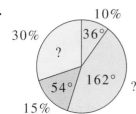

6.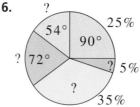

7.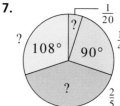

8. *Writing* Suppose you take two surveys asking people what they consider important safety features on a car. In one, people can give more than one safety feature. In the other, they give only the safety feature they consider most important. Which survey results can you show in a circle graph? Why?

Find the measure of the central angle that you would draw to represent each percent in a circle graph. Round to the nearest degree.

9. 25%   **10.** 28%   **11.** 30%   **12.** 11%   **13.** 12.5%   **14.** 14.5%

15. a. The data below show the percent of shoppers who prefer to shop on a specific day of the week. Use the data to draw a circle graph.

Day	Percent	Day	Percent
Monday	4	Friday	17
Tuesday	5	Saturday	29
Wednesday	12	Sunday	7
Thursday	13	No preference	13

b. If 1,200 people were interviewed for the survey, how many people gave each response?

16. a. *Research* Find a circle graph in a newspaper or magazine. Use the data in the graph to find the measure of each central angle.
b. Use a protractor to measure the central angles in the graph. Was the graph accurately made? Justify your answer.

17. The Miller family wants to buy a new car. Mr. Miller made a graph of how the family spends their monthly income of $2,400.
a. What percent of the budget is car expenses?
b. Mr. Miller estimates that payments on a new car will increase their monthly car expenses to $480. What percent of their monthly budget will car expenses be if the Millers buy a new car?
c. *Reasoning* What changes do you think the Miller family should make in their budget so that they can buy a new car? Make a circle graph that shows the changes you suggest.

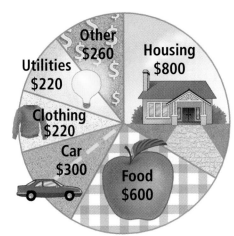

18. Use the data about how a group of students get to school to draw a circle graph.

Transportation Mode	Walk	Bicycle	Bus	Car
Number of Students	252	135	432	81

Mixed Review

Write each number as a percent. Round to the nearest tenth of a percent where necessary. *(Lesson 6-7)*

19. 0.07   **20.** 3.5   **21.** $\frac{3}{8}$ **22.** $\frac{9}{20}$ **23.** 0.099   **24.** $\frac{40}{125}$

Find each sum or difference. *(Lessons 5-2, 5-3)*

25. $\frac{2}{3} + \frac{3}{8}$ **26.** $4\frac{1}{6} + 6\frac{2}{9}$ **27.** $7\frac{3}{4} + \frac{11}{16}$ **28.** $\frac{7}{8} - \frac{1}{4}$ **29.** $9\frac{7}{10} - 4\frac{3}{5}$ **30.** $7\frac{1}{8} - 3\frac{1}{6}$

31. *Raffle Tickets* Melinda bought 9 more tickets than Lorissa. Together they bought 17. How many did each buy?
(Lessons 3-6, 3-8)

CHAPTER PROJECT

PROJECT LINK: MEASURING

Sketch a design of a tower that is at least 4 in. tall. How many toothpicks are needed? Build the tower using glue instead of raisins. Test it by gently placing a baseball on it. If your tower starts to buckle, reinforce it.

✓ CHECKPOINT 2

Lessons 7-4 through 7-8

Use dot or graph paper to draw each polygon.

1. a square   **2.** a trapezoid   **3.** a rhombus   **4.** a hexagon

5. Draw a circle graph to display the following results of a survey of favorite types of movies.

    Action-Adventure: 45   Comedy: 27   Science Fiction: 32   Other: 21

6. *Open-ended* Draw, label, and identify a circle, four radii, two diameters, an inscribed quadrilateral, and five chords.

7. Choose A, B, or C. Which triangle is *not* congruent to △*XYZ*?

  A.   **B.**   **C.**

What You'll Learn

▼ **1** To construct the perpendicular bisector of a segment

▼ **2** To construct the bisector of an angle

...And Why

Constructions made with only a straightedge and compass have been an important part of geometry since the time of the ancient Greeks.

Here's How

Look for questions that
▪ build understanding
✔ check understanding

Work Together
Folding Bisectors

Work with a partner. Draw a segment, $\overline{AB}$, on tracing paper. Fold the paper so that point A lies on point B. Unfold the paper and label the intersection of $\overline{AB}$ and the fold line as point M.

1. ▪ *Analyze* Compare your result with your partner's.
   a. What is the relationship between $\overline{AM}$ and $\overline{MB}$?
   b. What kind of angles does the fold line make with $\overline{AB}$?

Draw an angle, $\angle CDE$, on tracing paper. Fold the paper so that $\overrightarrow{DC}$ lies on $\overrightarrow{DE}$. Unfold the paper. Label any point of the fold line inside $\angle CDE$ as point F. Draw $\overrightarrow{DF}$.

2. ▪ *Analyze* Compare your result with your partner's. What is the relationship between $\angle CDF$ and $\angle FDE$?

THINK AND DISCUSS

▼ **1** Segment Bisectors

The **midpoint** of a segment is the point that divides a segment into two congruent segments. A **segment bisector** is a line (or segment or ray) that goes through the midpoint of the segment.

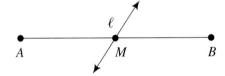

$\overline{AM} \cong \overline{MB}$
M is the midpoint of $\overline{AB}$.
Line ℓ is a segment bisector of $\overline{AB}$.

Perpendicular lines are lines that intersect to form right angles. A line that is perpendicular to a segment at its midpoint is the **perpendicular bisector** of the segment.

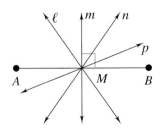

3. In the figure at the left, if M is the midpoint of $\overline{AB}$, which of the segment bisectors is the perpendicular bisector of $\overline{AB}$?

4. ▪ *Reasoning* How many bisectors does a segment have?

5. Point Z is the midpoint of $\overline{XY}$.
   a. If $\overline{XY}$ is 38 mm long, what is the length of $\overline{XY}$? of $\overline{ZY}$?
   b. If $\overline{XZ}$ is $\frac{3}{4}$ in. long, what is the length of $\overline{ZY}$? of $\overline{XY}$?

You can use a compass and *straightedge* (an unmarked ruler) to construct the perpendicular bisector of a given segment.

■ EXAMPLE 1

Use a compass and straightedge to construct the perpendicular bisector of $\overline{AB}$.

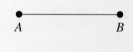

Step 1

Open the compass to more than half the length of $\overline{AB}$. Put the tip of the compass at A and draw an arc intersecting $\overline{AB}$.

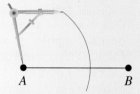

Step 2

Keeping the compass open to the same width, put the tip at B and draw another arc intersecting $\overline{AB}$. Label the points of intersection of the arcs as C and D.

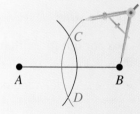

Step 3

Draw $\overleftrightarrow{CD}$. Label the intersection of $\overline{AB}$ and $\overleftrightarrow{CD}$ as point M.

$\overleftrightarrow{CD}$ is the perpendicular bisector of $\overline{AB}$. Point M is the midpoint of $\overline{AB}$.

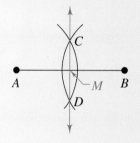

6. ✔ *Try It Out* Draw $\overline{XY}$. Construct the perpendicular bisector of $\overline{XY}$.

7. a. ■ *Think About It* Could you construct a different perpendicular bisector of $\overline{XY}$ in Question 6? Explain.
   b. How many perpendicular bisectors does a segment have?

▼ Angle Bisectors

The **bisector** of an angle is the ray that divides the angle into two congruent angles.

> ■ **EXAMPLE 2**
>
> Use a compass and straightedge to construct the angle bisector of ∠P.
>
>
>
> **Step 1**
>
> Put the tip of the compass at *P* and draw an arc that intersects the sides of ∠P. Label the points of intersection as *S* and *T*.
>
>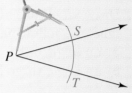
>
> **Step 2**
>
> With the compass tip at *S* and then at *T*, and with the same compass opening, draw intersecting arcs. Label the point where they intersect as *X*.
>
>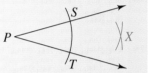
>
> **Step 3**
> Draw $\overrightarrow{PX}$.
> $\overrightarrow{PX}$ is the bisector of ∠SPT.
>
>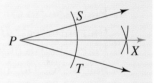

8. ✔ *Try It Out* Draw an obtuse angle. Construct its bisector.

EXERCISES *On Your Own*

Point B is the midpoint of $\overline{AC}$. Complete.

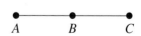

1. $AB = 4$ in., $AC = $ ▧

2. $AC = 9$ cm, $AB = $ ▧

3. $BC = 5$ ft, $AB = $ ▧

4. $AB = 17$ mm, $AC = $ ▧

5. $AC = 3$ in., $BC = $ ▧

6. $BC = 75$ cm, $AC = $ ▧

7. Draw a segment. Then construct its perpendicular bisector.

8. Draw an acute angle. Then construct its angle bisector.

9. The bisector of ∠JKL is $\overrightarrow{KN}$. If the measure of ∠JKN is 66°, what is the measure of ∠JKL?

10. Point A is the midpoint of $\overline{XY}$. Point Y is the midpoint of $\overline{XZ}$. Point Z is the midpoint of $\overline{AB}$. If $\overline{XA}$ is 2 cm long, how long is $\overline{XB}$? (*Hint:* Draw a diagram.)

11. Draw $\overline{CD}$ at least 3 in. long. Then construct and label the following.
    a. a segment half as long as $\overline{CD}$
    b. a segment one fourth as long as $\overline{CD}$

12. a. Construct a 90° angle.
    b. Construct a 45° angle.

13. Draw an obtuse angle, $\angle ABC$. Then construct and label the following two angles.
    a. an angle one fourth the measure of $\angle ABC$
    b. an angle three fourths the measure of $\angle ABC$

14. *Writing* How are a segment bisector and an angle bisector alike?

15. Construct an altitude of a triangle by following these steps.
    a. Draw a triangle about 2 in. high that is shaped like the one at the right.
    b. Place the tip of your compass on point A and draw an arc that intersects $\overline{BC}$ in two points. Label the points D and E.
    c. Place the tip of your compass on point D and draw an arc below $\overline{BC}$. Do the same from point E keeping the same compass setting.
    d. Label the intersection of the two arcs F. Draw $\overleftrightarrow{AF}$. Label the intersection of $\overleftrightarrow{AF}$ and $\overline{BC}$ as G. $\overline{AG}$ is an altitude of $\triangle ABC$.

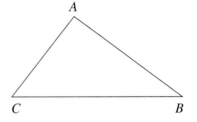

Mixed Review

Draw figures on 10 × 10 squares of graph paper to represent each of the following percents. (*Lesson 6-6*)

16. 150%   17. 98%   18. 310%   19. 75%   20. 27%

21. *Entertainment* Terick listens to the radio for two and a half hours every day after school. How many hours does he listen to the radio each week? (*Lesson 5-5*)

EXPLORATION

Constructing Congruent Angles and Parallel Lines

After Lesson 7-9

You can use a compass and straightedge to construct an angle congruent to a given angle.

1. Draw an angle like ∠A at the right. Also draw ray ℓ with endpoint B.

2. a. Place the tip of the compass at A. Make an arc that intersects the sides of ∠A. Label the points of intersection as C and D.
   b. With the same compass opening, place the tip of the compass at B and draw an arc that intersects ℓ at E.

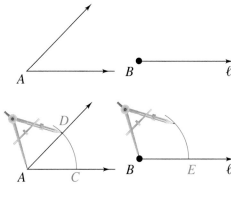

3. a. Change the compass opening to the length from C to D.
   b. Using this compass opening, place the tip of the compass at E. Draw an arc to determine point F.

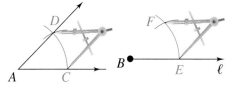

4. Draw $\overrightarrow{BF}$. ∠DAC ≅ ∠FBE.

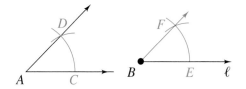

When a line intersects two parallel lines, congruent angles are formed. In the diagram at the right ∠1 ≅ ∠2. Now you can apply your ability to construct congruent angles to construct parallel lines.

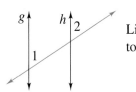

Line g is parallel to line h.

5. a. To construct a line parallel to m, first draw line n that intersects m at A as shown at the right. Then label point B on n.
   b. Follow the instructions for Questions 2 and 3 above to copy ∠1 at B.
   c. Draw $\overleftrightarrow{BF}$. $\overleftrightarrow{BF}$ is parallel to m.

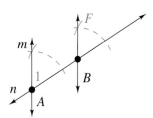

Read each question and choose the best answer.

1. Which best represents a pair of similar figures?

   A.

   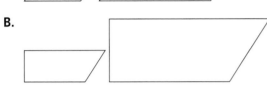

   B.

   C.

   D.

2. If $15c = 40$, what is the value of c?

   F. $2\frac{1}{3}$ G. $2\frac{1}{2}$

   H. $2\frac{2}{3}$ J. 3

3. During registration, 40% of the 500 students at Grove Middle School chose to take a foreign language. What fraction of the students are taking foreign language?

   A. $\frac{3}{10}$ B. $\frac{1}{3}$

   C. $\frac{2}{5}$ D. $\frac{3}{5}$

4. Which expression is equivalent to $2\frac{1}{5} \times 1\frac{1}{8} + 3\frac{1}{4}$?

   F. $2\frac{1}{5} \times (1\frac{1}{8} + 3\frac{1}{4})$

   G. $1\frac{1}{8} \times 3\frac{1}{4} \times 2\frac{1}{5}$

   H. $2\frac{1}{5} \times 3\frac{1}{4} + 1\frac{1}{8}$

   J. $3\frac{1}{4} + 2\frac{1}{5} \times 1\frac{1}{8}$

5. If the ratio of dogs to cats at a pet store is exactly 4 to 1, then the pet store could have—

   A. 15 dogs and 3 cats
   B. 18 dogs and 3 cats
   C. 20 dogs and 5 cats
   D. 12 cats and 4 dogs

Please note that items 6 and 7 have *five* answer choices.

6. A Fahrenheit temperature can be converted to a Celsius temperature by using the formula

   $$C = \frac{5}{9}(F - 32),$$

   where C is the Celsius temperature and F is the Fahrenheit temperature. The temperature on a summer day reached 104 degrees Fahrenheit. What is this temperature in degrees Celsius?

   F. 32 degrees Celsius
   G. 140 degrees Celsius
   H. 72 degrees Celsius
   J. 76 degrees Celsius
   K. Not Here

7. For an art project, a class is going to create a mural that contains an enlargement of this smaller drawing. If the building in the mural is 60 in. tall, what is its width?

   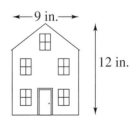

   A. 45 in.   B. 48 in.   C. 57 in.
   D. 72 in.   E. Not Here

CHAPTER PROJECT

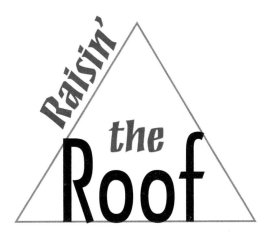

Raisin' the Roof

Build a Tower The Project Link questions on pages 295, 304, 312, and 322 should help you complete your project. Here is a checklist to help you gather together the parts of your project.

✔ pictures of structures built using triangles

✔ your description of how to strengthen a square

✔ your description of how to strengthen a cube

✔ your sketch for the design of a tower

✔ your completed tower

Try to make your tower attractive as well as strong. Demonstrate to the class that your tower will support a baseball.

Reflect and Revise
Show your tower to a friend, and discuss its design. Demonstrate its strength. Can you use fewer toothpicks without losing strength? If necessary, revise the design.

Web Extension
Prentice Hall's Internet site contains information you might find helpful as you complete your project. Visit www.phschool.com/mgm2/ch7 for some links and ideas related to construction and architecture.

1. Draw two figures that continue this pattern.

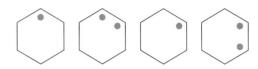

2. **Choose A, B, C, or D.** ∠1 and ∠2 are acute vertical angles. ∠1 and ∠3 are adjacent supplementary angles. What must be true?
   I. ∠1 is obtuse.
   II. ∠2 and ∠3 are complementary.
   III. $m\angle 1 = m\angle 3$
   IV. ∠2 and ∠3 are supplementary.

   A. I only   **B.** I and II
   C. III and IV   **D.** IV only

3. Two angles of a triangle are complementary. Describe the triangle.

4. **a.** The measures of two angles of a triangle are 54° and 26°. What is the measure of the third angle?
   b. Classify the triangle by its angles.

5. Describe the error that was made in constructing the perpendicular bisector of $\overline{AB}$.

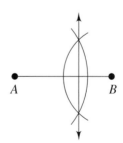

6. Construct a 45° angle.

7. *Writing* Write a definition for *square* that uses the word *rhombus*.

8. From home, Belinda walked half way to the playground. She continued on for $\frac{1}{4}$ mi and was then $\frac{5}{8}$ mi from home. How far is it from her home to the playground?

9. $\triangle ABC \cong \triangle ZYX$. Write six congruences involving corresponding sides and angles.

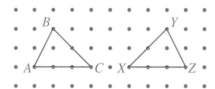

10. $\triangle ABC \cong \triangle EBD$. Find as many angle measures and side lengths as you can.

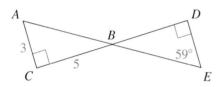

11. Name each of the following for circle O.
    a. a central angle
    b. three radii
    c. a chord that is not a diameter
    d. two semicircles

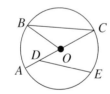

12. Students earned the following amounts of money to pay the transportation costs of a class trip. Make a circle graph for the data.

Fund Raiser	Money
Car wash	$150
Paper drive	$75
Book sale	$225
Food stand	$378

Choose the best answer.

1. In which set of numbers is 9 a factor of all the numbers?

  A. 36, 18, 21   **B.** 108, 252, 45
  C. 98, 81, 450   **D.** 120, 180, 267

2. ∠1 and ∠2 are complementary and the measure of ∠1 is four times the measure of ∠2. What is the measure of ∠2?

  A. 18°   **B.** 36°   **C.** 72°   **D.** 144°

3. Which kind of graph would best show the change in population of the United States from 1930 to 1990?

  A. line graph
  B. bar graph
  C. line plot
  D. stem-and-leaf plot

4. Find the *best* estimate for the perimeter of the shaded region.

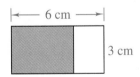

  A. 8 cm   **B.** 14 cm
  C. 12 cm   **D.** 18 cm

5. Which figure continues the pattern?

  A.   **B.**   **C.**   **D.**

6. Two angles of a triangle each measure 36°. Which classification is correct?

  A. acute triangle   **B.** right triangle
  C. obtuse triangle   **D.** scalene triangle

7. In parallelogram $ABCD$, the length of side $\overline{AB}$ is 9. The measure of ∠A is 40°. Which measure *cannot* be found?

  A. length of $\overline{BC}$ **B.** length of $\overline{CD}$
  C. $m\angle C$ **D.** $m\angle D$

8. The mean of six numbers is 9. Five of the numbers are 4, 7, 9, 10, and 11. What is the sixth number?

  A. 6   **B.** 9   **C.** 12   **D.** 13

9. Miki bought 4.4 lb of apples at $1.09/lb, 3.8 lb of pears at $1.29/lb, and two melons for $1.69 each. How much did she spend?

  A. $13.08   **B.** $11.39
  C. $12.16   **D.** $13.20

10. What is the solution of the equation $\frac{x}{4} + 8 = -1$?

  A. 28   **B.** −36   **C.** −9   **D.** −28

11. What is the name of this figure?

  A. hexagon
  B. regular polygon
  C. octagon
  D. pentagon

12. Which expression has the least value?

  A. $|12 - 10|$ **B.** $|10 - 12|$
  C. $|10| - |12|$ **D.** $|12| - |10|$

13. Find the mean of the data in the stem-and-leaf plot.

  A. 4.1
  B. 41
  C. 47
  D. 4.7

7	5
5	0 3
4	7
2	8
1	6 8

1|6 means 1.6

Geometry and Measurement

8

SHAPE UP AND SHIP OUT

Space is money! So before cargo is prepared for shipment in large containers, like those shown on a wharf in Houston, it is packaged in smaller containers, based on its size and shape.

Cans of tuna are examples of items you buy in cylindrical containers. Would you pack two cylinders side-by-side or one above the other? One arrangement wastes cardboard! But which one?

Design Boxes for Shipping Cylinders
For the chapter project, you will design boxes to hold cylindrical items. Your final product will be a model of a box that holds six cylinders.

• How to solve problems by guessing an answer and testing the guess

PROBLEM SOLVING

Estimating Length and Area

What You'll Learn

▼ To estimate lengths and perimeters

▼ To estimate areas

...And Why

Sometimes an estimate of length or area is all you need.

Here's How

Look for questions that
⊞ build understanding
✔ check understanding

Work Together
Measuring Length

1. ⊞ *Data Collection* Walk the length of your classroom heel-to-toe. Count the number of steps.

2. Measure your foot and determine the length of the room.

3. How close were the lengths found by members of your group? What accounts for the differences in the lengths?

4. Average the lengths found by the members of your group.

5. Which estimate do you think is the more accurate, the individual measurements or the average? Explain.

THINK AND DISCUSS

▼ *Estimating Length*

Measurements must include a unit in order to make sense. A height of 12 for a building is meaningless. However, if you know that a building is 12 in. tall, you know that the building is just a model.

■ EXAMPLE 1

What unit of measure would you use to estimate the width of a lake?

You might use meters or feet. For a large lake, you might use kilometers or miles.

Note that there is a table of metric measures and U.S. customary measures on page 525.

QUICKreview

Perimeter is the distance around an object or figure.

6. ✔ *Try It Out* What unit of measure would you use to estimate each of the following?
   a. the wingspread of a butterfly
   b. the perimeter of a picture frame
   c. the perimeter of an amusement park

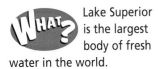

7. a. How could you use a piece of string to estimate the perimeter of the puzzle piece at the right?

b. Estimate the perimeter.

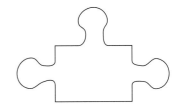

2 *Estimating Area*

When you find the number of square units inside a figure, you are finding the **area** of the figure.

■ **EXAMPLE 2**   *Real-World Problem Solving*

Geography Each square below represents 900 mi². Estimate the area of Lake Superior.

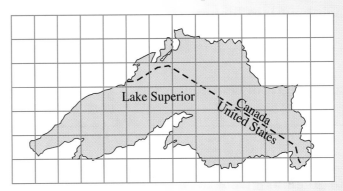

Count the number of squares that are filled or almost filled. Count the number of squares that are about half-filled.

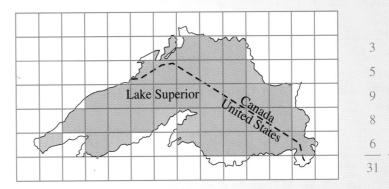

3	1
5	1
9	0
8	3
6	3
31	8

Estimate the number of squares filled: $31 + \frac{1}{2}(8)$, or 35.

Multiply 35 by 900 mi². The area is about 31,500 mi².

Lake Superior

8. ✔ *Try It Out* Each square below is 1 cm by 1 cm.
  a. Estimate the area of the figure.
  b. Suppose the figure is a map of a lake. Each square represents 25 km^2. Estimate the area of the lake.

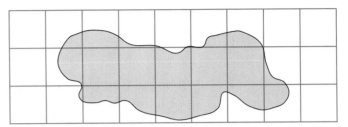

EXERCISES *On Your Own*

Estimate each length in inches.   1 in.

1. _____   **2.** _____

Estimate each length in centimeters.   1 cm

3. _____   **4.** _____

Choose the unit of measure listed that you would use to estimate the given length or area.

5. the height of a telephone pole:
   mm, cm, m, km

6. the perimeter of a picture frame:
   in., ft, yd, mi

7. the area of a swimming pool:
   in.^{2}, yd^2, ft^2, mi^2

8. the area of a soccer field:
   mm^2, cm^2, m^2, km^2

9. Each square below is 1 cm by 1 cm. Estimate the perimeter and area of the figure below.

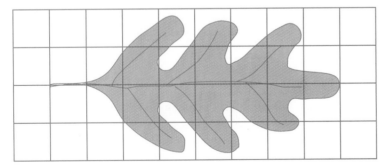

Use the article at the right for Exercises 10 and 11.

10. **a.** An acre contains 43,560 ft². Estimate the number of square feet in Tivoli Gardens.
    b. The area of a football field is 57,600 ft². Does a football field have more area or less area than an acre?
    c. About how many football fields are equal to the area of Tivoli Gardens?

11. Disneyland covers about 180 acres. About how many times larger than Tivoli Gardens is Disneyland?

OLDEST PARK INSPIRES

Tivoli Gardens in Copenhagen, Denmark, founded in 1833, is the world's oldest amusement park. The park covers about 20 acres and has 29 restaurants and 25 attractions.

The park features animated scenes from Hans Christian Andersen's fairy tales. After his visit there in the 1950s, Walt Disney began his plans for Disneyland.

Each square below represents 25 mi². Estimate the area of each region.

12.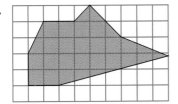

13.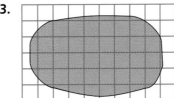

14. **a.** Measure the length of your *pace* (the distance you cover when you take a normal walking step).
    b. Use your pace to estimate the length and width of a room in your home. Then estimate the perimeter of the room.
    c. *Writing* Which would be more accurate, measuring the length of your room using your pace or the heel-to-toe method you used in the Work Together. Why?

Mixed Review

Solve each equation. *(Lesson 5-9)*

15. $4m = 416$

16. $\frac{72}{3} = 8n$

17. $\frac{p}{4} = \frac{325}{600}$

18. $\frac{-81}{3} = \frac{q}{9}$

19. $\frac{s}{2} = 5\frac{7}{8}$

20. Four test scores are 87, 80, 77, and 83. A fifth score makes the mean 82. Find the mode. *(Lesson 1-4)*

What You'll Learn

▼ To find the area and perimeter of parallelograms

...And Why

Area of a parallelogram is related to the areas of rectangles, squares, triangles, and trapezoids.

Here's How

Look for questions that
- ⬝ build understanding
- ✔ check understanding

THINK AND DISCUSS

You can use what you know about the area of a rectangle (a special parallelogram) to find the area of *any* parallelogram.

1. ⬝*Spatial Reasoning* What figures are formed by the perpendicular segment drawn as shown at the right?

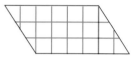

2. **a.** If you cut along the perpendicular segment and rearrange the two figures as shown, you will form a rectangle. What is its area?
   b. What is the area of the original parallelogram? Why?

3. **a.** How many units long are the *base b* and the *height h* of the parallelogram?
   b. ⬝*Explain* How are *b* and *h* related to the length and width of the rectangle that was formed?

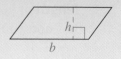

The formula for the area of a parallelogram follows from the formula for the area of a rectangle.

AREA OF A PARALLELOGRAM

The area of a parallelogram is the product of any base and the corresponding height.

$$A = bh$$

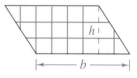

■ EXAMPLE

Find the area of the parallelogram.

Use $A = bh$ to find the area.

$$A = 47.5 \cdot 18.2$$
$$= 864.5$$

The area is 864.5 cm^2.

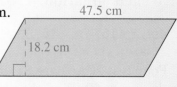

4. Suppose you want to find the perimeter of the parallelogram in the Example. What information do you need?

5. a. ✔ *Try It Out* Find the area of the parallelogram.
   b. Find the perimeter of the parallelogram.

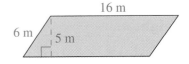

6. ⬩ *Estimation* The shape of the state of Tennessee is approximately a parallelogram. Find the area of the parallelogram to estimate the area of Tennessee.

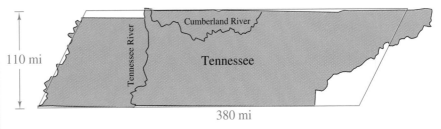

Surveyors are one of the many skilled workers involved in making a map. They measure distance, direction, and difference in elevation between points on Earth's surface.

Work Together

Exploring Similar Rectangles

If you double the dimensions of a rectangle, you get a rectangle similar to the original one. What do you think happens to the perimeter and area of a rectangle when you double each dimension?

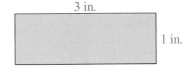

7. Find the perimeter and area of the rectangle shown.

8. Copy and complete the table by finding the perimeter and area of rectangles with the dimensions shown.

ℓ	w	P	A
3 in.	1 in.	▦	▦
6 in.	2 in.	▦	▦
9 in.	3 in.	▦	▦
12 in.	4 in.	▦	▦

9. ⬩ *Number Sense* What happens to the perimeter of a rectangle when you double, triple, or quadruple the dimensions?

10. ⬩ *Number Sense* What happens to the area of a rectangle when you double, triple, or quadruple the dimensions?

Find the area of a parallelogram with base length *b* and height *h*.

1. $b = 7$ ft, $h = 10$ ft

2. $b = 12$ in., $h = 7$ in.

3. $b = 8$ cm, $h = 0.5$ cm

 Choose **Use a calculator, pencil and paper, or mental math to find the area and perimeter of each parallelogram.**

4. square

5 in.

5. rectangle

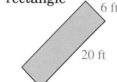

6 ft

20 ft

6.

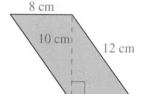

8 cm

10 cm

12 cm

7.

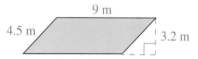

9 m

4.5 m

3.2 m

8.

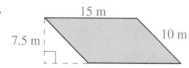

15 m

7.5 m

10 m

9.

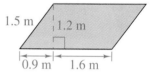

1.5 m

1.2 m

0.9 m   1.6 m

10. *Mental Math* The perimeter of a square is 28 in. What is the area?

11. Find the area of a parallelogram with base length 3 m and height 50 cm.

12. *Design* You can use parallelograms to make a design that gives the illusion of being three-dimensional. Do all of the parallelograms in this design have the same area? Why or why not?

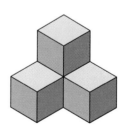

13. a. *Reasoning* What happens to the area of the rectangle in the Work Together activity if you multiply the dimensions by *n*?
   b. What happens to the perimeter of the rectangle if you multiply the dimensions by *n*?

14. The length of a rectangle is doubled and the width remains the same. What, if anything, can you say about the new area? About the new perimeter? Explain using examples.

15. The area of a certain rectangle is 20 in.^{2}. The perimeter is 21 in. If you double the length and width, what will be the area and perimeter of the new rectangle?

JOURNAL
Some parallelograms are rectangles. Explain why the formula $A = bh$ is the same as $A = \ell w$ for these special parallelograms.

16. a. Estimate the area of the pond.
   b. *Writing* Explain how you estimated the area.

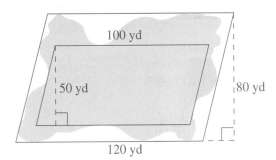

17. Find the area and perimeter of the figure.

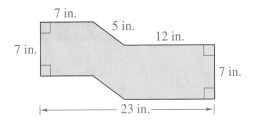

18. *Writing* Why is the area of the rectangle at the right greater than the area of the parallelogram even though they have the same perimeter?

19. The area of a rectangle is 120 cm^2. The width of the rectangle is 8 cm. What is the perimeter of the rectangle?

Mixed Review

Find the value of each expression. *(Lessons 3-3, 3-4)*

20. $120 + 43 - 95$ **21.** $28 - 9 + 35 + 14$ **22.** $37 + (-89)$ **23.** $(-5)^2 + 6(2 - 4)$

Find the percent of change. State whether the change is an increase or a decrease. Round to the nearest percent. *(Lesson 6-11)*

24. old: $3.95; new: $4.55   **25.** old: $180; new: $150   **26.** old: $32.50; new: $44

27. *Choose a Strategy* Whitney picked up twice as many books from the library as Lorena, who took 3 more than Amira. If Amira checked out 4 fewer books than Dominic, and he took 5 books, how many books did each person check out?

CHAPTER PROJECT

PROJECT LINK: ANALYZING

Choose an everyday item that is packaged in a cylinder. It is your job to design a rectangular box for shipping one such cylinder. Decide on the length, width, and height of the box. Remember, don't waste any cardboard.

What You'll Learn

▼ To find the area of triangles

▼ To find the area of trapezoids

...And Why

You will be able to find the area not only of triangles and trapezoids, but also of more complicated figures.

Here's How

Look for questions that
- build understanding
- ✔ check understanding

Work Together — *Finding the Area of a Triangle*

Step 1 Use centimeter graph paper to draw two congruent triangles.

Step 2 Cut out both triangles. Put them together to form a parallelogram.

1. What is the area of the parallelogram?

2. What is the area of each triangle? Explain your answer.

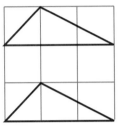

Sample

THINK AND DISCUSS

▼ 1 *Area of Triangles*

Any side of a triangle can be considered the *base* of the triangle, with length *b*. The *height h* is the length of the perpendicular segment from the opposite vertex to the line containing the base.

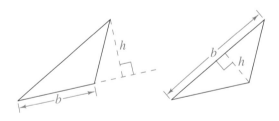

As you discovered in the Work Together activity, the formula for the area of a triangle follows from the area of a parallelogram.

AREA OF TRIANGLE

The area of a triangle is half the product of any base and the corresponding height.

$$A = \tfrac{1}{2}bh$$

Find the area and perimeter of the triangle.

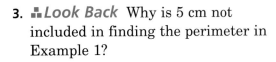
6 cm

5 cm

6.4 cm   5.4 cm

Use $A = \frac{1}{2}bh$ to find the area.

$$A = \frac{1}{2} \cdot 6 \cdot 5 = 15$$

Add the lengths of the sides to find the perimeter P.

$$P = 6.4 + 6 + 5.4 = 17.8$$

The area is 15 cm^2. The perimeter is 17.8 cm.

3. ■ *Look Back* Why is 5 cm not included in finding the perimeter in Example 1?

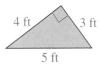
4 ft   3 ft

5 ft

4. Find the area and the perimeter of the triangle at the right.

5. a. ■ *Go a Step Further* The area of a triangle is 16 in.^{2}. The height of the triangle is 2 in. How would you find the length of the base of the triangle?
   b. Find the length of the base.

▼2 *Area of Trapezoids*

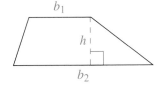
b_1

h

b_2

The two parallel sides of a trapezoid are the *bases* of the trapezoid, with lengths b_1 and b_2. The *height h* is the length of a perpendicular segment connecting the bases.

6. a. ■ *Modeling* Suppose you put a trapezoid and a copy of the trapezoid together to form a parallelogram. What will be the length of a base of the parallelogram?

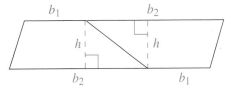
b_1 b_2

h h

b_2 b_1

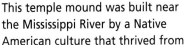

This temple mound was built near the Mississippi River by a Native American culture that thrived from 700 to 1700 A.D.

b. What will be the height of the parallelogram?
c. What is an expression for the area of the parallelogram?
d. What is an expression for the area of the trapezoid?

Find the area and perimeter of each figure.

22.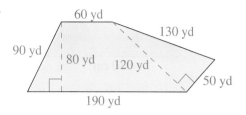

23.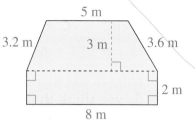

24.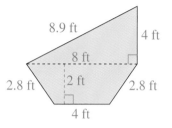

25.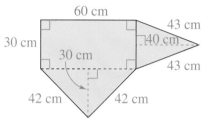

26. *Music* The hammer dulcimer at the right is a trapezoid. The top edge is 17 in. long, while the bottom edge is 39 in. long. The distance from the top edge to the bottom edge is 16 in. What is the area of the top of the dulcimer?

27. **a.** *Research* Use a map of the United States to name at least three states that resemble trapezoids.
    b. *Open-ended* Use the scale on the map to estimate the area of each of the three states.

Mixed Review

Classify each angle as acute, right, obtuse, or straight.
(Lesson 7-2)

28. $m\angle A = 84°$ 29. $m\angle C = 179°$ 30. $m\angle B = 91°$ 31. $m\angle P = 18°$ 32. $m\angle Q = 63°$

Find each sum or difference. *(Lessons 5-2, 5-3)*

33. $\frac{1}{10} + \frac{3}{4}$ 34. $\frac{7}{9} - \frac{1}{3}$ 35. $2 - \frac{3}{5}$ 36. $5\frac{1}{2} + 3\frac{7}{8}$ 37. $\frac{3}{10} - \frac{3}{15}$

38. *Cooking* Ms. Williams baked cookies for a bake sale. She sold 50% of them in the morning and $\frac{2}{3}$ of what was left in the afternoon. She had 4 cookies left. How many did she have at the beginning of the sale? *(Lesson 6-7)*

8-4 Circumference and Area of Circles

What You'll Learn

1 To find the circumference of a circle

2 To find the area of a circle

...And Why

Circles are all around you, from dinner plates to circus rings.

Here's How

Look for questions that
- ⚒ build understanding
- ✔ check understanding

Work Together
Finding the Ratio $\frac{C}{d}$ for a Circle

Use three cans that have bases of different sizes.

1. Measure the diameter d of a base of each can. Use string to measure the distance C around a base of each can. Record your results in a table.

2. Use a calculator to find the quotient $\frac{C}{d}$ for each can. Round each quotient to the nearest tenth.

3. ⚒ *Draw a Conclusion* What seems to be true about each quotient $\frac{C}{d}$?

THINK AND DISCUSS

1 *Circumference of a Circle*

Circumference is the distance around a circle. The ratio of every circle's circumference C to its diameter d is always the same, a number that is close to 3.14. Mathematicians use the symbol π, read as "pi," for this ratio. So, $\pi = \frac{C}{d}$.

If you multiply both sides of the equation $\pi = \frac{C}{d}$ by d, you get a formula for the circumference of a circle.

CIRCUMFERENCE OF A CIRCLE

The circumference of a circle is π times the diameter.

$$C = \pi d = 2\pi r$$

Many calculators have a $\boxed{\pi}$ key.

4. ⚒ *Calculator* Press the $\boxed{\pi}$ key on your calculator. What is the result?

Approximations such as 3.14 and $\frac{22}{7}$ are often used for π.

■ **EXAMPLE 1** *Real-World Problem Solving*

Entertainment A standard circus ring has a diameter of 13 m. What is the circumference?

Use $C = \pi d$ to find the circumference.

$\boxed{\pi}$ $\boxed{\times}$ 13 $\boxed{=}$ *40.8407045* ⟵ Use a calculator.

The circumference is about 40.8 m.

5. a. ⚏ *Go a Step Further* The circumference of a circle is about 50 cm. How would you find the diameter?
   b. ⚏ *Calculator* Find the diameter to the nearest unit.
   c. Is your answer reasonable? Explain.

▼2 *Area of a Circle*

6. ⚏ *Estimation* For each circle below, do the following:
   • Find the radius r.
   • Estimate the area A.
   • Use a calculator to find the ratio $\frac{A}{r^2}$.

a.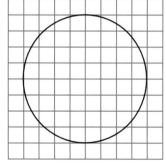

b.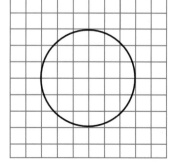

Did you find that in each case the quotient was a little more than 3? In fact, the quotient is equal to π!

$$\frac{A}{r^2} = \pi$$

If you multiply both sides of the equation $\frac{A}{r^2} = \pi$ by r^2, you get the following formula.

AREA OF A CIRCLE

The area of a circle is the product of π and the square of the radius.

$$A = \pi r^2$$

7. ▪ *Explain* How would you find the area of a circle if you know its diameter?

■ EXAMPLE 2

The diameter of a circle is 25 cm. Find the area of the circle to the nearest unit.

Use $A = \pi r^2$ to find the area.
$$r = 25 \div 2 = 12.5$$

⟵ **First divide the diameter by 2 to find r.**

π ✕ 12.5 x² ▤ *490.8738521*

The area is about 491 cm².

8. ✔ *Try It Out* The diameter of the inside of a basketball hoop is 18 in. What is the area enclosed by a basketball hoop? Round to the nearest tenth.

9. ▪ *Explain* How would you find the area of a circle if you know its circumference?

EXERCISES *On Your Own*

▦ *Calculator* **Find the circumference of each circle to the nearest unit.**

1.
7 cm

2.
50 cm

3.
9 m

4.
40 in.

5.
17 mm

⊞ Calculator **Find the area of each circle to the nearest unit.**

6.
7 cm

7.
50 cm

8.
9 m

9.
40 in.

10.
17 mm

Mental Math **Use 3 for π to estimate the circumference and area of each circle.**

11. $d = 2$ cm

12. $r = 10$ ft

13. $r = 6$ in.

14. $d = 4$ m

⊞ 15. a. *Calculator* Use the ⊡π key to find the area of this circle to the nearest hundredth.
b. *Calculator* Find the area of the circle to the nearest hundredth, using 3.14 for π.
c. *Writing* Kenny said that the area of the circle is about 99 m². Lynn said that the area is about 98 m². Which answer would you give for the area? Explain.

5.6 m

16. **Choose A, B, C, or D.** If you double the radius of a circle, what happens to the area?

   A. It remains the same.   **B.** It is doubled.
   C. It is tripled.   **D.** It is quadrupled.

Use $\frac{22}{7}$ for π to find the circumference and area of a circle with the given radius or diameter.

17. $r = 14$ ft

18. $d = 9$ cm

19. $r = 3\frac{1}{2}$ yd

20. $d = 7$ in.

21. $r = 11$ mm

Given the circumference of a circle, find the radius to the nearest tenth.

22. $C = 58$ m

23. $C = 41$ ft

24. $C = 35$ in.

25. $C = 93$ mm

26. $C = 12$ cm

27. *Sports* The track shown has two lanes separated by a dashed white line. Each lane is 1 m wide.
  a. What is the difference between the inside perimeter and the outside perimeter of the inner lane? How does that compare to the difference between the perimeters of the outer lane?
  b. The runner in the inner lane is to run once around the track. Where should the runner in the outer lane start if both runners are to run equal distances? Explain.

74 m
40 m

28. Social Studies Tipis of the Sioux and Cheyenne tribes were often over 12 ft tall. The circular base had a diameter of about 15 ft. What was the area of a base? Round to the nearest unit.

29. The diameter of the large circle shown below is 3.6 cm. The diameter of each of the small circles is 0.9 cm. Find the area of the shaded region to the nearest tenth.

Mixed Review

Find each answer. *(Lessons 6-9, 6-10)*

30. What is 40% of 360?   **31.** 45 is what percent of 360?   **32.** 36 is 12% of what number?

Solve each equation. *(Lesson 3-9)*

33. $13 + 3x = 7$ **34.** $16 + 2y = 9$ **35.** $1.1a + 2 = 7.5$ **36.** $\frac{1}{2}b - 16 = 10$

✓ CHECKPOINT 1   *Lessons 8-1 through 8-4*

1. Choose the unit you would use to estimate the area of your classroom: in., ft, mi, in.^{2}, ft^2, mi^2.

Find the area and perimeter of each figure.

2. triangle

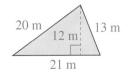

20 m   12 m   13 m
21 m

3. parallelogram

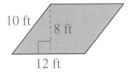

10 ft   8 ft
12 ft

4. triangle

7 cm   8 cm
10.6 cm

5. trapezoid

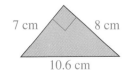

10 in.
6 in.   10 in.
18 in.

6. Calculator The radius of a circle is 75 cm. Find the circumference and area to the nearest unit.

8-5 Exploring Square Roots

What You'll Learn

1 To find perfect squares and square roots of perfect squares

2 To estimate square roots

...And Why

You will be able to find the length of a side of a square whose area is a perfect square.

Here's How

Look for questions that
- ⊹ build understanding
- ✔ check understanding

Work Together _____ *Investigating Square Numbers*

Look at the diagram at the right. If you form a square with 3 tiles on each side, you will use 9 tiles. This shows that $3^2 = 9$.

1. Use square tiles to form squares with 1, 2, . . . , 12 tiles on each side.

2. Make a table that shows the number of tiles needed for each square. Label the columns of the table n for side lengths and n^2 for number of tiles.

3. Extend your table for side lengths 13 through 20.

THINK AND DISCUSS

1 *Finding Square Roots of Perfect Squares*

A number like 9 that is the square of an integer is a **perfect square**. The inverse of squaring a number is finding its **square root**. Because $3^2 = 9$, the (positive) square root of 9 is 3.

■ **EXAMPLE 1**   *Real-World Problem Solving*

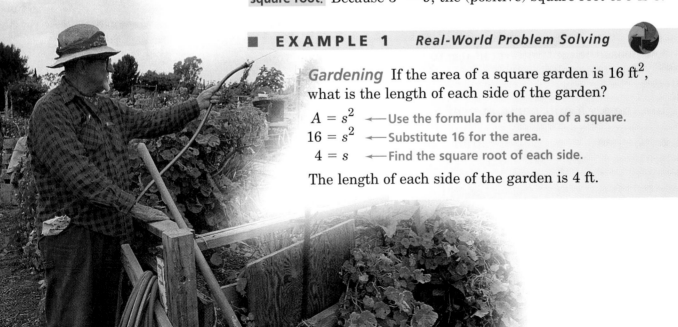

Gardening If the area of a square garden is 16 ft^2, what is the length of each side of the garden?

$A = s^2$ ⟵ Use the formula for the area of a square.
$16 = s^2$ ⟵ Substitute 16 for the area.
$4 = s$ ⟵ Find the square root of each side.

The length of each side of the garden is 4 ft.

The symbol $\sqrt{}$ is used to indicate nonnegative square roots.

4. ✔ *Try It Out* What is $\sqrt{4}$?

5. a. What is 7^2?
   b. What is $\sqrt{49}$?
   c. ⁙ *Reasoning* What other number, besides 7, can you square to get 49?

Every nonnegative number has two square roots. *Note*: In this book when we talk about *the* square root, we will mean the nonnegative square root.

You can use what you know about the perfect squares to find the square roots of some larger perfect squares.

6. ⁙ *Patterns* Find each perfect square.
   a. 20^2 b. 30^2 c. 40^2 d. 50^2 e. 60^2

7. a. How are 6^2 and 60^2 related?
   b. How are $\sqrt{6^2}$ and $\sqrt{60^2}$ related?
   c. What is $\sqrt{900}$? How is it related to $\sqrt{9}$?
   d. ⁙ *Number Sense* Why does $\sqrt{90}$ not fit in the pattern with $\sqrt{9}$ and $\sqrt{900}$?

▼2 *Estimating Square Roots*

When a number is not a perfect square, you can estimate its square root.

■ **EXAMPLE 2**

Estimation Find two consecutive whole numbers that $\sqrt{33}$ is between.

The consecutive perfect squares that 33 is between are 25 and 36.

$$\sqrt{25} < \sqrt{33} < \sqrt{36}$$
$$5 < \sqrt{33} < 6$$

$\sqrt{33}$ is between 5 and 6.

8. ✔ *Try It Out* Find two consecutive whole numbers that each square root is between.
   a. $\sqrt{50}$ b. $\sqrt{88}$ c. $\sqrt{150}$ d. $\sqrt{340}$

Find each of the following. Use mental math as much as possible.

1. 8^2 2. 13^2 3. 15^2 4. 18^2 5. 90^2 6. 100^2

7. 14^2 8. 16^2 9. 17^2 10. 20^2 11. $\sqrt{64}$ 12. $\sqrt{169}$

13. $\sqrt{81}$ 14. $\sqrt{36}$ 15. $\sqrt{144}$ 16. $\sqrt{25}$ 17. $\sqrt{100}$ 18. $\sqrt{196}$

19. $\sqrt{16}$ 20. $\sqrt{289}$ 21. $\sqrt{256}$ 22. $\sqrt{2,500}$ 23. $\sqrt{4,900}$ 24. $\sqrt{10,000}$

25. *Writing* Describe the difference between finding the square of a number and finding the square root of a number.

Find the length of a side of a square with the given area.

26. 64 cm^2 27. 121 km^2 28. 225 mm^2 29. 169 ft^2 30. $1,600 \text{ m}^2$

31. 900 in.^2 32. 289 mi^2 33. 400 cm^2 34. 196 mm^2 35. $8,100 \text{ ft}^2$

36. **Choose A, B, C, or D.** Which figure has an area twice the area of the figure at the right?

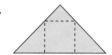

A.   B.   C.   D.

37. **a.** Find $\frac{1}{2} \times \frac{1}{2}$.
   b. What is the square root of $\frac{1}{4}$?
   c. What is the square root of $\frac{4}{9}$?

Estimation **Find two consecutive whole numbers that each square root is between.**

38. $\sqrt{95}$ 39. $\sqrt{61}$ 40. $\sqrt{42}$ 41. $\sqrt{125}$ 42. $\sqrt{200}$

43. $\sqrt{38}$ 44. $\sqrt{119}$ 45. $\sqrt{220}$ 46. $\sqrt{175}$ 47. $\sqrt{390}$

48. *Open-ended* Write two whole numbers whose square roots are between 9 and 10.

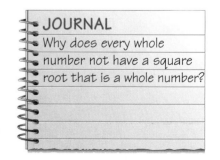

JOURNAL
Why does every whole number not have a square root that is a whole number?

49. *Gardening* The area of a square garden is 170 ft². Estimate the perimeter of the garden.

Mixed Review

Solve each proportion. *(Lesson 6-3)*

50. $\dfrac{13}{x} = \dfrac{39}{60}$ **51.** $\dfrac{4}{9} = \dfrac{7}{y}$ **52.** $\dfrac{2}{3} = \dfrac{n}{12}$ **53.** $\dfrac{x}{8} = \dfrac{6}{15}$ **54.** $\dfrac{18}{25} = \dfrac{y}{100}$

55. $\overrightarrow{QS}$ bisects $\angle PQR$. The measure of $\angle PQR$ is 102°. Find the measure of $\angle SQR$. *(Lesson 7-9)*

56. *Choose a Strategy* Jeshaun stopped at a rung one half of the way up a ladder. After climbing four more rungs, he was three fourths of the way up the ladder. How many rungs are there?

CHAPTER PROJECT

PROJECT LINK: DRAWING

Use the cylinders you chose in the Project Link on page 343. Sketch two ways that you could package two of the cylinders in rectangular boxes. Label the dimensions of both boxes. Estimate which box uses less cardboard.

Math at Work

FARM OPERATOR

Today's farm operator usually has a bachelor's degree in agriculture. A farm operator manages and trains farm workers who work with crops and livestock. Factors that influence a farm operator's job include weather, changes in prices of farm products, and federal farm programs. Farm operators use math and accounting skills to manage inventory and control budgets.

Visit this Web site for current information on farming: http://www.agriculture.com

Choose the best answer.

1. Kevin's yard measures 60 feet by 40 feet. Kevin will plant bushes and flowers at the front of his yard. He will plant grass in the rest of his yard.

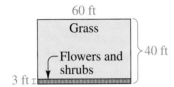

   How many square feet will Kevin plant with grass?

   A. 180 ft^2 B. 2,220 ft^2
   C. 2,400 ft^2 D. 2,580 ft^2

2. On Wednesday, $\frac{3}{5}$ of the students at school bought a hot lunch. What percent of the students bought a hot lunch?

   F. 65%   G. 60%   H. 40%   J. 20%

3. A beauty parlor charges $15 for a haircut and $10 for styling hair. If c represents the number of customers who have their hair cut and styled, then the money the beauty parlor will make is represented by this expression.

$$15c + 10c$$

   How much money will the beauty parlor make if 12 customers have their hair both cut and styled?

   A. $350   B. $300   C. $180   D. $120

4. The price of a coat is $114 before sales tax. The sales tax is 7%. To find the tax on the coat, multiply $114 by —

   F. 7.0   G. 0.7   H. 0.07   J. 0.007

5. The instructions for making puppets require $1\frac{1}{3}$ feet of ribbon for 4 puppets. How many feet of ribbon will be needed to make 14 puppets?

   A. $4\frac{2}{3}$ ft   B. $5\frac{1}{3}$ ft
   C. $18\frac{2}{3}$ ft   D. 56 ft

6. $\triangle QRS$ and $\triangle TUV$ are similar. What is the value of x?

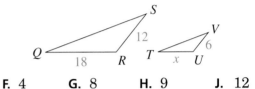

   F. 4   G. 8   H. 9   J. 12

Please note that items 7–9 have *five* answer choices.

7. The top of a large birthday cake is 10 in. wide and 18 in. long. "Happy Birthday!" is written in a rectangular section that is 5 in. by 6 in. Which number sentence could be used to find d, the amount of space left for decorations?

   A. $d = (18 \times 10) - (5 \times 6)$
   B. $d = (18 + 10) - (5 + 6)$
   C. $d = 18 \times 10 \times 5 \times 6$
   D. $d = (18 - 6) + (10 - 5)$
   E. $d = \frac{18}{6} \times \frac{10}{5}$

8. The diameter of the top of a jar of pickles is 3 in. What is the area of the top of the jar to the nearest hundredth? Use 3.14 for π.

   F. 28.26 in.^{2} G. 14.13 in.^{2}
   H. 9.12 in.^{2} J. 7.07 in.^{2}
   K. Not Here

9. Which fraction equals 3.4?

   A. $\frac{22}{7}$ B. $\frac{15}{4}$ C. $\frac{23}{6}$ D. $\frac{17}{5}$ E. $\frac{10}{3}$

8-6 Exploring the Pythagorean Theorem

What You'll Learn

1. To use the Pythagorean theorem
2. To determine whether a triangle is a right triangle

...And Why

When you know the lengths of two sides of a right triangle, you can find the length of the third side.

Here's How

Look for questions that
- ⁂ build understanding
- ✔ check understanding

Work Together   *Building Squares on Right Triangles*

Work with a partner to investigate a right triangle.

Step 1 Use centimeter graph paper to draw a right triangle with the right angle included between sides that are 3 cm and 4 cm long.

Step 2 Draw squares that have the horizontal and vertical sides of the right triangle as sides.

Step 3 Use another piece of the graph paper to make a square on the side opposite the right angle, as shown below.

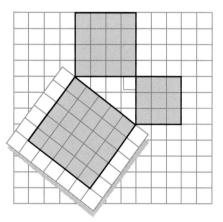

1. **a.** What is the length of each side of the square made on the side opposite the right angle?
   b. What is the area of each of the three squares?

2. ⁂*Modeling* Draw a right triangle on centimeter graph paper with the right angle included between sides that are 8 cm and 15 cm long. Repeat Steps 2 and 3 above.
   a. What is the length of each side of the square made on the side opposite the right angle?
   b. What is the area of each of the three squares?

3. ⁂*Reasoning* Look for a pattern. What seems to be the relationship of the areas of the smaller two squares and the third square built on the sides of a right triangle?

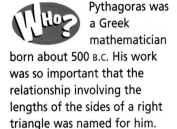
THINK AND DISCUSS

▼ *Using the Pythagorean Theorem*

The two shorter sides of a right triangle are the **legs.** The side opposite the right angle is the **hypotenuse.**

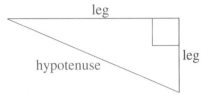

PYTHAGOREAN THEOREM

In any right triangle, the sum of the squares of the lengths a and b of the legs is equal to the square of the length c of the hypotenuse.

$$a^2 + b^2 = c^2$$

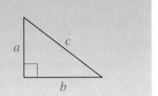

If you know the lengths of two sides of a right triangle, you can use the Pythagorean theorem to find the length of the third side.

■ EXAMPLE 1

Find the length of the hypotenuse of the figure at the right.

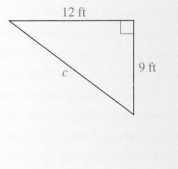

$$a^2 + b^2 = c^2$$
$$9^2 + 12^2 = c^2 \quad \longleftarrow \text{Substitute.}$$
$$81 + 144 = c^2$$
$$225 = c^2$$
$$\sqrt{225} = c \quad \longleftarrow \text{Find the value of } c.$$
$$15 = c$$

The length of the hypotenuse is 15 ft.

4. ✔ Try It Out Find the hypotenuse of each figure below.

a.   **b.**

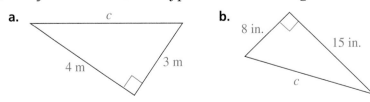

EXAMPLE 2   *Relating to the Real World*

Construction A wheelchair ramp 626 cm long covers a horizontal distance of 624 cm. What is the vertical rise of the ramp?

Draw a diagram.

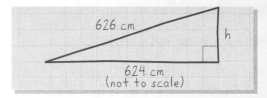

626 cm

h

624 cm
(not to scale)

Use the Pythagorean theorem.

$$a^2 + b^2 = c^2$$
$$624^2 + b^2 = 626^2 \qquad \longleftarrow \text{Substitute.}$$
$$b^2 = 626^2 - 624^2 \qquad \longleftarrow \text{Solve for } b^2.$$
$$b^2 = 391{,}876 - 389{,}376$$
$$b^2 = 2{,}500$$
$$b = \sqrt{2{,}500} = 50 \qquad \longleftarrow \begin{array}{l}\text{50 is the square}\\ \text{root of 2,500.}\end{array}$$

The vertical rise is 50 cm.

5. ✔ *Try It Out* One leg of a right triangle is 40 in. long. The hypotenuse is 41 in. long. What is the length of the other leg?

6. ∷ *Reasoning* The sides of a right triangle are 30 in., 50 in., and 40 in. long. Which is the length of the hypotenuse? How do you know?

▼2 *Determining Right Triangles*

If the lengths a, b, and c of the sides of a triangle satisfy the equation $a^2 + b^2 = c^2$, then the triangle is a right triangle.

■ **EXAMPLE 3**

Is the triangle at the left a right triangle? Explain.

$$a^2 + b^2 \stackrel{?}{=} c^2$$
$$15^2 + 36^2 \stackrel{?}{=} 39^2 \qquad \longleftarrow \begin{array}{l}\text{The longest side is 39 ft}\\ \text{long. Substitute 39 for } c.\end{array}$$
$$225 + 1{,}296 \stackrel{?}{=} 1{,}521$$
$$1{,}521 = 1{,}521 \;✔$$

15 ft

36 ft

39 ft

The lengths of the sides satisfy the equation $a^2 + b^2 = c^2$. The triangle is a right triangle.

7. **a.** ✔ *Try It Out* Is a triangle with sides of length 15 cm, 20 cm, and 25 cm a right triangle? Why or why not?

b. Is a triangle with sides of length 3 ft, 5 ft, and 6 ft a right triangle? Why or why not?

EXERCISES *On Your Own*

Find the missing side length.

1.
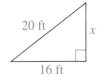

2.
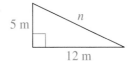

3.
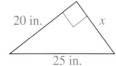

4.
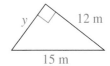

5. The hypotenuse of a right triangle is 37 ft long. One leg is 35 ft long. What is the length of the other leg?

6. The two longest sides of a right triangle are 60 m and 61 m long. What is the length of the third side?

7. *Camping* A large tent has an adjustable center pole. A rope 26 ft long connects the top of the pole to a peg 24 ft from the bottom of the pole. What is the height of the pole?

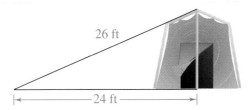

8. **a.** $\overline{AC}$ is the diameter of circle O. Find $\overline{AC}$.

b. Find the circumference and area of the circle.

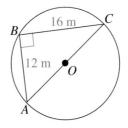

9. *History* The ancient Egyptians used a knotted rope to help them relocate property lines after the annual flooding of the Nile River. They divided a rope into 12 equal parts by tying knots. Then they used the rope to form a right triangle. The right angle helped them re-establish the square corners of boundary lines.

a. Draw a sketch to show how the knotted rope could be used to form a right triangle.

b. *Writing* Explain why the triangle must be a right triangle.

Determine whether each triangle is a right triangle. Explain your answer.

10.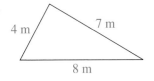

11.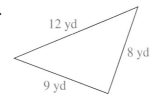

12.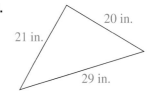

The lengths of the sides of a triangle are given. Is the triangle a right triangle? Explain your answer.

13. 15 in., 18 in., 24 in.

14. 10 m, 8 m, 13 m

15. 28 mm, 53 mm, 45 mm

16. 12 yd, 13 yd, 20 yd

17. 16 ft, 30 ft, 34 ft

18. 42 cm, 56 cm, 70 cm

19. *Home Repair* What is the height at which the ladder touches the side of the house?

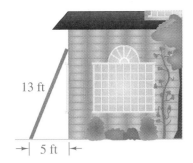

20. *Carpentry* The rectangular section of wood fencing shown below is reinforced with a piece of wood nailed across the diagonal of the rectangle. What is the length of the diagonal?

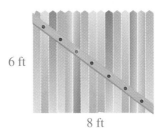

Mixed Review

The table shows the results of a survey in which seventh graders named their favorite pet. *(Lesson 7-8)*

21. Make a circle graph to show this information.

22. What percent of the students do not prefer dogs as pets?

23. *Choose a Strategy* Elicia, Michelle, and Cary are an engineer, a teacher, and a salesperson. Elicia and the engineer drove Cary to her company's main office on Saturday. Who is the teacher?

Pet	Number of Students
Dog	26
Cat	21
Fish	9
Rabbit	5
Other	11

8-7 Applying the Pythagorean Theorem

What You'll Learn

▼ To use a calculator to apply the Pythagorean theorem

...And Why

You can use a calculator to find lengths that are not square roots of perfect squares.

Here's How

Look for questions that
- build understanding
- ✔ check understanding

THINK AND DISCUSS

The water splashes around you as you rocket down the longest slide at the water park. As soon as you reach the bottom, you're up and set to go again.

Suppose you know that a slide starts 9 m above the water and covers 7 m horizontally. You want to find the length of the slide.

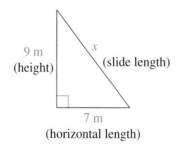

9 m
(height)

x
(slide length)

7 m
(horizontal length)

1. a. Use the Pythagorean theorem to write an equation involving the lengths of the sides of the triangle.
   b. Solve the equation for x^2.
   c. Is x^2 a perfect square? Explain.

You can use the square root key on your calculator to find the square root of any nonnegative number.

2. ▪ *Calculator* Use your calculator to find the value of x in the figure above. Round the result to the nearest tenth of a meter.

3. a. ▪ *Reasoning* How could you use your calculator to determine whether a number is a perfect square?
   b. Is 18,769 a perfect square? Why or why not?
   c. Is 7,925 a perfect square? Why or why not?

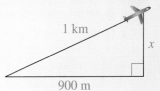

📟 *Aviation* A jet airplane takes off in a straight path. When it has traveled 1 km, it has covered a horizontal distance of 900 m. To the nearest meter, what is the height of the jet at that point?

Need Help? For practice converting metric units, see Skills Handbook page 541.

Use the Pythagorean theorem.

$$1{,}000^2 = 900^2 + x^2$$

← 1 km = 1,000 m

$$1{,}000^2 - 900^2 = x^2$$

1000 $\boxed{x^2}$ $\boxed{-}$ 900 $\boxed{x^2}$ $\boxed{=}$ $\boxed{\sqrt{}}$ **435.8898944**

The jet is about 436 m high.

4. a. ✔ *Try It Out* The legs of a right triangle are 80 cm and 1.5 m long. What is the length of the hypotenuse?

   b. The leg of a right triangle is 80 cm long. The length of the hypotenuse is 1.5 m. What is the length of the other leg?

EXERCISES *On Your Own*

Find the missing side length to the nearest tenth.

1.

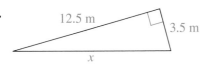

2.

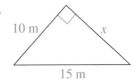

3.

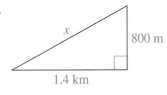

4.

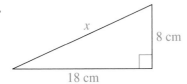

5.

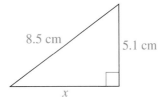

6.

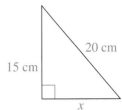

The lengths of two sides of a right triangle are given. Find the length of the third side to the nearest tenth of a unit.

7. legs: 8 m and 11 m

8. legs: 10 cm and 14 cm

9. leg: 25 in.; hypotenuse: 35 in.

10. legs: 6 m and 15 m

11. legs: 12 ft and 20 ft

12. leg: 18 yd; hypotenuse: 28 yd

13. **a.** Find the perimeter and area of this quadrilateral.
    b. *Writing* Which of the following is the best name for this quadrilateral: square, parallelogram, rhombus, trapezoid? Explain your choice.

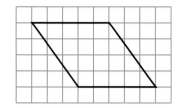

14. A rectangular park is 600 m long and 300 m wide. Tomi walked diagonally across the park from corner to corner. How far did he walk, to the nearest meter?

15. A support wire is attached to the top of a 60-m tower. It meets the ground 25 m from the base of the tower. How long is the support wire?

16. *Home Repair* A ladder is 6 m long. How much farther up a wall does it reach when the foot of the ladder is 2 m from the wall than when it is 3 m from the wall? Give the answer to the nearest tenth of a meter.

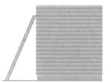

17. *Reasoning* The length of two sides of a right triangle are 9 cm and 14 cm. What are the two possible lengths for the third side? Round to the nearest tenth.

18. The area of $\triangle RSW$ is 216 cm^2.
    The area of $\triangle TSW$ is 540 cm^2.
    a. Find the lengths of $\overline{RW}$ and $\overline{WT}$.
    b. Find the lengths of $\overline{RS}$ and $\overline{ST}$.
    c. Find the perimeter of $\triangle RST$.

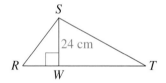

THE TILTING TOWER

Building began on the bell tower at Pisa, Italy, in 1173. Shortly after that, the builders realized the tower was beginning to lean. They tried to fix the problem, but the tower has continued to tilt even more over the centuries.

The tower leans because the foundation lies on a mixture of sand, clay, and water.

The tower now tilts southward about 5.5° from vertical. That means that a point 150 ft up the south side of the tower is about $149\frac{1}{4}$ ft above the ground.

19. If someone dropped a weight from 150 ft up the south side of the Leaning Tower of Pisa, about how far would it land from the base of the tower?

20. a. *Hobbies* If the area of a chessboard is 144 in.^{2}, what is the length of a side of the chessboard?
   b. What is the length of a diagonal of the chessboard?

21. *Sports* A softball diamond is a square 60 ft by 60 ft. A baseball diamond is a square 90 ft by 90 ft.
   a. How far is it from home plate to second base on a softball diamond? (*Hint:* Draw a diagram.)
   b. How far is it from home plate to second base on a baseball diamond?
   c. A baseball right fielder catches a fly ball on the first base line, 30 ft beyond first base. If he throws it to second base, how far does he throw the ball?
   d. A baseball right fielder catches a fly ball on the first base line, 30 ft beyond first base. If he throws it to third base, how far does he throw the ball?

Find the area of each triangle to the nearest tenth.

22.
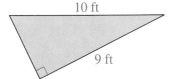
10 ft
9 ft

23.
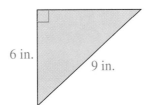
6 in.
9 in.

24.
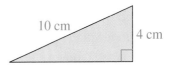
10 cm
4 cm

Mixed Review

Write the prime factorization of each number. (*Lesson 4-5*)

25. 28   **26.** 57   **27.** 72   **28.** 108   **29.** 156   **30.** 200

Compare using <, >, or =. (*Lesson 2-1*)

31. 1.72 ▩ 1.7   **32.** 10.1 ▩ 100.0   **33.** 0.02 ▩ 0.0002   **34.** 6.211 ▩ 6.21

Architecture **A floor plan has the scale 1.5 in. : 1 ft.** (*Lesson 6-5*)

35. What are the actual dimensions of a room that measures 21 in. × 24 in. on the floor plan?

36. What are the floor plan dimensions of a room measuring 12 ft × 15 ft?

Three-Dimensional Figures

What You'll Learn

1 To identify prisms

2 To identify other three-dimensional figures

...And Why

Architects use many different three-dimensional shapes in buildings.

Here's How

Look for questions that
- build understanding
- ✔ check understanding

THINK AND DISCUSS

1 *Identifying Prisms*

What geometric figures do you see in the entrance to the Louvre in Paris, France? In the Jomo Kenyatta Conference Center in Nairobi, Kenya? Figures that do not lie in a plane, such as these buildings, are *three-dimensional figures.*

Louvre

Jomo Kenyatta Conference Center

Some three-dimensional figures have only flat surfaces. The flat surfaces, called **faces,** are shaped like polygons.

face

1. **Draw a Conclusion** Which building has faces?

Prisms are three-dimensional figures with two parallel and congruent polygonal faces, called **bases.** The other faces are rectangles. A prism is named for the shape of its bases.

■ EXAMPLE 1

Give the best name for the prism.

The only parallel and congruent faces are triangular. The figure is a triangular prism.

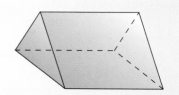

Notice in Example 1 that the bases of a prism are not necessarily at the "top" and "bottom."

2. ✔ *Try It Out* Match each prism with one of the following names: rectangular prism, pentagonal prism, hexagonal prism.

a.   b.   c.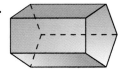

3. ▪ *Analyze* Each segment formed by the intersection of two faces is an *edge*. Why are some of the edges of the prisms in Question 2 dashed?

4. ▪ *Think About It* A *cube* is a rectangular prism whose faces are squares. Are the edges of a cube congruent? Explain.

▼2 *Other Three-Dimensional Figures*

A **pyramid** is a three-dimensional figure with only one base. The base is a polygon and the other faces are triangles. A pyramid is named for the shape of its base.

5. ▪ *Visual Thinking* Match each pyramid with one of the following names: triangular pyramid, rectangular pyramid, pentagonal pyramid, hexagonal pyramid.

a.  b. 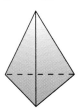 c.

6. ▪ *Think About It* Which of the three-dimensional figures below have bases? Describe the bases.

cylinder   cone   sphere

You can use graph paper to draw three-dimensional figures.

■ **EXAMPLE 2**

Draw a hexagonal prism.

Step 1
Draw a hexagon.

Step 2
Draw a second hexagon.

Step 3
Connect the vertices.

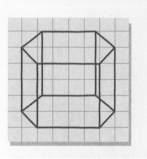

7. ✔ *Try It Out* Draw a triangular prism on graph paper.

EXERCISES *On Your Own*

Visual Thinking **Give the best name for each figure.**

1.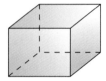

2.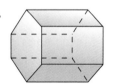

3.

4.

5.

6.

7.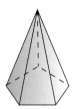

8.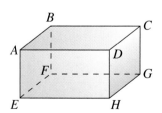

Use the rectangular prism at the right.

9. Name the four edges that intersect $\overline{AB}$.

10. Name the three edges that are parallel to $\overline{AB}$.

11. Name the four edges that are *not* parallel to $\overline{AB}$ and do *not* intersect $\overline{AB}$.

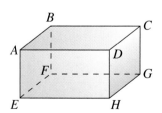

Architecture **Name some three-dimensional figures in each photograph on page 368.**

12. the Louvre

13. the Jomo Kenyatta Conference Center

Architecture **Name the three-dimensional figures in each photograph.**

14.

15.

16.

Drafting **Use graph paper to draw each figure.**

17. a rectangular prism

18. a rectangular pyramid

19. a triangular prism

Sketch each three-dimensional figure.

20. a television set

21. a container of salt

22. a tipi

23. How are a cylinder and a cone alike? How are they different?

Analyze **Classify as *true* or *false*. Explain.**

24. Every rectangular prism is a cube.

25. Some pyramids are prisms.

Mixed Review

Solve. *(Lesson 3-6)*

26. $4 + x = -6$

27. $x - 8 = 5$

28. $10 = y - (-2)$

29. $h + (-3) = -5$

Order from least to greatest. *(Lesson 4-3)*

30. $\dfrac{3}{8}, \dfrac{2}{12}, \dfrac{2}{3}$

31. $\dfrac{5}{9}, \dfrac{7}{12}, \dfrac{43}{81}$

32. $\dfrac{11}{24}, \dfrac{17}{42}, \dfrac{12}{36}$

33. $\dfrac{4}{6}, \dfrac{10}{18}, \dfrac{18}{24}$

34. $\dfrac{25}{27}, \dfrac{5}{7}, \dfrac{2}{5}$

35. *Photography* April must enlarge a 3 in. by 5 in. photograph so it is 185% of the original size. What will be the dimensions of the enlarged photograph? *(Lesson 6-9)*

Extra Practice, Lesson 8-8, page 521

EXPLORATION

Three Views of an Object

After Lesson 8-8

Three-dimensional objects can be drawn to show that they have length, width, and height, as in the drawing at the right. You can also make drawings that show only one view of the blocks.

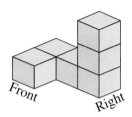

■ EXAMPLE

a. Make a drawing of the six blocks shown above. Draw them as if you are looking down on the blocks. This is called a *top view*.

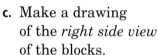

b. Make a drawing of the *front view* of the blocks.

c. Make a drawing of the *right side view* of the blocks.

Draw the top, front, and right side views of each figure.

1.

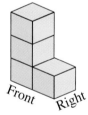

2.

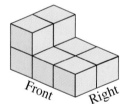

3.

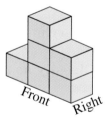

Use the top, front, and side views to draw each figure.

4. Top   Front   Right

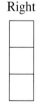

5. Top   Front   Right

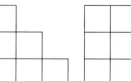

6. *Writing* Describe a solid you can build with blocks that has the same front, side, and top views.

8-9 Surface Area of Prisms and Cylinders

What You'll Learn

▼ 1 To find the surface area of prisms

▼ 2 To find the surface area of cylinders

...And Why

The surface area of prisms and cylinders determines the amount of material needed to cover their surfaces.

Here's How

Look for questions that
- ⁂ build understanding
- ✔ check understanding

THINK AND DISCUSS

▼ 1 Finding the Surface Area of Prisms

The centimeter graph paper covering a rectangular prism has been cut along the edges and folded flat.

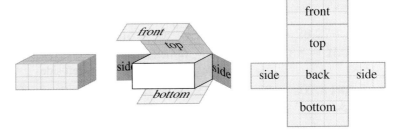

A pattern that can be folded to cover a solid figure is called a **net** for that figure.

1. ⁂ **Choose A, B, or C.** Which pattern is *not* a net for the rectangular solid above?

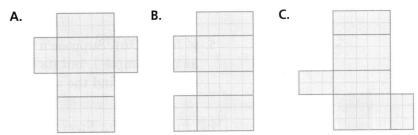

A. B. C.

The **surface area** of a prism is the sum of the areas of its faces. So, the surface area of a rectangular prism equals the sum of the areas of the six rectangles that make up its net.

2. What is the surface area of the rectangular prism above?

3. a. ⁂ *Modeling* This rectangular prism has been covered with inch graph paper. Draw a net for the prism.

   b. Draw a different net for the prism.

   c. Find the surface area of the prism.

6. Draw two different nets for a rectangular prism 3 units by 4 units by 7 units.

7. *Open-ended* Draw a net for a prism that has a surface area of 80 cm^2.

8. Which of these patterns is a net for a cylinder?

A.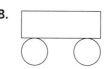

B.

C.

Draw a net for each cylinder. Then find its surface area. Round to the nearest unit.

9.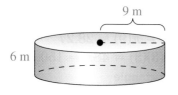
9 m
6 m

10.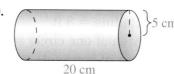
5 cm
20 cm

11.
7 ft
2 ft

12. The interior of a cylindrical water tank needs resurfacing. Its diameter is 60 ft and its height is 35 ft. What is the area of the interior to the nearest unit?

13. *Reasoning* Which has the greater effect on the surface area of a cylinder: doubling the base radius or doubling the height? Explain using examples.

Mixed Review

Which unit is best for measuring each of the following? *(Lesson 8-1)*

14. the perimeter of your desk: in., ft, yd, mi

15. the area of the gym floor: cm^2, m^2, km^2

Estimate each answer. *(Lessons 2-3, 2-5, 2-6)*

16. 25.5986×3.598

17. $12.3 \div 4.3$

18. $21.6 + 7.8$

19. $39.7 - 5.24$

20. *Choose a Strategy* A club has 100 members. Each of the 5 officers gets 6 other members to help them decorate for a party. What percent of the club members do the decorating?

CHAPTER PROJECT

PROJECT LINK: WRITING

Describe at least three different ways you can pack four of your cylinders in rectangular boxes. Which box has the least surface area? Calculate the surface area of the box.

Extra Practice, Lesson 8-9, page 521

Volume of Rectangular Prisms and Cylinders

What You'll Learn

1 To find the volume of a prism

2 To find the volume of a cylinder

...And Why

The volume of prisms and cylinders determines the amount of material needed to fill them.

Here's How

Look for questions that
- build understanding
- ✔ check understanding

THINK AND DISCUSS

1 Finding the Volume of Prisms

The **volume** of a three-dimensional figure is the number of cubic units needed to fill the space inside the figure. A **cubic unit** is a cube whose edges are one unit long.

a cubic centimeter ($1\ cm^3$)

■ **EXAMPLE 1**

Find the volume of the rectangular prism.

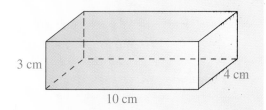

There are
$10 \cdot 4 = 40$ cubes in the bottom layer.

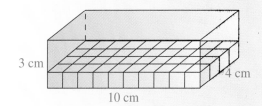

Three layers of cubes fit in the prism.

$40 \cdot 3 = 120$

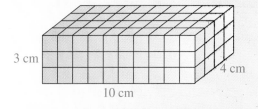

The volume is $120\ cm^3$.

1. a. ■ *Analyze* Find the area of the bottom of the prism at the right.
   b. How many unit cubes one inch on an edge would fit in the bottom layer?
   c. Find the volume of the prism.

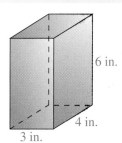

Niagara Falls

You can calculate the volume V of a rectangular prism by multiplying the area of a base B by the height h.

VOLUME OF A RECTANGULAR PRISM

V = area of base × height

$= Bh$

$= \ell wh$

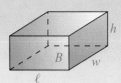

2. ✔ *Try It Out* The length of each edge of a cube is 7 m. What is the volume of the cube?

2 *Finding the Volume of a Cylinder*

You can calculate the volume of a cylinder in much the same way as you calculate the volume of a prism.

VOLUME OF A CYLINDER

V = area of base × height

$= Bh$

$= (\pi r^2)h$

■ EXAMPLE 2

A cylinder is 8.2 m high and has a base radius of 2.1 m. Estimate the volume. Then use a calculator to find the volume.

Use $V = \pi r^2 h$. Use 3 to estimate π.

Estimate: $V \approx 3 \cdot 2 \cdot 2 \cdot 8 = 96$ m³

π ⊗ 2.1 ⊡ ⊗ 8.2 ▤ *113.6062735* ←—Use a calculator.

The volume is about 113.6 m³.

3. ✔ *Try It Out* The base radius of a cylinder is 4.8 cm. The height is 15 cm. Estimate the volume. Then use a calculator to find the volume. Round to the nearest tenth.

▦ *Choose* **Use a calculator, paper and pencil, or mental math to find the volume of each rectangular prism.**

1.

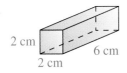

2 cm

6 cm

2 cm

2.

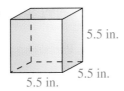

5.5 in.

5.5 in.

5.5 in.

3.

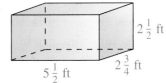

$2\frac{1}{2}$ ft

$5\frac{1}{2}$ ft

$2\frac{3}{4}$ ft

4. Choose A, B, C, or D. Which expression represents the volume of the rectangular prism at the right?

A. $9x$ **B.** $24x$ **C.** $24x^2$ **D.** $24x^3$

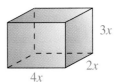

$3x$

$2x$

$4x$

5. Find the volume of a rectangular prism with length 11 ft, width 5 ft, and height 2 yd.

6. A gallon of milk occupies 231 in.^{3} of space. Can a container 15 in. by 6 in. by 8 in. hold 3 gallons? Why or why not?

7. a. The volume of a rectangular prism is 60 m^3. Find all possible whole number triples that could be the dimensions of the prism. For example, 2 m, 3 m, 10 m is a possible triple.

     b. *Writing* Explain how you solved the problem in part (a).

Find the volume of each cylinder. Round to nearest tenth.

8.

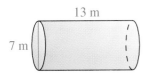

13 m

7 m

9.

11 ft

5 ft

10.

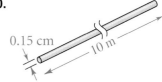

0.15 cm

10 m

11. Find the volume of a cylinder with a base radius of 2 cm and a height of 4 cm to the nearest unit.

Mental Math **Estimate each volume.**

12.

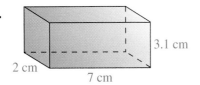

3.1 cm

2 cm

7 cm

13.

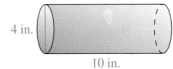

4 in.

10 in.

14. **a.** A cylinder has a base diameter and height of 5.5 cm. A cube has edges 5.5 cm long. Compare the volumes.
    b. *Reasoning* What accounts for the difference in the volumes?

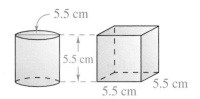

15. **a.** The triangular prism at the right was formed by cutting a rectangular prism in half. Find the volume of the rectangular prism and of the triangular prism.
    b. *Writing* Show that the volume of this triangular prism equals the area of its base times its height.

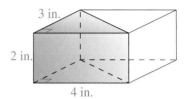

Mixed Review

Write the unit rate for each situation. *(Lesson 6-2)*

16. 18 mi in 3 h   17. $32.00 for 8 CDs   18. 12 lb in 5 wk   19. 4 c for 3 loaves

Write each decimal as a fraction in simplest form. *(Lesson 4-9)*

20. 1.25   21. 0.00215   22. 5.55   23. 0.429   24. 8.95   25. 0.003

26. *Choose a Strategy* Diego can mow Mrs. Jones' lawn twice as fast as Peter. Jody can mow the same lawn in 45 min. How long does it take Diego to mow the lawn? What do you need to know to solve the problem?

✓ CHECKPOINT 2   *Lessons 8-5 through 8-10*

Find the length of the third side of each right triangle. Round to the nearest tenth if necessary.

1. legs: 9 ft and 12 ft   2. leg: 5 cm; hypotenuse: 25 cm   3. legs: both 6 in.

Draw and label a figure for each description. Find the surface area and the volume of each. Use 3.14 for π.

4. a rectangular prism with dimensions 6 ft, 10 ft, and 5 ft
5. a cylinder with radius 8 m and height 20 m

6. **Choose A, B, C, or D.** A cylinder has a radius of 1 ft and a height of 3 ft. If you double the radius, the volume is ___?___.

   A. doubled   **B.** tripled   **C.** quadrupled   **D.** unchanged

8-11

Guess and Test

Problem Solving Strategies

Draw a Diagram
✓ Guess and Test
Look for a Pattern
Make a Model
Make a Table
Simulate a Problem
Solve a Simpler Problem
Too Much or Too Little
 Information
Use Logical Reasoning
Use Multiple Strategies
Work Backward
Write an Equation

THINK AND DISCUSS

Sometimes the best way to solve a problem is to make a guess and then test your guess. Using what you learn from testing your guess, you make another guess and test it. You repeat this process until you are able to solve the problem.

SAMPLE PROBLEM...

At a pet store, Alani decided on the number and kinds of fish she would like to have. The salesperson helped her figure that those fish would need an aquarium with a capacity of 10,648 cm^3. She wants a cubic aquarium. What should be the length of each edge of the cube?

 READ

Read for understanding. Summarize the problem.

1. Think about the information you are given and what you are asked to find.
   a. What type of three-dimensional figure is involved?
   b. What dimensions are important in the figure?

 PLAN

Decide on a strategy.

Guess and Test is a good strategy to use here. You can guess the length of each edge of the cube. Then test your guess by using a calculator to multiply the dimensions. If the test reveals that you guessed too high or too low, you can make a better guess and try again. A table can help you organize your guesses and the results.

 SOLVE

Try the strategy.

2. Suppose you start with a guess of 30 cm.
   a. Find the volume of the cube.
   b. Is the volume too high or too low?

3. a. What number would you use for your next guess for the length of each edge? Why?
   b. What will be the volume of the cube with this edge length? Make a table like the one below to record your guesses.

Length of Each Edge	Volume	Too High or Too Low?
30 cm	▪	▪
▪	▪	▪

Continue your guesses if necessary and add them to your table.

4. What length of each edge of the cube will give a volume of 10,648 cm^3?

LOOK BACK

Think about how you solved the problem.

5. Explain how the results of previous guesses helped you to make the next guess.

EXERCISES *On Your Own*

Solve using the Guess and Test strategy.

1. What are two whole numbers whose product is 147 and whose quotient is 3?

2. The volume of a rectangular prism is 2,058 cm^3. The length of the prism is three times the width. The height is twice the width. Find the width, length, and height of the prism.

Solve if possible. If not, tell what information is needed. Show all your work.

3. Find the next two numbers in the pattern below.
   100, 25, 50, 12.5, 25, ■, ■

4. *Jobs* After selling food during a soccer game, the cashier at the concession stand has some $1 bills, $5 bills, and $10 bills. She has 13 bills worth a total of $69. How many $1 bills, $5 bills, and $10 bills does she have?

5. Adam and Pablo each made a purchase at the bookstore. Adam bought 1 pencil and 2 pens for 86¢. Pablo bought 2 pencils and 1 pen for 67¢. How much does 1 pencil cost?

6. The width of a rectangle is 4 cm less than the length of the rectangle. The area of the rectangle is 96 cm^2. Find the length and width of the rectangle.

7. Mr. Quarles has cartons that measure 3 ft × 2 ft × 6 in. He wishes to store them in a 15 ft × 9 ft × 24 ft space. He can only stack the cartons on top of each other, not inside one another. How many cartons can he store?

8. a. Which is the longest segment shown in the rectangular prism at the right?

b. What measurements do you need to use to find x? To find y?

c. Find x and then find y.

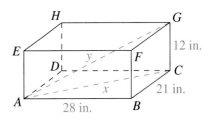

9. Suppose you have 12 square tiles that measure 1 in. by 1 in. What are the dimensions of the rectangle you can make that has the greatest perimeter? The least perimeter?

10. The sum of the digits of a certain two-digit number equals the square root of the number. What is the number?

11. *Science* The mass of 8 cm^3 of aluminum is 22 g. The mass of the same volume of gold is 154.4 g. Name two sets of dimensions that could give an 8 cm^3 rectangular prism.

 12. a. Use a calculator to find the following products.

$15 \cdot 15 \quad 25 \cdot 25 \quad 35 \cdot 35 \quad 45 \cdot 45$

b. *Writing* Look for patterns in part (a). Describe any patterns that you find.

c. Use the patterns you found to write each of the following products without multiplying the given numbers.

$55 \cdot 55 \quad 65 \cdot 65 \quad 75 \cdot 75 \quad 85 \cdot 85$

Mixed Review

Estimation **Find two consecutive whole numbers that each square root is between.** *(Lesson 8-5)*

13. $\sqrt{95}$　　**14.** $\sqrt{117}$　　**15.** $\sqrt{59}$　　**16.** $\sqrt{160}$　　**17.** $\sqrt{75}$　　**18.** $\sqrt{200}$

19. *Geography* The actual distance from San Francisco to Mexico City is about 1,890 mi. What is the map distance if the scale of the map is 2 in. : 420 mi? *(Lesson 6-5)*

CHAPTER PROJECT

PROJECT LINK: CALCULATING

Give at least three ways you can pack six of your cylinders in rectangular boxes. Find the surface area and volume of each box. Build a model of the box that uses the least cardboard.

EXPLORATION

Exploring Cubes

After Lesson 8-11

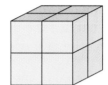

You can explore number patterns using unit cubes.

1. **Visual Thinking** Suppose you use unit cubes to make a larger cube. You paint the outside of a cube formed with two unit cubes on an edge.
   a. How many unit cubes are used to form the larger cube?
   b. How many sides of each unit cube are painted?

2. Make a chart like the one below for cubes formed by the given number of unit cubes on an edge.

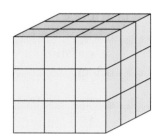

Number of Unit Cubes on an Edge	Total Number of Unit Cubes	Total Number Expressed as a Power	Number of Unit Cubes with Given Number of Sides Painted			
			0	1	2	3
2	8	2^3	0	0	0	8
3	■	■	■	■	■	■
4	■	■	■	■	■	■
5	■	■	■	■	■	■
6	■	■	■	■	■	■
7	■	■	■	■	■	■

3. **Patterns** Describe the number pattern you see in each of the last four columns of your table.

4. Use the number patterns you found for Question 3. Extend the table for 8 number cubes on an edge.

5. a. **Predict** What would be the total number of unit cubes in a cube that had 10 unit cubes on an edge?
   b. If there are 15 unit cubes on one edge of a cube, how many unit cubes will have no sides painted? One side? Two sides? Three sides?
   c. **Reasoning** If 144 unit cubes have two sides painted, how many unit cubes are on one edge of the cube?

6. **Writing** Can you tell the number of unit cubes on one edge of a cube if you know that eight unit cubes have three sides painted? Explain.

CHAPTER PROJECT

SHAPE UP AND SHIP OUT

Design Boxes for Shipping Cylinders The Project Link questions on pages 343, 357, 376, and 383 should help you complete your project. Here is a checklist to help you gather together the parts of your project.

- ✔ the dimensions of your cylinder
- ✔ the dimensions of rectangular boxes that hold one, two, four, and six cylinders using the least cardboard
- ✔ a model of the box that holds six cylinders

Your job calls for boxing shipments of cylinders. You don't want to waste cardboard, so design the boxes wisely! Remember, there can be lots of different ways to pack the cylinders, so pick the best arrangement for the six cylinders.

Reflect and Revise

Show your model to a friend. See if your friend agrees that you have thought of the best arrangement of six cylinders. If necessary, improve on your model.

Web Extension

Prentice Hall's Internet site contains information you might find helpful as you complete your project. Visit www.phschool.com/mgm2/ch8 for some links and ideas related to containers, surface area, and volume.

Area
8-1, 8-2, 8-3

Area is the number of square units inside a figure. Area is measured in square units such as square inches (in.^{2}), square meters (m^2), and square feet (ft^2).

1. Choose the unit you would use to estimate the area of a wall of a room: in., ft, mi, in.^{2}, ft^2, mi^2

Find the perimeter and area of each parallelogram, triangle, or trapezoid.

2.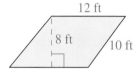
12 ft, 8 ft, 10 ft

3.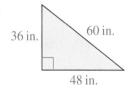
36 in., 60 in., 48 in.

4.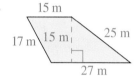
15 m, 15 m, 17 m, 25 m, 27 m

5.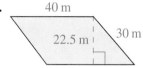
40 m, 22.5 m, 30 m

Circumference and Area of Circles
8-4

Circumference is the distance around a circle. The ratio of the circumference to the diameter of any circle is represented by π, which is close to the values 3.14 and $\frac{22}{7}$.

🖩 *Calculator* **Find the circumference and area of each circle to the nearest unit.**

6.
12 cm

7.
8 in.

8.
40 ft

9.
9 mm

Square Roots and the Pythagorean Theorem
8-5, 8-6, 8-7

A **perfect square** is a square of an integer. The opposite of squaring a number is finding its **square root**.

The **Pythagorean theorem** states that in any right triangle the sum of the squares of the lengths a and b of the legs is equal to the square of the length c of the hypotenuse.

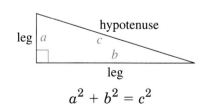
$$a^2 + b^2 = c^2$$

Mental Math **Find each of the following.**

10. 11^2 **11.** 7^2 **12.** $\sqrt{16}$ **13.** $\sqrt{64}$ **14.** $\sqrt{144}$ **15.** $\sqrt{400}$

16. *Estimation* Find two consecutive whole numbers that $\sqrt{87}$ lies between.

17. Choose A, B, C, or D. Which of the following could *not* be the lengths of sides of a right triangle?

   A. 3 m, 4 m, 5 m   **B.** 2 cm, 2 cm, 4 cm   **C.** 51 in., 85 in., 68 in.   **D.** 16 ft, 20 ft, 12 ft

The lengths of two sides of a right triangle are given. Find the length of the third side. Round to the nearest tenth if necessary.

18. leg: 12 mm; hypotenuse: 15 mm   **19.** legs: both 1 m   **20.** leg: 8 in.; hypotenuse: 14 in.

Surface Area and Volume of Three-Dimensional Figures 8-8, 8-9, 8-10

The **surface area** of a prism is the sum of the areas of the faces.

The **volume** of a three-dimensional figure is the number of cubic units needed to fill the space inside the figure.

21. The dimensions of a rectangular prism are 7 ft, 5 ft, and 3 ft.
   a. Sketch the rectangular prism.
   b. Find the volume of the rectangular prism.
   c. Draw a net for the rectangular prism.
   d. Find the surface area of the rectangular prism.

22. A cylinder is 14 cm high and has a base radius of 8 cm.
   a. Sketch the cylinder.
   b. Find the volume of the cylinder to the nearest tenth.
   c. Draw a net for the cylinder.
   d. Find the surface area of the cylinder to the nearest tenth.

Problem Solving Strategies   8-11

You can use the problem-solving strategy *Guess and Test* to solve many problems.

23. The volume of a rectangular prism is 24 m^3. The surface area is 52 m^2. Find the whole number dimensions of the prism.

1. Choose the unit you would use to estimate the length of an automobile: mm, cm, m, km, mm^2, cm^2, m^2, km^2

2. Find the area of a parallelogram with base length 14 m and height 9 m.

3. Find the area of a triangle with base length 12 cm and height 10 cm.

4. Find the area and perimeter of the trapezoid.

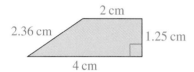

5. The area of a piece of land shaped like a rectangle is 114 yd^2. One dimension is 19 yd. Find the perimeter.

6. *Calculator* The diameter of a circle is 21 cm. Find the circumference and area of the circle to the nearest unit.

7. *Mental Math* Find each of the following.
   a. 8^2 b. 10^2 c. $\sqrt{25}$ d. $\sqrt{81}$

8. *Writing* Explain what a perfect square is.

9. Find x.

10. **Choose A, B, C, or D.** Suppose you want to estimate the number of bricks you could store in a shed. Which must you know about the shed?

    A. perimeter   **B.** area
    C. surface area   **D.** volume

11. *Calculator* Find the missing side length to the nearest tenth.

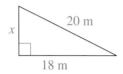

12. A rectangular garden is 40 m long and 30 m wide. Find the length of a diagonal walkway across the garden.

13. Give the best name for each shape.

    a.

    b.

    c.

    d.

14. **Choose A, B, C, or D.** The surface area of a cube is 150 cm^2. Find the volume.

    A. 15 cm^3 **B.** 30 cm^3
    C. 125 cm^3 **D.** 150 cm^3

15. Rectangular prism A has dimensions 10 cm, 2 cm, and 3 cm. Rectangular prism B has dimensions 5 cm, 2 cm, and 6 cm. Use $<$, $>$, or $=$ to compare the volumes of A and B.

16. *Estimation* The base radius of a cylinder is 9.7 cm. The height is 20 cm. To make a quick mental estimate of the volume, what would you use for a value of π? What is your estimate?

17. A cylinder-shaped tank is 12 ft long. It has a base diameter of 18 ft. Find the volume of the tank to the nearest unit.

Choose the best answer.

1. Which number has the greatest value?

   A. 2^5 **B.** 3^3

   C. 5^2 **D.** 20^1

2. Rectangle $ABCD$ is 3 ft × 4 ft. What is the area and the perimeter of $ABCD$?

   A. $A = 12$ ft^2, $P = 12$ ft
   B. $A = 12$ ft^2, $P = 14$ ft
   C. $A = 6$ ft^2, $P = 12$ ft
   D. $A = 12$ ft^2, $P = 7$ ft

3. The rectangles are similar. Which proportion could *not* be used to find the value of x?

   A. $\frac{7}{5} = \frac{2}{x}$ **B.** $\frac{x}{2} = \frac{7}{5}$

   C. $\frac{x}{5} = \frac{2}{7}$ **D.** $\frac{2}{7} = \frac{x}{5}$

4. Which of the following could *not* be the sides of a right triangle?

   A. 8, 15, 17   **B.** 10, 24, 26
   C. 15, 35, 40   **D.** 12, 16, 20

5. Which expression equals 8.23?

   A. $6.584 \div 0.8$
   B. $74.34 \div 9$
   C. $1{,}152.2 \div 14$
   D. $57.61 \div 7.1$

6. Which expression does *not* equal -12?

   A. $-3 \cdot 4$
   B. $-10 - 2$
   C. $-48 \div (-3)$
   D. $-16 - (-4)$

7. Which expression could you use to find the area of the cylinder's base?

   A. $(2 \cdot \pi \cdot 5)$
   B. $(\pi \cdot 2.5 \cdot 2.5)$
   C. $(\pi \cdot 5 \cdot 5)$
   D. $(2 \cdot \pi \cdot 2.5 \cdot 6)$

8. Which container has the greatest volume?

   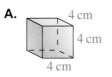
   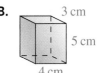
   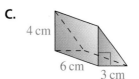
   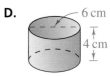

9. Which equation could you use to represent the following problem: Five more than half of the people (p) on the bus were students (s)?

   A. $\frac{p}{2} + 5 = s$
   B. $(p - 5) \div 2 = s$
   C. $\frac{p}{2} - 5 = s$
   D. $(p - 5) \div 2 = s$

10. Which expression does *not* have the same value as the other expressions?

    A. $\sqrt{144}$
    B. $\sqrt{36} + \sqrt{36}$
    C. $\sqrt{4} + \sqrt{64}$
    D. $\sqrt{81} + \sqrt{9}$

11. What is the value of x to the nearest tenth?

    A. 17.0   **B.** 12.7
    C. 7.0   **D.** 8.5

    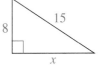

9

Using Probability

Everybody Wins

Remember the game "Rock, Paper, Scissors"? It is an unusual game because paper wins over rock, rock wins over scissors, and scissors win over paper. You can use mathematics to create and investigate a situation with similar characteristics.

Make Three Number Cubes For this chapter project, you will design three number cubes A, B, and C, which have a surprising property: A usually beats B, B usually beats C, and C usually beats A. Your final product will be to construct your cubes.

- **How to solve problems by doing a simulation**

PROBLEM SOLVING

9-1 Experimental Probability

THINK AND DISCUSS

1 *Finding Experimental Probability*

Suppose you play a game that includes tossing a coin and rolling a number cube. These are the results of eight turns.

Coin	heads	heads	tails	heads	tails	heads	tails	heads
Cube	2	5	1	2	3	2	3	5

Probability measures how likely it is that an event occurs. One or more results of an experiment make an **event.** In the game described above, "heads and a 2" is an example of an event.

For **experimental probability,** you collect data through observations or experiments. To find the experimental probability of the event "heads and a 2," use this ratio.

$$P(\text{event}) = \frac{\text{number of times an event occurs}}{\text{total number of experiments}}$$

$$P(\text{heads and a 2}) = \frac{\text{number of times "heads and a 2" occurs}}{\text{total number of experiments}} = \frac{3}{8}$$

■ EXAMPLE 1

Suppose you toss a coin 50 times. You get heads 20 times. Find the experimental probability that you get heads.

$$P(\text{heads}) = \frac{20}{50} \quad \begin{array}{l}\leftarrow\text{number of heads} \\ \leftarrow\text{number of tosses}\end{array}$$

$$= \frac{2}{5} \quad \leftarrow\textbf{Simplify the fraction.}$$

The probability that the result is heads is $\frac{2}{5}$.

1. a. ✔ *Try It Out* Suppose you toss a coin 60 times, and you get tails 25 times. Find the experimental probability of tails.

b. Suppose you plan to toss the same coin 10 more times. About how many times would you expect to get tails?

You can write a probability as a fraction, decimal, or percent.

■ **EXAMPLE 2**   *Real-World Problem Solving*

Manufacturing An employee of the Great Toys Manufacturing Company checked 400 toy cars. He found 12 defective cars. What is the experimental probability a toy car is defective?

$P(\text{defective toy car}) = \dfrac{12}{400}$ ← number of times "defective car" occurs
                                    ← total number of cars checked

$= \dfrac{3}{100} = 0.03 = 3\%$

The probability of a defective toy car is $\dfrac{3}{100}$, or 0.03, or 3%.

2. ◾*Predict* How many defective toy cars would you predict in 1,250 toy cars?

3. ✔ *Try It Out* Madison High School ordered 64 new soccer balls. The students found leaks in 5 of the balls. Write the experimental probability of finding a leaky soccer ball as a percent.

▼② *Simulating Events*

You can simulate situations in order to find probabilities.

■ **EXAMPLE 3**   *Real-World Problem Solving*

Science In a family of three children, what is the likelihood that the first two children are girls?

Simulate the situation by tossing three coins at the same time. Let "heads" represent a girl and "tails" represent a boy. The results of twenty tosses are at the left.

$P(\text{first two children girls}) = \dfrac{6}{20} = 30\%$

Using the data from this simulation, there is a 30% probability that the first two children are girls.

4. a. ✔ *Try It Out* Use the data in Example 3. What is the probability of all boys in a family of three children?
   b. About how many families would you predict have all boys in 200 families of three children?

5. ◾*Reasoning* Is it reasonable to expect that every simulation of 20 tosses will give exactly the same results as those in Example 3? Explain.

girl, girl, boy
girl, boy, boy
boy, girl, girl
girl, boy, girl
girl, boy, boy
boy, boy, girl
boy, boy, boy
boy, girl, girl
girl, boy, boy
girl, girl, girl

girl, girl, girl
boy, boy, boy
boy, boy, boy
girl, girl, boy
boy, boy, boy
boy, girl, boy
girl, girl, boy
girl, girl, girl
boy, boy, girl
boy, girl, boy

21. **Choose A, B, C, or D.** Suppose each of the following are the results of tossing a coin. Which result has the probability of 40% heads?

   A. heads, heads, tails, tails, heads   **B.** tails, heads, heads, tails, tails
   C. tails, heads, tails, tails, tails   **D.** heads, tails, heads, heads, heads

22. **a.** *Language* Find the probability that a randomly selected word in this book contains the letter *e*.

   b. *Writing* How many words did you sample to find $P(e)$? If you looked at twice as many words, would your results be different? Explain.

23. There are 15 boys and 15 girls in a group of 30 students. Five are selected at random.

   a. *Reasoning* Would you prefer to toss one coin five times or five coins once to simulate the situation? Explain.

   b. Simulate the situation 20 times. Record your results.

   c. Use your results from part (b). What is the probability that three of the five are boys? What is the probability that all five are girls?

24. *Open-ended* Give an example of a probability that you can find by conducting a simulation. Describe the simulation.

Mixed Review

Find the area of each triangle. *(Lesson 8-3)*

25.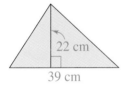

26.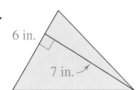

27.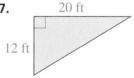

28.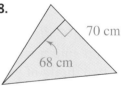

Evaluate for *x* = 2. *(Lesson 4-4)*

29. $5x^2 - 2x$ 30. $x^3 + 5x$ 31. $3x^2 \div x$ 32. $-4x(-2x)^2$ 33. $-16x^2 - 5$

34. *Real Estate* An agent sells a property for $140,000. The broker's commission is 6%. The agent receives 60% of the broker's commission. How much does the agent receive? *(Lesson 6-10)*

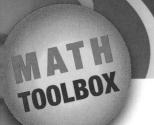

TECHNOLOGY

Using Random Numbers

◀ **After Lesson 9-1**

You can use a *random number table* to simulate some situations. Some calculators and computer programs can generate random number tables.

To generate a random number table in a spreadsheet, follow these steps.

Step 1 Set the number format to four digits.

Step 2 Use the formula RAND()*10,000. This will create groups of 4 digits in each cell of a spreadsheet. (*Note:* Each time you generate a random number table, you will get a different group of digits.)

	A	B	C	D
1	2660	1927	7807	0912
2	8879	6235	5897	8068
3	8121	4646	8368	1613
4	0821	8911	3022	0307
5	9393	5403	4930	4898

■ EXAMPLE

Suppose a rare lily bulb has a 50% chance of growing. You plant four bulbs. What is the probability that all four will grow?

Use the random number table. Let all the even digits represent "grow" and all the odd digits represent "does *not* grow."

The probability of four bulbs growing is $\frac{3}{20}$ or 15%.

2660 1927 7807 0912
8879 6235 5897 8068 ◀— Any group with
8121 4646 8368 1613   4 even digits
0821 8911 3022 0307   represents
9393 5403 4930 4898   "four bulbs grow."

Choose **Use the random number table above or generate your own to simulate each problem.**

1. Use the information in the Example. Find the probability that exactly three out of four bulbs will grow.

2. **a.** Suppose there is a 30% probability of being stopped by a red light at each of four stop lights. What is the probability of at least two red lights? Let 0, 1, and 2 represent red lights.

   b. *Reasoning* Suppose there is a 60% chance of a red light at each stop light. How many numbers would you use to represent getting a red light? Justify your answer.

3. *Writing* Write a probability problem you could solve using a random number table. Solve your problem.

Simulate a Problem

THINK AND DISCUSS

You can use simulations to act out some real-world situations. First develop a model. Then conduct experiments.

SAMPLE PROBLEM...

Kayley Karl wants to collect the six different model dinosaurs being given as prizes in boxes of Crispy Crunchy cereal. Each box of cereal contains one model, and there is an equally likely chance of any one of the prizes being in any one box. Kayley has enough money to buy 20 boxes. Is she likely to get all six prizes in those 20 boxes?

 READ

Read for understanding. Summarize the problem.

Think about the problem.

1. **a.** What is the least number of boxes of cereal Kayley may need to buy to collect all six dinosaurs?
   b. After buying 20 boxes of cereal, what is the least number of types of dinosaurs that she could have collected?
   c. Guess the number of boxes you think she may need to buy.

2. **⬤Reasoning** Why is it important to know that there is an equally likely chance of a prize being in any one box?

 PLAN

Decide on a strategy.

Kayley can simulate the problem to estimate how many boxes she will need to buy to get all six dinosaurs.

3. Suppose Kayley uses a standard number cube to simulate the problem. Rolling a 1 means Kayley gets a brontosaurus model. Rolling a 2 means Kayley gets a stegosaurus, and so on. How many different numbers will Kayley have to roll to receive the six different dinosaur models?

One *trial* for a simulation is completed when you get all possible responses once. You may get some responses more than once.

4. Kayley simulated the problem by rolling a number cube. The tally she made during the first trial is at the right.

   a. How many times did she have to roll the number cube to get all six numbers?

   b. According to this trial, how many boxes of cereal would Kayley have to buy to get all six model dinosaurs?

Rolls of a Number Cube

Number	Roll
1	||
2	||||
3	|
4	||
5	||
6	|||
Total	■

SOLVE

Try the strategy.

Simulate the problem by rolling a number cube.

5. a. Roll a number cube as many times as necessary to receive all six dinosaurs. Keep a tally of your results.

   b. Conduct 10 trials. Find the mean of the number of boxes Kayley would need to buy.

LOOK BACK

Think about how you solved the problem.

6. How close was your guess in Question 1(c) to the mean number of boxes you found in Question 5(b)?

7. The more trials you have the better your estimate is. Find the mean number of boxes Kayley needs to buy based on the results of the trials for your class.

8. a. ⁂*Reasoning* Do you think Kayley is likely to get all six prizes if she buys 20 boxes of cereal? Explain.

   b. Do you know for sure that Kayley will have all six prizes after she buys 20 boxes of cereal?

EXERCISES *On Your Own*

Describe a simulation you could use to solve each problem.

1. A restaurant gives away a model car with each purchase. You are equally likely to get any of three different cars. Estimate the number of purchases you would need to make to get all the cars.

2. Suppose you are given a matching quiz in a language you do not know. There are six questions and six answers. Find the average number of guesses you need to make to get a match.

Use any strategy to solve each problem. Show your work.

3. The Booster Club hired a rock band for a fund-raiser. The club guaranteed the band a fee of $1,500 plus $4.50 for each ticket sold. There are 1,132 seats in the auditorium. What is the greatest possible amount of money the band can earn?

4. The largest window in the world is in Paris, France, at the Palace of Industry and Technology. The window measures 715.2 ft wide by 164 ft high. How many square yards of glass are in this window?

5. The longest-lived comic strip is "The Katzenjammer Kids." It was created by Rudolph Dirks and first published in the *New York Journal* on December 12, 1897. Use today's date to calculate the age of this comic strip.

6. There are five different letters under the bottle caps for Sparky Juice: J, U, I, C and E. To win a prize, you must collect all five caps to spell JUICE. Estimate the number of juice bottles you will need to buy to win a prize.

7. *Writing* During a sale a store manager reduces a sweater's price by 30%. After the sale, the manager increases the price of the sweater by 30%. Is the price before and after the sale the same? Explain.

Mixed Review

Geometry **Find the circumference and area of each circle with diameter *d* or radius *r*. Round to the nearest hundredth.** *(Lesson 8-4)*

8. $r = 5$ cm   **9.** $d = 8$ in.   **10.** $r = 22$ cm   **11.** $d = 18$ ft   **12.** $r = 38$ yd

Express as unit rates. *(Lesson 6-2)*

13. 560 words typed in 8 min   **14.** 450.5 km driven in 9 h   **15.** $68 earned in 8 h

16. *Library* The public library charges $.50 for the first day a book is overdue and $.25 for each day after that. What is the charge for a book that is 10 days overdue? *(Lesson 2-5)*

9-3 Theoretical Probability and Proportional Reasoning

What You'll Learn

▼ **1** To find the theoretical probability of an event

▼ **2** To find the probability of a complement

...And Why

You can use theoretical probability to determine when games are fair.

Here's How

Look for questions that
- ⁜ build understanding
- ✔ check understanding

THINK AND DISCUSS

▼ 1 Finding Theoretical Probability

In Lesson 9-1, you found the experimental probability of "heads and a 2" by tossing a coin and rolling a number cube. Another way to find probability is to list the possible results, or **outcomes.**

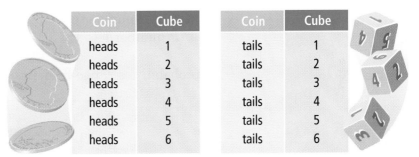

Coin	Cube
heads	1
heads	2
heads	3
heads	4
heads	5
heads	6

Coin	Cube
tails	1
tails	2
tails	3
tails	4
tails	5
tails	6

All of the outcomes are *equally likely*. Therefore, you can use the formula below to find the **theoretical probability** of "heads and a 2."

$$P(\text{event}) = \frac{\text{number of favorable outcomes}}{\text{number of possible outcomes}}$$

$$P(\text{heads and a 2}) = \frac{\text{number of outcomes with heads and a 2}}{\text{number of possible outcomes}} = \frac{1}{12}$$

■ EXAMPLE 1

A letter is selected at random from the letters A, E, I, O, and U. Find the theoretical probability that the letter is an E.

There are five possible outcomes. The event E has one favorable outcome.

$$P(\text{E}) = \frac{1}{5} \quad \longleftarrow \text{number of favorable outcomes} \atop \longleftarrow \text{number of possible outcomes}$$

The probability of selecting an E is $\frac{1}{5}$.

1. ✔ *Try It Out* Use the letters E, X, A, M, P, L, and E. Suppose you select one letter at random.
   a. How many possible outcomes are there?
   b. How many outcomes are there for the event E?
   c. Find the probability of selecting an E.

An event can be a combination of several outcomes.

■ EXAMPLE 2

Find the probability of rolling an even number using a
standard number cube.

The event of an even number has three outcomes: 2, 4, and 6.

$P(\text{even}) = \dfrac{3}{6}$ ◀— number of favorable outcomes
 ◀— number of possible outcomes

$\qquad = \dfrac{1}{2}$

The probability of rolling an even number is $\dfrac{1}{2}$.

2. ✔*Try It Out* Find the probability of each event using a
standard number cube.
 a. $P(\text{number less than 5})$ **b.** $P(\text{multiple of 3})$

All probabilities range from 0 to 1.

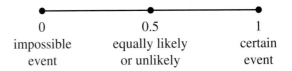

0	0.5	1
impossible event	equally likely or unlikely	certain event

3. ⬛ *Open-ended* Give an example of a certain event.

4. ⬛ *Open-ended* Give an example of an impossible event.

▽ *Finding the Probability of a Complement*

The event *no rain* is the **complement** of the event *rain*. The
probability of an event plus its complement equals 1, or 100%.

■ EXAMPLE 3   *Real-World Problem Solving*

Science In the United States, there is a 2.3% chance that a
child is a twin. Find $P(\text{not a twin})$.

$2.3\% = 0.023$ ◀—**Write the percent as a decimal.**

total probability — P(twin) = P(not a twin)

$\qquad 1 \quad - \quad 0.023 \quad = \quad 0.977$ **or 97.7%**

There is a 97.7% chance that a child is not a twin.

5. a. ✔*Try It Out* When rolling a number cube,
what is $P(6)$? What is $P(\text{not }6)$?
 b. What is $P(1, 2, 3, 4, \text{ or } 5)$?

Work Together

Work with a partner. A game is *fair* if all the players are equally likely to win. Play the following game.

- Take turns rolling two standard number cubes. Find the product of the two numbers. If the product is even, Player A scores a point. If the product is odd, Player B scores a point.

Product Chart

	1	2	3	4	5	6
1	1	2	3	■	■	■
2	2	4	■	■	■	■
3	■	■	■	■	■	■
4	■	■	■	■	■	■
5	■	■	■	■	■	■
6	■	■	■	■	■	■

- After 15 rolls each, the player with more points wins.

6. Play the game twice. Based on your results, do you think the game is fair? Explain.

7. a. Copy and complete the product chart at the left.
   b. What is the total number of even products? What is the total number of odd products?
   c. Find $P(\text{even})$ and $P(\text{odd})$.

8. Create a game using two number cubes. Make sure the game is fair.

EXERCISES *On Your Own*

Reasoning **For each of the following, decide whether the probability is *theoretical* or *experimental*. Explain.**

1. The letters C, I, R, C, L, and E are written on cards and put in a hat. One letter is selected at random. The probability of selecting a C is $\frac{2}{6}$ or $\frac{1}{3}$.

2. A coin is tossed 100 times. Fifty-two outcomes are heads. The probability of heads is $\frac{52}{100}$ or $\frac{13}{25}$.

3. A number cube is rolled 60 times. Twelve outcomes are the number 3. The probability of a 3 is $\frac{12}{60}$ or $\frac{1}{5}$.

4. There are 20 students in a class, 8 boys and 12 girls. The probability of selecting a girl's name from a basket containing all of the students' names is $\frac{12}{20}$ or $\frac{3}{5}$.

Find each probability for one roll of a standard number cube.

5. $P(4)$

6. $P(\text{multiple of 2})$

7. $P(\text{number less than 3})$

8. $P(1 \text{ or } 2)$

9. $P(\text{number less than 7})$

10. $P(7)$

Use the spinner at the right. Write each probability as a fraction, a decimal, and a percent.

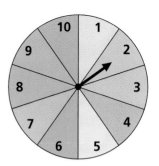

11. $P(5)$

12. $P(\text{odd})$

13. $P(\text{number less than 11})$

14. $P(\text{multiple of 3})$

15. $P(\text{number greater than 6})$

16. $P(\text{multiple of 4})$

A box contains cards numbered from 1 to 100. Suppose you pull a card at random. Express each probability as a percent.

17. $P(1)$

18. $P(\text{multiple of 10})$

19. $P(\text{number less than 12})$

20. $P(\text{prime number})$

21. $P(\text{even number})$

22. $P(\text{factor of 100})$

23. $P(\text{multiple of 15})$

24. $P(\text{factor of 51})$

25. $P(\text{number greater than 65})$

Use the spinner at the right to find each probability.

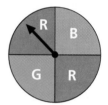

26. $P(\text{not green})$

27. $P(\text{red or blue})$

28. $P(\text{white})$

29. Your teacher selects one student at random from your class.
   a. What is the probability that you are selected?
   b. What is the probability that a girl is *not* selected?
   c. Find $P(\text{girl or boy is selected})$.

30. a. Suppose $P(E) = 0.3$. Find $P(\text{not } E)$.
   b. Suppose $P(\text{not } E) = 65\%$. Find $P(E)$.

Suppose you draw a marble at random from the bag.

31. Find each probability.
   a. $P(\text{red})$
   b. $P(\text{blue})$
   c. $P(\text{red}) + P(\text{blue})$
   d. $P(\text{red or blue})$

32. Complete: $P(\text{not red}) = P(\underline{\ ?\ })$, and $P(\text{not blue}) = P(\underline{\ ?\ })$.

33. a. You add six yellow marbles to the bag. What is $P(\text{yellow})$?
   b. What is the complement of the event "yellow"?

34. *Reasoning* A bag contains an unknown number of marbles. You know $P(\text{red}) = \frac{1}{4}$ and $P(\text{green}) = \frac{3}{4}$.
   a. Are all the marbles either red or green? How do you know?
   b. How many marbles of each color might be in the bag? Is your answer the only possibility? Explain.

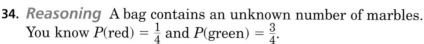

Use the letters C, O, M, P, L, E, M, E, N, and T. Find each probability.

35. P(not a consonant)

36. P(not a vowel)

37. P(not E)

38. P(not T)

39. P(not Z)

40. P(not E or M)

41. *Writing* Suppose you have 3 nickels, 3 dimes, and 3 quarters in your pocket. Are you equally likely to select a dime as a quarter from your pocket? Explain.

42. *Open-ended* Make up a probability problem in which you find the probability of the complement of an event.

43. **Choose A, B, C, or D.** The forecast for tomorrow is an 80% chance of rain. Which conclusion is most appropriate?

  A. 80% of the region will receive rain.
  B. It will rain on 8 of the next 10 days.
  C. It will rain for 9.6 h of the next 24 h.
  D. On similar days in the past, 8 out of 10 have had rain.

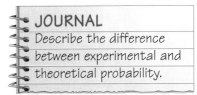

JOURNAL
Describe the difference between experimental and theoretical probability.

Mixed Review

Geometry **Find the measure of the central angle that would represent each percent in a circle graph.** *(Lesson 7-8)*

44. 40%   **45.** 15%   **46.** 5%   **47.** 9.5%   **48.** 34%   **49.** 49%

Find each difference. *(Lessons 2-3, 5-2)*

50. $1 - \frac{5}{6}$ **51.** $1 - 0.52$ **52.** $1 - \frac{5}{12}$ **53.** $1 - 0.39$ **54.** $1 - \frac{2}{7}$ **55.** $1 - 0.937$

56. *Choose a Strategy* A gas tank holds 18 gallons. The tank is one-quarter full. How many gallons will it take to fill it?

CHAPTER PROJECT

PROJECT LINK: ANALYZING

Suppose you have two number cubes, A and B. Cube A has two 1s and four 4s, and Cube B has six 3s. What is the probability of rolling a 4 on Cube A? What is the probability of rolling a 3 on Cube B? Suppose both number cubes are rolled. Which cube will usually beat the other by having a higher number? Why?

Odds

After Lesson 9-3

You can compare favorable outcomes to unfavorable outcomes using *odds*.

To calculate odds, you need to know how many of each type of outcome are possible.

$$\text{odds in favor of an event} = \frac{\text{number of favorable outcomes}}{\text{number of unfavorable outcomes}}$$

■ EXAMPLE

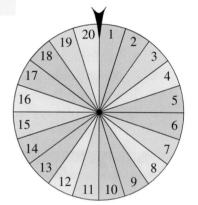

Use the spinner at the right. What are the odds in favor of spinning an 11?

There is one favorable outcome. There are 19 unfavorable outcomes.

$$\text{Odds} = \frac{\text{number of favorable outcomes}}{\text{number of unfavorable outcomes}} = \frac{1}{19}.$$

The odds in favor of spinning an 11 are 1 to 19.

1. **Reasoning** What are the odds *against* spinning an 11 on the spinner in the Example?

2. **a.** In the Example, what is the sum of the number of favorable and unfavorable outcomes?
   b. Use your answer to part (a) to find the probability of spinning an 11.

Calculate the odds for and against each event.

3. Spin a spinner lettered A–Z; the spinner lands on the first letter of your name.

4. Roll a standard number cube; the number is a multiple of 3.

5. You buy a raffle ticket to win a computer. One of 200 tickets will be drawn from a box to determine the winner.
   a. Find the odds that you win.
   b. Find the probability that you win.

6. **Writing** You are given a choice of two medical treatments, A and B. The odds in favor of recovery are 5 to 4 for A and 4 to 3 for B. Which treatment would you choose? Explain.

9-4 Sample Spaces

What You'll Learn

▼ To find a sample space

▼ To use the counting principle

...And Why

You can find probabilities once you know the number of possible outcomes.

Here's How

Look for questions that
- build understanding
- ✔ check understanding

THINK AND DISCUSS

▼ *Finding a Sample Space*

You win a million dollars—if you choose the right two letters from A, B, C, D, E. What are the possibilities?

A, B A, C A, D A, E B, C B, D B, E C, D C, E D, E

This list shows the **sample space,** the set of all possible outcomes.

1. Give the sample space for each situation. How many possible outcomes are there?
   a. You toss a coin.
   b. You spin the spinner once.
   c. You toss a coin and spin the spinner once.

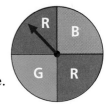

You can make a table to find a sample space.

■ EXAMPLE 1

Make a table to find the sample space for rolling two number cubes. Write the outcomes as ordered pairs.

	1	2	3	4	5	6
1	(1, 1)	(2, 1)	(3, 1)	(4, 1)	(5, 1)	(6, 1)
2	(1, 2)	(2, 2)	(3, 2)	(4, 2)	(5, 2)	(6, 2)
3	(1, 3)	(2, 3)	(3, 3)	(4, 3)	(5, 3)	(6, 3)
4	(1, 4)	(2, 4)	(3, 4)	(4, 4)	(5, 4)	(6, 4)
5	(1, 5)	(2, 5)	(3, 5)	(4, 5)	(5, 5)	(6, 5)
6	(1, 6)	(2, 6)	(3, 6)	(4, 6)	(5, 6)	(6, 6)

There are 36 possible outcomes.

2. ■*Think About It* What is the probability of rolling "doubles" (the same number on both number cubes)?

3. a. ✔*Try It Out* Give the sample space for tossing two coins.
   b. Find the probability of tossing two heads.

Another way to show a sample space is by using a tree diagram.

■ **EXAMPLE 2**

You toss three coins. What is the sample space?

Make a tree diagram in which you consider the outcomes one coin at a time.

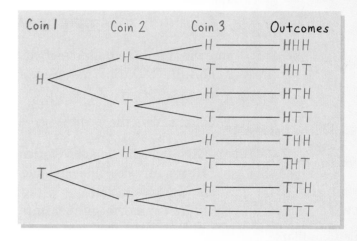

There are eight possible outcomes: HHH, HHT, HTH, HTT, THH, THT, TTH, and TTT.

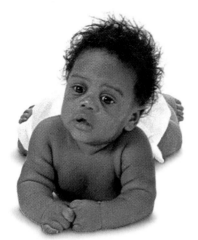

 In 1995, there were 3,848,000 children under the age of one in the United States. In this age group, $P(girl)$ is 0.488 and $P(boy)$ is 0.512.

Source: *Statistical Abstract*

4. Use the tree diagram in Example 2.
   a. Find P(at least two heads).   **b.** Find P(exactly two heads).

5. ▪ *Error Alert* Sarah used the tree diagram in Example 2 to find that P(one head and two tails) $= \frac{1}{8}$. What is her error?

6. **a.** ✔ *Try It Out* Four coins are tossed. Draw a tree diagram to show the sample space.
   b. Find P(three heads and one tail).

▼ *Using the Counting Principle*

When you have many outcomes, you can use the **counting principle** to find the number of outcomes.

THE COUNTING PRINCIPLE

If there are m ways of making one choice and n ways of making a second choice, then there are $m \times n$ ways of making the first choice followed by the second.

■ **EXAMPLE 3**   *Real-World Problem Solving*

Food Service To order a Deli-Button sandwich, a customer chooses one bread and one meat. Use the menu at the left. How many different sandwiches are available at the Deli-Button?

Bread		**Meat**	
number of choices	×	number of choices	
5	×	6	= 30

There are 30 different sandwiches available.

7. ▲ *Reasoning* Why is it helpful to use the counting principle instead of a tree diagram to solve this problem?

8. ✔ *Try It Out* The manager of the Deli-Button decides to add chicken to the list of meat choices. How many different sandwiches are now available?

9. ▲ *Think About It* What information does a tree diagram or a table give you that the counting principle does not?

EXERCISES *On Your Own*

Choose **Make a list, a table, or a tree diagram to show all the outcomes in the sample space.**

1. tossing a coin and spinning a number from 1 to 4

2. rolling a standard number cube and tossing a coin

3. choosing from two colors of shirts and three colors of pants

4. choosing from two sets of letters, A, B, C, D and X, Y, Z

5. *Education* Cuong is taking art and music. There are 4 art teachers and 3 music teachers. How many possible outcomes are there for the two teachers Cuong will have?

6. *Fashion* Ardell has four shirts (white, blue, green, and tan) and four pairs of socks in the same colors.
   a. How many different shirt–socks outfits does Ardell have?
   b. Suppose he grabs a shirt and a pair of socks without looking. What is the probability that they will *not* be the same color?

Find the number of outcomes for each situation.

7. Toss five coins.

8. Roll three number cubes.

9. Pick one of 7 boys and one of 12 girls.

10. Toss two coins and roll a number cube.

11. Choose three letters from A, B, C, and D. Use each letter only once.

12. Roll two number cubes and spin a two-part spinner.

13. Choose one letter from A to J and roll a number cube.

14. Pick a day of the week and a number 1 to 31.

Entertainment **Use the information at the right for Exercises 15–19.**

15. List all the possible beverage orders.

16. You order lemonade and popcorn at the City Movie Theater. Draw a tree diagram to show the sample space.

17. How many possible orders are there for popcorn and a beverage?

18. *Reasoning* The theater manager used the counting principle to find that P(small popcorn, medium lemonade) $= \frac{1}{24}$. Do you agree? Explain.

19. Suppose the popcorn choices are plain, buttered, and cheese. Find P(medium plain popcorn, medium fruit punch).

20. *Writing* Explain how to use the counting principle to find the number of outcomes in a sample space.

21. Seven people are eligible for three different positions on the student council. Their names are placed in a bag.
    a. How many people are eligible for the first position?
    b. How many people are eligible for the second position once the first has been selected? The third position once the first two have been selected?
    c. Use the counting principle to find the number of ways three people out of seven can be selected for the three positions.

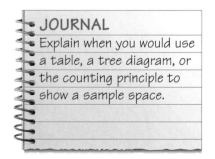

JOURNAL
Explain when you would use a table, a tree diagram, or the counting principle to show a sample space.

Find the square root. *(Lesson 8-5)*

22. 225   **23.** 8,100   **24.** 676   **25.** 289   **26.** 625   **27.** 196

Geometry **Classify each angle as acute, right, or obtuse.**
(Lesson 7-2)

28. $m\angle A = 90°$ **29.** $m\angle B = 122°$ **30.** $m\angle C = 74°$

31. *Environment* Approximately 107 million aluminum cans
are made on an average day. Of these, about 50% are
recycled. *(Lessons 5-8, 6-7)*
   a. To the nearest million, how many aluminum cans are
   recycled each day?
   b. One aluminum can weighs about 0.5 oz. How many
   pounds of aluminum are recycled each day?

✓ CHECKPOINT 1   *Lessons 9-1 through 9-4*

**Use the spinner at the right. Write each probability as a
fraction, a decimal, and a percent.**

1. $P(\text{not } 4)$ **2.** $P(2 \text{ or } 3)$ **3.** $P(\text{prime number})$

4. $P(6)$ **5.** $P(5)$ **6.** $P(\text{whole number})$

7. Choose A, B, C, or D. Use the wheel from Exercises 1–6.
   Which probability is *not* the same as the others?
   A. $P(\text{even number})$ **B.** $P(3 \text{ or } 5)$
   C. $P(\text{factor of } 3)$ **D.** $P(\text{multiple of } 1)$

8. a. A teacher uses a seating chart for students. Rows are
      numbered 1 through 6, and columns are lettered
      A through D. One possible seat for a student is 3A.
      Make a table to display the sample space for the seats.
   b. Use the counting principle to find the number of seats.
      Does your answer agree with the total in your table?

9. Simulate the problem. A true/false quiz has 10 questions.
   How likely are you to get at least seven answers right if you
   guess every answer?

What You'll Learn

▼ 1 To find the probability of independent events

▼ 2 To find the probability of dependent events

...And Why

You can make predictions about winning multiple-part games.

Here's How

Look for questions that

▪ build understanding

✔ check understanding

Work Together   *Exploring Multiple Events*

Work in pairs. Suppose you have a bag of marbles like the one at the right, and you draw a marble at random.

1. **a.** What is the probability that you draw a red marble?

   b. Suppose you drop the first marble back in the bag. Find $P(\text{red})$ for the second draw.

   c. Suppose that you draw a red marble and do not replace it. Describe the sample space for the second draw. What is $P(\text{red})$ on your second draw?

THINK AND DISCUSS

▼ 1 Finding Probability of Independent Events

Two events are **independent** if the outcome of one event does not affect the outcome of a second event.

PROBABILITY OF INDEPENDENT EVENTS

If A and B are independent events,
$$P(A \text{ and } B) = P(A) \times P(B).$$

■ **EXAMPLE 1**   *Real-World Problem Solving*

Games "Spin Your Initials" uses a wheel lettered A–Z. Suppose you spin it twice. Find $P(\text{B and Z})$.

The two events are independent.

$P(\text{B and Z}) = P(\text{B}) \times P(\text{Z})$ ⟵ Selecting B is the first event. Selecting Z is the second event.

$= \dfrac{1}{26} \times \dfrac{1}{26}$ ⟵ Substitute.

$= \dfrac{1}{676}$ ⟵ Multiply.

The probability is $\dfrac{1}{676}$.

 The chances of a fair coin landing heads up 50 times in a row are very low. If one million coins were tossed 10 times/min for 40 h/wk, then 50 consecutive heads would happen about once every 9 centuries.

2. ⊹ *Open-ended* Describe two events that are independent.

3. ✔ *Try It Out* Two number cubes are rolled. Find $P(6 \text{ and } 6)$.

② *Finding Probability of Dependent Events*

Two events are **dependent** if the outcome of the first event affects the outcome of a second event. In the Work Together, when the first marble is not returned to the bag before the second marble is drawn, the events (red, then red) are dependent.

PROBABILITY OF DEPENDENT EVENTS

If A and B are dependent events, then
$$P(A, \text{ then } B) = P(A) \times P(B \text{ after } A).$$

■ **EXAMPLE 2** *Real-World Problem Solving*

Games To play "Draw Your Initials," you draw a card from a bucket that contains cards lettered A–Z. Without replacing the first card, you draw a second one. Find the probability of winning if your initials are C and M.

The two events are dependent.

$$P(C, \text{ then } M) = P(C) \times P(M \text{ after } C) \quad \longleftarrow \text{Use the formula.}$$
$$= \frac{1}{26} \times \frac{1}{25} \quad \longleftarrow \text{Substitute.}$$
$$= \frac{1}{650} \quad \longleftarrow \text{Multiply.}$$

The probability of winning is $\frac{1}{650}$.

4. ⊹ *Reasoning* Explain why the probability of selecting M second is $\frac{1}{25}$.

5. ⊹ *Analyze* You remove a flower from a flower arrangement. Then you remove another flower without replacing the first. Why are these events dependent?

6. ✔ *Try It Out* Suppose the names of all the students in your class are in a basket. Your teacher draws one name, then draws a second name without replacing the first. Choose two students in your class. Find $P(\text{one student, then the other})$.

7. ⊹ *Open-ended* Describe two dependent events.

You roll one number cube twice. Find each probability.

1. P(1 and odd)   2. P(3 and even)   3. P(odd and even)

4. P(6 and 4)   5. P(5 and 5)   6. P(6 and 7)

You draw a letter from the group at the right, then replace it. Then you draw a second letter. Find each probability.

7. P(A and B)   8. P(G and vowel)

9. P(consonant and A)   10. P(vowel and vowel)

11. P(red and Z)   12. P(consonant and blue)

13. *Reasoning* For the cards at the right, is it reasonable to find P(two Zs) by multiplying 2 times $\frac{1}{8}$? Explain.

You draw two marbles from the bag at the right.

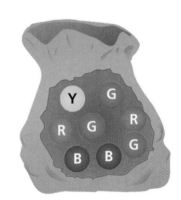

14. Suppose you replace the first marble before drawing the second one. What is P(two green marbles)?

15. Suppose you do *not* replace the first marble before drawing the second one. What is P(two green marbles)?

16. **Choose A, B, C, or D.** Suppose you do *not* replace the first marble before drawing the second. Find P(yellow, then red).
    A. $\frac{1}{8}$ B. $\frac{1}{14}$ C. $\frac{1}{28}$ D. $\frac{1}{32}$

17. *Theater Arts* Five girls and seven boys want to be the two announcers for a variety show. To be fair, a teacher put the names of the twelve students in a hat and drew two.
    a. Find P(boy, then boy).   b. Find P(girl, then girl).
    c. *Writing* One of the girls suggests separate hats for the girls' names and the boys' names. Is this a better method? Explain.

18. A box contains the letters M I S S I S S I P P I. What is the probability of selecting an S first and a P second, if:
    a. the first letter *is not* replaced?   b. the first letter *is* replaced?

Are the two events *independent* or *dependent*?

19. You toss a nickel, then you toss a dime.

20. You draw a card, then you draw another.

21. You grab a sock from the dryer, then grab another sock from the dryer.

22. You open this math book to a page, close it, then open it again.

A box contains cards with the numbers 1–20. You draw two cards. Find each probability.

23. $P(7 \text{ and } 2)$ if the first card is replaced

24. $P(7, \text{ then } 7)$ if the first card is not replaced

25. $P(7, \text{ then } 2)$ if the first card is not replaced

26. $P(\text{multiple of 3 and multiple of 7})$ if the first card is replaced

27. Suppose you have cards with the numbers 1, 2, and 3.
   a. Make a tree diagram showing the sample space for selecting a card, replacing it, then selecting a second card.
   b. Make a tree diagram for selecting a card, *not* replacing it, then selecting a second card.
   c. Find the probability of the independent events of selecting 1 on the first draw and 2 on the second draw.

Mixed Review

Geometry **Two legs of a right triangle are given. Find the hypotenuse to the nearest tenth of a unit.** *(Lesson 8-7)*

28. 12 ft, 25 ft   **29.** 15 yd, 24 yd   **30.** 4 mm, 6 mm   **31.** 5 cm, 8 cm   **32.** 14 m, 18 m

Solve each equation. *(Lesson 5-9)*

33. $\frac{3}{4}b = 21$ **34.** $\frac{1}{2}x = 4.5$ **35.** $28q = 36$ **36.** $5y = \frac{15}{7}$ **37.** $8z = \frac{1}{2}$

38. *Choose a Strategy* Start with a number, subtract 7, then divide by 13. The result is 21. What was the original number?

CHAPTER PROJECT

PROJECT LINK: CALCULATING

Show a sample space of all the possible outcomes for Cubes A and B from the project link on page 405. What is the probability that A beats B when each cube is rolled once?

Permutations

What You'll Learn

▼ To find permutations

...And Why

You can find all the arrangements of items in a group.

Here's How

Look for questions that
- build understanding
- ✔ check understanding

Work Together

Exploring Arrangements

Play the game STOP with your group. You have one minute in which to write as many words as possible that use all four letters in the word STOP. A word counts only if it is in a dictionary. The player who has the greatest number of words wins.

1. What strategies did you use to find every possible arrangement of the four letters?

2. Make an organized list of all arrangements of the letters.
   a. How many of these arrangements are in your list?
   b. How many of these arrangements are real words?

THINK AND DISCUSS

An arrangement in which order is important is a **permutation.** The permutation STOP is different from the permutation POTS because the order of the letters is different.

■ EXAMPLE 1

Use the counting principle to find the number of arrangements of the letters S, T, O, and P.

| first letter 4 | × | second letter 3 | × | third letter 2 | × | fourth letter 1 | = 24 |

There are 24 different arrangements.

QUICKreview

To use the counting principle, multiply by the number of choices for each decision.

3. **Reasoning** Why are there 4 choices for the first letter but only 3 choices for the second letter?

4. a. ✔ **Try It Out** Use the four letters S, T, O, and P. Make an organized list of all the three-letter permutations.
   b. **Go a Step Further** What do you notice about the number of permutations when you use all 4 items and when you use 3 of 4 items? Explain why this makes sense.

■ EXAMPLE 2

Use the counting principle to find the number of three-letter permutations of the five letters S, L, I, D, and E.

first letter 5	×	second letter 4	×	third letter 3	= 60

There are 60 three-letter permutations of the five letters.

5. ✔ *Try It Out* Use the counting principle to find the number of two-letter permutations of the letters S, T, O, and P. To check your work, make an organized list of all possible arrangements.

EXERCISES *On Your Own*

Use the counting principle to find the number of permutations for each group of letters. Use all the letters.

1. W, O, R, L, D
2. H, U, M, A, N, I, T, Y
3. P, I, C, K, L, E

Find the number of two-letter permutations of each group.

4. C, A, T
5. P, A, C, K
6. I, N, C, L, U, D, E
7. D, E, P, A, R, T

Find the number of four-letter permutations of each group.

8. R, E, P, S
9. Q, I, E, R, T, Y, U
10. G, D, X, Z, C
11. A, E, I, O, U, Y

COUNTING AREA CODES

THREE-DIGIT AREA CODES were first developed in 1947. At that time the first digit could not be 0 or 1 because 0 and 1 were used for contacting telephone operators. The second digit was always 0 or 1 to indicate a long distance phone call.

In the 1990s, new technology was developed so that the second digit could be any digit. The new area codes were put into use in 1995.

12. How many different area codes were available in 1947?

13. How many area codes were available in 1995?

14. A club of 10 students chooses officers. One student will be president and another student will be vice president. How many different outcomes are possible?

15. The combination to open your lock has three numbers: 10, 45, and 6. You cannot remember the order of the numbers.
  a. List all the possible arrangements of the numbers.
  b. You decide to try different arrangements. If you are as unlucky as possible, how many will you have to try before you open the lock?

16. *Writing* Explain how to find the number of permutations of all the letters C, H, E, M, I, S, T, R, Y. Then explain how to find the number of permutations of five of the letters.

17. Suppose you scramble the letters P, E, T, and S.
  a. Make an organized list of the sample space.
  b. How many of the groups form real words? What are they?
  c. Find the probability that a real word is formed when the letters P, E, T, and S are scrambled.

18. Dan, Eugene, Fran, and Gabi are in line for movie tickets.
  a. Make a list to show the sample space.
  b. What is the probability that they line up boy-girl-boy-girl?
  c. What is the probability that they line up girl-girl-boy-boy?

Mixed Review

Geometry **Classify each polygon by the number of sides. Judging by appearance, state whether it appears to be a regular polygon.** *(Lesson 7-6)*

19.   **20.**   **21.**   **22.**

Find each sum or difference. *(Lesson 5-3)*

23. $6\frac{1}{2} + 5\frac{2}{3}$ **24.** $12\frac{1}{8} + 4\frac{3}{4}$ **25.** $9\frac{2}{5} - 8\frac{5}{6}$ **26.** $17\frac{2}{9} - 6\frac{5}{12}$ **27.** $12\frac{3}{5} + 14\frac{7}{12}$

28. *Business* A can of frozen juice is in the shape of a cylinder. It has a radius of 1.5 in. and is 6 in. high. Find the amount of paper necessary to make a label for the can. *(Lessons 8-9)*

9-7 Combinations

THINK AND DISCUSS

In some arrangements, order does not matter. For example, suppose you choose LeVar, Ramon, and May to be on a committee. That is the same as choosing Ramon, May, and LeVar or May, LeVar, and Ramon. An arrangement in which order does *not* matter is a **combination.**

■ **EXAMPLE 1**   *Real-World Problem Solving*

Clothing Suppose you are packing for a hiking trip. You are choosing two T-shirts from the list at the right. In how many ways can you choose them?

T-shirts

Color	Letter
blue	b
yellow	y
green	g
red	r
purple	p

Let the letters represent the five T-shirts. List all the possible arrangements.

(b, y) (b, g) (b, r) (b, p) (y, b) (y, g) (y, r) (y, p), (g, b) (g, y) (g, r) (g, p) (r, b) (r, y) (r, g) (r, p), (p, b), (p, y), (p, g), (p, r)

Cross out the duplicate arrangements.

(b, y) (b, g) (b, r) (b, p) (y, b) (y, g) (y, r) (y, p), (g, b) (g, y) (g, r) (g, p) (r, b) (r, y) (r, g) (r, p), (p, b), (p, y), (p, g), (p, r)

(y, b) is the same group as (b, y), so keep only one.

You have 10 different choices.

Another way to find combinations is to make an organized list.

(b, y)	(b, g)	(b, r)	(b, p)
	(y, g)	(y, r)	(y, p)
		(g, r)	(g, p)
			(r, p)

1. **Think About It** Describe the organization of the list above.

2. ✔ **Try It Out** In how many ways can a camp counselor choose a relay team of three swimmers from a group of five?

3. Use the letters A, B, C, D, and E.
  a. Find the number of three-letter permutations.
  b. Find the number of three-letter combinations.
  c. ▪*Reasoning* Which is greater, the number of permutations or the number of combinations? Explain.

EXERCISES *On Your Own*

Find the number of combinations.

1. Choose 2 people from 3.   **2.** Choose 3 people from 5.   **3.** Choose 2 people from 6.

Use the letters B, E, O, P, R, W. Make a list of all the combinations.

4. 2 vowels   **5.** 3 consonants   **6.** any 3 letters

7. 1 consonant and 1 vowel   **8.** any 4 letters   **9.** any 5 letters

Use the poster for Exercises 10–14. Find the number of combinations for each situation.

10. participate in 2 track events

11. participate in 1 game, 1 track event, and 1 field event

12. participate in 2 field events

13. participate in 2 track events and 2 field events

14. *Open-ended* Write a combination problem from the information on the poster. Solve your problem.

15. Twelve students volunteer to help organize a class trip. Two of them are assigned to collect money for the trip. In how many ways can these two students be chosen?

16. *Music* Suppose you have five different CDs to play. Your CD player can hold three CDs. How many different sets of three CDs can you select?

17. *Writing* Use your own words and an example to explain the difference between a permutation and a combination.

Track and Field Day

Games
Baseball throw
Run the Bases relay

Track Events
50-m run
100-m relay
100-m hurdles
200-m run

Field Events
high jump
long jump
disc throw

18. **Choose A, B, C, or D.** Andrea plans to buy a bicycle, a helmet, a water bottle, and a lock. Today she will buy some of the accessories. How many different sets of two accessories can she select?

    A. 3   **B.** 5   **C.** 4   **D.** 7

Tell whether each of the following is a permutation or a combination problem. Explain your choice.

19. You select three books from a bookshelf that holds eight books. How many different sets of books could you choose?

20. You select three books to read over summer vacation. In how many different orders can you read the books?

21. Four students stand beside each other for a photograph. How many different orders are possible?

22. A committee of four people is chosen from your class. How many different committees may be chosen?

Mixed Review

Complete. *(Lesson 5-8)*

23. 12,000 lb = ▪ T   24. 2.5 gal = ▪ fl oz   25. 3 qt 1 pt = ▪ c   26. 15 in. = ▪ ft

Write a proportion and solve. *(Lessons 6-9, 6-10)*

27. 54 is 40% of what number?   28. 99 is what percent of 150?

29. What number is 65% of 200?   30. What number is 15.5% of 45?

31. *Geometry* A rectangle has a perimeter of 48 m. Make a list of all of the possible dimensions that are whole meter units. Which dimensions give you the greatest area? *(Lesson 8-2)*

CHAPTER PROJECT

PROJECT LINK: DESIGNING

Construct three cardboard number cubes A, B, and C. Design your cubes so that A usually beats B, B usually beats C, and C usually beats A. Use sample spaces to support your work.

The letters M A T H E M A T I C S are written on cards.

1. Find the probability of selecting a vowel, replacing it, then selecting another vowel.

2. Find the probability of selecting an A, then a T, if the first letter *is not* replaced before selecting the second one.

3. Find the probability of selecting any two vowels, if the first letter *is not* replaced before selecting the second one.

Use the numbers 1, 2, 3, 4, 5, and 6. Find the number of permutations and the number of combinations.

4. two odd numbers

5. three even numbers

6. all multiples of 3

7. all numbers less than 5

8. any two numbers

9. any four numbers

10. You decide to pin the pictures of six friends in a row on a bulletin board. In how many ways can you arrange the pictures?

11. *Calculator* Find the number of ways to arrange nine books on a shelf.

Math at Work

TEACHER

In addition to traditional classroom responsibilities, teachers plan lessons, supervise after-school activities, and meet with parents. Today's teachers use mathematics skills to help their students solve problems, understand concepts, and develop critical-thinking skills. Telecommunications technology is now opening a whole new world for teachers and students alike.

Find out more about working as a teacher at the Web site for the National Education Association: http://www.nea.org/

PROBLEM SOLVING PRACTICE

Read each question and choose the best answer.

1. $\triangle XYZ \cong \triangle MON$. Which statement is *not necessarily* true?

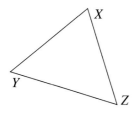

A. $\overline{YX} \cong \overline{NO}$
B. $m\angle N = m\angle Z$
C. $\angle Y \cong \angle O$
D. $\overline{MN} \cong \overline{XZ}$

2. A game uses a spinner that is divided into 10 equal sections that are labeled with the following numbers: 2, 4, 5, 5, 8, 10, 10, 11, 12, and 15. What is the probability of spinning an even number?

F. $\frac{2}{5}$ G. $\frac{4}{5}$ H. $\frac{3}{5}$ J. $\frac{1}{10}$

3. Cans of peas are sold 3 for $.75. How much will 6 cans of peas cost?

A. $1.80   B. $1.50   C. $1.35   D. $.90

4. This drawing shows how to —

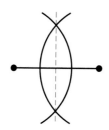

F. construct a line segment congruent to a given line segment
G. construct the perpendicular bisector of a line segment
H. construct complementary angles
J. bisect an angle

Please note that items 5–8 have *five* answer choices.

5. Latisha and her sister are standing next to each other. Latisha is 6 feet tall and casts an 8-foot shadow. How long is the shadow cast by Latisha's younger sister?

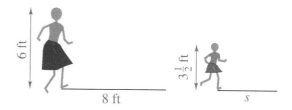

A. 28 ft   B. $16\frac{5}{8}$ ft   C. $10\frac{1}{2}$ ft
D. $4\frac{2}{3}$ ft   E. Not Here

6. A storage chest is a rectangular prism 4.5 feet long, 1.5 feet wide, and 2 feet tall. What is the volume of the chest?

F. 15.75 ft^3 G. 12 ft^3 H. 13.5 ft^3
J. 8 ft^3 K. 6.75 ft^3

7. Cards with the letters A through H are placed in a bag. Ken selects a card from the bag at random. He doesn't put the card back. Then he chooses a second card. What is the probability that both of the cards will be vowels?

A. $\frac{1}{16}$ B. $\frac{1}{14}$ C. $\frac{10}{56}$
D. $\frac{5}{16}$ E. Not Here

8. In a survey about pets, 30 out of 80 students questioned said that their families owned a dog. If 500 were surveyed, what is a good prediction for the number of students whose families own a dog?

F. 20   G. 50   H. 100
J. 200   K. 320

9-8 Estimating Population Size

What You'll Learn

▼ To estimate the size of a population using the capture/recapture method

...And Why

Park rangers can estimate the size of animal populations.

Here's How

Look for questions that
- build understanding
- ✔ check understanding

THINK AND DISCUSS

From 1979 to 1986, the Montana Department of Fish, Wildlife, and Parks monitored the mule deer population in the mountains near Bozeman. They used the *capture/recapture* method to estimate the number of deer each winter.

Researchers placed a visible collar on a number of deer to "mark" them. Later, the researchers flew over an area and counted the number of marked deer and the total number of deer they saw. They used the proportion below to estimate the deer population.

$$\frac{\text{marked deer counted}}{\text{total deer counted}} = \frac{\text{number of marked deer}}{\text{estimate of deer population}}$$

■ **EXAMPLE** *Real-World Problem Solving*

Biology Suppose researchers knew that there were 55 marked deer in an area. On a flight over the area, they counted 48 marked deer and a total of 638 deer. Estimate the deer population.

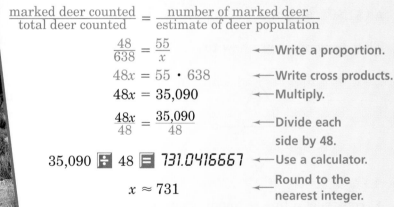

$$\frac{\text{marked deer counted}}{\text{total deer counted}} = \frac{\text{number of marked deer}}{\text{estimate of deer population}}$$

$\dfrac{48}{638} = \dfrac{55}{x}$ ←Write a proportion.

$48x = 55 \cdot 638$ ←Write cross products.

$48x = 35{,}090$ ←Multiply.

$\dfrac{48x}{48} = \dfrac{35{,}090}{48}$ ←Divide each side by 48.

$35{,}090 \; \boxed{\div} \; 48 \; \boxed{=} \; 731.0416667$ ←Use a calculator.

$x \approx 731$ ←Round to the nearest integer.

There are about 731 deer in the area.

1. ✔ **Try It Out** There are 20 marked sea otters in one coastal region. In one survey, marine biologists counted 42 sea otters, of which 12 were marked. About how many sea otters are in the area?

Work Together

Work in a group to use the capture/recapture method.

2. **a.** Place some square tiles in a bag without counting them.
   b. Decide how many tiles to mark. Remove them from the bag and mark each tile with an X. Then replace the marked tiles in the bag and shake it.
   c. Take a sample from the bag. Record the number of marked tiles in the sample. Record the total number of tiles in the sample.
   d. Write and solve a proportion to estimate the number of tiles in the bag.
   e. ▪*Reasoning* Do you think the number of tiles you decided to mark affects your estimate of the total number of tiles? Explain.
   f. Count the actual number of tiles. How close was your estimate?

EXERCISES *On Your Own*

Use a proportion to estimate the total number of deer for each year.

	Date	Total Deer Counted	Marked Deer Counted	Total Marked Deer
1.	3/79	1,173	65	101
2.	3/80	1,017	42	83
3.	3/81	1,212	32	60
4.	3/82	1,707	30	36
5.	3/83	1,612	68	89
6.	3/84	1,590	37	59
7.	3/85	1,417	42	54
8.	3/86	1,608	85	110
9.	3/87	1,469	52	83

10. *Analyze* Use your answers to Exercises 1–9 on page 425. Describe how the deer population changed over time.

11. Some researchers calculate the ratio of marked deer counted to the number of marked deer.
    a. Calculate this ratio for each year from 1979 to 1987. Write each ratio as a decimal rounded to the nearest thousandth.
    b. *Writing* Explain how counting a high percent of the marked deer might affect the estimate of the deer population.

12. In a study of catfish in Beaver Lake, the state extension service caught, tagged, and set free 124 catfish. A few weeks later they caught and set free 140 catfish. Thirty-five had tags. Estimate the number of catfish in the lake.

13. a. An ecology class is helping the local conservation society determine the squirrel population in a city park. In early October, the students and society members captured, tagged, and set free 68 squirrels. Three weeks later, of 84 squirrels captured, 16 had tags. Estimate the number of squirrels in the park.
    b. *Reasoning* Suppose some squirrels lost their tags. How would this affect your estimate of the squirrel population?

PORTFOLIO
For your portfolio, choose one or two items from your work for this chapter. Here are some possibilities:
• a journal entry
• corrected work
• part of your project
Explain why you have included each selection.

Mixed Review

14. *Geometry* $\triangle PQR \cong \triangle XYZ$. Find the angle measures and side lengths of $\triangle XYZ$. *(Lesson 7-5)*

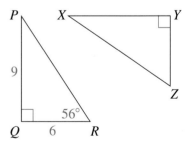

Write each decimal as a fraction in simplest form. *(Lesson 4-9)*

15. 0.096   16. 0.875   17. 0.26   18. 1.85

19. 8.5   20. 6.04   21. 0.18   22. 0.05

23. *Shopping* A $75 dollar coat is on sale for $52.50. What percent of the regular price is the sale price? *(Lesson 6-7)*

24. *Choose a Strategy* The manager of a cafeteria ordered three times as many plain bagels as onion bagels. He ordered the same number of onion and garlic bagels. He ordered 285 bagels in all. How many of each kind of bagel did he order?

CHAPTER PROJECT

Everybody Wins

Make Three Number cubes The Project Link questions on pages 405, 415, and 421 should help you complete your project. Here is a checklist to help you gather together the parts of your project.

✔ the sample space for Cubes A and B from the Project Link on page 415

✔ the cubes you designed

✔ the sample spaces for each pair of cubes

Your number cubes should have the property that A usually beats B and B usually beats C, yet C usually beats A. Roll your cubes several times to verify they have this property. How would you use them if you were in charge of a booth at a carnival?

Reflect and Revise

Review your project with a friend or someone at home. Are your sample spaces clear? Are your calculations correct? If necessary, make revisions in the design of your cubes.

Web Extension

Prentice Hall's Internet site contains information you might find helpful as you complete your project. Visit www.phschool.com/mgm2/ch9 for some links and ideas related to probability.

Probability 9-1, 9-3

You can find the **experimental probability** of an event using this formula.

$$P(\text{event}) = \frac{\text{number of times an event occurs}}{\text{total number of experiments}}$$

You can find the **theoretical probability** of an event using this formula.

$$P(\text{event}) = \frac{\text{number of favorable outcomes}}{\text{number of possible outcomes}}$$

The sum of the probability of an event and the probability of its **complement** is 1.

A card is drawn at random. Find each probability.

$$\boxed{T}\,\boxed{R}\,\boxed{U}\,\boxed{M}\,\boxed{P}\,\boxed{E}\,\boxed{T}$$

1. selecting a P

2. selecting a T

3. not selecting a P

Use the cards above to find the complement of each event.

4. selecting a T

5. selecting an E

6. selecting a consonant

7. a. *Games* You draw 10 marbles from a bag that contains 60 marbles. Three are blue, four red, one yellow, and two green. Find $P(\text{blue})$, $P(\text{red})$, $P(\text{yellow})$, $P(\text{green})$.

   b. Based on your answers to part (a), predict the number of marbles of each color in the bag.

Sample Space and the Counting Principle 9-4

The **sample space** is the set of all possible outcomes of an event. You can use the **counting principle** to find the number of outcomes for an event with more than one step by multiplying the number of outcomes for each step.

8. a. At the China Panda, if you order the Family Dinner, you choose one appetizer, one soup, and one main dish from the menu at the right. Use a tree diagram to find the sample space of all the possible dinners.

   b. Use the counting principle to find the number of possible dinners.

Appetizers	Soups
Egg Rolls	Won-ton
Fried Won-tons	Sizzling Rice

Main Dishes
Almond Chicken
Sweet & Sour Pork
Beef with Broccoli

9. Use the counting principle. Find the number of ways the offices of president, secretary, and treasurer can be filled from the 12-member student council.

Two events are **independent** if the outcome of the first event *does not* affect the outcome of the second event.

You can find the probability of two independent events using this formula.

$$P(A \text{ and } B) = P(A) \times P(B).$$

Two events are **dependent** if the outcome of the first event *does* affect the outcome of the second event.

You can find the probability of two dependent events using this formula.

$$P(A, \text{ then } B) = P(A) \times P(B \text{ after } A)$$

Classify each pair of events as *independent* or *dependent*.

10. You select a card from a set of cards. Without returning the card you select a second card.

11. You roll a standard number cube once. Then you roll it again.

12. Choose A, B, C, or D. A jar contains 5 blue, 3 red, and 2 green marbles. What is the probability of choosing a red marble and then another red marble when the first marble is *not* replaced?

  A. $\frac{1}{5}$ **B.** $\frac{1}{15}$ **C.** $\frac{3}{10}$ **D.** $\frac{3}{100}$

A **permutation** is an arrangement of a set of objects where order is important. A **combination** is an arrangement of objects where order does not matter.

13. Five students compete on a relay team. Only four of them can race at a time. How many different teams are possible?

14. Four students are selected for a relay team. In how many ways can they line up for the race?

You can simulate some problems by tossing a coin or rolling a number cube. To estimate population size, you can use the *capture/recapture* method.

15. *Writing* In a basketball game, Charlie usually makes one out of two baskets. Describe a simulation to find the probability that he will make four out of five baskets.

16. *Biology* Researchers marked 22 lions in an area. They make an aerial count of 68 lions, 16 of which are marked. Estimate the lion population.

1. Use the data at the right. Write each probability as a fraction, a decimal, and a percent.

Marker Color	Number Drawn
purple	6
green	2
white	3
black	5

   a. P(purple)
   b. P(green)
   c. P(orange)

2. Factory workers test 80 batteries. Four batteries are defective. Find the probability that a battery from the factory is defective. Write the probability as a percent.

3. There are six open containers arranged as shown. A ball is tossed and falls into one of the containers. Find the probability of each event.

   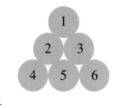

   a. P(4)   b. P(even number)
   c. P(a number greater than 4)

4. Suppose you have a bag that contains 6 blue, 3 red, 2 green, and 1 white marble. All marbles are equally likely to be drawn from the bag. Find each probability.

   a. P(blue)   b. P(white)
   c. P(blue or white)   d. P(red or blue)
   e. P(blue, then white when blue is not replaced)

5. The letters of the word HALLOWEEN are written on a set of cards. You are equally likely to get any card. What is the probability of selecting an L, then a W? The first card is *not* replaced before selecting the second card.

6. Suppose that the probability that you make a basket each time you shoot is 0.2. What is the probability that you will *not* make a basket?

7. Javier is buying a new car. He has a choice of 3 models, 8 colors, and 2 interiors. How many different car choices does he have?

8. a. Find the number of two-letter permutations of the letters A, B, C.
   b. Find the number of two-letter combinations of the letters A, B, C.

9. *Writing* Fifty students chosen at random were asked what kind of pizza crust they liked best. Fifteen preferred thick crust. There are 940 students in the school. What would you do to estimate the number of students in the school who prefer thick crust?

10. **Choose A, B, C, or D.** You are equally likely to get one of four prizes when you buy Good Morning cereal. You want to find out how many boxes of cereal you should buy to get all four prizes. Which of the following is *not* a true statement?

    A. You can simulate buying the cereal by using a spinner divided into four equal sections. One trial ends when the spinner has stopped in each of the sections at least once. Average the results of several trials.
    B. The result of the simulation is the exact number of boxes you will need to buy.
    C. The more trials you have, the better your results.
    D. A possible answer is 4 boxes.

Choose the best answer.

1. Which jar of peanut butter is the best buy?

   A. an 18-oz jar for $1.69
   B. a 30-oz jar for $2.59
   C. a 32-oz jar for $2.89
   D. a 24-oz jar for $2.09

2. Sarah bought a remnant of fabric $5\frac{1}{8}$ yards long to make pennants for the school fair. How many pennants can she make if $\frac{3}{4}$ yd is needed for each pennant?

   A. 5   **B.** 6   **C.** 7   **D.** 8

3. *Estimation* If the area of the shaded region is 4 in.^{2}, what is the best estimate for the area of the unshaded region?

   A. 4 in.^{2}
   B. 8 in.^{2}
   C. 12 in.^{2}
   D. 16 in.^{2}

   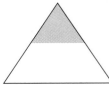

4. Which event does *not* have a 50% theoretical probability of occurring?

   A. getting heads on one toss of a coin
   B. drawing a red marble from a bag that has 3 red, 2 blue, and 1 yellow marble
   C. rolling a number cube and getting an even number
   D. rolling a number cube and getting either a 5 or a 6

5. Rectangle *ABCD* and rectangle *AXYZ* are similar. How long is $\overline{XY}$?

   A. 2.5 cm
   B. 2 cm
   C. 1.6 cm
   D. 1.5 cm

   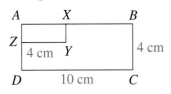

6. Which one does *not* equal the others?

   A. 4% of 3,000   **B.** 40% of 30
   C. 40% of 300   **D.** 30% of 400

7. If the two spinners are each spun once, what is the probability that the sum of the numbers spun is 10?

   A. 0   **B.** $\frac{1}{4}$ **C.** $\frac{1}{2}$ **D.** 1

8. The least common denominator of three fractions is 42. Two of the fractions are $\frac{5}{3}$ and $\frac{6}{7}$. Which fraction could be the third one?

   A. $\frac{10}{21}$ **B.** $\frac{1}{35}$ **C.** $\frac{17}{284}$ **D.** $\frac{9}{14}$

9. What is the volume of a rectangular prism that has dimensions 1 in., 2 in., and 3 in.?

   A. 27 in.^{3} **B.** 18 in.^{3}
   C. 6 in.^{3} **D.** 12 in.^{3}

10. A circle has circumference 56.52 ft. What is its area? Use 3.14 for π.

    A. 254.34 ft^2 **B.** 56.52 ft^2
    C. 28.26 ft^2 **D.** 1,017.36 ft^2

11. What is 64 written in exponential form?

    A. 2^6 **B.** 4^3 **C.** 8^2
    D. All of the above are correct.

12. In the diagram at the right, which two angles are adjacent angles?

    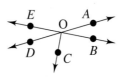

    A. $\angle EOD$, $\angle DOC$ **B.** $\angle BOC$, $\angle BOD$
    C. $\angle AOE$, $\angle BOC$ **D.** $\angle AOB$, $\angle EOD$

Algebra: Patterns and Functions

10

WHAT YOU WILL LEARN IN THIS CHAPTER

• How to use patterns to find sequences

• How to write numbers in scientific notation

• How to graph functions and write function rules

happy landings

Imagine this—you have just opened your parachute and you are floating through the air. Exciting, huh? How long it takes you to come to the ground can be predicted because the change in height versus time occurs in a predictable pattern. Many other things change in a predictable pattern, for instance, the height of a burning candle and the growth of money in a bank account.

Graphing Data For the chapter project, you will find how fast a container of water will empty if there is a hole in it. Your final project will be a graph of the data you collect.

• **How to use simpler problems to solve more complex problems**

Number Patterns

What You'll Learn

▼ 1 To identify and continue arithmethic sequences

▼ 2 To identify and continue geometric and other sequences

...And Why

A sunflower is just one place where you can see number patterns in nature.

Here's How

Look for questions that
⬛ build understanding
✔ check understanding

Work Together

Exploring Patterns

Work with a partner to find a number pattern.

1. **a.** Use pattern blocks to make the next two figures in the pattern at the right.
   b. How many blocks do you add to each figure to make the next figure in the pattern?
   c. Copy and complete the table.

Figure 1   Figure 2   Figure 3

Figure	1	2	3	4	5	6	7	8
Total Blocks in Figure	⬛	⬛	⬛	⬛	⬛	⬛	⬛	⬛

THINK AND DISCUSS

▼ 1 Arithmetic Sequences

A **sequence** is a set of numbers that follow a pattern. In the Work Together, the list of numbers that tell the total blocks in a figure is a sequence. Each number in a sequence is a **term.**

You find each term of an **arithmetic sequence** by adding the same number to the preceding term. The three dots ". . . " in a sequence indicate that the pattern continues.

You pronounce arithmetic sequence as
ar ith MEH tik SEE kwens.

⬛ EXAMPLE 1

a. Write a rule to describe the sequence 6, 13, 20, 27, ...

The rule is *Start with 6 and add 7 repeatedly.*

b. Find the next three terms in the sequence.

$27 + 7 = 34 \longrightarrow 34 + 7 = 41 \longrightarrow 41 + 7 = 48$

The next three terms are 34, 41, and 48.

2. a. ☒*Reasoning* What is added to each term to find the next term in the sequence 35, 29, 23, 17, . . . ?

   b. Write a rule for the sequence. Find the next three terms.

▼2 *Geometric and Other Sequences*

In a **geometric sequence,** you multiply the preceding term by the same number repeatedly.

■ **EXAMPLE 2**

  a. Write a rule to describe the sequence 1, 3, 9, 27, ...

    The rule is *Start with 1 and multiply by 3 repeatedly.*

  b. Find the next three terms in the sequence.

    $27 \times 3 = 81 \longrightarrow 81 \times 3 = 243 \longrightarrow 243 \times 3 = 729$

    The next three terms are 81, 243, and 729.

3. ✔ *Try It Out* Write a rule for the sequence 800, 400, 200, 100, ... Then find the next three terms.

Some sequences are neither arithmetic nor geometric.

■ **EXAMPLE 3**

  Is 1, 2, 6, 24, . . . arithmetic, geometric, or neither? Explain.

  The sequence is neither arithmetic nor geometric because you do not add or multiply by the same number.

4. ✔ *Try It Out* Is each sequence arithmetic, geometric, or neither?

  a. 1, 3, 6, 10, . . .   **b.** 2, 3, 6, 11, . . .   **c.** 3, 6, 12, 24, . . .

5. A sequence that often occurs in nature is the *Fibonnaci sequence,* which is 1, 1, 2, 3, 5, 8, . . .

  a. Is it arithmetic, geometric, or neither?

  b. ✔ *Try It Out* Find the next three terms of the sequence.

The sunflower is an example of the Fibonacci sequence. The number of seed pods in each ring equals the sum of the pods in the two preceding rings.

Write a rule for each arithmetic sequence. Then find the next three terms.

1. 5, 10, 15, 20, . . .   **2.** 3, 7, 11, 15, . . .   **3.** 34, 29, 24, 19, . . .

4. 25, 21, 17, 13, . . .   **5.** 63, 54, 45, 36, . . .   **6.** −8, −1, 6, 13, . . .

7. Use the pattern at the right.
   a. How many red tiles would be in the ninth figure?
   b. How many yellow tiles would be in the ninth figure?

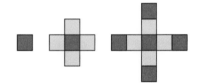

8. *Business* Suppose an employer starts employees at $6/h and raises the wage $.50/h every six months. What kind of sequence is this? Write a rule to describe the sequence.

9. Many people draw a dollar sign as an S-shape with one line through it. The line divides the S into four parts, as shown at the right. Other people draw two lines, dividing the S into seven parts. Suppose you drew the S with 15 vertical lines through it. Into how many parts would the S be divided?

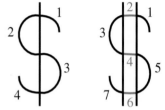

10. *Reasoning* What is the rule for an arithmetic sequence whose terms are all 37?

Write a rule for each geometric sequence. Then find the next three terms.

11. 1, 2, 4, 8, . . .   **12.** 2, 6, 18, 54, . . .   **13.** 600, 300, 150, 75, . . .

14. 0.1, 0.3, 0.9, 2.7, . . .   **15.** $\frac{1}{4}, \frac{1}{12}, \frac{1}{36}, \frac{1}{108}, \cdots$ **16.** 0.5, 1.5, 4.5, 13.5, . . .

17. *Geometry* Draw a 16 × 16 square on graph paper.
   a. Find its area.
   b. Join the midpoints of the sides of the square. Find the area of the inner square.
   c. Join the midpoints of the sides of the inner square. Find the area of the innermost square.
   d. What would be the area of the innermost square in the sixth figure in this sequence?

18. **Choose A, B, C, or D.** What are the next two numbers in the sequence 1, 64, 2, 32, 4, 16, . . . ?
   A. 16, 8   **B.** 8, 16   **C.** 8, 8   **D.** 32, 64

Identify each sequence as arithmetic, geometric, or neither. Then find the next three terms.

19. 2, 5, 10, 17, 26, . . .

20. 0.2, 0.4, 0.6, 0.8, . . .

21. 1, 4, 9, 16, 25, . . .

22. 7, 14, 28, 56, . . .

23. 1, 2, 4, 7, 11, . . .

24. 300, 60, 12, 2.4, . . .

25. A pattern of numbers is shown at the right.
   a. List the numbers in rows 4, 5, 6, and 7.
   b. Find the sum of the numbers in each of the first 7 rows.
   c. Write a rule to find the sum of the numbers in each row.
   d. Predict the sum of the numbers in the twentieth row.

row 1			1			
row 2		1	2	1		
row 3	1	2	3	2	1	

26. a. Write a rule for the geometric sequence 2, 4, 8, 16, ...
   b. Write a rule for the geometric sequence -2, 4, -8, 16, ...
   c. Find the next three terms of each sequence.

27. *Biology* A female bee has two biological parents, a female and a male. A male bee has one biological parent, a female.
   a. Make a "family tree" showing seven generations of ancestors of a female bee. Find the number of ancestors in each of the seven generations.
   b. The numbers of ancestors form a number sequence. Is the sequence arithmetic, geometric, or neither?

28. *Writing* Is the sequence 1, 1, 1, . . . arithmetic, geometric, both, or neither? Explain.

Mixed Review

Solve. *(Lesson 3-6)*

29. $4 + x = -6$

30. $x - 8 = 5$

31. $10 = y - (-2)$

32. $h + (-3) = -5$

Classify each angle as acute, right, obtuse, or straight. *(Lesson 7-2)*

33. $m\angle A = 100°$

34. $m\angle B = 76°$

35. $m\angle C = 26°$

36. $m\angle D = 179°$

37. A party store sells paper plates at $3.45 for 300 and paper cups at $2.94 for 50. At the supermarket, the same plates cost $1.98 for 200, and cups are $1.45 for 30. *(Lesson 6-2)*
   a. Find the unit price for each item at each store.
   b. Which store has a better buy for plates and for cups?

10-2 Scientific Notation

What You'll Learn

1 To write numbers in scientific notation

2 To write numbers in standard form

...And Why

Astronomers use scientific notation to express great distances.

Here's How

Look for questions that
⊞ build understanding
✔ check understanding

Need Help? For practice with powers of 10, see Skills Handbook page 538.

THINK AND DISCUSS

▼**1** *Scientific Notation*

The seventh of Jupiter's moons, Ganymede, orbits Jupiter 1,070,000 km from the planet. **Scientific notation** is a shorthand method for writing very large numbers like this. A number in scientific notation is written as the product of two factors.

$$1,070,000 = 1.07 \qquad \times \qquad 10^6$$

The first factor is greater than or equal to one, but less than 10.

The second factor is a power of 10.

1. a. Copy and complete each statement.

$10^1 = 10$
$10^2 = 10 \times 10 = \blacksquare$
$10^3 = 10 \times 10 \times 10 = \blacksquare$
$10^4 = 10 \times 10 \times 10 \times 10 = \blacksquare$

b. ⊞*Patterns* What patterns do you see in part (a)?

c. Write 100,000,000 using a power of 10.

■ EXAMPLE 1 *Real-World Problem Solving*

Astronomy The moon orbits Earth at a distance of 384,400 km. Write this number in scientific notation.

384,400. ← Move the decimal point to get a factor greater than 1 but less than 10.

5 places

3.844×10^5 ← The decimal point moved 5 places to the left. Use this number as the exponent of 10.

The moon orbits Earth at 3.844×10^5 km.

2. ⊞*Explain* Why is the scientific notation for 1,070,000 *not* 107×10^4?

3. ✔*Try It Out* Write each number in scientific notation.
a. 396,000,000   **b.** 43,000,000   **c.** 2,700,000,000

2 *Standard Form*

You can change a number from scientific notation to **standard form** by multiplying the two factors.

■ **EXAMPLE 2** *Real-World Problem Solving*

Astronomy The mean distance from Earth to the sun is about 1.5×10^8 km. Write this number in standard form.

$10^8 = 100,000,000$

$1.5 \times 10^8 = 150,000,000.$

Multiplying by 100,000,000 moves the decimal point **8** places to the right.

The mean distance is about 150,000,000 km.

4. ✔ *Try It Out* Write 5.6×10^6 in standard form.

WHAT? The distance from Earth to the sun varies between 1.47×10^8 km and 1.52×10^8 km.

Source: *Atlas of the Solar System*

EXERCISES *On Your Own*

Write each number in scientific notation.

1. 7,500　　　**2.** 75 million　　　**3.** 125　　　**4.** 3,400,000

5. 102 thousand　　**6.** 61,300,000　　**7.** 490 billion　　**8.** 44,000

9. There are about 350,000 different kinds of plants on Earth.

10. The Folsom Dam in California holds 326 billion gallons of water in a reservoir.

11. A light-year is how far light travels in one year. This distance is 5,880 trillion miles.

12. The tallest mountain in our solar system is on Mars. Olympus Mons is 78,000 ft tall.

13. *Writing* Explain how you find the power of 10 to write 725,000,000 in scientific notation.

Explain why each number is *not* in scientific notation.

14. 35.4×10^6　　**15.** 8×2^{10}　　**16.** 0.387×10^7　　**17.** 75.5×10^7

Write each number in standard form.

18. 8.6×10^7　　**19.** 5×10^{11}　　**20.** 7.02×10^1　　**21.** 8.3×10^5

22. 2.25×10^3　　**23.** 9.3×10^6　　**24.** 3.02×10^4　　**25.** 6.678×10^2

Write each number in standard form.

26. The first balloon to carry passengers weighed 1.6×10^3 lb.

27. There are about 2×10^{13} red blood cells in a 125-lb person.

28. In 2001, the world population will be about 6.128×10^9.

29. A CD-ROM can store about 6×10^8 bytes of information.

30. Suppose a science museum plans to make a model of the solar system. The distance from the sun to Mercury is about 3.6×10^7 mi. The distance from the sun to Pluto is about 3.7×10^9 mi.
    a. Write each number in standard form.
    b. About how much greater is the distance from the sun to Pluto than the sun to Mercury?
    c. Is using 1 mm : 1,000,000 mi as a scale for this model reasonable? Explain.

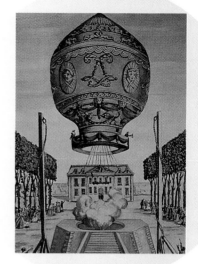

 The first balloons were flown by the Montgolfier brothers, Joseph and Etienne, in France in 1783.

Mixed Review

Find the number of two-letter permutations and combinations of each set. *(Lessons 9-6, 9-7)*

31. B, D, E, Y   32. E, M, O, R, S   33. K, O, L   34. A, E, I, R, V, Z

Find the percent of change. State whether the change is an increase or decrease. *(Lesson 6-11)*

35. old: $35; new: $70   36. old: $275; new: $150   37. old: $9.80; new: $10

38. Find two whole numbers whose sum is 23 and whose product is 132. *(Lessons 3-6, 3-7)*

CHAPTER PROJECT

PROJECT LINK: MEASURING

Select a plastic container for the project. Measure the height of the water level when the container is full. If you put a hole in the bottom, do you think the level will drop at a steady rate? Explain.

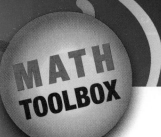

EXPLORATION

Scientific Notation with Negative Exponents

After Lesson 10-2

Scientists also use scientific notation to write very small numbers. Remember that a number in scientific notation has two factors, one greater than or equal to 1 and less than 10, and the other a power of 10.

■ EXAMPLE 1

Write 0.0084 in scientific notation.

0.0084 ←—— Move the decimal point to get a factor greater than 1 but less than 10.

3 places

8.4×10^{-3} ←—— The decimal point moved 3 places to the right so the exponent of 10 is –3.

In scientific notation, 0.0084 is 8.4×10^{-3}.

■ EXAMPLE 2

Write 3.52×10^{-5} in standard form.

$10^{-5} = 0.00001$

$3.52 \times 10^{-5} = 0.0000352$

Multiplying by 0.00001 moves the decimal point 5 places to the left.

The standard form of 3.52×10^{-5} is 0.0000352.

Write each number in scientific notation.

1. 0.0008   2. 0.0037   3. 0.00000691   4. 0.00000307   5. 0.005006

Write each number in standard form.

6. The width of a hair is about 3×10^{-7} in.   7. A flea weighs 4.9×10^{-3} g.

8. *Writing* Explain how to write the numbers 4,500,000 and 0.0000045 in scientific notation.

2. *Geometry* How many diagonals can you draw in a regular 8-sided figure?

Use any strategy to solve each problem. Show your work.

3. Suppose you are numbering 248 tickets for the class play by hand. How many digits do you have to write?

4. In this section of the city of Gridville, the streets are either one-way going east or one-way going south. A section of the city is shown at the right. How many possible routes are there from point *A* to point *B*?

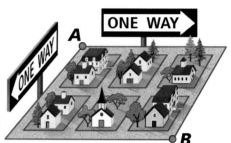

5. *Geometry* The measure of the first of three angles of a triangle is three times the measure of the second angle. The measure of the third angle is twice the measure of the second angle. What is the measure of each angle?

6. The houses on Main Street are numbered from 1 to 140. How many house numbers contain the digit 6 at least once?

7. You have three 29-cent stamps and two 23-cent stamps. How many different amounts of postage do you have?

8. A fruit seller has three weights that can be used to weigh any whole number of pounds from 1 lb to 13 lb on a balance scale. What are the weights?

Mixed Review

Find each product. *(Lesson 5-5)*

9. $3 \cdot 4\frac{5}{8}$ 10. $2\frac{1}{2} \cdot 3\frac{3}{4}$ 11. $\frac{4}{5} \cdot 2\frac{3}{4}$ 12. $4\frac{1}{3} \cdot 7\frac{1}{5}$ 13. $3\frac{2}{5} \cdot 2\frac{5}{6}$

Find the volume of each rectangular prism. *(Lesson 8-10)*

14. $\ell = 6$ m, $w = 3.5$ m, $h = 7$ m   15. $\ell = 3$ ft, $w = 2$ ft, $h = 9$ ft

16. Suppose it takes 18 min to cut a board into 6 pieces. How long would it take to cut the board into 8 pieces? *(Lesson 6-3)*

17. *Choose a Strategy* Darcy has $1.35 in dimes and quarters. How many different combinations of coins might she have?

Identify each sequence as arithmetic, geometric, or neither. Write a rule for each sequence. Then find the next three terms.

1. 3, 6, 9, 12, . . .   **2.** 53, 45, 37, 29, . . .   **3.** 3, 6, 12, 24, . . .

4. 4, 11, 18, 25, 32, . . .   **5.** 87, 77, 66, 54, . . .   **6.** 0.5, 1.5, 4.5, 13.5, . . .

Write each number in scientific notation.

7. 738,000,000   **8.** 29 thousand   **9.** 78.6×10^5 **10.** 1,807,000

Write each number in standard form.

11. 8.06×10^5 **12.** 1.74×10^3 **13.** 8.3×10^9 **14.** 1.008×10^7

15. Choose A, B, C, or D. What is 9 trillion in scientific notation?

     A. 9×10^9 **B.** 9×10^{10} **C.** 9×10^{11} **D.** 9×10^{12}

16. a. The figures at the right show the first three *pentagonal numbers*. How many dots will be on each side of the fourth figure? Include the endpoints.
     b. What is the tenth pentagonal number?

1   5   12

Math at Work

ARTIST

Artists use a variety of materials such as oils, watercolors, plaster, clay, or even computers to create images. Graphic artists work for businesses. Fine artists display their works in galleries or museums. Artists use angles and lines when they draw in perspective, an important skill for any aspiring artist.

 Visit this Web site for more information: http://www.yahoo.com/Arts/Artists/

10-4 Simple and Compound Interest

What You'll Learn

1 To find simple interest

2 To find compound interest

...And Why

When you invest money or borrow money, you earn or pay interest.

Here's How

Look for questions that
- build understanding
- ✔ check understanding

THINK AND DISCUSS

1 *Simple Interest*

Money may not grow on trees, but it can grow in a bank! A bank pays you interest on your deposit because they use your money to earn more money.

Simple interest is interest paid only on your original deposit, or **principal.** To calculate simple interest, you can use the formula $I = p \cdot r \cdot t$, where I is the interest,

p is the principal,

r is the interest rate per year,

and t is the time in years.

The **balance** of an account is the principal plus the interest earned.

■ EXAMPLE 1

Find the simple interest earned on $200 invested at 4% annual interest for three years.

$I = p \cdot r \cdot t$
$I = 200 \cdot 0.04 \cdot 3$ ⟵ Substitute. Use 0.04 for 4%.
$ = 24$

The account earns $24 in interest for three years.

1. ✔ *Try It Out* Suppose you borrow $2,500 to buy a car. The annual interest rate is 8%. Find the amount of simple interest that you will pay for one year.

2. **a.** ▪ *Reasoning* You deposit $150 into an account at the beginning of the year. The balance in the account at the beginning of the next year is $156.75. How much interest did your money earn?

   b. What was the interest rate?

▼2 Compound Interest

Finding simple interest is the first step in computing compound interest. **Compound interest** is interest paid on both the principal and the interest earned in previous interest periods.

You can use a spreadsheet to calculate compound interest.

■ **EXAMPLE 2**   *Real-World Problem Solving*

Banking Suppose someone put $1,000 in the bank for you the day you started first grade. The interest rate is 5% compounded annually. How much will be in the account after seven years?

Make a spreadsheet.

	A	B	C	D	E
1	Year	Start of Year	Rate	Interest	Balance at End of Year
2	1st	$1,000.00	0.05	$50.00	$1,050.00
3	2nd	$1,050.00	0.05	$52.50	$1,102.50
4	3rd	$1,102.50	0.05	$55.13	$1,157.63
5	4th	$1,157.63	0.05	$57.88	$1,215.51
6	5th	$1,215.51	0.05	$60.78	$1,276.28
7	6th	$1,276.28	0.05	$63.81	$1,340.10
8	7th	$1,340.10	0.05	$67.00	$1,407.10

The account has $1,407.10 at the end of seven years.

3. **a.** Why is the amount in cell B3 the same as that in cell E2?
   b. How was the amount in cell E2 calculated?

4. **a.** ✔*Try It Out* Suppose the annual interest on $1,000 principal is 6%. What is the balance after seven years?
   b. How much more interest was earned with 6% annual interest rather than 5% annual interest after seven years?

At the end of a year, the balance in Example 2 is 105% of the amount at the start of the year. 105% is the same as $1 + 0.05$. This sum is part of the following formula to find a balance with compound interest.

$B = p(1 + r)^t$, where B is the balance in the account,
p is the principal,
r is the annual interest rate,
and t is the time in years.

Consider the problem in Example 2 once again.

■ EXAMPLE 3   *Real-World Problem Solving*

Banking Suppose you deposit $1,000 in a bank account paying 5% annual interest. Use the formula to find your balance after 7 years.

$B = p(1 + r)^t$
$\quad = 1,000(1 + 0.05)^7$ ←——Substitute. Use 0.05 for 5%.
$\quad = 1,000(1.05)^7$ ←——Evaluate within the parentheses.
$\quad = 1,000(1.407100423)$ ←——Use a calculator to find $(1.05)^7$.
$\quad \approx 1,407.10$ ←——Multiply. Round to the nearest cent.

There is $1,407.10 in the account after seven years.

5. ✔ *Try It Out* You deposit $1,000 for 21 years. The bank pays 5% interest compounded annually. What is your balance?

Work Together _____ *Investigating Compound Interest*

Work in a group to investigate compound interest.

6. Suppose you invest $2,000 for 5 years. Your interest rate is 4% compounded annually. What will your balance be?

7. ⊞ *Technology* For the account in Question 6, predict which of the three changes below would increase the balance the most. Then calculate each balance to check your prediction.
   a. doubling the starting amount from $2,000 to $4,000
   b. doubling the interest rate to 8% annual interest
   c. doubling the time from 5 years to 10 years

EXERCISES *On Your Own*

⊞ *Choose* Use a calculator or pencil and paper to find the simple interest earned by each account.

1. $500 principal
   4% annual interest rate
   3 years

2. $2,000 principal
   6.5% annual interest rate
   7 years

3. $1,400 principal
   5.5% annual interest rate
   11 years

4. $900 principal
   6% annual interest rate
   5 years

5. $1,900 principal
   4.5% annual interest rate
   10 years

6. $3,500 principal
   7% annual interest rate
   9 years

7. When you use a credit card and leave a balance, you owe interest. If you leave a $500 balance for a year on a card with 18% simple interest, how much will you owe after one year?

8. You invest $2,000 in an account earning simple interest. The balance after 8 years is $2,720. What was the interest rate?

Choose Use a spreadsheet or a calculator to find the balance of each account earning compound interest.

9. $500 principal
4% annual interest rate
3 years

10. $1,200 principal
5.5% annual interest rate
9 years

11. $1,400 principal
6.5% annual interest rate
8 years

12. $1,800 principal
6% annual interest rate
11 years

13. $900 principal
5% annual interest rate
14 years

14. $1,500 principal
4.7% annual interest rate
6 years

15. **Choose A, B, C, or D.** Which expression would you use to find the balance of $200 invested for 6 years at 5% interest compounded annually?

   A. $200 \cdot 0.05 \cdot 6$ **B.** $200(1 + 0.05)^6$ **C.** $200 \cdot 0.06 \cdot 5$ **D.** $200(1 + 0.06)^5$

16. *Writing* Which would you prefer, $2,000 at 6% interest compounded annually for 5 years or $2,000 at 5% interest compounded annually for 6 years? Explain your choice.

17. **a.** *Research* Find the interest rate of savings accounts at three banks.
   b. *Open-ended* Decide on an amount as the principal. Using interest that compounds annually, calculate the balance after four years at each bank.

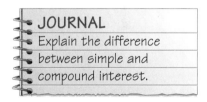

JOURNAL
Explain the difference between simple and compound interest.

Mixed Review

Solve. *(Lesson 3-7)*

18. $w \div 13 = 5$ 19. $-8z = 56$ 20. $27 = -3x$ 21. $16 = t \div (-4)$ 22. $5y = -20$

Determine whether the given sides form a right triangle. *(Lesson 7-3)*

23. $3, 4, 5$ 24. $12, 13, 17$ 25. $6, 5, 2$ 26. $6, 8, 10$ 27. $20, 15, 12$ 28. $3, 8, 12$

29. The length of a rectangle is twice the width. The area is 32 cm^2. Find the dimensions of the rectangle. *(Lesson 8-2)*

What You'll Learn

▼ **1** To represent functions with tables and rules

▼ **2** To graph functions

...And Why

You can use functions to describe many real-world relationships, such as time and distance.

Here's How

Look for questions that
- ▪ build understanding
- ✔ check understanding

THINK AND DISCUSS

▼ **1** Using Tables and Rules

Suppose your family is planning a sight-seeing vacation by car. You expect to drive at an average speed of 50 mi/h.

1. ▪ *Mental Math* How many miles will you drive in 1 h? 2 h?

2. ▪ *Reasoning* How many hours will it take to drive 200 mi?

You can represent the relationship between the time you drive and the distance you drive using a function machine like the one at the right. You say that the distance is a **function** of time, since each input value (time) has exactly one output value (distance).

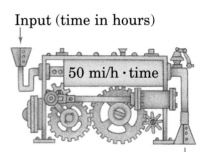

Input (time in hours)

50 mi/h · time

Output (mi)

3. When the input is 3, what is the output?

4. If the output is 300, what is the input?

You can represent functions using a table or a rule.

■ **EXAMPLE 1** *Real-World Problem Solving*

a. Make a table to represent the relationship between the time and distance you drive.

Input (hours)	1	2	3	4
Output (miles)	50	100	150	200

b. Write a rule to represent the relationship between the time and distance you drive.

distance = **50** · time

$d = 50t$ ◀— Variables represent the input (*t*) and output (*d*).

---

5. ⬛ *Look Back* What kind of sequence is the number pattern you see in the output row of the table in Example 1?

6. ✔ *Try It Out* Use the rule to find the miles you drive in 3.5 h.

❷ Graphing Functions

You can make a graph to represent a function.

⬛ **EXAMPLE 2**

Graph the input and output data from the table in Example 1. Draw a line through the points on your graph.

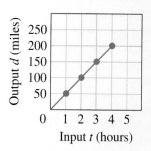

7. ⬛ *Predict* Use the graph to predict the miles traveled in 5 h.

8. ✔ *Try It Out* Make a table of values for the function rule output = 3 · input. Then graph the data.

Work Together   *Investigating Functions*

Work with a partner to investigate a function.

9. a. ⬛ *Data Collection* Count the number of times you or your partner breathes in one minute. Record the result.
b. Repeat the experiment four times. Then find the mean of your results.

10. a. Use your mean number of breaths per minute. Copy and complete this table.

Input t (minutes)	1	2	3	4	5	6
Output b (number of breaths)	⬛	⬛	⬛	⬛	⬛	⬛

b. Graph the data in your table.
c. Write a rule for the function.

Most people can hold their breath for about 1 min. Experienced skin divers can hold their breath for about $2\frac{1}{2}$ min. A beaver can stay under water for about 15 min.

Source: *Encyclopedia Britannica*

Write a function rule for each table of values.

1.

Hours Worked	Salary
1	$6.50
2	$13.00
3	$19.50
4	$26.00

2.

Number of CDs	Price Paid
1	$11.99
2	$23.98
3	$35.97
4	$47.96

3.

Weeks	Plant Height
1	3 in.
2	5 in.
3	7 in.
4	9 in.

4. *Writing* Explain when you would use a table to represent a function, and when you would use a rule.

Input

5. *Algebra* Use the function machine at the right.
   a. Make an input/output table for input values from -5 to 5.
   b. What two inputs result in an output of 22?

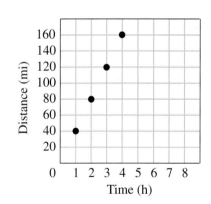

$x^2 + x + 2$

Output

Make a table of values for each function rule. Use input values of 1, 2, 3, 4, and 5.

6. Output = 5 · Input

7. Output = Input + 3

8. Output = 2 · Input + 1

9. Output = Input ÷ 2

10. *Open-ended* Describe a situation for each rule in Exercises 6–9.

11. *Cars* The graph at the right shows the relationship between distance and time for a car driven at a constant speed.
    a. What is the speed? Explain.
    b. Use the graph to find the number of hours it takes to drive 120 miles.
    c. Make a table for the function. Use input (time) for 1, 2, 3, and 4 hours.
    d. Write a rule to represent the function.

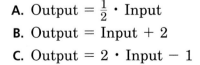

Match the graph with the rule.

12.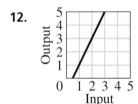

13.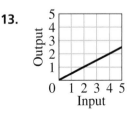

14.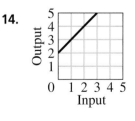

A. Output = $\frac{1}{2}$ · Input

B. Output = Input + 2

C. Output = 2 · Input − 1

15. **a.** Copy and complete the function table at the right.
   b. Use the data from your table to make a graph.
   c. Write a rule for the function.
   d. List three more input/output pairs for the function.

Change from a $5.00 Purchase

Input p (cost)	Output c (change)
$ .50	■
$1.00	■
$1.50	■
. . .	. . .
$5.00	■

16. *Geometry* The formula $A = s^2$ is a function rule. It shows that the area of a square is a function of the length of a side.
   a. Using the rule, make a table for the area of a square with sides of length 1, 2, 3, and 4.
   b. Use the data from your table to graph the function.
   c. Describe what your graph looks like.

17. **a.** *Jobs* Use the function machine at the right. Suppose you work six hours (input). What are your wages (output)?
   b. Make a table of five inputs and outputs for this machine.
   c. Make a graph of the function using the data in your table.

Input

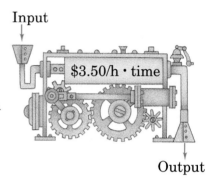

$3.50/h · time

Output

18. A function has only one output for each input. Explain if each situation represents a function.
   a. Input: the number of pounds a turkey weighs
      Output: the number of $\frac{1}{3}$-lb servings of turkey
   b. Input: the number of days in a month
      Output: the number of holidays in the month

Mixed Review

Find the value of each expression. *(Lessons 2-5, 2-6)*

19. 95.26×110 **20.** 0.23×8.45 **21.** $4\overline{)1.988}$ **22.** $0.384 \div 9.6$ **23.** $19.563 \div 6$

Compare. Use <, >, or =. *(Lesson 4-3)*

24. $\frac{7}{9}$ ■ $\frac{3}{4}$ **25.** $\frac{5}{14}$ ■ $\frac{2}{6}$ **26.** $\frac{7}{30}$ ■ $\frac{1}{3}$ **27.** $\frac{8}{24}$ ■ $\frac{2}{6}$ **28.** $\frac{11}{49}$ ■ $\frac{12}{42}$

29. Suppose that January 1 is a Monday. What are the dates of the other Mondays in January? *(Lesson 10-1)*

CHAPTER PROJECT

PROJECT LINK: COLLECTING DATA

Put a small hole in the bottom of the container. Measure the height of the water level every 30 seconds. How long does it take to empty? Use your data to make a table of the height of the water level at each time.

10-6 Function Rules

What You'll Learn

▼1 To make a table given a function rule

▼2 To find a function rule given a table

...And Why

Different views of functions are useful in different situations.

Here's How

Look for questions that

▪ build understanding

✔ check understanding

Work Together   *Viewing Functions*

Use the function table below. Consider these three rules.

Input	Output
1	2
2	3
3	4
4	5

I. Output = 2 × Input

II. Output = Input + 1

III. Output = 2 × Input − 1

1. a. ▪*Analyze* Which rule(s) describes the relationship between the first input and output?
   b. Which rule(s) describes the relationship between the input and output when the input is 2?
   c. Which rule(s) describes the relationship between the input and output in all of the rows?

2. Use the variable n to represent any input in the table. Write a variable expression to represent the related output.

THINK AND DISCUSS

▼1 *Making Tables*

Input	Output
1	4
2	5
3	6
4	7

Here are two ways you can describe the relationship of the values in the table at the left.

Each output is three greater than the input

Output = Input + 3

Another way to state the rule is using function notation.

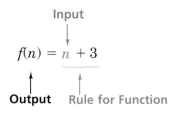

You read the function rule above as "f of n equals n plus three."

You also use function notation to find input/output pairs.

■ EXAMPLE 1

Use the function rule $f(n) = -3n + 5$. Find $f(0)$, $f(1)$, $f(2)$, and $f(3)$. Then make a table for the function.

Use the expression $-3n + 5$. Replace n with 0, 1, 2, and 3.

Put the inputs and outputs in a table.

$$f(0) = -3(0) + 5 = 5$$
$$f(1) = -3(1) + 5 = 2$$
$$f(2) = -3(2) + 5 = -1$$
$$f(3) = -3(3) + 5 = -4$$

n	$f(n) = -3n + 5$
0	5
1	2
2	-1
3	-4

Fractals, like the one pictured below, are created using a feedback process. This means that an output is used for the next input. For example, suppose you used $n = 0.8$ as the first value for n in $f(n) = n^2$. The output is 0.64. You would use the output 0.64 as the second input value for n.

Source: *The Beauty of Fractals*

3. ✔ **Try It Out** Use the function rule in Example 1. Find $f(4)$.

▼❷ Looking for Patterns

When you have a function table, you can find a function rule by looking for patterns.

■ EXAMPLE 2

Write a rule for each function represented by a table below.

a.

n	$f(n)$
0	0
1	-4
2	-8
3	-12

+ 1 ( ) - 4
+ 1 ( ) - 4
+ 1 ( ) - 4

When $n = 0$, $f(n) = 0$.
Each number in the second column is $n \cdot (-4)$.

The function rule is $f(n) = n \cdot (-4)$, or $f(n) = -4n$.

b.

n	$f(n)$
0	2
1	5
2	8
3	11

+ 1 ( ) + 3
+ 1 ( ) + 3
+ 1 ( ) + 3

When $n = 0$, $f(n) = 2$. Then as inputs increase by 1, outputs increase by 3.

The function rule is $f(n) = 3n + 2$.

n	0	1	2	3
f(n)	1	5	9	13

4. a. What is $f(n)$ when $n = 0$? How much do the outputs increase when the inputs increase by 1?

b. ✔ *Try It Out* Write a rule for the function represented by the table.

EXERCISES *On Your Own*

Use the function rule $f(n) = 2n + 7$. Find each output.

1. $f(3)$ **2.** $f(0)$ **3.** $f(-1)$ **4.** $f(-4)$ **5.** $f(0.5)$ **6.** $f\left(\frac{1}{4}\right)$

Make a table for the function represented by each rule. Find $f(0)$, $f(1)$, $f(2)$, and $f(3)$.

7. $f(n) = n + 2$ **8.** $f(n) = 12 - 2n$ **9.** $f(n) = 4n$ **10.** $f(n) = n \div 2$

11. $f(n) = 9 - n$ **12.** $f(n) = -3n$ **13.** $f(n) = 2n + 1$ **14.** $f(n) = n^2 + 1$

15. a. Make a table of input/output pairs for the graph at the right.

b. Use your table to write a rule for the function.

16. You pay \$.05 for each day a library book is overdue. A rule that describes this is $f(n) = 0.05n$, where n represents the number of days overdue.

a. What is the charge for a book that is nine days overdue?

b. A book has a fine of \$1.05. How many days is it overdue?

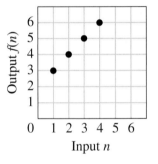

Write a rule for the function represented by each table.

17.

n	f(n)
0	0
1	5
2	10
3	15

18.

n	f(n)
0	4
1	5
2	6
3	7

19.

n	f(n)
0	-6
1	-5
2	-4
3	-3

20.

n	f(n)
0	-2
1	0
2	2
3	4

21.

n	f(n)
0	0
1	-8
2	-16
3	-24

22.

n	f(n)
0	5
1	8
2	11
3	14

23.

n	f(n)
0	5
1	9
2	13
3	17

24.

n	f(n)
0	1
1	-8
2	-17
3	-26

25. *Writing* Explain how you found the rule you wrote for one of the tables in Exercises 17–24.

26. *Money* Suppose you put $.50 in your piggy bank on July 1, $1.00 on July 2, $1.50 on July 3, and so on. Use *n* to represent the date in July. Write a function rule for the amount you put in the piggy bank on any date in July.

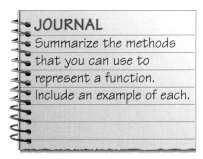

JOURNAL
Summarize the methods that you can use to represent a function. Include an example of each.

Mixed Review

Write each number as a percent. *(Lesson 6-7)*

27. 0.455   **28.** $\frac{7}{8}$ **29.** 9.25   **30.** $\frac{209}{400}$ **31.** $6\frac{1}{2}$ **32.** 2

Find the circumference and area of each circle. Round your answers to the nearest tenth. *(Lesson 8-4)*

33. $r = 1.75$ ft   **34.** $d = 17$ yd   **35.** $r = 1.5$ m   **36.** $d = 9.5$ km   **37.** $r = 1$ in.

38. The three sides of a right triangle are 6 in., 8 in., and 10 in. What is the area of the triangle? *(Lesson 8-3)*

✓ CHECKPOINT 2　　　　　　　　　　　*Lessons 10-4 through 10-6*

Make a table of values for each function. Then graph the function.

1. $f(n) = 3n$ **2.** $f(n) = 2n - 4$ **3.** $f(n) = 8 - n$ **4.** $f(n) = n + 7$

Write a rule for the function represented by each table.

5.

n	f(n)
0	0
1	−12
2	−24
3	−36

6.

n	f(n)
0	4
1	3
2	2
3	1

7.

n	f(n)
0	1
1	4
2	7
3	10

8.

n	f(n)
0	0
1	7
2	14
3	21

9. *Writing* You invest $600 for three years. The interest rate is 4% compounded annually. Explain how to find your balance.

Extra Practice, Lesson 10-6, page 523

MATH TOOLBOX

Three Views of a Function

After Lesson 10-6

When you input a function in a graphing calculator, you can view the graph of the function or a table of values.

■ EXAMPLE

Graph $f(x) = 9 - x$ and make a table of values.

Step 1 Use WINDOW to set the range.

```
WINDOW FORMAT
Xmin = 0
Xmax = 10
Xscl = 1
Ymin = 0
Ymax = 10
Yscl = 1
```

Step 2 Use Y= to enter the function.

```
Y1 ■ 9–X
Y2 =
Y3 =
Y4 =
Y5 =
Y6 =
Y7 =
Y8 =
```

Step 3 Use the GRAPH feature to view the graph.

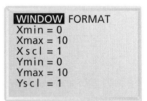

Step 4 Use the TABLE feature to make a table of values.

X	Y1
0	9
1	8
2	7
3	6
4	5
5	4
6	3

X=0

Step 5 Sketch the graph and copy the table of values.

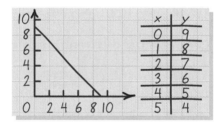

Use a graphing calculator to graph each function and make a table of values. Sketch the graph and copy the table of values.

1. $f(x) = 2x$

2. $f(x) = x - 3$

3. $f(x) = 13 - 2x$

4. $f(x) = x + 1$

5. $f(x) = 3x - 4$

6. $f(x) = 0.5x + 6$

7. $f(x) = 7$

8. $f(x) = x^2 - 8x + 16$

10-7

Interpreting Graphs

What You'll Learn

1 To write a description for a graph

2 To sketch a graph from a description

...And Why

You can use graphs to analyze events.

Here's How

Look for questions that
- build understanding
- ✔ check understanding

THINK AND DISCUSS

1 *Describing Graphs*

In some situations, a visual description such as a graph can be more helpful than a verbal description.

■ **EXAMPLE 1**   *Real-World Problem Solving*

A trip to the supermarket combines riding your bike with time spent shopping. The graph at the right relates time and your distance from home. Describe what the graph shows.

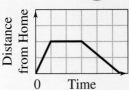

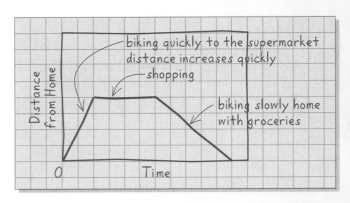

1. ✔ *Try It Out* Suppose you live six blocks from school. The graphs show your walk home on a sunny and a rainy day. Describe what each graph shows.

a.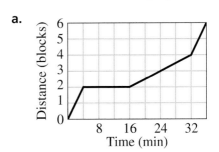

b.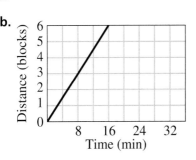

2 Drawing Graphs

You can sketch a graph to describe real-world situations.

■ **EXAMPLE 2** *Real-World Problem Solving*

Tedrick's mother drove him part of the way to school. After he got out of the car, he waited for a friend. Then they walked the rest of the way to school. Tedrick took a bus home. Sketch a graph to show the distance Tedrick traveled. Label each section.

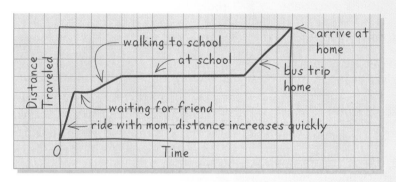

2. a. ✔ *Try It Out* Sketch a graph of the situation in Example 2, but use "Distance from Home" instead of "Distance Traveled" for one axis.

b. How is your graph different from the one in Example 2?

3. ⬚ *Go a Step Further* Make a graph that represents the height above the ground of one car on a Ferris wheel during three turns of the wheel. You can use a coin to simulate the Ferris wheel as it turns.

EXERCISES *On Your Own*

Match each graph with its situation. Explain your choices.

1.
Time

2.
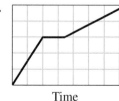
Time

3.
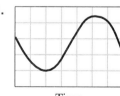
Time

A. distance in a hurdles race, falling over a hurdle

B. air temperature in the 24-h period starting from midnight

C. height of a person from birth to age 20

4. Lee, Paulo, and Mary each walked six blocks from school to the library. The graphs at the right show the time and distance for each person's walk.

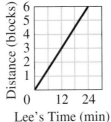
Lee's Time (min)

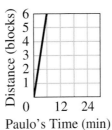
Paulo's Time (min)

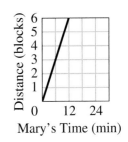
Mary's Time (min)

a. Who walked fastest? Slowest? Explain how you know.

b. How is the steepness of the line related to the speed?

Sketch a graph for each situation. Label each section and your axes.

5. You run the first three blocks from the library to your house, then walk the remaining five blocks.

6. You ride your bike slowly up a steep hill, then quickly down the other side.

7. You climb a jungle gym, then slide down the slide.

8. Suppose you are steadily pouring sand into the container at the right. Which graph below better shows the relationship of the height of the sand with the amount you have poured? Why?

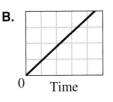

A.
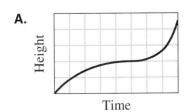
Time

B.
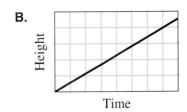
Time

9. *Reasoning* A driver sets a car's cruise control to 50 mi/h. Which graph shows the speed of the car? Which graph shows the distance traveled? Explain your reasoning.

A. 0 Time B. 0 Time

10. *Estimation* The graph at the right shows what happens when a ball is thrown into the air.

a. What is the greatest height that the ball reaches?

b. How long does it take for the ball to hit the ground?

c. Why are there two times when the height of the ball is 20 ft? What are the times?

d. When the time is 0, why is the height of the ball *not* 0?

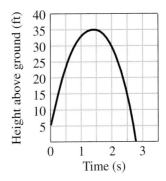

The Population EXPLOSION

From A.D. 1 to A.D. 1650, the world population grew by 300 million. This translates to an average of just 180,000 people per year, or about 21 people per hour. In contrast, today nine babies are born every two seconds, but only three people die. This means that the population is growing by about 10,800 people per hour, 259,200 per day, 1.8 million per week, 7.2 million per month, and 86.4 million per year. By the year 2000, the population will increase 94 million per year, and by 2020 that number will be 98 million per year.

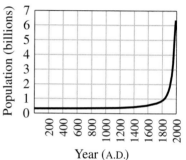

World Population

11. **a.** Explain how the graph at the right illustrates the numbers mentioned in the article.
    b. At what time in history would you say that the rate of population growth began a dramatic increase?

12. *Sports* The graph at the right shows the results of a 50-m race. In this race Edwin had a 15-m head start over Carl.
    a. Who won the race?
    b. By how many seconds did he win?
    c. Predict what might happen in another race between Edwin and Carl if Edwin does not have a head start.

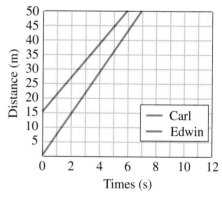

13. *Reasoning* Fares for Sunshine Taxi fares are $.90 for the first 0.2 mi and $.40 for each additional 0.2 mi or less. Carmen and Brian graphed the taxi fares. Which graph would you use to find the cost of a 0.5 mi trip? Explain your choice.

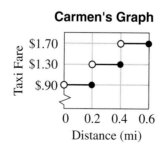

Carmen's Graph

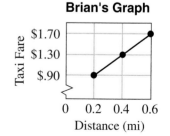

Brian's Graph

14. *Open-ended* Sketch a graph that represents your trip home from school yesterday.

15. *Writing* Describe a situation that the graph below might represent.

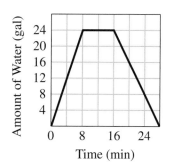

Mixed Review

Complete. *(Lesson 5-8)*

16. ▓ kg = 157 g **17.** 8 c = ▓ pt **18.** 50 in. = ▓ ft **19.** 9 lb = ▓ oz **20.** $2\frac{1}{4}$ m = ▓ cm

Make a stem-and-leaf plot. *(Lesson 1-5)*

21. 34 46 50 48 53 33 20 44 48 45 34 **22.** 9.6 9.2 7.3 8.1 7.4 8.1 7.8 7.5 8.5 9.6

23. A florist can create an arrangement in 14 min. An order arrives for 124 arrangements for a large banquet. How long will it take the florist to make the arrangements, to the nearest hour? *(Lesson 6-2)*

24. The six members of the Estrella family walked a total of 60 mi in 5 days. What is the average number of miles each family member walked each day? *(Lesson 3-5)*

CHAPTER PROJECT

PROJECT LINK: GRAPHING

Make a graph of your table from the Project Link on page 453. Label the horizontal axis "Time" and the vertical axis "Water Level." Begin with time zero when the container is full, and end when the water level is zero. Connect the points and give your graph a title. Explain how the graph reflects the shape of your container.

Read each question and choose the best answer.

1. This drawing shows how to—

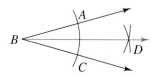

   A. construct a right angle
   B. construct an angle
   C. construct an angle bisector
   D. construct complementary angles

2. One ride at an amusement park requires that passengers be at least 40 inches tall. Which number line shows the range of heights for people who can go on this ride?

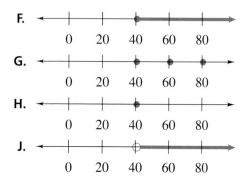

3. Anoki, Moy, Carmisha, and Ellen run the 100-m dash. In how many different orders could the four runners finish the race?

   A. 4   **B.** 12   **C.** 16   **D.** 24

4. The farthest distance that Earth is from the sun is 9.45×10^7 miles. This distance is—

   F. 945,000,000 miles
   G. 94,500,000 miles
   H. 9,450,000 miles
   J. 945,000 miles

5. Ears of corn are sold 3 for \$.45. How much will 10 ears of corn cost?

   A. \$1.80   **B.** \$1.50   **C.** \$1.35   **D.** \$.90

6. The winner of a contest will be chosen by drawing a name out of a bag without looking. The bag holds the names of 4 sixth graders, 5 seventh graders, and 6 eighth graders. What is the probability that the winner will *not* be in the seventh grade?

   F. $\frac{2}{3}$ **G.** $\frac{3}{5}$ **H.** $\frac{1}{3}$ **J.** $\frac{4}{15}$

Please note that items 7–9 have *five* answer choices.

7. The outside edge of a circular window measures 88 in. What is the diameter of the window? Use $\frac{22}{7}$ for π.

   A. 12 in.   **B.** 14 in.   **C.** 21 in.
   D. 28 in.   **E.** 56 in.

8. A large box will be used to hold school supplies. All of the sides of the box will be decorated except the top and the bottom. The box is 15 in. long, 7 in. wide, and 5 in. tall. How many square inches of paper are needed to decorate the box?

   F. 110 in.^{2} **G.** 220 in.^{2} **H.** 280 in.^{2}
   J. 360 in.^{2} **K.** Not Here

9. A survey of 125 customers showed that 35 customers were extremely happy with the Super Speedy bicycle manufactured by the Roadster Company. If 1,000 customers have purchased the Super Speedy bicycle, what is a good prediction for the number of customers who are extremely happy with the bicycle?

   A. 70   **B.** 105   **C.** 210
   D. 280   **E.** 560

happy *landings*

Graphing Data The Project Link questions on pages 440, 453, and 463 should help you to complete your project. Here is a checklist to help you gather together the parts of your project.

✓ the container

✓ the table of the height of water level at different times

✓ the graph of your data

✓ the explanation of how your graph reflects the shape of your container

Your graph should be large, clear, and neat. Did the container empty at a steady rate? Be prepared to explain how the graph helps you answer this question.

Reflect and Revise

Review your project with a friend or someone at home. Is your table complete? Is your graph accurate? Is your explanation clear? If necessary, make changes to improve your project.

Web Extension
Prentice Hall's Internet site contains information you might find helpful as you complete your project. Visit www.phschool.com/mgm2/ch10 for some links and ideas related to science.

Number Patterns 10-1

A **sequence** is a set of numbers arranged according to some pattern. Each number in a sequence is a **term.**

You find each term of an **arithmetic sequence** by adding the same number to the preceding term.

You find each term of a **geometric sequence** by multiplying the preceding term by the same number.

Identify each sequence as arithmetic, geometric, or neither. Then find the next three terms of each sequence.

1. 7, 11, 15, 19, . . .   2. 48, 24, 12, 6, . . .   3. 3, 9, 27, 81, . . .   4. 20, 16, 11, 5, . . .

5. Write a rule for each sequence in Exercises 1–3.

6. **Choose A, B, C, or D.** What is the seventh term of the sequence 1, 3, 7, 15, . . .?

   A. 127   **B.** 99   **C.** 64   **D.** 101

Scientific Notation 10-2

A number in **scientific notation** is the product of two factors. The first factor is greater than or equal to 1 and less than 10. The second factor is a power of 10. Multiply the two factors to write the number in **standard form.**

Write each number using scientific notation.

7. 1,524,000,000   8. 250,000   9. 383 million   10. 87,600

11. The population of the United States in 1990 was about 2.49×10^8. Write this number in standard form.

Problem Solving Strategies 10-3

Sometimes you can solve a problem by solving a simpler problem.

12. You have a game that uses the board at the right. How many triangles with sides on the gridlines are on the board?

Simple interest is earned only on the beginning **principal.** You use the formula $I = p \cdot r \cdot t$ to find the interest earned.

Compound interest is earned on the principal and any interest already earned. You use the formula $B = p(1 + r)^t$ to find the **balance** of an account.

13. You deposit $1,500 in an account earning 6% simple interest. How much interest is earned after 5 years?

14. You leave a $600 balance for a year on a credit card charging 20% simple interest. How much will you owe after one year?

15. You deposit $1,500 in an account that pays 5% interest compounded annually. What is the balance after 5 years?

Functions   10-5, 10-6

You can represent a **function** using a table, a rule, or a graph.

16. a. Write a rule for the function represented by the table at the right.
b. Graph the function.

n	f(n)
0	2
1	4
2	6
3	8

17. a. Make an input/output table for the graph at the right.
b. Write a rule for the function.

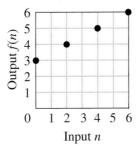

18. A rule for a function is $f(n) = 2n + 5$. Find $f(-1)$, $f(0)$, $f(1)$, and $f(2)$.

Interpreting Graphs   10-7

You can use graphs to represent real-world situations.

19. *Writing* Describe a situation that the graph at the right might represent.

20. Tani walks at a rate of about 3 mi/h. She leaves home and walks for 3 h. She stops and spends 1 h eating lunch. Then she walks one more hour. Sketch a graph that represents the distance she has walked over the 5-h period.

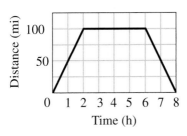

1. Identify each sequence as arithmetic, geometric, or neither. Then find the next three terms.
   a. 1, 3, 9, 27, . . .   b. 4, 9, 14, 19, . . .
   c. 3, 4, 6, 9, . . .   d. 10, 8, 6, 4, . . .
   e. −1, 3, 7, 11, . . . f. 1.5, 3, 6, 12, . . .

2. Write rules for the arithmetic and geometric sequences in Exercise 1.

3. Write each number in scientific notation.
   a. 175,000,000   b. 600
   c. 9,600,000,000 d. 22 million

4. Write each number in standard form.
   a. 4×10^2 b. 6.72×10^7
   c. 7.80×10^4 d. 1.046×10^9

5. An amusement park costs $12/person. The park offers special rates for groups. Admission charges are $40 for four people, $49 for five, $57 for six, $64 for seven, and so on. How much does each member of a group of twelve save by getting a group rate?

6. Suppose you deposit $2,000 in an account that earns 6.5% simple interest each year. How much interest is earned after 10 years?

7. Suppose you deposit $1,000 in an account that earns 6% interest compounded annually. What is the balance in the account after four years? Use the formula $B = p(1 + r)^t$.

8. Make a table of the input/output pairs for each of the following.
   a. the cost of 1 to 5 books at $2.95 each
   b. the perimeter of a square with sides 5 in., 6 in., 7 in., 8 in., and 9 in. long

9. Find $f(-2)$, $f(0)$, and $f(5)$ for each function represented by a rule below.
   a. $f(n) = n - 5$ b. $f(n) = 9 + n$
   c. $f(n) = 2n + 1$ d. $f(n) = n^2 - 1$

10. **Choose A, B, C, or D.** Which is *not* an output for $f(n) = 2n^2 - 5$?

    A. −3   B. 45   C. 27   D. −8

11. *Writing* Tori earns $4.50/h. How can she use a function to find her earnings for any number of hours she works?

12. Write a function rule for each table.

    a.
n	f(n)
0	0
1	3
2	6
3	9

    b.
n	f(n)
0	1
1	3
2	5
3	7

    c.
n	f(n)
0	−2
1	−7
2	−12
3	−17

13. Use the graph for the questions below.

    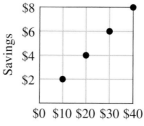

    a. Make a table of input/output pairs.
    b. Write a rule for the function.
    c. Find how much money is saved when $100 is earned.

14. Sketch a graph describing the height of a basketball as it is dribbled down the court and a basket is made. Label the sections of your graph.

Choose the best answer.

1. Which number is written in scientific notation?

   A. 0.2×10^9 **B.** 9.14×2^5

   C. 10×10^8 **D.** 7.12×10^{11}

2. Which equation has the same solution as $2x + 7 = 9$?

   A. $x + 3 = 2$ **B.** $-3x = -2$

   C. $x - 3 = -2$ **D.** $x + 3 = -2$

3. The A-One Hotel charges \$88/day for two people in a room, plus \$7 for each additional person. Which equation could you use to find the cost c for n people to stay in a room one day?

   A. $c = 88 + n(7)$

   B. $c = 88 + (n - 2)(7)$

   C. $c = (n + 2)(88 + 7)$

   D. $c = 88 + (n + 2)(7)$

4. What could the graph below represent?

   Time

   A. height of a ball t seconds after it is thrown upward

   B. temperature of an oven t minutes after it is turned on

   C. temperature of hot water while cooling for t minutes

   D. distance a car has traveled at 45 mi/h after t hours

5. Which expression has the greatest value?

   A. $4^2 - 3$ **B.** $22 - |-5|$

   C. $(8 - 6)^2 + 10$ **D.** $11 - (-7)$

6. Florisa earns \$16/week. Which equation can you use to find how many weeks it will take her to earn \$400?

   A. $16 + w = 400$ **B.** $16w = 400$

   C. $\frac{16}{w} = 400$ **D.** $\frac{16}{400} = w$

7. Find the median of the data in the stem-and-leaf plot.

7	0 0 5 8
8	1 5 6 9 9
9	4

   $9 \mid 4$ means 94

   A. 81.7   **B.** 89

   C. 85   **D.** 83

8. Find two numbers whose sum is 10 and whose product is -24.

   A. -6 and 4   **B.** 12 and -2

   C. -8 and -3 **D.** 6 and -4

9. Which type of graph would best display the following data on the number of viewers (in millions) watching television during prime time?

   Mon., 91.9   Tue., 89.8   Wed., 93.9
   Thu., 93.9   Fri., 78.0   Sat., 77.1
   Sun., 87.7

   A. line   **B.** double line

   C. bar   **D.** double bar

10. An obtuse triangle has one angle whose measure is 30°. What is the measure of the other acute angle?

    A. any measure between 0° and 60°

    B. any measure less than 90°

    C. any measure between 30° and 60°

    D. any measure between 60° and 90°

Graphing in the Coordinate Plane

11

THEME:
BUSINESS

People's *choice*

You're an advertising executive, and you want to know which of three television shows is the most popular. So you plan to conduct a poll of viewers.

But how many viewers do you survey? Polling is expensive, so you don't want to poll too many. Polling too few viewers might give you the wrong information. Here's your chance to explore the process!

Find a Sample Size Fill a container with three different kinds of beans. Use the beans to find the sample size that best predicts the percent of each kind of bean in the container.

Steps to help you complete the project:

• How to solve problems by writing an equation

PROBLEM SOLVING

What You'll Learn

1. To graph points on the coordinate plane
2. To identify quadrants

...And Why

Computer programmers and robotics engineers use the coordinate plane to describe locations.

Here's How

Look for questions that
- build understanding
- ✔ check understanding

To direct a robot/computer like this one, programmers use coordinates.

THINK AND DISCUSS

1 Graphing Points

René Descartes (1596–1650) was a French mathematician and philosopher. An old legend says that he looked up at the ceiling one day and noticed a fly crawling across it. Descartes began thinking about how to describe the exact position of the fly on the ceiling. His thoughts generated the *coordinate plane*.

A **coordinate plane** is formed by a horizontal number line called the *x*-axis and a vertical number line called the *y*-axis.

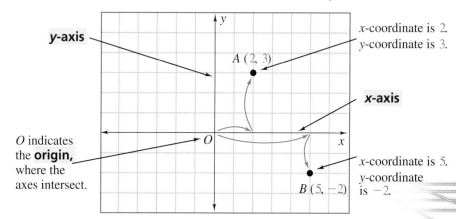

y-axis

x-coordinate is 2.
y-coordinate is 3.

A (2, 3)

x-axis

O indicates the **origin,** where the axes intersect.

x-coordinate is 5.
y-coordinate is −2.

B (5, −2)

An **ordered pair** identifies the location of a point. The ordered pair (2, 3) identifies point *A*.

1. a. ■ *Think About It* On the *x*-axis, which direction is positive? Negative?
   b. On the *y*-axis, which direction is positive? Negative?

The *x*-coordinate of an ordered pair shows the position left or right of the origin. The *y*-coordinate shows the position up or down. You can use this information to write coordinates.

■ EXAMPLE 1

Write the coordinates for the fly on the coordinate plane at the right.

The fly is 2 units to the right of the *y*-axis. So the *x*-coordinate is 2.

The fly is 1 unit above the *x*-axis. So the *y*-coordinate is 1.

The ordered pair for the location of the fly is (2, 1).

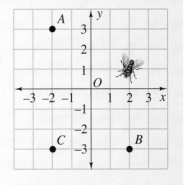

2. ✔ *Try It Out* Use the graph in Example 1. What are the coordinates of points *A*, *B*, and *C*?

3. ⁂ *Go a Step Further* Find the coordinates of the origin.

You can use an ordered pair to graph a point on a plane.

■ EXAMPLE 2

Graph the point with coordinates $(3, -5)$.

Step 1
Start at the origin.

Step 2
Move 3 units to the right.

Step 3
Then move 5 units down. Draw a dot. Label it *A*.

4. ✔ *Try It Out* Graph the points on the same plane.
   a. $B(3, 5)$ b. $C(-3, -5)$ c. $D(-3, 5)$

5. a. Graph the points $G(0, 4)$, $H(-2, 0)$, $J(0, -3)$ and $K(5, 0)$. Tell on which axis each point lies.
   b. ⁂ *Draw a Conclusion* On which axis does the point $(m, 0)$ lie? On which axis does the point $(0, n)$ lie?

✌ Identifying Quadrants

The *x*- and *y*-axes divide the coordinate plane into four **quadrants.**

■ EXAMPLE 3

In which quadrant is the point $(-4, -1)$ located?

Start at the origin (O). Move 4 units to the left and 1 unit down.

The point $(-4, -1)$ is in the third quadrant.

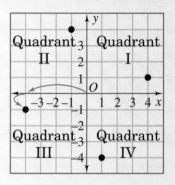

6. ✔ *Try It Out* Identify the quadrant in which each point lies.

   a. $(4, 5)$ **b.** $(-1, 7)$ **c.** $(10, -13)$

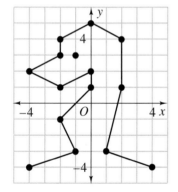

Work Together

Exploring the Coordinate Plane

Work with a partner.

7. Make a dot-to-dot drawing (such as the one at the left). On a separate sheet of paper, write the coordinates of the dots in the order in which you connected them.

8. Exchange lists of ordered pairs with your partner. Recreate your partner's drawing by graphing the coordinates.

EXERCISES *On Your Own*

Name the point with the given coordinates.

1. $(-5, 3)$ **2.** $(4, 0)$ **3.** $(-6, 2)$

4. $(5, -3)$ **5.** $(0, 5)$ **6.** $(6, 2)$

Write the coordinates of each point.

7. G **8.** K **9.** J

10. H **11.** M **12.** L

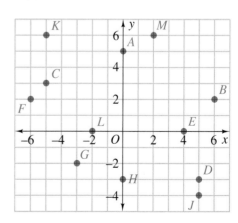

13. a. *Patterns* Graph the points $(-3, -2)$, $(-3, 2)$, $(-3, -6)$, and $(-3, 6)$.
    b. What do you notice about these four points?
    c. Give the coordinates of two other points that fit the pattern.

14. a. A horizontal line is shown in red at the right. List the ordered pairs of 3 points that are on the line.
    b. Which coordinate of an ordered pair stays the same for all points on the line? Which coordinate changes?

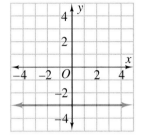

15. *Writing* Describe how to find the point $(5, -1)$ on a coordinate plane.

16. Four of these points are the vertices of a square. Which one is not?
    $(-1, -3)$ $(-1, 0)$ $(2, -3)$ $(4, -2)$ $(2, 0)$

17. **Choose A, B, C, or D.** Which of the following groups of ordered pairs are *not* the vertices of a rectangle?
    A. $(-4, 1)$, $(4, 1)$, $(-4, -1)$, and $(4, -1)$ **B.** $(-1, 0)$, $(-5, -3)$, $(-1, -4)$, and $(-5, 0)$
    C. $(3, 6)$, $(6, 6)$, $(3, 9)$, and $(6, 9)$ **D.** $(-3, 8)$, $(3, 8)$, $(3, -8)$, and $(-3, -8)$

Identify the quadrant in which each point lies.

18. $(-3, 7)$ 19. $(9, 5)$ 20. $(6, -2)$ 21. $(-1, -9)$

22. $(3, -15)$ 23. $(-2,000, 12)$ 24. $(-0.05, -0.39)$ 25. $\left(\frac{17}{2}, \frac{3}{21}\right)$

Open-ended **Draw each quadrilateral on a coordinate grid such that each vertex is in a different quadrant. Label each vertex and identify which quadrant it is in.**

26. square   27. parallelogram   28. trapezoid

29. *Open-ended* A robot arm must move the black peg in the diagram onto the white square, but the peg must be moved around—not over— the red walls. List the coordinates of the vertices of a path the robot arm might follow to move the peg.

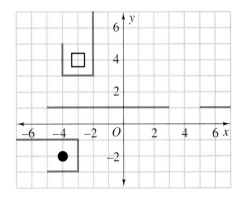

30. The robot arm at the right is moving the computer chip from the point $(-2, 5)$ to a point three units up and seven units to the right. In which quadrant will the chip be placed?

31. *Analyze* For each quadrant, identify the signs of the *x*- and *y*-coordinates of an ordered pair in the quadrant.

Mixed Review

32. Find the number of two-letter permutations for the group of letters M, A, R, S. *(Lesson 9-6)*

Choose **Use a calculator or pencil and paper to find the simple interest earned by each account.** *(Lesson 10-4)*

33. $3,000 principal
4.5% annual interest rate
2 years

34. $1,500 principal
5.25% annual interest rate
5 years

35. $3,150 principal
6% annual interest rate
4 years

36. *Choose a Strategy* Carla used her baby-sitting money and $15 she received on her birthday to go shopping. She bought film for $12.49, a flash for $29, and batteries for $2.99. She had $3.91 left. How much money did Carla earn baby-sitting?

Math at Work

AUTOMOTIVE ENGINEER

Automotive engineers design, develop, test, and produce all kinds of vehicles. They also test and evaluate a design's cost, reliability, and safety.

An automotive engineer has many opportunities to use math skills. Engineers apply problem-solving skills to determine causes of breakdowns and to test for quality. And they use computer-aided design systems to create the cars of the future!

Vist the Web site www.sqe.org to find out more about automotive engineering.

What You'll Learn

1 To find ordered pairs that are solutions of equations in two variables

2 To graph a linear equation

...And Why

You can use linear equations to model business situations.

Here's How

Look for questions that
- build understanding
- ✔ check understanding

THINK AND DISCUSS

1 *Finding Ordered Pairs*

Ronelle Moore makes tire swings for local day-care centers. Each swing requires enough rope to reach the tree branch plus another 5 ft for tying the rope around the tire and the branch.

1. **Mental Math** Suppose you want a swing to hang 8 ft below the branch. How much rope do you need?

2. **Reasoning** Suppose you have 17 ft of rope. How far below the branch will the swing hang?

Ronelle let x represent the distance the swing hangs below a branch and y represent the length of rope. She wrote the equation $y = x + 5$, which is an equation in two variables. Any ordered pair that makes the equation true is a **solution** of the equation.

■ **E X A M P L E 1**   *Real-World Problem Solving*

Find three solutions of Ronelle's equation $y = x + 5$ and explain what one solution represents.

Choose three values for x. Then make a table.

x	$x + 5$	y	(x, y)
8	$8 + 5$	13	(8, 13)
10	$10 + 5$	15	(10, 15)
12	$12 + 5$	17	(12, 17)

The ordered pairs (8, 13), (10, 15), and (12, 17) are solutions of the equation $y = x + 5$.

The solution (8, 13) means that Ronelle needs 13 ft of rope to make a swing that will hang 8 ft from a branch.

3. Find one other solution of the equation in Example 1.

4. ✔ *Try It Out* Find three solutions of $y = 2x$.

■ **EXAMPLE 2**

Tell whether each ordered pair is a solution of $y = x + 5$.

a. $(40, 45)$ **b.** $(21, 27)$

$$y = x + 5$$
$$45 \stackrel{?}{=} 40 + 5 \quad \longleftarrow \begin{array}{c}\text{Substitute for } x \text{ and } y \\ \text{in the equation.}\end{array} \longrightarrow \quad \begin{array}{c} y = x + 5 \\ 27 \stackrel{?}{=} 21 + 5 \end{array}$$
$$45 = 45 \text{ ✔ yes} \qquad\qquad\qquad\qquad\qquad\qquad 27 \neq 26 \text{ no}$$

5. ✔ *Try It Out* Is $(10, 15)$ a solution of $y = 2x - 7$? Explain.

6. ▪ **Choose A, B, C, or D.** Which ordered pair is *not* a solution of the equation $y = 3x - 1$?

A. $(4, 11)$ **B.** $(7, 22)$ **C.** $(\frac{1}{3}, 0)$ **D.** $(-2, -7)$

▼2 *Graphing a Linear Equation*

The **graph of an equation** is the graph of all the points whose coordinates are solutions of the equation. An equation is a **linear equation** if all its solutions lie on a line.

■ **EXAMPLE 3**

Graph the equation $y = x + 1$. Is it a linear equation?

Choose values for x. Then make a table of values.

Graph the points. Then draw a line through the points.

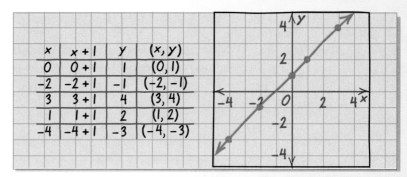

x	x + 1	y	(x, y)
0	0 + 1	1	(0, 1)
-2	-2 + 1	-1	(-2, -1)
3	3 + 1	4	(3, 4)
1	1 + 1	2	(1, 2)
-4	-4 + 1	-3	(-4, -3)

Since the solutions lie on a line, $y = x + 1$ is a linear equation.

7. ▪ **Look Back** Use the graph from Example 3 to find two more solutions of the equation $y = x + 1$.

8. ✔ *Try It Out* Graph the equation $y = 2x$. Is this equation a linear equation?

EXERCISES *On Your Own*

Open-ended **Find three solutions of each equation.**

1. $y = x - 2$ **2.** $y = 5x$ **3.** $y = 3x + 1$ **4.** $y = -2x + 4$ **5.** $y = x + 9$

Tell whether each ordered pair is a solution of $y = x + 12$. Explain how you know.

6. $(-12, 24)$ **7.** $(12, 24)$ **8.** $(0, -12)$ **9.** $(-12, 0)$ **10.** $(-24, -12)$

On which of the following lines does each point lie?
(*Hint*: A point may lie on more than one line.)

11. $(-2, -1)$ **12.** $(-6, 0)$ **A.** $y = x + 6$

13. $(-3, -3)$ **14.** $(0, -6)$ **B.** $y = -x - 6$

15. $(0, 0)$ **16.** $(3, 9)$ **C.** $y = 2x + 3$

17. *Error Analysis* LaVonna said that $(-1, -5)$ is a solution of $y = -3x - 2$. Explain why her answer is incorrect.

Match each equation with a line on the graph below.

18. $y = x - 3$

19. $y = 2x$

20. $y = -x$

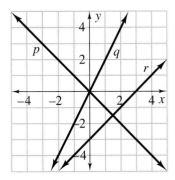

21. a. Copy and complete the table at the right to find three solutions of $y = x - 7$.
  b. Graph the ordered pairs on a coordinate plane.
  c. Is this a linear equation? Explain how you know.

x	$x - 7$	y	(x, y)
0	■	■	■
-3	■	■	■
10	■	■	■

22. *Reasoning* How many solutions does a linear equation have? Explain your reasoning.

23. **Choose A, B, C, or D.** The graph of which equation passes through the second quadrant?

   A. $y = x - 5$ **B.** $y = 2x$ **C.** $y = x + 3$ **D.** $y = x$

Use the graph at the right for Exercises 24 and 25.

24. *Reasoning* Substitute the x- and y-coordinates for point P into the equation for line j to show that this ordered pair is *not* a solution of the equation.

25. What are the coordinates of the point that is a solution of the equations of both lines j and k?

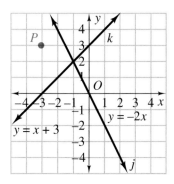

Graph each equation on a coordinate plane.

26. $y = x - 5$ 27. $y = 3x$ 28. $y = 2x + 1$ 29. $y = -2x$

30. $y = x + 3$ 31. $y = 2x - 4$ 32. $y = -x + 2$ 33. $y = \frac{1}{2}x$

CUSHIONS *of* CORN

The Popcorn Institute reports that sales of popcorn have increased recently. One reason is that many companies now use popcorn instead of Styrofoam to cushion packages.

Environmentally friendly popcorn is easy to produce. A hot-air popper about the size of a microwave oven can make about $\frac{1}{2}$ pound of popcorn in 1 minute, or about 30 pounds in 1 hour.

34. **a.** *Food Preparation* Let x represent the number of minutes the popper is on and let y represent the popper's output in pounds. Then the equation $y = \frac{1}{2}x$ describes the relationship between x and y. Make a table for the equation. Find three solutions.

   b. Graph the points from your table. Draw the line that represents the equation.

   c. *Reasoning* Does it make sense to extend the line into the third quadrant? Why or why not?

35. *Writing* When you graph the equation of a line, you could use any two points. Explain why graphing a third point is a good idea.

36. *Money* Adin had $35 saved at the beginning of the year. He planned to save $5 each week. He modeled his savings plan with the equation $y = 5x + 35$.
   a. Graph the equation.
   b. How many weeks will it take him to save $60?

37. a. Graph the equations $y = x$ and $y = -x$ on the same axes.
   b. Find the ordered pair that is a solution of both equations.
   c. *Geometry* Do these lines appear to be perpendicular or parallel?

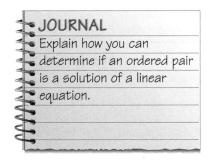
JOURNAL
Explain how you can determine if an ordered pair is a solution of a linear equation.

Mixed Review

Write a function rule for each table of values. *(Lesson 10-5)*

38.

Hours	Salary
0	$0.00
1	$5.25
2	$10.50
3	$15.75

39.

Hours	Service Cost
0	$35
1	$60
2	$85
3	$110

40.

Weeks	Plant Height
1	42 mm
2	84 mm
3	126 mm
4	168 mm

Use the Pythagorean theorem to determine if a triangle with the given side lengths is a right triangle. *(Lesson 8-7)*

41. 4 cm, 5 cm, 7 cm   **42.** 12 ft, 16 ft, 20 ft   **43.** 20 m, 21 m, 29 m   **44.** 7 in., 8 in., 12 in.

45. *Cooking* Larry is making a casserole for dinner. For every 2 onions, his recipe requires 3 tomatoes. How many onions should Larry use when he has 15 tomatoes? *(Lesson 6-3)*

CHAPTER PROJECT

PROJECT LINK: COLLECTING DATA

Sample the beans in the container ten times. Make each sample larger than the previous one. Remember to mix the sampled beans back into the container each time. Keep track of the size of each sample and the percent of each type of bean.

11-3 Finding the Slope of a Line

What You'll Learn

- To calculate the slope of a line

...And Why

You can use the slope of a line to describe real-world relationships.

Here's How

Look for questions that
- build understanding
- ✔ check understanding

Work Together

Exploring Slope

Work with a partner. Notice the rise and run of the stair steps. You can use rise and run to describe the steepness of a line.

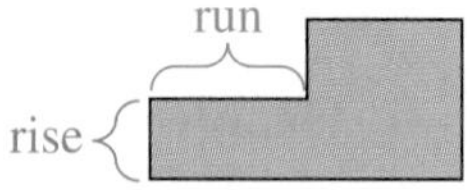

1. Use the ratio $\frac{\text{rise}}{\text{run}}$ to express the steepness of the graph of each line.

a.

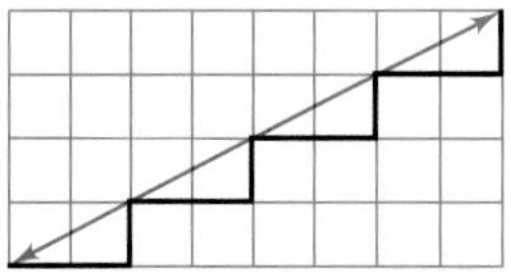

b.

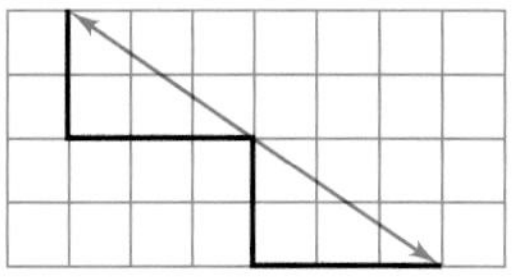

2. *Reasoning* Going from left to right, the graph on the left goes upward. The one on the right goes downward. How can you indicate this when describing the steepness of these lines?

THINK AND DISCUSS

Slope describes the steepness of the graph of a line.

slope of a line $= \frac{\text{rise}}{\text{run}}$

■ EXAMPLE 1

Find the slope of each line.

a.

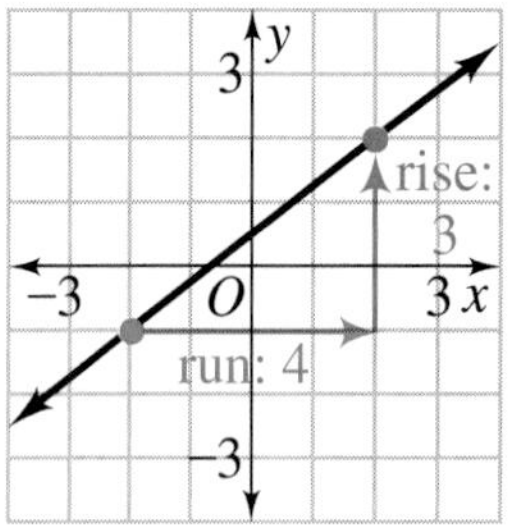

$$\text{slope} = \frac{\text{rise}}{\text{run}} = \frac{3}{4}$$

The slope is $\frac{3}{4}$.

b.

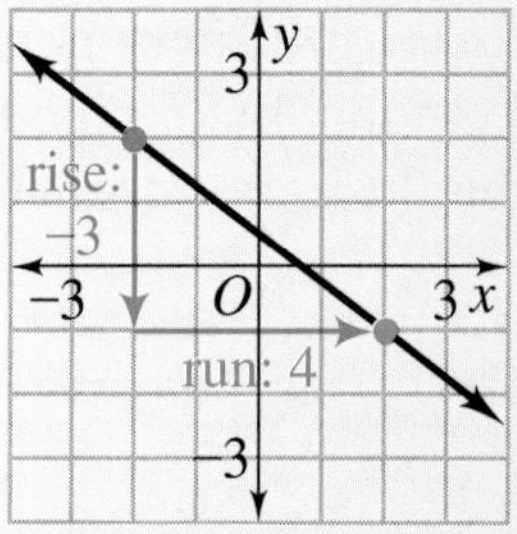

$$\text{slope} = \frac{\text{rise}}{\text{run}} = \frac{-3}{4} = -\frac{3}{4}$$

The slope is $-\frac{3}{4}$.

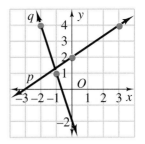

3. ✔ *Try It Out* Find the slope of line *q* and line *p*.

4. ▪*Look Back* Use the graphs and slopes of the lines in Example 1 and in Question 2 to answer the questions below.
   a. Does a line that goes upward from left to right have *positive* or *negative* slope?
   b. Does a line that goes downward from left to right have *positive* or *negative* slope?

The slope of a line tells you how fast one variable is changing in relation to the other variable.

▪ **EXAMPLE 2**   *Real-World Problem Solving*

Science The graph shows the relationship between the time a candle burns and the candle's height. Find the slope of the line. How does the candle's height change in relation to the time it has been burning?

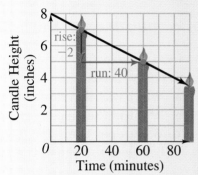

slope of the line $= \frac{-2}{40} = -\frac{1}{20}$

The candle gets 1 in. shorter every 20 min.

5. a. ▪*Look Back* Could you find the slope by starting at (60, 5) and going to (20, 7)? What would be the rise and the run?
   b. Does this affect the value of the slope?

EXERCISES *On Your Own*

Find the slope of each line.

1.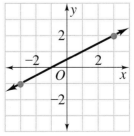

2.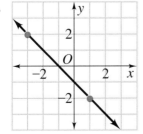

3.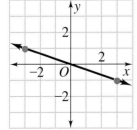

For each exercise, graph the given points. Find the slope of the line through the points.

4. (4, 8), (5, 10)   **5.** (2, 2), (1, 1)   **6.** (4, −1), (−4, 1)   **7.** (2, 7), (3, −1)

8. a. Use the graph at the right to name two points on line *j* and two points on line *k*.
   b. Find the slope of lines *j* and *k*.
   c. Which line has a negative slope?

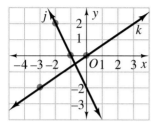

9. *Error Analysis* Suppose Kenji found the slope of a line through the points (4, 2) and (5, −1) to be 3. His friend Kelton found the slope to be −3. Who is correct? What mistake was made?

10. *Writing* Describe how to find the slope of a line.

11. *Cars* The graph at the right shows the value of a car for the first seven years of ownership.
   a. What was the value of the car when it was new?
   b. What is the slope of the graph?
   c. What does the slope tell you about the relationship between the age of the car and its value?

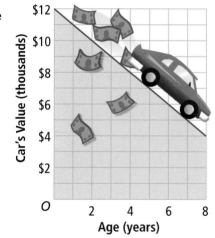

12. a. Graph a line through the points (0, 4) and (3, −3). Find the slope of the line.
   b. Graph a line through the points (1, 5) and (4, −2). Find the slope of the line.
   c. *Geometry* What do you notice about the slopes? Look at the lines. What seems to be true about the two lines?

Mixed Review

Identify each number sequence as an arithmetic sequence, geometric sequence, or neither. Then find the next three terms. *(Lesson 10-1)*

13. 4, 9, 14, 19, . . .   **14.** 6, 12, 24, 48, . . .   **15.** 6, 13, 20, 27, . . .   **16.** 5, 7, 10, 14, . . .

Identify the quadrant in which each point lies. *(Lesson 11-1)*

17. (−3, 2)   **18.** (1, −8)   **19.** (5, 11)   **20.** (−12, −7)   **21.** $\left(-\frac{6}{7}, \frac{2}{3}\right)$ **22.** (0.16, −0.3)

23. Make a tree diagram to show the outcomes for tossing three coins. *(Lesson 9-4)*

Exploring Slope

After Lesson 11-3

There is a relationship between the slope of a line and its equation. At the right is the graph of the equation $y = -\frac{3}{5}x$.

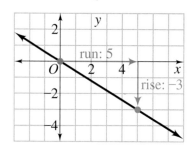

1. **a.** What is the slope of the line?
   b. How does the equation for the graph express the slope of the line?

2. What is the slope of each line?
   a. $y = \frac{2}{3}x$ **b.** $y = -4x$ **c.** $y = \frac{7}{2}x$

You can explore the effect slope has on a line using a graphing calculator.

3. **a.** Use the window values at the right. Graph the equations $y = x$, $y = 3x$, and $y = 4x$.
   b. Which line is steepest? Which line is the least steep?
   c. How does the value of the slope affect the steepness of the line?
   d. *Predict* Describe where you would expect the graph of $y = 5x$ to be. Check your prediction.

```
WINDOW  FORMAT
Xmin=-10
Xmax=10
Xscl=1
Ymin=-10
Ymax=10
Yscl=1
```

4. **a.** Graph the lines $y = x$, $y = \frac{1}{3}x$, and $y = \frac{1}{4}x$.
   b. *Analyze* What happens to the steepness of the graph as the value of the slope gets closer to zero?

5. *Open-ended* Write the equation of a line that is less steep than $y = \frac{1}{4}x$. Verify that your line is less steep by graphing your equation and $y = \frac{1}{4}x$.

6. *Writing* Explain how you can determine which of two lines with positive slope is steeper without graphing them.

7. **a.** Graph the line $y = -x$.
   b. Through what quadrants does the graph of this line pass?
   c. Graph the lines $y = -3x$ and $y = -4x$. Are these lines steeper than $y = -x$?
   d. *Open-ended* Write the equation of a line steeper than $y = -7x$ that passes through the same quadrants as $y = -7x$.

What You'll Learn

▼**1** To draw graphs of parabolas

▼**2** To draw graphs of absolute value functions

...And Why

Nonlinear equations are models for many applications such as the path of a thrown object.

Here's How

Look for questions that

⊞ build understanding

✔ check understanding

THINK AND DISCUSS

▼**1** *Graphing Parabolas*

Not all equations in two variables have graphs that are straight lines (linear). The nonlinear graph of $y = x^2$ is a curve called a *parabola*. A parabola is U-shaped.

■ **EXAMPLE 1**

Make a table of values for the equation $y = x^2$. Graph the ordered pairs and draw a smooth curve through them.

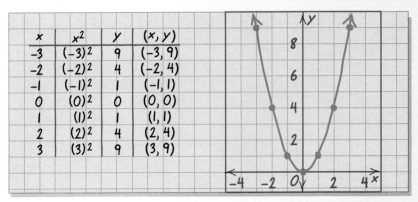

x	x^2	y	(x, y)
-3	$(-3)^2$	9	$(-3, 9)$
-2	$(-2)^2$	4	$(-2, 4)$
-1	$(-1)^2$	1	$(-1, 1)$
0	$(0)^2$	0	$(0, 0)$
1	$(1)^2$	1	$(1, 1)$
2	$(2)^2$	4	$(2, 4)$
3	$(3)^2$	9	$(3, 9)$

1. **a.** ✔ *Try It Out* Make a table of values for the equation $y = 2x^2$. Include both positive and negative values for x.

  b. Graph the ordered pairs. Draw a smooth curve through the points.

  c. ⊞ *Think About It* How does the parabola that is the graph of $y = 2x^2$ differ from the graph of $y = x^2$?

When you throw or kick a ball, the path that the ball follows is in the shape of a parabola.

▼2 *Graphing an Absolute Value Equation*

The equation $y = |x|$ is an absolute value equation in two variables. The graphs of absolute value equations are V-shaped.

■ **EXAMPLE 2**

Make a table of values for the equation $y = |x|$. Graph the ordered pairs. Connect the points.

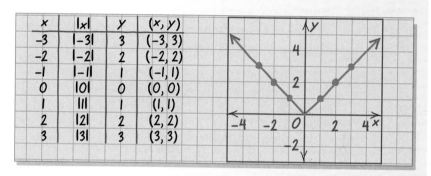

x	$|x|$	y	(x, y)
-3	$|-3|$	3	$(-3, 3)$
-2	$|-2|$	2	$(-2, 2)$
-1	$|-1|$	1	$(-1, 1)$
0	$|0|$	0	$(0, 0)$
1	$|1|$	1	$(1, 1)$
2	$|2|$	2	$(2, 2)$
3	$|3|$	3	$(3, 3)$

2. Which of the following points are on the graph of $y = |x|$?
   a. $(4, 4)$ b. $(-4, 4)$ c. $(4, -4)$
   d. $(-4, -4)$ e. $\left(\frac{1}{2}, \frac{1}{2}\right)$ f. $\left(-\frac{1}{2}, \frac{1}{2}\right)$

3. ▪*Reasoning* Will the graph of $y = |x|$ ever have points in quadrant III? In quadrant IV? Justify your answer.

4. ✔ *Try It Out* Make a table of values for the equation $y = 2|x|$. Graph the equation.

EXERCISES *On Your Own*

Make a table of values. Then graph each parabola.

1. $y = \frac{1}{2}x^2$ 2. $y = 3x^2$ 3. $y = x^2 - 4$ 4. $y = x^2 + 4$

Make a table of values. Then graph each absolute value equation.

5. $y = 3|x|$ 6. $y = \frac{1}{2}|x|$ 7. $y = |x| + 1$ 8. $y = |x| - 1$

What is the shape of the graph of each equation?

9. $y = 5x^2$ 10. $y = 5x - 2$ 11. $y = 10|x|$ 12. $y = -\frac{1}{10}x + 7$

13. **Physics** When an object (with little air resistance) is dropped, you can use the equation $d = 16t^2$ to find the distance in feet the object has dropped in t seconds.
   a. Suppose a ball is dropped from the top of a tall tower. How far has it dropped after 1 second? 2 seconds? 3 seconds?
   b. *The Tower of the Americas* in San Antonio, Texas, is 650 ft tall. About how many seconds will it take an object dropped from the tower to hit the ground?

14. **Writing** Suppose you were paid by the hour for stuffing pillows. Which of the equations below would you prefer to use to calculate your salary? Explain.

Salary Options
Option 1 $y = x$
Option 2 $y = x^2$
(x = hours worked; y = dollars earned)

15. a. Make a table of values for $y = -x^2$. Use at least 7 values for x, some positive and some negative. Include 0.
   b. Draw a graph of the equation.
   c. How is this parabola different from the others you have seen?

16. a. **Geometry** What kind of angle is formed when you graph $y = |x|$?
   b. What kind of angle is the graph of $y = 2|x|$?
   c. **Reasoning** Describe the absolute value equations whose graphs are obtuse angles.

Match each graph with an equation. (*Hint*: Substitute values for x into the equations to find coordinates of points.)

17.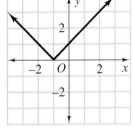

18.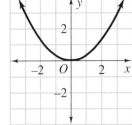

19.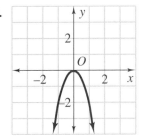

A. $y = |x + 1|$

B. $y = |x| - 1$

C. $y = \frac{1}{2}x^2$

D. $y = \frac{1}{3}x^2$

E. $y = x^2 - 8$

F. $y = -2x^2$

20. a. Make a table of values for $y = -|x|$. Use at least 7 values for x, some positive and some negative. Include 0.
   b. Graph the ordered pairs and connect them.
   c. How is this graph different from the graph of other absolute value equations you have seen?
   d. Will the graph of $y = -|x|$ ever have points in quadrants I and II? Why or why not?

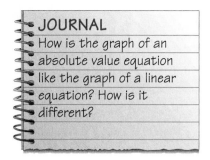

JOURNAL
How is the graph of an absolute value equation like the graph of a linear equation? How is it different?

Mixed Review

Suppose you have cards numbered consecutively from 1 through 25. A card is drawn and is *not* replaced. What is the probability of each of the events? *(Lesson 9-5)*

21. $P(4 \text{ and } 5)$ **22.** $P(\text{two even numbers})$ **23.** $P(\text{odd and even})$

Tell whether each ordered pair is a solution of $y = 2x - 3$. Explain how you know. *(Lesson 11-2)*

24. $(-2, -1)$ **25.** $(4, 5)$ **26.** $(-3, -3)$ **27.** $(0, -5)$ **28.** $(2, 1)$ **29.** $(3, 9)$

30. *Working* This week, Lena worked $2\frac{1}{3}$ times the 15 hours she worked last week. How many hours did she work? *(Lesson 5-9)*

✓ CHECKPOINT 1   *Lessons 11-1 through 11-4*

Name the point with the given coordinates.

1. $(-4, 1)$ **2.** $(3, -3)$ **3.** $(0, 2)$

Name the coordinates of each point.

4. F **5.** C **6.** A **7.** E

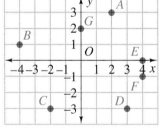

8. Choose A, B, or C. The graph of which equation passes through the first quadrant?
   A. $y = -\frac{2}{3}x - 1$ **B.** $y = -x$ **C.** $y = 4 + x$

9. a. Make a table of values and graph $y = x - 2$.
   b. What is the slope of the line?

10. a. Make a table of values for $y = x^2 - 5$.
   b. Graph the equation.

11-5 Write an Equation

READ PLAN LOOK BACK SOLVE

Problem Solving Strategies

Draw a Diagram
Guess and Test
Look for a Pattern
Make a Model
Make a Table
Simulate a Problem
Solve a Simpler Problem
Too Much or Too Little
 Information
Use Logical Reasoning
Use Multiple Strategies
Work Backward
✔ Write an Equation

Sometimes you can write an equation to solve a problem.

SAMPLE PROBLEM

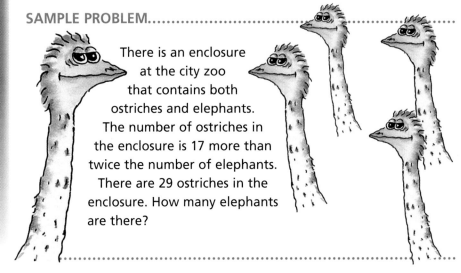

There is an enclosure at the city zoo that contains both ostriches and elephants. The number of ostriches in the enclosure is 17 more than twice the number of elephants. There are 29 ostriches in the enclosure. How many elephants are there?

READ

Read for understanding. Summarize the problem.

1. Think about the information and what you are asked to find.
 a. What information are you given about the ostriches?
 b. What do you need to find?

PLAN

Decide on a strategy.

Since you are given the relationship between the numbers, an equation may help solve the problem.

Let *e* represent the number of elephants. A number sentence that relates the number of ostriches and the number of elephants is

$$\text{number of ostriches} = 17 + 2e.$$

Since there are 29 ostriches, you can write

$$29 = 17 + 2e.$$

SOLVE

Try the strategy.

You can solve the equation for *e*.

$$29 = 17 + 2e$$
$$29 - 17 = 17 - 17 + 2e \quad \longleftarrow \text{Subtract 17 from each side.}$$
$$12 = 2e \quad \longleftarrow \text{Simplify.}$$
$$\frac{12}{2} = \frac{2e}{2} \quad \longleftarrow \text{Divide each side by 2.}$$
$$6 = e \quad \longleftarrow \text{Simplify.}$$

2. How many elephants are there?

LOOK BACK

Think about how you solved the problem.

Another advantage of using an equation to solve a problem is that if any aspect of the problem changes, only a small adjustment needs to be made to the equation.

3. Suppose there were 33 ostriches in the enclosure, not 29.
   a. How would the original equation change?
   b. Write and solve the new equation.

4. Suppose the number of ostriches was 11 more than twice the number of elephants instead of 17 more.
   a. How would the original equation change?
   b. Write and solve the new equation.

EXERCISES *On Your Own*

Write and solve an equation for each problem.

1. *Money* A pair of boots costs $5 more than twice the cost of a pair of shoes. The boots cost $42.90. How much do the shoes cost?

2. *Geometry* The perimeter of a rectangle is 64 cm. The length is 20 cm. Find the width.

3. *Entertainment* Daheem and Judy read mystery novels. Judy has read 3 less than 5 times as many as Daheem. She has read 17 mysteries. How many has Daheem read?

4. *Fund-raising* The booster club sold $\frac{3}{4}$ of their raffle tickets. They had 175 tickets left. How many tickets were printed?

5. A piggy bank contains $4.30 in dimes and quarters. The bank has $2.80 in dimes. How many quarters does the bank contain? (*Hint*: Let n be the number of quarters. Since each quarter has a value of $.25, the value of n quarters is $0.25n$.)

Use any strategy to solve each problem.

6. *Money* With the $5.75 in her pocket, Tia decided to treat herself to lunch. How much can she spend on lunch so she still has enough to leave a 15% tip for the waitress?

7. Paloma, Jasper, and Holly are each less than 45 years old. The mode of their ages is 35. The range is 14. What is the mean of their ages? What is the median of their ages?

8. **Architecture** JoAnne's kitchen measures 11 ft by $13\frac{1}{2}$ ft. She wants to tile the floor using square ceramic tiles that are 6 in. on each side. How many tiles does she need?

9. **Geometry** The area of the square at the right is 64 square units. Point C is the midpoint of $\overline{AD}$. Point B is the midpoint of $\overline{AC}$. What fraction of the square is shaded?

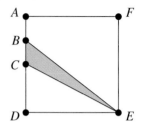

10. A worm is at the bottom of a 40-m hole. It can crawl upward at the rate of 4 m in one day, but at night it slips back 3 m. How long will it take the worm to crawl out of the hole?

Mixed Review

Suppose you flip a coin 1,000 times and get 548 heads. *(Lessons 9-1, 9-3)*

11. What is the experimental probability of getting heads? Tails?

12. What is the theoretical probability of getting heads?

Calculator **Use the formula $B = p(1 + r)^t$ to find the balance of each account earning compound interest. Recall that B is the balance, p is the principal, r is the annual interest rate, and t is the time in years.** *(Lesson 10-4)*

13. $4,000 principal
    4.5% annual interest rate
    1 year

14. $12,500 principal
    5.25% annual interest rate
    5 years

15. $3,870 principal
    6% annual interest rate
    4 years

16. Sketch a graph of your height above ground as you swing four times on a swing. Include labels. *(Lesson 10-7)*

17. **Choose a Strategy** The water at Limestone Cove is 5 ft deep. Every $\frac{1}{4}$ mile out to sea, the water is 3 ft deeper. How deep is the water $\frac{1}{2}$ mi from Limestone Cove?

CHAPTER PROJECT

PROJECT LINK: GRAPHING

For each type of bean, make a graph relating the different sample sizes to the percents you found in each sample. Put *sample size* on the x-axis and *percent* on the y-axis. Use your graphs to decide the smallest sample size you need to predict the percent of each kind of bean in the jar.

Slides, Flips, and Turns

Before Lesson 11-6

There are many transformations you can do with geometric figures. Three of these are *slides*, *flips*, and *turns*.

A *slide* moves a figure so that every point moves the same direction and the same distance.

A *turn* rotates a figure around a point.

A *flip* reflects a figure over a line.

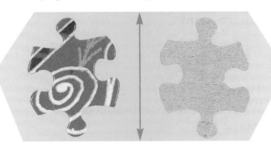

Describe each transformation from the black figure to the red figure as a *slide*, *flip*, or *turn*.

1.
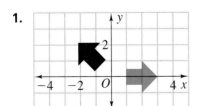

2.
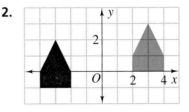

3.
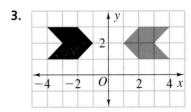

4. *Writing* Describe how two flips can have the same effect as a slide. Include a drawing to illustrate your example.

11-6 Translations

What You'll Learn

▼ 1 To graph translations

▼ 2 To write a rule for a translation

...And Why

Fabric designers and artists use translations to create repeating designs.

Here's How

Look for questions that

▪ build understanding

✔ check understanding

THINK AND DISCUSS

▼ 1 Graphing Translations

Movements of figures on a plane are **transformations.** A transformation can be a slide, a flip, or a turn. The pattern in the tie is created by sliding a single, purple shape into new positions on the fabric. Another name for a slide is a **translation.**

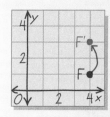

1. ▪*Patterns* Describe the other figure that has been translated on the tie.

The figure you get after a translation is the **image** of the original. You use *prime notation* (A') to identify an image point.

■ EXAMPLE 1

Translate point $F(4, 1)$ up 2 units. What are the coordinates of the image F'?

The coordinates of F' are $(4, 3)$.

2. ✔ *Try It Out* Point G has coordinates $(-4, 1)$. Graph it and its image G' after a translation three units to the left.

To show a translation, you can use arrow notation. For the translation of F to F' in Example 1, you can write $F(4, 1) \longrightarrow F'(4, 3)$.

3. Use the points you graphed in Question 2. Write the translation of G to G' using arrow notation.

To translate a geometric figure, first translate the vertices of the figure. Then connect the new points to form the translated image of the original figure.

■ **EXAMPLE 2** *Real-World Problem Solving*

Fabric Design To make the tie design on page 494, the designer translated figure *ABCD*. Draw its image after a translation four units to the right and one unit down. Use prime notation to label the image.

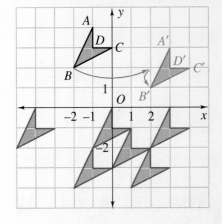

4. a. ▪ *Look Back* What are the coordinates of points *A*, *B*, *C*, and *D*? What are the coordinates of their images, points *A′*, *B′*, *C′*, *D′*?

   b. Use arrow notation to describe the translation of point *A* to point *A′*; point *B* to point *B′*; point *C* to point *C′*; point *D* to point *D′*.

5. a. ✔ *Try It Out* Graph △*PAT* with vertices *P*(0, 4), *A*(−2, 3), and *T*(−4, 5). Then graph its image *P′A′T′* after a translation two units right and five units down.

   b. Complete:
   $P(0, 4), A(-2, 3), T(-4, 5) \rightarrow P'(\blacksquare, \blacksquare), A'(\blacksquare, \blacksquare), T'(\blacksquare, \blacksquare)$

❷ *Writing a Rule for a Translation*

To find the coordinates of a translated image, you can add or subtract the amount of movement from the coordinates of the original figure.

6. ▪ *Think About It* Suppose you translate a point to the left two units and up one unit. Would you add or subtract to find the *x*-coordinate of the image? Would you add or subtract to find the *y*-coordinate of the image?

■ **EXAMPLE 3**

Write a rule for the translation of △*MNP*. Use arrow notation.

The horizontal → change from *N* to *N'* is 4 units to the right, so *x* → *x* + 4.

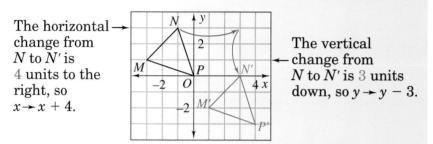

The vertical ← change from *N* to *N'* is 3 units down, so *y* → *y* − 3.

The rule for the translation is $(x, y) \rightarrow (x + 4, y - 3)$.

7. ✔ **Try It Out** Suppose a figure is translated to the right 2 units and up 6 units. Complete the general rule to show how to find the image: $(x, y) \rightarrow (x + \blacksquare, y + \blacksquare)$.

Work Together

Exploring Tessellations

Art A *tessellation* is a repeating pattern of figures that has no gaps or overlaps, like the pattern in the tie. The pattern at the right shows how you can create a design for fabric or wrapping paper.

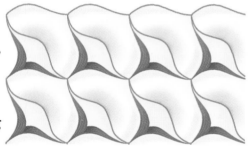

Work with a partner. Start with a cardboard cutout of a square.

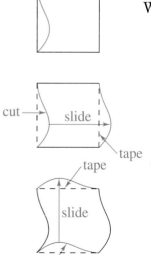

8. **a.** As shown at the left, draw a curve from one vertex of the square to a neighboring vertex.
   b. Cut along the curve you drew in part (a). Slide the cut-out piece to the opposite side of the square. Tape the flat edge of the cut-out piece to that side of the square.
   c. Repeat the process using the other two sides of the square.

9. **a.** Trace around your figure on a piece of paper. Carefully translate the figure so that the edges touch. Continue tracing until you have covered a large area of the paper.
   b. Congratulations! You've created a tessellation! Now decorate your tessellation to create a work of art.

Use the graph at the right for Exercises 1 and 2.

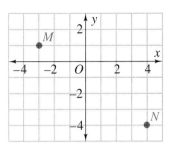

1. Give the coordinates of point M after it is translated right 5 units.

2. Give the coordinates of point N after it is translated up 4 units.

3. Suppose $P(3, 4) \rightarrow P'(-2, -3)$. What is the horizontal change? What is the vertical change?

For Exercises 4–6, use graph paper to graph each image of figure $ABCD$. Name the coordinates of A', B', C', and D'.

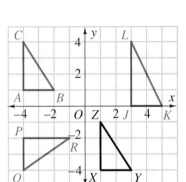

4. left 3 units   5. up 2 units   6. right 1 unit, down 4 units

7. The vertices of $\triangle DEF$ are $D(-1, 2)$, $E(-1, -1)$, and $F(2, -1)$.
   a. Graph the triangle.
   b. Graph its translation right 2 units and down 1 unit.
   c. Write the coordinates of $\triangle D'E'F'$.

8. **Choose A, B, or C.** On the graph at the right, which shape is a translation of $\triangle XYZ$?

   A. $\triangle ABC$ B. $\triangle JKL$ C. $\triangle PQR$

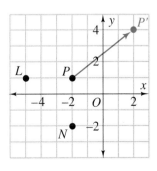

9. *Reasoning* $\triangle RST$ has coordinates $R(2, -5)$, $S(1, 1)$, $T(-3, -1)$. Point $R(2, -5) \rightarrow R'(5, -7)$. If $\triangle RST$ is translated to $\triangle R'S'T'$, give the coordinates of S' and T'.

Find the horizontal change and the vertical change for each translation.

10. $P(4, 6) \rightarrow P'(0, 8)$ 11. $A(-1, 3) \rightarrow A'(2, 4)$

12. $F(2, -2) \rightarrow F'(1, -7)$ 13. $M(0, -1) \rightarrow M'(2, -4)$

14. *Aviation* Three airplanes are flying in a triangular formation. In 1 min, airplane P moves as shown in the graph at the right. The planes remain in formation as they fly.
   a. Give the original coordinates and the new coordinates of each airplane.
   b. How far in each direction did the airplanes move?

15. Suppose you translated a figure to the left 2 units and up 1 unit. Complete the general rule to show how to find the image: $(x, y) \rightarrow (x - \blacksquare, y + \blacksquare)$.

Write the rule for the translation shown in each graph.

16.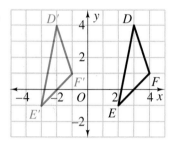

17.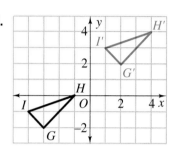

Graph the point and its translated image. Then write a rule to describe the translation.

18. $M(3, 5)$; right 3 units, down 1 unit

19. $T(-1, 6)$; right 4 units, up 2 units

20. $H(4, 0)$; left 1 unit, up 4 units

21. $C(-2, -5)$; right 5 units, down 2 units

22. $W(3, -1)$; left 1 unit, up 5 units

23. $B(0, 6)$; left 3 units, down 4 units

24. a. *Geometry* Graph $\triangle CAT$ with vertices $C(4, 6)$, $A(0, 8)$, and $T(-6, -4)$.
   b. Graph the image of $\triangle CAT$ after the transformation $(x, y) \rightarrow \left(\frac{1}{2}x, \frac{1}{2}y\right)$. Write the coordinates of the image.
   c. Graph the image of $\triangle CAT$ after the transformation $(x, y) \rightarrow (2x, 2y)$. Write the coordinates of the image.
   d. *Writing* Look at $\triangle CAT$ and its images. Are the triangles congruent? Are they similar? Justify your reasoning.

Mixed Review

Write each number in standard form. *(Lesson 10-2)*

25. 4.31×10^5 26. 5.36×10^6 27. 8.596×10^3 28. 2.001×10^8

29. a. Make a table of values for the equation $y = 2x^2$.
   b. Graph the equation. *(Lesson 11-4)*

30. *Choose a Strategy* Pilar recycled 6 fewer than 5 times the number of boxes of newspaper that Alice recycled. Pilar recycled 34 boxes. How many boxes did Alice recycle?

11-7 Symmetry and Reflections

What You'll Learn

1. To identify lines of symmetry
2. To graph reflections

...And Why

Reflections occur in art, architecture, and nature.

Here's How

Look for questions that
- build understanding
- ✔ check understanding

THINK AND DISCUSS

1 Identifying Lines of Symmetry

When water vapor freezes, it becomes a snowflake. Scientists think that each snowflake is one of a kind. Every snowflake has *symmetry*.

A figure is **symmetrical** when one side is a mirror image of the other side. The red line drawn through the snowflake is a **line of symmetry.**

1. Some objects have more than one line of symmetry. How many lines of symmetry do you see in the snowflake?

■ **EXAMPLE 1**   *Real-World Problem Solving*

Photography Identify the lines of symmetry in each photograph.

a.

The mask has one line of symmetry.

b.

The flower has five lines of symmetry.

2. ✔ *Try It Out* Name four capital letters of the alphabet that have a line of symmetry. Write the letters and show the line of symmetry.

✌ *Graphing Reflections*

A **reflection,** or flip, is a transformation you can use to create symmetry on the coordinate plane. The line you reflect a figure across is called the **line of reflection.**

■ EXAMPLE 2

Draw the reflected image of △ABC. Use the y-axis as the line of reflection. Use arrow notation to describe the original triangle and its reflection.

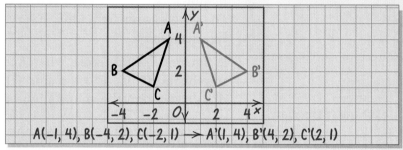

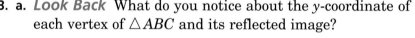
A(−1, 4), B(−4, 2), C(−2, 1) → A'(1, 4), B'(4, 2), C'(2, 1)

3. **a.** *Look Back* What do you notice about the y-coordinate of each vertex of △ABC and its reflected image?

4. **a.** ✔ *Try It Out* Draw △ABC from Example 2 on graph paper. Reflect △ABC across the x-axis. Use arrow notation to describe △ABC and its reflected image.
   b. What do you notice about the y-coordinate of each vertex of △ABC and its reflected image?

Work Together _____ *Exploring Symmetry*

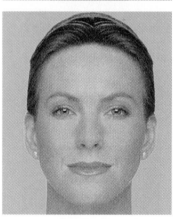

A person's face is not perfectly symmetrical. These photographs are of the same woman. The top one is the right side of the woman's face and its reflection. The bottom is the left side and its reflection.

Work with a partner. Fold a rectangular piece of paper into sixths by first folding into thirds and then folding in half as shown at the right.

Use scissors to cut a heart shape into the folded paper. Do not cut the edges of the paper.

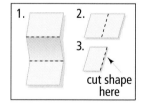
1.
2.
3.
cut shape here

5. Mark the line or lines of symmetry on paper.

6. **a.** What transformations relate the middle and bottom figures to the top figure?
   b. Repeat this activity by folding a rectangular piece of paper into eighths instead of sixths. How does this affect the cut-out figures?

**Trace each figure and draw the line(s) of symmetry. If
there are no lines of symmetry, write *none*.**

1.

2.

3.

4.

5.

Nature **Describe the line(s) of symmetry for each figure.**

6.

7.

8.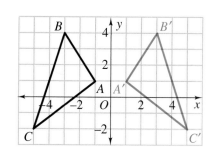

9. *Open-ended* Name two items in your classroom that have a
line of symmetry. Explain your choice.

10. *Research* Photocopy or cut out a picture in a magazine that
has symmetry. Draw the line(s) of symmetry.

Use the graph at the right for Exercises 11–13.

11. For which two points is the *x*-axis the line of reflection?

12. For which two points is the *y*-axis the line of reflection?

13. Point *C* is *not* a reflection of Point *E* over the *x*-axis. Why?

**Graph each point and its reflection. Write the coordinates
of each reflected point.**

14. $(3, 8)$ across the *x*-axis   15. $(-5, 7)$ across the *y*-axis   16. $(-3, -6)$ across the *x*-axis

**$\triangle A'B'C'$ is a reflection of $\triangle ABC$ over the *y*-axis.
Complete each statement.**

17. $A(-1, 1) \rightarrow A'(\blacksquare, \blacksquare)$

18. $B(-3, 4) \rightarrow B'(\blacksquare, \blacksquare)$

19. $C(-5, -2) \rightarrow C'(\blacksquare, \blacksquare)$

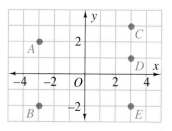

20. a. *Geometry* The vertices of $\triangle LMN$ are $L(0, 0)$, $M(0, 5)$, and $N(4, 0)$. Graph $\triangle LMN$ on a coordinate plane.

   b. Graph the reflection of $\triangle LMN$ over the x-axis.

   c. Use $\triangle LMN$ and its image. Reflect both triangles over the y-axis.

   d. Outline the perimeter of the figure formed by the four triangles. What type of polygon is formed?

21. *Writing* Explain the difference between a translation and a reflection. Use examples.

Tell whether the graph shows a reflection or a translation. Name the line of reflection or describe the translation.

22.

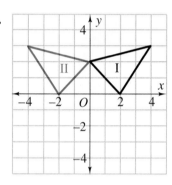

23.

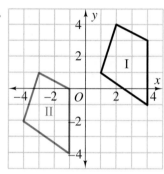

24.

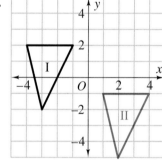

25.

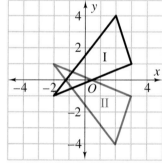

26. a. Graph the line $y = -2x$.

   b. Draw the reflection of this line across the y-axis.

27. a. *Language* Some of the following words have a line of symmetry. Trace the words that show symmetry. Draw the lines of symmetry.

Artist Scott Kim uses reflections in the creation of his calligraphy.

BIKE CODE BOY MOM FOOD HIKE EXIT

   b. *Open-ended* Find another word that has a line of symmetry.

Make a table for the function represented by each rule.
Find $f(0)$, $f(1)$, $f(2)$, and $f(3)$. *(Lesson 10-6)*

28. $f(n) = 2n^2 - 1$ **29.** $f(n) = 3n + 32$ **30.** $f(n) = -5n + 4$ **31.** $f(n) = 6 - n$

Write *always*, *sometimes*, or *never*. *(Lesson 7-7)*

32. A chord is ▨ a radius.   **33.** A diameter is ▨ a chord.   **34.** A chord is ▨ a diameter.

35. *Biology* Researchers tagged 1,250 black bears in an area of Canada. The researchers made an aerial count of 120 black bears, of which 75 were tagged. Estimate the black bear population. *(Lesson 9-8)*

CHAPTER PROJECT

PROJECT LINK: WRITING

Connect your findings about sample sizes to a real situation. Do you need to survey everyone who watches television to get an idea about which shows are most popular? Explain.

✓ CHECKPOINT 2   *Lessons 11-5 through 11-7*

For Exercises 1–2, $\triangle DEF$ has vertices $D(2, 6)$, $E(1, 2)$, and $F(4, 5)$.

1. Graph $\triangle DEF$ and its image after a translation 6 units left and 4 units down.

2. Graph $\triangle DEF$ and its image after a reflection across the x-axis.

3. *Writing* Do a line and its image after a translation have the same slope? Explain.

4. *Open-ended* Draw two figures. Be sure the first figure has one line of symmetry, the second has two lines of symmetry.

5. Samantha delivers pizzas for Alfonso's Pizza. Alfonso pays Samantha $2 for each pizza she delivers.
  a. Samantha uses $10 worth of gas each week. Write an equation to find Samantha's weekly profit.
  b. How many pizzas must Samantha deliver to make a profit of $70 in a week?

Choose the best answer.

1. The approximate weight of the largest blue whale ever measured was 160,000 kilograms. This weight expressed in scientific notation is —

   A. 1.6×10^6 kg   B. 0.16×10^6 kg
   C. 16×10^4 kg   D. 1.6×10^5 kg

2. David is planting a row of 5 rosebushes in his garden. Each bush has a different color rose. In how many ways could David plant the rosebushes?

   F. 10   G. 25   H. 60   J. 120

3. For a social studies project, students will prepare a presentation about the culture of two different countries. If students have six countries to choose from, how many different groups of two countries can be chosen?

   A. 69   B. 30   C. 15   D. 12

4. Which word has a line of symmetry?

   F. B O O T   G. T I E
   H. H I K E   J. B A C K

5. The number of visitors in one year to the Grand Canyon National Park were 4.4×10^6. The number of visitors is —

   A. 440,000   B. 4,400,000
   C. 44,000,000   D. 440,000,000

6. The Outdoor Store had a sale. All clothing was sold for 30% off the marked price. Esteban bought a jacket marked $58.90 and a pair of jeans marked $29.95. Estimate the total amount he spent.

   F. $30   G. $60   H. $90   J. $120

7. Which ordered pair is *not* a solution to the linear equation $y = 2x + 5$?

   A. $(2, 9)$ B. $(5, 15)$
   C. $(3, 12)$ D. $(4, 13)$

Please note that items 8–10 have *five* answer choices.

8. Which linear equation is graphed?

   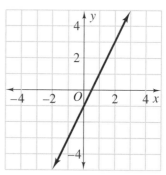

   F. $y = -2x - 1$ G. $y = 2x + 1$
   H. $y = 2x - 1$ J. $y = -2x + 1$
   K. $y = \frac{1}{2}x - 1$

9. For a party of 50 people, 29 people chose chicken for their main course. For a banquet of 300 people, what is a good prediction for the number of people who would choose chicken as their main course?

   A. 89   B. 145   C. 174
   D. 203   E. 205

10. Lupe picked a letter out of a bag 50 times and replaced it each time. She drew the letter A 20 times, the letter B 10 times, the letter C 15 times, and the letter D 5 times. If there are 10 letters in the bag, how many letters would you expect to have the letter C?

    F. 6   G. 5   H. 4
    J. 3   K. 2

11-8 Rotations

What You'll Learn

▼ To identify figures that have rotational symmetry

▼ To rotate a figure about a point

...And Why

Many artistic designs use rotational symmetry.

Here's How

Look for questions that
■ build understanding
✔ check understanding

THINK AND DISCUSS

1 Identifying Rotational Symmetry

The blades of this windmill revolve counterclockwise. One full turn brings the blade at position A back to its original position.

1. How much of a turn brings the blade at position A to the A′ position? The A″ position? The A‴ position?

A **rotation** is a transformation that turns a figure about a fixed point (O). Point O is the **center of rotation.** In this book, all rotations are counterclockwise.

A figure has **rotational symmetry** when an image after a rotation of 180° or less fits exactly on top of the original figure. In the photo, windmill blades show 90° rotational symmetry because after a turn of 90° the blades look like they did before the turn. They also have 180° symmetry.

■ **EXAMPLE 1**   *Real-World Problem Solving*

Nature Does the flower at the right have rotational symmetry?

To determine if the flower has rotational symmetry, rotate petal 1 to the position of each of the other petals.

Since the flower looks the same at each position, the flower has rotational symmetry.

2. a. ✔ *Try It Out* Does star A at the right have rotational symmetry? How do you know?

b. Does star B have rotational symmetry? Explain.

A B

3. ⬝ *Think About It* Name a capital letter in the alphabet that has rotational symmetry. Name one that does not have rotational symmetry.

▼ *Rotating a Figure*

In the figure below, $\triangle TRO$, has been rotated 90° around point O. The center of rotation is point O. The image of $\triangle TRO$ is $\triangle T'R'O'$.

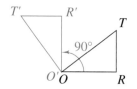

■ EXAMPLE 2

Draw the image of $\triangle TRO$ after a rotation of:

a. 180° about O.

b. 270° about O.

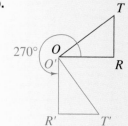

a.

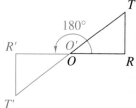

b.

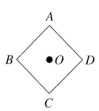

4. a. ✔ *Try It Out* In the square at the right, what rotation will move point A to the position held by point B? What rotation will move A to C? What rotation will move A to D?

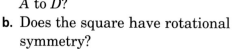

b. Does the square have rotational symmetry?

Which figures below have rotational symmetry? Explain.

1.

2.

3.

4.

5.

6.

7.

8. *Writing* Describe an object in your classroom that has rotational symmetry. Explain how it shows rotational symmetry.

Trace and shade each figure in Exercises 9–12. Draw the image of each figure after a rotation of 90°, 180°, and 270° about point O.

9.

10.

11.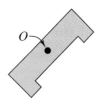

12.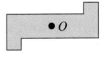

13. Which figures in Exercises 9–12 have rotational symmetry?

14. *Engineering* In a rotary gasoline engine, a "triangular" rotor moves in a specially shaped chamber. The three tips of the rotor always touch the walls of the chamber. This divides the chamber into three parts which change in volume as the rotor rotates. Does the rotor have rotational symmetry? Explain.

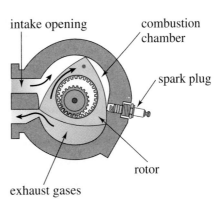

intake opening

combustion chamber

spark plug

rotor

exhaust gases

Figure II is the image of Figure I. Identify each transformation as a translation, a reflection, or a rotation.

15.

16.

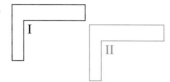

17.

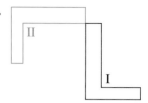

18.

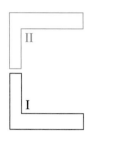

19.

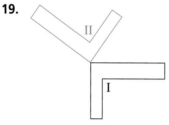

20. **a.** On graph paper, draw rectangle *ABCD* with vertices at *A*(0, 0), *B*(0, 2), *C*(4, 2), and *D*(4, 0).
   b. What are the coordinates of the center of the rectangle?
   c. Draw three images formed by rotating the rectangle 90°, 180°, and 270° about its center.
   d. Draw three images formed by rotating the rectangle 90°, 180°, and 270° about the origin.

> **PORTFOLIO**
> Select one or two items from your work for this chapter. Consider:
> • cooperative work
> • work you found challenging
> • part of your project
> Explain why you have included each selection.

Mixed Review

▦ *Calculator* **Find the length of the third side of each right triangle to the nearest unit.** *(Lesson 8-6)*

21.

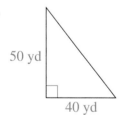

50 yd

40 yd

22.

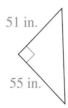

51 in.

55 in.

23.

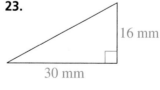

16 mm

30 mm

24.

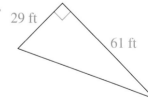

29 ft

61 ft

25. The ratio of vowels to consonants in the word *bear* is 2 : 2. List ten more animal names, then write a ratio for each that compares the vowels to consonants. *(Lesson 9-1)*

26. *Choose a Strategy* At a museum, each adult pays $3 and each student pays $2. A group of 20 people paid a total of $44. How many are adults and how many are students?

CHAPTER PROJECT

People's *choice*

Find a Sample Size The Project Link questions on pages 481, 492, and 503 should help you complete your project. Here is a checklist to help you gather together the parts of your project.

✔ the table of data from all ten samples

✔ a graph for each sample

✔ a paragraph about sampling

Plan a presentation to show your results. Explain the connection between the size of a sample and how accurately that sample represents the container of beans.

Reflect and Revise

Show your graphs to a friend or family member, and practice your presentation. If necessary, make revisions that make your ideas more forceful or your graphs more clear.

Web Extension

Prentice Hall's Internet site contains information you might find helpful as you complete your project. Visit www.phschool.com/mgm2/ch11 for some links and ideas related to sampling.

The Coordinate Plane and Graphing Linear Equations   11-1, 11-2

The **coordinate plane** is formed by a horizontal number line called the **x-axis** and a vertical number line called the **y-axis.** Every point on the plane is described by an *ordered pair* of numbers (x, y) called **coordinates.** An equation is linear if its solutions lie on a straight line.

Use the graph for Exercises 1 and 2.

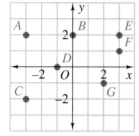

1. Name the point with the given coordinates.
   a. $(-3, 2)$ **b.** $(2, -1)$ **c.** $(3, 1)$

2. Write the coordinates of each point.
   a. B **b.** C **c.** D

3. Tell whether each ordered pair is a solution of $y = 3x - 5$.
   a. $(5, 10)$ **b.** $(-2, -1)$ **c.** $(1, -2)$

4. **a.** Find four solutions of the equation $y = x + 4$.
   b. Graph the ordered pairs on a coordinate plane.

Finding the Slope of a Line   11-3

The **slope** of a line is the ratio $\frac{rise}{run}$.

5. **Choose A, B, C or D.** What is the slope of the line graphed at the right?

   A. $\frac{3}{1}$ **B.** $\frac{-3}{1}$ **C.** $\frac{1}{3}$ **D.** $\frac{-1}{3}$

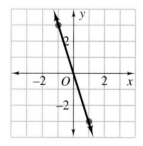

Graph each set of points and find the slope of the line through the points.

6. $(-2, 6), (4, 3)$ 7. $(-3, 2), (-1, 5)$

8. $(0, 5), (9, 8)$ 9. $(6, 2), (-3, 4)$

Exploring Nonlinear Relationships   11-4

The graph of a parabola is U-shaped. The graph of an absolute value function is V-shaped.

10. **a.** Graph $(-2, 0)$, $(0, -4)$, $(2, 0)$, and $(-4, 12)$.
    b. *Writing* Explain whether $y = x^2 - 4$ or $y = |2x| - 4$ is a better model for the data.

11. Which equation has the greatest value for y when $x = 3$? When $x = 12$?

    I. $y = |3x + 5|$ **II.** $y = x^2 - 6$ **III.** $y = -2x^2 + 26$

Problem Solving Strategies   11-5

Some problems describe relationships between numbers. You can write an equation to find a solution.

12. The school band made a profit of $352 on their spring concert. They sold 116 tickets and spent $25 on photocopying. How much did each ticket cost?

Geometric Transformations and Symmentry   11-6, 11-7, 11-8

You can move a figure in three ways. You can slide it, flip it, or turn it. The names for these *transformations* are **translations, reflections,** and **rotations.**

A figure has a **line of symmetry** when one side is a mirror image of the other side.

13. On graph paper, draw $\triangle SUN$ and its image after the translation $(x, y) \longrightarrow (x + 3, y - 4)$.

14. *Open-ended* Draw an everyday object that has at least two lines of symmetry. Show the lines of symmetry.

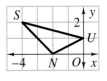

Figure II is the image of Figure I. Is the transformation a *translation*, a *reflection*, or a *rotation*?

15.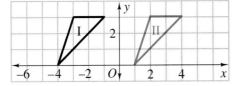

16.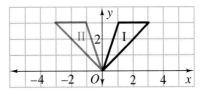

17.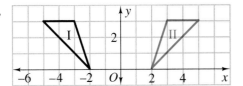

18.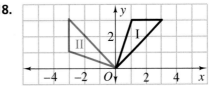

1. Name the point with the given coordinates.

   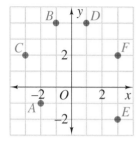

   a. (1, 4)
   b. (−2, −1)
   c. (3, −2)
   d. (−3, 2)

2. Identify the quadrant in which each point lies.

   a. (−3, 3)   b. (−9, 4)
   c. (5, −12)   d. (1, 11)

3. Determine whether each ordered pair is a solution of the equation $y = -2x + 5$.

   a. (3, −5)   b. (0, 5)
   c. (4, −3)   d. (2.5, 0)

4. Graph each pair of points. Determine the slope of the line through the points.

   a. $E(7, 1), F(-3, 3)$
   b. $G(-2, 6), H(0, 0)$
   c. $L(-4, 0), M(0, 2)$
   d. $S(8, 5), T(1, -1)$

5. **Choose A, B, C, or D.** Which set of ordered pairs does *not* describe the vertices of a parallelogram?

   A. (2, 4), (3, 4), (2, −1), (−3, −1)
   B. (0, 5), (5, 5), (0, 0), (−5, 0)
   C. (4, 3), (6, −2), (1, −2), (−1, 3)
   D. (5, −1), (−3, −1), (2, 5), (10, 5)

6. In which quadrant(s) are both coordinates of a point negative?

7. Match each equation with its graph.

   a. $y = -x + 2$
   b. $y = x + 2$
   c. $y = 2$
   d. $x = 2$

   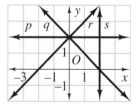

8. Graph each equation.

   a. $y = x - 3$
   b. $y = 3x + 1$

9. Find four solutions of each equation. Then graph each equation.

   a. $y = x^2$
   b. $y = |x|$

10. a. Graph $\triangle ABC$ with vertices $A(1, 3)$, $B(5, 8)$, and $C(7, 1)$. Then connect the vertices in order.

    b. Graph the image of $\triangle ABC$ after a reflection over the x-axis.

    c. Graph the image of $\triangle ABC$ after a translation 12 units left and 10 units down.

11. Draw the image of the triangle after a rotation of 90°, 180°, and 270° about point O.

    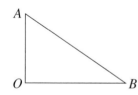

12. Make a table and graph the equation $y = \frac{1}{2}x + 4$. Use the graph to find the slope of the line.

13. *Writing* Give an example of a rotation, a reflection, and a translation you might see in the real world.

14. Inez paid $185 for car repairs. The garage charged $65 for parts and $30 per hour for the mechanic's labor. Write and solve an equation to find the number of hours the mechanic worked on her car.

Choose the best answer.

1. Which rule best describes the function in the table?

n	f(n)
0	0
1	1
2	4
3	9

   A. $f(n) = n + 2$
   B. $f(n) = n$
   C. $f(n) = 2n$
   D. $f(n) = n^2$

2. How many two-letter permutations of the letters C, A, R contain the letter R?

   A. 2   **B.** 3   **C.** 4   **D.** 6

3. Which situation is described by the linear equation $P = 7.5x - 150$?

   A. A bus company's profit if x people buy tickets for a trip at $7.50 each, but it costs $150 to run the bus.
   B. The total price of renting a restaurant for a party if the restaurant charges $150 plus $7.50 per person, and x people attend.
   C. The price of a home video game machine if it costs $150, but you have x coupons, each of which says, "deduct $7.50."
   D. The total profit made by putting on a concert if the profit is $7.50 per person and x people more than 150 attend.

4. A muffin recipe uses $2\frac{1}{4}$ c of flour and makes 12 muffins. How many muffins can you make with 6 c of flour?

   A. 24   **B.** 30   **C.** 32   **D.** 45

5. What percent of the letters of the alphabet are vowels?

   A. about 15%   **B.** about 21%

   C. about 30%   **D.** about 33%

6. What is the ones digit of 7^{23}?

   A. 3   **B.** 5   **C.** 7   **D.** 9

7. What is the best estimate for the percent of the figure that is shaded?

   A. 10%   **B.** 25%
   C. 60%   **D.** 75%

8. For which linear equation is $(-3, 0.5)$ *not* a solution?

   A. $x - 2y = -4$
   B. $4y = 3x + 11$
   C. $x = -6y$
   D. $-x + 6y = 0$

9. What is the probability of spinning red or blue on the spinner?

   A. $P(\text{red}) - P(\text{blue})$
   B. $P(\text{red}) + P(\text{blue})$
   C. $P(\text{blue}) - P(\text{red})$
   D. $P(\text{red}) \times P(\text{blue})$

10. Which translation takes $\triangle ABC$ to $\triangle A'B'C'$?

    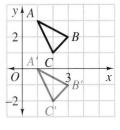

    A. $(x, y) \longrightarrow (x - 3, y)$
    B. $(x, y) \longrightarrow (x + 3, y)$
    C. $(x, y) \longrightarrow (x, y + 3)$
    D. $(x, y) \longrightarrow (x, y - 3)$

11. Write the numbers 0.361×10^7, 4.22×10^7, and 13.5×10^6 in order from least to greatest.

    A. $13.5 \times 10^6, 0.361 \times 10^7, 4.22 \times 10^7$
    B. $4.22 \times 10^7, 13.5 \times 10^6, 0.361 \times 10^7$
    C. $0.361 \times 10^7, 13.5 \times 10^6, 4.22 \times 10^7$
    D. $13.5 \times 10^6, 4.22 \times 10^7, 0.361 \times 10^7$

12. Which expression has the greatest value?

    A. $\frac{3}{4}(8)$ **B.** $2 \cdot 3.3$ **C.** 2^3 **D.** $\frac{2}{3} \cdot \frac{6}{5}$

The stem-and-leaf plot shows daily high temperatures on Mt. Washington, NH, during three weeks in January.

1. Create a frequency table for the data.

2. Create a line plot for the data.

3. How many days was the temperature above 10 degrees?

■ **LESSON 1-1**

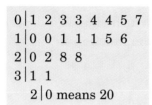

```
0 | 1 2 3 3 4 4 5 7
1 | 0 0 1 1 1 5 6
2 | 0 2 8 8
3 | 1 1
    2 | 0 means 20
```

Exercises 4–7 refer to the graph at the right.

4. Which team has won the most matches?

5. Which team has won the fewest matches?

6. Which team has won almost the same number of matches as they lost?

7. About how many more matches has Team A won than Team D?

■ **LESSONS 1-2, 1-3**

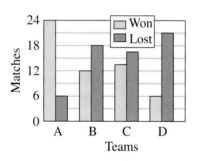

The data set at the right shows the number of stories of some tall buildings in the United States.

8. Display the data in a stem-and-leaf plot.

9. Find the mean, median, and mode of the data.

10. Find the range of the data.

■ **LESSONS 1-4, 1-5**

Number of Stories				
73	44	57	64	48
60	55	51	77	40
80	72	60	82	57

11. *Open-ended* Write a fair and a biased survey question.

■ **LESSON 1-7**

12. *Writing* The graph at the right shows the growth of personal computer purchases for home use.
    a. Describe the data as presented in the graph.
    b. Is the graph misleading or fair? Justify your answer.

13. The data in the table below represent the heights and weights of some 7-year-olds.

Height	40 in.	39 in.	42 in.	45 in.	48 in.	43 in.	41 in.
Weight	56 lb	52 lb	62 lb	75 lb	72 lb	67 lb	62 lb

   a. Make a scatter plot of the data.
   b. Describe any trend you see in the data.

■ **LESSONS 1-8, 1-9**

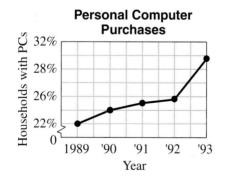

Extra Practice

Order from least to greatest.

■ **LESSON 2-1**

1. 0.092, 0.095, 0.102, 0.099   **2.** 1.01, 1.12, 1.02, 1.101   **3.** 0.55, 0.505, 0.52, 0.56

4. 4.301, 4.29, 4.30, 4.297, 3.40 **5.** 0.708, 0.712, 0.699, 0.7   **6.** 10.1, 10.01, 11.01, 11.101

Compare. Use <, >, or =.

7. 0.101 ■ 0.10   **8.** 15.55 ■ 15.555   **9.** 1.16 ■ 1.160   **10.** 29.08 ■ 29.10

11. 10.4 ■ 1.04   **12.** 6.049 ■ 6.40   **13.** 37.02 ■ 37.2   **14.** 8.721 ■ 8.712

***Estimation* Use any method to estimate.**

■ **LESSON 2-2**

15. 2.7236 − 0.6512   **16.** 1.2 + 2.4 + 0.86   **17.** $34.50 − $10.80 + $2.10

18. 0.054 + 0.901 + 0.62   **19.** $18.95 × 3.5   **20.** $32.13 ÷ 6.15

Find each sum or difference.

■ **LESSON 2-3**

21. 5.87 + 2.41   **22.** 9.31 − 4.08   **23.** 7.2 + 1.907   **24.** 4.86 − 2.161

25. 11.46 − 10.64   **26.** 2.1 + 3.62 + 1.003   **27.** 10 − 5.98   **28.** 12.3 + 118.42

Find each product.

■ **LESSON 2-5**

29. 2.9 × 1.7   **30.** 3.5 × 4.4   **31.** 5.01 · 3.2   **32.** 0.56 × 8.21

33. 6.09 × 1.3   **34.** 0.09 · 0.35   **35.** 4.17 · 7.1   **36.** 10.05 × 0.9

***Choose* Use a calculator or paper and pencil to find each answer. Use a bar to show repeating decimals.**

■ **LESSONS 2-6, 2-7**

37. 3.2 ÷ 1.2   **38.** 6.3 ÷ 2.1   **39.** 9.4 ÷ 3   **40.** 30.6 ÷ 3.6

41. 44.856 ÷ 7.12   **42.** 127 ÷ 2.4   **43.** 37 ÷ 11.1   **44.** 3.64 ÷ 9.1

Find the value of each expression.

■ **LESSON 2-8**

45. 2(8 − 4.5)   **46.** 24 − (3 + 1.9)   **47.** 3.14(2.1 + 7.5)   **48.** 3(6.1 + 0.461)

49. (18 − 2.4)(0.7)   **50.** 8.3 · 6.9 − 4.7   **51.** (5.3 − 0.9) ÷ 1.1   **52.** 2.7 · (3.1 − 0.7)

Write a variable expression for each word phrase.　■ **LESSON 3-1**

1. the difference of a number and 3

2. 17 increased by a number

3. 5 less than twice a number

4. 6 more than a number divided by 2

5. Copy and complete the table at the right. Substitute the value indicated on the left for the variable in the expression at the top of each column. Then evaluate.

	$3(x - 1)$	$3x - 1$	$3x + 1$
$x = 5$	■	■	■
$x = 2$	■	■	■

Write *true* or *false*.　■ **LESSON 3-2**

6. $|5| > |-5|$

7. $|6| < |8|$

8. $|-3| \leq |-2|$

9. $|10| = |-10|$

Order each group of numbers from least to greatest.

10. $-10, 8, 9, 0, -5, 3$

11. $|-8|, -1, 3, |10|, -11$

12. $|12|, |-3|, 22, -14, |5|, 0$

Write the integer represented by each model.　■ **LESSONS 3-3, 3-4, 3-5**

13.

14.

15.

16.

Simplify each expression.

17. $-110 + 5 - (-5)$

18. $3(-6 \div 3)$

19. $(-3)(-2)(-1)$

20. $2(-2) - 4$

21. $|-9| + 8 - (-1)$

22. $-7 + |12 - 8|$

23. $4 + 11 - (-13)$

24. $-14 \div (-7) + (-2)$

Solve.　■ **LESSONS 3-6, 3-7**

25. $t - 3 = -10$

26. $7 + x = -7$

27. $\frac{m}{5} = -15$

28. $-7y = -42$

29. $-4a = 12$

30. $\frac{x}{2} = -8$

31. $-2x = -4$

32. $\frac{y}{-6} = 3$

Write an equation. Then solve.　■ **LESSON 3-8**

33. Fifty-one is three times what number?

34. What number increased by eight is 35?

Solve.　■ **LESSON 3-9**

35. $\frac{r}{-6} + 4 = -3$

36. $12m + 24 = 0$

37. $3x + 1 = -11$

38. $\frac{k}{-3} - 2 = -20$

Extra Practice

Write a fraction for the part of each model that is shaded. ■ LESSON 4-1

1.

2.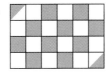

3.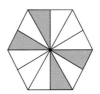

4.

Write two fractions equivalent to each fraction. Then write each fraction in simplest form. ■ LESSONS 4-2, 4-6

5. $\frac{21}{24}$

6. $\frac{65}{100}$

7. $\frac{6}{9}$

8. $\frac{40}{80}$

9. $\frac{12}{36}$

10. $\frac{18}{54}$

11. $\frac{15}{75}$

12. $\frac{16}{36}$

13. $\frac{110}{225}$

14. $\frac{72}{108}$

15. $\frac{45}{315}$

16. $\frac{54}{96}$

Compare. Use <, >, or =. ■ LESSON 4-3

17. $\frac{1}{4}$ ■ $\frac{2}{9}$

18. $\frac{3}{7}$ ■ $\frac{1}{2}$

19. $\frac{2}{5}$ ■ $\frac{4}{10}$

20. $\frac{5}{6}$ ■ $\frac{7}{8}$

21. $\frac{3}{5}$ ■ $\frac{2}{3}$

Choose **Use a calculator, paper and pencil, or mental math to find the value of each expression.** ■ LESSON 4-4

22. 100^1

23. 5^3

24. 3^5

25. 15^2

26. 8^4

27. 4^3

Use prime factorization to find the GCF of each pair of numbers. ■ LESSON 4-5

28. 35, 49

29. 11, 12

30. 28, 40

31. 17, 34

32. 16, 26

33. 10, 30

Write each mixed number as an improper fraction. ■ LESSON 4-8

34. $7\frac{7}{8}$

35. $3\frac{5}{7}$

36. $3\frac{1}{4}$

37. $4\frac{2}{5}$

38. $10\frac{1}{6}$

39. $2\frac{2}{5}$

Write each improper fraction as a mixed number.

40. $\frac{45}{8}$

41. $\frac{24}{5}$

42. $\frac{33}{8}$

43. $\frac{29}{4}$

44. $\frac{35}{6}$

45. $\frac{56}{9}$

Write each fraction as a decimal. Write each decimal as a fraction. Use a bar to show repeating decimals. ■ LESSON 4-9

46. $\frac{4}{5}$

47. 0.365

48. $\frac{7}{8}$

49. 0.42

50. $\frac{9}{11}$

51. 0.7

52. $\frac{76}{15}$

53. $\frac{136}{12}$

54. $\frac{76}{4}$

55. $\frac{13}{4}$

56. $\frac{28}{8}$

57. $\frac{100}{6}$

Extra Practice

Estimate each sum, difference, product, or quotient. ■ LESSON 5-1

1. $\frac{2}{5} + \frac{7}{9}$ 2. $15\frac{1}{5} - 5\frac{4}{7}$ 3. $\frac{3}{5} - \frac{1}{8}$ 4. $99\frac{9}{10} + \frac{1}{5}$ 5. $7\frac{4}{5} \div 1\frac{2}{3}$

6. $9\frac{2}{3} \cdot 4\frac{2}{3}$ 7. $6\frac{1}{8} \cdot 12\frac{2}{3}$ 8. $62\frac{1}{2} \div 8\frac{3}{4}$ 9. $10\frac{3}{4} \div 5\frac{1}{5}$ 10. $71\frac{1}{5} \div 5\frac{2}{3}$

Find each sum or difference. Write the answer in simplest form. ■ LESSON 5-2

11. $\frac{2}{3} + \frac{2}{3}$ 12. $\frac{7}{10} - \frac{3}{10}$ 13. $\frac{2}{5} + \frac{1}{3}$ 14. $\frac{1}{4} + \frac{3}{8}$ 15. $\frac{2}{3} - \frac{1}{6}$

16. $\frac{7}{12} - \frac{1}{4}$ 17. $\frac{2}{3} - \frac{3}{8}$ 18. $\frac{1}{3} + \frac{3}{4}$ 19. $\frac{3}{4} + \frac{3}{10}$ 20. $\frac{1}{6} + \frac{3}{4}$

Find each sum or difference. Write the answer in simplest form. ■ LESSON 5-3

21. $4\frac{3}{8} + 2\frac{5}{8}$ 22. $5\frac{2}{5} - 1\frac{4}{5}$ 23. $2\frac{2}{3} + 3\frac{1}{4}$ 24. $4\frac{1}{2} - 2\frac{3}{4}$ 25. $7\frac{3}{8} - 1\frac{3}{4}$

26. $8\frac{3}{4} + 2\frac{5}{8}$ 27. $11 - 3\frac{1}{8}$ 28. $2\frac{1}{6} + 3\frac{3}{8}$ 29. $10\frac{2}{3} - 4\frac{1}{2}$ 30. $7\frac{2}{5} + 3\frac{1}{4}$

Find each product. Write the answer in simplest form. ■ LESSON 5-5

31. $\frac{3}{8} \cdot \frac{2}{5}$ 32. $\frac{1}{4}$ of $\frac{4}{5}$ 33. $\frac{3}{10} \cdot \frac{5}{6}$ 34. $\frac{2}{5} \cdot 40$ 35. $\frac{5}{6}$ of 30

36. $4\frac{2}{5} \cdot 2\frac{1}{2}$ 37. $2\frac{3}{4} \cdot 1\frac{1}{2}$ 38. $3\frac{2}{3} \cdot 4\frac{3}{5}$ 39. $3 \cdot 5\frac{3}{8}$ 40. $2\frac{7}{8} \cdot \frac{4}{5}$

Find each quotient. Write the answer in simplest form. ■ LESSON 5-6

41. $\frac{3}{5} \div \frac{1}{5}$ 42. $4 \div \frac{1}{4}$ 43. $\frac{4}{5} \div \frac{4}{5}$ 44. $9 \div \frac{3}{4}$ 45. $\frac{5}{6} \div \frac{3}{8}$

46. $2\frac{1}{5} \div \frac{5}{6}$ 47. $2\frac{3}{8} \div 1\frac{1}{4}$ 48. $\frac{3}{4} \div 6$ 49. $3\frac{2}{3} \div 2\frac{1}{2}$ 50. $\frac{3}{4} \div 4\frac{1}{8}$

Complete. ■ LESSON 5-8

51. $\frac{3}{4}$ gal = ■ c   52. 4,500 lb = ■ T   53. $\frac{3}{8}$ mi = ■ yd   54. $12\frac{2}{3}$ lb = ■ oz

55. $6\frac{1}{8}$ T = ■ lb   56. 2 yd 1 ft = ■ yd   57. ■ gal = 18 pt   58. 2 lb 2 oz = ■ lb

Solve each equation. ■ LESSONS 5-4, 5-9

59. $j + \frac{1}{4} = \frac{5}{8}$ 60. $1\frac{1}{3} + m = 2\frac{5}{6}$ 61. $\frac{2}{7} = y - \frac{1}{2}$ 62. $\frac{4}{5} = t + \frac{3}{10}$

63. $38 = \frac{1}{4}b$ 64. $164t = 16$ 65. $121 = 11c$ 66. $\frac{n}{3} = 18$

Extra Practice

Write each ratio in two other ways.　　　　　　　　　■ **LESSON 6-1**

1. $\frac{2}{3}$　　　　**2.** 3 : 5　　　**3.** 4 to 7　　**4.** 17 to 3　　**5.** $\frac{25}{50}$　　　　**6.** 66 : 99

Find each unit rate. Then determine the better buy.　■ **LESSON 6-2**

7. 32 oz for $2.29　　　　**8.** 3 yd for $12.48　　　**9.** 2 lb for $4.17
48 oz for $3.19　　　　　5 yd for $20.30　　　　10 lb for $20.80

Find the value of *n* in each proportion.　　　　■ **LESSON 6-3**

10. $\frac{12}{n} = \frac{3}{5}$　　　**11.** $\frac{n}{12} = \frac{4}{16}$　　　**12.** $\frac{7}{8} = \frac{n}{4}$　　　**13.** $\frac{7}{10} = \frac{14}{n}$　　　**14.** $\frac{7}{n} = \frac{17.5}{5}$

15. $\frac{15}{3} = \frac{n}{5}$　　　**16.** $\frac{17}{3} = \frac{51}{n}$　　　**17.** $\frac{18}{n} = \frac{3}{4}$　　　**18.** $\frac{65}{n} = \frac{5}{1}$　　　**19.** $\frac{n}{2} = \frac{5}{20}$

Find the missing lengths in each pair of similar figures.　■ **LESSON 6-4**

20.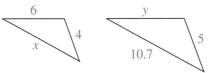

21.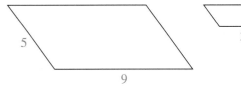

22. *Architecture* The scale on an architectural drawing is　■ **LESSON 6-5**
0.5 in. : 15 ft. If the dimensions of a room in the drawing are
0.75 in. by 1.2 in., how big is the actual room?

Write each fraction or decimal as a percent. Write each　■ **LESSONS 6-6, 6-7**
percent as a fraction in simplest form and as a decimal.

23. $\frac{5}{6}$　　　**24.** 37.5%　　**25.** $\frac{11}{5}$　　　**26.** 87.5%　　**27.** 64%　　**28.** 0.12

29. 27.3　　**30.** 225%　　**31.** 0.000975　**32.** 1%　　　**33.** 0.1　　**34.** $\frac{3}{2}$

Write a proportion and solve.　　　　　　　　■ **LESSONS 6-9, 6-10**

35. 54 is 40% of what number?　**36.** What is 5% of 48?　**37.** What percent of 200 is 120?

38. What percent of 150 is 27?　**39.** Find 25% of 130.　**40.** 8 is 40% of what number?

Find each percent of change. State whether the change is　■ **LESSON 6-11**
an *increase* or a *decrease*.

41. 25 to 40　　**42.** 95 to 45　　**43.** 108 to 110　　**44.** 50 to 95　　**45.** 125 to 75

1. Draw the next figure in the pattern.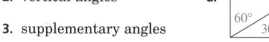

■ **LESSON 7-1**

Match each description with a figure.

■ **LESSON 7-2**

2. vertical angles

3. supplementary angles

4. complementary angles

5. nonadjacent angles

a.

b.

c.

d.

Find each missing angle measure. Then classify each triangle by its angles.

■ **LESSON 7-3**

6.

7.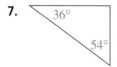

8.

9. △*ABD* ≅ △*CED*. Which of the following are true?

■ **LESSON 7-5**

   a. $\overline{AB} \cong \overline{CE}$

   b. $\overline{AD} \cong \overline{ED}$

   c. ∠*A* ≅ ∠*C*

   d. ∠*BDA* and ∠*EDC* are congruent angles.

   e. $\overline{BD} \cong \overline{EC}$

Judging by appearance, classify each figure. Then name the congruent sides and angles.

■ **LESSON 7-6**

10.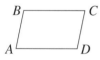

11.

12.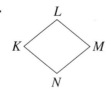

13.

14. Draw a circle *O*. Draw, label, and identify a diameter, a chord, a radius, and an arc that is not a semicircle.

■ **LESSON 7-7**

15. In a survey of 500 people, 86 of them preferred Brand A. Find the measure of the central angle that you would draw to represent Brand A in a circle graph.

■ **LESSON 7-8**

16. Draw an obtuse angle. Then construct its bisector.

■ **LESSON 7-9**

1. Each square represents 100 ft².
   Estimate the perimeter and area
   of the figure.

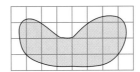

■ **LESSON 8-1**

Find the area and perimeter of each figure.

■ **LESSONS 8-2, 8-3**

2.

5 cm
2 cm

3.

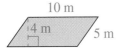

10 m
4 m · 5 m

4.

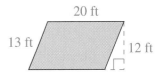

20 ft
13 ft · 12 ft

5.

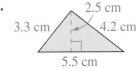

2.5 cm
3.3 cm · 4.2 cm
5.5 cm

6.

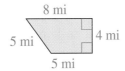

8 mi
5 mi · 4 mi
5 mi

7.

28 mm
22 mm · 20 mm · 34 mm
62 mm

8. The diameter of a circle is 40 cm. Find its circumference and
   area to the nearest unit.

■ **LESSON 8-4**

Find each square root.

■ **LESSON 8-5**

9. $\sqrt{1}$ 10. $\sqrt{4}$ 11. $\sqrt{49}$ 12. $\sqrt{81}$ 13. $\sqrt{900}$ 14. $\sqrt{3,600}$

Find each missing side length.

■ **LESSON 8-6**

15.

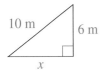

10 m
6 m
x

16.

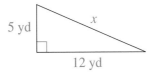

5 yd
x
12 yd

17.

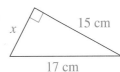

x
15 cm
17 cm

18. The lengths of the legs of a right triangle are 9 m and 14 m.
    How long is the third side to the nearest tenth of a unit?

■ **LESSON 8-7**

**Give the best name for each figure. Then find its surface
area. Round to the nearest whole number if necessary.**

■ **LESSONS 8-8, 8-9**

19.

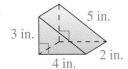

5 in.
3 in.
4 in.
2 in.

20.

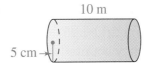

10 m
5 cm →

21.

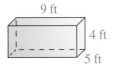

9 ft
4 ft
5 ft

22. Find the volumes of the figures in Exercises 20 and 21.

■ **LESSON 8-10**

Extra Practice

1. A quality control engineer at a factory inspected 300 glow sticks for quality. She found 15 defective glow sticks. ■ **LESSON 9-1**
   a. What is the probability that a glow stick is defective?
   b. The factory can produce 1,400 glow sticks in one shift. Predict how many glow sticks will be defective.

Find each probability for one roll of a number cube. ■ **LESSON 9-3**

2. P(3 or 4)   3. P(not 3)   4. P(5)   5. P(1 or 7)   6. P(not 3 or 4)

7. a. Toss two coins and spin a spinner with three congruent sections colored red, white, and blue. Draw a tree diagram to find the sample space. ■ **LESSON 9-4**
   b. Find P(2 heads and blue) and P(at least 1 tails and red).

Events A and B are independent. Find $P(A \text{ and } B)$. ■ **LESSON 9-5**

8. $P(A) = \frac{1}{5}, P(B) = \frac{3}{4}$ 9. $P(A) = \frac{1}{6}, P(B) = \frac{5}{6}$ 10. $P(A) = 1, P(B) = 0$

A bag contains 6 green marbles, 8 blue marbles, and 3 red marbles. Find $P(B)$ after A has happened.

11. A: Draw a green marble. Keep it. B: Draw a red marble.

12. A: Draw a blue marble. Replace it. B: Draw a red marble.

13. A: Draw a red marble. Keep it. B: Draw a red marble.

14. A box contains the letters S T A T I S T I C S. Suppose you select two letters, one after the other without replacement. Find P(S, then T).

State whether the situation is a *permutation* or a *combination*. Then answer the question. ■ **LESSONS 9-6, 9-7**

15. In how many ways can a committee of 2 be chosen from a club of 5 members?

16. In how many ways can a president and a treasurer be selected from a club of 5 members?

17. Members of an environmental group marked 25 sea gulls in a nesting area. Later that summer they counted 500 gulls, 19 of which were marked. Estimate the sea gull population. ■ **LESSON 9-8**

Extra Practice

Identify each sequence as *arithmetic, geometric,* or *neither.* Then find the next three terms in the sequence.

■ LESSON 10-1

1. 7, 10, 13, 16, . . .   **2.** 800, 400, 200, 100, . . .   **3.** 50, 25, 48, 24, . . .

4. 1, 2, 5, 6, 9, . . .   **5.** 18.1, 17.5, 16.9, 16.3, . . .   **6.** 2, 3, 4.5, 6.75, . . .

Write each number in scientific notation.

■ LESSON 10-2

7. 70,000   **8.** 2,654,000   **9.** 610,000   **10.** 250   **11.** 2,200   **12.** 20,000,000

Write each number in standard form.

13. 7.03×10^4 **14.** 1.02×10^2 **15.** 2.56×10^7 **16.** 2.8×10^5 **17.** 8.2901×10^3

Choose Use a calculator or pencil and paper to find the balance of each account earning compound interest. Use the formula $B = p(1 + r)^t$.

■ LESSON 10-4

18. $1,000 principal
5% annual interest rate
4 years

19. $700 principal
4% annual interest rate
12 years

20. 1,500 principal
5.5% annual interest rate
7 years

Write a function rule for each table of values.

■ LESSONS 10-5, 10-6

21.

n	$f(n)$
0	0
1	6
2	12
3	18

22.

n	$f(n)$
0	−2
1	−1
2	0
3	1

23.

n	$f(n)$
0	1
1	4
2	7
3	10

24.

n	$f(n)$
0	10
1	8
2	6
3	4

Find $f(0)$, $f(1)$, $f(2)$, and $f(3)$ for each function rule. Make a table of values, then graph the function.

25. $f(n) = n + 5$ **26.** $f(n) = 3n - 2$ **27.** $f(n) = 8 - n$ **28.** $f(n) = n^2$

29. On her trip to the library, Arlene walked two blocks to the bus stop in five minutes. She rode the bus for 15 min. The bus stopped three times, for one minute each time. Sketch a graph to represent Arlene's trip.

■ LESSON 10-7

Extra Practice

Use the graph at the right for Exercises 1–12.

■ LESSONS 11-1, 11-3

Name the point with the given coordinates.

1. $(-2, -1)$ **2.** $(1, 1)$ **3.** $(3, -4)$

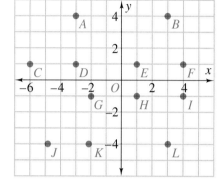

Write the coordinates of each point.

4. A **5.** I **6.** J

7. C **8.** F **9.** B

Find the slope of the line through the points.

10. A and E **11.** G and E **12.** B and F

Tell whether each ordered pair is a solution of $y = x + 18$. Explain how you know.

■ LESSON 11-2

13. $(2, 20)$ **14.** $(22, 4)$ **15.** $(36, -18)$ **16.** $(-20, -2)$

Make a table of values. Then graph each function.

■ LESSON 11-4

17. $y = x^2 + 3$ **18.** $y = x^2 - 4$ **19.** $y = 2|x|$ **20.** $y = |x + 1|$

Use the graph above right to answer Exercises 21 and 22.

■ LESSONS 11-6, 11-7

21. *Writing* Write a rule for the translation of the triangle formed by points C, A, and D to the triangle formed by points J, G, and K.

22. Is the triangle formed by points E, B, and F a reflection, a rotation, or a translation of the triangle formed by points H, L, and I? Explain.

23. a. Graph the square $ABCD$ with vertices $A(2, -3)$, $B(4, -5)$, $C(6, -3)$, and $D(4, -1)$. Then connect the vertices in order.

■ LESSON 11-8

   b. Draw the image of square $ABCD$ after a rotation of $180°$ about point A.

   c. Write the coordinates of the vertices of the image of square $ABCD$.

Tables

TABLE 1 *Measures*

Metric

Length

10 millimeters (mm) = 1 centimeter (cm)

100 cm = 1 meter (m)

1,000 m = 1 kilometer (km)

Area

100 square millimeters (mm^2) = 1 square centimeter (cm^2)

10,000 cm^2 = 1 square meter (m^2)

Volume

1,000 cubic millimeters (mm^3) = 1 cubic centimeter (cm^3)

1,000,000 cm^3 = 1 cubic meter (m^3)

Mass

1,000 milligrams (mg) = 1 gram (g)

1,000 g = 1 kilogram (kg)

Liquid Capacity

1,000 milliliters (mL) = 1 liter (L)

United States Customary

Length

12 inches (in.) = 1 foot (ft)

3 feet = 1 yard (yd)

36 in. = 1 yd

5,280 ft = 1 mile (mi)

1,760 yd = 1 mi

Area

144 square inches ($in.^2$) = 1 square foot (ft^2)

9 ft^2 = 1 square yard (yd^2)

4,840 yd^2 = 1 acre

Volume

1,728 cubic inches ($in.^3$) = 1 cubic foot (ft^3)

27 ft^3 = 1 cubic yard (yd^3)

Weight

16 ounces (oz) = 1 pound (lb)

2,000 lb = 1 ton (T)

Liquid Capacity

8 fluid ounces (fl oz) = 1 cup (c)

2 c = 1 pint (pt)

2 pt = 1 quart (qt)

4 qt = 1 gallon (gal)

Time

1 minute (min) = 60 seconds (s)

1 hour (h) = 60 min

1 day (da) = 24 h

1 year (yr) = 365 da

TABLE 2   *Formulas*

Circumference of a circle

$C = \pi d$ or $C = 2\pi r$

Area		
	parallelogram:	$A = bh$
	rectangle:	$A = bh$
	trapezoid:	$A = \frac{1}{2}h(b_1 + b_2)$
	triangle:	$A = \frac{1}{2}bh$
	circle:	$A = \pi r^2$

Volume		
	cylinder:	$V = \pi r^2 h$
	rectangular prism:	$V = lwh$

TABLE 3   *Symbols*

$>$	is greater than	$\perp$	is perpendicular to
$<$	is less than	$\cong$	is congruent to
$\geq$	is greater than or equal to	$\sim$	is similar to
$\leq$	is less than or equal to	$\approx$	is approximately equal to
$=$	is equal to	$\overline{AB}$	segment AB
$\neq$	is not equal to	$\overrightarrow{AB}$	ray AB
$^\circ$	degrees	$\overleftrightarrow{AB}$	line AB
$\%$	percent	$\triangle ABC$	triangle ABC
$f(n)$	f of n	$\angle ABC$	angle ABC
$a : b$	ratio of a to b, $\frac{a}{b}$	$m\angle ABC$	measure of angle ABC
$|-5|$	absolute value of negative 5	AB	length of segment AB
$P(E)$	probability of an event E	$\overset{\frown}{AB}$	arc AB
π	pi		

TABLE 4 *Squares and Square Roots*

N	N^2	$\sqrt{N}$	N	N^2	$\sqrt{N}$
1	1	1	51	2,601	7.141
2	4	1.414	52	2,704	7.211
3	9	1.732	53	2,809	7.280
4	16	2	54	2,916	7.348
5	25	2.236	55	3,025	7.416
6	36	2.449	56	3,136	7.483
7	49	2.646	57	3,249	7.550
8	64	2.828	58	3,364	7.616
9	81	3	59	3,481	7.681
10	100	3.162	60	3,600	7.746
11	121	3.317	61	3,721	7.810
12	144	3.464	62	3,844	7.874
13	169	3.606	63	3,969	7.937
14	196	3.742	64	4,096	8
15	225	3.873	65	4,225	8.062
16	256	4	66	4,356	8.124
17	289	4.123	67	4,489	8.185
18	324	4.243	68	4,624	8.246
19	361	4.359	69	4,761	8.307
20	400	4.472	70	4,900	8.367
21	441	4.583	71	5,041	8.426
22	484	4.690	72	5,184	8.485
23	529	4.796	73	5,329	8.544
24	576	4.899	74	5,476	8.602
25	625	5	75	5,625	8.660
26	676	5.099	76	5,776	8.718
27	729	5.196	77	5,929	8.775
28	784	5.292	78	6,084	8.832
29	841	5.385	79	6,241	8.888
30	900	5.477	80	6,400	8.944
31	961	5.568	81	6,561	9
32	1,024	5.657	82	6,724	9.055
33	1,089	5.745	83	6,889	9.110
34	1,156	5.831	84	7,056	9.165
35	1,225	5.916	85	7,225	9.220
36	1,296	6	86	7,396	9.274
37	1,369	6.083	87	7,569	9.327
38	1,444	6.164	88	7,744	9.381
39	1,521	6.245	89	7,921	9.434
40	1,600	6.325	90	8,100	9.487
41	1,681	6.403	91	8,281	9.539
42	1,764	6.481	92	8,464	9.592
43	1,849	6.557	93	8,649	9.644
44	1,936	6.633	94	8,836	9.695
45	2,025	6.708	95	9,025	9.747
46	2,116	6.782	96	9,216	9.798
47	2,209	6.856	97	9,409	9.849
48	2,304	6.928	98	9,604	9.899
49	2,401	7	99	9,801	9.950
50	2,500	7.071	100	10,000	10

Comparing and Ordering Whole Numbers

The numbers on a number line are in order from least to greatest.

298 299 300 301 302 303 304 305 306

You can use a number line to compare whole numbers. Use the symbols > (is greater than) and < (is less than).

■ EXAMPLE 1

Use > or < to compare the numbers.

a. 303 ■ 299

303 is to the right of 299.

300 > 299

b. 301 ■ 305

301 is to the left of 305.

301 < 305

The value of a digit depends on its place in a number. Compare digits starting from the left.

■ EXAMPLE 2

Use > or < to compare the numbers.

a. 12,060,012,875 ■ 12,060,012,675

8 hundreds > 6 hundreds, so

12,060,012,875 > 12,060,012,675

b. 465,320 ■ 4,653,208

0 millions < 4 millions, so

465,320 < 4,653,208

EXERCISES *On Your Own*

Use > or < to compare the numbers.

1. 3,660 ■ 360

2. 74,328 ■ 74,238

3. 88,010 ■ 8,101

4. 87,524 ■ 9,879

5. 295,286 ■ 295,826

6. 829,631 ■ 842,832

7. 932,401 ■ 932,701

8. 60,000 ■ 500,009

9. 1,609,372,002 ■ 609,172,002

10. 45,248,315,150 ■ 45,283,718,150

Write the numbers from least to greatest.

11. 3,747; 3,474; 3,774; 3,347; 3,734

12. 70,903; 70,309; 73,909; 73,090

13. 32,056,403; 302,056,403; 30,265,403; 30,256,403

14. 884,172; 881,472; 887,142; 881,872

Rounding Whole Numbers

You can use number lines to help you round numbers.

■ **EXAMPLE 1**

a. Round 7,510 to the nearest thousand.

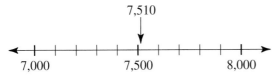

7,510 is between 7,000 and 8,000.
7,510 rounds to 8,000.

b. Round 237 to the nearest ten.

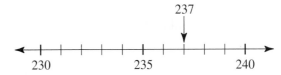

237 is between 230 and 240.
237 rounds to 240.

To round a number to a particular place, look at the digit to the right of that place. If the digit is less than 5, round down. If the digit is 5 or more, round up.

■ **EXAMPLE 2**

Round to the place of the underlined digit.

a. 3,4<u>6</u>3,280
The digit to the right of the 6 is 3, so 3,463,280 rounds down to 3,460,000.

b. 28<u>9</u>,543
The digit to the right of the 9 is 5, so 289,543 rounds up to 290,000.

EXERCISES *On Your Own*

Round to the nearest ten.

1. 42   **2.** 89   **3.** 671   **4.** 3,482   **5.** 7,029   **6.** 661,423

Round to the nearest thousand.

7. 5,800   **8.** 3,100   **9.** 44,280   **10.** 9,936   **11.** 987   **12.** 313,591

13. 5,641   **14.** 37,896   **15.** 82,019   **16.** 808,155   **17.** 34,501   **18.** 650,828

Round to the place of the underlined digit.

19. 68,<u>8</u>52   **20.** <u>4</u>51,006   **21.** 3,40<u>6</u>,781   **22.** 2<u>8</u>,512,030   **23.** 71,2<u>2</u>5,003

24. 96,<u>3</u>59   **25.** 4<u>0</u>1,223   **26.** <u>8</u>,902   **27.** 3,6<u>7</u>7   **28.** 2,551,<u>7</u>50

29. 68,<u>6</u>63   **30.** 70<u>1</u>,803,229   **31.** 56<u>5</u>,598   **32.** 32,<u>8</u>10   **33.** 1,<u>4</u>46,300

Multiplying Whole Numbers

When you multiply by a two-digit number, first multiply by the
ones and then multiply by the tens. Add the products.

■ EXAMPLE 1

Multiply 62×704.

Step 1

$$\begin{array}{r} 704 \\ \times\ 62 \\ \hline 1408 \end{array}$$

Step 2

$$\begin{array}{r} 704 \\ \times\ 62 \\ \hline 1408 \\ 42240 \end{array}$$

Step 3

$$\begin{array}{r} 704 \\ \times\ 62 \\ \hline 1\,408 \\ +\ 42\,240 \\ \hline 43,648 \end{array}$$

■ EXAMPLE 2

Find each product.

a. 93×6

$$\begin{array}{r} 93 \\ \times\ 6 \\ \hline 558 \end{array}$$

b. 25×48

$$\begin{array}{r} 48 \\ \times\ 25 \\ \hline 240 \\ +\ 960 \\ \hline 1,200 \end{array}$$

c. 80×921

$$\begin{array}{r} 921 \\ \times\ 80 \\ \hline 73,680 \end{array}$$

EXERCISES *On Your Own*

Find each product.

1. $\begin{array}{r} 74 \\ \times\ 6 \end{array}$
2. $\begin{array}{r} 35 \\ \times\ 9 \end{array}$
3. $\begin{array}{r} 53 \\ \times\ 7 \end{array}$
4. $\begin{array}{r} 80 \\ \times\ 8 \end{array}$
5. $\begin{array}{r} 98 \\ \times\ 4 \end{array}$
6. $\begin{array}{r} 65 \\ \times\ 8 \end{array}$

7. $\begin{array}{r} 512 \\ \times\ 3 \end{array}$
8. $\begin{array}{r} 407 \\ \times\ 9 \end{array}$
9. $\begin{array}{r} 225 \\ \times\ 6 \end{array}$
10. $\begin{array}{r} 340 \\ \times\ 5 \end{array}$
11. $\begin{array}{r} 816 \\ \times\ 7 \end{array}$
12. $\begin{array}{r} 603 \\ \times\ 3 \end{array}$

13. $\begin{array}{r} 70 \\ \times\ 36 \end{array}$
14. $\begin{array}{r} 41 \\ \times\ 55 \end{array}$
15. $\begin{array}{r} 38 \\ \times\ 49 \end{array}$
16. $\begin{array}{r} 601 \\ \times\ 87 \end{array}$
17. $\begin{array}{r} 271 \\ \times\ 34 \end{array}$
18. $\begin{array}{r} 450 \\ \times\ 67 \end{array}$

19. 6×82
20. 405×5
21. 81×9
22. 3×274
23. 552×4

24. 60×84
25. 52×17
26. 31×90
27. 78×52
28. 43×66

29. 826×3
30. 702×4
31. 8×180
32. 6×339
33. 781×7

Dividing Whole Numbers

First estimate the quotient by rounding the divisor, the dividend, or both. When you divide, after you bring down a digit, you must write a digit in the quotient.

■ **EXAMPLE**

Find each quotient.

a. $741 \div 8$

Estimate:

$720 \div 8 \approx 90$

$$\begin{array}{r} 92 \text{ R}5 \\ 8\overline{)741} \\ -72 \\ \hline 21 \\ -16 \\ \hline 5 \end{array}$$

b. $838 \div 43$

Estimate:

$800 \div 40 \approx 20$

$$\begin{array}{r} 19 \text{ R}21 \\ 43\overline{)838} \\ -43 \\ \hline 408 \\ -387 \\ \hline 21 \end{array}$$

c. $367 \div 9$

Estimate:

$360 \div 9 \approx 40$

$$\begin{array}{r} 40 \text{ R}7 \\ 9\overline{)367} \\ -360 \\ \hline 7 \end{array}$$

EXERCISES *On Your Own*

Divide.

1. $4\overline{)61}$
2. $8\overline{)53}$
3. $7\overline{)90}$
4. $3\overline{)84}$
5. $6\overline{)81}$

6. $6\overline{)469}$
7. $3\overline{)653}$
8. $8\overline{)645}$
9. $9\overline{)231}$
10. $4\overline{)415}$

11. $60\overline{)461}$
12. $40\overline{)213}$
13. $70\overline{)517}$
14. $30\overline{)432}$
15. $80\overline{)276}$

16. $43\overline{)273}$
17. $52\overline{)281}$
18. $69\overline{)207}$
19. $38\overline{)121}$
20. $81\overline{)433}$

21. $94\overline{)1,368}$
22. $62\overline{)1,147}$
23. $55\overline{)2,047}$
24. $85\overline{)1,450}$
25. $46\overline{)996}$

26. $94 \div 4$
27. $66 \div 9$
28. $90 \div 5$
29. $69 \div 6$
30. $58 \div 8$

31. $323 \div 5$
32. $849 \div 7$
33. $404 \div 8$
34. $934 \div 3$
35. $619 \div 6$

36. $777 \div 50$
37. $528 \div 20$
38. $443 \div 70$
39. $312 \div 40$
40. $335 \div 60$

41. $382 \div 72$
42. $580 \div 68$
43. $279 \div 43$
44. $232 \div 27$
45. $331 \div 93$

46. $614 \div 35$
47. $423 \div 28$
48. $489 \div 15$
49. $1,134 \div 51$
50. $1,103 \div 26$

Place Value and Decimals

Each digit in a decimal has both a place and a value. The value of any place is one tenth the value of the place to its left. In the chart below, the digit 5 is in the hundredths place. So, its value is 5 hundredths.

thousands	hundreds	tens	ones	.	tenths	hundredths	thousandths	ten-thousandths	hundred-thousandths
2	8	3	6	.	7	5	0	1	4

■ EXAMPLE

a. In what place is the digit 8?
   hundreds

b. What is the value of the digit 8?
   8 hundred

EXERCISES *On Your Own*

Use the chart above. Write the place of each digit.

1. 3   **2.** 4   **3.** 6   **4.** 7   **5.** 1   **6.** 0

Use the chart above. Write the value of each digit.

7. 3   **8.** 4   **9.** 6   **10.** 7   **11.** 1   **12.** 0

Write the value of the digit 6 in each number.

13. 0.162   **14.** 0.016   **15.** 13.672   **16.** 1,640.8   **17.** 62.135

18. 26.34   **19.** 6,025.9   **20.** 0.6003   **21.** 2,450.65   **22.** 615.28

23. 3.16125   **24.** 1.20641   **25.** 0.15361   **26.** 1.55736   **27.** 0.20516

Write the value of the underlined digit.

28. 2<u>4</u>.0026   **29.** 14.9<u>31</u>   **30.** 5.78<u>94</u>   **31.** 0.<u>8</u>7   **32.** 10.056<u>3</u>

Reading and Writing Decimals

A place value chart can help you read and write decimals. When there are no ones, write a zero before the decimal point.

billions	hundred millions	ten millions	millions	hundred thousands	ten thousands	thousands	hundreds	tens	ones	.	tenths	hundredths	thousandths	ten-thousandths	hundred-thousandths	millionths	Read
									0	.	0	7					7 hundredths
								2	3	.	0	1	4				23 and 14 thousandths
3	0	0	0	0	0	0	0	0	0	.	8						3 billion and 8 tenths
									5	.	0	0	0	1	0	2	5 and 102 millionths

■ **EXAMPLE**

a. Write thirteen ten-thousandths in numerals.

Ten-thousandths is 4 places after the decimal point. So, the decimal will have 4 places after the decimal point. The number is 0.0013.

b. Write 1.025 in words.

The digit 5 is in the thousandths place. So, 1.025 is one and twenty-five thousandths.

EXERCISES *On Your Own*

Write a number for the given words.

1. three hundredths

2. twenty-one millions

3. six and two hundredths

4. two billion and six tenths

5. two and five hundredths

6. five thousand twelve

7. seven millionths

8. forty-one ten-thousandths

9. eleven thousandths

10. one and twenty-five millionths

11. three hundred four thousandths

Write each number in words.

12. 5,700.4   13. 3,000,000.09   14. 12.000069   15. 900.02   16. 25.00007   17. 0.00015

Rounding Decimals

You can use number lines to help you round decimals.

■ EXAMPLE 1

a. Round 1.627 to the nearest tenth.

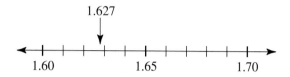

1.627 is between 1.6 and 1.7.
1.627 rounds to 1.6.

b. Round 0.248 to the nearest hundredth.

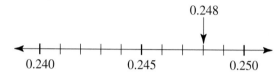

0.248 is between 0.24 and 0.25.
0.248 rounds to 0.25.

To round a number to a particular place, look at the digit to the right of that place. If the digit is less than 5, round down. If the digit is 5 or more, round up.

■ EXAMPLE 2

a. Round 2.4301 to the nearest whole number.

The digit to the right of 2 is 4, so 2.4301 rounds down to 2.

b. Round 0.0515 to the nearest thousandth.

The digit to the right of 1 is 5, so 0.0515 rounds up to 0.052.

EXERCISES *On Your Own*

Round to the nearest tenth.

1. 2.75   **2.** 3.816   **3.** 19.72   **4.** 401.1603   **5.** 499.491   **6.** 3.949

7. 4.67522   **8.** 20.397   **9.** 399.956   **10.** 129.98   **11.** 96.4045   **12.** 125.66047

Round to the nearest hundredth.

13. 31.723   **14.** 14.869   **15.** 1.78826   **16.** 0.1119   **17.** 736.941   **18.** 9.6057

19. 0.699   **20.** 4.231   **21.** 12.09531   **22.** 5.77125   **23.** 0.9195   **24.** 4.0033

Round to the nearest thousandth.

25. 0.4387   **26.** 0.0649   **27.** 3.4953   **28.** 8.07092   **29.** 0.6008   **30.** 6.0074

Round to the nearest whole number.

31. 3.942   **32.** 10.4   **33.** 79.52   **34.** 105.3002   **35.** 431.23   **36.** 0.4962

Multiplying Decimals

When you multiply with decimals, first multiply as if the factors were whole numbers. Then, count the decimal places in both factors to find how many places are needed in the product.

■ EXAMPLE 1

Multiply 2.5×1.8.

$$
\begin{array}{r}
1.8 \quad \leftarrow \text{ one decimal place} \\
\times\ 2.5 \quad \leftarrow \text{ one decimal place} \\
\hline
90 \\
+\ 360 \\
\hline
4.50 \quad \leftarrow \text{ two decimal places}
\end{array}
$$

■ EXAMPLE 2

Find each product.

a. 0.7×1.02

$$
\begin{array}{r}
1.02 \\
\times\ 0.7 \\
\hline
0.714
\end{array}
$$

b. 0.03×407

$$
\begin{array}{r}
407 \\
\times\ 0.03 \\
\hline
12.21
\end{array}
$$

c. 0.62×2.45

$$
\begin{array}{r}
2.45 \\
\times\ 0.62 \\
\hline
490 \\
+\ 14700 \\
\hline
1.5190
\end{array}
$$

d. 75×3.06

$$
\begin{array}{r}
3.06 \\
\times\ 75 \\
\hline
1530 \\
+\ 21420 \\
\hline
229.50
\end{array}
$$

EXERCISES *On Your Own*

Multiply.

1.
$$
\begin{array}{r} 0.3 \\ \times\ 8 \\ \hline \end{array}
$$

2.
$$
\begin{array}{r} 5 \\ \times\ 0.06 \\ \hline \end{array}
$$

3.
$$
\begin{array}{r} 0.04 \\ \times\ 7 \\ \hline \end{array}
$$

4.
$$
\begin{array}{r} 6 \\ \times\ 0.8 \\ \hline \end{array}
$$

5.
$$
\begin{array}{r} 3.1 \\ \times\ 0.05 \\ \hline \end{array}
$$

6.
$$
\begin{array}{r} 14 \\ \times\ 0.2 \\ \hline \end{array}
$$

7.
$$
\begin{array}{r} 3.1 \\ \times\ 6 \\ \hline \end{array}
$$

8.
$$
\begin{array}{r} 0.05 \\ \times\ 43 \\ \hline \end{array}
$$

9.
$$
\begin{array}{r} 0.27 \\ \times\ 5 \\ \hline \end{array}
$$

10.
$$
\begin{array}{r} 72 \\ \times\ 0.6 \\ \hline \end{array}
$$

11.
$$
\begin{array}{r} 0.8 \\ \times\ 312 \\ \hline \end{array}
$$

12.
$$
\begin{array}{r} 4.56 \\ \times\ 7 \\ \hline \end{array}
$$

13. 5×2.41

14. 704×0.3

15. 9×1.35

16. 1.2×0.3

17. 0.04×2.5

18. 6.6×0.3

19. 15.1×0.02

20. 0.8×31.3

21. 0.07×25.1

22. 42.2×0.9

23. 0.6×30.02

24. 0.05×11.8

25. 71.13×0.4

26. 48×2.1

27. 6.3×85

28. 0.42×98

29. 76×3.3

30. 0.77×51

31. 5.2×4.8

32. 0.12×6.1

Zeros in the Product

When you multiply with decimals, start at the right of the product to count the number of decimal places. Sometimes you need to write extra zeros to the left of a product before you can place the decimal point.

■ EXAMPLE 1

Multiply 0.03 × 0.51.

Step 1

$$
\begin{array}{r}
0.51 \\
\times\ 0.03 \\
\hline
1\,53
\end{array}
$$

←—two decimal places—→
←—two decimal places—→
←—four decimal places—→

Step 2

$$
\begin{array}{r}
0.51 \\
\times\ 0.03 \\
\hline
0.01\,53
\end{array}
$$

← Put extra zeros to the left. Then place the decimal point.

■ EXAMPLE 2

Find each product.

a. 0.2 × 0.3

$$
\begin{array}{r}
0.3 \\
\times\ 0.2 \\
\hline
0.06
\end{array}
$$

b. 0.5 × 0.04

$$
\begin{array}{r}
0.04 \\
\times\ 0.5 \\
\hline
0.020
\end{array}
$$

c. 4 × 0.02

$$
\begin{array}{r}
0.02 \\
\times\ 4 \\
\hline
0.08
\end{array}
$$

d. 0.02 × 0.45

$$
\begin{array}{r}
0.45 \\
\times\ 0.02 \\
\hline
0.0090
\end{array}
$$

EXERCISES *On Your Own*

Multiply.

1. 0.1 × 0.6

2. 0.4 × 0.2

3. 0.05 × 0.06

4. 0.01 × 8

5. 0.7 × 0.02

6. 0.03 × 0.4

7. 0.03 × 0.9

8. 0.06 × 0.5

9. 0.2 × 0.02

10. 7 × 0.01

11. 0.05 × 0.05

12. 0.6 × 0.06

13. 0.4 × 0.08

14. 0.07 × 0.05

15. 0.03 × 0.03

16. 0.09 × 0.05

17. 0.5 × 0.08

18. 0.06 × 0.7

19. 0.07 × 0.01

20. 0.16 × 0.2

21. 0.01 × 0.74

22. 0.47 × 0.08

23. 0.76 × 0.1

24. 0.19 × 0.3

25. 0.5 × 0.17

26. 0.31 × 0.08

27. 0.14 × 0.05

28. 0.07 × 0.85

29. 0.45 × 0.06

30. 0.4 × 0.23

31. 0.17 × 0.06

32. 0.3 × 0.24

33. 0.67 × 0.09

34. 0.08 × 0.39

35. 0.3 × 0.27

36. 0.19 × 0.05

37. 0.06 × 0.11

Dividing a Decimal by a Whole Number

When you divide a decimal by a whole number, first divide as if the numbers were whole numbers. Then put a decimal point in the quotient directly above the decimal point in the dividend.

■ EXAMPLE 1

Divide $0.256 \div 8$.

Step 1

$$
\begin{array}{r}
32 \\
8)\overline{0.256} \\
-24 \\
\hline
16 \\
-16 \\
\hline
0
\end{array}
$$

Step 2

$$
\begin{array}{r}
0.032 \\
8)\overline{0.256} \\
-24 \\
\hline
16 \\
-16 \\
\hline
0
\end{array}
$$

← Put extra zeros to the left. Then place the decimal point.

■ EXAMPLE 2

Find each quotient.

a. $12.6 \div 6$

$$
\begin{array}{r}
2.1 \\
6)\overline{12.6} \\
-12 \\
\hline
0\,6 \\
-\,6 \\
\hline
0
\end{array}
$$

b. $37.26 \div 81$

$$
\begin{array}{r}
0.46 \\
81)\overline{37.26} \\
-32\,4 \\
\hline
4\,86 \\
-4\,86 \\
\hline
0
\end{array}
$$

c. $0.666 \div 9$

$$
\begin{array}{r}
0.074 \\
9)\overline{0.666} \\
-\,63 \\
\hline
36 \\
-\,36 \\
\hline
0
\end{array}
$$

EXERCISES *On Your Own*

Divide.

1. $4)\overline{28.56}$
2. $5)\overline{16.5}$
3. $9)\overline{6.984}$
4. $6)\overline{91.44}$
5. $4)\overline{35.16}$

6. $81)\overline{33.291}$
7. $22)\overline{2.42}$
8. $26)\overline{1723.8}$
9. $83)\overline{15.272}$
10. $39)\overline{26.91}$

11. $22.2 \div 3$
12. $1.2 \div 4$
13. $4.65 \div 5$
14. $7.11 \div 9$

15. $17.52 \div 2$
16. $10.53 \div 9$
17. $14.49 \div 7$
18. $37.14 \div 6$

19. $0.0324 \div 9$
20. $0.1352 \div 8$
21. $0.0882 \div 6$
22. $0.8682 \div 6$

23. $79.599 \div 13$
24. $45.918 \div 18$
25. $59.7 \div 15$
26. $74.664 \div 12$

27. $12.342 \div 22$
28. $29.792 \div 32$
29. $22.568 \div 26$
30. $11.340 \div 36$

Powers of Ten

You can use shortcuts when multiplying and dividing by powers of ten.

When you multiply by	Move the decimal point
1,000	3 places to the right
100	2 places to the right
10	1 place to the right
0.1	1 place to the left
0.01	2 places to the left

When you divide by	Move the decimal point
1,000	3 places to the left
100	2 places to the left
10	1 place to the left
0.1	1 place to the right
0.01	2 places to the right

■ EXAMPLE

Multiply or divide.

a. 0.3×0.01

0.00.3 ⟵ Move the decimal point 2 places to the left.

$0.3 \times 0.01 = 0.003$

b. $0.18 \div 1,000$

0.000.18 ⟵ Move the decimal point 3 places to the left.

$0.18 \div 1,000 = 0.00018$

EXERCISES *On Your Own*

Multiply.

1. 3.2×0.01

2. $1,000 \times 0.12$

3. 0.7×0.1

4. 0.01×6.2

5. 0.09×100

6. 23.6×0.01

7. 5.2×10

8. $0.08 \times 1,000$

9. 100×0.05

10. 0.1×0.24

11. 18.03×0.1

12. 6.1×100

Divide.

13. $82.3 \div 0.1$

14. $0.4 \div 1,000$

15. $5.02 \div 0.01$

16. $16.5 \div 100$

17. $236.7 \div 0.1$

18. $45.28 \div 10$

19. $0.9 \div 1,000$

20. $1.03 \div 0.01$

21. $42.6 \div 0.1$

22. $203.05 \div 0.01$

23. $4.7 \div 10$

24. $0.07 \div 100$

Multiply or divide.

25. 0.32×0.1

26. $0.03 \div 100$

27. $2.6 \div 0.1$

28. $12.6 \times 1,000$

29. $0.8 \div 1,000$

30. 0.01×6.7

31. 100×0.15

32. $23.5 \div 10$

Zeros in Decimal Division

When you are dividing by a decimal, sometimes you need to use extra zeros in the dividend, the quotient, or both.

■ **EXAMPLE**

Find each quotient.

a. $0.14 \div 0.04$

Multiply by 100.

$$
\begin{array}{r}
3.5 \\
0.04\overline{)0.14.0} \\
-12 \\
\hline
2\ 0 \\
-2\ 0 \\
\hline
0
\end{array}
$$

b. $0.00434 \div 0.07$

Multiply by 100.

$$
\begin{array}{r}
0.062 \\
0.07\overline{)0.00.434} \\
-42 \\
\hline
14 \\
-14 \\
\hline
0
\end{array}
$$

c. $0.045 \div 3.6$

Multiply by 10.

$$
\begin{array}{r}
0.0125 \\
3.6.\overline{)0.0.4500} \\
-36 \\
\hline
90 \\
-72 \\
\hline
180 \\
-180 \\
\hline
0
\end{array}
$$

EXERCISES *On Your Own*

Divide.

1. $0.4\overline{)0.001}$
2. $0.05\overline{)0.0023}$
3. $0.02\overline{)0.000162}$
4. $0.6\overline{)0.0015}$

5. $1.2\overline{)0.078}$
6. $0.34\overline{)0.00119}$
7. $0.12\overline{)0.009}$
8. $2.5\overline{)0.021}$

9. $0.0017 \div 0.02$
10. $0.003 \div 0.6$
11. $0.01099 \div 0.7$
12. $0.104 \div 0.05$

13. $0.0945 \div 0.09$
14. $0.00045 \div 0.3$
15. $0.052 \div 0.8$
16. $0.142 \div 0.04$

17. $0.034 \div 0.05$
18. $0.0019 \div 0.2$
19. $0.9 \div 0.8$
20. $0.000175 \div 0.07$

21. $0.0084 \div 1.4$
22. $0.259 \div 3.5$
23. $0.00468 \div 0.52$
24. $0.00056 \div 0.16$

25. $0.0612 \div 7.2$
26. $0.17701 \div 3.1$
27. $0.00063 \div 0.18$
28. $0.011 \div 0.25$

29. $0.3069 \div 9.3$
30. $0.000924 \div 0.44$
31. $0.058023 \div 0.63$
32. $0.00123 \div 8.2$

33. $0.03225 \div 0.75$
34. $0.006 \div 0.75$
35. $0.73 \div 0.25$
36. $0.68 \div 0.002$

37. $0.398 \div 0.05$
38. $0.0004 \div 0.002$
39. $0.125 \div 0.005$
40. $0.000096 \div 0.04$

Adding and Subtracting Fractions with Like Denominators

When you add or subtract fractions with the same denominator, first add or subtract the numerators. Write the answer over the denominator. If necessary, change the answer to simplest form.

■ EXAMPLE 1

Add or subtract. Write the answer in simplest form.

a. $\frac{5}{16} + \frac{3}{16}$

$$\frac{5}{16}$$
$$+ \frac{3}{16}$$
$$\frac{8}{16} = \frac{1}{2}$$

b. $\frac{7}{8} - \frac{1}{8}$

$$\frac{7}{8}$$
$$- \frac{1}{8}$$
$$\frac{6}{8} = \frac{3}{4}$$

c. $\frac{3}{5} + \frac{2}{5}$

$$\frac{3}{5} + \frac{2}{5} = \frac{5}{5} = 1$$

To add or subtract mixed numbers, add or subtract the fractions first. Then add or subtract the whole numbers. If necessary, change the answer to simplest form.

■ EXAMPLE 2

Add or subtract. Write the answer in simplest form.

a. $2\frac{5}{8} + 3\frac{1}{8}$

$$2\frac{5}{8}$$
$$+ 3\frac{1}{8}$$
$$5\frac{6}{8} = 5\frac{3}{4}$$

b. $4\frac{3}{4} - 1\frac{1}{4}$

$$4\frac{3}{4}$$
$$- 1\frac{1}{4}$$
$$3\frac{2}{4} = 3\frac{1}{2}$$

c. $5\frac{5}{6} + 2\frac{5}{6}$

$$5\frac{5}{6} + 2\frac{5}{6} = 7\frac{10}{6}$$
$$= 7 + 1 + \frac{4}{6}$$
$$= 8\frac{2}{3}$$

EXERCISES *On Your Own*

Add or subtract. Write the answers in simplest form.

1. $\frac{2}{5}$
$+ \frac{2}{5}$

2. $\frac{2}{6}$
$- \frac{1}{6}$

3. $\frac{2}{7}$
$+ \frac{2}{7}$

4. $9\frac{1}{3}$
$- 8\frac{1}{3}$

5. $8\frac{6}{7}$
$- 4\frac{2}{7}$

6. $3\frac{1}{10}$
$+ 1\frac{3}{10}$

7. $\frac{2}{8} + \frac{2}{8}$

8. $\frac{3}{6} - \frac{1}{6}$

9. $\frac{6}{8} - \frac{3}{8}$

10. $\frac{2}{9} + \frac{1}{9}$

11. $\frac{4}{5} - \frac{1}{5}$

12. $\frac{3}{4} + \frac{1}{4}$

13. $\frac{9}{10} - \frac{3}{10}$

14. $8\frac{7}{10} + 2\frac{3}{10}$

15. $1\frac{4}{5} + 3\frac{3}{5}$

16. $2\frac{2}{9} + 3\frac{4}{9}$

17. $3\frac{2}{5} + 8\frac{1}{5}$

18. $8\frac{5}{8} - 3\frac{3}{8}$

19. $1\frac{1}{12} + 5\frac{5}{12}$

20. $9\frac{7}{10} - 2\frac{3}{10}$

21. $9\frac{3}{4} + 1\frac{3}{4}$

Metric Units of Length

The basic unit of length in the metric system is the meter. All the other units are based on the meter. In the chart below, each unit is 10 times the value of the unit to its left.

Unit	millimeter	centimeter	decimeter	meter	decameter	hectometer	kilometer
Symbol	mm	cm	dm	m	dam	hm	km
Value	0.001 m	0.01 m	0.1 m	1 m	10 m	100 m	1,000 m

To change a measure from one unit to another, start by using the chart to find the relationship between the two units.

■ EXAMPLE

Complete each equation.

a. $0.8 \text{ km} = \blacksquare \text{ m}$

$1 \text{ km} = 1,000 \text{ m}$

$0.8 \times 1,000 = 800$ ⟵ To change km to m, multiply by 1,000.

$0.8 \text{ km} = 800 \text{ m}$

b. $17.2 \text{ mm} = \blacksquare \text{ cm}$

$1 \text{ mm} = 0.1 \text{ cm}$

$17.2 \times 0.1 = 1.72$ ⟵ To change mm to cm, multiply by 0.1.

$17.2 \text{ mm} = 1.72 \text{ cm}$

c. $\blacksquare \text{ cm} = 2.1 \text{ km}$

$1 \text{ km} = 100,000 \text{ cm}$

$2.1 \times 100,000 = 210,000$ ⟵ To change km to cm, multiply by 100,000.

$210,000 \text{ cm} = 2.1 \text{ km}$

d. $\blacksquare \text{ m} = 5,200 \text{ cm}$

$1 \text{ m} = 0.01 \text{ cm}$

$5,200 \times 0.01 = 52$ ⟵ To change cm to m, multiply by 0.01.

$52 \text{ m} = 5,200 \text{ cm}$

EXERCISES *On Your Own*

Complete each equation.

1. $1 \text{ mm} = \blacksquare \text{ cm}$

2. $1 \text{ m} = \blacksquare \text{ km}$

3. $1 \text{ mm} = \blacksquare \text{ m}$

4. $1 \text{ cm} = \blacksquare \text{ m}$

5. $1.2 \text{ cm} = \blacksquare \text{ km}$

6. $\blacksquare \text{ km} = 45,000 \text{ mm}$

7. $\blacksquare \text{ m} = 30 \text{ km}$

8. $6.2 \text{ cm} = \blacksquare \text{ mm}$

9. $3.3 \text{ km} = \blacksquare \text{ m}$

10. $0.6 \text{ mm} = \blacksquare \text{ cm}$

11. $72 \text{ cm} = \blacksquare \text{ m}$

12. $180 \text{ m} = \blacksquare \text{ mm}$

13. $\blacksquare \text{ cm} = 13 \text{ km}$

14. $\blacksquare \text{ m} = 530 \text{ cm}$

15. $4,900 \text{ mm} = \blacksquare \text{ m}$

16. $\blacksquare \text{ cm} = 24 \text{ m}$

17. $\blacksquare \text{ km} = 106,000 \text{ cm}$

18. $259,000 \text{ mm} = \blacksquare \text{ m}$

19. $1,200,000 \text{ mm} = \blacksquare \text{ km}$

Metric Units of Capacity

The basic unit of capacity in the metric system is the liter. All the other units are based on the liter. In the chart below, each unit is 10 times the value of the unit to its left. Note that we use a capital L as the abbreviation for liters to avoid confusion with the number 1.

Unit	milliliter	centiliter	deciliter	liter	decaliter	hectoliter	kiloliter
Symbol	mL	cL	dL	L	daL	hL	kL
Value	0.001 L	0.01 L	0.1 L	1 L	10 L	100 L	1,000 L

To change a measure from one unit to another, start by using the chart to find the relationship between the two units.

■ **EXAMPLE**

Complete each equation.

a. 245 mL = ■ L

   1 mL = 0.001 L

   245 × 0.001 = 0.245 ← To change mL to L, multiply by 0.001.

   245 mL = 0.245 L

b. ■ mL = 4.5 kL

   1 kL = 1,000,000 mL

   4.5 × 1,000,000 = 4,500,000 ← To change kL to mL, multiply by 1,000,000.

   4,500,000 mL = 4.5 kL

EXERCISES *On Your Own*

Complete each equation.

1. 1 L = ■ mL

2. 1 mL = ■ kL

3. 1 kL = ■ L

4. 1 kL = ■ mL

5. 200 L = ■ kL

6. 1.3 kL = ■ mL

7. ■ L = 30 kL

8. ■ kL = 5.2 L

9. 180 mL = ■ L

10. ■ kL = 240 L

11. 0.6 mL = ■ L

12. ■ kL = 106,000 L

13. 72 kL = ■ mL

14. ■ mL = 1.5 kL

15. ■ kL = 450,000 mL

16. 4,900 L = ■ kL

17. ■ kL = 200,000 mL

18. ■ L = 8 mL

19. 4.2 L = ■ mL

20. 57,000,000 mL = ■ L

21. 28,000 kL = ■ L

22. ■ mL = 9,000 L

23. 4,000 L = ■ mL

24. 870 L = ■ kL

Metric Units of Mass

The basic unit of mass in the metric system is the gram. All the other units are based on the gram. In the chart below, each unit is 10 times the value of the unit to its left.

Unit	milligram	centigram	decigram	gram	decagram	hectogram	kilogram
Symbol	mg	cg	dg	g	dag	hg	kg
Value	0.001 g	0.01 g	0.1 g	1 g	10 g	100 g	1,000 g

To change a measure from one unit to another, start by using the chart to find the relationship between the two units.

■ EXAMPLE

Complete each equation.

a. $2.3 \text{ kg} = \blacksquare \text{ g}$

$1 \text{ kg} = 1,000 \text{ g}$

$2.3 \times 1,000 = 2,300$ ◄— To change kg to g, multiply by 1,000.

$2.3 \text{ kg} = 2,300 \text{ g}$

b. $\blacksquare \text{ g} = 250 \text{ mg}$

$1 \text{ mg} = 0.001 \text{ g}$

$250 \times 0.001 = 0.25$ ◄— To change mg to g, multiply by 0.001.

$0.25 \text{ g} = 250 \text{ mg}$

EXERCISES *On Your Own*

Complete each equation.

1. $1 \text{ mg} = \blacksquare \text{ g}$

2. $1 \text{ g} = \blacksquare \text{ kg}$

3. $1 \text{ mg} = \blacksquare \text{ kg}$

4. $1 \text{ g} = \blacksquare \text{ mg}$

5. $1 \text{ kg} = \blacksquare \text{ g}$

6. $1 \text{ kg} = \blacksquare \text{ mg}$

7. $\blacksquare \text{ g} = 8 \text{ mg}$

8. $1,500 \text{ mg} = \blacksquare \text{ kg}$

9. $\blacksquare \text{ kg} = 200,000 \text{ g}$

10. $72 \text{ g} = \blacksquare \text{ kg}$

11. $\blacksquare \text{ mg} = 5.2 \text{ kg}$

12. $180 \text{ mg} = \blacksquare \text{ g}$

13. $\blacksquare \text{ mg} = 3.7 \text{ g}$

14. $0.6 \text{ mg} = \blacksquare \text{ g}$

15. $370 \text{ g} = \blacksquare \text{ kg}$

16. $\blacksquare \text{ kg} = 300,000 \text{ mg}$

17. $900 \text{ g} = \blacksquare \text{ mg}$

18. $\blacksquare \text{ kg} = 5.7 \text{ mg}$

19. $120 \text{ g} = \blacksquare \text{ kg}$

20. $\blacksquare \text{ kg} = 440 \text{ g}$

21. $\blacksquare \text{ kg} = 1,006,000 \text{ mg}$

22. $0.009 \text{ kg} = \blacksquare \text{ mg}$

23. $0.2 \text{ mg} = \blacksquare \text{ g}$

24. $8.6 \text{ kg} = \blacksquare \text{ g}$

25. $800 \text{ g} = \blacksquare \text{ mg}$

26. $1.7 \text{ kg} = \blacksquare \text{ g}$

27. $\blacksquare \text{ mg} = 6.2 \text{ kg}$

Glossary / Study Guide

Examples

Absolute value (p. 98)   The absolute value of a number is its distance from zero on a number line.

-7 is 7 units from 0, so $|-7| = 7$.

Acute angle (p. 292)   An acute angle is any angle that measures less than 90°.

$0° < m\angle 1 < 90°$

Acute triangle (p. 297)   A triangle that contains all acute angles is an acute triangle.

Example: In the triangle, $\angle 1$, $\angle 2$, and $\angle 3$ are acute.

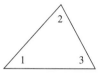

Addition Property of Equality (p. 120)   If the same number is added to each side of an equation, the results are equal.

Since $\frac{20}{2} = 10$, $\frac{20}{2} + 3 = 10 + 3$.
If $a = b$, then $a + c = b + c$.

Adjacent angles (p. 292)   Adjacent angles are two angles that share a vertex and one side but have no interior points in common.

Example: $\angle 1$ and $\angle 2$ are adjacent angles.

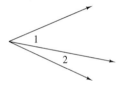

Angle (p. 291)   An angle is made up of two rays with a common endpoint.

Example: $\angle 1$ is made up of $\overrightarrow{GP}$ and $\overrightarrow{GS}$ with common endpoint G.

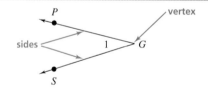

Angle bisector (p. 325)   An angle bisector is the ray that divides the angle into two congruent angles.

Example: $\overrightarrow{DB}$ bisects $\angle ADC$ so $\angle 1 \cong \angle 2$.

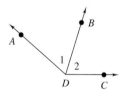

Arc (p. 315)   An arc is part of a circle. A semicircle is an arc that is half of a circle.

Example: $\overset{\frown}{AB}$ is an arc of circle O. $\overset{\frown}{ABC}$ is a semicircle of circle O.

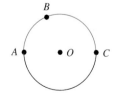

Area (p. 337) The number of square units inside a figure is the area.

Example: $\ell = 6$ ft, and $w = 4$ ft, so the area is 24 ft^2.

Each square equals 1 ft^2.

Arithmetic sequence (p. 434) In an arithmetic sequence, you add the same number to each term to find the next term.

The sequence 4, 10, 16, 22, 28, 34, . . . is an arithmetic sequence. You add 6 to each term to find the next term.

Associative Property of Addition (p. 60) Changing the grouping of the addends does not change the sum.

$(2 + 3) + 7 = 2 + (3 + 7)$
$(a + b) + c = a + (b + c)$

Associative Property of Multiplication (p. 68) Changing the grouping of the factors does not change the product.

$(3 \times 4) \times 5 = 3 \times (4 \times 5)$
$(a \times b) \times c = a \times (b \times c)$

B

Balance (p. 446) The balance of an account is the principal plus the interest earned.

You deposit $100 and earn $5 in interest. Your balance is $105.

Bar graph (p. 8) A bar graph compares amounts.

Example: This bar graph represents class sizes for grades 6, 7, and 8.

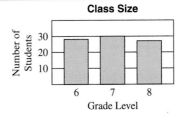

Base (p. 155) When a number is written in exponential form, the number that is used as a factor is the base.

$5^4 = 5 \times 5 \times 5 \times 5$
$\quad\llcorner$ base

Bases of two-dimensional figures (pp. 340, 344, 345)
See *Parallelogram, Triangle,* and *Trapezoid.*

Bases of three-dimensional figures (pp. 368, 369)
See *Cone, Cylinder, Prism,* and *Pyramid.*

Biased question (p. 31) A question is biased if it makes assumptions about the person being questioned or if it makes one answer seem better than another.

"Do you prefer good food or junk food?"

Box-and-whisker plot (p. 26) A box-and-whisker plot shows the distribution of data in each quartile, that is, in each quarter of the data.

Example: The box-and-whisker plot uses these data: 16   19   26
26   27   29   30   31   34   34   38   39   40

The lower quartile is 26. The median is 30. The upper quartile is 36.

C

Capacity (p. 75) Capacity is a measure of the amount of space a liquid or dry ingredient occupies.

A juice bottle has a capacity of about 1 liter.

Central angle (p. 314) A central angle is an angle whose vertex is the center of a circle.

Example: ∠AOB is a central angle of circle O.

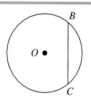

Chord (p. 314) A chord is a segment that has both endpoints on the circle.

Example: $\overline{CB}$ is a chord of circle O.

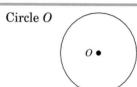

Circle (p. 314) A circle is the set of points in a plane that are all the same distance from a given point, called the center.

Circle O

Circle graph (p. 318) A circle graph presents data as percents or fractions of a total. The total must be 100% or 1.

Example: This circle graph represents the types of plays William Shakespeare wrote.

Shakespeare's Plays

Histories 26%
Tragedies 26%
Romances 13%
Comedies 35%

Circumference (p. 349) Circumference is the distance around a circle. You calculate the circumference of a circle by multiplying the diameter by pi, or π, ($C = \pi d$). Pi is approximately equal to 3.14.

Example: The circumference of a circle with a diameter of 10 cm is approximately 31.4 cm.

10 cm   about 31.4 cm
O

Combination (p. 419) An arrangement in which order does not matter is a combination.

You choose two vegetables from carrots, peas, and spinach. The possible combinations are carrots and peas, carrots and spinach, and peas and spinach.

Commutative Property of Addition (p. 60) Changing the order of the addends does not change the sum.

$3 + 1 = 1 + 3$

$a + b = b + a$

Commutative Property of Multiplication (p. 68) Changing the order of the factors does not change the product.

$6 \times 3 = 3 \times 6$

$ab = ba$

Compass (p. 316) A compass is a geometric tool you can use to draw circles and arcs.

Compatible numbers (p. 55) Compatible numbers are numbers close in value to the numbers you want to multiply or divide. Estimating products or quotients is easier when you use compatible numbers. Compatible numbers are easy to multiply or divide mentally.

Estimate $151 \div 14.6$.

$151 \approx 150$
$14.6 \approx 15$
$150 \div 15 = 10$
$151 \div 14.6 \approx 10$

Compensation (p. 63) A sum remains the same if you add a number to one addend and subtract it from another addend. A difference remains the same if you add the same number to both numbers or subtract the same number from both numbers.

$7 + 5 = (7 + 3) + (5 - 3)$

$22 - 8 = (22 + 2) - (8 + 2)$

Complement of an event (p. 402) The complement of an event is all the other possible events for that situation. The probability of an event plus the probability of its complement equals 1.

The event *no rain* is the complement of the event *rain*.

Complementary angles (p. 292) Two angles are complementary if the sum of their measures is 90°.

Example: $\angle BCA$ and $\angle CAB$ are complementary angles.

Composite number (p. 160) A whole number that has more than two factors is a composite number.

24 is a composite number that has 1, 2, 3, 4, 6, 8, 12, and 24 as factors.

Glossary/Study Guide

Compound interest (p. 447)   Compound interest is interest paid on both the principal and the interest earned in previous interest periods. To calculate compound interest, you can use the formula $B = p(1 + r)^t$, where B is the balance in the account, p is the principal, r is the annual interest rate, and t is the time in years that the account earns interest.

You deposit $500 in an account earning 5% annual interest.

The balance after six years is $500(1 + 0.05)^6$ or $670.05.

Cone (p. 369)   A cone is a three-dimensional figure with one circular base and one vertex.

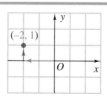
base

Congruent angles (p. 297)   Congruent angles are angles that have the same measure.

$\angle B \cong \angle C$

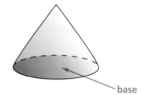
C 60°   60° B

Congruent figures (p. 305)   Figures that have the same size and shape are congruent. Congruent polygons have congruent corresponding sides and congruent corresponding angles.

Example: $\overline{AB} \cong \overline{QS}$, $\overline{CB} \cong \overline{RS}$, and $\overline{AC} \cong \overline{QR}$.
$\angle A \cong \angle Q$, $\angle C \cong \angle R$, and $\angle B \cong \angle S$.
$\triangle ABC \cong \triangle QSR$.

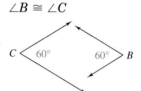

Congruent segments (p. 297)   Congruent segments are segments that have the same length.

$\overline{AB} \cong \overline{WX}$

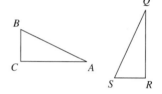
$A \bullet$————————$\bullet B$
$W \bullet$————————$\bullet X$

Coordinate plane (p. 472)   A coordinate plane is formed by a horizontal number line called the x-axis and a vertical number line called the y-axis.

Coordinates (p. 473)   Each point on the coordinate plane is identified by a unique ordered pair of numbers called coordinates. The first coordinate tells you how far from the origin to move along the x-axis. The second coordinate tells you how far from the origin to move along the y-axis.

Example: The ordered pair $(-2, 1)$ describes the point that is 2 units to the left of the y-axis and one unit above the x-axis.

Corresponding angles of polygons (pp. 245, 305)
The matching angles of similar or congruent figures are
corresponding angles.

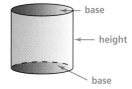

corresponding
angles of
similar trapezoids
corresponding
angles of
congruent triangles

Corresponding sides of polygons (pp. 245, 305)
The matching sides of similar or congruent figures are
corresponding sides.

corresponding
sides of
similar rectangles
corresponding
sides of
congruent triangles

Counting principle (p. 408)   If there are m ways of
making one choice and n ways of making a second choice,
then there are $m \times n$ ways of making the first choice followed
by the second.

Toss a coin and roll a standard number
cube. The total number of possible
outcomes is $2 \times 6 = 12$.

Cross products (p. 241)   In the proportion $\frac{a}{b} = \frac{c}{d}$, the cross
products are ad and bc. Cross products of a proportion are
equal.

In the proportion $\frac{2}{5} = \frac{10}{25}$, the cross
products are $2(25)$ and $5(10)$.

Cube (p. 369)   A cube is a rectangular prism whose faces
are squares.

Cylinder (p. 369)   A cylinder is a three-dimensional figure
with two circular, parallel, and congruent bases.

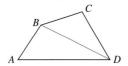

base

height

base

D

Dependent events (p. 413)   Two events are dependent if
the outcome of the first event affects the outcome of the
second event.

Suppose you draw two marbles, one
after the other, from a bag. If you do
not replace the first marble before
drawing the second marble, the events
are dependent.

Diagonal (p. 310)   A diagonal of a polygon is a segment that
connects two vertices that are not next to each other.
Example: $\overline{BD}$ is a diagonal of quadrilateral *ABCD*.

C
B
A
D

Diameter (p. 314)   A diameter is a segment that passes through the center of a circle and has both endpoints on the circle.

Example: $\overline{RS}$ is a diameter of a circle O.

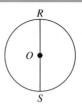

Distributive Property (p. 81)   If a, b, and c are any numbers, then
   $a\,(b + c) = ab + ac$ and $a\,(b - c) = ab - ac$.

$2(3 + \frac{1}{2}) = 2 \cdot 3 + 2 \cdot \frac{1}{2}$

$8(5 - 3) = 8(5) - 8(3)$

Divisible (p. 159)   A number is divisible by another if the remainder is zero.

16 is divisible by 1, 2, 4, 8 and 16.

Division Property of Equality (p. 124)   If both sides of an equation are divided by the same nonzero number, the results are equal.

Since $3(2) = 6$, $3(2) \div 2 = 6 \div 2$.

If $a = b$ and $c \neq 0$, then $\frac{a}{c} = \frac{b}{c}$.

Double bar graph (p. 12)   A double bar graph compares quantities of two sets of data.

Example: This double bar graph shows class sizes for grades 6, 7, and 8 for both boys and girls.

Double line graph (p. 12)   A double line graph compares two sets of data over time.

Example: This double line graph represents seasonal air conditioner and snow blower sales (in thousands of dollars) for a large chain of department stores.

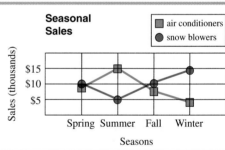

E

Edge (p. 369)   An edge is a segment where two faces of a three-dimensional figure meet.

See *Three-dimensional figure.*

Equation (p. 118)   A mathematical sentence that contains an equal sign, =, is an equation.

$27 \div 9 = 3$

$x + 10 = 8$

Equilateral triangle (p. 297)   An equilateral triangle is a triangle with three congruent sides.

Example: $\overline{SL} \cong \overline{LW} \cong \overline{WS}$

Equivalent decimals (p. 50)   Decimals that name the same amount are equivalent decimals.

$0.6 = 0.60$

Equivalent fractions (p. 148)   Fractions that are equal to each other are equivalent fractions.

$\frac{1}{2}$ and $\frac{25}{50}$ are equivalent fractions.

Evaluate an expression (p. 92)   To evaluate an expression, replace each variable with a number. Then follow the order of operations.

To evaluate the expression $3x + 2$ for $x = 4$, substitute 4 for x.

$3x + 2 = 3(4) + 2 = 12 + 2 = 14$

Event (p. 392)   An event is one or more results of an experiment.

In a game that includes tossing a coin and rolling a standard number cube, "heads and a 2" is an event.

Experimental probability (p. 392)   You find the experimental probability of an event by repeating an experiment many times and using this ratio.

$P(\text{event}) = \dfrac{\text{number of times an event happens}}{\text{number of times the experiment is done}}$

Suppose a basketball player makes 19 baskets in 28 attempts. The experimental probability that she makes a basket is $\frac{19}{28} \approx 68\%$.

Exponent (p. 155)   You can use an exponent to show repeated multiplication. An exponent tells you how many times a base is used as a factor.

exponent

$3^4 = 3 \times 3 \times 3 \times 3$

F

Face (p. 368)   A flat surface on a three-dimensional figure is called a face.

See *Three-dimensional figure*.

Factor (p. 148)   A factor is a whole number that divides another whole number with no remainder.

1, 2, 3, 4, 6, 9, 12, 18, and 36 are factors of 36.

Factor tree (p. 160)   A factor tree is used to find a number's prime factors.

Fair game (p. 403)   A game is fair if all players are equally likely to win.

Players A and B roll a number cube. Player A gets a point if the number is even; player B gets a point if the number is odd. This game is fair.

Glossary/Study Guide

Frequency table (p. 4)   A frequency table lists items together with the number of times, or frequency, that they occur.

Example: This frequency table shows the number of household telephones for a class of students.

Household Telephones

Phones	Tally	Frequency
1	ꟼꟼ ꟼꟼꟼ	8
2	ꟼꟼ ꟼ	6
3	ꟼꟼꟼꟼ	4

Front-end estimation (p. 54)   You can use front-end estimation to estimate a sum. First add the front-end digits. Then adjust by estimating the sum of the remaining digits. Add the two values.

Estimate $\$3.49 + \$2.29$.

$3 + 2 = 5$

$0.49 + 0.29 \approx 1$

$\$3.49 + \$2.29 \approx \$5 + \$1 = \$6$

Function (p. 450)   A function is a relationship in which each input value has exactly one output value.

Earned income is a function of the number of hours worked (w). If you earn $\$6$/h, then your income is expressed by the function $f(w) = 6w$.

G

Geometric sequence (p. 435)   In a geometric sequence, you multiply each term by the same number to find the next term.

The sequence 1, 3, 9, 27, 81, . . . is a geometric sequence. You multiply each term by 3 to find the next term.

Graph of an equation (p. 478)   The graph of an equation in two variables is the graph of all the points whose coordinates are solutions of the equation.

Example: The coordinates of all of the points on the graph satisfy the equation $y = |x| - 1$.

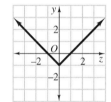

Greatest common factor (GCF) (p. 161)   The greatest common factor of two or more numbers is the greatest number that is a factor of all the numbers.

The GCF of 12 and 30 is 6.

H

Height of two-dimensional figures (pp. 340, 344, 345)
See *Parallelogram, Triangle,* and *Trapezoid.*

Height of three-dimensional figures (p. 378)
See *Cylinder* and *Prism.*

Histogram (p. 5)   A histogram is a special type of bar graph used to show frequency. The height of each bar gives the frequency of the data. Information on the horizontal axis is grouped into *intervals*.

Example: This histogram gives the frequency of board game purchases at a local toy store.

Board Game Purchases

Hypotenuse (p. 360)   The hypotenuse is the longest side of a right triangle. It is the side opposite the right angle.

Example: $\overline{AC}$ is the hypotenuse of $\triangle ABC$.

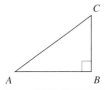

I

Identity Property of Addition (p. 60)   The sum of zero and any number a is a.

$7 + 0 = 7$
$a + 0 = a$

Identity Property of Multiplication (p. 68)   The product of one and any number a is a.

$5 \times 1 = 5$
$a(1) = a$

Image (p. 494)   A point, line, or figure that has been transformed to a new set of coordinates is the image of the original point, line, or figure.

Example: $A'B'C'D'$ is the image of $ABCD$.

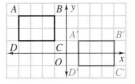

Improper fraction (p. 172)   An improper fraction has a numerator that is greater than or equal to the denominator.

$\frac{24}{15}$ and $\frac{16}{16}$ are improper fractions.

Independent events (p. 412)   Two events are independent if the outcome of one event does not affect the outcome of the other.

Suppose you draw two marbles, one after the other, from a bag. If you replace the first marble before drawing the second marble, the events are independent.

Inequality (p. 101)   An inequality is a comparison of two expressions that uses one of the symbols $<, \leq, >,$ or $\geq$.

$0 \leq 2, k > -3, 10 < t, m + 2 \geq -5$

Integers (p. 98)   Integers are the set of whole numbers and their opposites.

$\ldots -3, -2, -1, 0, 1, 2, 3, \ldots$

Inverse operations (p. 113)   Operations that undo each other, such as addition and subtraction, are inverse operations.

$15 + 3 = 18$ and $18 - 3 = 15$

Glossary/Study Guide

Examples

Isosceles triangle (p. 297) An isosceles triangle is a triangle with at least two congruent sides.

$\overline{LM} \cong \overline{LB}$

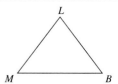

L

Least common denominator (LCD) (p. 152) The least common denominator of two or more fractions is the least common multiple of their denominators.

The least common denominator of $\frac{1}{5}$ and $\frac{2}{3}$ is 15.

Least common multiple (LCM) (p. 147) The least common multiple of two numbers is the least number that is a multiple of both.

The LCM of 10 and 6 is 30.

Legs of a right triangle (p. 360) The two shorter sides of a right triangle form a right angle and are the legs of the triangle.

Example: $\overline{AB}$ and $\overline{BC}$ are the legs of $\triangle ABC$.

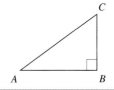

Line graph (p. 9) A line graph shows how an amount changes over time.

Example: This line graph shows the amount of time a student spends reading each night for a week.

Line plot (p. 4) A line plot uses a number line to display data. An ✗ represents each data item.

Example: This line plot shows the number of pets owned by each of 12 students.

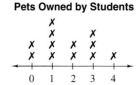

Line of reflection (p. 500) A line over which a figure is reflected

See *Reflection.*

Line of symmetry (p. 499) A line that divides a figure into mirror images

See *Symmetry.*

Linear equation (p. 478) An equation is a linear equation when the graph of all its solutions is a line.

Example: $y = \frac{1}{2}x + 3$ is a linear equation because the graph of its solutions is a line.

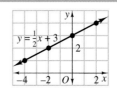

Mean (p. 17)   The mean of a set of data is the sum of the data divided by the number of items in the set of data.

The mean temperature (°F) for the set of temperatures 44, 52, 48, 55, 61, 67 and 58 is

$$\frac{44 + 52 + 48 + 55 + 61 + 67 + 58}{7} = 55°F$$

Median (p. 17)   The median is the middle number in a set of ordered data. If there is an even number of data items, the median is the mean of the two middle items.

Temperatures (°F) for one week arranged in numerical order are 44, 48, 52, 55, 58, 61, and 67. The median is 55 because it is the middle number in the set of data.

Midpoint (p. 323)   The midpoint of a segment is the point that divides the segment into two congruent segments.

Example: $\overline{XM} \cong \overline{MY}$. M is the midpoint of $\overline{XY}$.

Mixed number (p. 172)   A mixed number is the sum of a whole number and a fraction.

$3\frac{11}{16}$ is a mixed number.

$$3\frac{11}{16} = 3 + \frac{11}{16}$$

Mode (p. 18)   The mode of a set of data is the data item that occurs most often.

The mode of the set of prices $2.50, $3.75, $3.60, $2.75, $2.75, and $3.70 is $2.75.

Multiple (p. 147)   A multiple of a number is the product of that number and a nonzero whole number.

Some multiples of 13 are 13, 26, 39, and 52.

Multiplication Property of Equality (p. 124)   If each side of an equation is multiplied by the same number, the results are equal.

Since $\frac{12}{2} = 6$, $\frac{12}{2} \cdot 2 = 6 \cdot 2$.
If $a = b$, then $a \cdot c = b \cdot c$.

N

Net (p. 373)   A pattern that can be folded to cover a solid figure is a net for the figure.

Example: These are nets for a cube.

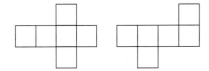

O

Obtuse angle (p. 292)   An obtuse angle is any angle whose measure is greater than 90° and less than 180°.

Obtuse triangle (p. 297)   A triangle that contains one obtuse angle is an obtuse triangle.

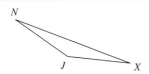

Glossary/Study Guide

Odds (p. 406)   You can calculate the odds in favor of an event by using the ratio $\frac{\text{number of favorable outcomes}}{\text{number of unfavorable outcomes}}$.

Suppose you roll a standard number cube. The odds in favor of getting a 4 are $\frac{1}{5}$.

Opposites (p. 98)   Numbers that are the same distance from zero on the number line but in opposite directions are opposites.

-17 and 17 are opposites.

Order of operations (pp. 80, 150)
1. Do all operations within grouping symbols.
2. Evaluate any term with exponents.
3. Multiply and divide in order from left to right.
4. Add and subtract in order from left to right.

$2^3(7 - 4) = 2^3 \cdot 3 = 8 \cdot 3 = 24$

Ordered pair (p. 472)   An ordered pair is a pair of numbers that describe the location of a point on a coordinate plane. The first value is the x-coordinate and the second value is the y-coordinate.

Example: $(-2, 1)$ is an ordered pair. The x-coordinate is -2; the y-coordinate is 1.

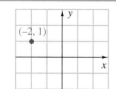

Origin (p. 472)   The point of intersection of the x- and y-axes on a coordinate plane is the origin.

Example: The ordered pair that describes the origin is $(0, 0)$.

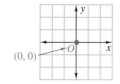

Outcomes (p. 401)   Outcomes are the possible results or consequences of an action.

The outcomes of rolling a standard number cube are 1, 2, 3, 4, 5, and 6.

Outlier (p. 18)   A data item that is far apart from the rest of the data is an outlier.

An outlier in the data set 6, 7, 9, 10, 11, 12, 14, and 52 is 52.

P

Parabola (p. 486)   A parabola is a U-shaped graph of an equation like $y = x^2 - 2$.

Example: This parabola is the graph of the equation $y = x^2 - 2$.

Parallel lines (p. 296)   Parallel lines are lines in the same plane that do not intersect.

$\overleftrightarrow{EF}$ is parallel to $\overleftrightarrow{HI}$.

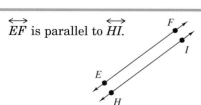

S

Sample (p. 30) A sample of a group is a subgroup selected from within the group.

Your English teacher might read one or two poems from the poems written by your class.

Sample space (p. 407) The set of all possible outcomes of a situation is called the sample space.

The sample space for tossing two coins is HH, HT, TH, TT.

Scale drawing (p. 251) A scale drawing is an enlarged or reduced drawing of an object that is proportional to the original object.

A map is a scale drawing.

Scalene triangle (p. 297) A scalene triangle is a triangle with no congruent sides.

Scatter plot (p. 39) In a scatter plot two related sets of data are graphed as points.

Example: This scatter plot shows amounts spent by several companies on advertising (in dollars) versus product sales (in thousands of dollars).

Scientific notation (p. 438) A number is expressed in scientific notation when it is written as the product of two factors. The first is a number greater than or equal to 1 and less than 10, and the second is a power of 10.

37,000,000 is written as 3.7×10^7 in scientific notation.

Segment bisector (p. 323) A segment bisector is a line (or segment or ray) that goes through the midpoint of a segment.
Example: $GM = MH$. $\overleftrightarrow{FD}$ is a bisector of $\overline{GH}$.

Semicircle (p. 315) A semicircle is half a circle.
Example: $\overarc{ABC}$ is a semicircle of circle O.

Sequence (p. 434) A sequence is a set of numbers that follow a pattern.

3, 6, 9, 12, 15, . . . is a sequence.

Sides of an angle (p. 291) The sides of an angle are its two rays.

See *Angle*.

Glossary/Study Guide

Similar figures (p. 245)   In similar figures, corresponding angles are congruent and the ratios of the lengths of corresponding sides are equal.

$\triangle ABC \sim \triangle RTS$

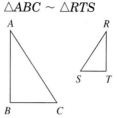

Simple interest (p. 446)   Simple interest is paid only on the original deposit. Use the formula $I = prt$ where I is the simple interest, p is the principal, r is the annual interest rate, and t is the number of years that the account earns interest.

The simple interest earned on $200 invested at 5% annual interest for three years is $200 × 0.05 × 6 or $30.

Simplest form of a fraction (p. 164)   A fraction is in simplest form when the only common factor of the numerator and the denominator is 1.

$\frac{1}{3}$ is the simplest form of $\frac{27}{81}$.

Simulation (p. 393)   A simulation is a model of a real-world situation.

A baseball team has an equal chance of winning or losing its next game. You can toss a coin to simulate the situation.

Slope (p. 482)   Slope is a ratio that describes the steepness of a line.

$$\text{Slope} = \frac{\text{rise}}{\text{run}}$$

Example: The slope of the given line $= \frac{2}{4} = \frac{1}{2}$.

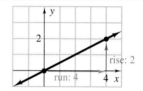

Solution (pp. 118, 477)   Any value or values that make an equation true

4 is the solution of $x + 5 = 9$.

$(8, 4)$ is a solution of $y = -1x + 12$ because $4 = -1(8) + 12$.

Sphere (p. 369)   A sphere is the set of points in space that are the same distance from a given point called the center.

Spreadsheet (p. 12)   A spreadsheet is a tool used for organizing and analyzing data. Spreadsheets are arranged in rows and columns. A cell is the box on a spreadsheet where a row and a column meet. The names of the row and column determine the name of the cell.

	A	B	C	D	E
1	0.50	0.70	0.60	0.50	2.30
2	1.50	0.50	2.75	2.50	7.25

Example: In the spreadsheet shown, column C and row 2 meet at the shaded box, cell C2. The value in cell C2 is 2.75.

Square (p. 309) A square is a parallelogram with four right angles and four congruent sides.

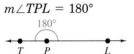

Square root (p. 354) The square root of a number is a number which when multiplied by itself equals the given number.

$\sqrt{9} = 3$ because $3^2 = 9$.

Standard form of a number (p. 439) When you multiply the factors of a number in scientific notation, the number is in standard form.

The standard form of 2.5×10^6 is 2,500,000.

Stem-and-leaf plot (p. 22) A stem-and-leaf plot displays data items in order. A leaf is a data item's last digit on the right. A stem represents the digits to the left of the leaf.

Example: This stem-and-leaf-plot displays recorded times in a race. The stem represents the number of seconds. The leaves represent tenths of a second.

```
stem  leaves
 27 | 7
 28 | 5 6 8
 29 | 6 9
 30 | 8
```
27 | 7 means 27.7

Straight angle (p. 292) An angle that measures 180° is a straight angle.

$m\angle TPL = 180°$

Subtraction Property of Equality (p. 120) If the same number is subtracted from each side of an equation, the results are equal.

Since $\frac{20}{2} = 10$, $\frac{20}{2} - 3 = 10 - 3$.
If $a = b$, then $a - c = b - c$.

Supplementary angles (p. 292) Two angles are supplementary if the sum of their measures is 180°.

Example: $\angle A$ and $\angle D$ are supplementary.

Surface area of a prism (p. 373) The surface area of a prism is the sum of the areas of the faces.

Example: $4 \times 12 \text{ in.}^2 + 2 \times 9 \text{ in.}^2 = 66 \text{ in.}^2$

Each square = 1 in.²

Symmetry (p. 499) A figure is symmetrical when one side of a figure is the mirror image of the other side.

Example: The left and right sides of the mask are mirror images of each other.

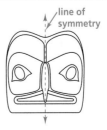

line of symmetry

Glossary/Study Guide

Term (p. 434) Each number in a sequence is a term.

In the sequence 2, 4, 6, 8, . . ., the numbers 2, 4, 6, and 8 are terms.

Terminating decimal (p. 76) A terminating decimal is a decimal that stops, or terminates.

Both 0.6 and 0.7265 are terminating decimals.

Tessellation (p. 496) A tessellation is a repeated pattern of figures without gaps or overlaps.

Example: This tessellation consists of small and large squares.

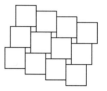

Theoretical probability (p. 401) You can compute the theoretical probability of an event using this formula.

$P(\text{event}) = \dfrac{\text{number of favorable outcomes}}{\text{number of possible outcomes}}$

Suppose you select a letter from the letters H, A, P, P, and Y. The theoretical probability of selecting a P is $\frac{2}{5}$.

Three-dimensional figure (p. 368) Figures, such as buildings, that do not lie in a plane are three-dimensional.

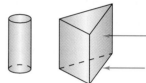

Transformation (p. 494) Movements of figures on a plane are transformations. A transformation can be a translation, reflection, or rotation.

Example: $K'L'M'N'$ is a reflection of $KLMN$.

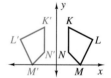

Translation (p. 494) A translation slides a figure.

Example: $ABCD$ has been translated to $A'B'C'D'$.

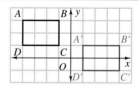

Transversal (p. 296) A transversal is a line that intersects two other coplanar lines in different points.

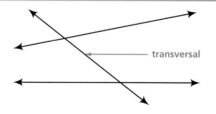

Trapezoid (p. 309) A trapezoid is a quadrilateral that has exactly one pair of parallel sides.

$\overline{UV}$ is parallel to $\overline{WY}$.

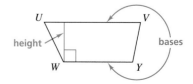

Tree diagram (p. 408)   A tree diagram shows the total number of possible outcomes in a probability experiment.

Example: This tree diagram shows the possible outcomes of tossing two coins.

Trend (p. 40)   Two sets of related data have a *positive trend* if, in general, as the values of one set of data increase, the values of the other set increase also. Two sets of related data have a *negative trend* if, in general, as the values of one set increase, the values of the other set decrease. Two sets of related data have little or *no trend* if the data show no relationship.

Triangle (p. 297)   A triangle is a polygon with three sides.

base

height

 U

Unit price (p. 238)   A unit price is the price per unit of an item.

$$\frac{\$5.98}{10.2 \text{ fl oz}} = \$.59/\text{fl oz}$$

Unit rate (p. 237)   A unit rate is a rate that has a denominator of 1.

If you drive 165 mi in 3 h, your unit rate of travel is $\frac{55 \text{ mi}}{1 \text{ h}}$ or 55 mi/h.

V

Variable (p. 92)   A variable is a symbol, usually a letter, that stands for a number.

x is a variable in the equation $9 - x = 3$.

Variable expression (p. 92)   A variable expression is a group of numbers, variables, and operations.

$7 + x, 2y - 4, \frac{3}{5}g, \frac{7}{k}$

Vertex of an angle (p. 291)   The vertex of an angle is the common endpoint of its two rays.

See *Angle*.

Vertex of a polygon (p. 305)   The vertex of a polygon is any point where two sides of a polygon meet.

See *Polygon*.

Volume (p. 377)   The volume of a three-dimensional figure is the number of cubic units needed to fill the space inside the figure.

Example: The volume of the rectangular prism is 36 in.^{3}.

Each cube = 1 in.^{3}

Glossary/Study Guide

W

Examples

Whole numbers (p. 98) The whole numbers are 0, 1, 2, 3, ...

4, 125, and 3,947 are whole numbers; -4, 17.5, and $2\frac{1}{2}$ are *not* whole numbers.

X

x-axis (p. 472) The x-axis is the horizontal number line that, together with the y-axis, forms the coordinate plane.

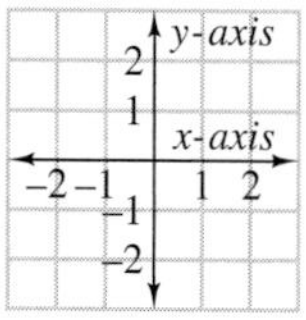

Y

y-axis (p. 472) The y-axis is the vertical number line that, together with the x-axis, forms the coordinate plane.

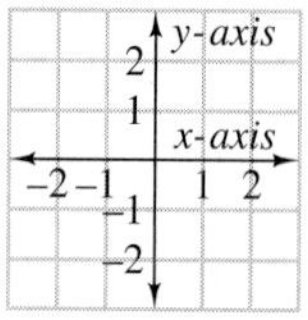

Z

Zero pair (p. 102) A positive tile and a negative tile make a zero pair.

Zero Property of Multiplication (p. 68) The product of zero and any number is a zero.

$6 \times 0 = 0$

$a \times 0 = 0$

Selected Answers

TOOLS FOR PROBLEM SOLVING

The Four-Step Approach — page xxii

ON YOUR OWN **1.** 3 small and 8 large tables or 11 small and 3 large tables **3.** 16 triangles **5.** troposphere, stratosphere, mesosphere, thermosphere

Using Strategies — page xxv

ON YOUR OWN **1.** Kim made $15, Petra made $32 **3.** 16 **5.** 3:55 A.M. **7.** 22,500

Working Together — page xxvii

ON YOUR OWN **1.** 75 different amounts **3.** 32 min **5.** at noon on March 7, if there is no leap year

Preparing for Standardized Tests — page xxix

ON YOUR OWN **1.** D **3.** E **5.** B

CHAPTER 1

Lesson 1-1 — pages 4–7

ON YOUR OWN
1. Tickets Sold

Number of Tickets	Frequency
45	2
46	4
47	0
48	2
49	1
50	3
51	2
52	0
53	1

3. Number of TVs per Household

TVs	Frequency
1	6
2	6
3	5
4	1

Number of TVs in Household

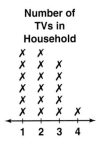

5a. 16 people **b.** 4 people **7.** 16 people
9a. 12 people **b.** 4–5; 15 people **c.** 14 people
d. 50 people
11.

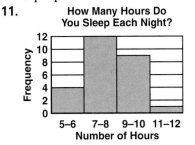

13a. What Time Do You Get Up?

Time	Frequency
5:30–5:59	2
6:00–6:29	5
6:30–6:59	1
7:00–7:29	3
7:30–7:59	3
8:00–8:29	2

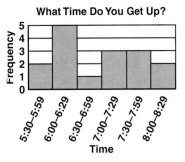

b. 6:00–6:29

MIXED REVIEW **15.** < **17.** > **19.** 310 **21.** 490

Lesson 1-2 — pages 8–11

ON YOUR OWN
1.

Number of Movies Made in One Year

3. Los Angeles, Memphis, and Tokyo **5.** Memphis, Tokyo, Los Angeles, Kennedy, Frankfurt **7.** Bar graph; two quantities are being compared. **9.** The number of CD singles is rapidly increasing.

11a.

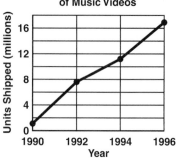

Wholesale Shipments of Music Videos

b. The number of music videos is increasing by about 5 million units every 2 years.
13. B

MIXED REVIEW   **15.** 32 students   **17.** 13   **19.** 6
21. 56

Lesson 1-3   *pages 12–15*

ON YOUR OWN   **1.** 28   **3.** 9 calories   **5a.** 1965
7. Corpus Christi, TX
9.

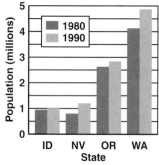

State Population

1980
1990

MIXED REVIEW   **11a.** no

Toolbox   *page 16*

1. 15   **3.** 13 R1   **5.** 13   **7.** 217 R2   **9.** 25 R6
11. 6 R15   **13.** 3   **15.** 5 R28   **17.** 7 R3   **19.** 11 R2
21. 5 R22   **23.** 6 R21   **25.** 3 R52

Lesson 1-4   *pages 17–21*

ON YOUR OWN   **1.** 2; 2; 1 and 2   **3.** 63; 62; 62
5. 28.9; 28.5; 25   **7a.** Always   **b.** No; people may
give to charity in other ways than contributing
their aluminum cans.   **9a.** 21 students
b. 10 students   **11a.** 84; 81; 79   **b.** Yes; 102.
13. C   **15a.** 12.7 years   **b.** 12 years; 12 and
15 years

Mixed Review   **17.** Double bar graph; the graph
compares two sets of quantities at one time.
19. 800   **21.** 60   **23.** 27 and 3

CHECKPOINT

Number	Frequency
1	2
2	2
3	2
4	2
5	3
6	1
7	2
8	2
9	1

2. 120; 119; 117
3. 25; 25; 25

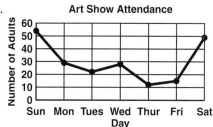

4.

Art Show Attendance

Use a line graph to show change over time.

Lesson 1-5   *pages 22–25*

ON YOUR OWN
1. 1 | 3 3 4 4 4 4
      2 | 3 4 5 5
      3 | 6 9

      2 | 3 means $2.3 million

3. 9 | 8 9   **5.** 12   **7.** 6
     10 | 0 1 3 4 8 9   **9.** tenths   **11.** 6
     11 | 1 2 2 3 3 8

      11 | 1 means 111°F
13. Count ten items up from 16 | 1 or down from
19 | 9. The median is 18.4.
15a. 3 | 5 8   **b.** 53
       4 | 2 2 7
       5 | 0 5 7
       6 |
       7 |
       8 | 2 8

      8 | 2 means 82

MIXED REVIEW   **17.** 360   **19.** 1,200   **21.** =
23. <   **25.** 47

Toolbox — page 26

1. The data in the second quartile are closer together than in the third.

3.

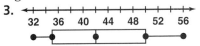

5.

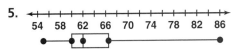

Lesson 1-6 — pages 27–29

ON YOUR OWN   1. The locker marked "basketballs" has soccer balls. The locker marked "soccer balls" has footballs.   **3.** 7 students
5. 7 zebras

MIXED REVIEW   7. 10   **9.** mode   **11.** 192
13. 333

Lesson 1-7 — pages 30–32

ON YOUR OWN   1. Survey bus drivers at the end of each shift.   **3.** No; only teenagers from the nearby school are likely to be surveyed, and some of them you might ask more than once.   **5.** Yes; each visitor has an equal chance of being surveyed.
7. Biased; the terms "invigorating" and "couch potato" may influence responses.   **9.** Fair; the question does not give preference to one answer or the other.   **11.** Words are used to make one choice seem better than the other.

MIXED REVIEW   13. 56; 50; 50; 99; the outlier significantly increases the mean.

Problem Solving Practice — page 33

1. D   **3.** A   **5.** B   **7.** C

Lesson 1-8 — pages 34–38

ON YOUR OWN
1a.

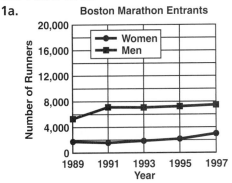

Boston Marathon Entrants

b.

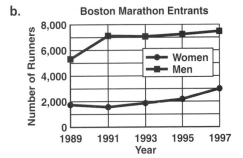

Boston Marathon Entrants

c. Second; the sponsors want to see an increasing number of participants.   **5a.** mean   **b.** mode
7. The number of bald eagle pairs increased a lot from 1987 to 1995   **9.** about 2,500 pairs

MIXED REVIEW   11. Biased; would you prefer to vacation in Florida or Maine?   **13.** 300   **15.** 70
17. 2,000

CHECKPOINT   1. Elsa carried the pink towel and a beach ball; Anna carried the blue towel and sandwiches; LaTonya carried the striped towel and iced tea.   **2.** Mode; although the mode does not represent the data well, it is greater than the mean and the median.
3.

```
0 | 9
1 | 0 3 7
2 | 1 1 7

  2 | 1 means 21
```

5. A

Lesson 1-9 — pages 39–42

ON YOUR OWN   1. The moose population is generally increasing; there does not seem to be a pattern in the wolf population.   **3.** None; there is no relationship between the number of children and the number of pets in a family.   **5.** None; the number of governors a state has had depends on the age of the state, not its area.   **7.** C; as temperature rises, more people go to the beach.

MIXED REVIEW
9.

```
1 | 5 9 9
2 | 2 4 5 7 7 9 9
3 | 0 4

  1 | 5 means 15 students
```

11. No; the question shows no preference to either choice.

1.   How Often
Do You Cook?   **2a.** 70.3   **b.** C4

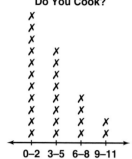

X
X
X
X   X
X   X
X   X
X   X
X   X   X
X   X   X
X   X   X   X
X   X   X   X

0–2 3–5 6–8 9–11

3a.   Selected United States Population

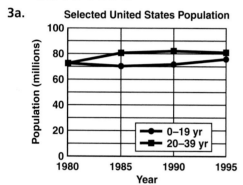

4a. 27.5; 25; 40 and 15   **b.** 75 is an outlier; it increases the mean.   **c.** the mode 40

5.

0	0
1	0 5 5 5
2	0 5 5
3	0 5
4	0 0 0
5	
6	
7	5

6. Sam was the spider and brought apples; Katie was the fish and brought popcorn; Martin was the fox and brought cookies.

4 | 0 means 40 min

9a.   Average Weights and Pulse Rates
of 9 Animals

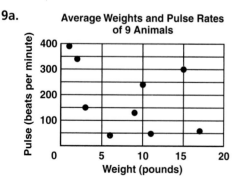

b. No; there is no clear trend in the data.   **10.** B

1. A   **3.** A   **5.** B   **7.** C   **9.** A   **11.** C

CHAPTER 2

ON YOUR OWN   1a. fifty-two hundredths or 0.52; thirty-six hundredths or 0.36; sixty-four hundredths or 0.64   **b.** 0.36 < 0.52 < 0.64   **3.** 9.4, 9.42, 9.7   **5.** 0.29, 0.32, 0.38   **7.** 1.30, 1.6, 1.74   **9.** 5.42, 5.43, 5.51   **11.** John Olerud, Paul O'Neill, Alex Rodriguez, Edgar Martinez (1995), Edgar Martinez (1992), Julio Franco   **17.** >   **19.** >   **21.** <   **25.** No; the next digit is 4, so you round down.   **27.** ten-thousandths; 5.1944   **29.** hundredths; 0.61   **31.** ones; 416   **33.** ten-thousandths; 15.6194

MIXED REVIEW   37. 0.4; 0.4; 0.2   **39.** 231

ON YOUR OWN   1. $11.50   **3.** $18.50   **5.** $3   **7.** 8   **9.** 8   **11a.** You missed the decimal point in 42.8.   **15.** $56   **17.** 8 boxes   **19.** about $2.80   **29a.** 2 in.   **b.** 1.5 in.   **31a.** 160 noodles   **b.** Round 8,192 to 8,000. Round 59.29 to 50. Divide 8,000 by 50.

MIXED REVIEW   33. 7.681, 7.6801, 7.618, 7.0681   **35.** 6,187   **37.** 244

ON YOUR OWN   1. 7.46   **3.** 5.26   **5.** 4.46   **7.** 2.212   **9.** 105.8   **11.** 0.0645   **13a.** 4 cm   **15.** 29.66 m   **17a.** $1.75   **b.** $8.75   **c.** $8.25   **19.** identity   **21.** associative   **23.** 43.5; commutative, then associative   **25.** 39.5; identity   **27.** 11; identity   **29.** 16.3; commutative, then associative   **31.** 13.2; commutative, then associative

MIXED REVIEW   33. biased   **35.** 5   **37.** 12

CHECKPOINT   1. =   **2.** >   **3.** >   **4.** <   **5a.** $10.50   **b.** $11   **6.** C   **7.** 66.247   **8.** 24.6342   **9.** 5.1388

1. 2.3   **3.** 20.5   **5.** 11.6   **7.** 87.1   **9.** 27   **11.** 25   **13.** 4.8   **15.** 132   **17.** 203   **19.** 8.2

On Your Own   1. 1 yd   **3.** You need to know the average speed with which the Coy family traveled.

5. $28.50   **7.** James Johnson is writing; Emily Wong is interviewing; Marcia Brown is researching.

MIXED REVIEW   9. 1   **11.** 9.5
13. 1 | 3 3 4 7
    2 | 2

        2 | 2 means 2.2

ON YOUR OWN   1. $1.2 \times 49 = 58.8$ **3.** $3.7 \times 6.4 = 23.68$ **5.** 0.24   **7.** 22,059   **9.** 0.065   **11.** 307.5   **13.** 3.915   **15.** 0.675   **19.** 4.2 mi   **21a.** Multiply the numbers as whole numbers. Then place the decimal point before the three digits on the right.   **b.** 196.875 ft^2 **23.** 25.5; identity   **25.** 1; identity   **27.** 6.5; associative   **29.** 0   **31.** 21.5   **33.** B

MIXED REVIEW   35. 0.619   **37.** 10.5
39. 60 packages

1. C   **3.** C   **5.** D   **7.** C   **9.** D

ON YOUR OWN   1. 7.4   **3.** 2.07   **5.** 6.123   **7.** 0.868   **9.** $4.75   **11.** 4   **13.** 452   **15.** 74   **17.** 0.0035   **19.** 0.065   **21.** 2.5   **23a.** 4; 40; 400   **b.** For each place the decimal point moves to the left in the divisor, the quotient increases 10-fold.   **25.** 2,367   **27.** 0.07   **29.** No; the quotient is about 17.5 mi/gal.   **31.** No; $1 \div 10$ is not the same as $10 \div 1$.

MIXED REVIEW   33. 18.043   **35.** 20.19

1. 0.09   **3.** 0.0006   **5.** 0.0012   **7.** 58,000   **9.** 8.5   **11.** 2,460,000   **13.** 3.09   **15.** 0.007

ON YOUR OWN   1. 0.75   **3.** 0.5   **5.** $0.\overline{5}$ **7.** 1   **9.** 0.375   **11.** $3.\overline{3}$ **13.** $0.\overline{285714}$ **15.** $5.\overline{45}$ **17.** $8.\overline{3}$ **19a.** Each successive divisor is one tenth of the one before it.   **b.** 0.0001; 0.00001; 0.000001; 0.5; 5; 50; 500; 5,000; 50,000; 500,000; 5,000,000; 50,000,000   **21a.** 11, 12, 13, 14, 15, 18; 10, 16, 20   **b.** 17, 19; digits in the calculator display do not repeat, but fill all spaces.   **23.** $223 \div 71$ **25.** No; the numbers in the pattern do not repeat in the same order.

MIXED REVIEW   27. 2.78   **29.** 8.83   **31.** <
33. <   **35.** $1.60

CHECKPOINT   1. 49.2   **2.** 1.5   **3.** 21.84   **4.** 2.175   **5.** $1.558\overline{3}$ **6.** 58.71   **7.** $1.458\overline{3}$ **8.** 10.37   **9.** $2.6\overline{48}$ **10.** 12.1584   **11.** $136.\overline{36}$ **12.** $3.8\overline{3}$ **14.** 63 students

ON YOUR OWN   1. 11   **3.** 3   **5.** 1   **7.** 12.5   **11.** ×   **13.** ÷   **15.** ÷   **17.** $4 + (4 \div 4) - 4 = 1$ **19.** $(4 + 4 + 4) \div 4 = 3$ **21.** $(4 + 4) \times 4 - 4 = 28$ **23a.** $20 \times (30 - 1.5)$ **b.** 570 in.^{2} **25.** 3; 3   **27.** 7   **29.** 23.4   **31.** 18.2   **33.** $8 \times (3 + 1)$; $8 \times 3 + 8 \times 1$; 32   **35.** $5 \times (2 + 3)$; $5 \times 2 + 5 \times 3$; 25   **37.** $3.56

MIXED REVIEW   39. 1.3   **41.** 24.8   **43.** 8.875   **45.** 29   **47.** 42; 420; 4,200; 4,200,000

1. =   **2.** >   **3.** <   **4.** >   **5.** 17.85   **6.** 0.104   **7.** 110   **8.** 1.4   **9.** 5   **10.** 8.1947   **11.** 7; compatible numbers   **12.** 6; front-end   **13.** 51.5; rounding   **14.** 63; rounding   **15.** $5; compatible numbers   **16.** 1; rounding   **17.** 5; front-end   **18.** 160; rounding   **19.** Use compatible numbers to estimate a quotient.   **20.** 18.02   **21.** 3.97   **22.** 0.73   **23.** 17.14   **24.** 16.6   **25.** 2.44   **26.** 0.567   **27.** 0.115   **28.** 260.7569 m^2 **29.** You need to know the original price of the jeans.   **30.** 5.5   **31.** 7.89   **32.** 3.425   **33.** 41.24645   **34.** 7.397   **35.** 2.84   **36.** C   **37.** 1.96   **38.** $5.8\overline{6}$ **39.** $1.11\overline{3}$ **40.** $1.5\overline{90}$ **41.** 33   **42.** 0.396875   **43.** $0.48\overline{90}$ **44.** $5.25\overline{5681}$

1. A   **3.** D   **5.** C   **7.** E

CHAPTER 3

ON YOUR OWN   1. 23   **3.** 8   **5.** $\frac{3}{2}$ **7.** 0   **9.** 5

11.

	$t + 2$	$2t - 1$	$2(t - 1)$	$2(2t)$
$t = 1.7$	3.7	2.4	1.4	6.8
$t = 2.04$	4.04	3.08	2.08	8.16

13. 25.2   **15.** 0.2   **17.** 4   **19.** 5.8   **21.** 9.3   **23.** 6.9   **25a.** y **b.** 20,064 movies   **27.** 14   **29.** 2   **31.** 54   **33.** 4   **35.** 35   **41.** $r + c$ **43.** $7t$ **45.** $x - 9$

51. p = number of pages in the directory, $440p$
53a. $599.4h$ **b.** 14,385.6 gallons of blood   **55.** C

MIXED REVIEW   57. 45   **59.** 50   **61.** 40   **63.** 62

Lesson 3-2 pages 97–100

ON YOUR OWN   1. 7   **3.** -2 **5.** C and D   **7.** 83
9. $-1,312$ **11.** $|7|$ **13.** $>$ **15.** $<$ **17.** $>$ **19.** $=$
25.

27.

   29. 11   **31.** 1
   33. 7   **35.** 4
37. 4   **47.** 22; -43; the absolute value of -43 is 43.
The absolute value of 22 is 22. $43 > 22$

MIXED REVIEW   49. 37   **51.** 74   **53.** 562

Toolbox page 101

1. -3 **3.** 0, 6
5.

  7.

Lesson 3-3 pages 102–105

ON YOUR OWN   1. $-3 + 4$; 1   **3.** $3 + 6$; 9   **5.** 11
7. -6 **9.** 5   **11.** -9 **13.** -9 **15.** -3 **23.** 35 ft
25. 9   **27.** -10 **29.** 2.6   **31.** -9.4 **33.** 12
35. -4 **37.** $-12 + 19 = 7$; 7°F   **39.** 0   **41.** -6
43. 34   **45.** 38   **47.** 49

MIXED REVIEW
49. 24 | 3 4 8 9   **51.** $>$ **53.** $<$
       25 | 0 3 7
       26 | 2

       26 | 2 means 2.62

Lesson 3-4 pages 106–110

ON YOUR OWN   1. -2 **3.** -6 **5.** -6 **7.** 12
9. 16   **11.** -17 **13.** -3 **15.** 4   **17.** -104 **19.** 25
21. 0   **23.** 8   **25.** -219 **27.** -136 **29.** B
31. $-9 + 6$; -3 **33.** $5 + 3$; 8   **35.** $1 + 9$; 10
37a. $30   **b.** $13   **c.** $2.60   **39.** -6 **41.** 6   **43.** 0
45. 0   **47.** 14   **49.** 12   **51.** positive   **53.** positive
67. 218.95°C   **69.** 234.334°C

MIXED REVIEW   73. 11   **75.** -72 **77.** 2   **79.** 4.2
81. 56.2

CHECKPOINT   1a. $6p$ **b.** 24; 60   **2.** $10a + 8t$
3. 20   **4.** 0   **5.** 3   **6.** 41.6   **7.** 4   **8.** -9 **9.** 4
10. -23 **11.** -9 **12.** 5   **13.** -3 **14.** -29
15. -5 **16.** 6

Toolbox page 111

1. $224.02, = D2 - C3; -$15.38, = D3 - C4;
$106.62, = D4 + B5; $51.97, = D5 - C6; $401.97,
= D6 + B7; $238.17, = D7 - C8   **3.** Check in C9;
the balance decreased.

Lesson 3-5 pages 112–116

On Your Own   1. -28 **3.** -36 **5.** -6
7. 26   **9.** 30   **11.** -48 **13.** -72 **15.** -840
17. 6 min   **27.** -2 **29.** -8 **31.** -3
33. -13 **35.** 8   **37.** 10   **39.** -9 **41.** $-21 \div 7 = -3$;
$-21 \div (-3) = 7$ **53.** D **55.** E **57.** B

MIXED REVIEW   61. 7   **63.** 5   **65.** -32 **67.** 25.6
69. 21.28   **71.** 24 ways

Problem Solving Practice page 117

1. C   **3.** D   **5.** E   **7.** B

Lesson 3-6 pages 118–121

ON YOUR OWN   1. $x + 2 = 1$; -1
3. $x + 4 = -3$; -7 **5.** 1   **7.** -5 **9.** 8   **11.** -5
13. -1 **15.** 4   **17.** -12 **19.** 0   **21.** 3   **23.** 10
25. 3   **27.** 16   **29.** 21   **31.** 17   **33.** -13 **35.** -12
37. 5   **39.** 4   **41.** 119   **43.** -9 **45a.** computer
engineer; directory assistance operator
b. $n - 17 = 5$ **c.** physician   **47.** Add -15 to each
side of the equation.

MIXED REVIEW   49. -8 **51.** -30

Lesson 3-7 pages 122–125

ON YOUR OWN   1. $3x = -12$; -4 **3.** -4 **5.** -4
7. 2   **9.** -9 **11.** 28   **13.** -60 **15.** 28   **17.** 960
19. about 198 plays per year   **21.** -3 **23.** -6
25. -55 **27.** -150 **29.** 2   **31.** -1 **33.** -56
35. 45   **37.** 416   **39.** -720 **41.** Susan divided
12 by -6; you find the solution by multiplying
12 by -6 to get -72.   **43.** C

MIXED REVIEW   45. identity property of
multiplication   **47.** commutative property of
addition   **49.** 77   **51.** 84   **53.** 12:44 P.M.

Lesson 3-8 pages 126–129

ON YOUR OWN   1. Sixty-seven is fifteen more
than a number.   **3.** Half a number is seventeen.
5. Eighteen is a number divided by three.
7. Negative fifty-five is five times a number.

9. $52 + x = 75; 23$ **11.** $5n = 45; 9$ **13.** $10x = 60; 6$
15. $-1n = 8; -8$ **17.** $7d = 72.5;$ about 10 ft
19. $4n = 52; 13$ **21.** $x + 12 = 61; 49$

23. $3 + n = -2; -5$ **25.** $13x = 91; 7$

27. 40 constellations **29.** 4 shelves

MIXED REVIEW **31.** eight hundred thirty-six thousand, one **33.** three hundred twelve million, two hundred ninety-one thousand, seven hundred forty-five **35.** twenty-five million, seven hundred eighty-five thousand, four hundred fifty-six
37. 5.4 **39.** 3 **41a.** about $2.50 **b.** Each book is about $2.50. The total cost is about 3×2.50.

CHECKPOINT **1.** -42 **2.** 12 **3.** -5 **4.** -7
5. -54 **6.** 4 **7.** 72 **8.** 3 **9.** 53 **10.** -88
11. 48 **12.** -7 **13.** 64 **14.** 10 **15.** 18 **16.** -7
17. -42 **18.** -9 **19.** 21 **20.** -7 **21.** B
22. $20 = 9 + n; 11$ **23.** $x - 6 = 15; 21$
24. $2n = 62; 31$ **25.** $\frac{x}{13} = 7; 91$

Lesson 3-9   *pages 130–133*

ON YOUR OWN **1.** $3x - 2 = -5; -1$ **3.** $2x + 2 = 4; 1$ **5.** $12; 2 \times 12 - 6 = 18$ ✓ **7.** $2; 3 \times 2 - 2 = 4$ ✓ **9.** 2 **11.** 10 **13.** 4 **15.** 10 **17.** $-3; 8(-3) - 8 = -32$ ✓ **19.** $-3; -9(-3) + 5 = 32$ ✓ **21.** $121; \frac{121}{-11} + 1 = -10$ ✓ **23.** $-14; 7(-14) - 6 = -104$ ✓
25. $-3; 3(-3) - 6 = -15$ ✓ **27.** $-3; 10(-3) + 3 = -27$ ✓ **29.** $3; 8 \times 3 - 1 = 23$ ✓ **31.** $35; \frac{35}{-7} + 3 = -2$ ✓ **33.** ⬚ 12 +/− ⊞ 6 ⬚ ÷ 4 ⊟; -1.5
35. ⬚ 10 ⊟ 5 ⬚ ⊠ 3 ⊟; 15 **37.** E **39.** A **41.** G
43. 4.4 h **45.** 3 extra nights **47.** $3n - 51 = 0; 17$
49. $\frac{n}{2} - 5 = -15; -20$

MIXED REVIEW **51.** 19 **53.** 26 **55.** 22

Lesson 3-10   *pages 134–136*

ON YOUR OWN **1a.** 9 combinations **3.** 4 paperback and 2 hardcover books **5a.** Lundberg, Chester, Topson, Dornville **b.** 16.5 mi **9.** 42 ft
11. 15th floor

MIXED REVIEW **13a.** about $41,167; $25,000; $14,000 **b.** Mean; the gap between your salary and the mean is the greatest. **15.** 0.3, 0.36792, 0.368, 0.3681

Wrap Up   *pages 138–139*

1. 27 **2.** 43 **3.** 15 **4.** 11 **5.** 4 **6.** 1 **7.** $8 - n$
8. $6c$ **9.** $6 + 2n$ **10.** -9

11. **12a.** 5 **b.** 2 **c.** 17 **13.** $-6, -3, 0, 1, 7$
14. $<$ **15.** $=$ **16.** $<$ **17.** $>$ **18.** $>$
19. B **20.** $-4 + (-6); -10$

21. $5 + (-4); 1$ **22.** $-6 + 7; 1$ **23.** 3 **24.** -22
25. -5 **26.** 29 **27.** -3 **28.** -30 **29.** 84
30. -25 **31.** 2 **32.** -5 **34.** -6 **35.** 4 **36.** 35
37. -2 **38.** -9 **39.** -14 **40.** 3 **41.** 7
42. $4 + n = -7; -11$
43.

Large	Small
0 ($0)	16 ($20)
5 ($8.75)	9 ($11.25)
10 ($17.50)	2 ($2.50)

Cumulative Review   *page 141*

1. C **3.** D **5.** B **7.** D **9.** C **11.** C

CHAPTER 4

Lesson 4-1   *pages 144–146*

ON YOUR OWN **1.** $\frac{1}{2}$ **3.** $\frac{3}{8}$ **7.** $\frac{5}{6}$ **9.** $1\frac{6}{10}$

MIXED REVIEW **11.** $2n - 4$ **13.** $=$ **15.** $>$
17. about 0.31 m

Lesson 4-2   *pages 147–151*

ON YOUR OWN **1.** 1, 17 **3.** 1, 2, 4, 8, 16, 32
5. 1, 23 **7.** 7, 14, 21, 28, 35 **9.** 9, 18, 27, 36, 45
11. 18, 36, 54, 72, 90 **15.** 6 people **17.** 12 **19.** 40

21. 24 **23.** 10 **25.** 30 **27.** 48 **33a.** $\frac{5}{20}$ of the problems **b.** $\frac{1}{4}$ **35.** 20 **37.** 45 **39.** 1
41. 24 **43.** 63 **45.** 40 **47.** 40 **49.** 24 **51.** D

MIXED REVIEW **55.** 2 **57.** 30 **59.** 17.62
61. 43.49 **63.** 17.09

Lesson 4-3   *pages 152–154*

ON YOUR OWN **1.** $\frac{3}{5} < \frac{4}{5}$ **3.** $<$ **5.** $<$ **7.** $<$
9. $>$ **11.** $<$ **13.** $<$ **15.** $<$ **17.** $>$ **23.** $\frac{2}{3}, \frac{3}{4}, \frac{5}{6}$
25. $\frac{4}{9}, \frac{1}{2}, \frac{2}{3}$ **27.** $\frac{1}{9}, \frac{1}{8}, \frac{1}{6}$ **29.** $\frac{3}{15}, \frac{3}{10}, \frac{3}{5}$ **31.** $\frac{1}{3}, \frac{2}{5}, \frac{2}{3}$
33. $\frac{3}{4}, \frac{4}{5}, \frac{5}{6}$ **35.** B **37.** C **39.** Cheese, since that was the pizza with the least amount of left-overs.

MIXED REVIEW **41.** 3 **43.** -13 **45.** -4 **47.** 3.4
49. 17.9 **51.** on the 27th day

Lesson 4-4   *pages 155–158*

ON YOUR OWN **1.** 7^3 **3.** 0.3^5 **5.** $5 \times 5 \times 5; 125$
7. $0.2 \times 0.2 \times 0.2 \times 0.2; 0.0016$ **9.** $9 \times 9 \times 9 \times$

$9 \times 9 \times 9$; 531,441 **11.** $6 \times 6 \times 6 \times 6 \times 6$; 7,776
13. $8 \times 8 \times 8 \times 8$; 4,096 **15.** 0.6×0.6; 0.36
17a. 10, 100, 1,000, 10,000, 100,000; 2, 3, 4, 5
b. The number of zeros is the same as the
exponent. **c.** 1,000,000,000,000 **19.** Answers
may vary. Sample: 4^3, 6^2 **21.** C **23.** A **25.** 512
27. −2,401 **29.** −3,125 **31.** 256 **33.** 18 **35.** 66
37. 13 **39.** −64 **41.** 65 **43a.** $(7 - 9)$; 4 **b.** 16

MIXED REVIEW **45.** −43 **47.** 1 **49.** >
51. 1,750,000

Toolbox   *page 159*

1. 2, 3, 4, 9 **3.** 2, 3, 5, 10 **5.** 3, 5 **7.** 2, 3, 4, 8
9. 2, 3, 4, 8 **11.** 3, 9 **13.** 5 **15.** 2, 3, 4, 8, 9
17. 3, 5, 9 **19a.** 6

Lesson 4-5   *pages 160–163*

ON YOUR OWN **1.** composite **3.** composite
5. composite **7.** 2, 3, 5, 7, 11, 13, 17, 19, 23, 29,
31, 37, 41, 43, 47 **9.** 2^6 **11.** $3 \cdot 37$ **13.** $2^2 \cdot 13$
15. $2^2 \cdot 3 \cdot 11$ **17.** $2^2 \cdot 3 \cdot 5$ **19.** $5^2 \cdot 3$
21. $2n$ is composite unless $n = 1$. Since 2 is a factor
of $2n$, it is not prime. **23.** 15 **25.** 25 **27.** 11 **29.** 2
31. 16 **33.** 7 **35a.** 6; GCF **b.** 72; LCM **37.** No

MIXED REVIEW **39.** 21 **41.** −45

CHECKPOINT **7.** D **8.** 75 **9.** 76 **10.** 36 **11.** 16
12. −125 **13.** −81 **14.** composite, composite; 3
15. composite, prime; 11 **16.** composite, prime; 3
17. composite, composite; 2 **18.** composite,
composite; 9 **19.** prime, composite; 3

Lesson 4-6   *pages 164–167*

ON YOUR OWN **1.** $\frac{3}{4}$ **3.** $\frac{5}{6}$ **5.** $\frac{11}{13}$ **7.** $\frac{4}{7}$ **9.** $\frac{3}{5}$
11. $\frac{3}{5}$ **13.** $\frac{9}{16}$ **15.** school $\frac{7}{24}$, delivering papers $\frac{1}{24}$,
homework $\frac{1}{12}$, reading or talking on the phone $\frac{1}{8}$,
sleep $\frac{1}{3}$ **17.** 21; $\frac{2}{3}$ **19.** 3; $\frac{4}{25}$ **21.** 15; $\frac{1}{7}$ **23.** 4; $\frac{7}{24}$
25. 12; $\frac{9}{10}$ **27.** 25; $\frac{5}{8}$ **29.** 5; $\frac{7}{19}$ **31.** 6; $\frac{3}{8}$
33. 17; $\frac{1}{3}$ **35.** B **37.** Asia $\frac{121}{200}$, Africa $\frac{16}{125}$,
Europe $\frac{63}{500}$, Latin America $\frac{21}{250}$, North America $\frac{13}{250}$,
Australia and New Zealand $\frac{1}{200}$

MIXED REVIEW **45.** 49 **47.** 31 **49.** 8 **51.** $3.\overline{6}$
53. $6.1\overline{6}$ **55.** in 60 months

Lesson 4-7   *pages 168–170*

ON YOUR OWN **1a.** The sequence of ones digits

repeats the pattern 7, 9, 3, 1. **b.** 7 **3.** −1 **5.** 15
combinations **7.** 8 school days **9.** 6 minutes
11. **13.** 13 strawberries

MIXED REVIEW **17.** 6 **19.** −1 **21.** $9 **23.** 7

Problem Solving Practice   *page 171*

1. C **3.** A **5.** C **7.** D **9.** C

Lesson 4-8   *pages 172–175*

ON YOUR OWN **1.** $\frac{19}{8}$ **3.** $\frac{13}{12}$ **5.** $\frac{10}{7}$ **7.** $\frac{17}{5}$ **9.** $\frac{17}{3}$
11. $\frac{22}{9}$ **13.** $\frac{39}{8}$ **15.** $\frac{59}{7}$ **17.** $\frac{43}{7}$ **21.** $2\frac{3}{8}$, $\frac{19}{8}$
23. $2\frac{5}{8}$, $\frac{21}{8}$ **25.** $5\frac{1}{3}$ **27.** $10\frac{1}{2}$ **29.** 4 **31.** 12 **33.** 6
35. $4\frac{1}{2}$ **37.** $4\frac{2}{5}$ **39.** $6\frac{3}{4}$ **41.** $4\frac{1}{2}$ **43.** 7 **45.** $3\frac{3}{4}$ h,
$\frac{15}{4}$ h **47.** C **49.** $\frac{95}{2}$, $47\frac{1}{2}$

MIXED REVIEW **51.** 13 **53.** −24 **55.** 21 in.

CHECKPOINT **1.** $\frac{3}{4}$ **2.** $\frac{2}{3}$ **3.** $\frac{2}{3}$ **4.** $\frac{9}{10}$ **5.** $\frac{2}{9}$ **6.** $\frac{7}{10}$
7. $4\frac{5}{6}$ **8.** $16\frac{2}{5}$ **9.** $\frac{37}{9}$ **10.** $\frac{19}{10}$ **11.** $2\frac{3}{4}$ **12.** $\frac{17}{6}$ **14.** 42

Lesson 4-9   *pages 176–180*

ON YOUR OWN **1.** 0.4 **3.** 0.15 **5.** $0.91\overline{6}$ **7.** 0.75
9. $0.41\overline{6}$ **11.** $0.1\overline{6}$ **13.** $0.\overline{75}$ **15.** 0.7 **17.** 0.9
19a. $\frac{3}{100}$ **b.** 0.03 **c.** $\frac{97}{100}$ **21.** C **25.** $\frac{3}{5}$ **27.** $\frac{33}{50}$
29. $3\frac{3}{4}$ **31.** $\frac{19}{100}$ **33.** $\frac{193}{200}$ **35.** $4\frac{61}{200}$ **37.** $\frac{13}{20}$
39. $1\frac{69}{100}$ **41.** $\frac{71}{125}$ **43.** $\frac{5}{9}$, 0.58, $\frac{7}{12}$, $\frac{2}{3}$, 0.67
45. $2\frac{63}{100}$, $\frac{263}{100}$

MIXED REVIEW **47.** $\frac{14}{5}$ **49.** $\frac{37}{12}$ **51.** $\frac{25}{11}$ **53.** 0.8
55. 10.2

Wrap Up   *pages 182–183*

1. $\frac{2}{5}$ **2.** $\frac{4}{7}$ **3.** $\frac{3}{4}$ **4.** $\frac{1}{4}$, $\frac{3}{8}$, $\frac{1}{2}$ **5.** $\frac{1}{6}$, $\frac{7}{12}$, $\frac{3}{4}$ **6.** $\frac{1}{3}$, $\frac{2}{5}$, $\frac{7}{15}$
7. $\frac{8}{20}$, $\frac{6}{10}$, $\frac{4}{5}$ **8.** $\frac{3}{4}$, $\frac{8}{10}$, $\frac{6}{7}$ **9.** $\frac{3}{5}$, $\frac{4}{6}$, $\frac{9}{12}$ **10.** B
11. $2 \times 2 \times 2$; 8 **12.** $-(3 \times 3 \times 3)$; −81
13. 6×6; 36 **14.** $0.2 \times 0.2 \times 0.2$; 0.008
15. 0.12×0.12; 0.0144 **16.** $-3 \times -3 \times -3 \times -3$;
81 **17.** prime; $1 \cdot 73$ **18.** composite; $2 \cdot 5 \cdot 11$
19. composite; $2 \cdot 2 \cdot 2 \cdot 2$ **20.** composite; $3 \cdot 29$
21. composite; $11 \cdot 11$ **22.** composite; $2 \cdot 2 \cdot 7$

23. $\frac{1}{2}$　**24.** $\frac{1}{4}$　**25.** $\frac{3}{4}$　**26.** $\frac{2}{5}$　**27.** $\frac{8}{9}$　**28.** $\frac{7}{12}$　$\frac{1}{12}$

29. 210 boxes　**30.** $\frac{37}{8}$　**31.** $4\frac{3}{5}$　**32.** $\frac{52}{9}$　**33.** $\frac{11}{3}$

34. $1\frac{7}{8}$　**35.** $4\frac{2}{3}$　**37.** $\frac{1}{20}$　**38.** 0.75　**39.** $\frac{6}{25}$

40. 0.875　**41.** $2\frac{24}{25}$　**42.** $0.8\overline{3}$

CUMULATIVE REVIEW　**1.** D　**3.** C　**5.** D　**7.** D
9. B　**11.** C

CHAPTER 5

ON YOUR OWN　**1.** $\frac{1}{2}$　**3.** 5　**5.** 3　**7.** 5　**9.** 2

11. 2 tons　**13.** $\frac{1}{2}$ ton　**15.** 8　**17.** 3　**19.** 21　**21.** 9

23. 18　**27.** 2　**29.** 2　**31.** 25　**33.** 1　**35.** 60

37. $\frac{1}{2}$　**39.** 0　**41.** 1　**43.** No; $2\frac{3}{4}$ is almost 3, so the triple recipe will use almost 9 c of flour.　**45.** C

MIXED REVIEW　**47.** 0.91　**49.** 2,001　**51.** Positive trend; as people grow older, they grow taller. After you stop growing, the height remains the same.　**53.** Positive trend; you are likely to get better income with greater experience.

1. $\frac{4}{5} - \frac{2}{5} = \frac{2}{5}$　**3.** $\frac{3}{4}$　**5.** $\frac{1}{5}$　**7.** $\frac{9}{10}$　**9.** $\frac{3}{10}$　**11.** $\frac{4}{3}$　**13.** $\frac{1}{2}$

ON YOUR OWN　**1.** $\frac{5}{7}$　**3.** $1\frac{1}{6}$　**5.** $1\frac{5}{8}$　**7.** $1\frac{3}{10}$

9. $1\frac{3}{4}$　**11a.** $\frac{7}{12}$　**b.** yes; $\frac{7}{12} > \frac{1}{2}$　**13.** No; $\frac{1}{2} + \frac{2}{3} + \frac{3}{4} = 1\frac{11}{12}$, so 2 c is enough.　**15.** $\frac{3}{5}$　**17.** $\frac{1}{2}$　**19.** $\frac{5}{12}$

21. $\frac{1}{6}$　**23.** $\frac{5}{12}$　**25. a.** your friend; $\frac{2}{15}$ mi

b. Subtraction; to find the difference of the distances, you subtract.　**27.** $\frac{7}{12}$　**29.** $\frac{1}{12}$　**31.** $1\frac{7}{12}$

33. $\frac{3}{8}$　**35.** $\frac{5}{12}$　**37.** $1\frac{7}{20}$　**39.** $\frac{23}{40}$　**41.** $\frac{9}{20}$ mi

43. positive; $\frac{2}{3} < \frac{5}{6}$　**45.** negative; $\frac{7}{8} > \frac{3}{4}$

47a. 7 ⊡ 8 ⊟ 3 ⊡ 5 ⊟　**b.** 0.275

MIXED REVIEW　**49.** -7　**51.** -65　**53.** 37　**55.** 38

ON YOUR OWN　**1.** $8\frac{1}{5}$　**3.** $18\frac{5}{6}$　**5.** $11\frac{1}{3}$　**7.** $14\frac{8}{9}$

9. $21\frac{1}{8}$　**11.** $3\frac{3}{4}$ in.; $7\frac{1}{2}$ in.　**13.** $4\frac{3}{5}$　**15.** $6\frac{1}{2}$　**17.** $7\frac{3}{8}$

19. $8\frac{4}{5}$　**21.** $5\frac{5}{6}$　**23.** $14\frac{7}{8}$ in.　**25.** $2\frac{4}{5}$　**27.** $3\frac{5}{6}$

29. $7\frac{1}{12}$　**31.** $9\frac{1}{6}$　**33.** $8\frac{3}{8}$　**35.** $14\frac{2}{5}$　**37.** $13\frac{17}{20}$

39. $16\frac{3}{40}$　**41.** $6\frac{11}{15}$　**43.** $\frac{53}{60}$　**45.** $2\frac{7}{16}$ in.

47a. ⊏ 4 ⊞ 1 ÷ 8 ⊐ ⊟ ⊏ 1 ⊞ 3 ÷ 4 ⊐ ⊟　**b.** 2.375

MIXED REVIEW　**49.** $2^3 \times 13$　**51.** $2 \times 5 \times 7$
53. 0.4, 0.43, 0.431, 0.438　**55.** 75.09, 75.3, 75.98

ON YOUR OWN　**1.** $x - \frac{3}{4} = \frac{1}{12}; \frac{5}{6}$　**3.** $2\frac{3}{8}$　**5.** $\frac{7}{12}$

7. $d - 1\frac{3}{4} = 10\frac{1}{3}; 12\frac{1}{12}$ ft　**9.** $\frac{1}{8}$　**11.** $7\frac{1}{3}$

13a. $51\frac{1}{2} + h = 52\frac{1}{4}$　**b.** $\frac{3}{4}$ in.　**15.** $1\frac{1}{24}$　**17.** $3\frac{5}{8}$

19. $2\frac{1}{8}$　**21.** $\frac{8}{9}$　**23.** 0　**25.** $7\frac{1}{3}$　**27.** $\frac{1}{2}$　**29.** 0

31. $3\frac{2}{9}$　**33.** $\frac{5}{9}$　**35.** $b + 3\frac{3}{4} = 5\frac{1}{4}; 1\frac{1}{2}$ ft

37. $\frac{1}{4} + r = \frac{2}{3}; \frac{5}{12}$ of trash

MIXED REVIEW　**41.** 24　**43.** -13　**45.** 27

CHECKPOINT　**1.** 1　**2.** $\frac{1}{2}$　**3.** 3　**4.** 24　**5.** 32

6. $1\frac{5}{8}$　**7.** $\frac{1}{24}$　**8.** $\frac{13}{24}$　**9.** $\frac{13}{18}$　**10.** $\frac{2}{3}$　**11.** $4\frac{1}{14}$

12. $4\frac{7}{15}$　**13.** $5\frac{7}{8}$　**14.** $5\frac{11}{15}$　**15.** $13\frac{1}{8}$　**16.** $\frac{1}{2} + \frac{1}{4} = \frac{3}{4}$

17. $\frac{1}{3} - \frac{1}{4} = \frac{1}{12}$　**18.** $\frac{1}{2} + \frac{2}{5} = \frac{9}{10}$　**19.** $1\frac{1}{8}$

20. $1\frac{7}{15}$　**21.** $1\frac{4}{5}$　**22.** $18\frac{7}{8}$　**23.** $\frac{1}{10}$　**24.** $\frac{5}{24}$　**25.** $7\frac{17}{20}$

26. $10\frac{2}{15}$

ON YOUR OWN　**1.** $\frac{3}{8} \cdot \frac{2}{3} = \frac{6}{24}$　**3.** $\frac{5}{6} \cdot \frac{3}{4} = \frac{15}{24}$

5. $\frac{3}{20}$　**7.** $\frac{5}{18}$　**9.** $\frac{7}{10}$　**11.** 4　**13.** $1\frac{1}{8}$　**15.** $\frac{4}{25}$　**17.** 15

19. $\frac{3}{8}$　**21.** 18　**23a.** 140,000,000 mi^2

b. 12,000,000 mi^2　**25.** $7\frac{1}{8}$　**27.** 18　**29.** $7\frac{1}{3}$　**31.** $\frac{4}{5}$

33. $\frac{2}{5}$　**35.** $3\frac{1}{8}$　**37.** $11\frac{5}{8}$　**39.** 1　**41.** $34\frac{2}{9}$ yd^2

43. ⊏ 1 ⊞ 1 ÷ 4 ⊐ ⊠ ⊏ 3 ⊞ 1 ÷ 5 ⊐ ⊟
45. $34\frac{1}{2}$ lb

MIXED REVIEW　**47.** 76　**49.** 270　**51.** 400

ON YOUR OWN　**1.** $\frac{4}{3}$　**3.** 7　**5.** $\frac{6}{13}$　**7.** 16　**9.** 18

11. 3　**13.** 20　**15.** $\frac{1}{3}$　**17.** $1\frac{1}{4}$　**19.** $\frac{5}{8}$　**21.** 54

25. $\frac{1}{4}$　**27.** $3\frac{4}{5}$　**29.** $\frac{12}{23}$　**31.** $\frac{8}{49}$　**33.** $\frac{12}{23}$　**35.** $1\frac{1}{2}$

37. $1\frac{23}{27}$　**39.** 32 mi　**41.** ⊏ 13 ⊞ 7 ÷ 8 ⊐ ÷
⊏ 6 ⊞ 1 ÷ 6 ⊐ ⊟; 2.25

MIXED REVIEW　**43.** 0.375　**45.** $2.\overline{6}$　**47.** $0.291\overline{6}$

49. $\frac{5}{8}$　**51.** $2\frac{19}{50}$　**53.** $4\frac{61}{200}$

1. $17\frac{9}{10}$ **3.** $20\frac{1}{20}$ **5.** $3\frac{1}{46}$ **7.** $78\frac{7}{12}$ **9.** $382\frac{31}{32}$

Lesson 5-7 pages 214–216

ON YOUR OWN **1a.** 6:15 P.M. **b.** 6:10 P.M. **3.** 14
5a. 132 tiles; 108 tiles **7.** $9.60 **9.** 7th year
11. $59

MIXED REVIEW **13.** $1\frac{1}{8}$ **15.** $9\frac{5}{24}$ **17.** 44.8
19. 1.4 **21.** 3.2 **23a.** $18.96 **b.** $6.32

Problem Solving Practice page 217

1. B **3.** B **5.** D **7.** A **9.** C

Lesson 5-8 pages 218–221

ON YOUR OWN **1.** multiply **3.** multiply **5.** $4\frac{1}{2}$
7. $\frac{1}{4}$ **9.** $4\frac{1}{4}$ lb **11.** $2\frac{5}{8}$ **13.** $4\frac{1}{2}$ **15.** 32 **17.** $2\frac{1}{4}$
19. $5\frac{1}{3}$ **21.** $1\frac{2}{5}$ **23.** $\frac{7}{8}$ **25.** $3\frac{1}{2}$ **27.** Yes; 1 gal = 16 c,
so 4 gal = 64 c. **31a.** about $6\frac{1}{4}$ mi **b.** about $\frac{3}{4}$ mi

MIXED REVIEW **33.** 41 **35.** 230 **37.** $3.85

CHECKPOINT **1.** $\frac{1}{2}$ **2.** $\frac{3}{4}$ **3.** $\frac{1}{8}$ **4.** $26\frac{11}{14}$ **5.** 34
6. 7:05 A.M. **7.** $2\frac{1}{3}$ **8.** 136 **9.** $3\frac{3}{4}$ **10.** $7\frac{2}{3}$

Lesson 5-9 pages 222–224

ON YOUR OWN **1.** 30 **3.** $18\frac{1}{2}$ **5.** $52\frac{1}{2}$ **7.** 8 mi/h
9. $2\frac{1}{4}$ **11.** $2\frac{2}{3}$ **13.** $1\frac{7}{8}$ **15.** 3 **17.** 36 **19a.** Ed's;
49 is about 50, so the solution is $\frac{50}{20} = 2\frac{1}{2}$. **b.** Carl
divided 20 by 50 instead of 50 by 20. **21.** $2\frac{2}{9}$
23. $\frac{1}{7}$ **25.** $4\frac{2}{7}$ **27.** 4 **29.** $\frac{1}{9}$ **31.** 4,290 **33.** 1,053
41. 13.7 times

MIXED REVIEW **45.** 17 **47.** 63 **49.** < **51.** =
53. >

Wrap Up pages 226–227

1. 1 **2.** 2 **3.** $\frac{1}{2}$ **4.** 30 **5.** 3 **6.** $1\frac{1}{5}$ **7.** $\frac{5}{8}$ **8.** $\frac{9}{10}$
9. $\frac{7}{16}$ **10.** $1\frac{5}{12}$ **11.** $3\frac{1}{12}$ **12.** $7\frac{2}{15}$ **13.** $15\frac{5}{12}$
14. $6\frac{11}{24}$ **15.** $\frac{7}{12}$ **16.** $1\frac{7}{8}$ **17.** $8\frac{1}{2}$ **18.** $1\frac{1}{10}$ **19.** $4\frac{19}{20}$
20. $1\frac{1}{10}$ **21.** $8\frac{7}{12}$ **22.** $7\frac{7}{12}$ **23.** $1\frac{9}{10}$ **24.** $\frac{3}{10}$ **25.** $\frac{1}{4}$
26. $\frac{9}{10}$ **27.** 9 **28.** $94\frac{23}{24}$ **29.** $\frac{1}{2}$ **30.** $\frac{1}{2}$ **31.** 6
32. $3\frac{3}{5}$ **33.** $\frac{5}{18}$ **34.** 6:00 A.M. **35.** $39.76 **36.** $2\frac{1}{2}$
37. $3\frac{3}{8}$ **38.** 60 **39.** 28 **40.** $4\frac{2}{3}$ **41.** 7,500 **42.** $2\frac{1}{4}$

---

43. $6\frac{1}{2}$ **44.** 50 **45.** $\frac{1}{4}$ **46.** $3\frac{3}{5}$ **47.** $1\frac{1}{4}$ **48.** $3\frac{1}{2}$
49. 21 **50.** $6\frac{1}{2}$ **51.** $14\frac{1}{2}$ **52.** $\frac{5}{6}$ **53.** 4
54. $\frac{1}{5}s = 70$; 350 students

Cumulative Review page 229

1. C **3.** D **5.** B **7.** B **9.** A **11.** D

CHAPTER 6

Lesson 6-1 pages 232–236

ON YOUR OWN **1.** Sample: 1 : 4, 1 to 4, $\frac{1}{4}$
3. 12 to 4, $\frac{12}{4}$ **5.** 5 to 4, 5 : 4 **7.** 21 to 28, $\frac{21}{28}$ **9.** B
11a. 23 : 19, 23 to 19, $\frac{23}{19}$ **b.** 19 : 42, 19 to 42, $\frac{19}{42}$
13. 0.9 **15.** 2.7 **17.** 0.5 **19a.** 225 : 3, 455 : 7
b. 75, 65 **27.** 5 : 2 **29.** $\frac{1}{50}$ **31.** 1 : 2 **33.** 25 to 1
35a. 8 : 4 **b.** 10 qt antifreeze, 5 qt water

MIXED REVIEW **37.** 650 ÷ 50 = 13 **39.** 23 +
23 + 23 = 69 **41.** 45 **43.** −54 **45.** $28.50

Lesson 6-2 pages 237–240

ON YOUR OWN **1.** 300 mi/h **3.** $5.80/h
5. 4.3 m/s **7.** $3/yd **9.** $3.29/gal **11.** $2.50/m
13. $.95/oz **15.** $.14/min **17.** $.06/oz, $.05/oz;
50 fl oz **19.** $.04/oz, $.05/oz; 48 fl oz **21.** $.49/yd,
$.65/yd; 1 yd **23a.** 1 person/mi^2
25a. 10.35 m/s, 9.24 m/s, 7.90 m/s
27a. 64-oz bottle **b.** 12-oz bottle

MIXED REVIEW **29.** 4.88 **31.** 21.46 **33.** 1.00
35.
37.

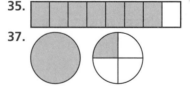

Lesson 6-3 pages 241–244

ON YOUR OWN **1.** yes **3.** no **5.** yes **7.** $\frac{27}{18} = \frac{9}{6}$
9. no **11.** 25 **13.** 3 **15.** $1.\overline{3}$ **17.** 28 **19.** 15
21. 19.2 **23.** 30.25 **25a.** 6 h
27. about 17,100,000 votes

MIXED REVIEW **31.** 5.1; 5 **33.** < **35.** = **37.** >

CHECKPOINT **7.** 152 **8.** 28 **9.** 12.5 **10.** 24
11. 5.3 **12.** 60 **13.** C **14.** 196 min

ON YOUR OWN   1. No; the sides are not proportional.   **3.** Not similar; number of sides is different.   **5.** Not similar; the ratios of the lengths of corresponding sides are not equal.   **9.** 2.8   **11.** 24.7   **13.** 99 cm

MIXED REVIEW   15. -14 **17.** -6 **19.** $\frac{11}{4}$ **21.** $\frac{13}{6}$ **23.** $\frac{25}{7}$

1. The triangle changes its shape and stays similar to $\triangle ABC$.   **3a.** Each line passes through a vertex of $\triangle ABC$ and its image.   **b.** Every line connecting a point and its image passes through D.

ON YOUR OWN   1. 60 km   **3.** 3.75 km   **5.** 6 km   **7.** 1 in.   **9.** $\frac{1}{4}$ in.   **11.** 0.075 in.   **13.** 1 in. : 1.2 mi   **17a.** 4.7 in.   **b.** 1 in. : 194.3 mi   **19.** 3 in.   **21.** 1 in. : 1,865 mi

MIXED REVIEW   23. 40, 32   **25.** 80   **27.** $1.45, $1.65

1. B   **3.** D   **5.** B   **7.** B   **9.** B

ON YOUR OWN   1. 64%   **3.** 45%   **5.** 80%   **7.** 10%   **9.** 50%   **11.** 100%   **13.** about 25%   **15.** about 25%

17. 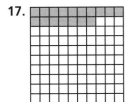   **19.**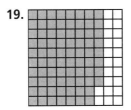

31. 60%   **33.** 84%   **35.** 35%   **37.** 80%   **39.** 30%   **41.** 20%   **43.** 87.5%   **45.** 40%   **47.** 14%   **49.** 0.6%   **51.** 176%

MIXED REVIEW   53. $4\frac{8}{9}$ **55.** $36\frac{13}{20}$ **57.** -4 **59.** 0   **61.** 42 matches

ON YOUR OWN   1. $\frac{9}{20}$ **3.** $\frac{9}{5}$ **5.** $\frac{3}{50}$ **7.** $\frac{3}{40}$ **9.** $\frac{1}{1000}$ **11.** $\frac{17}{20}$ **13.** B   **15.** 85%   **17.** 62.5%

19. 475%   **21.** 101%   **23.** 87.5%   **25.** 60%   **27.** 8%   **29.** 83.3%   **31.** No; 0.4% is 0.004, which is less than 0.4.   **33.** 0.32   **35.** 0.88   **37.** 3.45   **39.** 0.03   **41.** 0.12   **43.** 0.0009   **45.** 50%   **47.** 0.28%   **49.** 0.33%   **51.** 37.5%   **53.** 98.7%   **55.** 0.9%   **57.** 1,000%   **59.** 6,780%   **61a.** $\frac{1}{10}$, 0.1; $\frac{3}{20}$, 0.15; $\frac{1}{25}$, 0.04; $\frac{1}{50}$, 0.02; $\frac{3}{100}$, 0.03   **b.** 25 servings

MIXED REVIEW   63. 1,225   **65.** 3,250   **67.** 75   **69.** 6   **71.** -4.5 **73.** 2

ON YOUR OWN   1a. 10   **b.** 8 ft $\times$ 12 ft or 4 ft $\times$ 16 ft   **3.** 91   **5.** 36   **7.** $1\frac{7}{8}$c   **9a.** 1 3 5 7 9 11   **b.** 21; 45   **c.** 16; 100   **d.** The sum is the square of the row number.   **11.** Alvin is the conductor, Breon is the banker, and Carl is the artist.

MIXED REVIEW   13. $\frac{1}{6}$ **15.** $6\frac{3}{7}$ **17.** 6   **19.** 2 : 11, 2 to 11, $\frac{2}{11}$ **21a.** 2   **b.** 7

ON YOUR OWN   1. 5.4   **3.** 7   **5.** 180   **7.** 0.36   **9.** 21   **11.** 13.31   **13.** 63.7   **15.** 6.75   **17.** 2   **19.** 23.75   **21.** 4   **23.** 3.96   **25a.** $\frac{500}{100} \times 63,000$ **b.** 315,000   **27a.** 35 students; 23.3%   **b.** French, 23.3%; German, 11.3%; Spanish, 45.3%   **c.** French, 583; German, 283; Spanish, 1,133   **29.** D   **31.** $2.49   **33.** the calico fabric; $.21 per yd

MIXED REVIEW   37. $\frac{4}{5}$ **39.** $\frac{1}{20}$ **41.** $\frac{1}{7}$ **43.** $6\frac{1}{4}$ **45.** 44   **47.** $48

CHECKPOINT   1. 80%   **2.** 0.4%   **3.** $33\frac{1}{3}$%   **4.** 56%   **5.** 52%   **6.** 20%   **7.** 0.17, $\frac{17}{100}$ **8.** 0.29, $\frac{29}{100}$ **9.** 1.35, $1\frac{7}{20}$ **10.** 0.77, $\frac{77}{100}$ **11.** 0.98, $\frac{49}{50}$ **12.** 0.45, $\frac{9}{20}$ **13.** 16.82   **14.** 171%   **15.** 14.4   **16.** 10, 6   **17.** 52.5 mi   **18.** 35%

ON YOUR OWN   1. $\frac{n}{100} = \frac{12}{15}$; $n = 80$ **3.** $\frac{75}{100} = \frac{6}{n}$; $n = 8$ **5.** A   **7.** 10%   **9.** $33\frac{1}{3}$%   **11.** 125%   **13.** 40%   **15.** 7%   **17.** A   **19.** $\frac{225}{100} = \frac{n}{48}$, 108   **21.** $\frac{80}{100} = \frac{15}{n}$, 18.75   **23.** $\frac{12}{100} = \frac{42}{n}$, 350   **25.** 459 students   **27a.** 6.25%   **b.** $479.95

MIXED REVIEW **29.** $6\frac{3}{10}$ **31.** about 68,000,000
33. 4 mi

1. $2.25 **3.** $3.00

ON YOUR OWN **1.** 25% **3.** 100% **5.** 133.3%
7. 425% **9.** 4.2% **11.** 300% **13.** 25% **15.** 85.2%
17. 44.5% **19.** 16.5% **21.** 2% **23.** 66.7% **25.**
37.5% **27.** 52% **29.** 40% **31.** 77.8% **33.** 35.7%
35. 10% **37.** 41.8% **39.** 20.1% **41.** 10% decrease
43. 13.2% increase **45.** 15.4% increase **47.** 30%
decrease **49.** 23.6% increase **51.** 25.9% decrease
53. 27.6% decrease **55.** 46.7% decrease

MIXED REVIEW **59.** 0 **61.** -7 **63.** 0.2 **65.** $0.1\overline{6}$
67. $0.\overline{6}$ **69.** $2.35/lb

1. 44 : 101, 44 to 101, $\frac{44}{101}$ **2.** $.28/oz, $.31/oz;
10 oz box **3.** 12 **4.** 25 **5.** 3 **6.** 136 **7.** 4
8a. $\frac{5}{3} = \frac{n}{250,000}$; 416,667 board feet **b.** $\frac{3}{250,000} = \frac{8}{n}$;
666,667 board feet **9.** 45 **10.** 45, 36 **11.** 4,000 mi
12. 0.75 in. **13.** 37.5% **14.** 0.018 **15.** $\frac{5}{8}$
16. $\frac{x}{100} = \frac{28}{40}$; 70% **17.** $\frac{38}{x} = \frac{80}{100}$; 47.5 **18.** $\frac{60}{100} = \frac{x}{420}$; 252 **19.** $\frac{80}{100} = \frac{x}{15}$; 12 **20.** $\frac{54}{x} = \frac{75}{100}$; 72
21. $\frac{36}{180} = \frac{x}{100}$; 20% **22.** $300 **23.** D **24.** 17%
decrease **25.** 20% increase **26.** 15% increase
28. 32.5% decrease **29.** 31% decrease

1. D **3.** B **5.** C **7.** A **9.** C **11.** D **13.** C
15. B

CHAPTER 7

ON YOUR OWN **1a.**

b. 20 × 20 square array of dots **3.** C

MIXED REVIEW **7.** $\frac{2}{5}$ **9.** $\frac{3}{7}$ **11.** $\frac{4}{5}$
13. 9% increase **15.** 8% increase

ON YOUR OWN **1.** acute **3.** right **5.** 50°; acute
7. 130°; obtuse **9.** about 65° **11.**

13. **17.** $\angle ABF$, $\angle FBC$, $\angle CBG$,
$\angle ABG$ **23.** 165°

25. **27.** 75° **29.** reasonable
31. 140° **33a.** mammoth
b. elephant

MIXED REVIEW **35.** $\frac{1}{2}$ **37.** $\frac{22}{27}$ **39.** $\frac{2}{3}$

1. $m\angle 1 = 132°$, $m\angle 2 = 48°$, $m\angle 3 = 48°$, $m\angle 4 = 132°$, $m\angle 5 = 132°$, $m\angle 6 = 48°$, $m\angle 7 = 48°$,
$m\angle 8 = 132°$ **3.** $\angle 2$, $\angle 3$, $\angle 6$, $\angle 7$ **5.** $\angle 3$; $\angle 2$, $\angle 4$
7. $\angle 2$, $\angle 3$; $\angle 4$ **9.** $m\angle 1 = 122°$, $m\angle 2 = 58°$,
$m\angle 3 = 122°$

ON YOUR OWN **1.** isosceles; $\overline{XY}$, $\overline{YZ}$ **3.** scalene
5. right; $\angle Y$ is right. **7.** obtuse; $\angle B$ is obtuse.
9. equilateral triangle **11.** 80° **13.** 44° **15.** 60°
17. The two green triangles are scalene right
triangles. The other triangles are acute isosceles
triangles. **19a.** acute **b.** No; the angles of an
equilateral triangle are congruent. **c.** No; two
angles of an isosceles triangle are congruent.
d. Yes; since it is not equilateral or isosceles, it
must be scalene. **21.** 50°, 50° **23.** 59°, 62°

MIXED REVIEW **25.** 64 **27.** 49 **29.** 78,125
31. $1.\overline{6}$ **33.** $0.8\overline{3}$ **35.** 2.625

CHECKPOINT **1.**   **2.** acute **3.** obtuse
4. right **5.** straight
6. equilateral, acute
7. isosceles, obtuse
8. scalene, right

ON YOUR OWN **1.** 8:36 A.M.; he walks one block
in 4 min and has 3 blocks, or 12 min, to go at
8:24 A.M. **3a.** 84 toothpicks **b.** row 8

5. 225 tulip bulbs   **7.** Rosa plays piano, Alberto plays drums, and Vernesha plays guitar.
9. 6 angles; 3 obtuse angles   **11.** 13 triangles

MIXED REVIEW   **13.** $\frac{9}{2}$, or $4\frac{1}{2}$ **15.** $\frac{2}{3}$ **17.** 1
19. $2\frac{1}{2}$ **21.** bicycling

Lesson 7-5   pages 305–307

ON YOUR OWN   **1.** a and f, b and e, c and d
3. △FDE   **5a.** ∠C   **b.** ∠L   **c.** ∠K   **d.** $\overline{CL}$
e. $\overline{LK}$ **f.** $\overline{CK}$ **7.** $\overline{XY} \cong \overline{RB}$, $\overline{YZ} \cong \overline{BP}$, $\overline{XZ} \cong \overline{RP}$,
∠X ≅ ∠R, ∠Y ≅ ∠B, ∠Z ≅ ∠P   **9.** △DJK, △DKJ
11. D

MIXED REVIEW   **13.** 0.8   **15.** 0.$\overline{3}$ **17.** 1.5
19. $n + 15 = 45$; 30

Lesson 7-6   pages 308–312

ON YOUR OWN   **1.** hexagon; regular
3. quadrilateral; not regular   **5.** polygon,
quadrilateral, $\boxed{\text{parallelogram}}$ **7.** polygon,
quadrilateral, parallelogram, $\boxed{\text{rhombus}}$

9.    **11.**

21. Yes; a square is a rhombus and a rectangle.
25. trapezoid   **27.** rectangle; $\overline{AB} \cong \overline{DC}$, $\overline{BC} \cong \overline{AD}$,
∠A ≅ ∠B ≅ ∠C ≅ ∠D   **29.** $m\angle C = 65°$, $DC =$
6 cm   **31.** $XY = 4$ cm, $YZ = 4$ cm, $WZ = 4$ cm
33. No additional measures can be found.

MIXED REVIEW   **39.** composite; $3 \cdot 5$
41. composite; $3 \cdot 3 \cdot 37$ **43.** composite; $2 \cdot 73$

Toolbox   page 313

1a. The sum should be 540°.   **b.** 540°   **c.** 540°
5. It is always 720°.   **7.** The number of triangles that can be formed from one vertex is 2 less than the number of sides of the polygon.

Lesson 7-7   pages 314–317

ON YOUR OWN   **3.** $\overline{FH}$ **5.** $\overset{\frown}{FEH}$, $\overset{\frown}{FGH}$ **7.** $\overline{FH}$
9. radii: $\overline{OE}$, $\overline{OF}$, $\overline{OG}$, $\overline{OH}$; diameters: $\overline{EG}$, $\overline{FH}$;
chords: $\overline{EG}$, $\overline{FH}$, $\overline{FG}$ **11.** D   **13.** The triangle is right.

MIXED REVIEW   **15.** $5\frac{9}{14}$ **17.** $2\frac{7}{30}$ **19.** 10   **21.** 9
23. 5

Lesson 7-8   pages 318–322

ON YOUR OWN   **1b.** 18 yr; 23 states
3. 30 vehicles; you can have only a whole number of vehicles.   **5.** 108°, 45%   **7.** $\frac{3}{10}$, 18°,
144°   **9.** 90°   **11.** 108°   **13.** 45°
15a.

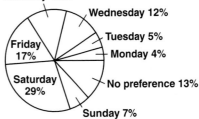

b. Monday: 48, Tuesday: 60, Wednesday: 144, Thursday: 156, Friday: 204, Saturday: 348, Sunday: 84, No preference: 156   **17a.** $12\frac{1}{2}\%$
b. 20%

MIXED REVIEW   **19.** 7%   **21.** 37.5%   **23.** 9.9%
25. $1\frac{1}{24}$ **27.** $8\frac{7}{16}$ **29.** $5\frac{1}{10}$ **31.** Lorissa, 4 tickets;
Melinda, 13 tickets

CHECKPOINT
1.   **2.**

5. 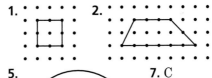   **7.** C

Lesson 7-9   pages 323–326

ON YOUR OWN   **1.** 8 in.   **3.** 5 ft   **5.** $1\frac{1}{2}$ in.
7. 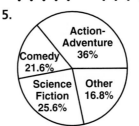   **9.** 132°

11.

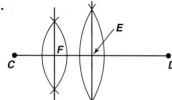

11a. $\overline{CE}$ and $\overline{ED}$ are half as long as $\overline{CD}$. **b.** $\overline{CF}$ and $\overline{FE}$ are $\frac{1}{4}$ as long as $\overline{CD}$.

22.

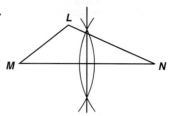

1. B   **3.** A   **5.** C   **7.** A   **9.** A   **11.** D   **13.** A

CHAPTER 8

13.

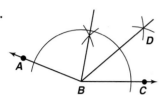

13a. $m\angle CBD = \frac{1}{4}m\angle ABC$
b. $m\angle ABD = \frac{3}{4}m\angle ABC$

15a–d.

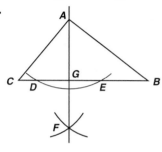

MIXED REVIEW

17.

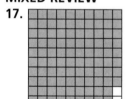

19.

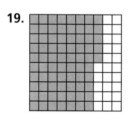

21. $12\frac{1}{2}$ h

Problem Solving Practice   **page 328**

1. B   **3.** C   **5.** C   **7.** A

Wrap Up   **pages 330–331**

1.

2. $\angle 1, \angle 4$ **3.** $\angle 1, \angle 2$ **6.** 23°; 113°
7a. 97°   **b.** obtuse   **8.** D   **9.** $\overline{UV} \cong \overline{YX}, \overline{VW} \cong \overline{XZ}, \overline{UW} \cong \overline{YZ}, \angle U \cong \angle Y,$
$\angle V \cong \angle X, \angle W \cong \angle Z$ **10.** Yes; if the largest angle is obtuse, the triangle is obtuse. If the largest angle is a right angle, the triangle is a right triangle. If the largest angle is acute, the triangle is acute.   **11.** 32° and 116°, 74° and 74°   **17.** $\widehat{ABC}$, $\widehat{ADC}$ **19.** ABCD   **21.**

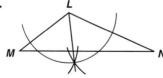

Lesson 8-1   **pages 336–339**

ON YOUR OWN   **1.** about 2 in.   **3.** about 5 cm
5. m   **7.** ft^2 or yd^2 **11.** about 9 times
MIXED REVIEW   **15.** 104   **17.** $\frac{13}{6}$, or $2\frac{1}{6}$ **19.** $11\frac{3}{4}$

Lesson 8-2   **pages 340–343**

ON YOUR OWN   **1.** 70 ft^2 **3.** 4 cm^2 **5.** 120 ft^2;
52 ft   **7.** 28.8 m^2; 27 m   **9.** 3 m^2; 8 m   **11.** 1.5 m^2, or 15,000 cm^2 **13a.** You multiply the area by n^2.
b. You multiply the perimeter by n.   **15.** 80 in.^{2};
42 in.   **17.** 161 in.^{2}; 62 in.   **19.** 46 cm

MIXED REVIEW   **21.** 68   **23.** 13   **25.** about 17% decrease   **27.** Whitney: 8 books; Lorena: 4 books; Amira: 1 book; Dominic: 5 books

Lesson 8-3   **pages 344–348**

ON YOUR OWN   **1.** 75 ft^2 **3.** 27.5 m^2
5. 24.96 mm^2 **7.** 15 m^2 **9.** 42.3 cm^2 **11.** D
13. 5 ft   **15.** 7.5 ft^2; 17.5 ft   **17.** 22 ft^2; 20 ft
19. 150 in.^{2}; 60 in.   **21.** $\frac{1}{2} \cdot 6(b + 3b) = 48$;
12 cm, 4 cm   **23.** 35.5 m^2; 23.8 m   **25.** 3,300 cm^2;
260 cm

MIXED REVIEW   **29.** obtuse   **31.** acute   **33.** $\frac{17}{20}$
35. $1\frac{2}{5}$ **37.** $\frac{1}{10}$

Lesson 8-4   **pages 349–353**

ON YOUR OWN   **1.** 44 cm   **3.** 28 m   **5.** 53 mm
7. 1,963 cm^2 **9.** 5,027 in.^{2} **11.** 6 cm; 3 cm^2
13. 36 in.; 108 in.^{2} **15a.** 98.52 m^2 **b.** 98.47 m^2
c. 99 m^2 **17.** 88 ft; 616 ft^2 **19.** 22 yd; $38\frac{1}{2}$ yd^2
21. $69\frac{1}{7}$ mm; $380\frac{2}{7}$ mm^2 **23.** 6.5 ft   **25.** 14.8 mm

27a. About 6.3 m; the differences are the same.
b. About 6.3 m forward; the outer lane is 6.3 m longer. **29.** 7.6 cm^2

MIXED REVIEW   31. 12.5%   **33.** -2 **35.** 5

CHECKPOINT   1. ft^2 **2.** 126 m^2; 54 m   **3.** 96 ft^2; 44 ft   **4.** 28 cm^2; 25.6 cm   **5.** 84 in.^{2}; 44 in.
6. 471 cm; 17,671 cm^2

Lesson 8-5	pages 354–357

ON YOUR OWN   1. 64   **3.** 225   **5.** 8,100   **7.** 196
9. 289   **11.** 8   **13.** 9   **15.** 12   **17.** 10   **19.** 4
21. 16   **23.** 70   **27.** 11 km   **29.** 13 ft   **31.** 30 in.
33. 20 cm   **35.** 90 ft   **37a.** $\frac{1}{4}$ **b.** $\frac{1}{2}$ **c.** $\frac{2}{3}$
39. 7 and 8   **41.** 11 and 12   **43.** 6 and 7
45. 14 and 15   **47.** 19 and 20   **49.** 52 ft

MIXED REVIEW   51. 15.75   **53.** 3.2   **55.** 51°

Problem Solving Practice	page 358

1. B   **3.** B   **5.** A   **7.** A   **9.** D

Lesson 8-6	pages 359–363

ON YOUR OWN   1. 12 ft   **3.** 15 in.   **5.** 12 ft
7. 10 ft   **9a.**   **b.** The lengths of the sides are 3, 4, and 5, and $3^2 + 4^2 = 5^2$. So the sides must form a right triangle.
11. no; $8^2 + 9^2 \neq 12^2$ **13.** no; $15^2 + 18^2 \neq 24^2$
15. yes; $28^2 + 45^2 = 53^2$ **17.** yes; $16^2 + 30^2 = 34^2$
19. 12 ft

MIXED REVIEW   23. Elicia

Lesson 8-7	pages 364–367

ON YOUR OWN   1. 19.7 cm   **3.** 13.2 cm   **5.** 6.8 cm
7. 13.6 m   **9.** 24.5 in.   **11.** 23.3 ft   **13a.** 20 units; 20 square units   **b.** rhombus   **15.** 65m
17. 10.7 cm, 16.6 cm   **19.** about 15 ft
21a. about 85 ft   **b.** about 127 ft   **c.** about 95 ft
d. 150 ft   **23.** 20.1 in.^{2}

MIXED REVIEW   25. $2^2 \cdot 7$ **27.** $2^3 \cdot 3^2$
29. $2^2 \cdot 3 \cdot 13$ **31.** >   **33.** >   **35.** 14 ft × 16 ft

Lesson 8-8	pages 368–371

ON YOUR OWN   1. rectangular prism
3. triangular prism   **5.** cone   **7.** pentagonal pyramid   **9.** $\overline{AD}, \overline{AE}, \overline{BC}, \overline{BF}$ **11.** $\overline{CG}, \overline{DH}, \overline{EH}, \overline{FG}$ **13.** cone and cylinder   **15.** cylinders and rectangular prisms

17.   **19.**

25. False; pyramids have only one base and prisms have two.

MIXED REVIEW   27. 13   **29.** -2 **31.** $\frac{43}{81}, \frac{5}{9}, \frac{7}{12}$
33. $\frac{10}{18}, \frac{4}{6}, \frac{18}{24}$ **35.** 5.55 in. by 9.25 in.

Toolbox	page 372

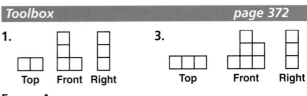

1. Top   Front   Right   **3.** Top   Front   Right

5.

Lesson 8-9	pages 373–376

ON YOUR OWN   1. B   **9.** 848 m^2 **11.** 121 ft^2
13. doubling the radius

MIXED REVIEW   15. m^2

Lesson 8-10	pages 377–380

ON YOUR OWN   1. 24 cm^3 **3.** $37\frac{13}{16}$ ft^3
5. 330 ft^3 **9.** about 1,900.7 ft^3 **11.** about 50 cm^3
13. 120 in.^{3} **15a.** 24 in.^{3}; 12 in.^{3} **b.** The area of the triangular base is 6 in.^{2}. The height is 2 in. So, 6 in.^{2} × 2 in. = 12 in.^{3}.

MIXED REVIEW   17. $4.00 for 1 CD   **19.** $1\frac{1}{3}$ c per loaf   **21.** $\frac{43}{20,000}$ **23.** $\frac{429}{1,000}$ **25.** $\frac{3}{1,000}$

CHECKPOINT   1. 15   **2.** 24.5 cm   **3.** 8.5 in.
4. 280 ft^2; 300 ft^3 **5.** 1,406.72 m^2; 4,019.2 m^3 **6.** C

Lesson 8-11	pages 381–383

ON YOUR OWN   1. 7, 21   **3.** 6.25, 12.5   **5.** 16¢
7. 1,080 cartons   **9.** 1 in. by 12 in.; 3 in. by 4 in.

MIXED REVIEW   13. 9 and 10   **15.** 7 and 8
17. 8 and 9   **19.** 9 in.

Toolbox	page 384

1a. 8 unit cubes   **b.** 24 unit cube sides
5a. 1,000 unit cubes   **b.** 2,197 cubes; 1,014 cubes;

156 cubes; 8 cubes **c.** 14 unit cubes

Wrap Up   pages 386–387

1. ft^2 **2.** 44 ft; 96 ft^2 **3.** 144 in.; 864 in.^{2}
4. 84 m; 315 m^2 **5.** 140 m; 900 m^2 **6.** 38 cm; 113 cm^2
7. 50 in.; 201 in.^{2} **8.** 126 ft; 1,257 ft^2 **9.** 57 mm;
254 mm^2 **10.** 121 **11.** 49 **12.** 4 **13.** 8 **14.** 12
15. 20 **16.** 9 and 10 **17.** B **18.** 9 mm
19. 1.4 m **20.** 11.5 in. **21a.**

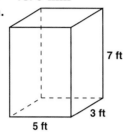

7 ft
3 ft
5 ft

b. 105 ft^3 **c.** 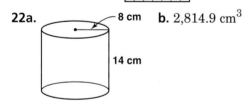 **d.** 142 ft^2

22a.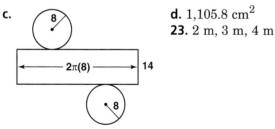

8 cm
14 cm

b. 2,814.9 cm^3

c.

8
2π(8)   14
8

d. 1,105.8 cm^2
23. 2 m, 3 m, 4 m

Cumulative Review   page 389

1. A 3. B 5. A 7. B 9. A 11. B

Lesson 9-1   pages 392–396

ON YOUR OWN **1.** $\frac{4}{13}$ **3.** $\frac{3}{26}$ **5.** 0 **7.** 12%
9. 20% **11.** 72% **13a.** 13.$\overline{3}$% **c.** 2,081 wrenches
15a. $\frac{1}{2}$ or 50% **b.** 6 free throws **c.** No; probability
cannot predict exact outcomes. **17.** A **19.** B
21. B

MIXED REVIEW **25.** 429 cm^2 **27.** 120 ft^2 **29.** 16
31. 6 **33.** −69

Toolbox   page 397

1. $\frac{1}{5}$ or 20%

Lesson 9-2   pages 398–400

ON YOUR OWN **3.** $6,594 **7.** No; the discount is
30% of a greater amount than the mark up.

MIXED REVIEW **9.** 25.13 in.; 50.27 in.^{2}
11. 56.55 ft; 254.47 ft^2 **13.** 70 words/min
15. $8.50/h

Lesson 9-3   pages 401–405

ON YOUR OWN **1.** theoretical probability
3. experimental probability **5.** $\frac{1}{6}$ **7.** $\frac{1}{3}$ **9.** 1
11. $\frac{1}{10}$; 0.1; 10% **13.** 1; 1; 100% **15.** $\frac{2}{5}$; 0.4; 40%
17. 1% **19.** 11% **21.** 50% **23.** 6% **25.** 35%
27. $\frac{3}{4}$ **31a.** $\frac{2}{7}$ **b.** $\frac{5}{7}$ **c.** 1 **d.** 1 **33a.** $\frac{6}{13}$
b. "red or blue" **35.** 0.3 **37.** 0.8 **39.** 1 **43.** D
MIXED REVIEW **45.** 54° **47.** 34.2° **49.** 176.4°
51. 0.48 **53.** 0.61 **55.** 0.063

Toolbox   page 406

1. 19 to 1 **3.** 1 to 25; 25 to 1 **5a.** 1 to 199 **b.** $\frac{1}{200}$
or 0.5%

Lesson 9-4   pages 407–411

ON YOUR OWN **1.** H1, H2, H3, H4, T1, T2, T3,
T4 **3.** s1p1, s1p2, s1p3, s2p1, s2p2, s2p3
5. 12 outcomes **7.** 32 **9.** 84 **11.** 24 **13.** 60
15. S punch, M punch, L punch, J punch, S
lemonade, M lemonade, L lemonade, J lemonade
17. 24 orders **19.** $\frac{1}{72}$ **21a.** 7 people **b.** 6 people;
5 people **c.** 210 ways

MIXED REVIEW   **23.** 90   **25.** 17   **27.** 14   **29.** obtuse
31a. 54 million cans   **b.** about 1.7 million lb
CHECKPOINT   **1.** $\frac{4}{5}$; 0.8; 80%   **2.** $\frac{2}{5}$; 0.4; 40%
3. $\frac{3}{5}$; 0.6; 60%   **4.** 0; 0; 0%   **5.** $\frac{1}{5}$; 0.2; 20%

6. 1; 1; 100%   **7.** D
8a.

	A	B	C	D
1	1A	1B	1C	1D
2	2A	2B	2C	2D
3	3A	3B	3C	3D
4	4A	4B	4C	4D
5	5A	5B	5C	5D
6	6A	6B	6C	6D

b. 24 seats; yes

Lesson 9-5   *pages 412–415*

ON YOUR OWN   **1.** $\frac{1}{12}$ **3.** $\frac{1}{4}$ **5.** $\frac{1}{36}$ **7.** $\frac{1}{64}$ **9.** $\frac{5}{64}$
11. $\frac{3}{64}$ **13.** No; the probability does not double.
The probability is $\frac{1}{8} \cdot \frac{1}{8} = \frac{1}{64}$.   **15.** $\frac{3}{28}$ **17a.** $\frac{7}{22}$
b. $\frac{5}{33}$ **c.** No; each girl has $\frac{1}{5}$ chance of being
selected. Each boy has $\frac{1}{7}$ chance of being selected.
19. independent   **21.** dependent   **23.** $\frac{1}{400}$ **25.** $\frac{1}{380}$
27c. $\frac{1}{9}$
MIXED REVIEW   **29.** 28.3 yd   **31.** 9.4 cm   **33.** 28
35. $1\frac{2}{7}$ **37.** $\frac{1}{16}$

Lesson 9-6   *pages 416–418*

ON YOUR OWN   **1.** 120 permutations
3. 720 permutations   **5.** 12 permutations
7. 30 permuatations   **9.** 840 permutations
11. 360 permutations   **13.** 800 area codes
15a. 6, 10, 45; 6, 45, 10; 10, 6, 45; 10, 45, 6; 45, 6, 10;
45, 10, 6   **b.** 6 arrangements   **17b.** 4 words;
PETS, PEST, SEPT, STEP   **c.** $\frac{1}{6}$
MIXED REVIEW   **19.** triangle; no
21. quadrilateral; yes   **23.** $12\frac{1}{6}$ **25.** $\frac{17}{30}$ **27.** $27\frac{11}{60}$

Lesson 9-7   *pages 419–422*

ON YOUR OWN   **1.** 3   **3.** 15   **5.** BPR, BPW,
BRW, PRW   **7.** BE, BO, PE, PO, RE, RO, WE, WO
9. BEOPW, BEOPR, BEORW, BEPRW, BOPRW,
EOPRW   **11.** 24 combinations
13. 18 combinations   **15.** 66 ways
19. Combination; the order in the set is not
important.   **21.** Permutation; the order in the
photograph is important.

MIXED REVIEW   **23.** 6   **25.** 14   **27.** 135   **29.** 130
CHECKPOINT   **1.** $\frac{16}{121}$ **2.** $\frac{2}{55}$ **3.** $\frac{6}{55}$ **4.** 6; 3

5. 6; 1   **6.** 2; 1   **7.** 24; 1   **8.** 30; 15   **9.** 360; 15
10. 720 ways   **11.** 362,880 ways

Problem Solving Practice   *page 423*

1. A   **3.** B   **5.** D   **7.** E

Lesson 9-8   *pages 424–426*

ON YOUR OWN   **1.** about 1,823 deer   **3.** about
2,273 deer   **5.** about 2,110 deer   **7.** about 1,822
deer   **9.** about 2,345 deer   **11.** 0.644, 0.506, 0.533,
0.833, 0.764, 0.627, 0.778, 0.773, 0.627
13. 357 squirrels
MIXED REVIEW   **15.** $\frac{12}{125}$ **17.** $\frac{13}{50}$ **19.** $8\frac{1}{2}$ **21.** $\frac{9}{50}$
23. 70%

Wrap Up   *pages 428–429*

1. $\frac{1}{7}$ **2.** $\frac{2}{7}$ **3.** $\frac{6}{7}$ **4.** $\frac{5}{7}$ **5.** $\frac{6}{7}$ **6.** $\frac{2}{7}$ **7a.** $\frac{3}{10}$; $\frac{2}{5}$; $\frac{1}{10}$; $\frac{1}{5}$
b. 18 blue, 24 red, 6 yellow, and 12 green marbles

8a.

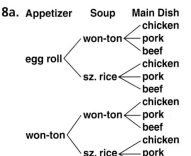

b. 12 dinners
9. 1,320 ways
10. dependent
11. independent
12. B   **13.** 5 teams
14. 24 ways
16. about 94 lions

Cumulative Review   *page 431*

1. B   **3.** C   **5.** C   **7.** B   **9.** C   **11.** D

CHAPTER 10

Lesson10-1   *pages 434–437*

ON YOUR OWN   **1.** Start with 5 and add 5
repeatedly; 25, 30, 35.   **3.** Start with 34 and add
−5 repeatedly; 14, 9, 4.   **5.** Start with 63 and add
−9 repeatedly; 27, 18, 9.   **7a.** 17 red tiles
b. 16 yellow tiles   **9.** 46 parts   **11.** Start with 1
and multiply by 2 repeatedly; 16, 32, 64.

13. Start with 600 and multiply by $\frac{1}{2}$ repeatedly;

$37\frac{1}{2}$, $18\frac{3}{4}$, $9\frac{3}{8}$. **15.** Start with $\frac{1}{4}$ and multiply by $\frac{1}{3}$ repeatedly; $\frac{1}{324}$, $\frac{1}{972}$, $\frac{1}{2,916}$. **17a.** 256 units^2
b. 128 units^2 **c.** 64 units^2 **d.** 8 units^2
19. neither; 37, 50, 65 **21.** neither; 36, 49, 64
23. neither; 16, 22, 29 **25b.** 1, 4, 9, 16, 25, 36, 49
c. The sum of the numbers in each row is the square of the row number. **d.** 400 **27a.** 2; 3; 5; 8; 13; 21; 34 **b.** neither

MIXED REVIEW **29.** -10 **31.** 8 **33.** obtuse
35. acute **37a.** $0.0115 per plate, $0.0588 per cup; $0.0099 per plate, about $0.048 per cup **b.** The supermarket has a better buy on each item.

Lesson10-2	pages 438–440

ON YOUR OWN **1.** 7.5×10^3 **3.** 1.25×10^2
5. 1.02×10^5 **7.** 4.9×10^{11} **9.** 3.5×10^5
11. 5.88×10^{15} **13.** Count the number of digits. Then subtract 1. **15.** The second factor must be a power of 10. **17.** The first factor must be greater than or equal to 1 but less than 10.
19. 500,000,000,000 **21.** 830,000 **23.** 9,300,000
25. 667.8 **27.** 20,000,000,000,000 cells
29. 600,000,000 bytes

MIXED REVIEW **31.** 12 permutations; 6 combinations **33.** 6 permutations; 3 combinations
35. 100% increase **37.** about 2% increase

Toolbox	page 441

1. 8×10^{-4} **3.** 6.91×10^{-6} **5.** 5.006×10^{-3}
7. 0.0049

Lesson10-3	pages 442–445

ON YOUR OWN **1.** 31 games **3.** 636 digits
5. 90°, 30°, 60° **7.** 11 amounts

MIXED REVIEW **9.** $13\frac{7}{8}$ **11.** $2\frac{1}{5}$ **13.** $9\frac{19}{30}$
15. 54 ft^3 **17.** 3 combinations

CHECKPOINT **1.** Arithmetic; start with 3 and add 3 repeatedly; 15, 18, 21. **2.** Arithmetic; start with 53 and add 128 repeatedly; 21, 13, 5.
3. Geometric; start with 3 and multiply by 2 repeatedly; 48, 96, 192. **4.** Arithmetic; start with 4 and add 7 repeatedly; 39, 46, 53. **5.** Neither; start with 87 and subtract 10, then subtract 11, then subtract 12 and continue the subtraction pattern; 41, 27, 12. **6.** Geometric; start with 0.5 and multiply by 3 repeatedly; 40.5, 121.5, 364.5.

7. 7.38×10^8 **8.** 2.9×10^4 **9.** 7.86×10^6
10. 1.807×10^6 **11.** 806,000 **12.** 1,740
13. 8,300,000,000 **14.** 10,080,000 **15.** D **16a.** 4
b. 145

Lesson10-4	pages 446–449

ON YOUR OWN **1.** $60 **3.** $847 **5.** $855
7. $590 **9.** $562.43 **11.** $2,316.99 **13.** $1,781.94
15. B

MIXED REVIEW **19.** 127 **21.** 1264 **23.** yes
25. no **27.** no **29.** 8 cm long and 4 cm wide

Lesson10-5	pages 450–453

ON YOUR OWN **1.** $s = 6.5h$ **3.** $h = 2w + 1$
5a.

Input	Output
−5	22
−4	14
−3	8
−2	4
−1	2
0	2
1	4
2	8
3	14
4	22
5	32

b. −5 and 4
7.

Input	Output
1	4
2	5
3	6
4	7
5	8

9.

Input	Output
1	0.5
2	1
3	1.5
4	2
5	2.5

11a. 40 mi/h **b.** 3 **c.**

Input	Output
1	40
2	80
3	120
4	160

d. $d = 40t$ **13.** A
15a.

Input p	Output c
$.50	$4.50
$1.00	$4.00
$1.50	$3.50
$2.00	$3.00
$2.50	$2.50
$3.00	$2.00
$3.50	$1.50
$4.00	$1.00
$4.50	$.50
$5.00	$.00

b.

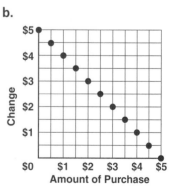

c. $c = 5 - p$ **17a.** $21

b.

Input t	Output d
1	$3.50
2	$7.00
3	$10.50
4	$14.00
5	$17.50

c.

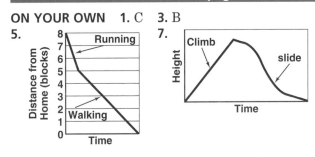

MIXED REVIEW **19.** 10,478.6 **21.** 0.497
23. 3.2605 **25.** > **27.** = **29.** January 8, 15, 22, 29

Lesson10-6 — pages 454–457

ON YOUR OWN 1. 13 **3.** 5 **5.** 8 **7.**

n	$f(n)$
0	2
1	3
2	4
3	5

9.

n	$f(n)$
0	0
1	4
2	8
3	12

11.

n	$f(n)$
0	9
1	8
2	7
3	6

13.

n	$f(n)$
0	1
1	3
2	5
3	7

15a.

n	$f(n)$
1	3
2	4
3	5
4	6

b. $f(n) = n + 2$
17. $f(n) = 5n$
19. $f(n) = n - 6$
21. $f(n) = -8n$
23. $f(n) = 4n + 5$

MIXED REVIEW **27.** 45.5% **29.** 925% **31.** 650%
33. 11.0 ft; 9.6 ft^2 **35.** 9.4 m; 7.1 m^2 **37.** 6.3 in.; 3.1 in.^{2}

CHECKPOINT **1.**

n	$f(n)$
0	0
1	3
2	6
3	9

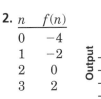

2.

n	$f(n)$
0	-4
1	-2
2	0
3	2

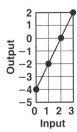

5. $f(n) = -12n$
6. $f(n) = 4 - n$
7. $f(n) = 3n + 1$
8. $f(n) = 7n$

Toolbox — page 458

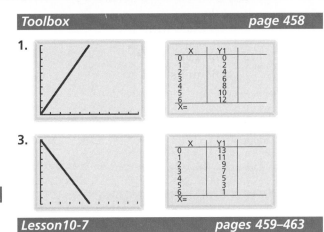

1.

X	Y1
0	0
1	2
2	4
3	6
4	8
5	10
6	12
X=	

3.

X	Y1
0	13
1	11
2	9
3	7
4	5
5	3
6	1
X=	

Lesson10-7 — pages 459–463

ON YOUR OWN **1.** C **3.** B
5.

[graph: Distance from Home (blocks) vs Time, labeled Running and Walking]

7.

[graph: Height vs Time, labeled Climb and slide]

9. A; B; graph A shows speed because it shows a quantity that is not changing with time. The quantity in graph B increases at a constant rate.
11b. about 1800 **13.** Carmen's graph

MIXED REVIEW **17.** 4 **19.** 144
21.

```
2 | 0
3 | 3 4 4
4 | 4 5 6 8 8
5 | 0 3

    5 | 0 means 50
```

23. 29 h

Problem Solving Practice — page 464

1. C **3.** D **5.** B **7.** D **9.** D

Wrap Up — pages 466–467

1. arithmetic; 23, 27, 31 **2.** geometric; 3, $\frac{3}{2}$, $\frac{3}{4}$

3. geometric; 243; 729; 2,187 **4.** neither; -2, -10, -19 **5.** Start with 7 and add 4 repeatedly; start with 48 and multiply by $\frac{1}{2}$ repeatedly; start with 3 and multiply by 3 repeatedly. **6.** A
7. 1.52×10^9 **8.** 2.5×10^5 **9.** 3.83×10^8
10. 8.76×10^4 **11.** 249,000,000 **12.** 110 triangles
13. $450 **14.** $720 **15.** $1,914.42
16a. $f(n) = 2n + 2$

b.

Output / Input graph

17a.

Input n	Output $f(n)$
0	3
2	4
4	5
6	6

b.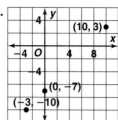

c. Yes; the solutions lie on one line.   **23.** C
25. $(-1, 2)$ **27.**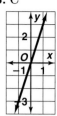

b. $f(n) = \frac{1}{2}n + 3$ **18.** 3; 5; 7; 9

Cumulative Review   **page 469**

1. D   **3.** B   **5.** D   **7.** D   **9.** A

CHAPTER 11

Lesson 11-1   **pages 472–476**

ON YOUR OWN   **1.** C   **3.** F   **5.** A   **7.** $(-3, -2)$
9. $(5, -4)$ **11.** $(2, 6)$ **13a.** 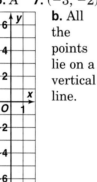   **b.** All the points lie on a vertical line.

15. Starting from the origin, move 5 units right. Then move 1 unit down.   **17.** B   **19.** I   **21.** III
23. II   **25.** I   **31.** I: (+ , +); II: (− , +);
III: (− , −); IV: (+ , −)

MIXED REVIEW   **33.** $270   **35.** $756

Lesson 11-2   **pages 477–481**

ON YOUR OWN   **7.** yes; $24 = (12) + 12$ **9.** yes;
$0 = (-12) + 12$ **11.** C   **13.** B, C   **15.** none
17. If you substitute -1 for x and -5 for y, the equality is not true.   **19.** line q

21a.

x	$x - 7$	y	(x,y)
0	$0 - 7$	-7	$(0, -7)$
-3	$-3 - 7$	-10	$(-3, -10)$
10	$10 - 7$	3	$(10, 3)$

b.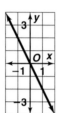

29.

35. The third point serves as a check that you graphed the first two points correctly.

37a.

b. $(0, 0)$
c. perpendicular

MIXED REVIEW   **39.** $f(x) = 25x + 35$ **41.** no
43. yes   **45.** 10 onions

Lesson 11-3   **pages 482–484**

ON YOUR OWN   **1.** $\frac{1}{2}$ **3.** $-\frac{1}{3}$ **5.** 1   **7.** -8
9. Kelton; Kenji thought the rise was positive.
11a. $12,000   **b.** -1 **c.** The car loses $1,000 in value each year.

MIXED REVIEW   **13.** arithmetic; 24, 29, 34
15. arithmetic; 34, 41, 48   **17.** II   **19.** I   **21.** II
23.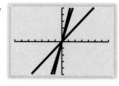

Toolbox   **page 485**

1a. $-\frac{3}{5}$ **b.** The value that multiplies x has the same value as the slope.
3a.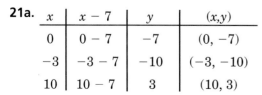

b. $y = 4x$; $y = x$
c. For lines with positive slopes, the greater the value of the slope, the steeper the graph of the line.

d. closer to the y-axis

7a. 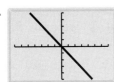 **b.** II and IV   **c.** yes

Toolbox	page 493

1. turn   **3.** flip

Lesson 11-4	pages 486–489

ON YOUR OWN

1.   **3.** 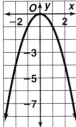   **9.** parabola
11. V-shape
13a. 16 ft;
64 ft; 144 ft
b. about 6.4 s

15b.   **c.** The graph of $y = -x^2$ is a reflection of the graph of $y = x^2$ in the x-axis.
17. A   **19.** F

MIXED REVIEW **21.** $\frac{1}{600}$ **23.** $\frac{156}{600}$ or $\frac{13}{50}$ **25.** yes;
$5 = 2(4) - 3$ **27.** no; $-5 \neq 2(0) - 3$ **29.** no;
$9 \neq 2(3) - 3$

CHECKPOINT **1.** B **2.** D **3.** G **4.** $(4, -1)$
5. $(-2, -3)$ **6.** $(2, 3)$ **7.** $(4, 0)$ **8.** C

9b. 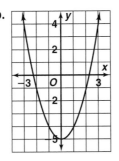   **c.** 1   **10b.**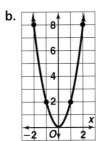

Lesson 11-5	pages 490–492

ON YOUR OWN   **1.** $42.9 = 5 + 2x$; $18.95
3. $17 = 5D - 3$; 4 mystery novels   **5.** $2.8 + 0.25n = 4.3$; 6 quarters   **7.** $30\frac{1}{3}$ yr; 35 yr   **9.** $\frac{1}{8}$

Lesson 11-6	pages 494–498

ON YOUR OWN   **1.** $(2, 1)$ **3.** 5 units left; 7 units down

5. 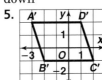 $A'(-3, 2), B'(-2, -1), C'(2, -1),$ $D'(1, 2)$

7a–b. 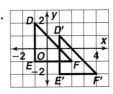   **c.** $D'(1, 1), E'(1, -2),$ $F'(4, -2)$ **9.** $S'(4, -1),$ $T'(0, -3)$ **11.** right 3 units, up 1 unit   **13.** right 2 units, down 3 units   **15.** 2; 1

17. $(x, y) \longrightarrow (x + 5, y + 4)$ **19.** $(x, y) \longrightarrow (x + 4, y + 2)$ **21.** $(x, y) \longrightarrow (x + 5, y - 2)$ **23.** $(x, y) \longrightarrow (x - 3, y - 4)$

MIXED REVIEW   **25.** 431,000   **27.** 8,596

29a.

x	-2	-1	0	1	2
y	8	2	0	2	8

b.

Lesson 11-7	pages 499–503

ON YOUR OWN

1.   **3.** none   **5.**

7. Three lines of symmetry, one down the center of each petal.   **11.** A, B **13.** It is not the same distance from the x-axis. **15.** $(5, 7)$ **17.** $(1, 1)$ **19.** $(5, -2)$ **21.** The image of a translation has the same orientation as the original figure, and the distance between any point and its image is the same. The image of a reflection faces in the opposite direction, and the farther away a point is from the line of reflection, the greater the distance between the point and its image. **23.** translation; $(x, y) \longrightarrow (x + 5, y + 3)$ **25.** reflection; x-axis

27a.

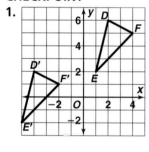

MIXED REVIEW **29.**

x	0	1	2	3
$f(x)$	32	35	38	41

31.

x	0	1	2	3
$f(x)$	6	5	4	3

33. always **35.** 2,000 black bears

CHECKPOINT

1.

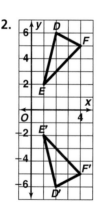

2.

3. Yes; the rise and run do not change when you translate a line, so the slope does not change. **5a.** $y = 2p - 10$ **b.** 40 pizzas

Problem Solving Practice page 504

1. D **3.** C **5.** B **7.** C **9.** C

Lesson 11-8 pages 505–508

ON YOUR OWN **1.** No; you cannot rotate the figure $180°$ or less so that the image fits on top of the original figure. **3.** Yes; the image after $180°$ or $90°$ rotation fits exactly on top of the original figure. **5.** No; you cannot rotate the figure $180°$ or

less so that the image fits on top of the original figure. **7.** Yes; the image after $72°$ rotation fits exactly on top of the original figure.

9.

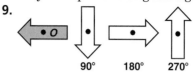

11.

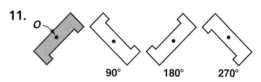

13. The figures in exercises 10 and 12 have rotational symmetry because each can be fit exactly on top of itself after a rotation of $180°$ or less. **15.** reflection **17.** rotation **19.** rotation

MIXED REVIEW **21.** 64 yd **23.** 34 mm

Wrap Up pages 510-511

1a. A **b.** G **c.** F **2a.** $(0, 2)$ **b.** $(-3, -2)$ **c.** $(-1, 0)$ **3a.** yes; $(10) = 3(5) - 5$ **b.** no; $(-1) \neq 3(-2) - 5$ **c.** yes; $(-2) = 3(1) - 5$

4b.

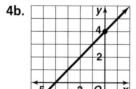

5. B

6.

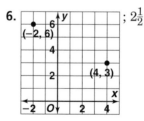

$; 2\frac{1}{2}$ **7.**

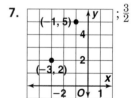

$; \frac{3}{2}$

10a.

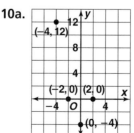

b. $y = x^2 - 4$; all four points lie on its graph. **11.** I; II **12.** $3.25

13.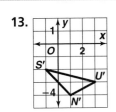

15. translation
16. reflection
17. reflection
18. rotation

1. D   **3.** A   **5.** B   **7.** B   **9.** B   **11.** C

EXTRA PRACTICE

CHAPTER 1   **3.** 11   **5.** D   **7.** 18   **9.** 61.33; 60; 60

CHAPTER 2   **1.** 0.092, 0.095, 0.099, 0.102
3. 0.505, 0.52, 0.55, 0.56   **5.** 0.699, 0.7, 0.708,
0.712   **7.** >   **9.** =   **11.** >   **13.** <   **15.** 2
17. \$27   **19.** \$60   **21.** 8.28   **23.** 9.107   **25.** 0.82
27. 4.02   **29.** 4.93   **31.** 16.032   **33.** 7.917
35. 29.607   **37.** $2.\overline{6}$ **39.** $3.1\overline{3}$ **41.** 6.3   **43.** $3.\overline{3}$
45. 7   **47.** 30.144   **49.** 10.92   **51.** 4

CHAPTER 3   **1.** $x - 3$ **3.** $2x - 5$ **5.** 12; 14; 16; 3;
5; 7   **7.** T   **9.** T   **11.** $-11, -1, 3, |-8|, |10|$
13. 6   **15.** 0   **17.** -100 **19.** -6 **21.** 18   **23.** 28
25. -7 **27.** -75 **29.** -3 **31.** 2   **33.** $51 = 3x,$
$x = 17$ **35.** 42   **37.** -4

CHAPTER 4   **1.** $\frac{4}{8}$ or $\frac{1}{2}$ **3.** $\frac{4}{12}$ or $\frac{1}{3}$ **5.** $\frac{7}{8}$ **7.** $\frac{2}{3}$
9. $\frac{1}{3}$ **11.** $\frac{1}{5}$ **13.** $\frac{22}{45}$ **15.** $\frac{1}{7}$ **17.** >   **19.** =   **21.** <
23. 125   **25.** 225   **27.** 64   **29.** 1   **31.** 17   **33.** 10
35. $\frac{26}{7}$ **37.** $\frac{22}{5}$ **39.** $\frac{12}{5}$ **41.** $4\frac{4}{5}$ **43.** $7\frac{1}{4}$ **45.** $6\frac{2}{9}$
47. $\frac{73}{200}$ **49.** $\frac{21}{50}$ **51.** $\frac{7}{10}$ **53.** $11.\overline{3}$ **55.** 3.25   **57.** $16.\overline{6}$

CHAPTER 5   **1.** 1   **3.** $\frac{1}{2}$ **5.** 4   **7.** 78   **9.** 2   **11.** $\frac{4}{3}$
13. $\frac{11}{15}$ **15.** $\frac{1}{2}$ **17.** $\frac{7}{24}$ **19.** $\frac{21}{20}$ **21.** 7   **23.** $5\frac{11}{12}$
25. $5\frac{5}{8}$ **27.** $7\frac{7}{8}$ **29.** $6\frac{1}{6}$ **31.** $\frac{3}{20}$ **33.** $\frac{1}{4}$ **35.** 25
37. $4\frac{1}{8}$ **39.** $16\frac{1}{8}$ **41.** 3   **43.** 1   **45.** $2\frac{2}{9}$ **47.** $1\frac{9}{10}$
49. $1\frac{7}{15}$ **51.** 12   **53.** 660   **55.** 12,250   **57.** $2\frac{1}{4}$
59. $\frac{3}{8}$ **61.** $\frac{11}{14}$ **63.** 152   **65.** 11

CHAPTER 6   **1.** 2 : 3, 2 to 3   **3.** 4 : 7, $\frac{4}{7}$ **5.** 25 : 50,
25 to 50   **7.** 48 oz   **9.** 10 lb   **11.** 3   **13.** 20   **15.** 25
17. 24   **19.** $\frac{1}{2}$ or 0.5   **21.** $x = \frac{5}{3}$ **23.** 83%   **25.** 220%
27. $\frac{16}{25}$, 0.64   **29.** 2,730%   **31.** 0.0975%   **33.** 10%
35. 135   **37.** 60%   **39.** 32.5   **41.** 60% increase
43. about 2% increase   **45.** 40% decrease

CHAPTER 7   **1.**   **3.** d   **5.** b   **7.** 90°   **9a.** T
b. F   **c.** T   **d.** T   **e.** F
11. regular pentagon

13. rectangle   **15.** 61.92°

CHAPTER 8   **1.** 180 ft, 1,400 ft^2 **3.** 40 m^2, 30 m
5. 6.875 cm^2, 13 cm   **7.** 900 mm^2, 146 mm   **9.** 1
11. 7   **13.** 30   **15.** 8 m   **17.** 8 cm   **19.** triangular
prism, 36 in.^{2} **21.** rectangular prism, 202 ft^2

CHAPTER 9   **1a.** $\frac{15}{300}$ **b.** 70   **3.** $\frac{5}{6}$ **5.** $\frac{1}{6}$
7b. $\frac{1}{12}$, $\frac{3}{12}$ or $\frac{1}{4}$ **9.** $\frac{5}{36}$ **11.** $\frac{3}{16}$ **13.** $\frac{2}{16}$
15. combination; 10 ways   **17.** 658

CHAPTER 10   **1.** arithmetic; 19, 22, 25   **3.** neither;
46, 23, 44   **5.** arithmetic; 15.7, 15.1, 14.5   **7.** 7 ×
10^4 **9.** 6.1 × 10^5 **11.** 2.2 × 10^3 **13.** 70,300
15. 25,600,000   **17.** 8,290.1   **19.** \$1,120.72
21. $f(n) = 6n$ **23.** $f(n) = 3n + 1$
25. 5, 6, 7, 8   **27.** 8, 7, 6, 5

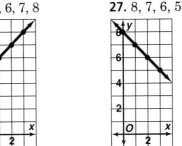

CHAPTER 11   **1.** G   **3.** L   **5.** (4, −1)   **7.** (−6, 1)
9. (3, 4)   **11.** $\frac{2}{3}$ **13.** yes; 2 + 18 = 20   **15.** no;
$36 + 18 \neq -18$

17.

x	y
−2	7
−1	4
0	3
1	4
2	7

19.

x	y
−2	4
−1	2
0	0
1	2
2	4

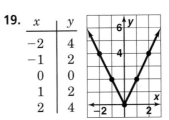

23a–b.

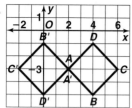

c. $(2, -3)$, $(0, -1)$, $(-2, -3)$, $(0, -5)$

SKILLS HANDBOOK

PAGE 528 **1.** > **3.** > **5.** < **7.** < **9.** > **11.** 3,347; 3,474; 3,734; 3,747; 3,774 **13.** 30,256,403; 30,265,403; 32,056,403; 302,056,403

PAGE 529 **1.** 40 **3.** 670 **5.** 7,030 **7.** 6,000 **9.** 44,000 **11.** 1,000 **13.** 6,000 **15.** 82,000 **17.** 35,000 **19.** 68,900 **21.** 3,407,000 **23.** 71,230,000 **25.** 400,000 **27.** 3,680 **29.** 69,000 **31.** 566,000 **33.** 1,400,000

PAGE 530 **1.** 444 **3.** 371 **5.** 392 **7.** 1,536 **9.** 1,350 **11.** 5,712 **13.** 2,520 **15.** 1,862 **17.** 9,214 **19.** 492 **21.** 729 **23.** 2,208 **25.** 884 **27.** 4,056 **29.** 2,478 **31.** 1,440 **33.** 5,467

PAGE 531 **1.** 15 R1 **3.** 12 R6 **5.** 13 R3 **7.** 217 R2 **9.** 25 R6 **11.** 7 R41 **13.** 7 R27 **15.** 3 R36 **17.** 5 R21 **19.** 3 R7 **21.** 14 R52 **23.** 37 R12 **25.** 21 R30 **27.** 7 R3 **29.** 11 R3 **31.** 64 R3 **33.** 50 R4 **35.** 103 R1 **37.** 26 R8 **39.** 7 R32 **41.** 5 R22 **43.** 6 R21 **45.** 3 R52 **47.** 15 R3 **49.** 22 R12

PAGE 532 **1.** tens **3.** ones **5.** ten-thousandths **7.** 3 tens **9.** 6 ones **11.** 1 ten-thousandths **13.** 6 hundredths **15.** 6 tenths **17.** 6 tens **19.** 6 thousands **21.** 6 tenths **23.** 6 hundredths **25.** 6 ten-thousandths **27.** 6 hundred-thousandths **29.** 3 hundredths **31.** 8 tenths

PAGE 533 **1.** 0.03 **3.** 6.02 **5.** 2.05 **7.** 0.000007 **9.** 0.011 **11.** 0.304 **13.** three million and nine hundredths **15.** nine hundred and two hundredths **17.** fifteen hundred-thousandths

PAGE 534 **1.** 2.8 **3.** 19.7 **5.** 499.5 **7.** 4.7 **9.** 400.0 **11.** 96.4 **13.** 31.72 **15.** 1.79 **17.** 736.94 **19.** 0.70 **21.** 12.10 **23.** 0.92 **25.** 0.439 **27.** 3.495 **29.** 0.601 **31.** 4 **33.** 80 **35.** 431

PAGE 535 **1.** 2.4 **3.** 0.28 **5.** 0.155 **7.** 18.6 **9.** 1.35 **11.** 249.6 **13.** 12.05 **15.** 12.15 **17.** 0.1 **19.** 0.302 **21.** 1.757 **23.** 18.012 **25.** 28.452 **27.** 535.5 **29.** 250.8 **31.** 24.96

PAGE 536 **1.** 0.06 **3.** 0.003 **5.** 0.014 **7.** 0.027 **9.** 0.004 **11.** 0.0025 **13.** 0.032 **15.** 0.0009 **17.** 0.04 **19.** 0.0007 **21.** 0.0074 **23.** 0.076 **25.** 0.085 **27.** 0.007 **29.** 0.027 **31.** 0.0102 **33.** 0.0603 **35.** 0.081 **37.** 0.0066

PAGE 537 **1.** 7.14 **3.** 0.776 **5.** 8.79 **7.** 0.11 **9.** 0.184 **11.** 7.4 **13.** 0.93 **15.** 8.76 **17.** 2.07 **19.** 0.0036 **21.** 0.0147 **23.** 6.123 **25.** 3.98 **27.** 0.561 **29.** 0.868

PAGE 538 **1.** 0.032 **3.** 0.07 **5.** 9 **7.** 52 **9.** 5 **11.** 1.803 **13.** 823 **15.** 502 **17.** 2,367 **19.** 0.0009 **21.** 426 **23.** 0.47 **25.** 0.032 **27.** 26 **29.** 0.0008 **31.** 15

PAGE 539 **1.** 0.0025 **3.** 0.0081 **5.** 0.065 **7.** 0.075 **9.** 0.085 **11.** 0.0157 **13.** 1.05 **15.** 0.065 **17.** 0.68 **19.** 1.125 **21.** 0.006 **23.** 0.009 **25.** 0.0085 **27.** 0.0035 **29.** 0.033 **31.** 0.0921 **33.** 0.043 **35.** 2.92 **37.** 7.96 **39.** 25

PAGE 540 **1.** $\frac{4}{5}$ **3.** $\frac{4}{7}$ **5.** $4\frac{4}{7}$ **7.** $\frac{1}{2}$ **9.** $\frac{3}{8}$ **11.** $\frac{3}{5}$ **13.** $\frac{3}{5}$ **15.** $5\frac{2}{5}$ **17.** $11\frac{3}{5}$ **19.** $6\frac{1}{2}$ **21.** $11\frac{1}{2}$

PAGE 541 **1.** 0.1 **3.** 0.001 **5.** 0.000012 **7.** 30,000 **9.** 3,300 **11.** 0.72 **13.** 1,300,000 **15.** 4.9 **17.** 1.06 **19.** 1.2

PAGE 542 **1.** 1,000 **3.** 1,000 **5.** 0.2 **7.** 30,000 **9.** 0.18 **11.** 0.0006 **13.** 72,000,000 **15.** 0.45 **17.** 0.2 **19.** 4,200 **21.** 28,000,000 **23.** 4,000,000

PAGE 543 **1.** 0.001 **3.** 0.000001 **5.** 1,000 **7.** 0.008 **9.** 200 **11.** 5,200,000 **13.** 3,700 **15.** 0.37 **17.** 900,000 **19.** 0.12 **21.** 1.006 **23.** 0.0002 **25.** 800,000 **27.** 6,200,000

Index

Index

Rotational symmetry, 505–507

Rounding
    decimals, 51–52, 86, 534
    as estimation strategy, 54, 55, 56,
        86, 188–191
    percents, 278
    whole numbers, 529

Rules, function, 450–451, 454–457,
    467

Sample, random, 30–32, 45

Sample size, 471, 481, 492, 503,
    509

Sample space, 407–411
    counting principle and, 408–411,
        428
    defined, 407
    finding, 407–411

Scale drawing, 251–254, 282
    defined, 251
    finding scale of, 252–254
    making, 252

Scale factor, 250

Scalene triangle, 297

Scatter plot, 39–42, 45

Scientific calculator, 76, 156–158,
    177–180, 213, 349, 364, 378

Scientific notation, 438–440, 441,
    445, 466
    defined, 438
    with negative exponents, 441

Segment bisector, 323–326, 331

Semicircle, 315–316

Sequence
    arithmetic, 434–437, 466
    defined, 434
    geometric, 435–437, 466

Sides, corresponding, 245–249,
    305–307

Similar figures, 245–250
    creating, 250
    defined, 246
    finding missing measures in,
        246–249, 282
    properties of, 245–249
    symbol for, 246

Simple interest, 446–449

Simpler problem, solving, 442–445,
    466

Simplest form of fraction, 164–167,
    178, 182

Simulation
    of events, 393–396, 397, 398–400
    as problem solving strategy,
        398–400

Skills Handbook, 528–543

Slide, 493

Slope, 482–484, 485, 510
    defined, 482
    equation and, 485
    negative, 483
    positive, 483

Solid figures. *See* Three-dimensional
    figures

Solution
    defined, 118
    of equations, 118–125, 130–133,
        139, 200–204, 222–224, 226, 227,
        477–481
    estimating, 223, 224
    of proportions, 241–244, 282, 283
    reasonableness of, 5, 19, 33, 54–58,
        151, 155, 164, 185, 193, 194, 197,
        198, 213, 294, 350, 393, 414

Spatial reasoning, 245, 288–290,
    330, 369, 370, 384

Specific gravity, 66, 79, 85

Sphere, 369

Spreadsheet, 12–15, 44, 111, 397,
    447, 449

Square, 157, 331
    area of, 354, 359, 453
    defined, 309
    diagonal of, 367
    perfect, 354, 364, 386
    perimeter of, 342, 357

Square numbers, 156, 157, 354

Square root
    calculator key for, 364
    estimating, 355–357
    finding, 354–357, 386
    symbol for, 355

Standard form, 439–441, 466

Standardized Test Preparation,
    xxviii–xxix, 11, 20, 24, 33, 38, 42,
    47, 56, 62, 70, 71, 87, 89, 93, 96,
    108, 111, 117, 125, 129, 132, 138,
    141, 150, 163, 166, 169, 171, 175,
    179, 185, 191, 202, 217, 229, 234,
    244, 255, 262, 269, 273, 276, 283,
    285, 300, 307, 311, 317, 320, 322,
    328, 330, 332, 333, 347, 352, 356,
    358, 373, 375, 379, 380, 387, 388,
    389, 396, 405, 411, 414, 421, 423,
    429, 430, 431, 436, 445, 464, 466,
    468, 469, 475, 478, 480, 489, 497,
    504, 510, 512, 513

Statistics. *See* Data Analysis

Stem, 22

Stem-and-leaf plot, 22–25, 44

Straight angle, 292

Straightedge, 324–325, 327

Subtraction
    of decimals, 59–62, 86

estimating differences, 54–55,
    188–191, 194, 198, 226
of fractions, 194–196, 226, 540
of integers, 106–110, 138–139
as inverse of addition, 200
of mixed numbers, 198–199, 226
modeling, 106–107, 192, 193
order of operations in, 80, 156
for solving equations, 118–121, 139,
    200–204, 226, 276–277, 293,
    298–299
using compensation, 63

Subtraction property of equality,
    120

Sum
    estimating, 54–55, 188–191, 193,
        194, 197, 198, 226
    using compensation, 63
    See also Addition

Supplementary angles, 292, 293,
    294, 296

Surface area
    of cylinders, 374–376, 387
    defined, 373
    of prisms, 373–376, 387

Survey, 30–32

Symbols
    for right angles, 292
    in comparisons, 52, 152
    for congruence, 305
    grouping, 80–84
    for multiplication, 68
    for similarity, 246
    for square root, 355

Symmetrical figure, 499

Symmetry
    lines of, 499–503, 511
    rotational, 505–507

Table
    frequency, 4–7, 18, 44
    as problem solving strategy, xxiii,
        28, 134–136, 139
    random number, 397
    to represent functions, 450–457
    of values, 450–452, 457

Tally, 20

Technology connections
    creating similar figures, 250
    fraction calculator, 213
    Math Toolboxes, 111, 213, 250, 313,
        397, 458, 485
    measuring angles of polygons, 313
    spreadsheets and data displays,
        12–15, 44, 111, 397, 447, 449
    See also Calculator; Computer;
        Internet

Index

Acknowledgments

Cover Design: Bruce Bond; Martucci Studio

Cover Photos: Martucci Studio

Book Design: Olena Serbyn; Brown Publishing Network

Page Design and Design Management: Brown Publishing Network

Technical Illustration: GTS Graphics; Brown Publishing Network

ILLUSTRATION

Annie Bissett: 199, 203, 392, 395, 401, 460, 484, 491

Dan Brawner: 35, 410, 437

Daniel Collins: 151, 308, 450, 452, 453

Andrea Golden: 34, 146, 153, 244, 494

Tom Klare: xxviii, 28, 64, 168, 409, 448, 486, 490

Tom Lochray: 39, 249, 277

Karen Minot: 69, 97, 134, 164, 208, 220, 239, 251, 321, 345, 420, 444, 472, 496

Michael Moran: 236

Outlook/ANCO: 57, 66, 156, 178, 242, 248, 300, 337, 378

Steve Pica: 14, 382

Matthew Pippin: 315

Gary Torrisi: 303

Camille Venti: 54, 172, 214, 216, 219, 262, 263, 268, 269, 398

Rose Zgodzinski: 51, 115, 121, 169, 196, 254, 267, 318, 414

PHOTOGRAPHY

Photo Research: Brown Publishing Network

Front Matter

vii, David Young-Wolff/Photo Edit; **viii,** Superstock; **ix,** M. Siluk/The Image Works; **x,** AP/Wide World; **xi,** Superstock; **xii,** David Young-Wolff/Photo Edit ; **xiv,** Thomas Craig/FPG; **xv,** David Young-Wolff/Tony Stone Images**; xvi,** Chris Marona/Photo Researchers; **xvii,** The Image Bank; **xviii,** Lawrence Migdale; **xix t,** Bob Daemmrich/The Image Works; **xix c,** Prentice Hall photo by Irene Perlman; **xx,** Alan & Linda Detrick/Photo Researchers; **xxiii,** Uniphoto; **xxiv,** Kindra Clineff/The Picture Cube; **xxvi,** Prentice Hall photo by Ken O'Donoghue

Chapter One

2–3, Superstock; **5t,** David Young-Wolff/Photo Edit; **5b,** Al Tielemans/Duomo; **6,** David Young-Wolff/Photo Edit; **8,** Superstock; **13,** Archive Photos; **18,** Lee Snyder/Photo Researchers; **20,** AP/Wide World; **23,** Tom Stack & Assoc.; **25,** Jose Pelaez/Stock Market; **30,** Corbis-Bettmann; **32,** AP/Wide World; **34,** Grant Heilman; **36,** Steve Sutton/Duomo; **39,** Tom Stewart/Stock Market; **41,** Gary Milburn/Tom Stack & Assoc.

Chapter Two

48–49, Domainede Bellevue/Stock Boston; **50,** Brock Peter/Gamma Liaison; **53,** Brian Kenney/Natural Selection; **57,** Superstock; **58,** Frank Siteman/Monkmeyer; **61,** Prentice Hall photo by Ken O'Donoghue; **59,** Photo Image Tech.; **65,** Prentice Hall photo by Ken O'Donoghue; **66,** Superstock; **72,** David Young-Wolff/Photo Edit; **83,** Jim Amos/ Photo Researchers

Chapter Three

90–91, Jeffrey W. Meters/Uniphoto; **92 all,** Prentice Hall photo by Ken O'Donoghue; **93 all,** Prentice Hall photo by Russ Lappa; **98,** Skjold/Image Works; **99,** Agence France Presse/Corbis-Bettmann; **107,** Superstock; **113,** Michael K. Nichols/National Geographic Society; **116,** Gupton/Uniphoto; **118 all,** Prentice Hall photo by Ken O'Donoghue; **119,** Prentice Hall photo by Tracy Wheeler; **123,** Prentice Hall photo by Ken O'Donoghue; **126,** Superstock; **128,** Sky and Telescope; **131,** UPI/Corbis-Bettmann; **133,** M. Siluk/Image Works; **135 all,** Prentice Hall photo by Russ Lappa; **136,** Animals, Animals

Chapter Four

142–143, Dennis O'Clair/Tony Stone Images; **144 all,** Prentice Hall photo by Russ Lappa; **151,** Michelle Bridwell/Photo Edit; **147,** Laima Druskis/Stock Boston; **153,** Grace Davies; **156,** Prentice Hall photo by Russ Lappa; **156,** Hans Wolf/Image Bank; **160,** Prentice Hall photo by Tracy Wheeler; **165 all,** AP/Wide World;

166, Will & Deni McIntyre/Photo Researchers;
170, Bob Daemmrich/Stock Boston; 176, Athletic
Dept., University of Georgia; 178, Bob Daemmrich

Chapter Five

186–187, Prentice Hall photo by Ken O'Donoghue;
188, L. Rorke/Image Works; 190, Tom Bross/Stock
Boston; 194, Addison Geary; 197, Superstock; 201,
David Wilbeck/Picture Cube; 204, Paul
Conklin/Monkmeyer; 206, Robert Tyrell;
206, Anthony Mercieco/Photo Researchers;
211, Steven Peters/Tony Stone Images;
212, Superstock; 222, Eric Poggenpohl/Folio

Chapter Six

230–231, Courtesy of Paramount Parks; 232, Bob
Daemmrich/Stock Boston; 233, Peter Beck/
Uniphoto; 234, Alan Nelson/Animals, Animals;
238, Vandystadt; 242, Eric Schnakenberg/FPG;
243, UPI/Corbis-Bettmann; 248, Francis Lepine/
Animals, Animals, Earth Scenes; 253, NASA;
254, Cindy Charles/Photo Edit; 257, Leo
Keeler/Animals, Animals; 261, Animals, Animals;
265, John Neubauer/Photo Edit; 265, Bob
Daemmrich/Stock Boston; 271, David Young-
Wolff/Photo Edit; 276, Uniphoto

Chapter Seven

286–287, Uniphoto; Lewellyn/Uniphoto;
288, Eastcott/Momatiuk/Image Works;
290, Superstock; 293, Prentice Hall photo by Ken
O'Donoghue; 295t, E.R. Degginger/Earth Scenes;
295bl, National Fish and Wildlife Forensics Lab;
295br, National Fish and Wildlife Forensics Lab;
298, William S. Helsel/Tony Stone Images;
300, Prentice Hall photo by Ken O'Donoghue;
305, Prentice Hall photo by Ken O'Donoghue;
308, Superstock; 311t, Animals, Animals;
311b, Joyce Photographics/Photo Researchers;
316, Prentice Hall photo; 324, Courtesy of Wellesley
College Library, Special Collections. Photo by George
McLean

Chapter Eight

334–335, Winston Fraser; 337, S. J. Krasemann/DRK
Photo; 339, Matsumoto/Explorer/Photo Researchers;

341, Bob Daemmrich/Stock Boston; 348, David
Frazier; 350, Mike Peters/FPG; 353, D & I
MacDonald/Picture Cube; 354, Deborah Davies/Photo
Edit; 357, Bob Daemmrich/Stock Boston; 359, Terry
Qing/FPG; 362, Prentice Hall photo by Russ Lappa;
364, M. Antman/Image Works; 366, Joe Cornish/Tony
Stone Images; 367, Prentice Hall photo by Russ
Lappa; 368r, Derek Berwin/ Image Bank;
368l, Chuck Zsymanski/International Stock;
369, Thomas Craig/FPG; 371l, John Gerlach/DRK;
371c, Cathlyn Melloan/Tony Stone Images;
371r, Will & Deni McIntyre/Photo Researchers;
375, Greig Cranna/Stock Boston; 378, Peter
Gridley/FPG

Chapter Nine

390–391, Prentice Hall photo by Ken O'Donoghue;
393l, Michael Newman/Photo Edit; 393r, J. Gerard
Smith/ Monkmeyer; 402, Bill Bachmann/Photo
Researchers; 408, Superstock; 413, Prentice Hall
photo by Tracy Wheeler; 417, Corbis- Bettmann;
419, Superstock; 422, David Young-Wolff/Tony Stone
Images; 424, Phil Dotson/ Photo Researchers;
425, Ralph Reinhold/Animals, Animals

Chapter Ten

432–433, Mark Reinstein/Uniphoto; 435, Superstock;
435i, Peter G. Aitken/Photo Researchers;
438, Superstock; 440, Corbis-Bettmann; 445, Chris
Marona Photo Researchers; 446, Rhoda Sidney/Stock
Boston; 451, Dennis O'Clair/Tony Stone Images;
455, Stephen Gerard/Photo Researchers; 461, Lowe Art
Museum, University of Miami/Superstock

Chapter Eleven

470–471, Courtesy MSNBC; 472, Corbis Bettmann;
476, John Madere/The Stock Market; 477, David
Young-Wolff/Photo Edit; 480, Annie Hunter;
488, Bob Daemmrich; 493 all, Prentice Hall photo by
Russ Lappa; 499t, A & F Michler; 499bl, Charles
Kennard/Stock Boston; 499br, Jerome Wexler/Photo
Researchers; 500 all, Roy Morsch/The Stock Market;
501l, Corel; 501r, Jeff Lepore/Photo Researchers;
501c, Don & Pat Valenti/DRK; 505t, Foto World/The
Image Bank; 505b, Rod Planck/Tom Stack; 507m,
Alfred Pasieka/SPL/Photo Researchers; 507r, Prentice
Hall Photo